ORGANIZATIONAL BEHAVIOR 5

ORGANIZATIONAL BEHAVIOR 5

FROM UNCONSCIOUS MOTIVATION TO ROLE-MOTIVATED LEADERSHIP

JOHN B. MINER

M.E.Sharpe
Armonk, New York
London, England

Library of Congress Cataloging-in-Publication Data

Miner, John B.
Organizational behavior 1. Essential theories of motivation and leadership
Organizational behavior 2. Essential theories of process and structure
Organizational behavior 3. Historical origins, theoretical foundations, and the future
Organizational behavior 4. From theory to practice
Organizational behavior 5. From unconscious motivation to role-motivated leadership
by John B. Miner.
p. cm.
Includes bibliographical references and index.
Vol. 1: ISBN 0-7656-1523-1 (cloth : alk. paper)
Vol. 2: ISBN 0-7656-1525-8 (cloth : alk. paper)
Vol. 3: ISBN 0-7656-1527-4 (cloth : alk. paper)
Vol. 4: ISBN 978-0-7656-1529-9 (cloth : alk. paper)
Vol. 5: ISBN 978-0-7656-1990-7 (cloth : alk. paper)
1. Employee motivation. 2. Leadership. 3. Organizational behavior. I. Title: Organizational behavior one. Essential theories of motivation and leadership. II. Title: Organizational behavior. 1. Essential theories of motivation and leadership. III. Title: Essential theories of motivation and leadership. IV. Title.

HF5549.5.M63M5638 2005
302.3′5—dc22 2005003746

Printed in the United States of America

The paper used in this publication meets the minimum requirements of
American National Standard for Information Sciences
Permanence of Paper for Printed Library Materials,
ANSI Z 39.48-1984.

BM (c) 10 9 8 7 6 5 4 3 2 1

DEDICATION

To the authors who contributed their research in one way or another to the creation of this volume—

Frederic E. Berman
Jeffrey S. Bracker
Richard P. Butler
Kenneth P. Carson
Chao-Chuan Chen
Donald P. Crane
Alice H. Eagly
Debora J. Gilliard
Dorothy N. Harlow
James W. Hill
Blair T. Johnson
Steven J. Karau
Charles L. Lardent
Jennifer L. Miner
John E. Oliver
Nambury S. Raju
John R. Rizzo
Norman R. Smith
Robert J. Vandenberg
Celeste P. M. Wilderom
K. C. Yu

Building on Miner's *Organizational Behavior: Foundations, Theories, and Analyses,* the M.E. Sharpe Organizational Behavior series consists of the following volumes—

1. Essential Theories of Motivation and Leadership (2005)
2. Essential Theories of Process and Structure (2006)
3. Historical Origins, Theoretical Foundations, and the Future (2006)
4. From Theory to Practice (2007)
5. From Unconscious Motivation to Role-Motivated Leadership (2008)

CONTENTS

LIST OF TABLES

PREFACE

My intentions in preparing this volume are twofold. First, I would like to make available in one place the large body of research that has accumulated over the years on role motivation theory. This research has developed from its origins in motivation theory to its current status as a major contributor to leadership theory. Consistent with my own training in personality theory and psychoanalysis, this research activity has always been concerned with unconscious factors in human experience and behavior.

Thus one of my reasons for writing this book is to bring together and update writings on role motivation subjects that have been available previously, if at all, only in scattered locations. In this process my intent is to provide an introduction to the role of unconscious motivation in organizational behavior. Since the advent of the field, the primary concern has been to consider conscious processes both in theoretical formulations and in measurement (such as the five-factor model). The objective here is to help correct this imbalance, and to bring unconscious factors into the domain of organizational behavior; I want to try to fill some of the void that has existed heretofore in this regard.

The selections presented report original research with which I have been involved in one way or another, either with faculty colleagues, with graduate students, with other organizational behavior scholars, or on my own. This work is of a scholarly nature focused on the unconscious and contributions to research in that field and utilizing an approach that attempts to emphasize good science and equally good scholarly contributions to knowledge. My desire—as I present these selections and from the outset, when the research began at the Atlantic Refining Company—is and has been to demonstrate that the field of unconscious motivation can be a source of effective theorizing at least the equal of what conscious motivation has achieved previously in organizational behavior.

This volume is modeled after various books that have appeared in the past, often in the area of decision making, and that review of the research and writings of a single author, or set of authors. I have in mind such books as:

- James March's *Decisions and Organizations* (1988) and *The Pursuit of Organizational Intelligence* (1999)
- Karl Weick's *Making Sense of the Organization* (2001)
- Lee Roy Beach's *Image Theory: Theoretical and Empirical Foundations* (1998)
- Richard Scott and John Meyer's *Institutional Environments and Organizations* (1994)

I, myself, have prepared little by way of books of this kind, in one instance many years ago. This publication, dealing with early research and theory on hierarchic role motivation primarily, is:

- John Miner's *Motivation to Manage: A Ten-Year Update on the "Studies in Management Education" Research* (1977b)

That volume overlaps only minimally with the present one.

My second objective in preparing this book, beyond making available key research contributions on role motivation topics, is to provide background for the book to follow in this organizational behavior series, titled *Integrated Theory Development and the Role of the Unconscious.* This sixth book will attempt to integrate the various theories considered previously in the series, and it will do this by pointing up the role of unconscious factors in these theories. Thus, a knowledge of role motivation research will prove beneficial. For those who may wish more information on the theoretical context of the research I recommend Miner (1993); more succinct and up-to-date resentations are contained in Chapter 5 of Miner (2002), Chapter 17 of Miner (2005), and Chapter 28 of Thomas and Segal (2006). Book Six uses organizational forms, roles, unconscious motives and affective states from role motivation theorizing as the building blocks.

To provide a better idea of whether this book is one that would be of interest to you, and from which you might learn, let me outline the contents. Part I contains two chapters that set the scene for what follows and provides an introduction. They are concerned with the current status of projective techniques and what is now known about the operation of unconscious factors. Of the references noted 79 percent are from the year 2000 onward and 45 percent from 2005 onward. Much of this is new data, insofar as the field of organizational behavior is concerned. It may contain some major surprises for many. The evidence for the validity of projective measures has become increasingly convincing, and with it the data to support a role for the unconscious. Part I is not concerned with role motivation theory per se, but it does provide an underpinning that should help elucidate the research on that theory that follows.

Part II contains twenty-one chapters and thirty selections. Of these, one is original to this volume; the rest are reprinted from various sources, most of them journal articles. These publications are presented in chronological order and are introduced with a commentary that indicates their source as well as their context.

Part III consists of nine chapters that involve psychometric data analyses, meta-analyses, and factor analysis. Four of these are original to this volume, and thus have never been published in any other source. The other five are republished here, primarily from various journals.

The references represent all of those cited previously in this book. These vary in date of origin with the year the selection was published, ranging from the 1950s, and even before, to 2007. They provide a comprehensive reference guide to sources that have over the years been tied to role motivation theory. More on these sources may be obtained from Organizational Measurement Systems Press, P.O. Box 70586, Eugene, Oregon, 97401.

John B. Miner
Eugene, Oregon

ACKNOWLEDGMENTS

A major debt in preparing this book is acknowledged in the dedication. These are the people who have helped author the material contained in this volume; I owe them a considerable debt.

Harry Briggs at M.E. Sharpe has shown himself to be both a very helpful person and a highly proficient editor as well. It has been a pleasure to work with him. Stacey Victor, my project editor, has been equally helpful.

In the absence of university support, my wife, Barbara, has taken on all of the numerous tasks involved in the preparation of this book, other than writing it. I thank her not only for her dedication and efficiency, but for her support and love.

I also want to acknowledge the contributions of the following organizations and publishers who have granted permission to incorporate material from the indicated sources in this volume:

Academy of Management
American Psychological Association
American Personnel and Guidance Association (American Counseling Association)
Blackwell Publishing
The British Psychological Society
Cornell University—Johnson Graduate School of Management
Elsevier
Institute for Operations Research and the Management Sciences
Sage Publications
Taylor and Francis Limited
John Wiley & Sons

PART I

UNCONSCIOUS MOTIVATION

CHAPTER 1

UNCONSCIOUS MOTIVATION AS VIEWED FROM THE PROJECTIVE PERSPECTIVE

INTRODUCTION

In large part the study of organizational behavior has failed to embrace two approaches to its subject matter that are important to its advance. These missing emphases are (1) a concern with the organizational context within which behavior occurs and (2) the unconscious (or subconscious) motivation that drives this behavior. The research program described in this volume deals with these matters. Before proceeding, however, we must first document the underrepresentation of these two variables in organizational behavior's research and theory.

The Missing Organizational Context

Porter and McLaughlin (2006) surveyed the leadership literature for the period 1990–2005 to assess how articles in twenty-one major journals dealt with matters of organizational context. They say:

> . . . the basic premise of this article is: Leadership in organizations does not take place in a vacuum. It takes place in organizational contexts. The key issue, therefore, is whether, and

> to what extent, the organizational context has been front and center in recent leadership literature (Porter and McLaughlin 2006, 559).

Based on their data they conclude that 16 percent of the leadership articles they reviewed gave moderate or strong attention to some aspect of the organizational context as a factor affecting conclusions. Another 19 percent placed only slight emphasis on organizational context. Thus 65 percent of the articles fell into the no emphasis category. This void was most pronounced among the empirical articles surveyed (74 percent), as opposed to the conceptual articles. Accordingly these authors conclude that the organizational context is indeed missing from research on leadership, and to a somewhat lesser extent from the theoretical or conceptual literature.

Porter and McLaughlin (2006) extend their discussion of this deficiency in the field beyond leadership to organizational behavior more broadly, contending that for some reason the organization has been omitted in large part from our research studies. Johns (2006) does an even more extensive job of documenting the ways in which contextual factors tend to be ignored in organizational behavior as a whole. All in all, there can be no question that there is indeed a missing organizational context in the field that stems primarily from certain historical circumstances surrounding the way in which research into organizational behavior has developed (see Miner 2006a).

The Missing Unconscious (or Subconscious)

A substantially different type of neglect occurs in the case of unconscious motivation. Here the problem is both more pronounced and arguably more important, and the documentation derives from clear instances of omission. As an example let us consider a recent issue of the *American Psychologist.* This issue deals with the leadership field and is predicated on the view that many psychologists are relatively unfamiliar with the leadership literature. To remedy this situation six contributions were solicited from leading theorists—Warren Bennis (2007), Stephen Zaccaro (2007), Victor Vroom and Arthur Jago (2007), Bruce Avolio (2007), Robert Sternberg (2007), and Richard Hackman and Ruth Wageman (2007).

None of these leadership theorists makes any mention of unconscious (or subconscious) factors, or of procedures used to assess or measure unconscious motivation; the word unconscious is simply not used. There are, to be sure, references to theories that include in their repertoires unconscious considerations—references to McClelland's achievement motivation theory (by Zaccaro), to Lord's information processing theory (by Zaccaro and Avolio), and even to Miner's role motivation theory (by Zaccaro). Yet even in these instances the concept of the unconscious is not specifically invoked. We will consider shortly why this kind of omission occurs.

THE NATURE OF UNCONSCIOUS MOTIVATION

In discussing the reactions of the executives he counsels, Manfred Kets de Vries has the following to say:

> If you study executives, you quickly see that they don't behave rationally all the time. Indeed irrational behavior is common in organizational life . . . When I analyze them, I usually find that their drives spring from childhood patterns and experiences that have carried

over into adulthood. Executives don't like to hear this; they like to think they're totally in control. They're insulted to hear that certain things in their minds are unconscious (Coutu 2004, 67).

Uses to Which the Idea of an Unconscious May Be Devoted

Definitions employed to enunciate unconscious factors may vary considerably. The following listing is not intended to include all possibilities, but it does introduce many of the alternatives to be found in the recent literature.

> Unconscious thought refers to object-relevant or task-relevant cognitive or affective thought processes that occur while conscious attention is directed elsewhere (Dijksterhuis and Nordgren 2006, 96).

> The unconscious was the subterranean strata of the psyche that consisted of previous experiences, memories, feelings, and urges, of which the individual was not actively aware due to defensive mechanisms—the most common of which was repression—or other active psychodynamic processes (Carr 2002, 344).

> . . . most central, much of mental life—including thoughts, feelings, and motives—is unconscious, which means that people can behave in ways or develop symptoms that are inexplicable to themselves (Westen 1998, 334).

> . . . there can be no doubt that the subconscious is a storehouse of knowledge and values beyond that which is in focal awareness at a given time. People can take action without being fully aware of what is motivating them or what stored knowledge is affecting their choices (Locke and Latham 2002, 714).

> The concept of the subconscious is not a "hypothetical construct" but a fully objective one. It refers to information that is "in consciousness," but not at a given time, in focal awareness. . . . We validate the concept of the subconscious by observing that we can draw knowledge out of memory without any additional learning (Locke and Latham 2004, 395).

> The psychoanalytic unconscious is to most lay people and those in the arts and humanities, the only unconscious. It has many more characteristics (besides operating outside of awareness) than can be reviewed here. It includes the id . . . and most . . . of the superego . . . and ego. . . . But it does not provide an influential framework for understanding unconscious processes in academic or scientific circles (see Westen 1998 for a dissenting view). Unlike the psychoanalytic unconscious, the cognitive unconscious has no innate drives. . . . So what is new about the new unconscious? It is basically cognitive, firmly embedded in cognitive science and historically beholden to the computer as a metaphor . . . the new unconscious is much more concerned with affect, motivation, and even control and metacognition . . . goals, motives, and self-regulation are prominent (Hassin, Uleman, and Bargh 2005, 4–6).

> The unconscious is, in the first place, the state of ideas and desires which have undergone repression. . . . The idea that repression is a form of mental defense against threatening psychic

> phenomena lies at the heart of Freudian psychology. . . . Repressed ideas do not disappear without a trace from a person's life, but they seek expression in various subterfuges. . . . Dreams represent fulfillment of unconscious desires and they are censored to the extent that they may contradict the contents of consciousness (Gabriel 1999, 6–7).

There is research to support many of these formulations. It seems likely that all of these statements may prove to be correct as knowledge evolves; thus I believe that a definition of unconscious motivation at present should encompass all of these propositions. Note in this connection the following quotes—

> With regard to career decisions—once the self-concept has been formed, it functions as a stabilizing force, an anchor, and can be thought of as the values and motives that the person will not give up if forced to make a choice. Most of us are not aware of our career anchors (Hall 2002, 186). With regard to organizational identification—whether individuals believe they are part of the organization involves both subconscious and conscious processes (Leana and Rousseau 2000, 159).

Thus, some major contributors to the organizational behavior field do recognize unconscious considerations and find such constructs useful; the missing unconscious is not a universal phenomenon.

Harry Levinson on the Missing Unconscious

One writer who has made abundant use of the unconscious terminology is Harry Levinson (see Miner 2002b). As an example he describes organizations as tending to recapitulate the family structure; members evolve conscious and unconscious contracts with organizations to maintain psychological equilibria (Levinson 1973, 28). In the same vein he says "A leader should understand the meaning of the unconscious psychological contract" (Levinson 1998, 236).

Levinson and his colleagues have also directed their attention to the missing unconscious and the reasons for its prevalence:

> We get the sense that even those scholars who would like to speak of unconscious needs and psychological development may be reluctant to do so in the face of collegial skepticism regarding clinical themes . . . One reason organizational scholars tend to fall back on agency theory and transactional elements is that concepts of unconscious needs and personality are no longer in vogue. . . . Terms such as "unconscious motivation," "ego ideals," and "dependency needs" have been eliminated from our working language. . . . Contemporary articles stay away from the language of unconscious needs, self-identity, and developmental aspects of psychology (Meckler, Drake, and Levinson 2003, 219–221).

In short, unconscious motivation and its associated terminology have become taboo words for organizational behavior, something on the order of four-letter words. As we will see later in this chapter and in the next chapter, this taboo is not attributable to a lack of scientific substantiation, although such has been claimed. More likely it derives from certain processes (presumably often of an unconscious nature) that have come to permeate the field. I have demonstrated such processes as they apply to leadership. Meckler, Drake, and Levinson (2003) have done the same in the case of the psychological contract.

THE STATUS OF RESEARCH, MEASUREMENT, AND ASSESSMENT OF UNCONSCIOUS MOTIVATION

Psychoanalysis as promulgated by Sigmund Freud has been the driving force behind the study of unconscious motivation historically, although there have been inputs from other areas of psychology for many years, in particular from experimental psychology. Psychoanalysis has at present made its greatest contribution to measurement in the area of projective techniques and their use in assessment. Research data of a scientific nature has increasingly infiltrated the study of projective techniques, yet—like psychoanalysis as a theory and as an application—measurement of the unconscious motivation that derives from psychoanalysis remains largely part of the clinical process. However, the new unconscious as it has emerged in recent years has come out of experimental psychology. This new unconscious has developed increasing force; it will be considered in Chapter 2, after we take up the research, the measurement procedures, and the assessment processes involving projectives considered here in Chapter 1.

There have been two major milestones in the evaluation of research related to psychoanalytic theory. The first of these was the Sears (1943; 1944) analysis which tells us little about the outcomes of research at the present time, but much about the overall evaluation of the theory itself at an early point:

> The experiments and observations examined in this report stand testimony that few investigators feel free to accept Freud's statements at face value. The reason lies in the same factor that makes psychoanalysis a bad science—its method. Psychoanalysis relies upon techniques that do not admit of the repetition of observation, that have no self-evident or denotative validity, and that are tinctured to an unknown degree with the observer's own suggestions. . . . When the method is used for uncovering psychological facts that are required to have objective validity it simply fails. This does not mean that all psychoanalytic findings are false. . . . In spite of these various difficulties and qualifications, a few conclusions relative to specific concepts and principles can be reached (Sears 1943, 133–135).

This scientific evaluation of the original theory, derived as it is from clinical origins, still stands today, but the "few conclusions" have continued to expand over the years to the point where much greater credibility has arrived; increasing research findings have made the difference.

The second evaluation of psychoanalytic theory of a major nature was of Westen (1998), which was considered previously in this chapter. Westen takes the position that—

> Many aspects of Freudian theory are indeed out of date, and they should be. Freud died in 1939, and he has been slow to undertake further revisions. His critics, however, are equally behind the times, attacking Freudian views of the 1920s as if they continue to have some currency in their original form. . . . Many psychoanalytic writings are obscure, muddleheaded, and ignorant of relevant empirical work. . . . Was Freud wrong in some of his ideas about human nature? Without doubt (Westen 1998, 333, 362).

Yet Westen (1998, 334–335) is able to set forth five postulates that define contemporary psychodynamic theory:

1. much of mental life—including thoughts, feelings and motives—is unconscious, which means that people can behave in ways or develop symptoms that are inexplicable to themselves.
2. mental processes, including affective and motivational processes, operate in parallel so that, toward the same person or situation, individuals can have conflicting feelings that motivate them in opposing ways and often lead to compromise solutions.
3. stable personality patterns begin to form in childhood, and childhood experiences play an important role in personality development.
4. mental representations of the self, others, and relationships guide peoples' interactions with others and influence the ways they become psychologically symptomatic.
5. personality development involves not only learning to regulate sexual and aggressive feelings, but also moving from an immature, socially dependent state to a mature, interdependent one.

PROJECTIVE TECHNIQUES AND THE UNCONSCIOUS

One line of research leading from psychoanalysis ran out through projective measurement; this is the line I have followed, and the studies reported in this volume take this tack. Thus we need to become familiar with these projective techniques, and see what they can and cannot accomplish. Roy Schafer has been a major contributor to the literature, linking the unconscious, psychoanalysis, and projective measurement. His work in this regard is detailed in Schafer (2006). His formulations are best set forth in Schafer (1967).

Projective techniques present people with a stimulus, or some other activity, in pictorial or word form and ask them to react to it. In their response people unconsciously project aspects of themselves. The sample of behaviors elicited in the process becomes the subject of questions put by the interpreter. Thus the theory is not in the test, but in the interpreter's own mind. To varying degrees the stimulus is ambiguous, unstructured, and impersonal. The tests encourage fantasy and creative "regression in the service of the ego" (Schafer 1967, 52), and thus the manifestation of unconscious material. There is little constraint placed on the response, as would be the case with multiple choice alternatives, but considerable demand upon the skills of the interpreter, as aided by whatever guides or manuals are available.

The processes that operate in the case of projective techniques may be likened to what happens in psychoanalysis when patients bring their memories of dreams to the therapy session, and then provide free associations to these ambiguous stimuli (Reiser 1990). Dream interpretation of this kind has much in common with the procedures used to score and interpret projective techniques.

A number of projective techniques have been developed, some of which do not fully qualify for description using that label (Bell 1948). In this volume I will concentrate on the Rorschach, the Thematic Apperception Test (TAT), and various sentence completion measures; and more tangentially on the Picture Arrangement Test (PAT). These are the procedures that have particular relevance for the purposes at hand.

Evaluations—Primarily Negative

Projective techniques have come under a substantial amount of criticism over the years, and have suffered from the same kind of treatment as has unconscious motivation, largely because this motivation is what they indeed measure. James and Mazerolle (2002) indicate that up to the present, "interrater reliabilities and construct validity of the scoring systems designed to score the free response, fantasy-based projective tests have long been, and continue to be, of concern to psychometricians" (134). They cite a number of quotes to back up their views:

> Apparently most projective techniques do a rather poor job of measuring personality traits, tend to have unacceptably low reliabilities, are rather unstandardized, and are psychometrically unsound vehicles for measuring anything (Nunnally 1978).
>
> Aside from their questionable theoretical rationales, projective techniques are clearly found wanting with regard to standardization of administration and scoring procedures, adequacy of norms, reliability, and validity (Anastasi 1982).
>
> Among their shortcomings are inadequacies of administration, scoring, and standardization. The lack of objectivity in scoring and the paucity and deficiency of representative normative data are particularly bothersome to specialists in psychometrics (Aiken 1994).

A number of publications that have consistently attacked the validity of projective techniques began emerging some twelve years ago from a combination of authors. Of these the more significant publications are Lilienfeld, Wood, and Garb (2000) and Wood, Garb, Lilienfeld, and Nezworski (2002), although there have been a number of others of the same ilk.

This attack has been directed most extensively against the Rorschach, but extends to the TAT and human figure drawing methods. The concern regarding the Rorschach is directed specifically at the Comprehensive System that was introduced to provide greater coherence and psychometric precision to a long-time, largely clinical instrument (Exner 1974). This measure is said to possess inadequate norms, insufficient evidence of differential validity with minorities, and problematic scorer reliability and test-retest reliability, as well as inadequate corrections for response frequency effects, deviation from predicted factor structures, validities of 0.30, and insufficient incremental validity. "The scientific status of this system appears to be less than convincing" (Lilienfeld, Wood and Garb 2000, 38). In line with the 0.30 validity, some Rorschach indexes were found to be adequate.

Most of the criticisms leveled against the Rorschach are repeated in the case of the TAT. In particular the lack of a standardized set of pictures represents a problem, especially for norming purposes. Some critics have acknowledged the value of attempts to introduce scoring systems based on standardized guides, but this has not prevented further attacks. David McClelland's scoring system for achievement motivation receives passing marks (see Miner 2005, Chapter 4), but confounds with intelligence are said to plague all TAT scoring approaches.

Human figure drawing is described as weak in terms of its overall scientific status. Although the condemnation of projective techniques as a whole is not universal, it is extensive. Where validity is achieved, it appears to derive from following three guidelines:

1. By aggregating across a number of items designed to assess the same construct, measurement error is typically averaged out, thereby resulting in a more reliable and construct valid index.
2. Many successful projective techniques consist of ambiguous stimuli that are especially relevant to the construct being assessed.
3. Future development of projective instruments would benefit from an approach . . . in which the test developer begins with a tentative formulation of the constructs to

> be assessed and then progressively revises these constructs . . . on the basis of new data (Lilienfeld, Wood, and Garb 2000, 55).

Replies to the Negative Evaluations

The main thrust of a reply by Hibbard (2003) is that Lilienfeld, Wood, and Garb (2000) are often in error, frequently seem to be mistaken, and tend to misunderstand, inappropriately report, or fail to cite relevant information. As to the last point a count of references indicates that only 50 percent of the 78 citations in Hibbard (2003) that could have been used by Lilienfeld et al. (2000) were used; this out of 384 references noted by Lilienfeld et al. Clearly the two sources are dealing with substantially different literature even though their subjects are the same. In general the other points made in this reply seem justified. Accordingly:

> If as is argued herein, there is a large aggregation of errors in their report, then the reasonableness of their recommendations may require some rethinking. I contend that it would not be reasonable to implement their recommendations in the light of their criticisms. This said, it needs also to be acknowledged that Lilienfeld et al. made some reasonable criticisms (Hibbard 2003, 269).

Another reply, by Masling (2006), concentrates on the recent book *What's Wrong with the Rorschach?* by Wood, Nezworski, Lilienfeld, and Garb (2003), which largely echoes these authors' past position. This reply gives considerable attention to what is omitted by the authors and to how these omissions tend to be self-serving. Particularly noteworthy is their failure to cite and provide meaningful discussion of scoring systems that introduce objective approaches to responses, and thus utilize a manualized procedure. Masling's (2006) view of the Rorschach critics points to their proclivity for ignoring literature that fails to align with their favored position. Hibbard says the same thing, but in a different way, and such an approach is in line with Harry Levinson's concerns about the ways in which unconscious factors often are handled.

The following treatment of individual projective procedures contains much additional information that indicates when and how these techniques operate effectively. In demonstrating their effectiveness, I have marshaled additional data to rebut the negative evaluations. At this point I cease to talk in terms of the global term "projective techniques" and follow the advice given by Meyer and Kurtz (2006) in speaking with reference to specific measures of this kind.

The Rorschach Inkblot Method

The Rorschach (1942) consists of ten inkblot cards, half of which are in black and white, and half with color. Those taking the test respond to each card by indicating what they think it resembles. Scoring takes considerable time, and is carried out by the examiner using various designations dealing with content, location, and determinants of the responses such as color or movement. Several different scoring systems were integrated by John Exner (see Erdberg and Weiner 2007), thus contributing to the route to standardization and psychometric refinement that has continued up to the present. Exner published a number of books on the subject, conducted workshops, and was a prime mover in the development of the Rorschach over the thirty years before his death in 2006.

Most of the use of the test, and the research too, has been in connection with clinical and forensic practice. The major contribution to the field of organizational behavior has been in its implications for, and possible future applications to, measuring unconscious motivation. There is one study, moreover, that deserves special mention—an investigation of how the Rorschach may be applied in executive selection (Piotrowski and Rock 1963). This study compared successful and unsuccessful top managers, and constructed a specific scale consisting of differentiating signs from the Rorschach. Initial findings proved positive. Important findings associated with success were a drive for power, foresight and anticipation of challenge, self-confidence and mental health, friendly cooperation and competition, integration and spontaneity, mental productivity, and controlled aggressiveness. However, the study does not include a necessary cross-validation effort.

Evidence of the Rorschach's value in a psychometric sense has been evolving steadily as each new study is conducted. Thus, one has to concentrate on the truly most recent research if one is to capture the present scene. An evaluation of the perceptual thinking index, a new scale of Rorschach designations intended to replace previous characteristics indicating schizophrenia, yielded a median interrater reliability of 0.84 and an internal consistency figure of 0.75 (Dao and Prevatt 2006). Further evidence of the reliability of the Rorschach comes from meta-analytic data provided by Grønnerød (2006, 225) who concludes that "with sufficient attention to methodological issues the Rorschach method is as stable as other assessment methods and can capture personality changes as well as other methods." Other analyses ranging across the spectrum of types of reliability indicate consistently sizable figures (Hilsenroth and Strickler 2004; Meyer, Mihura, and Smith 2005; Liebman, Porcerelli, and Abell 2005). Recent data clearly indicate that the concerns expressed previously with regard to Rorschach reliability indexes no longer hold.

Validity has been assessed in a large number of studies. What Masling (2006, 67) labels "a blue ribbon panel of nine experts," appointed by the American Psychological Association, reports on over 125 meta-analyses of various measurement indexes (Meyer, Finn, Eyde, Kay, Moreland, Dies, Eisman, Kubiszyn, and Reed 2001). Their findings indicate that "the validity of psychological tests is comparable to the validity of medical tests" (155), and with regard to the Rorschach specifically the reported correlations were as follows:

- with conceptually meaningful criterion measures .35
- with dependent behavior (Rorschach dependency measure) .37
- with psychotherapy outcome (Rorschach prognostic rating) .44

A subsequent official statement (from the Society for Personality Assessment 2005) includes the above data plus additional findings. It says: "the Rorschach possesses reliability and validity similar to that of other generally accepted personality assessment instruments, and its use in personality assessment is appropriate and justified" (219).

Much of the research dealing with validity uses as its criterion some type of diagnostic condition. Nowhere is this illustrated more clearly than in Huprich's (2006) recent book on the Rorschach, which provides (1) diagnostic predictions for a wide range of mental disorders, (2) indexes derived from the Rorschach, and (3) special purpose Rorschach scales such as the Suicide Constellation developed by Exner that accurately predicts suicides completed within two months. This book is particularly helpful in indicating gaps in knowledge, as is the case with passive-aggressive personalities. It also stresses the role of psychoanalytic theory and unconscious motivation in Rorschach interpretation.

A sampling of recent research using a variety of criteria and designs indicates that the validity of the Rorschach is substantial (Berant, Mikulincer, Shaver, and Segal 2005; Elfhag, Rössner, Lindgren, Andersson, and Carlsson 2004; Hartmann, Wang, Berg, and Saether 2003; Janson and Stattin 2003; Viglione, Perry, and Meyer 2003). Evidence of the same kind comes from new meta-analyses (see Grønnerød 2004). These studies also attest to improved reliability. It becomes increasingly apparent that greater attention to reliability does pay off, especially interrater reliability. Equally important is the construction of multi-sign standardized scales for the Rorschach. There are many indications that improved psychometrics have been producing major advances in the past few years.

Murray's Thematic Apperception Test (TAT)

The Thematic Apperception Test grew out of work by Henry Murray (1943) and his collaborators at the Harvard Psychological Clinic in the 1930s and 1940s. Of these collaborators Christiana D. Morgan was the most significant contributor. The selection of picture stimuli was in constant flux over almost ten years prior to the formal publication (Morgan 2002, 2003). The standard procedure followed by Murray utilized some twenty cards with ten additional pictures intended to be substituted into the twenty when females were to be tested. Thus the test for males was deliberately different from the one for females. However, many other variations on the original set of cards have appeared over the years, most containing much fewer pictures. If a scoring system is complex and diversified and, the responses are often sparse in content, there is a real possibility that the range of any particular score may be seriously restricted, with the result that reliability and validity may suffer. This need not happen, but it can, especially when less than twenty cards are administered. Such a process may have operated to restrict validity and reliability in the case of the AT&T studies described by Howard (see Latham 2007). These studies used only a limited number of cards; but it is also possible that theoretical constraints may have been activated as well.

The TAT's critics gave relatively favorable grades to the test as compared with other projectives, especially when McClelland's applications were involved. This fits well with my own views (see Chapter 4 of Miner 2005 and Chapter 4 of Miner 2007). I find that the evidence in favor of McClelland's theory, much of which derives from TAT studies, is predominantly supportive. This result was achieved largely because of the development of a scoring procedure that emphasized standardization and systematic procedures. Recent research building on these strengths has introduced further improvements in reliability and validity along with certain changes in the format and conduct of the TAT (see Langan-Fox and Grant 2006; Blankenship, Vega, Ramos, Romero, Warren, Keenan, Rosenow, Vasquez, and Sullivan 2006; and Schmalt 2005).

Various Sentence Completion Tests

Holaday, Smith, and Sherry (2000) report on fifteen sentence completion measures currently used in clinical practice, but there are more than that. The usual procedure is to use these tests in an informal, clinical, global way, rather than to undertake any formal scoring. However, there are sentence completion tests that have formal scoring systems, with manuals and examples of how to score particular responses. Chief among these is the Rotter Incomplete Sentence Blank, said to be the most widely used method of this type, an indicator of maladjustment. This test contains 40 incomplete sentence stems and scorer reliabilities having a median of 0.93; test-retest figures were at 0.82 (Logan and Wachler 2001).

A second such measure is the Washington University Sentence Completion Test (Loevinger 1998, 2002). This projective measure is the only one that the critics actually endorse. It (1) aggregates scores across multiple items, (2) focuses on the relevant construct, and (3) begins with a tentative formulation and then progressively revises based on new data. Based on these guidelines this sentence completion test has "demonstrated impressive construct validity" (Lilienfeld, Wood, and Garb 2000, 56) and (on the same page) "is arguably the most extensively validated projective technique." Similarly Manners and Durkin (2001, 56) say that "there is substantial support for the validity of the ego development theory and its measurement" as reflected in the Loevinger measure.

The Miner Sentence Completion Scales used in the research reported in this volume—although devoted primarily to organizational behavior objectives, not clinical ones, and failing of mention by the critics—also are based on the threefold criteria of aggregation, construct focus, and data-based development. I agree that these are among the ways to create a scientifically appropriate projective method.

The Tomkins-Horn Picture Arrangement Test

I introduce this particular projective measure, now largely outdated, in part because of my familiarity with it, but also because it presents methods of dealing with some of the concerns that have plagued projective techniques in general. The PAT has been discussed, and data derived from it explained, in Miner 2006a, Chapter 19. The test contains both picture arrangements (six per plate across twenty-five plates) and brief verbal descriptions for each arrangement selected. Scoring of the latter (in a manner similar to the TAT) has yielded evidence of validity as against criteria provided by high-level, presumably successful executives (Miner and Culver 1955). Studies of IBM tabulating machine operators used keys developed from the arrangements for the PAT and based on the normative material, as well as the verbal responses, to predict performance ratings These studies yielded very strong validities for work motivation, super-ego strength and overconformity (Miner 1960c; 1961b). A similar validity study using sales data as criteria was conducted with oil company dealer salesmen (Miner 1962a). Although the predictor characteristics found to work differed substantially from those of the machine operators, validity again was high.

Research was also conducted using the PAT on the effects of a caste system within the United States as of 1954. These studies identified such effects for both blacks (Karon 1958) and whites (Karon 1973), thus giving further credence to the PAT's validity.

The work with the PAT was important for a number of reasons. There was good evidence for validity, often using performance criteria, rather than clinical, thus bringing the test into the domain of organizational behavior. Little such research involving a projective measure existed at the time. The PAT, consisting of line drawings, was only semi-ambiguous and served to focus attention on specific topics, work motivation and social relations in particular. The stimuli were standardized and sufficient in number (twenty-five) so that reliable measures could be derived (this in contrast to many versions of the TAT). The PAT norms (based on a representative sample of the United States population with N = 1,500) were to my knowledge the first such to be developed for a projective test. The keys for the arrangements provided a unique method for scoring the PAT that involved the derivation of rare scores.

Given that the development of the PAT and the creation of the original Miner Sentence Completion Scale that came to be known as Form H were in large part overlapping, I had the benefit of learning from these facets of the PAT experience in constructing the MSCSs. This overlap provided a great many inputs that have served me well as I carried out the research contained in this volume.

PROJECTIVE TECHNIQUES IN CONTRAST TO SELF-REPORT (OR OBJECTIVE) MEASURES

Two types of personality tests are often differentiated—projective techniques, which we have considered at length in the last section, and self-report measures (often termed objective). Meyer and Kurtz (2006) refer to the latter in the following way:

> For personality tests, the term *objective* typically refers to instruments in which the stimulus is an adjective, proposition, or question that is presented to a person who is required to indicate how accurately it describes his or her personality using a limited set of externally provided response options (true vs. false, yes vs. no, Likert scale, etc.). What is *objective* about such a procedure is that the psychologist administering the test does not need to rely on judgment to classify or interpret the test-taker's response; the intended response is clearly indicated and scored according to a pre-existing key. As a result, however, the necessity for judgment is passed on to the test taker. She must interpret the question, consider her personal characteristics, evaluate herself relative to others as best she can, decide the extent to which the characteristics fit her personality, and then choose whether to honestly convey this information in her response (223).

Terming such a measure "objective" is, in the context of science, clearly intended to introduce a value-laden label. Accordingly I will retain the more descriptive self-report measure; all personality tests have some potential for error of one kind or another.

Now that we have some indication of the difference between projectives, with the potential to encompass unconscious motivation, and self-report measures, with less of this type of motivation, we need to look for other differentiating factors. This does not take us far afield: The dominant motives on the projective side are achievement, power, and affiliation as reflected in the TAT; on the self-report side they are the big five personality characteristics—extraversion, agreeableness, conscientiousness, emotional stability, and openness to experience (intellect) as reflected in the lexical studies (Saucier and Goldberg 2003). These variables indicate little by way of a common ground.

The McClelland, Koestner, and Weinberger (1989) Theory

In further pursuit of these differences let us look into the theorizing that emerged from McClelland, Koestner, and Weinberger (1989) appearing in the *Psychological Review:*

> Implicit motives [projectives] generally sustain spontaneous behavioral trends over time because of the pleasure derived from the activity itself, whereas the self-attributed motives predict immediate responses to structured situations (690).
>
> . . . implicit motives have generally been found to predict operant behaviors and self-attributed motives have been found to predict respondent behaviors (695).
>
> . . . self-attributed motives result in better performance if they are explicitly aroused by appropriate incentives. . . . Implicit motives may energize behavior more in the sense that

> they lead to more frequent activity of a certain type because it is pleasurable, even in the absence of specific social demands (296–297).
>
> This . . . suggests a number of important implications:
>
> 1. The implicit motives seem most likely to be built on affective experiences with natural incentives early in life.
> 2. It should be possible for implicit motives like n Achievement or n Power to develop in animals without language so long as the species responds to the natural incentives on which these motives are based.
> 3. Because the implicit motives are apparently built on direct experiences of affect also characteristic of animals, it seems likely that these motives are mediated by more primitive midbrain structures than are the self-attributed motives that would be subserved by the highly developed cerebral cortex, in which language is processed.
> 4. Even though stories written to pictures obviously involve the use of language (and hence the cerebral cortex), it seems likely that they are more successful than self-reports in reflecting implicit motives because they provide a more direct readout of motivational and emotional experiences than do self-reports.
> 5. The cognitive, information-processing model of human motivation in terms of needs, plans, and goals describes the way self-attributed motives function much better than the way implicit motives function.
> 6. The distinction between the two types of motives is very similar to a distinction made by memory theorists . . . between explicit and implicit, or episodic and semantic memory (697–698).

All this is predicated on the assumption that the two types of motives are uncorrelated with each other, a finding consistent with the evidence cited by the authors. Thus when both types of measures are incorporated in a prediction equation the result will be to "improve prediction of performance" (692).

The essentially uncorrelated nature of the relationship between implicit and explicit measures seems to be well-established (see Schultheiss and Brunstein 2001). Yet there are situations where the overlap is sufficient to indicate a positive relationship (Bornstein 2002); such results cannot be ruled out.

Comparisons with the Minnesota Multiphasic Personality Inventory (MMPI)

The MMPI and the Rorschach measures ostensibly deal with the same constructs, yet they do not converge statistically (Meyer 1996). These two nonoverlapping instruments when used together yield a multiple correlation of 0.35; thus both contribute in their own way to the diagnostic process (Huprich 2006, 238). The Board of Trustees for the Society for Personality Assessment (2005) had the following to say in this regard:

> In a meta-analytic comparison of criterion-related validity coefficients for the MMPI and for the Rorschach, we found both instruments to have validity effect sizes of substantial magnitude (unweighted mean *r* of .30 and .29 for the MMPI and Rorschach, respectively). Validity estimates for the MMPI and Rorschach were not reliably different from each other (221).

The MMPI is a self-report measure; it has undergone several revisions in scoring, norming, and item content over the years (Meyer 2006). The latest revisions have introduced some uncertainty into what was long a widely accepted instrument. The current feeling is that these newest scales should be used with caution, that they may mislead clinical inference, and that further studies are needed (Nichols 2006; Simms 2006). Thus, while projective techniques are providing widespread evidence of advance and moving toward stability, this particular self-report measure is undergoing a period of instability. Indeed some evidence is beginning to emerge to the effect that while the Rorschach can operate to demonstrate diagnostic value, the MMPI fails in this regard under similar circumstances (Ritsher 2004).

Comparisons with the Big Five Personality Characteristics

I have noted that the big five characteristics typify the self-report approach to measuring personality. In general five-factor tests are applied in the domain occupied by organizational behavior and not in the clinical area. Yet exceptions exist. For instance psychopathic individuals have been found to be characterized by low agreeableness, low conscientiousness, high extraversion, and both elevations and depressions on facets of neuroticism (Miller and Lynam 2003). A need exists for studies that duplicate the MMPI research in that projective-big five relationships are established.

Various approaches to measuring the five characteristics exist; there is no one test involved (see Paunonen and Nicol 2001). The model is predicated on the idea that the degree of representation of an attribute in language (not just English) has some degree of correspondence with the general importance of that attribute in real world transactions. When such a lexical approach is applied, variable selection is not so much a matter for the expert, but is entrusted to a disinterested source (the dictionary). The big five factors have substantial bandwidth and are clearly important dimensions of personality; there is general, though not total, agreement as to their nature, but at a more specific level, as it were, reporting to them, are a host of facets. These facets vary from test to test and this constitutes a real scientific problem (Saucier and Goldberg 2003).

Thus what appears to be a very orderly variable structure (with five factors) breaks down at the next hierarchic level into a raging controversy involving alternative facets. This disorganization raises serious problems of construct validity, and what was a high level of reliability at the superordinate level now becomes much more diluted (McGrath 2005). The problem here is whether there is some particular justifiable lower order structure to follow upon the big five (Roberts, Walton, and Viechtbauer 2006). The answer at present appears to be that there is not. At the same time the usefulness of the big five themselves (in predicting leadership behaviors, for example) does not appear to be in doubt (Judge, Bono, Ilies, and Gerhardt 2002).

On the Imperfections of Self-report Measures

I have noted some of the problems that have arisen as particular self-report approaches are researched and applied, but here my concern is to deal with problems inherent in the self-report concept itself. My goal is not to imply that such an approach is too error-laden to be viable; we know this is not the case. Rather my objective is to point up certain inherent limitations.

First, it is well-established that self-assessments of skill, expertise, knowledge, and character are often flawed in substantive and systematic ways. In empirical fact their relationship to actual behavior and even to internal experience is often tenuous and at best modest (Dunning, Heath, and Suls 2004). In part erroneous self-assessments occur because people lack the information needed to make more accurate determinations. Furthermore error often occurs because people neglect relevant information that is in fact available to them; they could take steps to overcome their flaws in judgment, but they do not. Self-report techniques can only be as effective as the capabilities of the person permit.

To some degree these errors reflect a desirability bias, a tendency to be overoptimistic about some future outcome. An analysis of the evidence on this phenomenon yields the following conclusion:

> Although our review indicates that research findings on the desirability bias are mixed, we are not suggesting that this bias does not exist or that desires do not influence predictions (Krizan and Windschitl 2007, 116).

It seems evident that desirability bias can operate on occasion to distort self-reports.

A second factor in the imperfections of self-report measures is that evidence is beginning to accumulate in support of the McClelland, Koestner, and Weinberger (1989) theory of implicit motivation (Rudman 2004). Implicit attitudes do appear to stem from past and largely forgotten experiences; explicit attitudes from recent, more accessible events. Implicit attitudes, in contrast with explicit, are more sensitive to affective experience, and they appear to be more subject to influence by aspects of the cultural milieu.

A third consideration reflects more conscious motivational factors. One study compared self-report test data obtained under selection conditions (where the desire to look good is paramount) with data obtained under development conditions (where the motivation to distort is minimal). It indicates that "applicant response distortion increases personality scale means" (Ellingson, Sackett, and Connelly 2007, 393)—not to a large extent, but significantly so. This study was not designed to consider big five characteristics and thus does not assess the effects on items of this type. It focuses on intentional distortion, although self-deception, which is described as being unconscious in nature, may also operate in such cases. Self-deception is said to be constant in this research and to be independent of the assessment purpose; the study cannot shed light on unconscious motivation of this kind. To the authors' credit there is no "missing unconscious" here, but any method of measurement that does not tap into unconscious factors (such as self-reports) is inevitably at a disadvantage in contrast to measurement methods that do (such as projectives).

CHAPTER 2

UNCONSCIOUS MOTIVATION AS VIEWED FROM THE NEW UNCONSCIOUS PERSPECTIVE

In the last chapter I noted a number of definitions and uses applied to the case of unconscious motivation, some of which derive from the new unconscious perspective. Among these formulations are those proposed by Dijksterhuis and Nordgren (2006), Locke and Latham (2002; 2004), and Hassin, Uleman, and Bargh (2005), which set forth the new unconscious perspective in various ways.

Also in Chapter 1 this new unconscious was attributed to a research stream that had its origins in experimental psychology. However, this line of research is also associated with social psychology on occasion (see Stajkovic, Locke, and Blair 2006) and much of it is closely allied with personality theory. Thus it seems appropriate to conclude that all three disciplinary orientations are often involved.

How new is this new unconscious? It appears to have gotten started in the early 1980s, and has been gathering steam since (see Bargh and Pietromonaco 1982). A recent book, *The New Unconscious,* edited by Hassin, Uleman, and Bargh (2005) surveys important developments that have occurred within the framework of this new unconscious perspective. This book provides a useful overview of the subject matter, and I use it to introduce this particular perspective on research on the unconscious (in addition to the projective perspective as presented in Chapter 1). In general this approach tends to consider the formulations of psychoanalysis regarding the unconscious as somewhat antiquated and unscientific, even though the terminology of psychoanalysis is incorporated on occasion.

FUNDAMENTAL QUESTIONS

The book starts with a discussion of how controlled processes of the type initiated by unconscious motivation might be explained (see Daniel Wegner in Hassin, Uleman, and Bargh 2005, 19–36). Either explicitly or implicitly such explanations often carry with them the assumption of a kind of homunculus within the head—a little person within the person, who does the controlling. This supposition is, however, rejected because it "undermines the possibility of a scientific theory of psychology by creating an explanatory entity that cannot itself be explained" (20). Rather the operation of controlled processes is part of the mental mechanism that creates the sense of a conscious will. "The way the mind seems to its owner is the owner's best guess at its method of operation, not a revealed truth" (33). What is really involved, however, is the activation of unconscious motivation processes by patterns of environmental features. More on this may be found in Bargh (1990).

The next chapter of the book presents the essence of the new unconscious view (John Bargh in Hassin, Uleman, and Bargh 2005, 37–58). The major point is as follows:

> The priming and the patient studies do complement and support each other in demonstrating the same two principles: that an individual's behavior can be directly caused by the current environment, without the necessity of an act of conscious choice or will; and that this behavior can and will unfold without the person being aware of its external determinants (39).

Human behavior cannot be explained in terms of conscious processes alone because it is too complex and requires much greater capacity than is possible within a conscious agenda; thus unconscious phenomena must be brought into play. "The classic phenomenon demonstrating a disassociation between conscious will and behavior is hypnosis" (48). Actually consciousness tends to drop out of the cognitive process when it is no longer needed; a primary reason for deploying consciousness only as needed is its limited capacity aspect as demonstrated in research on ego-depletion in the face of conscious choice. One of the reasons for conscious processing may in fact be the elimination of the need for it later on. "The evolved purpose of consciousness turns out to be the creation of even more complex nonconscious processes" (53).

BASIC MECHANISMS

Subcortical Brain Mechanisms

A subsequent chapter presents the evidence from neuroscience regarding the locus of unconscious processes. The amygdala in the lower brain appears to be in large part specialized to emotions and their operations; much of the research deals with fear reactions, but it goes beyond that.

In addition the amygdala influences cognitive awareness in various ways:

- the amygdala alters our ability over time to consciously recollect events that are emotional and important.
- the amygdala can modulate perception and attention by increasing the likelihood that emotional information in the environment will break through to cognitive awareness (Elizabeth Phelps in Hassin, Uleman, and Bargh 2005, 73).

Subliminal Perception

The idea of subliminal perception, like unconscious motivation in general, makes many people uncomfortable (see the discussion of the missing unconscious in Chapter 10 of this volume). Considerable evidence in support of subliminal perception has accumulated, however (see Ap Dijksterhuis, Henk Aarts, and Pamela Smith in Hassin, Uleman, and Bargh 2005, 77–106). Going back to Bargh and Pietromonaco (1982) clear evidence has existed that subliminally activated trait characteristics (for example, hostility) influence the impression we have of others. Both supraliminal and subliminal exposures have the same effects. The impact is most pronounced for attitudes, much less for behavior; and it is more likely for visual than for auditory stimuli. "Evidence is definitely strong enough to say that commercial applications of subliminal stimulation can, in principle, work" (97). Based on this type of evidence Dijksterhuis and Nordgren (2006) have proposed a theory of unconscious thought indicating that in large part unconscious thought is superior to the more limited-capacity conscious processes; a case in point is said to be creative thinking.

Similarity Processing

A great deal of research has been conducted on the influences exerted by similarities, often in an unconscious manner (see Arthur Markman and Dedre Gentner in Hassin, Uleman, and Bargh 2005, 107–137). These similarity processes remain active at all times and the comparison processes involved need not be under conscious control; in fact, they may produce results that are not available to consciousness. When similarities among items exist, they may unintentionally influence cognitive processes, in that attention may be devoted to activities selected by other than intentional similarities.

Unconscious Volition

Evidence from research on automatic emotional reactions indicates that—

> the human mind is capable of maintaining unconscious vigilance over its own automatic processes. This suggests a volitional nature of the unconscious. . . . People can unconsciously monitor and correct for bias in judgments, just as they might consciously. . . . Demonstrations of the effects of chronic ideological goals (e.g. egalitarianism) on suppressing automatic, and therefore previously presumed uncontrollable, responses bolster the thesis of unconscious volition. . . . This thesis, and the findings supporting it, represents a departure from traditional conceptions of the unconscious as passive and reactive, suggesting an unconscious that is paradoxically, "aware" (Jack Glaser and John Kihlstrom in Hassin, Uleman, and Bargh 2005, 189–190).

Unconscious Control and Working Memory

Working memory is most closely associated with controlled, conscious mental processes. It is the home base of conscious awareness, or at least it has been assumed to be. Yet implicit insights that are of an unconscious nature have been found to derive from working memory. Thus these results indicate that the "cognitive components of working memory can, at least under some circumstances, operate outside of conscious awareness" (Ran Hassin in Hassin, Uleman, and Bargh 2005, 211). It follows that cognitive control may operate in the same manner. The evidence is clear that motivational aspects of working memory can engage other than conscious processes. The conclusion appears to be that unconscious control, as well as conscious, serves to permit flexibility in adjusting both behavior and thought to the surrounding environment and to the pursuit of goals.

PERCEIVING AND ENGAGING OTHERS

Unintended Communication and Perception

In their everyday social interactions people give off many signals that permit others to make numerous inferences about them. Displaying such characteristics via nonverbal behavior is essentially an automatic process. The research leads to a conclusion that "the interpretation of cues to others' personality traits can occur without effort, intention, or awareness" (Susan Choi, Heather Gray and Nalini Ambady in Hassin, Uleman, and Bargh 2005, 311). Furthermore, attempts to exercise conscious control in such situations can have negative consequences. In a research setting, subjects asked to deliberate in detail demonstrated reduced judgment; by contrast, judges in social contexts were more accurate when required to provide instant reactions under conditions that fostered the use of intuition. Certainly people do exert conscious control in social situations, but the evidence indicates that a great deal of what happens is achieved unconsciously.

Automatic Imitation

There is considerable research to indicate that often people mimic one another without being aware of it; they do this using words, facial expressions, mannerisms, moods, and emotions:

> Merely perceiving another person saying, feeling, or doing something makes us more likely to say, feel, and do the same thing. . . . Mimicry . . . expresses similarity which in turn builds empathy, liking, rapport, and affiliation. . . . This occurs regardless of whether the goal is temporary or chronic, consciously pursued or nonconsciously primed. . . . People use nonconscious mimicry to further their own goals. This suggests that on an implicit level, individuals know of the affiliative function that mimicry serves (Tanya Chartrand, William Maddux, and Jessica Lakin in Hassin, Uleman, and Bargh 2005, 356–357).

Implicit Impressions

Let us start with the following assumptions:

- Implicit impressions exist, and there is good experimental support for them.
- Implicit impressions affect trait judgments of others.
- Implicit and explicit impressions of the same person can be held simultaneously, and their

> effects can be empirically distinguished (James Uleman, Steven Bladder, and Alexander Todorov in Hassin, Uleman, and Bargh 2005, 363).

Thus implicit (nonconscious) impressions do exist, and there is considerable support to be found for them. Errors and biases can occur in the case of intentional impressions, but they are equally likely in the case of implicit impressions; indeed some errors are inherent in implicit impressions per se. Thus incorrectly attributing certain traits seems more likely to occur under implicit than intentional (conscious) circumstances: "Rigorous demonstrations [exist] that incidental encounters with others leave impressions that persist long after the details of the encounter have faded from memory. . . . After an encounter trait ratings of actors were based on both explicitly remembered (controlled) and implied (automatic) impressions. Two days later, only implicit impressions had any effect" (388). Further research on such matters is contained in Willis and Todorov (2006).

Accessibility Bias in Perception

A further chapter of Hassin, Uleman, and Bargh (2005) deals with a process dissociation approach whereby implicit attitudes serve as a basis for guessing that enters into perception and thus produces an accessibility bias (Keith Payne, Larry Jacoby, and Alan Lambert in Hassin, Uleman, and Bargh 2005, 393–420). Essentially this is a matter of the interplay or separation between conscious processes and unconscious. The former have been measured in the research with self-report indexes; the latter with measures such as sentence completion tests. More often than not the two prove to be uncorrelated (see Chapter 1) and thus to provide independent measures of conscious and unconscious processes.

Under certain circumstances individuals may become aware of what is initially unconscious. Accordingly it can be possible to exercise control over previously unconscious processes. This, of course, is what psychoanalysis has been predicated on for many years, and is the reason for resorting to the interpretation process in psychotherapy. Making the unconscious conscious can help serve to get it under control. The research to this effect is quite convincing.

Significant Others, Transference, and the Unconscious Relational Self

Significant others are conceptualized as those having an impact on a person and with whom that person is emotionally invested—parents, siblings, certain members of any extended family, lovers, spouses, best friends, mentors, close colleagues, and psychotherapists. Aspects of such relationships tend to be called to the fore in new relationship situations and this is called transference (a term derived from psychoanalysis wherein therapists are seen to take on the positive and negative emotionality invested in a parent).

The authors of a chapter on these phenomena report the following:

> we present a wide array of findings that address these issues and support four main conclusions about the unconscious self:
>
> 1. Significant-other representations are activated automatically in transference.
> 2. Affect arises relatively automatically in transference when the significant-other representation is activated.
> 3. The relational self is activated automatically when the significant-other representation is activated.

4. Some self-regulatory processes in the relational self are evoked in response to "threat" (e.g., negative cues) in transference and may be automatic (Susan Anderson, Inga Reznick, and Noah Glassman in Hassin, Uleman, and Bargh 2005, 423).

The authors indicate that they have direct evidence that significant-other representations can be activated unconsciously and with little or no effort; these representations have a high level of activation readiness. Unconscious transferences can operate to produce rigidity, however, and become maladaptive. At such times the introduction of conscious processes to achieve control may well become desirable.

SELF-REGULATION

Implementation Intentions

Implementation intentions create a link between some specific future situation and a particular response in the service of goal achievement. They are in fact plans with the added benefit that they provide heightened accessibility. "By forming implementation intentions people can strategically switch from conscious and effortful action initiation (guided by goal intentions) to having their goal-directed actions effortlessly elicited by the specified situational cues" which serve to prime the activities in pursuit of goals unconsciously (Peter Gollwitzer, Ute Bayer, and Kathleen McCulloch in Hassin, Uleman, and Bargh 2005, 488).

In this way individuals protect themselves against any negative consequences of ego depletion. Goal pursuits planned with the aid of implementation intentions run off in an automatic manner, invulnerable to adverse influences either in the environmental situation or in the individual. Research has shown that they operate in an unconscious manner, and provide "an effective way to bridge the gap that exists between our best intentions and the successful attainment of our goals" (511).

Sources of Conflict and Unconscious Motivation

Two additional chapters take up research into how unconscious factors may arise out of conscious strivings. One example is described as follows:

> I have presented evidence for the conclusion that unintended thought is also a product of the rational use of basic self-regulatory strategies. Motivation strategies like eagerness and vigilance have critical benefits that people would not want to give up. However, our use of motivational strategies has unintended side effects of which we are unaware (Tory Higgins in Hassin, Uleman, and Bargh 2005, 533).

A second instance deals with counteractive control as follows:

> It is necessary to take into account self-control processes in predicting the motivational and behavioral consequences of priming a motive. When the primed motive threatens the attainment of long-term goals, people may engage in counteractive control that shields these goals against the primed motive. . . . Counteractive control is an effortful process. . . . Exercising self-control in one task depletes a person's ability to exercise self-control in a subsequent task. . . . Evidence for implicit counteractive self-control has been obtained. . . .

Counteractive control strategies may be automatized (Yaacov Trope and Ayelet Fishback in Hassin, Uleman, and Bargh 2005, 545, 555, 559, 561).

ADDENDUM ON THE NEW UNCONSCIOUS PERSPECTIVE

The sum total of the various chapters in Hassin, Uleman, and Bargh (2005) is that evidence pointing from many directions indicates that unconscious motivation is a recurring reality. However, there is even more evidence. An analysis of various types of projections, as considered in Chapter 1 of this volume, indicates that these processes occur independent of conscious awareness; "the results of the three studies reported provide evidence that people project their implicit and explicit goals onto others" (Kawada, Oettingen, Gollwitzer, and Bargh 2004, 553). The findings indicate that both positive and negative goals may be projected, suggesting that goal projection may well act to serve self-defensive and self-enhancing purposes. Thus the data are consistent with hypotheses derived from psychoanalysis, although they may be derived from other sources as well.

This matter of goal pursuit has been the subject of considerable research (see Bargh, Gollwitzer, Lee-Chai, Barndollar, and Trötschel 2001; Fitzsimons and Bargh 2004). Goals need not be activated only by conscious choices. Rather they may be primed unconsciously by environmental cues. Whatever the source, once activated these goals continue to operate in accordance with procedures known to apply when the activation is entirely conscious. Shifting goal pursuit from conscious to unconscious mechanisms serves an adaptive purpose in that the goal continues to govern even when new and difficult circumstances exist.

Nonconscious processes of this kind may guide both memory and attention. They may qualify as self-regulation; thus—

> To claim the existence of "automatic self-regulation," we must show both that the phenomenon is automatic by standard criteria and also qualifies as self-regulation. For it to be truly *automatic,* it must not require conscious, intentional, interventions, neither in the selection of the goal to pursue in the situation nor in the guidance of behavior toward that goal. The experimental evidence . . . is consistent with this claim. For it to be truly *self-regulation,* it must adapt thought, emotion, or behavior to the demands of both the current situation and the individual's own goal(s) within that situation. The evidence supports this part of the claim as well (Fitzsimmons and Bargh 2004, 156).

Self-regulation of this kind occurs more efficiently and also more consistently than its conscious counterpart. Similar processes serve to activate behaviors in pursuit of social norms and other aspects of culture.

> Research bearing on these matters includes the following: Subtle priming of the stereotype of the elderly (which includes the notions that the elderly are forgetful, as well as physically slow and weak) caused college students to walk more slowly when leaving the experimental session . . . and to subsequently have poorer memory for the features of a room (in another)—both effects predicted from the content of that stereotype. Stereotypes associated with social roles produce similar effects: Priming the professor stereotype led to students answering a greater number of questions correctly in a trivia game. . . . Other people, their characteristic features, the groups they belong to, the social roles they fill, and whether or not one has a close relationship with them have all been found to be automatic triggers of important psychological and behavioral processes (Bargh and Williams 2006, 2–3).

At this writing the most up-to-date compendium on the new unconscious is a book by Bargh (2007). This volume is intended as a sourcebook for researchers; it contains chapters on the component features of automaticity, the effects of priming, close relationships, emotions, evaluations, and on various methodological approaches used to distinguish automatic and controlled processes.

In contrast with the 2005 volume the 2007 version is less wide-ranging in its coverage of the evidence for unconscious mechanisms, with somewhat greater depth on particular topics. It continues the practice of using individual chapters written by experts in the various areas, and indeed these contributors are also represented in the 2005 book in a third of the instances. There is considerable overlap in content; the chapters are much fewer and the pages less. All in all this presentation makes an ideal supplement to the material contained in Hassin, Uleman, and Bargh (2005).

ORGANIZATIONAL BEHAVIOR RESEARCH ON UNCONSCIOUS GOAL SETTING

All of what has been described is a product of psychology—experimental, social, and personality theory—but this research has begun to coalesce with organizational behavior. I have noted the uses to which the idea of an unconscious may be devoted proposed by Locke and Latham (2002; 2004) in Chapter 1. But there is more, in the form of specific research investigations, concerned with the matter of goal setting as related to task performance.

Two studies are reported in Stajkovic, Locke, and Blair (2006): a pilot study designed to determine whether priming was effective on tasks used previously in goal-setting research, and a main study conducted to link unconscious and conscious goals by examining the interaction involved.

The Pilot Study

The participants in this first study were seventy-six MBA students. Under priming conditions the requirement was that thirteen words be located, seven of which were achievement-related, in a 10 x 10 word matrix. Under control conditions all thirteen words were achievement-neutral. Performance was measured with a task, used frequently in previous goal-setting research, which required listing various uses for a common object within a five-minute period. Subsequently participants indicated their memory for the words in the puzzle and their awareness of any theme in these words (based on Bargh and Chartrand 2000). Students were eliminated from the study when—

- they failed to circle the prime words.
- they provided evidence that they were aware of the priming.

This left sixty-five usable participants, who were randomly assigned to experimental (prime) and control groups.

As hypothesized, priming had a positive impact on performance at the $p < .05$ level. The mean in the prime condition was 13.70 listed uses and in the control condition 10.72 uses. Accordingly evidence was found to exist that priming worked when applied to a task typically used in prior goal-setting research.

The Main Study

This design was extended to include consciously and unconsciously set goals in the main study, the hypothesis being that both approaches would have a significant impact. The initial sample was ninety-six undergraduate and graduate business students. Priming was via a scrambled sentence test (constructing a correct four-word sentence from a scrambled set). There were twenty sentences of which twelve included, once again, words that were achievement-related. The control condition used a test in which all words were achievement-neutral.

Performance was measured as in the pilot study. Conscious goal-setting involved conditions where the goals were (1) easy, (2) do your best, or (3) difficult as utilized in previous research. In accord with the criteria applied in the pilot research, seventy-eight participants qualified.

The results indicated a significant effect for unconscious goals ($p < .05$) and a similarly significant conscious goal effect ($p < .01$). Thus, both studies support the existence of a priming effect. The means for both difficult goals and for do-best goals were significantly above easy goals, but the two higher goals did not differ. Unconscious "goals significantly enhanced the effect of do-best and difficult goals but not that of easy goals" (Stajkovic, Locke, and Blair 2006, 1175).

Using an available sample of fifty-seven, neither conscious nor unconscious goals provided any change in results over a one-day interval. The findings from this research as a whole are discussed further in Latham (2007). Also priming effects obtained independent of conscious awareness have now been observed over much longer time intervals; in the latest study up to seventeen years (Mitchell 2006).

Preliminary Results of a Goal Conflict Study

In Locke and Latham (2006) the authors provide partial results of a study involving a proofreading task where primed speed goals and primed accuracy goals were crossed with conscious, assigned speed and accuracy goals, thus putting the two types of goals in conflict. When speed was the dependent variable, both conscious and unconscious goals showed significant main effects, but under conflict conditions partial neutralization was apparent. Also the effects of conscious speed goals were the most manifest. Unconscious priming had no apparent impact on accuracy while conscious goals had a pronounced effect.

MEMORY RESEARCH AND THE DYNAMICS OF REPRESSION

Among the descriptions of the unconscious given in Chapter 1 of this volume are several that derive from a psychoanalytic orientation and that make specific reference to repression (see Carr 2002 and Gabriel 1999). This term is rarely used by the proponents of the new unconscious and it does not appear in the index to Hassin, Uleman, and Bargh (2005). Yet it clearly has reference to unconscious processes; it needs to be considered here.

Sears (1943), in his review of the experimental evidence on psychoanalytic concepts, appears to be somewhat ambivalent on the subject of repression. Characteristically his overall assessment is a negative one; he uses words such as "trivial" and "discouraging" to describe the research and he indicates that the future of studies on the subject is not promising. Yet he offers some hope for research on the artificial creation of repression in a laboratory setting. Certainly the process does exist. Sears (1944) reiterates this conclusion.

In actual fact, over the years since, laboratory studies on facets of memory have begun to yield evidence on the workings of repression, and the unconscious processes that often underlie it. The best such evidence comes from Michael Anderson and his colleagues at the Memory Control Laboratory at the University of Oregon (see in particular Anderson 2006).

Memory and Forgetting

Research by those at the University of Oregon on memory and forgetting is quite extensive (Levy, McVeigh, Marful, and Anderson 2007; Anderson 2005; Johnson and Anderson 2004; Anderson, Ochsner, Kuhl, Cooper, Robertson, Gabrieli, Glover, and Gabrieli 2004; Anderson 2003; Levy and Anderson 2002). The consequence of this research has been a number of statements regarding its implications for repression:

- Repression has remained controversial for nearly a century on account of the lack of well-controlled evidence validating it. Here we argue that the conceptual and methodological tools now exist for a rigorous scientific examination of repression. . . . Repression is, in fact, a scientifically tractable problem. . . . Experimental psychology will no longer sweep repression under the rug (Anderson and Levy 2006, 512–513).
- What are the mechanisms by which human beings willfully control awareness of unwanted memories? . . . Although my colleagues and I view this question through the lens of cognitive psychology, the situation bears a strong resemblance to repression. . . . The resulting theory may not be identical to Freudian repression, but it clearly speaks to the situation characterized by Freud. . . . The end result may be impaired memory for the things that people avoid thinking about. This suggests that the think/no think paradigm of Anderson and Green (2001) may provide a useful laboratory model of the repression proposed by Freud. . . . It is now no longer possible to say that there is no mechanism that could possibly support repression. . . . If the proper experiments are conducted the current phenomena may have most of the core characteristics of repression envisioned by Freud (Anderson 2006, 328, 336, 340, 345).
- Our results establish a direct link between internal operations that control phenomenal awareness of a memory and its later accessibility. These findings thus support a suppression mechanism that pushes unwanted memories out of awareness, as posited by Freud (Anderson and Green 2001, 368).
- Our work does not demonstrate unconscious repression (Anderson and Levy 2002, 503).

Brain Mechanisms

Evidence in support of the activation of neural systems in the brain concomitant with the suppression of unwanted memories and thus keeping them from awareness has been obtained (Anderson, Ochsner, Kuhl, Cooper, Robertson, Gabrieli, Glover, and Gabrieli 2004; Anderson 2006). Functional magnetic resonance was used for this purpose. As hypothesized, prefrontal cortical and right hippocampal activity combined to predict the extent of forgetting. Thus a neurobiological process underlying motivated forgetting was demonstrated; "people suppress consciousness of unwanted memories by recruiting lateral prefrontal cortex to disengage the hippocampal processing that supports recollection" (Anderson 2006, 337).

The Controversy

A major disagreement with the Anderson et al. findings and interpretations has been mounted by Kihlstrom (2002), who feels that the Oregon researchers claim too much. This dissent is important because Kihlstrom is one of the more influential advocates of the new unconscious position (Hassin, Uleman, and Bargh 2005). Thus a controversy surrounds the evidence regarding repression. This controversy is developed further by Winerman (2005). This article describes research indicating that motivated forgetting works better when emotional content is involved than when it is absent. Winerman notes an instance of a failure to replicate the original results, but also presents results from a meta-analysis supporting the motivated forgetting position. On balance this report on the controversy achieves a level of objectivity that is to be applauded. Yet all parties are in agreement that unconscious repression has not to date actually been demonstrated. The mechanism to accomplish this has been identified, but not the fact of the matter, at least not as yet. A report on the state of this controversy subsequent to the article by Anderson et al. (2004) that appeared in *Science* is contained in O'Connor (2004).

CONCLUSIONS

Experimental research in the laboratory has moved a long way since the early Sears reports on repression. Over time we have come to accept a great deal more of the psychoanalytic position. Yet we are not fully home; the unconscious processes involved have not been completely explicated. A meeting of the minds between the new unconscious perspective and the Oregon perspective, and thus a melding of the research orientations advocated by the two groups, seems needed. But there are also disagreements regarding the role of psychoanalytic interpretations that appear to impede collaboration.

PART II

STUDIES THAT CONSIDER UNCONSCIOUS MOTIVE PATTERNS

CHAPTER 3

MANAGERS AT THE ATLANTIC REFINING COMPANY

INTRODUCTION

The Atlantic Refining Company research was published originally in the *Journal of Applied Psychology* (Miner 1960a), and supplemented later in Chapters 3, 4, 7, and 8 of a book (Miner 1965a). The latter materials supersede what is presented in the original article on occasion, and are given primary attention here. For one thing the experimental group was increased from fifty-five to fifty-six with the addition of an individual whose posttest was considerably delayed. Second, the concurrent validity sample was increased from eighty-one to one hundred in computing relationships with job grade, as new data became available. Third, rare scores were calculated using a normative sample of 160 managers from the same company rather than the original 120, thus producing more stable results and a number of changes. Finally item score findings were incorporated in the presentation for the first time. In hindsight the original publication appears to have been somewhat premature, and that situation is corrected in what follows.

This research represented the birth of the Miner Sentence Completion Scale (MSCS) which has come to be designated as Form H (for hierarchic); the scoring procedures for this measure are presented in a scoring guide (Miner 1964). It also represented the origination of managerial role motivation training, described briefly here, but elaborated in much more detail elsewhere (Miner 1963, 1966, 1975, 1985a). The Atlantic Refining Company research is considered in several other publications, and in particular publications aimed at practitioners and managers (Miner 1973a, 1974a).

The reader needs to be alerted that the following material derives from a period, the 1950s, in which the culture of the United States was considerably different than it is today. In particular in that culture men held almost all of the management positions in American industry, and The Atlantic Refining Company was no exception. In fact there was only one woman involved in any of the studies to be reported. This cultural reality is manifest in the company's staffing and in the wording of the instrument employed. In presenting the research I make no effort to hide this fact or to apologize for the cultural context in which the material was written; this is the way it was fifty years ago. The presentation is distinctively authentic.

The theory that developed from this research was in the grounded theory tradition (Glaser and Strauss 1967; Locke 2001); I was serving as a psychologist in the personnel research area at Atlantic at the time, and was very much a participant observer, not only in conducting the training but in guiding the research as well (Miner 2006a).

* * *

A number of studies (Asch 1951; Laughlin 1954; Mann 1957) have pointed to the effectiveness of group discussion and nondirective procedures in promoting attitude change and improved emotional adjustment. These findings are further supported by DiVesta's (1954) evaluation of a human relations course for military hospital administrators. This latter study is unique, however, in that both directive (lecture) and nondirective approaches to the subject matter seemed to produce similar positive effects. There is the suggestion here that nondirective procedures do not constitute a necessary condition for change. Apparently, training courses based on the lecture method can also have an effect on the attitudes of a group.

An opportunity to investigate this conclusion further was presented to the author when he was asked to conduct a course in psychology for seventy-two supervisors in the Research and Development (R&D) Department of a large corporation. Management appraisals carried out in the department had pointed to a situation which is apparently not uncommon in research groups of this type. A number of the supervisors had achieved their positions largely as a result of scientific accomplishments. Lacking interest in supervisory work, many had continued to emphasize individual research at the expense of supervisory responsibility. As a result, their subordinates were frequently given only a bare minimum of guidance, and the general level of performance in several of the research groups was below a satisfactory level. It was hoped that a course in psychology dealing with various facets of supervision might serve to foster a more favorable attitude toward supervisory work among these scientists, many of whom held graduate degrees in chemistry and engineering.

THE COURSE

Training was carried out during ten one-and-a-half-hour sessions given at weekly intervals. There were four groups. However, the membership of these groups tended to fluctuate somewhat as men shifted from one to another in accordance with the demands of their work. Participation in the course was not on a strictly voluntary basis. Most of the seventy-two men were asked to attend and attendance was recorded. The average man failed for one reason or another to participate in one of the ten sessions. There was no reading material either required or recommended and no examinations covering the content of the course were administered.

Although the course was primarily lecture-based, the groups were small enough to allow facilitation of discussion. The interaction was, however, almost exclusively between instructor and supervisor; rarely between one supervisor and another. The majority of these discussions dealt with questions directed to the instructor, questions aimed at clarifying points made during the lectures and obtaining information relevant to a specific situation the supervisor had faced. In addition, the instructor spent an average of at least a half-hour after each session discussing specific problems with individuals and smaller groups.

The lecture content was focused on the various reasons why a man might fail to perform effectively in the work situation. In this respect the lectures followed closely the category scheme detailed in *Breakdown and Recovery* (Ginzberg, Miner, Anderson, Ginsburg, and Herma 1959). There were frequent references to theoretical formulations and specific research studies. Every effort was made to present the material in a way that would give the supervisors a feeling of being in a position of responsibility, faced with the necessity of diagnosing the reasons behind the ineffective performance of a subordinate and taking appropriate action. Thus, those participating in the course were constantly reminded of their supervisory role throughout the sessions. In addition they were given information ostensibly intended to improve their understanding of other people. Many, no doubt, as the course progressed, began to relate this information to their own performance failures. During the final session this latter emphasis was made quite explicit. The focus shifted from the ineffective subordinate to the ineffective supervisor. Here, for the first time, an attempt was made to explain the sources of anxiety inherent in the supervisory role. Reference was made to the physical anxiety so commonly experienced by top level executives of large corporations (Miner and Culver 1955). This lecture took a form in many ways analogous to an expanded psychoanalytic interpretation.

The general nature of the material covered in each lecture is outlined below.

Lecture 1

This lecture presented the results of various studies carried out by the Survey Research Center of the University of Michigan (Kahn 1956; Kahn and Katz 1953) dealing with the differences between highly productive and less productive industrial work groups. Particular emphasis was placed on the role of the supervisor in fostering effective performance.

Lecture 2

The relationship between physical and intellectual factors and performance was discussed, the latter receiving major attention. The subjects covered included motor dexterity, theory of intelligence, special abilities, and job placement. Studies and theoretical formulations were drawn largely from Vernon (1950) and Miner (1957).

Lecture 3

A brief survey of studies dealing with the relationship between emotional factors and performance was followed by a more detailed analysis of the Markowe (1953) and Miner and Anderson (1958) researches. There was also some discussion of various psychosomatic disorders based on studies presented in *Life Stress and Bodily Disease* (Association for Research in Nervous and Mental Disease 1950), of alcoholism, and of methods of identifying emotional pathology.

Lecture 4

Although some attempt was made to discuss the literature on motivation in a general way, the primary emphasis was on work motivation. Considerable time was devoted to the subject of unconscious motivation following generally the position taken by Pederson-Krag (1955). Additional material dealing with the law of effect was drawn from Haire (1956).

Lecture 5

With this lecture the emphasis shifted from individual factors that might produce ineffective performance to group factors. The matter of a man's relationship to his family was discussed, drawing heavily on material presented in Ginzberg, Miner, Anderson, Ginsburg, and Herma (1959). The major framework was, however, industrial rather than military with particular attention devoted to performance while on business trips and foreign assignments.

Lecture 6

This lecture covered some of the material discussed during the introductory session. However, the work group, rather than the supervisor, constituted the major focus. An attempt was made to show how various characteristics of, and relationships within, the group might contribute to the ineffective performance of a group member. Cohesion, informal leadership, and the social isolate were among the topics discussed. Much of the material was drawn from Brown (1954).

Lecture 7

The primary emphasis was on the various ways in which organizational policy may affect both the performance of individual members and the standards against which they are evaluated. The subject of training and its relationship to performance was covered, as were sick leave policy, the handling of grievances, and layoffs.

Lecture 8

After a rather brief discussion of cultural values and the manner of their transmission, an attempt was made to demonstrate how conflicting values may contribute to ineffective performance. Much of the material was drawn from the Ginzberg volume (1959), especially that dealing with values placed on equity, freedom of choice, and morality. In addition there was some discussion of the problems that may arise when the value placed on individual freedom of choice by those with scientific training comes in conflict with the demands of the industrial situation.

Lecture 9

With this lecture another major shift occurred. Previous lectures dealt with factors within the individual, and factors related to various groups, all of which might have a negative impact on performance. Here the focus changed to the third major type of determinant—the situational. Within this category, which also includes economic and political conditions, and geographical location, the general topic of situationally aroused fear reactions was given primary consideration. Subjects covered were subjective and objective fear reactions, types of situations that may arouse anxiety, and the psychodynamics of phobic reactions.

Lecture 10

As indicated previously this final session focused explicitly on ineffective performance in the supervisory job. Again the emphasis was on situational factors, but the framework was further narrowed. The instructor returned to the results of the University of Michigan studies presented in the first lecture and attempted to show how the differences in behavior characteristic of supervisors with highly productive and less productive work groups might be attributed to differences in emotional response to the supervisory situation itself. Special note was made of the fact that even though a man was well informed as to effective methods of supervision, he might still be quite unable to utilize this knowledge, due to anxiety aroused by the supervisory situation.

THE EVALUATION PROCEDURE

A measure of attitude toward various aspects of supervisory work was developed and administered in the usual pre- and posttest design with a single control group. Participation in the evaluation study was on a voluntary basis and as a result only fifty-six of the seventy-two supervisors who completed the course actually were included. The remaining 22 percent failed to return the initial test and thus could not be included in the experimental group. There is no reason to believe that the inclusion of these additional supervisors would have materially altered the findings obtained. Nevertheless this possibility cannot be completely ruled out. The control group consisted of thirty supervisors within the (R&D) department who did not attend the course in psychology and who volunteered to participate in the study.

The evaluation instrument was a specially developed sentence completion test designed to measure attitude toward a number of aspects of the supervisory job. The test contained forty stems, only thirty-five of which were scored. The stems were deliberately selected to yield information on certain attitudes without at the same time revealing the purpose of the test. Thus, stems intended to produce answers indicative of attitudes toward authority figures included: My family doctor . . . ; as well as, Top management. . . . Actually, the majority of items referred to situations outside the work environment or not specifically related to the work environment; this in spite of the fact that the test was intended to measure attitudinal reactions characteristic of the man's working situation. As far as could be determined, the supervisors had no idea of what the test really measured and thus were in no position to select their responses in such a way as to give a good impression; nor could they consciously manipulate their answers with a view to predetermining the outcome of the study. In several of the groups there was some discussion of the evaluation instrument during the introductory session and a number of guesses were offered as to its purpose. Although highly imaginative, these guesses had little relationship to the true objective.

Each individual item response was scored as positive, neutral, or negative depending on whether or not there was an expression of attitude toward the activity, event, or individual specified in the stem, and on the direction of the attitude if one was in evidence. The thirty-five scorable items were selected to fall in seven different categories, each of which contained five items. The seven categories, typical items, and the general characteristics of responses labeled positive or negative are indicated below. On the average, approximately half of the items in a record were scored neutral because no attitude was indicated, or, although this was relatively rare, because of skipping. Ambivalent responses were considered negative.

1. Attitude toward Authority Figures

(My family doctor . . . ; Policemen. . . .) Positive attitude was indicated by any expression of liking, praise, respect, appreciation, confidence, or a feeling that better treatment is deserved. Negative attitude was indicated by any expression of criticism, negative emotional reactions, or a feeling that the rewards received are greater than deserved.

2. Attitude toward Competitive Games

(Playing golf . . . ; When playing cards, I. . . .) Positive attitude was indicated by any reference to attempting to win, interest in participation, pleasant emotional reactions, or physical sensations, and expectation of success. Negative attitude was indicated by any reference to a lack of interest in participation, unpleasant emotional reactions or physical sensations, expectation of failure, and criticism of the activity.

3. Attitude toward Competitive Situations Generally

(Running for political office . . . ; Final examinations. . . .) Positive and negative attitudes were scored essentially in the same manner as for competitive games.

4. Attitude toward Taking a Masculine (Assertive) Role

(Shooting a rifle . . . ; Wearing a necktie. . . .) Positive attitude was indicated by any expression of liking, positive physical sensation or emotional reaction, favorable opinion, being helped, wish to participate, or a feeling of confidence in one's ability to perform well. Negative attitude was indicated by any expression of dislike, negative emotional reaction or physical sensation, unfavorable opinion, lack of interest, or a wish not to participate. This subscale was subsequently renamed Assertive Role.

5. Attitude toward Imposing One's Wishes on Others

(Punishing children . . . ; When one of my men asks me for advice. . . .) Positive attitude was indicated by references to positive emotional reactions, wishes for participation, liking or being interested in the activity, favoring participation, association of the activity with success, and any evidence that the man actually does impose his wishes on others. Negative attitude was indicated by references to negative emotional reactions, a wish not to participate, the undesirability of the activity, and any suggestion that the man either does not impose his wishes on others, or characteristically fails in attempting to do so.

6. Attitude toward Standing Out from the Group

(Presenting a report at a staff meeting . . . ; Making introductions. . . .) Positive attitude was indicated by reference to positive emotion, expectation of success, the helpfulness of the activity, favorable opinion, liking, interest, or a wish to participate. Negative attitude was indicated by reference to dislike, failure to function effectively in the situation, negative emotional reactions, criticism of the activity, or a wish not to participate.

7. Attitude toward Routine Administrative Functions

(Dictating letters . . . ; Decisions. . . .) Positive attitude was indicated by any expression of a wish to participate, positive emotions, favorable opinion, positive physical sensation, liking, and any evidence that the man either does participate in the activity or feels it to be helpful. Negative attitude was indicated by any expression of a wish not to participate, negative physical sensation or emotional reaction, criticism, or a suggestion of poor performance in the situation.

These characteristics were selected as being among those required for effective performance in the supervisory job. It was assumed that a supervisor should have a reasonably favorable attitude toward authority figures, should like competitive situations or at least not dislike them, should prefer the masculine role, should have no difficulty in bringing himself to impose his wishes on others, should not wish to avoid standing out from the group, and should be willing to perform routine administrative functions. The more positive his attitude toward such things the more effective his performance. Evidence on the validity of these assumptions will be presented after a brief discussion of the scoring procedure.

The responses of a normative group consisting of 160 managers employed by The Atlantic Refining Company in various functions including research, engineering, human resources, sales, accounting, and finance were categorized as positive, negative, or neutral. Keys consisting of all combinations of the five items in a category were then constructed. There were thirty-one such keys for each characteristic—those based on taking the items one at a time, two at a time, three at a time, four at a time, and five at a time. The responses of the normative group were then matched against the keys, and those keys—usually those with a larger number of items—that yielded rare frequencies, which were met by 5 percent or less of the normative sample, were noted. Each key was scored for positive and negative responses separately so that there were actually sixty-two keys for each of the seven characteristics. Any individual who gave a pattern of either positive or negative responses to a given set of five items that matched one of the keys previously found to be rare in the normative group was considered as possessing either a positive or negative attitude toward that particular aspect of the supervisory job. This procedure is similar to that employed in scoring the Tomkins-Horn Picture Arrangement Test. The rationale on which it is based has been presented elsewhere (Tomkins and Miner 1957, 1959).

In addition to the seven categories already noted, an eighth was developed, based on the patterning of responses throughout the total test. This might be considered a measure of attitude toward the supervisory job as a whole rather than some specific aspect. Within each of the seven categories the five items were ranked in the order of the frequency with which they elicited positive responses in the normative group. Five keys were then constructed—one for each level of rank—each containing seven items. These keys were then combined to form keys of 14, 21, 28, and 35 items in the same manner as individual items had been combined previously. There were thus 31 keys for positive attitudes and, after a similar procedure had been carried out based on the frequencies for negative responses in the normative group, 31 keys for negative attitudes. In the case of these more general keys the matching against an individual's response pattern was carried out to determine whether he had met the key on enough items to yield a rare. It was not a matter, as previously, of noting whether the key in toto was rare in the normative group. All of these keys were rare by this definition. Rather the matching was carried out to determine whether the individual had met the key a sufficient number of times to mark him as exceeding 95 percent of the normative group. This procedure is identical to that employed with the Tomkins-Horn Picture Arrangement Test.

For the purposes of this study no attempt was made to determine how many rares an individual might have obtained on keys within a given category. If a rare was found on at least one key that was enough to label his attitude as positive or negative. An individual's total score on the test was the sum of his positive rares (maximum possible, 8) minus the sum of his negative rares (maximum possible, 8). This total score could vary from –8 through 0 to +8; it is called the Rare Score.

The reliability of the scoring was checked by rescoring twenty MSCS records at a four-month interval. There was perfect agreement in assigning rares on 96.9 percent of the subscales; the average error within the Rare Scores was 0.25 per record. On individual items there was 95.4 percent agreement, and the average error in the Item Scores was 1.6.

An estimate of the overall reliability of the instrument was obtained by comparing pre- and posttest scores for the control group. The *r* obtained was .84 with the Item Scores and .82 with the Rare Scores. Subscale reliabilities, with fewer items (5), range from .44 to .63; median .48. All these values are without question underestimates considering the time interval involved and changes occurring during this interval. The Item-Rare Score correlation is .84.

Validity was evaluated by comparing the scores with management appraisal ratings obtained in the R&D department approximately a year and a half prior to the initial testing. The results of these comparisons are presented in Table 3.1 along with those based on job grades. The ratings represent the pooled judgment of the man's immediate supervisor, that man's superior, and a representative of the Industrial Relations Department. The performance rating was made on a 10-point scale and represented an overall judgment of the man's present job performance. In addition to leadership, the judges specifically considered such matters as technical competence, motivation, effective intelligence, and emotional stability prior to making their ratings. For this reason the ratings cannot be considered a pure measure of supervisory skill. Even if perfect validity were present they would not yield a high correlation with the sentence completion test. They contain too many components other than supervisory skill. The same must be said of the potential for advancement ratings. These, too, contain a variety of components. However, in the case of the rather large number of men whose present jobs required only a minimum of supervisory responsibility, the weighting given to supervisory skill is probably considerably greater in the potential ratings than in the performance ratings.

Table 3.1

Correlations between MSCS Rare and Item Scores and Various Indexes of Occupational Success in Samples of Research and Development Managers

	Indexes of Success		
MSCS Measures	Job Grade Level (N = 100)	Performance Rating (N = 81)	Potential Rating (N = 81)
Total Scores			
Item	.24*	.20	.31**
Rare	.40**	.24*	.43**
Subscale Item Scores			
Authority Figures	.12	.28**	.21*
Competitive Games	.10	.02	.20*
Competitive Situations	.45**	.21*	.36**
Masculine (Assertive) Role	.07	.05	–.04
Imposing Wishes	.06	.29**	.24*
Standing Out from Group	.12	.10	.32**
Routine Administrative Functions	.15	–.04	–.05

Note: MSCS = Miner Sentence Completion Scale.
$^*p < .05$; $^{**}p < .01$

RESULTS

The pre- and posttest comparisons (Table 3.2) reveal a significant rise in the scores obtained by the experimental group and a significant decline in the controls. Using the Rare Score as an indicator, 59 percent of the experimental subjects were higher at posttest, 20 percent remained the same, and 21 percent decreased. Among the latter group many may well have declined because of factors external to the course. It is doubtful that the experimental conditions themselves caused the decrease.

This interpretation is reinforced by the control group findings. From the Rare Score means it appears that the control managers actually declined in role-relevant motivation during the period of the course. Although the Item Score change does not quite reach significance at the .05 level, it tends to yield essentially the same conclusion. Among the 30, only 17 percent increased their Rare Scores during the pretest-posttest period, 43 percent stayed at an identical level, and 40 percent shifted in a negative direction.

When the two groups are compared it becomes evident that the Rare Scores differed by only a negligible amount at pretest ($t = 0.30$). At posttest a sizable difference had emerged ($t = 2.98$, $p < .01$). The Item Scores were somewhat farther apart at pretest ($t = 0.76$), and it is largely because of this fact that the posttest difference does not attain accepted levels of significance ($t = 1.77$, $p < .10$). From the evidence it would appear that the experimental course not only increased the MSCS scores of those exposed to it, but also served to ward off the effects of certain external environmental factors that produced a general decline in role-related motivation within the R&D department's management as a whole. Although it remains possible that the repeated administration of the measuring instrument, and not some extra-experimental aspect of the departmental milieu, might account for the decrease among the controls, this seems unlikely in view of the subscale findings.

A further breakdown of the Rare Score into its parts yields additional information on the change in the experimental group. The only reliable increase occurs in the number

Table 3.2

Mean MSCS Rare and Item Scores at Pretest and Posttest for Experimental and Control Groups of Research and Development Managers

	Experimental Group (N = 56)			Control Group (N = 30)		
MSCS Measures	Pretest Mean	Posttest Mean	*t*	Pretest Mean	Posttest Mean	*t*
Total Scores						
Item	4.66	6.77	3.35**	5.60	4.47	1.95
Rare	–.21	.80	3.48**	–.07	–.63	2.48*
Subscales Item Scores						
Authority Figures	.86	1.21	1.79*	1.43	1.33	
Competitive Games	1.32	1.52		1.30	1.27	
Competitive Situations	–.36	–.20		.10	–.50	2.61**
Masculine (Assertive) Role	.50	.75	1.50	.30	.07	
Imposing Wishes	.50	.89	1.79*	.47	.57	
Standing Out from Group	1.09	1.25		.80	.83	
Routine Administrative Functions	.77	1.34	2.48**	1.20	.90	

Note: MSCS = Miner Sentence Completion Scale.
$*p < .05$; $**p < .01$

of positive rares ($t = 3.91$, $p < .01$). The managers become more positively motivated to behave in accordance with managerial role requirements as a result of the course, but they did not characteristically lose any of their negative feelings. When the course was originally constructed, it was hoped that those individuals who had previously developed strong negative motivation with reference to certain aspects of the managerial role would gain insight into their emotional reactions as the training progressed, and consequently overcome many of their avoidant tendencies. This clearly did not occur on a widespread basis. At best, some of the managers may have been protected against certain external sources of negative motivation, which without the course would presumably have produced an even more negative attitude.

It is interesting to note, however, that this imbalance in the type of motivational change experienced does not characterize the control group. Unlike the experimentals, these subjects did not show a disproportionate modification of either a positive or a negative nature. While the number of positive rares went down and the number of negative rares up, the shifts were roughly equal and neither reliable alone.

The decline in scores among the controls was totally unexpected. It is conceivable that some factor associated with repeated measurement might be responsible, but this does not seem probable. An increase in scores as a result of a somewhat greater familiarity with the test would seem to be a possibility: Something comparable to a practice effect. But where a decrease of the kind found here occurs, it would seem more likely that some environmental factor, external to both the course and the measurement process, is responsible. This interpretation is reinforced by an analysis based on the individual MSCS subscales.

The data of Table 3.2 indicate that the only reliable change occurred on the Competitive Situations measure. Although with such a small sample this type of analysis is probably somewhat less sensitive than it should be, the difference between this one subscale and the others is striking. When Competitive Situations is excluded, the number of positive rares increases at posttest in two instances, stays the same in another two, and declines in three. Negative rares increase on three subscales, remain identical on one, and decrease on three. In no instance is the change greater than 10 percent. This pattern appears to be entirely consistent with what a chance model would predict.

The Competitive Situations measure, on the other hand, yields a decrease in the percentage of positive rares amounting to 17 percent and an increase in negative rares of 20 percent. These changes can hardly reflect the operation of chance factors, a conclusion which is further supported by the data of Table 3.2. When item scores are used to identify subscale changes, only Competitive Situations discriminates, and this time at the .01 level. Four of the other subscales decline and two increase, but none shift by more than .30. The Competitive Situations change is twice that large.

DISCUSSION

Although this study was originally designed to yield information regarding the impact of a course in psychology on attitudes toward supervisory work, it also appears to provide considerable insight into the effects of organizational change. Shortly after the course began, rumors of a shift in the organizational structure of the R&D department began to spread at a rather accelerated rate. These rumors had persisted over a period of several years, but without being given a great deal of credence. Now it became quite apparent that some change was inevitable. There was, however, no authoritative information available as to the exact nature of the reorganization, nor was there any clear-cut basis for predicting what personnel changes would be made. This state of uncertainty persisted until the end of the course. In fact it was not finally alleviated until a number of months later when several functions were shifted to another department.

It is, of course, possible that the increase in negative attitudes toward supervision found in the control group was totally unrelated to the prospect of organizational change. It seems probable, however, that the two were closely associated. One might hypothesize that a number of supervisors faced with a very uncertain future, sought a degree of security in increased allegiance to their present group. If such a banding together to ward off changes which might be introduced from the outside did occur, a reduction in the degree of emphasis on individual competition is not surprising. In fact the supervisors might well feel that individual competition was undesirable, since it would tend to break up the group's solidarity and make individual members more vulnerable. This is, of course, explanation after the fact. We do not know with certainty why competitive activity became so distasteful. Nevertheless, an explanation in terms of increased group solidarity in the face of external threat is not inconsistent with what we know of group dynamics.

Although the shift in control group scores provided the most unexpected outcome of the study, the persistence of negative attitudes within the experimental group was far from anticipated. Certainly the results of the present study cannot be taken as providing evidence for the efficacy of psychoanalytic interpretations in a lecture situation.

On the other hand there is considerable evidence that positive attitudes toward the supervisory job were aroused. Many who were previously neutral as regards certain aspects of their work developed more favorable viewpoints. In all probability this was a result of the way in which the men were treated. They were told again and again that they were supervisors and responsible for the performance of their subordinates. They were given some insight into the complexity that supervisory work could assume and into the difficulties associated with diagnosing the causal factors behind a given instance of ineffective performance. Many, apparently, began to view such things as getting others to do what they wanted and carrying out routine administrative functions with a new respect. It seems probable that this result is largely attributable to the specific type of lecture approach employed. Research studies and theoretical formulations which should be of value to those in supervisory jobs were emphasized. The material was specifically designed to appeal to the men in their supervisory role.

FOLLOW-UP WITHIN THE INITIAL STUDY

Although there is little question that attitude change was in fact produced by some aspect of the course, the question of permanency remains. Ever since the International Harvester studies (Fleishman, Harris, and Burtt 1955) it has been clear that attitude changes produced by a training program may well disintegrate under the impact of contradictory attitudes existing in the workplace. The possibility that the changes produced as a result of the present course were similarly short-lived cannot be ruled out. There are, however, two arguments suggesting that the favorable attitudes toward supervisory work had some permanency.

First, there is the manner in which the course was conducted. Contrary to the International Harvester situation, the men were not removed from their jobs and subjected to a period of concentrated training in a new location. The course was conducted in a conference room located in the same building as the offices where many of the men worked. Laboratories and pilot plant units were all nearby. The men left their work to attend sessions and returned to their jobs between one and a half and two hours later. Any attitude changes induced as a result of a given session had to meet the test of "job realities" for the ensuing week before the change could again be reinforced through training.

Secondly, due to certain exigencies of the industrial situation, it was not possible to administer the posttest questionnaire to all of the men immediately upon completion of the course. Within both experimental and control groups there was often considerable delay before the tests were filled out. Thirty-three of the experimental subjects did complete the questionnaire within two weeks of the time they finished the course; but the remaining twenty-three were delayed for various reasons, and the last test did not come in until the end of the seventh week. As a result there was a group of experimental subjects with posttests completed an average of approximately a week after training, and another group with an average interval of roughly a month. These were not randomly assigned samples. The men who completed the MSCS late were self-selected, and thus may have differed in a number of respects from those who responded with greater promptness. And these differences may have been such as to exert some influence on the MSCS scores. Yet, it does seem relevant to inquire into the results which emerge when these two groups of experimental subjects are compared.

The mean Rare Score change for the early posttest group was +1.06, and for the late group +0.96. The mean Item Score change for the early group was +2.15, and for the late subjects +2.05. In both cases the decreases are negligible and far from reliable. Thus, there is no reason to believe that the changes produced by the course had disappeared within the relatively brief period represented by the dispersion of posttest administration dates.

FOLLOW-UP OVER FIVE YEARS

A more satisfactory solution to this problem developed as a result of follow-up research carried out five and a quarter years after testing with the MSCS. This research permitted evaluating the experimental course against subsequent success data, and also carrying out predictive validity studies. No third round of MSCS testing was possible.

Predictive Validity

In order to study any possible causal relationships involved in the previous concurrent study, follow-up data were obtained from the company. For this predictive phase of the research MSCS scores of a posttest nature were used—thus from subsequent to the time when training was completed.

All changes in grade level occurring during the follow-up period had been recorded on the appropriate forms. These are the data used in Table 3.3, but reduced by separations since testing, and also by those whose promotions were instituted within the recently instituted scientist chain—Senior Research Physicist, Associate Research Chemist, Research Director, Research Associate, etc. The final sample thus contained 49 true managers who had started in the R&D department, although 40 percent had now shifted to other departments, largely as a result of reorganization. The grade changes varied from an increase of six levels to a decrease of three. At follow-up 75 percent were in positions one or more grade levels above that held at the time the MSCS was administered. The mean change was +1.6 grades. Because there had been a number of retirements and resignations among the company's upper level management, there was no restriction of opportunity to move up for those who had started out in the relatively higher grades. All had the experience of seeing numerous positions above them become vacant during the five-year period.

The data of Table 3.3 are consistent with the hypothesis that those who score relatively high on the MSCS will progress more rapidly to positions of power in business organizations. The correlations are not particularly sizable, but reliable relationships do appear to be present. Furthermore, these findings cannot be explained away as a possible result of bias introduced by virtue of the actual use of test data in reaching promotion decisions. The MSCS scores were not made available to the company's management and therefore could not have influenced the grade changes.

A degree of predictive validity is demonstrated by these R&D findings. There is some basis for concluding that those with role-relevant motivation, and thus a desire to exercise power, do gain satisfaction for their motives through promotion within a business organization.

As a result of a prior investigation, MSCS scores were available on a sizable group of men employed in the Marketing Department of the same company. At the time the follow-up data were collected, eighty-one of these individuals were still with the company, and all were in the same department where they had been employed when tested. Of these, twenty-five had already moved up to managerial positions by the time the MSCS was administered. The remainder were in various sales positions, but all were at the level from which promotions to supervision are normally made. They had been identified as candidates for managerial work and were eligible for promotion, but had not, when the MSCS was administered, actually made the move into management. As with the R&D department study, the test results had not been released; they could not have served to influence promotions and thus bias the research findings.

The MSCS had been administered individually to various members of the sample during a period extending over somewhat less than two years. As a result the follow-up period varied from three and a quarter to five years. The average was three years eleven months. Because

Table 3.3

Correlations between Rare and Item Scores and Various Indexes of Subsequent Success in Samples of Atlantic Refining Company Managers

	Indexes of Success		
	Job Grade Level Change		Rating at Separation
MSCS Measures	R&D (N = 49)	Marketing (N = 81)	Combined Sample (N = 61)
Total Scores			
Item	.29*	.32**	.57**
Rare	.25	.39**	.69**
Subscale Item Scores			
Authority Figures	.34**	.37**	.41**
Competitive Games	.28*	–.11	.27*
Competitive Situations	.17	.31**	.36**
Masculine (Assertive) Role	.12	.07	.41**
Imposing Wishes	.07	.26**	.42**
Standing Out from Group	.37**	.08	.15
Routine Administrative Functions	–.16	.15	.17

Note: MSCS = Miner Sentence Completion Scale.
$*p < .05$; $**p < .01$

of the differing periods since testing, it was necessary to use grade change per year as a criterion variable rather than the total amount of change. The values obtained ranged from –0.5 to +1.3. The average change per year was +0.3. During the follow-up period 49 percent of the men progressed by at least one grade.

The predictive correlations presented in the second column of Table 3.3 run somewhat higher than in the R&D department study, presumably because the confounding with research endeavor is clearly removed from the criterion. Yet once again predictive validity is distinctly in evidence.

Promotion rate was, unfortunately, the only criterion variable which could be used with those who were still employed in the R&D department and in the Marketing Department when the follow-up information was collected. Management appraisals had not been conducted in these departments subsequent to the time of testing. Certain data were available, however, on those who had separated during the follow-up period.

The form that the immediate superior was required to complete when one of his men resigned or was fired contained spaces for comments on the man's performance while with the company, on the reasons for separation, and on whether rehiring at a later date would be desirable. Although not all forms had been completed in their entirety, a majority had. Even when certain spaces had been left blank, it was usually not very difficult to determine whether the man's superior was sorry to see him go or glad to be rid of him. These statements on the separation forms were generally made with a great deal of care, since an indication that a man had done well and should be rehired if available might well result in the man's returning to his former position at a later date. Rehirings did occur and requests of this kind from former employees were rather frequent. Thus, the superior might well have to live with his recommendation at some future time. The common tendency to give nearly everyone favorable references was, therefore, minimized in this particular situation. The separation forms seemed to provide a rather accurate index of a man's performance on the job. The men who had been fired or forced out were not treated in a very favorable manner. Neither were those who had done rather poorly, but had nevertheless left on their own initiative. On the other hand the men who had performed effectively received positive recommendations, largely because their superiors were sorry to lose them and did not want to obviate any possibility of a return.

The analysis of these performance ratings at the time of separation was carried out using a combined sample from both departments, since neither alone provided a sufficient number of cases. There were a total sixty-one involved, most of whom had held supervisory positions when they left the company. Some in the Marketing Department were still in sales jobs, although definitely considered candidates for promotion into Management. Those in R&D whose last position had carried a research title were again excluded. In these latter cases the separation recommendations were more likely to be based on research competence than on skill as a manager. There were thirty-one instances where it seemed clear that the immediate superior thought well of the man's past performance, was sorry to lose him, and would have liked to have him back. In the remaining thirty cases the separation rating was unfavorable.

The time that had elapsed between testing and separation varied considerably. A few had left within the first month, while the longest period was three years and nine months; the average was one year and eight months. All but five were rated in the department where they had been tested. These five had transferred from R&D to either Manufacturing or Construction Engineering, and were separated from their new department. The MSCS scores used were, as in preceding analyses, the most recent available. This meant that among the R&D department subjects scores obtained at the time of posttest were employed.

In order to compute the biserial correlations of Table 3.3 it was necessary to view the separation report statements as providing a dichotomization of an otherwise continuous and normally distributed variable. This assumption seems justified since the ratings were made along what amounted to a performance effectiveness continuum—the distribution having been split at that point which differentiated between positive and negative rehiring recommendations.

The picture that emerges is quite striking. These are the highest validity coefficients obtained to date. Why this is so remains something of a mystery. Probably the ratings are as devoid of bias as any subjective criterion measure can be. Furthermore, although prediction is involved, the period over which it extends is considerably less than in the two preceding studies. Thus, there is less opportunity for actual change in the subjects themselves. Whether these factors are sufficient to account for the size of the relationships remains an open question, however. In any event, it is clear that those who scored high on the MSCS originally are much more likely to be given a good recommendation when they leave the company. A lack of role-relevant motivation seems to contribute subsequently to a much less favorable evaluation of managerial competence.

As a check on the results presented in Table 3.3 mean scores on the MSCS were computed for the thirty-one managers separated with favorable recommendations, for the thirty who left under negative circumstances, and for the 130 in the two departments who were still employed at the time of follow-up. According to the theory, men with high MSCS scores, and thus a strong desire to exercise power, should rise rapidly within the organization. If for some reason this is impossible and promotion is slowed, or blocked entirely, such an individual would be expected to leave in search of promotion and greater opportunity to exercise power elsewhere. At the time of separation these people ought to be considered effective managers, and therefore be recommended for rehire, should an opportunity present itself at a later date. Those who are more negatively motivated insofar as competition for power is concerned would be expected to do a much less effective job in management. In some instances the failure might be sufficiently acute to result in firing or forced resignation. In other cases these managers may find their work so onerous that resignation appears to be the only possible course open to them. Whatever the specific reason for leaving, those who separate and who also score low on the MSCS would be expected to receive few favorable recommendations insofar as rehiring is concerned. Thus, in accordance with the theory, the highest mean MSCS scores should be obtained by those who separate with a positive recommendation; next should come the managers who are still employed, some highly effective and others much less so; lowest would be the men who separate under unfavorable circumstances.

The data are generally consistent with these hypotheses. The Total Scores and many of the subscales yield significant results supporting them. The deficiencies in managerial motivation among those who left with a recommendation against rehiring are particularly pronounced. Given that testing had been carried out in this group an average of one year and five months prior to separation, these men did not decide that they disliked managerial work only *after* having been fired or encouraged to leave.

Career Success after Training

Data were available also on the subsequent careers of all men who were managers in the R&D department at the time the training was conducted. Thus, the retention question in its grossest form becomes: Did those managers who took the course perform more effectively later and achieve greater success than the managers who were in the department at the same time, but who were not exposed to training?

The follow-up period for this study was five years and three months. The basic sample consisted of those who were employed in management positions in the department at the time the experimental course was completed. From this total all managers holding positions designated with a research title at the time of follow-up, or when the man separated, were excluded. These latter individuals had presumably been promoted and rated largely on the basis of their research competence. Thus, their inclusion could only serve to obscure any positive results that might be present. The course was intended as an aid to the attainment of managerial skill only, and for this reason the follow-up had to be restricted to those who had been evaluated in terms of their performance as managers.

The resulting experimental sample contained the fifty-two non-research managers who had completed training. The control sample contained another forty-nine men who had not been exposed to the particular management development program, but who were in management positions in the department at the time, and who did not subsequently move into research jobs. These groups were to be compared in terms of the average change in grade level experienced over the follow-up period. This raises an obvious question regarding the opportunities available to the members of the two samples. If in one group the positions held were on the average of a somewhat higher level when the course was conducted, this particular group might quite possibly have less opportunity for promotion. The degree of matching on initial grade level, therefore, becomes an important consideration.

A check revealed that the average grade level in the experimental group at the time these men were taking the course was 11.6. This is on a 12-point scale, where the lowest possible managerial grade is 7. In the control group the mean grade level at the same point in time was 11.8. The difference is too small to have had any possible effect on promotional opportunities. Furthermore, as it turned out, there was probably very little differential restriction of opportunity associated with grade level over the follow-up period. As a result of separations, transfers, and opportunities that became available in other departments, promotions appear to have been as available to those who were initially in higher level positions as to those who were not.

Further evidence on the matching of experimental and control groups comes from the management appraisals that had been conducted in the R&D department some twelve to eighteen months prior to the training program. All but twenty of the individuals in the two samples had been assigned ratings on the five-point potential for advancement scale. Those who had not been formally appraised at this time were primarily in the lower management positions, serving as foremen over various groups of technicians and skilled workers. For a number of reasons these latter men had rather limited prospects for promotion. Thus, it was possible to assign them potential ratings even though they had not been through the formal appraisal process. The available data were not sufficient to permit a performance rating of these twenty individuals, however. Fortunately, the degree of matching achieved on the potential measure is the crucial factor when promotion rates are to be compared. And it was possible to obtain ratings that reflected the opinions of higher management regarding the chances for advancement of all members of both samples. Thus the experimental and control subjects could be compared in terms of their relative position vis-à-vis promotion prior to the introduction of the management development program.

Among those who subsequently took the course the average rating, where a value of 1.00 indicates the highest potential, was 2.86. Since the 49 control subjects had a 2.90 average, and the standard deviations were almost identical, the two groups appear to have had an equal rated chance of promotion prior to the advent of the management development program, as well as the same mean grade level. As far as can be determined the experimentals and controls not only began the race at the same starting line, but had also in other respects an equal prospect of winning, at least at the outset. The question is: Did one group achieve a special advantage by virtue of exposure to the management development program shortly after the race began?

The average grade change over the follow-up period provides one answer. Among the 36 experimentals who remained with the company this figure was +1.86; among the 39 controls it was +1.10 ($t = 2.00, p < .05$). Within the experimental group 86 percent had a least one promotion, while only 56 percent of the controls progressed in a like manner. Thus, the available evidence is entirely consistent with the hypothesis that exposure to the training experience did make the men better managers, and in this way facilitated their promotions.

It was also possible to check the rehiring recommendations for those who separated during the follow-up period. Among the controls ten men left the company, but only three of these were so well thought of that their superiors seemed sorry to lose them. Exposure to management education clearly did not contribute to retention, since sixteen of the experimental group separated. Yet, eleven of these were favorably recommended for rehire when they left. In other words, 30 percent of the controls and 69 percent of the experimental subjects who separated did so with a statement in their files indicating that their superiors were sorry to see them go. However, with samples this small the difference between the two groups yields a chi-square of only 2.36, which is not reliable.

Ideally, a comparison should also be made using the total experimental and control groups, without reference to whether the subjects separated or remained. In order to carry out such an analysis a dichotomy had to be used, since the men who had terminated employment with the company could only be divided into those who were considered good managers and those who were rated less favorably. A similar split was accordingly made within those who had maintained employment throughout the follow-up period. Those who moved up at least one grade level were placed in one category and those with no promotions, or a demotion, were put in the other. Thus, a successful grouping was constituted, consisting of men favorably recommended at separation plus those with a grade rise of at least one level. Individuals meeting these criteria were identified in both the experimental and the control samples.

The results demonstrate a clear and highly reliable difference. In the experimental group, 52, 81 percent, were successful; among the 49 controls only 51 percent were similarly successful ($x^2 = 8.70$, $p < .01$). There is little doubt that those who were exposed to training did in fact have a more successful subsequent career with the company. This in spite of the fact that the two groups started at the same grade level and with the same rated potential for advancement.

Although it would seem likely that the management development program was the major cause of this difference, there is another interpretation that must be considered. Promotions and favorable evaluations may have been awarded merely because of the fact of training, rather than because of the impact the course content had on job performance. No effort was made to restrict information regarding who had and had not participated in the development program. In fact, any such effort would inevitably have failed, even if it had been attempted. Thus, those making promotions and writing separation recommendations knew whether the men involved had been exposed to the course, or at least could have obtained such information without much trouble. It is possible, therefore, that this knowledge influenced their decisions.

Evidence that would conclusively rule out this interpretation is unfortunately not available. It is known, however, that a number of the men were promoted into other departments, and that the managers making these decisions probably did not have much information regarding the experimental course, if they knew anything of it at all. In addition, the writer doubts seriously that the training was generally considered of sufficient importance so that superiors would necessarily be inclined to give favorable evaluations to those who had been exposed. Certainly, there was no feeling in the department that the expense and effort involved in the program had to be justified after the fact. Various kinds of management development activities had been conducted in the company for many years, so that most managers had become rather used to this sort of thing, even if they had not been personally involved. In general, these activities were viewed as somewhat peripheral to the main stream of work, and for this reason were not consciously valued as highly as they might have been. It seems unlikely therefore, that one such course could serve to distort decisions over a five-year period.

CHAPTER 4

STUDENTS AT THE UNIVERSITY OF OREGON WITH MANAGERIAL CAREER GOALS

INTRODUCTION

This research from the University of Oregon was published in the *Personnel and Guidance Journal* (Miner and Smith 1969) on the recommendation that its subject matter was particularly relevant to vocational counselors. It was preceded by a similar study also conducted with University of Oregon business students, but exclusively at the graduate level (Miner 1968a). Research of a related nature was conducted within the University of Oregon School of Education (Miner 1968b) as part of an extension of the Miner Sentence Completion Scale (MSCS) research program into the field of education (Miner 1967). Data from these efforts are included here.

With this research thrust the MSCS studies moved specifically into the vocational guidance domain, an area that has remained of concern for a number of years. As part of this thrust, women became more conspicuously involved and in fact were the subject of several reports on their motivation to manage; and of additional reports dealing with business managers and educational administrators (Miner 1974b) and with college students (Miner 1974c).

* * *

Two research efforts into the identification of managerial talent have preceded this one. The first dealt with the prediction of success among practicing business managers (Miner 1965a). In three separate studies, scores obtained from the Miner Sentence Completion Scale (MSCS), a measure of managerial motivation, were found to be significantly correlated with subsequent success in management. From this research it was apparent that managers with potential for subsequent success in the business world could be identified at a relatively early stage in their careers. However, there was nothing to indicate whether these individuals could be identified much earlier, while still immersed in the educational process.

The second research effort was initiated to answer this latter question (Miner 1968a).

From John B. Miner and Norman R. Smith, *Personnel and Guidance Journal,* vol. 47 (1969), pp. 995–1000.

Although the ideal approach would have been to reapply the predictive design used previously with the managers to a student population, such a study would have taken many years to complete. As an alternative the students were measured with the MSCS and asked at the same time to indicate their occupational objectives. The hypothesis was that those who aspired to become managers would obtain test scores well above those who did not have such aspirations. Also, the students anticipating managerial careers were expected to score at a level at least equal to practicing managers. Thus, the assumption was that students should exhibit differentials in managerial motivation as measured by the MSCS that parallel those found among people already employed; that the future managers would respond to the test in much the same way as those already working in that capacity.

The findings supported these hypotheses. In the particular student group used, there was found to be a differentiation of managerial motivation at least the equal of that found among those already well into their business careers. These results were obtained within a group of over 100 graduate business students at the University of Oregon. The students were enrolled in both MBA and DBA programs. On the average they were in their second year of graduate study and were 26.6 years of age.

The present study attempts to extend this analysis further downward in the educational system. It seeks to answer the question: When undergraduate business students are used as subjects, are exceptionally high MSCS scores found among those who aspire to managerial careers?

THE MEASURE

The MSCS is a projective or indirect measure of managerial motivation. Each individual response is scored as positive, neutral, or negative in accordance with guidelines and examples that are presented in the Scoring Guide for the Miner Sentence Completion Scale (Miner 1964). The subscales of the test are intended to measure the component variables of a role motivation theory of managerial effectiveness (Miner 1965a).

When all of the subscale scores are combined into a single index, the Item Score is obtained. It reflects the overall positive-versus-negative trend of the responses and thus provides a measure of the extent to which an individual is motivated to fulfill the role requirements specified in the theory of managerial effectiveness. A second comprehensive measure, called the Rare Score, has been developed in accordance with the rationale for test interpretation described in the book, *The Tomkins-Horn Picture Arrangement Test* (Tomkins and Miner 1957). The primary requirement of this scoring procedure is that patterns of responses given by a subject be compared against frequencies obtained from a normative group—in this case, a sample of 160 managers drawn from a variety of business fields. This score cuts through the superficial content of responses and thus minimizes the influence of social desirability and conformity motivation. Repeat testings at two-to-three month intervals produced correlations of .83 for the item score and .78 for the rare score among business administration students (Miner 1965a).

STUDY DESIGN

The students selected for testing were enrolled in an introductory marketing course in the School of Business Administration at the University of Oregon during the 1967–1968 academic year. Since the course is required of all business majors, the group should be representative of undergraduate students at approximately the junior level in the school. It is thus comparable, in providing a cross-section of areas of specialization and interest, to the graduate student sample used in the earlier study (Miner 1968a). Both groups are from the same school although on the average the graduate students were tested two years earlier.

The students were asked to indicate in as specific a manner as possible what their career objectives were: what they were preparing for, what they were after and wanted to do in an occupational sense. There were thirty-three who clearly had managerial goals within business organizations of some size. Of these, 61 percent were in their junior year of college, 30 percent were seniors, and the remaining few were sophomores. The average age was 20.9 years. This contrasts with 25.5 for the forty-one graduate students with managerial objectives studied previously (Miner 1968a).

In the graduate study two additional groups were identified. One consisted of thirty-two students who were primarily interested in teaching business subjects. These averaged 29.7 years of age, and many were working toward doctorates. In the second group there were thirty-three who were headed for professional or technical careers in business. The average age of this group was 25.1. The business specialties noted were consultant, market research analyst, advertising specialist, security analyst, life insurance underwriter, accountant, forester, training representative, labor relations specialist, systems engineer, insurance salesman, commercial loan specialist, and production engineer.

Among the undergraduates only 7 of the 124 students tested had teaching objectives. Since within the graduate sample the teaching and specialist groups had almost identical scores on the MSCS, the prospective teachers were combined with the specialists in the undergraduate analysis. The resulting group numbered 75, and the average age was 20.7. Of these, 74 percent were juniors, 13 percent seniors, and 13 percent sophomores.

An additional twenty-one students were tested but not included in the analyses because they either failed to indicate a career objective or, in a few cases, were headed for non-business occupations.

The primary question was whether the undergraduates with managerial goals would score above the combined teaching and specialist group. In addition, comparisons were made between the undergraduates and graduates, and between the undergraduates and samples of practicing managers.

RESULTS

The mean scores for the two undergraduate groups are shown in Table 4.1.

As with the graduate students, the undergraduates with managerial goals score above those without such goals on both comprehensive measures. But in this younger group the differences are much less pronounced. Whereas among the graduate students the Item Score difference was roughly 6.5 and the Rare Score difference 2.5, these values shrink to 2.5 and 1.0 among the undergraduates. The *t*-values for the graduate student sample were significant at well beyond the .01 level; now they are just significant at the .05 level.

The subscale comparisons follow a similar pattern. Within the graduate group only two out of the fourteen comparisons failed to achieve significance in the expected direction; over half did so beyond the .01 level. This contrasts sharply with the undergraduates. In Table 4.1 there is only one clearly significant subscale difference. Those who desire to manage are more competitive.

Although these data do indicate some differentiation of managerial motivation as early as

Table 4.1

Comparison of MSCS Scores for Undergraduate Business Students Having Managerial Goals with Scores for Those Having Teaching or Specialist Goals

MSCS Measures	Managerial Goals (N = 33)	Teaching and Specialist Goals (N = 75)	*t*
Item Score	2.27	–.20	2.04*
Rare Score	–.94	–2.05	2.34*
Authority Figures	.24	.61	
Competitive Games	.85	.71	
Competitive Situations	–.42	–1.41	3.01**
Masculine (Assertive) Role	.42	–.19	1.70
Imposing Wishes	.70	.11	
Standing Out from Group	.64	.21	
Routine Functions	–.15	–.24	

Note: MSCS = Miner Sentence Completion Scale.
$*p < .05$; $**p < .01$

Table 4.2

Comparison of MSCS Scores for Undergraduate and Graduate Business Students with Managerial Goals

MSCS Measures	Undergraduate Students (N = 33)	Graduate Students (N = 41)	*t*
Item Score	2.27	7.71	4.35**
Rare Score	–.94	1.00	3.88**
Authority Figures	.24	1.54	3.82**
Competitive Games	.85	1.10	
Competitive Situations	–.42	.46	2.59*
Masculine (Assertive) Role	.42	1.12	1.79
Imposing Wishes	.70	1.44	2.11*
Standing Out from Group	.64	.83	
Routine Functions	–.15	1.22	4.03**

Note: MSCS = Miner Sentence Completion Scale.
$*p < .05$; $**p < .01$

age twenty, they say little about the overall strength of this motivation. Table 4.2 deals with this point. The undergraduates and graduate students with managerial aspirations are contrasted.

The graduate scores are consistently higher. Significance is obtained on both comprehensive scores and on four of the subscales. Thus, although the undergraduates headed for managerial work score above their current peers who do not have such objectives, they still are well below the graduates with similar aspirations.

Table 4.3 provides similar comparison data for those with teaching and business specialist goals. The scores for both the undergraduates and graduates are equally low compared to those who are more managerially oriented. Apparently if one does not aspire to managerial responsibilities, the motivation to meet the specific role requirements in this area is likely

Table 4.3

Comparison of MSCS Scores for Undergraduate Business Students Having Teaching or Specialist Goals with Graduate Business Students Having Teaching and Specialist Goals

	Undergraduates	Graduates		*t*	
	Teaching or Specialist Goals (N = 75)	Teaching Goals (N = 32)	Specialist Goals (N = 33)	Column 1 vs.	
MSCS Measures	Column 1	Column 2	Column 3	Column 2	Column 3
Item Score	–.20	.59	1.27		
Rare Score	–2.05	–1.72	–1.36		
Authority Figures	.61	.62	.42		
Competitive Games	.71	.03	.70	1.79	
Competitive Situations	–1.41	–.91	–.82		1.74
Masculine (Assertive) Role	–.19	–.53	.06		
Imposing Wishes	.11	.38	.40		
Standing Out from Group	.21	1.09	.03	3.03**	
Routine Functions	–.24	–.09	.48		1.80

Note: MSCS = Miner Sentence Completion Scale.
$^{**}p < .01$

to be minimal whether one is twenty or thirty. The only score that is at all elevated is the one for Standing Out from Group among the graduate students with teaching objectives. Since the teaching process involves standing out from a student group, this finding is not unexpected. The same pattern has emerged in studies of practicing business school professors (Miner 1965a).

Table 4.4 serves to complete the comparisons and utilizes data from the earlier Miner (1968a) study. This analysis was carried out at a considerably later date. It provides correlational information on the MSCS-managerial relationship. Rare score data are not included because of increasing doubts about the applicability of the Atlantic Refining Company norms to such student samples. The sample with non-managerial goals includes students with teaching and specialist goals (see Table 4.3) plus several other individuals who did not aspire to a managerial role.

Overall the findings indicate a hierarchy of managerial motivation with the lowest scores achieved by those who desire business specialist or teaching careers (undergraduate or graduate), the next highest scores by undergraduates desiring managerial positions, and the highest scores by graduates headed for management.

Within this ladder, the average for practicing business managers in general appears to be somewhere approximately midway between the undergraduates and the graduates with managerial aspirations. In the normative group of managers from Atlantic Refining the Item Score was 5.39 and the Rare Score 0.00. Among the managers of a large department store these values were 4.47 and –0.10. Among the sales managers of a wood products firm they were 5.52 and +0.22 (Miner 1965a, 1968a). These groups were all heavily weighted with members of the lower managerial ranks, although middle-level managers were included. Had top management been included as well, the means would undoubtedly have been higher and, therefore, closer to those for the graduate business students with managerial goals.

Table 4.4

Comparisons of MSCS Scores for Graduate Business Students Having Managerial Goals with Similar Students Possessing Nonmanagerial Goals

MSCS Measures	Managerial Goals (N = 41)	Nonmanagerial Goals (N = 68)	t	r_{pb}
Item Score	7.71	.84	6.47**	.52
Authority Figures	1.54	.51	3.73**	.34
Competitive Games	1.10	.37	1.98*	.19
Competitive Situations	.46	–.95	4.29**	.38
Masculine (Assertive) Role	1.12	–.25	4.10**	.36
Imposing Wishes	1.44	.41	3.30**	.30
Standing Out from Group	.83	.54	.99	.10
Routine Functions	1.22	.21	3.18**	.29

Note: MSCS = Miner Sentence Completion Scale.
$*p < .05$; $**p < .01$

In general the subscales follow the same pattern, but there are several noticeable exceptions. The unusually high Standing Out from Group scores among those with teaching aspirations have already been noted. In addition the graduate students desiring managerial careers score at roughly the same level as the practicing managers on Competitive Games and Standing Out from Group, rather than above them as on the other subscales. The most pronounced deviation, however, is in the very low Authority Figures score of the undergraduates with managerial aspirations. This group is also low on Routine Functions. There are hints here of a potential for conflict with superiors and of irresponsibility, both of which may well produce difficulties for many of these aspiring managers later as they embark upon their careers.

DISCUSSION

Short of a predictive study, which would involve a follow-up of the students extending well into their occupational lifetimes, these results are quite definitive. Combined with the predictive studies on managers, they indicate that managerial motivation is developed as early as twenty and that it can be a determinant of career success and career choice from that time on. Thus early identification of managerial talent does seem to be feasible. And consequently realistic vocational guidance and career planning in this regard are a possibility. Those who obtain high MSCS scores at an early age are likely to represent good bets for subsequent managerial success and obtain satisfaction in this type of work.

Yet there is a question remaining as to whether the marked difference between the undergraduates and graduates with managerial aspirations is to be explained in terms of a further development of managerial motivation or a shift in career objectives. Do those who wish to become managers develop even more pronounced managerial motives and go on to graduate work so that they may move directly into the ranks of management? Or do a number of undergraduates who are strongly motivated in areas related to managerial roles, but who do not as yet have actual aspirations to engage in managing, subsequently shift their career objectives so as to yield a better match between their motives and occupational behavior?

This is, of course, the type of problem that is best solved through a predictive study extending over time. Yet there are some data available which argue rather strongly for the second alternative. There are a number of undergraduates who do not as yet exhibit an interest in managing, but who nevertheless score at a relatively high level on the MSCS. Roughly a third of the undergraduate teaching and specialist group score above the mean for the currently managerially oriented undergraduates and a ninth score above the mean for the managerially oriented graduate students. Thus a pool of potential managers does exist, which, if added to those already headed for managerial careers, could raise the undergraduate mean considerably. Should some of the undergraduates who now aspire to management in spite of low MSCS scores change their vocational choices, the mean would be raised even further.

This, of course, says only that a selection process as the undergraduates move on to graduate school and/or business employment could account for the higher scores in the older managerially oriented groups. It by no means rules out the developmental hypothesis. Research has, in fact, demonstrated that appropriate educational procedures can increase managerial motivation as measured by the MSCS. Increases are particularly pronounced among those characterized by a high activity level; they do not occur among those who are highly dependent (Miner 1965a). Much of this research was done using University of Oregon undergraduates as subjects.

Yet this same research also indicated that under normal conditions, where students are not exposed to this role-motivation training, the undergraduate program in business at the University of Oregon does little to develop managerial motivation. Juniors and seniors score at approximately the same level. Other evidence points to the same conclusion. Without the introduction of some special stimulus, students as a group do not appear to increase their managerial motivation.

Thus, the most likely hypothesis is that much of the rise in MSCS scores in the older management groups is due to a gradual learning process whereby individuals come to recognize that certain of their strong motives can be satisfied within a management job. Other people with low MSCS scores, who may aspire to managerial positions because of status or other considerations, may come to view this original choice as inappropriate to their existing motivational pattern. Learning of this kind which yields a satisfying motivation-occupation match as an end product can, of course, be facilitated by effective vocational guidance and personnel selection.

REPLICATION AMONG EDUCATION STUDENTS

Subsequent to the conduct of the Miner (1968a) study a similar design was applied to graduate students in the School of Education at the University of Oregon. The MSCS was again administered and the students asked to provide an indication of their career goals as in the business school research. From these statements samples were constituted as follows—

57 with administrative goals
56 with teaching goals
28 with specialist goals (special education, student personnel work, instructional media coordination, research activities, educational consulting, school counseling, educational psychologist, school librarian)

Table 4.5 presents the results obtained for the administrative and specialist groups. The teaching sample had a mean item score of 1.32 and a rare score of –0.21. All rare scores were

Table 4.5

Comparisons of MSCS Scores for Graduate Education Students Having Administrative Goals with Scores for Those Having Specialist Goals

MSCS Measures	Administrative Goals (N = 57)	Specialist Goals (N = 28)	*t*
Item Score	3.09	–.96	3.05**
Rare Score	.18	–1.07	2.45*
Authority Figures	1.14	.39	2.34*
Competitive Games	1.31	.68	
Competitive Situations	–.75	–.71	
Masculine (Assertive) Role	.07	–.71	2.00*
Imposing Wishes	.16	–.82	3.06**
Standing Out from Group	.72	.36	
Routine Functions	.44	–.14	

Note: MSCS = Miner Sentence Completion Scale.
*$p < .05$; **$p < .01$

calculated using normative data derived from 219 school administrators from four school districts of varying size located in Oregon and Washington; thus an appropriate normative sample was used.

The students with teaching goals are not included in Table 4.5 because neither their total scores nor any of the subscales yield significant differences in comparisons with the students having administrative goals. In this respect the education research failed to replicate the business school findings. However, as Table 4.5 indicates, replication was achieved in the administrative-specialist comparisons.

Data to provide an indication of where the education students stand relative to practicing school administrators suggest few differences from what is given in Table 4.5. Administrators and students with administrative goals look much the same. The mean item score for 219 administrators in four Pacific Northwest districts was 1.51 and the rare score 0.01. Within this sample only the administrators from Portland, Oregon showed meaningful evidence of MSCS validity; this was the largest city studied by far (Miner 1967). In the Portland district the mean item score was 1.47 and the rare score –0.32. An overall rating of performance by superiors yielded the following validities—

Item score	0.39, $p < .01$
Rare score	0.33, $p < .01$

Validities against job grade level and salary as criteria were not significant at $p < .05$ or better in the Portland district or elsewhere. Subscale validities did occur, although again primarily in Portland, even there on a somewhat spotty basis, and where they did occur never at a level above the high .30s.

It is apparent that among graduate students in the field of education those with relatively high levels of managerial motivation are no more likely to seek administrative careers than careers in teaching, although they do tend to avoid the educational specialties. This is perhaps not too surprising in view of the finding that the kind of motivation they possess goes consistently unrewarded in the outside world of educational administration (Miner 1967).

It is tempting to move from this conclusion to the view that the theory of managerial motivation does not apply in the field of education at all, that the managerial role requirements do not operate there. Yet the data do not support this generalization. It is true that imposing one's wishes on subordinates so as to exercise power and direct their behavior does not appear to be an important consideration in the school systems studied, nor does the matter of carrying out routine administrative duties. But the other motives incorporated in the theory are important, particularly in Portland, but elsewhere as well. They are clearly valued, and people are considered outstanding or unsatisfactory administrators according to whether they possess them.

The Portland findings, as compared with the sparsity of results from Eugene and Beaverton, Oregon, and Vancouver, Washington, serve to point up that managerial motivation becomes really important in relatively large organizations with multiple levels of hierarchy and thus in true bureaucracies (see Miner 2006a). In the other districts, being smaller, professional or semiprofessional features seem to have prevailed, thus thwarting the effects of hierarchy (Etzioni 1964).

DATA FROM HIGH SCHOOL STUDENTS

We have seen that the effects of motivation to manage appear to persist, although at a reduced level, as one moves from graduate to undergraduate business administration students. But what happens at the high school level?

Evidence on this point comes from several studies conducted on high school students enrolled in a leadership program in the Washington, D.C. area. These students were self-selected into the program and appear to have averaged about fifteen years of age; they were quite diverse. These studies have been described elsewhere (Miner 2007) as follows:

A longitudinal study using the MSCS–Form H provides an example of how the research on role motivation theory is often reported. This study was conducted with high school students and used the hierarchic theory to predict either teacher ratings or peer ratings or both at intervals after testing. The first report (Schneider, Paul, White, and Holcombe 1999) was a one-year follow-up using teacher ratings of leadership behaviors and both total scores and subscale values for Form H. Only the subscale figures provided any evidence for validity and this was minimal; in their report the authors refer to "the relative failure of the Miner" (627) and its "out of date and sexist" nature (631); they do not recommend its use in future research.

The second report (Schneider, Ehrhart, and Ehrhart 2002), a two-year follow-up also using teacher ratings, continued to find little evidence of validity, but only the subscale data are reported. More importantly, peer ratings are now included (see Table 4.6), and these fellow students may well have been more knowledgeable on the matters of concern than the teachers. Total score data were not reported here either, but were obtained from the authors directly. As Table 4.6 indicates, the evidence for validity is much more robust with the inclusion of the peer data, especially the total score findings. Yet there is no mention at all of the now more positive performance of Form H, only of the previous failure.

The correlations in the first three columns of Table 4.6 would seem to be consistent with hypotheses from theory. The fourth column findings are more problematic, but it is not surprising that those with strong hierarchic motivation, especially involving power over others and standing out from the crowd, would be less attractive as friends.

Also, although these students appear to have been equally distributed across the high school years, it is not clear how representative they are of students at this level. A number

Table 4.6

Significant Correlations between MSCS–Form H Scores and Peer Nominations Obtained 24 Months Later (N = 53)

	Peer Nominations as Leader		Peer Nominations	
MSCS Measures	Task-goal	Socioemotional	for Popularity	as Friends
Item Score	.29	.26	.29	–.26
Authority Figures				
Competitive Games			.32	
Competitive Situations				
Assertive Role	.28		.37	
Imposing Wishes				–.32
Standing Out from Group	.30	.33		–.25
Routine Functions				

Note: MSCS = Miner Sentence Completion Scale.

were foreign nationals. In addition the specific nature of the "leadership program" in which the students were enrolled is not clear. Evidence, beyond that provided by the positive correlations in Table 4.6, is not available to the effect that this program promulgated hierarchic leadership, as opposed to group, task, or professional types (see Foti and Miner 2003). We need more research before extrapolating from managerial motivation down to the high school level with confidence.

CHAPTER 5

CONSULTANTS EMPLOYED BY McKINSEY & COMPANY

INTRODUCTION

This research, conducted at McKinsey & Company during the four years I served as consultant there, was published in two sources—*Personnel Psychology* (Miner 1971a) and the *Academy of Management Journal* (Miner 1973b). Other publications on McKinsey's selection procedures are (Miner 1970a, 1970b, 1971c, 1978a).

Among these, the ones dealing with the Miner Sentence Completion Scale (MSCS) represented an attempt to investigate the possible extension of hierarchic role motivation theory's domain into previously uncharted areas. These efforts subsequently led to the idea that certain research studies were congruent with their organizational context—as in the case where the MSCS–Form H was used in large bureaucratic organizations (see Chapter 3); and that other studies were noncongruent with the context—as in the McKinsey studies. Prediction would occur only in the congruent studies. Other attempts to extend the domain of the hierarchic role motivation theory in addition to this McKinsey research include (Miner, Rizzo, Harlow, and Hill 1974), (Miner 1980a), and (Smith and Miner 1983). The first two of these are included as chapters in this book.

* * *

Two previous articles have discussed the effectiveness of psychological evaluations (Miner 1970a) and executive and personnel interviews (Miner 1970b) as selection procedures used by consulting firms in hiring people for positions as consultants. In general the evidence has been that, in the forms most typically used in the past, these procedures have contributed very little toward predictive efficiency.

The studies considered here extend the prior analyses within the personality sphere. The original objective was to identify procedures that might supplement the psychological evaluations in this respect. At least as important as the objective of establishing predictors for use in selection, however, is the goal of learning about consulting success. What kinds of people, with what personality characteristics, perform effectively within the role structure of a successful management consulting firm?

PROCEDURE

Study One was concurrent in nature and utilized as subjects all twenty-four consultants below the managerial level who were employed in the San Francisco office of McKinsey & Company. All those studied were citizens of the United States. On the average the subjects had been employed by the organization in a consulting capacity for 2.3 years at the time the research was carried out; the average age was thirty.

Two measures were administered under controlled conditions during the regular workday. The first was the Tomkins-Horn Picture Arrangement Test (PAT) (Tomkins and Miner 1957); the second, the Miner Sentence Completion Scale (MSCS), a measure of managerial motivation (Miner 1965a). Given the focus of this book, the treatment which follows will be concerned primarily with the MSCS.

Four different criteria of consulting success were obtained at approximately the same time as the tests were administered. Ratings were made by managers in the same office, for whom the subjects had worked. On the average each consultant was rated 2.5 times on a form that contained items dealing with problem-solving skills, client relations, firm acceptance, managerial capability, overall effectiveness, and potential for advancement. The first four items were combined as one success criterion to yield an average rating, which had a reliability of .88 calculated by correlating pairs of ratings. The overall rating had a reliability of .84 and the potential rating .91. The other, more specific items produced considerably lower reliabilities (all below .65), and for that reason were not considered except as they contributed to the average rating. All three rating criteria were intercorrelated in the .90s.

A fourth success criterion was the individual's total annual compensation as of the time of the study. This reward index was reasonably well correlated with the three value indices—.67 with average rating, .59 with overall rating, and .58 with potential rating.

Study Two was undertaken as a replication of the first, with two major additions. First, the fifty-one subjects were employed in six different U.S. offices of the firm rather than only one. (As in the first study, all subjects were citizens of this country.) In addition, the research was predictive rather than concurrent in design. Testing was carried out an average of four months after hiring, during a centralized orientation program. Success criteria were collected an average of one year and seven months later. At this time the consultants were approximately twenty-nine and one-half years of age on the average.

The personality measures were correlated with success criteria that differed in several respects from those used in the initial study. The ratings were made by either two or three managers with whom the consultant had worked for an extended period of time. In general these managers were employed in the same office, but this was not always the case. Presumably because opportunities for a common value structure to develop among the raters were less, the correlations between raters were lower in this study than in the first. The overall rating had a reliability of .74 and the advancement potential rating .76; all others were below .70 and thus were excluded from further consideration. The two ratings used were correlated .94.

The compensation criteria were total annual compensation at the time of follow-up and compensation change per year from hiring to follow-up, both corrected for regional differences. These two were correlated .53 and correlations with the rating criteria ranged from .45 to .72. In addition, the per diem charge being made to clients for a consultant's services at the time of follow-up was also used as an index of success. This was most closely related to total compensation (.85), but none of the correlations with other criteria were below .50.

Study Three was also predictive and used the same success criteria, but the subjects differed in a number of respects. All thirty were employed in six offices of the firm located outside the United States, most of them in Europe. None were U.S. citizens. Ten were from Great Britain, five from Germany, four from France, three from Switzerland, two from the Netherlands and the rest from places as diverse as South Africa and Argentina.

As in Study Two, testing followed hiring by approximately four months, but the follow-up was later by some four months ($t = 2.91$, $p < .01$). Also these consultants employed in offices outside the United States tended to be older, thirty years and eight months as contrasted with twenty-nine years and six months ($t = 3.09$, $p < .01$) for the United States group.

In general the correlations among criteria were similar in Studies Two and Three. The two ratings correlated .95. The compensation measures correlated .60 with each other and in the range .56 to .69 with the ratings. The per diem charge to clients, which in this instance required correction for geographical variations, was again closely associated with total compensation with a value of .80. The correlations with ratings were much the same as in the prior study also—.47 and .60. But the correlation between the per diem charge and compensation change per year declined from .50 to .27.

RESULTS

Study One produced a large number of significant correlations with criteria for the PAT, but absolutely none for the MSCS, either total score or any subscale.

The data of Study Two provide a check on the findings of Study One, although because of its predictive nature and more extensive sampling, Study Two is not in the true sense a replication. Once again the PAT yields a number of significant correlations. The actual magnitude of the values is somewhat less (as one might expect with a predictive study), but significance levels are maintained. The MSCS correlations are once again generally low. There is consistent evidence across a number of criteria that the Imposing Wishes measure of power motivation is related to success, with correlations as high as .41 with total compensation, but no other subscale yields significance, nor does the total score. In view of the lack of results on Imposing Wishes in the first study generalization does not appear warranted.

The results from Study Three on the consultants employed in offices outside the United States depart in a number of respects from those for the two previous studies. With the PAT, significance is often obtained, yet these findings rarely support those for the U. S. consultants and quite frequently directly contradict them. The MSCS data do not attain acceptable levels of significance in any instance. The association between power motivation and success evident in Study Two is no longer present.

DISCUSSION

The results obtained with the personality tests are consistent with the interview study findings (Miner 1970b), while extending them in a number of respects. The focus on planning and thinking rather than doing, in particular, fits well with the interview findings indicating the importance of mental ability, imagination, and practical judgment. In the social sphere, the more successful consultants seem drawn to authority figures, they do not want to be alone when away from work, they prefer physically close relationships, and they move toward supportive relationships. But support is desired for its own sake, presumably in conjunction with the desire to be with authority figures, rather than as a means to getting "geared up" for action. These are people who are quite capable of acting independently even though they seek out close, approving relationships with those in positions of authority. In addition the successful consultants are not characterized by approach motivation insofar as groups of peers are concerned. They want to spend their time with those who are above them rather than with "their peers." Yet their attitudes toward these authority figures are not particularly positive.

These characteristics seem to make considerable sense in a group of people who spend their working hours, and many of their nonworking hours as well, in social interaction with the leaders of large corporations. And whose role in these relationships is to plan and think rather than actually carry out and do.

These conclusions regarding the successful consultant apply only in the United States context and they derive almost entirely from the PAT, not the MSCS. The evidence that success in consulting work can derive from other personality patterns—based on the results obtained with the sample from offices outside the United States—suggests that different consulting organizations, having different types of relationships with clients, may require different personality characteristics. It seems likely that these types of client relationships are particularly likely to vary from culture to culture.

In view of the trend of recent research findings with the MSCS, it does not appear surprising that this measure failed to predict in the consulting context. It has become increasingly clear that the MSCS variables are of particular significance for relatively large administrative or bureaucratic organizations. They are of much less importance in relation to the value and reward structures of professional organizations, such as consulting firms (Miner 1971b).

CONSULTANTS AS MANAGERS

For a number of years many companies have recruited from the professional staffs of major management consulting firms when seeking individuals to fill vacancies at the higher levels of management. The diversified experience of the consultant is viewed as an asset that lower-level managers in the company do not possess. Thus consultants, who may well have worked with the company in a client relationship, are often preferred to managers promoted from within. This movement into the higher levels of management appears to be most pronounced from the major consulting firms that provide a diverse spectrum of services to a wide range of corporate clients—the true generalists of which McKinsey & Company is one (Higdon 1969).

Findings indicate that approximately 75 percent of consultants at McKinsey & Company can expect to shift out of consulting into company management within a ten year period, and that a sizable proportion will be in high-level jobs. Experience in other consulting firms may be less pronounced, but the phenomenon is of sizable proportions generally throughout the profession. For a number of reasons this movement out into the ranks of top management tends to be encouraged by the consulting firms themselves. The question to which this research addresses itself is whether the process is desirable from the point of view of the companies involved. Do ex-consultants make particularly good managers?

The approach to the problem in this study is to compare groups of consultants and of lower-level company managers on a number of measures of motives, personality characteristics, and intelligence that are known to have a relationship to managerial effectiveness. Where statistically significant differences in mean scores are identified, it can be assumed that the ranks of management consulting will provide either a greater or lesser incidence of the particular characteristics than will the ranks of company management, depending on the direction of the difference. Whether these differences are of a kind that can be expected to relate to effective managerial performance can then be established by reference to previous research.

Measures

Four different tests were used in this research—the MSCS, the PAT, and two intelligence indexes. As previously, the concern here will be primarily with the MSCS measures.

Sample

It was not possible to use the same samples with all instruments. The MSCS and PAT were administered to practically all newly hired consultants at McKinsey over a period of a year. Approximately 90 percent of the new consultants had advanced degrees. Of these 85 percent had gone as far as a master's degree, usually in business, or a law degree. The remainder had continued on toward a doctorate, although not all had actually completed the degree requirements at the time of hire. All were thirty-five years of age or less when tested.

This group was divided into two samples on the basis of citizenship for use in what approximates a cross-validation design, in order to ensure an adequate basis for generalization. The first sample contained fifty-one United States citizens, all of whom were employed initially in one of six offices in this country. Their mean age was twenty-seven and one-half years. Significant differences obtained with this group were then tested further using the remaining forty-one consultants who were citizens of other countries. Approximately three-fourths of these consultants were employed initially outside the United States, primarily in Europe; the remainder were hired in five different locations in this country, although many eventually moved to foreign assignments This second consultant sample averaged just over twenty-nine years of age when tested.

Different managerial comparison samples were used for the two personality tests, the MSCS and PAT, although both samples contained only managers aged thirty-five or less. Also, in both cases the managers were below the officer level in their organizations, usually well below, and in positions from which movement upward could be anticipated. Educational attainment in these two managerial samples varied from the doctorate downward; some did not have a college education. Thus, as is typical of career managers, the company management samples contained a greater range of education than the consultant samples. As far as is known, none of the managers had ever worked for a consulting firm—and it seems very unlikely that any, indeed, had.

The MSCS comparison sample contained sixty-two managers drawn largely from the MSCS standardization study (see Chapter 3). These data were supplemented using managers from the Meier and Frank department store in Salem, Oregon and from Georgia Pacific Corporation.

Results

On the MSCS, significant results occur only on two subscales. There are no such differences on total score. On the Imposing Wishes measure (an index of dominance or power motivation) there does appear to be a consistent difference in that both consultant groups score below the managers. A similar pattern emerges for the Masculine Role measure (an index of desire to behave in accord with culturally prescribed norms of masculinity). In general the consultants appear to be less assertive and forceful.

A number of studies have been conducted relating the MSCS to success indexes for managers. These show a consistent, but by no means strong, tendency for high Masculine Role scores to be associated with success. The highest correlation with a success measure that has been obtained involves performance ratings by superiors and is .41. This evidence from large corporations is somewhat marginal, with only two of seven correlation values being significantly different from zero. Given the distinctly low scores of the consultants in contrast with those of managers, the Masculine Role findings provide weak negative evidence for the basic hypothesis.

Data on the relationship of the Imposing Wishes measure to managerial success are much more clear-cut. Studies have produced evidence of a sizable positive association with a high degree of consistency. The low scores of the consultants on the Imposing Wishes measure must be viewed as raising serious questions regarding the advisability of hiring ex-consultants for positions of major managerial responsibility.

Discussion

In the MSCS data, the consultants indicate a rejection of managerial work in large bureaucratic organizations—results of much the same kind as found among those who seek careers as faculty members in schools of business (Miner 1965a). Yet the PAT findings are somewhat more positive insofar as prospects for managerial success are concerned, and the intelligence tests do not provide a completely negative picture.

Do ex-consultants make particularly good managers? No, not *particularly* good. They are likely to have some assets and some liabilities. There is no reason based on the evidence obtained here to prefer them to those who come up through the management ranks, but no reason to reject them either. This is consistent with a frequent observation among experienced consultants that those among them who shift to managerial careers often take a while to settle in—they rarely achieve success in their first company; more often it takes several job changes before they really succeed. The breadth of experience provided by diverse consulting engagements may be an asset, but true managerial experience cannot be obtained in a consulting firm. And those who remain in the ranks of management, either with one company or several, can obtain breadth also.

All in all it would appear that those who are initially attracted to a major consulting firm may or may not prove out as managers, but the same is true with regard to a consulting career. They are as yet an untried and undifferentiated group. Only future events will determine whether managerial success, or consulting success, or no real success at all will come their way. A company may find outstanding managerial talent among the ranks of consulting firms, but the prospects are likely to be no better than in its own backyard, or in the vineyards of some other company. The view that ex-consultants make *particularly* good managers is not supported.

CHAPTER 6

STUDENTS AT WESTERN MICHIGAN UNIVERSITY (ORGANIZED ON A HIERARCHIC BASIS) AND AT THE UNIVERSITY OF SOUTH FLORIDA (ORGANIZED ON A GROUP BASIS)

INTRODUCTION

The South Florida study was a joint effort between Dorothy Harlow and myself conducted during my visiting appointment there. The Western Michigan study was an outgrowth of a consulting project working with the management department faculty including particularly John Rizzo and later James Hill. The two efforts were combined for this publication in the *Journal of Applied Psychology* (Miner, Rizzo, Harlow, and Hill 1974).

This is one of the few researches on role motivation theory that would qualify as a laboratory study; it is certainly the first. A frequent problem with research of this kind is that it is not possible to establish the type of organizational form being simulated (Foti and Miner 2003). Many such studies in the leadership area seem best labeled as "context free" (Boal and Hooijberg 2000). As I indicated in the exchange of letters with Roseanne Foti (Foti and Miner 2003, 92): "An example of the type of study in this vein that makes the appropriate distinctions, and that I would like to see more of, is the present research by Miner, Rizzo, Harlow, and Hill (1974)."

* * *

One approach to the study of human motivation in the organizational context involves an emphasis on the motivational requirements of tasks and of informal and formal role requirements, rather than on the specific needs and motives of individuals, which are the central focus of the

From John B. Miner, John R. Rizzo, Dorothy N. Harlow, and James W. Hill, "Role Motivation Theory of Managerial Effectiveness in Simulated Organizations of Varying Degrees of Structure," *Journal of Applied Psychology,* vol. 59, no. 1, 31–37.

various content theories of motivation. Such a role-based approach has as its major concern the sum total of motivational inputs needed to satisfy job requirements. What is important is that these motivational inputs make a difference in the performance of a particular kind of job rather than that they be of a particular type, such as the need for self-actualization or intrinsic job satisfaction.

To date this role-based approach has been developed most fully in the areas of entrepreneurship (McClelland and Winter 1969) and the management of bureaucracies (Miner 1965a). However, as has been noted elsewhere (Miner and Dachler 1973) the approach could be extended to cover a whole network of key jobs in varying organizational contexts. There is thus the possibility of creating a highly parsimonious but comprehensive theory of motivation at work, which would provide a base for meaningful organizational actions, long before the total complexity of human motivation is understood.

A basic problem in the development of such a theory relates to the generality or breadth of job definitions. Research to date indicates that a theory originally developed to apply to managerial positions in the context of a large, highly structured, hierarchic organization cannot be extended to less structured professional organizations where face-to-face relationships predominate (Miner 1971d). Thus the degree of structuring in the organizational environment where the job is performed appears to be an important variable in defining job categories for purposes of developing role-based theories of motivation at work. The present research attempts to shed further light on this matter by moving from the field situation typified by ongoing organizations to simulated situations where a greater degree of control of relevant variables is possible.

ROLE MOTIVATION THEORY OF MANAGERIAL EFFECTIVENESS

The theory that provided a stimulus to the studies reported in this article posits six types of role prescriptions for managerial jobs. These role prescriptions are assumed to be primarily of an informal nature in most organizations, although the fact that they are formally stated would not make the theory less applicable. The role requirements are hypothesized to have a high probability of occurrence across a broad range of managerial jobs, and their presence is expected to be positively related to organizational goal attainment and thus to contribute to organizational effectiveness. The theory as originally stated was viewed as applying to "business firms organized in accordance with the scalar principle" (Miner 1965a).

The six role requirements and their accompanying motivation may be described as follows:

(1) Managers are typically expected to behave in ways that do not provoke negative reactions from their superiors. In order to represent their groups upward in the organization and to obtain support for their actions managers should maintain good relationships with those above them. It follows that they should have a generally positive attitude toward those holding positions of authority.

(2) There is, at least insofar as peers are concerned, a strong competitive element built into managerial work. Managers must compete for the available rewards, both for themselves and for their groups. If they do not, they may lose ground as they and their functions are relegated to lower and lower status levels. Certainly without competitive behavior rapid promotion is very improbable. Thus, managers must characteristically strive to win for themselves and their groups. In order to meet this role requirement a person should be favorably disposed toward engaging in competition.

(3) There is a marked parallel between the requirements of the managerial role and the

more general demands of the masculine role as it is defined in our society. Both a manager and a father are supposed to take charge, to make decisions, to take such disciplinary action as may be necessary, and to protect others. Thus, one of the more common role requirements of the managerial job is that the incumbent behave in an assertive masculine manner. Even when women are appointed to managerial positions they are expected to follow an essentially masculine behavior pattern. It follows that a desire to meet the requirements of masculinity as it is typically defined will generally lead to success in meeting certain role prescriptions of the managerial job as well.

(4) This is the requirement that managers exercise power over subordinates and direct their behavior in a manner consistent with organizational, and presumably their own, objectives. They must tell others what to do when this becomes necessary, and enforce their words through appropriate use of positive and negative sanctions. The individual who finds such behavior difficult and emotionally disturbing would not be expected to meet this particular role prescription.

(5) The managerial job requires a person to stand out from the group and assume a position of high visibility. Managers cannot use the actions of their subordinates as a guide for their own behavior as a manager. Rather they must deviate from the immediate group and do things that will inevitably invite attention, discussion, and, perhaps criticism from those reporting to them. When this prospect is viewed as unattractive, when the idea of standing out from the group, of behaving in a different manner, and of being highly visible elicits feelings of unpleasantness, then behavior appropriate to the role will occur much less often than would otherwise be the case.

(6) The final role requirement refers to the process of getting the work out and keeping on top of routine demands. The things that have to be done must actually be done. There are administrative requirements of this kind in all managerial work, although the specific activities will vary somewhat from one situation to another. To meet these prescriptions managers must at least be responsible in dealing with this type of routine, and ideally they will gain some satisfaction from it (Miner 1965a).

In order to test this theory the Miner Sentence Completion Scale (MSCS) was developed. It provided measures of motivation relevant to the six role prescriptions. The Miner scale yields two total scores and seven subscale scores (two in the area of competitiveness).

Tests of this theory using the MSCS have produced positive results in the types of organizations and under the conditions where it was originally considered applicable (Gantz, Erickson, and Stephenson 1971; Miner 1965a). Criteria used have included supervisory performance ratings, peer ratings, promotion rates, and managerial level. However, the theory has not received support when extended to less structured organizations such as a management consulting firm that uses the professional form and three small school districts where the administrative process is largely of a face-to-face nature (Miner 1971a). Also, the criterion must be one of *managerial* performance; in the research and development context when promotion is heavily weighted with creative and professional components negative correlations may in fact be obtained (Gantz, Erickson, and Stephenson 1972; Miner 1965b).

In the hierarchically structured organization, which relies heavily on formalized procedures, relationships and communication of a vertical nature are of major importance; the very nature of the bureaucratic form makes this so. Thus it does not seem surprising that the Miner Sentence Completion Scale subscales dealing with role prescriptions in the areas of authority relationships, competition with peers, and exercising power over subordinates have contributed the most consistently significant correlations with criteria, although all the other subscales have produced significant results on occasion. In small face-to-face and professional organizations, on the other hand, horizontal relationships and communication tend to be emphasized to a much greater extent, relative to the vertical; the Miner Sentence Completion Scale variables should make little difference under such circumstances.

Furthermore, effectively functioning organizations should place high value on and bestow rewards for behavior that is in accordance with the role requirements of their particular organizational forms. Thus, both role performance evaluations and role assignments (managerial level) should be predictable from the variables of role-motivation theory. In addition, to the extent individuals are aware of the requirements of managerial work in hierarchic organizations and possess the motives required to perform in accordance with them, these individuals would be expected to seek out managerial positions in order to satisfy their strong motives. There is evidence that this does in fact occur (see Chapter 4).

Given these lines of reasoning and the results obtained from research on actual organizations, the role motivation theory of managerial effectiveness should prove applicable to any reasonably large organization of the administrative or bureaucratic type, and the very fact of structuring an organization in this manner should tend to elicit a positive value toward the role prescriptions of the theory. One method of investigating this hypothesis is to test the theory in temporary, simulated organizations having varying degrees of vertical structure. Where structuring is greater one would expect the Miner Sentence Completion Scale measures to correlate more highly with criterion variables. The approach involved here in moving from the field to the simulated situation is essentially the same as that used by Ghiselli and Lodahl (1958) in establishing the construct validity of the Ghiselli Self-Description Inventory (Ghiselli 1971).

METHOD

Low-structure Situation

The low-structure simulation used student teams that worked on various case projects throughout the spring quarter of 1972 at the University of South Florida. Each project team worked independently of the others on a separate and distinct problem; the teams were drawn from three different management courses. The groups formed on a voluntary basis, rather than with an assigned membership, and in some cases they formed well in advance of the start of the course. The amount of interaction was sizable with some teams spending as much as forty hours per week working together. At least 50% of the course grade derived from this group effort. There was no organizational structure above the project team level and there was no specification of a division of labor on either a horizontal or vertical basis within the teams. To the extent such internal structuring appeared it was entirely emergent.

In all there were nineteen teams studied with memberships ranging from four to seven. The total number of individuals in the teams was eighty-nine. Of these seventy-two completed the Miner Sentence Completion Scale during the spring quarter. These seventy-two constitute the sample for purposes of study.

At the end of the quarter when all projects were completed the team members filled out a brief questionnaire based on their experiences in working quite closely together over a two-month period. The questionnaire was designed to get at the nature and extent of emergent leadership; it was worded as follows:

> Assume you are a manager of the people listed above. You have received a request from your immediate superior to recommend one of them for a promotion as a manager of another group; that is, the person is not your replacement. What would your recommendation be in terms of who you think would be a good leader?

The assumption was that if role motivation theory applies at all, in such low structure situations, it should differentiate between those nominated for leadership positions as a result of their behavior in the project team context and those viewed as lacking leadership potential.

Emergent leadership potential scores were calculated by giving two points for a first choice and one point for a second choice. To correct for differences in group size and because only seventy-two of the eighty-nine group members completed the questionnaire, the score for each person was computed as a percentage of the total number of points that could have been obtained. Values of 60 or higher were taken as indicative of managerial potential. Using this criterion, seven groups had a single leader and twelve had dual leadership. Of these, four individuals did not complete the Miner Sentence Completion Scale; the total number of emergent leaders was thus twenty-seven. Their mean score was 80.

The dual leadership phenomenon appeared to be a function of a certain amount of clique formation within the groups. As would be expected the single leaders had a higher leadership score, 94 versus 76. However, the slight trend toward higher total Miner Sentence Completion Scale scores for the single leaders did not approximate significance and thus combining of the single and dual leaders for purposes of the analysis seemed justified. There was no significant difference between the mean total Miner Sentence Completion Scale scores of members of one-leader and of two-leader groups.

In addition to comparing the Miner Sentence Completion Scale scores of the twenty-seven leaders with those of the forty-five nonleaders, a further differentiation was made within the latter group. Those with leadership scores in the 20 to 59 range were designated as possible leaders; the mean score for these twenty individuals was 42. Those with the lowest scores were designated definite nonleaders; these twenty-five individuals had a mean score of 6. None had more than a single second choice nomination.

High-structure Situation

The high-structure simulation study used a student-managed simulated organization called the Management Development Corporation operated by individuals enrolled in management courses at Western Michigan University. Management Development Corporation was a six-level divisionalized organization established for training purposes. The hierarchical form was intended to provide peer, superior, and subordinate role experience.

The students worked on actual current problems. Often the output was in the form of services delivered to the management department as client (including computer printouts, data on several classes associated with grade records, and analyses of department studies). It could also be in the form of final plans (activities, costs, scheduling of resources and the like, toward the accomplishment of some objective to which the plan addressed itself); or of information to relevant publics about Western Michigan University, the management department, and the Management Development Corporation (such as brochures, newspaper articles, and newsletters); or of personnel and administrative records related to the Management Development Corporation itself. Operating procedures tended to vary somewhat from semester to semester depending on the problems dealt with and the particular management group.

The organization was headed by a president who reported to a three-man faculty board. The board reviewed and approved progress toward objectives and received final oral reports at the end of the semester. Performance appraisals were made by the students themselves without any direct faculty involvement. These appraisals were in the form of some type of superior rating and were subsequently converted into course grades.

Subordinate to the president were varying numbers of vice presidents, general managers, department managers, project managers, and staff analysts depending on course enrollments. The structure was in the form of a pyramid with decreasing numbers at each higher level. Leadership was appointive, with promotion decisions having been made by superiors. The organization could, and did, promote at any time, but larger changeovers occurred at the beginning of each semester. Each top management group selected its own successors.

All those who subsequently became managers in the Management Development Corporation started out at the lowest level as staff analysts who worked on project teams just as in the low-structure situation. After individuals had worked as a staff analyst for some time, they became candidates for selection as project managers. Based on observed performance and anticipated managerial role performance some were promoted to project manager and many were not. Thus, in both the low- and high-structure situations what was involved was picking a good leader based on observation of prior performance in similar situations. In both cases the choices were made by other students; but in one instance they were made in a manner typical of hierarchically structured organizations and in another in a manner typical of organizations with minimal structure. This structural variation was the experimental differentiation.

At a point subsequent to the first move into management as a project manager, factors other than observed performance at a lower level assumed increased significance in the promotion process. Seniority began to enter in the promotion process to a sizable degree; so did a personal decision as to whether continuing as a manager in the Management Development Corporation was preferable to other types of learning opportunities. Thus the promotion from staff analyst to project manager differed significantly from those to department manager, general manager, vice president, and president.

The staff analysts derived primarily from the introductory management course that was required of all business students. Participation in the Management Development Corporation was voluntary within the course; students could complete the course requirements in several different ways. However, the grading system was established so as to provide an incentive to work within the Management Development Corporation, and a relatively high proportion of the students did in fact include this alternative as one of their activities.

The Miner Sentence Completion Scale was administered in early 1971 to students enrolled in the introductory course in management and to the other more advanced students who had continued as members of the simulated organization. The response rate for the Miner Sentence Completion Scale was over 90 percent Three basic samples were established as follows: (1) leaders—seventy-three individuals who held management positions in the Management Development Corporation; (2) nonleaders—264 individuals who had elected to work in the Management Development Corporation as staff analysts to complete requirements for the introductory management course; (3) nonorganization—seventy-eight individuals who could have elected to work in the Management Development Corporation as staff analysts, but chose not to do so, and completed the management course requirements in other ways.

It was hypothesized that the Miner Sentence Completion Scale scores in the leader sample would exceed those in both the nonleader and the nonorganization groups. In addition it

Table 6.1

Mean MSCS Scores for Emergent Project Leaders and Nonleaders, and within the Nonleader Group for Possible Leaders and Definite Nonleaders (Low Structure Study)

MSCS measure	Possible Leaders (N = 20)	Definite Nonleaders (N = 25)	Total Nonleaders (N = 45)	Leaders (N = 27)
Total score—Item	–1.00	–.80	–.89	–.93
Total score—Rare	–2.20	–1.68	–1.91	–2.19
Authority Figures	–.05	–.12	–.09	.48
Competitive Games	.65	.92	.80	.85
Competitive Situations	–.95	–1.52	–1.27	–1.70
Masculine (Assertive) Role	–.70	–.52	–.60	–.48
Imposing Wishes	.20	.00	.09	.33
Standing Out from Group	.65	.60	.62	.26
Routine Functions	–.80	–.16	–.44	–.67

Note: MSCS = Miner Sentence Completion Scale.

seemed probable that if any differences existed between the two nonmanagement samples, those who chose the organization should score higher. Reasons for not electing membership in the Management Development Corporation were sufficiently obscure; therefore, this could not be considered a strong hypothesis.

A further differentiation was made within the leader sample on the basis of managerial level. The higher level group consisted of the president, the vice presidents, the general managers, and the department managers—a total of thirty-one individuals. The lower level group contained forty-two project managers, the first-line supervisors. Higher Miner Sentence Completion Scale scores were hypothesized for the higher level managerial sample than for the lower. In addition, comparisons were made between the two leader groups and the two nonleader groups to identify differences that would hold up over two samples of each type. This analysis provided approximations to replication.

RESULTS

Low-structure Study

Table 6.1 contains the mean Miner Sentence Completion Scale scores for the emergent leaders and the total nonleaders. None of the differences attained significance at even the $p < .10$ level. On five of the nine comparisons the total nonleader mean was higher than that for the leaders, in direct contradiction to the hypothesis.

It remained possible that the definite nonleaders within the total nonleader group might have exhibited very low scores. Data on this point are also given in Table 6.1. However, an examination of the mean Miner scale scores for the three levels of emergent project leadership (leaders, possible leaders, and definite nonleaders) indicated no support for the hypothesis. None of the comparisons among the three samples attained significance at $p < .10$. On four of the nine variables, including the two total score measures, the definite nonleaders had the highest score, in only one instance were they the lowest. The data provided no support for role motivation theory in a context of low organizational structure.

High-structure Study

Table 6.2 contains the comparisons involving the various groups. As indicated the major hypothesis was confirmed. The total leaders, who held managerial positions in the simulated organization, had significantly higher means on both the total score measures than both nonleader groups. The subscale comparisons indicated that—in the degree to which there was the potential for meeting managerial role requirements that involved competitiveness and in the performance of routine administrative functions—these factors distinguished the organizational leaders from those who did not hold managerial positions.

There was no evidence that those who elected organizational membership at the nonmanagerial level differed at all from those who did not elect membership. However, the low standing out from group score in the nonorganizational sample, as contrasted with that of the managers, did suggest a possible reason for not joining the Management Development Corporation. The Management Development Corporation, compared to other course options available to the students, required more interaction with other students, more group work, and the possibility of making informal and formal presentations to peers, superiors, and faculty. Students who preferred to work independently in more traditional academic roles (for example, reading, attending lectures, taking exams) may have avoided the Management Development Corporation, and its opportunity to stand out, as an option.

The comparison of managerial levels within the Management Development Corporation failed to yield any significant differences at $p < .10$ or better, although the trend of the data favored the higher level group. Furthermore, as indicated in Table 6.2 the higher level managers differed from both nonmanagerial groups at $p < .10$ on five of the nine Miner Sentence Completion Scale measures, while the lower level manager group yielded comparable differences on only two variables. Overall it seems quite likely that if larger managerial samples had been available, a small, but statistically significant difference between the two levels would have emerged on both total score and both competitiveness measures.

DISCUSSION

One of the most striking findings from the high-structure study was the consistent differentiation between managers and nonmanagers on the measure of motivation to perform routine administrative duties. Experience suggests that this measure reflected a type of conscientiousness, or perhaps a mild compulsiveness. In a student-run organization such as the Management Development Corporation, this role requirement would appear to be particularly important. There was a strong need to get someone to participate and do the work. Those who exhibited a desire to perform the necessary routine tasks were thus most likely to be selected by the existing managers for new managerial positions. Each group of managers that was promoted to higher levels perceived a need for help in getting its work accomplished and thus tapped a group that exhibited motivation to fill the role requirement to replace the lower level managerial positions that were vacated.

One of the major problems with the Management Development Corporation simulated organization as a teaching device noted by the management faculty at Western Michigan was that a number of students exhibited only minimal involvement. It appears from the present research that the hierarchic leadership selection process operates to provide a solution to this problem at least at the level of the organization, although not necessarily at the level of the individual.

Table 6.2

Mean MSCS Scores for Appointed Organizational Leaders, Nonleaders, and Those Choosing Not to Join the Organization and within the Leader Group for Higher Level Leaders and Lower Level Leaders

						t values					
						Higher level leaders vs.		Lower level leaders vs.		Total leaders vs.	
MSCS Measure	Higher level leaders (N = 31)	Lower level leaders (N = 42)	Total leaders (N = 73)	Non-leaders (N = 264)	Non-organization (N = 78)	Non-leaders	Non-organization	Non-leaders	Non-organization	Non-leaders	Non-organization
Total score—Item	2.14	.98	1.47	–.76	–1.12	2.98***	2.73***	1.78*	1.76*	3.01***	2.57**
Total score—Rare	–1.13	–1.52	–1.35	–2.12	–2.12	2.30**	2.06**	—	—	2.48**	2.03**
Authority Figures	.03	–.10	–.04	.09	.36	—	—	—	—	—	—
Competitive Games	1.68	1.00	1.29	.85	.85	2.18**	1.89*	—	—	1.83*	—
Competitive Situations	–.48	–.98	–.77	–1.36	–1.31	2.38**	2.08**	—	—	2.57**	1.93*
Masculine (Assertive) Role	–.33	–.33	–.33	–.64	–.73	—	—	—	—	—	—
Imposing Wishes	.55	.55	.55	.55	.49	—	—	—	—	—	—
Standing Out from Group	.61	.60	.60	.31	–.02	—	1.82*	—	2.21**	—	2.43**
Routine Functions	.09	.24	.18	–.55	–.76	2.06**	2.50**	2.93***	3.23***	3.40***	3.62***

Note: MSCS = Miner Sentence Completion Scale. *$p < .10$; **$p < .05$; ***$p < .01$, t values ($p < .10$) only.

Within the ranks of management there was some evidence that those who enjoyed competitive striving were particularly likely to move up into higher management positions. Actually the managers who reported to the president were selected from among those who volunteered for these positions in preference to some other form of independent or group work. Yet because the simulated organization was staffed and run by students who move from junior to senior standing and then graduate, it departed from most actual organizations in the rapidity with which turnover occurred and openings developed in the managerial ranks, most significantly at the upper levels. The result was that each year a high proportion of the existing project managers had to move up at least one managerial grade level, a much higher proportion than one would find being promoted that fast in most real organizations; seniority per se was a major factor in promotion. As a consequence, the degree of selectivity on the basis of observed performance tended to be much less when upper and lower management were contrasted, than when those promoted into management were contrasted with those who were not. It was presumably, at least in part, because of the artificially inflated turnover rate at the top that the managerial level differences were so small within the simulated organization.

Yet, in spite of this inherent difficulty with the particular simulation used, the evidence in support of role motivation theory as applied to highly structured administrative or bureaucratic organizations seems quite strong. Total score differences on the Miner Sentence Completion Scale emerged consistently between those appointed to management positions and those not appointed. On the other hand, the research provided no evidence in support of the applicability of the theory in a context of minimal organizational structure.

CHAPTER 7

HUMAN RESOURCE MANAGERS FROM A BUREAU OF NATIONAL AFFAIRS (BNA) PANEL

INTRODUCTION

This is the lead article among several dealing with the motivation to manage of human resource managers (previously known as personnel and industrial relations managers or some other combination of those terms, including employment managers). It was published initially in the *Journal of Applied Psychology* (Miner 1976a). Other articles of this genre include Miner and Miner (1976) and Miner (1979a) dealing with success relationships and Miner (1976b) dealing with alternative measures of managerial orientation. The results from all of these studies are considered in the following.

In addition this study introduces for the first time data on the hierarchic leadership characteristics of a group of managers (Miner 2002a). The concept is operationally defined and a group of managers is specified as pursuing a leadership career, not a whole career, but some part of one.

* * *

A reading of the historical literature in the field of personnel and industrial relations raises serious questions regarding the extent to which managers in this field are primarily interested in managing and are committed to managerial as opposed to other types of goals (Ling 1965; Milton 1970; Nash and Miner 1973). Throughout its history, personnel (now human resources) management has often been identified more strongly with employees than with management, and more strongly with organizational maintenance goals than with making a profit. These orientations are inherent in a number of interpretations of the human relations and participative management viewpoints, both of which have often been embraced by personnel managers;

they are also inherent in the current emphasis on a professional commitment to employee-clients and to society as a whole.

Patten (1972) has hypothesized that the net result of these essentially nonmanagerial orientations within the field has been to produce a function staffed by "managers" who lack the will to manage. Although he considers this unfortunate and predicts a change in the future, he nevertheless views the current deficiency in managerial motivation as the major factor keeping personnel and industrial relations managers from achieving their full potential as contributors to the managerial systems of most companies. It is this hypothesis—that personnel and industrial relations managers are lacking in motivation to manage relative to managers in other functional areas—that the present research seeks to test.

METHOD

The Measure

The Miner Sentence Completion Scale (MSCS) was used to measure managerial motivation (Miner 1964). All of the protocols for all samples used in the present study were scored by the author. For eight of these samples this presents no special problem, since the scoring was done prior to the conceptualization of the research. However, in the case of the two primary personnel and industrial relations manager samples, the scoring was done with knowledge of the hypothesis. Thus a check for unconscious bias in favor of the hypothesis is required.

To accomplish this, fifteen records were selected at random and submitted to an individual not otherwise involved in the research who had had some prior experience with the test for independent scoring.* The resulting Item Scores deviated in one direction or another by 1.60 from those of the author and the Rare Scores by 1.07. The mean Item Score was .40 *lower* and the mean Rare Score .13 *lower.* Individual subscale mean scores varied from .33 higher to .27 lower. Correlations were .91 for the Item Score and .71 for the Rare Score. Subscale correlations ranged from .79 for Standing Out from Group to .96 for Competitive Situations, with a median of .86. Overall there is no basis for concluding that the author's scoring of the personnel and industrial relations manager protocols led to a bias in favor of the hypothesis. What it does appear to have accomplished is a degree of comparability across the ten samples studied.

Tests of the seminal hypothesis—that motivation to manage as measured by the Miner Scale is positively related to *managerial* success as indicated by performance ratings, peer ratings, promotion rates, and managerial level in large hierarchic organizations—have consistently produced positive results (Gantz, Erickson, and Stephenson 1971; Lacey 1974; Miner 1965a, 1974b; Steger, Kelley, Chouiniere, and Goldenbaum 1975). In addition, a sufficient number of these studies are predictive in nature to justify a causal interpretation from motivation to performance. Furthermore, there are a number of studies indicating that the key conditions are *managing* rather than some other type of work (Gantz, Erickson, and Stephenson 1972; Miner 1962a, 1965b; 1971a) and managing in a *large hierarchic* organization rather than in a small organization with minimal hierarchy (Miner 1968b; Miner, Rizzo, Harlow, and Hill 1974). To the extent that individuals are aware of the requirements of managerial work in hierarchic organizations and possess the motives required to perform in accordance with

*I am most appreciative of the assistance given by Timothy Singleton, then Dean of Men at Georgia State, in rescoring these protocols.

them (motivation to manage), they would be expected to seek out managerial positions to satisfy their strong motives. This, too, appears to be true (Miner 1968b; Miner and Smith 1969). Finally, the Miner Scale is positively related to other indexes of managerial talent such as the Kuder Preference Record scale for supervisory interest (Miner 1960b), the Ghiselli Self Description Inventory measures (Miner 1976b), and the various managerial scales for the Strong Vocational Interest Blank (Gantz, Erickson, and Stephenson 1971). Taken as a whole, there is substantial evidence that the Miner Scale does measure a construct that is of importance in managerial work.

Samples

The major source of personnel and industrial relations managers (human resource managers) was a national panel used by one of the major reporting services in the area of personnel practices, the Bureau of National Affairs (BNA). This panel contained 234 managers who were sufficiently senior to have a comprehensive knowledge of personnel practices at their locations. They were employed by business firms with more than 100 employees and, in most cases, had spent the majority of their careers in the personnel field. The range of business types, company size, and geographical locations represented was very broad.

Panel members were contacted by mail and asked to complete the Miner Scale. After one follow-up, 101 respondents were obtained. A comparison of respondents and nonrespondents in terms of level of position and company size indicates no significant differences.

Because previous research has consistently shown a positive relationship between managerial motivation scores and managerial level (Miner 1965b), the 101 subjects were divided into two relatively homogeneous samples in terms of the level of their positions.

Personnel and Industrial Relations Samples

Top Managers. This sample contained fifty managers who met one of the following criteria: (1) the individual's position title contained the designation vice-president and the position was described by the respondent as being of a top management nature, (2) the individual reported either to the chief executive officer or one level lower and the position was described by the respondent as being of a top management nature, (3) the individual's position title contained the designation of vice-president and the individual reported either to the chief executive officer or one level lower. The relatively few people in this third category described their positions as being at the middle management level. However, they, like the other managers in this sample, met at least two of the three criteria used in defining top management. The data were collected in 1974.

Middle Managers. This sample contained the fifty-one managers who did not meet the criteria for inclusion in the top management sample. Of these, forty-four described their position as at the middle management level and three as in lower management (first-line supervision). The four individuals included here who said they were in top management did not have a vice-presidential title and reported at a relatively low level.

As a check on the extent to which these two primary personnel and industrial relations manager samples could be considered typical, two additional personnel samples were used for comparative purposes. Both of these samples contained a cross-section of personnel and industrial relations managers within a given company component. No attempt was made to control for differences in age, education, and intelligence between these samples and the two primary personnel and industrial relations samples, since these factors have consistently been found to be unrelated to the motivation to manage scores (Miner 1965a). No doubt age differences will appear at the management level eventually as the college students of the past ten years, who tend to have relatively low levels of managerial motivation, move up in the management hierarchy (Miner 1971d, 1974d). However, no such effect is currently in evidence.

Personnel and Industrial Relations Managers

General Electric Co. This sample contained twenty managers from the personnel component of a major division of a heavy manufacturing firm. All levels of management were represented. Average scores for this sample would be expected to be roughly the same as for the primary middle management sample, but below the top management sample. The data were collected in 1974.

The Atlantic Refining Co. This sample contained twenty-one managers from the corporate industrial relations department of a major oil company. All levels of management were represented, the sample being of essentially the same nature as that from the heavy manufacturing company. However, the data were collected in 1957. Thus this sample provides a check on the comparability of findings obtained over a seventeen-year interval. Assuming comparability, average scores for the oil company sample should approximate those for the middle management and heavy manufacturing samples but fall below those for the top management sample.

In order to establish the relationship between motivation to manage scores of personnel and industrial relations managers and those of managers in general, the two primary personnel samples were compared with six other managerial samples. These represent all the samples that could be constituted from the author's files where homogeneity of managerial level could be established with confidence and where the protocols had been scored by the author. There were no personnel and industrial relations managers in any of these samples. Three of the samples were made up of first-line supervisors and three of middle managers.

Lower Level Managers

General Motors Corp. This sample contained 117 foremen and first-level supervisors from the production, office, and, to a lesser degree, sales operations of the company. A wide range of locations and functions are represented; thus the sample is a particularly appropriate one for a comparison with managers in general. The data were collected in 1974.

The Atlantic Refining Co. This sample contained fifty foremen and first-level supervisors from various functional areas and locations, drawn from the same oil company as the personnel and industrial relations sample. The sample is of basically the same nature as that from the automobile company but represents a different industry. In addition, the data were collected in 1958–1959. Assuming comparability across industries and over an approximately sixteen-year time span, the automobile company and oil company subjects would be expected to score at roughly the same level.

Baking Company. This sample contained thirty supervisors of route salesmen for a regional baking company. Previous studies have tended to indicate that higher scores can be anticipated in the territorial sales area than in other functional components (Miner 1965a). This fact, combined with the restricted occupational and geographical range within the baking company sample, make this sample somewhat less valuable for comparative purposes than the preceding two. The data were collected in 1969.

Middle Level Managers

Georgia Pacific Co. This sample contained thirty regional managers for a major wood products company. The managers all had at least one level of supervision below them. The sample suffers from the fact that all the managers were in the same job. However, they were dispersed throughout the United States. In general, the average scores for this sample would be expected to be above those for lower management samples. The data were collected in 1965.

The Atlantic Refining Co. This sample contained thirty managers above the first level from the same company as the two preceding oil company samples. None of the managers were at the top level, but within the middle management range there was considerable dispersion. Also, a variety of functional areas and geographical locations were represented. The data were collected in 1958–1959. Given the fact that the company, dates of testing, range of functions, and range of locations were essentially constant between this sample and the lower management oil company sample, while managerial level varied, higher scores would definitely be expected from this middle management group. Also, this sample should be generally above other lower management samples and at the same level as other middle management samples, assuming comparability over time.

Meier & Frank Co. This sample contained thirty-seven managers, representing the total managerial component of the store, once first-level supervisors and the store manager were eliminated. Although a number of them were retail sales department managers, a variety of office functions were also included. Again, this sample would be expected to score generally at a level comparable to that of other middle management groups and above lower management samples. The data were collected in 1963, thus placing this sample between the other two middle management samples as to time of testing.

In order to identify significant differences between mean scores for the various samples, the data were first subjected to simple one-way analyses of variance, computed separately for each Miner Scale measure. This was done for the four personnel and industrial relations samples as a group and then for the six comparison samples, plus the top and middle level personnel and industrial relations samples derived from the national panel. In those instances where the F values achieved significance, t tests were performed to determine whether the particular differences that had been hypothesized were in fact present.

RESULTS

Comparisons involving the four personnel and industrial relations manager samples are given in Table 7.1. As anticipated, significant differences are present and the two primary samples do differ, with the top managers scoring at a higher level on both total scores and two subscales. In no case do the middle managers have a higher score.

When the top level personnel and industrial relations managers are compared with the Gen-

Table 7.1

Mean Miner Sentence Completion Scale Scores for Various Personnel and Industrial Relations Manager Samples

	BNA Panel				
MSCS Measures	Top managers (N = 50)	Middle managers (N = 51)	General Electric Co. (N = 20)	Atlantic Refining Co. (N = 21)	*F*
Item Score	4.92	1.28	1.90	2.10	3.17*
Rare Score	–.04	–1.55	–.40	–.86	2.83*
Authority Figures	1.47	.53	–.10	.86	4.80**
Competitive Games	1.55	.51	1.05	.62	2.70*
Competitive Situations	–.31	–.45	.40	–.71	1.29
Assertive Role	–.29	–.74	–.70	–.52	.66
Imposing Wishes	.88	.49	–.20	.76	3.43*
Standing Out from Group	.98	.98	.80	.90	.12
Routine Functions	.63	–.04	.65	.19	1.40

Note: MSCS = Miner Sentence Completion Scale.
*$p < .05$; **$p < .01$

Table 7.2

***t* Values for Hypothesized Differences Where *F* Is Significant**

	BNA Panel Top Managers vs.		
MSCS Measures	BNA Middle Managers	General Electric Co.	Atlantic Refining Co.
Item Score	3.10**	1.94*	2.17*
Rare Score	3.12**	.53	1.37
Authority Figures	2.84**	3.59**	1.47
Competitive Games	2.73**	1.05	2.09*
Imposing Wishes	1.37	2.91**	.37

Note: MSCS = Miner Sentence Completion Scale.
*$p < .05$; **$p < .01$

eral Electric and Atlantic groups, the results are somewhat less striking, but where significant differences are identified the top managers consistently have higher scores (see Table 7.2). In contrast, the basic middle management sample shows no clear-cut differences in comparison with either the manufacturing or oil company samples, thus tending to confirm the original interpretation that all three are on the average at the middle management level and that their scores are typical for personnel managers at this level.

The total score differences for the manufacturing company and oil company human resource components do not approximate significance. However, the General Electric group has a distinctly elevated score on Competitive Situations ($t = 2.19, p < .05$) and a very low score on Imposing Wishes ($t = 2.32, p < .05$). Overall, since these differences tend to cancel each other out, there does appear to be considerable stability of the scores over the seventeen-year period from 1957 to 1974.

Table 7.3 compares the two primary personnel and industrial relations manager samples with the three lower management and the three middle management groups, thus permitting a relative slotting of the human resource managers to determine whether their scores are indeed relatively low. Such a slotting requires, however, a degree of homogeneity *within* managerial levels and distinct differences *between* levels for the six comparison samples. As specified by these hypotheses, significant overall F values were obtained for both the total scores and for five of the subscales.

The homogeneity requirement is clearly met among the middle managers. The only significant differences obtained involve the elevated Competitive Situations score of the Atlantic managers. There are no total score differences and the only two subscale differences (both $ps < .05$) fall within the bounds of what might be expected to occur due to chance alone.

Within the lower management samples there are no significant differences at $p < .05$ between the General Motors and Atlantic samples. However, the baking company sales supervisors do score above the other two lower management groups. This is true for both total scores and for the Authority Figures subscale. However, other subscale score differences occur only on the comparisons involving the automobile company (Competitive Situations, Assertive Role, Imposing Wishes).

The elevation of the baking company managers' scores is of sufficient magnitude so that they do not differ from any of the middle manager samples on any measures. However, there is clear evidence of differentiation for the other two lower management groups. The automobile company managers are significantly below all three middle manager samples on both total scores and on the Authority Figures and Competitive Situations subscales. They are also lower than the wood products and oil company groups on Competitive Games, the department store managers on Assertive Role, and the wood products company sample on Imposing Wishes.

The comparisons involving the lower level oil company managers and their middle management counterparts are a key consideration insofar as differentiation is concerned. The lower managers do in fact score lower on both total scores, on Competitive Games, and on Competitive Situations. Also, the oil company lower managers are significantly below the other two middle management samples on the Rare Score and below the department store managers on Authority Figures.

The evidence from the six comparison samples, like that from the personnel and industrial relations samples, indicates considerable stability of scores within managerial levels when the different samples are compared with reference to the time of measurement. The middle managerial samples show little variation even though the different samples were tested over a seven-year span. The lower manager samples span sixteen years; yet the 1957–1959 and 1974 groups have very similar scores. The intermediate baking company group does vary, but this is more appropriately explained as a function of the particular occupational composition of that sample rather than as a consequence of widespread temporal changes.

With the exception of the baking company first-level supervisors, the comparison samples do appear to meet the requirements for slotting the two primary personnel and industrial relations manager samples (see Table 7.4). The top level human resource managers score somewhat higher than the lower managers in the automobile company, but otherwise there are few differences in the lower manager comparisons. The one striking exception is the unusually low Assertive Role score in the personnel sample. The comparisons with the middle management samples show some tendency for the top level personnel managers to score below the oil company managers and once again to be low on the Assertive Role subscale.

When the middle level personnel and industrial relations managers are fitted into the comparison groups, they emerge as distinctly below other middle managers and, in fact,

Table 7.3

Comparison of Personnel and Industrial Relation Managers with Various Other Managerial Groups

	BNA Panel		Lower Level Managers			Middle Level Managers			
MSCS Measures	Top (N = 50)	Middle (N = 51)	General Motors Co. (N = 117)	Atlantic Refining Co. (N = 50)	Baking Co. (N = 30)	Georgia Pacific Co. (N = 30)	Atlantic Refining Co. (N = 30)	Meier & Frank Co. (N = 37)	*F*
Item Score	4.92	1.28	3.07	4.62	7.13	5.90	7.20	5.73	6.23**
Rare Score	–.04	–1.55	–.74	–.44	.57	.33	.97	.35	6.53**
Authority Figures	1.47	.53	.87	1.18	1.90	1.70	1.33	1.73	4.60**
Competitive Games	1.55	.51	1.15	1.14	1.90	1.63	1.97	1.22	2.72**
Competitive Situations	–.31	–.45	–.90	–.48	–.17	–.40	.47	–.27	2.79**
Assertive Role	–.29	–.74	.14	.52	.90	.30	.67	.70	4.84**
Imposing Wishes	.88	.49	.51	.66	1.13	1.00	.73	.54	1.19
Standing Out from Group	.98	.98	.65	1.08	.73	.83	.97	.76	.81
Routine Functions	.63	–.04	.65	.52	.73	.83	1.07	1.05	2.04*

Note: MSCS = Miner Sentence Completion Scale.
$^{*}p < .05$; $^{**}p < .01$

Table 7.4

t Values for Hypothesized Differences Where F Is Significant

	BNA Top Human Resource Managers vs.					
	Lower Managers			Middle Managers		
MSCS Measures	Auto	Oil	Baking	Wood	Oil	Store
Item Score	2.00*	.29	1.98*	.84	1.84*	.75
Rare Score	1.94*	.97	1.24	.72	2.00*	.84
Authority Figures	2.24*	.90	1.19	.60	.39	.78
Competitive Games	1.25	1.18	.84	.22	1.00	.92
Competitive Situations	2.00*	.54	.36	.28	1.98*	.10
Assertive Role	1.43	2.35*	3.38**	1.34	2.47**	2.77**
Routine Functions	.36	.10	.50	.81	1.45	1.43
	BNA Middle Human Resource Managers vs.					
	Lower Managers			Middle Managers		
Item Score	1.79*	2.88**	4.87**	3.40**	4.16**	3.69**
Rare Score	2.17*	2.61**	4.51**	3.51**	4.84**	3.93**
Authority Figures	1.42	2.05*	3.88**	3.09**	2.35*	3.69**
Competitive Games	1.89*	1.72*	3.18**	3.13**	3.34**	1.84*
Competitive Situations	1.44	.09	.65	.13	2.15*	.47
Assertive Role	3.03**	3.86**	4.65**	2.51**	3.92**	4.32**
Routine Functions	2.46**	1.66	2.01*	2.38**	2.95**	2.97**

Note: MSCS = Miner Sentence Completion Scale.
* $p < .05$; ** $p < .01$

even below lower level managers. The same tendency to lower scores on the Assertive Role subscale, as found with the top managers, is strongly in evidence. But in addition, the middle level personnel managers have low scores on Authority Figures, Competitive Games, and Routine Functions.

A further check on these findings can be obtained by comparing the scores for the oil company personnel managers in Table 7.1 with those for lower and middle managers in the same company, as given in Table 7.3. On the two total scores the personnel sample is distinctly lower than the middle managers ($t = 3.42$, $p < .01$ and $t = 3.19$, $p < .01$, respectively). They are also lower on Competitive Games ($t = 2.89$, $p < .01$), Competitive Situations ($t = 2.80$, $p < .01$), Assertive Role ($t = 2.77$, $p < .01$), and Routine Functions ($t = 2.06$, $p < .05$). Only the substitution of a significantly low score on Competitive Situations for that on Authority Figures distinguishes these findings from those obtained with the primary group of middle level human resource managers.

In the oil company the personnel group, which averages out at the middle management level, is not as clearly below the first-line managers as in the previous comparisons. However, the Item Score difference is almost significant at the .05 level ($t = 1.97$) and the Assertive Role difference is once again pronounced ($t = 2.47$, $p < .05$).

DISCUSSION

The data support the hypothesis that motivation to manage is relatively low among personnel and industrial relations managers. At the maximum, middle managers in the field appear to be at the same level as the average first-line supervisor in other functional areas. Top managers appear to fall at a point roughly intermediate between lower and middle level managers in the other areas of the business.

Whether the historical factors noted at the beginning of this article are responsible for this situation cannot be determined from the data available. However, from what is known about age relationships and the long-term predictive validity of the Miner Scale (Lacey 1974; Miner 1965a), the hypothesis that the field attracts individuals who are relatively low in motivation to manage originally seems much more tenable than the alternative explanation that exposure to personnel and industrial relations work reduces this kind of motivation. Age is unrelated to Miner Scale scores in the total group of 101 personnel managers, as it has been in other managerial groups studied, and it can be assumed that the older managers have been in the personnel field longer. Thus, duration of exposure to the work is not likely to determine managerial motivation levels.

The finding of an overall depression in managerial motivation levels is somewhat surprising in view of the fact that the managers picked for top level personnel and industrial relations positions are more strongly motivated. One might have thought that rewarding motivation to manage in this way would have attracted more strongly motivated managers to the field generally. The top managers are not only higher than the middle managers on the two total scores but also on two of the four subscales where the middle level personnel managers turn out to be particularly low relative to managers in other functions. On a third such subscale, Routine Functions, the t value is 2.04 ($p < .05$) even though the overall F in Table 7.1 is not significant. Only on the Assertive Role measure, among those where the score depression is particularly pronounced, do the two levels of human resource managers clearly fail to differ significantly. A likely explanation is that people are selected for top level positions in the area on the basis of their *managerial* capabilities, and this selection process serves in many cases to compensate partially for the relatively low managerial motivation that seems to characterize the field in general.

In contrast, middle level human resource managers appear to be less positively oriented to authority figures, less competitive in the non-occupational sphere, less assertive, and less responsible in routine matters than other managers at their level. However, they are equally desirous of standing out in a differentiated manner, of exercising power, and probably of competing in the occupational arena. Very low assertiveness characterizes all four personnel and industrial relations samples and may provide a clue to the processes of occupational choice underlying entry into the field. However, an analysis of the developmental dynamics inherent in the present findings is beyond the capabilities of the data. Also, the data do not permit a determination of whether the motivational patterns identified might not be functional in some way for the total organization.

What does seem clear is that although personnel and industrial relations managers operate within a managerial system where rewards are allocated in relation to managerial motivation, they are somewhat less likely to possess these motivational requirements than other managers around them. This suggests that individuals with relatively high motivation to manage, who wish to achieve the rewards of promotion, might find it advantageous to seek careers in the personnel and industrial relations field at the present time. They would be competing with others who have relatively low managerial motivation level, and thus the chances of moving to the top management level are greater than in many other functional areas.

RELATIONSHIPS TO SUCCESS CRITERIA

The data to this point say nothing about the relationships between the MSCS measures and the success levels of the BNA panel members. Information of this kind does exist, however (Miner and Miner 1976; Miner 1979a). A composite success index was computed as follows:

Vice president in title	1 point
One level of management above position	1 point
Top management ascribed to position	1 point
Yearly income from position—	
$20,000–35,000	1 point
Over $35,000	2 points
Position level as a percent of management levels existing	
61 to 75 percent	1 point
Over 75 percent	2 points
Possible success score 0–7	

Table 7.5 shows the correlations between the MSCS variables and this success measure. In addition, to provide a basis for comparison, similar data for the Ghiselli Self Description Inventory (SDI) (Ghiselli 1971) are included. Both measures work about equally well to predict success; both provide significant, though not extremely pronounced, evidence of a relationship.

RELATIONSHIPS TO OTHER MANAGERIAL MEASURES

This study (Miner 1976b) used not only the BNA panel, but a sample of University of Maryland undergraduates (N = 110). The instruments involved were the MSCS, as previously

Table 7.5

MSCS and Ghiselli Self-Description Inventory Relationships to Composite Success Index in BNA Panel (N = 101)

	Expected Relationship	Composite Success Index
MSCS Measures		
Item Score	positive	.24**
Rare Score	positive	.28**
Authority Figures	positive	.30**
Competitive Games	positive	.13
Competitive Situations	positive	.18*
Masculine (Assertive) Role	positive	.04
Imposing Wishes	positive	.11
Standing Out from Group	positive	–.06
Routine Functions	positive	.13
Ghiselli SDI		
Supervisory Ability	positive	.18*
Occupational Achievement	positive	.15
Intelligence	positive	.20*
Self-actualization	positive	.15
Self-assurance	positive	.14
Decisiveness	positive	.03
Need for Security	negative	–.25**
Initiative	positive	.23**
Need for High Financial Reward	negative	–.16

Note: MSCS = Miner Sentence Completion Scale.
$^*p < .05$; $^{**}p < .01$

indicated the Ghiselli SDI, and a version of the F-Scale calculated to delete items that had clearly become outdated due to passage of time and thus were not culturally relevant (Adorno, Frenkel-Brunswik, Levinson, and Sanford 1950). Both MSCS total scores show many significant relationships with the managerial scales of the Ghiselli SDI in both samples, but more frequently in the BNA panel. The median of the significant correlations is in the .20s. Subscale findings vary, but are most pronounced for the Competitive Situations and Standing Out from Group components, again largely among the managers. Decisiveness on the Ghiselli SDI is most pronounced there. The F-Scale is clearly related to the MSCS variables among the students, but no such relationship is apparent within the BNA panel. The same pattern is evident on the Ghiselli, but to a much lesser extent.

As would be anticipated from Miner (1974a) the scores on both the MSCS and the Ghiselli SDI consistently follow the pattern of expectations set forth in Table 7.5 with the students showing a less managerial orientation than the BNA panel of personnel and industrial relations managers.

ROLE-MOTIVATED LEADERSHIP IN HIERARCHIC ORGANIZATIONS

A considerable number of years after the preceding analyses an investigation was conducted to establish leadership relations within the BNA panel. For this purpose top management was considered as indicative of hierarchic leadership, but the criteria applied were more stringent,

Table 7.6

Relationships between MSCS Measures and Hierarchic Leadership within BNA Panel

MSCS Measures	Hierarchic Leaders (N = 41)	Not Hierarchic Leaders (N = 60)	t	r_{bis}
Item Score	6.18	.95	4.64**	.54
Authority Figures	1.78	.46	4.08**	.49
Competitive Games	1.78	.52	3.44**	.41
Competitive Situations	.12	–.75	2.32*	.29
Masculine (Assertive) Role	–.10	–.80	1.99*	.25
Imposing Wishes	.85	.57	.97	.13
Standing Out from Group	1.07	.91	.54	.07
Routine Functions	.68	.04	1.93*	.25

Note: MSCS = Miner Sentence Completion Scale.
$^*p < .05$; $^{**}p < .01$

focusing on vice presidents and those who reported at the very highest level. This approach was consistent with leadership theory (Miner 2002) when applied to hierarchic organizations and reduced the top management sample to forty-one.

As might be expected, given the fact of overlapping components, leadership status was highly related to the composite success index with the leaders having a mean index of 5.20 and the nonleaders 1.83 on the scale of seven ($t = 11.58$, $p < .01$). As indicated in Table 7.6, leadership is also highly related to the MSCS measure. As previously, rare scores were not calculated in this analysis because of doubt about the appropriateness of available norms. However, the item score coefficient is .54 and the majority of the subscale values are significant. Using the Ghiselli SDI to predict leadership status yields significant values also, but with coefficients that top out in the mid-.30s. On the MSCS the highest subscale value is .49 on authority figures, a finding that seems consistent with the current emphasis on strategic human resource management in the field from which the BNA panel of managers derives. The median age of the leaders is in the high forties; for the nonleaders in the low forties.

CHAPTER 8

DIVERSITY AMONG GENERAL MOTORS CORPORATION MANAGERS

INTRODUCTION

This General Motors research was published originally in the *Journal of Applied Psychology* (Miner 1977a). It represents the most definitive evidence on the effects of race and gender differences on motivation to manage. Thus it takes up where Chapter 4 left off. Further research and discussion on diversity issues may be found in Miner (1977b) and Miner (1993). Eagly, Karau, Miner, and Johnson (1994) contains a meta-analysis of the Miner Sentence Completion Scale (MSCS) research on gender.

This research at General Motors resulted from my collaboration with J. Sterling Livingston (see Livingston 1971) in the conduct of a consulting engagement with the company. Efforts to supplement what is presented here by obtaining performance appraisal information on the managers, subsequent to the conduct of the research, proved unsuccessful.

* * *

Governmental actions since the passage of the Civil Rights Act of 1964 have put companies under increasing pressure to move females and minorities into positions of significant managerial responsibility (Lockwood 1974). Furthermore, the apparent decline in motivation to manage among the college-age population since the early 1960s has created the prospect of a major managerial talent shortage that will require the use of all possible manpower sources to meet the demand (Miner 1974a). These two considerations make it desirable from a company viewpoint that the lower supervisory ranks contain sizable numbers of females and minorities with the potential for effective performance at higher managerial levels. A considerable body of evidence now indicates that the motivation to manage may well be a major component of this potential. Individuals with a strong motivation to manage tend to move up faster and are more likely to perform effectively in managerial positions. This conclusion is supported

From John B. Miner, "Motivational Potential for Upgrading Among Minority and Female Managers," *Journal of Applied Psychology,* vol. 62, 691–697.

by at least fifteen independent studies, four of which are longitudinal (predictive) in nature (Miner 1965a, 1977b).

A review of the literature related to the motivation to manage led to the formation of the following hypotheses:

1. Minority managers tend to have a higher level of motivation to manage than white managers.
2. Female managers tend to have a lower level of motivation to manage than male managers.

The basis for the first hypothesis stems from studies by Crane (1971) and Fernandez (1975). Crane found that 55 percent of his black sample wanted to move up to the highest echelon of management as compared with only 24 percent of the whites. Fernandez found that black managers were more upwardly mobile; they placed more emphasis on income and advancement and wanted to be promoted sooner and to higher level positions than white managers of the same age in the same companies. Given these findings with regard to career aspirations and choices, it seems appropriate to hypothesize the existence of an underlying elevated level of motivation to manage among black managers.

The second hypothesis has its origins in the supposition that the early training of females fails to develop, or inhibits, managerial motivation. Given the culture-based differences in child-rearing practices historically applied to males and females in this society, it seems not at all unlikely that females would have less motivation to manage than their male counterparts, and that this difference would manifest itself among practicing managers.

This hypothesis has been tested previously with samples of department store supervisors and public school administrators (Miner 1977b). In neither case did the data support the hypothesis. However, the research suffered at various points because of organizationally heterogeneous samples, small sample sizes, lack of comparability between male and female groups, and diversity of managerial positions. The present research attempts to overcome many of these difficulties and is designed to test the hypothesis in a typical large corporation. It follows from the two stated hypotheses that minority male managers are expected to have a higher motivation to manage than white females.

METHOD

Measures

The measurement approach used in testing the hypotheses was the sentence completion method. This method can be traced back to at least 1928 and has served as a basis for a great variety of instruments used in both clinical and industrial practice (Bell 1948). These measures vary considerably, not only in the nature of the stems employed but also in the precision with which scoring categories for the completions have been specified. Nevertheless, there appears to be a general consensus among those knowledgeable on the subject that the sentence completion method is the most valid of the projective techniques (Shouval, Duck, and Ginton 1975). This combination of good validity and the power inherent in the projective approach make it particularly valuable for the present purposes.

The basic instrument used in this study was the Miner Sentence Completion Scale (MSCS; Miner 1964). The protocols were scored by the author. Although this is a frequently, and usually unquestioned, practice when multiple-choice or similar measures are used, it has been questioned when projective measures are employed. The approach was used here because the author is an experienced scorer. Thus, random error variance should be held to a minimum. In addition, a number of considerations argue against experimental bias.

Chief among these is the fact that the instruments used in this study were not initially scored with the hypotheses of the present research in mind. The original objective was to compare a variety of different versions of the MSCS (Miner 1977b); minority and female samples were included to investigate adverse impact. Only subsequent to the scoring of the protocols did the specific hypotheses of the study enter the picture. Thus bias in favor of these hypotheses, however unlikely on other grounds, seems particularly improbable in the present instance.

The Situation-specific MSCS

Data from a second, experimental version of the MSCS were also available for the samples of this study. This instrument was developed for purposes independent of those involved in the present research, and relatively little is known about its psychometric properties. Nevertheless, these data do provide an opportunity for independent substantiation of the main MSCS findings.

This second instrument is designated "situation specific" because, unlike the standard MSCS, it focuses directly on the work environment of the first-line supervisor. It is identical with the standard MSCS in all respects except for the actual content of the stems. It measures the same variables with the same number of items distributed through the measure in the same positions. Scoring was done using the same guidelines as for the regular MSCS.

The two scales have proved to be consistently significantly related in various subsamples based on occupation, sex, and race, as well as in the total subject sample of this study. Item score correlations range from .38 to .81, with a median value of .63. Subscale correlations are lower, averaging about .35. Although differences in mean item scores on the two measures have been found to be minimal, significant differences do appear on the various subscales; thus direct comparability from scale to scale cannot be assumed.

In the case of this situation-specific measure, as with the standard MSCS, the scoring was done by the author. Many of the arguments presented for the unbiased nature of the MSCS results hold here as well. However, it should be recognized that the situation-specific measure is experimental in nature and was used for the first time on the subjects of this study.

Subscale Correlations

Intercorrelations among the various subscales obtained in the present study are given in Table 8.1. The median value for the standard MSCS is .15, which compares favorably with the value of .12 obtained in previous investigations and with the .13 median for the situation-specific MSCS as given in Table 8.1. When the two versions are combined to double the test length, this median intercorrelation increases to .19, and seventeen of the twenty-one correlations increase in value over those for the regular MSCS. Yet even with such a sizable contribution to reliability, the intercorrelations remain quite low. The evidence from this study, as from others (Miner 1977b), indicates a consistently positive but very modest relationship among the various subscale measures.

Table 8.1

Correlations among Subscale Scores in Total Sample

Subscale	1	2	3	4	5	6	7
1. Authority Figures	—	.07	.17	–.01	.00	.16	–.01
2. Competitive Games	.28	—	.15	.28	.04	.19	.19
3. Competitive Situations	.34	.14	—	.18	.17	.10	.25
4. Assertive Role	.04	.12	.27	—	.10	.21	.08
5. Imposing Wishes	.04	.19	–.05	.13	—	.11	.24
6. Standing Out from Group	.06	.05	.13	.15	.15	—	.05
7. Routine Functions	.14	.17	.07	–.04	.05	.20	—

Note: Standard Miner Sentence Completion Scale (MSCS) intercorrelations are above the diagonal and situation-specific correlations below it.

Construct Validity

Any test of the hypotheses using MSCS measures must rest on the evidence of the measures' construct validity as indexes of motivation to manage. As indicated previously, the MSCS has consistently yielded evidence of criterion-related validity (concurrent and predictive) against criteria of managerial success. On the other hand, relationships with other types of success indexes such as course grades in college, sales performance, success as a management consultant, faculty rank achieved, and research accomplishment have consistently proven nonexistent or, as in the last instance, negative (Miner 1965a, 1977b).

As might be expected, managerial groups have been found to score above comparable nonmanagerial samples. In addition, business students aspiring to managerial careers tend to obtain relatively high scores, whereas students wishing to become teachers, accountants, counselors, and other types of professionals or specialists score low; thus the MSCS is predictive of career aspirations in the manner anticipated (Miner 1977b). Furthermore, a course designed specifically to increase motivation to manage has in fact raised MSCS scores significantly in nine out of ten trials. Among a wide range of other courses similarly measured, significant score increases have not been obtained.

In addition to the situation-specific version of the MSCS used in this study, a number of other variants of the test have been developed, including several multiple-choice measures. These different measures have invariably been found to be significantly positively related, and usually at a high level; the median correlation across measures and samples is .65 (Miner 1977b), a figure roughly comparable to that obtained when different measures of intelligence are intercorrelated.

Further evidence of construct validity derives from studies correlating the MSCS with other instruments (Miner 1977b). A special measure of supervisory interest developed for the Kuder Preference Record-Vocational Form C correlated .45 and .38 with the MSCS item score in two different managerial samples. Those scoring high on the MSCS also score high on the Adjective Check List (Gough 1965), measures of Dominance ($r = .38$), Favorable Self-Opinion ($r = .36$), Defensiveness ($r = .34$), Achievement ($r = .33$), and Self-Confidence ($r = .32$); they score low on Abasement ($r = -.39$), Counseling Readiness ($r = -.34$) and Succorance ($r = -.33$). On the Myers-Briggs Type Indicator (Myers 1962), they score low on introversion ($r = -.40$). Positive relationships with the various Strong Vocational Interest Blank scores (Strong and Campbell

1966) are most pronounced for Credit Manager ($r = .51$), Business Education Teacher ($r = .44$), Sales Manager ($r = .40$), Vocational Counselor ($r = .40$), Mortician ($r = .39$), Personnel Director ($r = .39$), YMCA Secretary ($r = .39$), YMCA Physical Director ($r = .38$), Army Officer ($r = .37$), and Interest Maturity ($r = .36$); negative relationships are greatest for Artist ($r = -.45$), Architect ($r = -.44$), Mathematician ($r = -.44$), Author-Journalist ($r = -.42$), Physicist ($r = -.42$), Chemist ($r = -.42$), and Dentist ($r = -.38$). On the Self-Description Inventory (Ghiselli 1971), high scores on the managerial talent indexes of Decisiveness ($r = .35$), Supervisory Ability ($r = .26$), and Self-Assurance ($r = .24$) are associated with high MSCS scores and the relationship is negative for Need Security ($r = -.26$). All of these correlations are significant, and most of them support a managerial motivation interpretation of the MSCS scores.

Data bearing on the differential construct validity of the individual subscales are limited, but certain findings are indicative (Miner 1965a, 1977b). In contrast with other subscale scores, Standing Out from Group (a desire for a differentiated role) has consistently been found to remain high among university professors. Assertive (Masculine) Role scores tend to be lower in female groups than among males. Although other subscale scores have declined steadily in successive college student groups since the early 1960s, Imposing Wishes (power motivation) and Standing Out from Group have held steady over many samples up to the present time. These and other findings indicate that the various subscale scores do not necessarily move in a lock-step fashion.

Samples

The two instruments were administered to a total of 138 managers with a large automobile manufacturing company (General Motors). They worked at a variety of company locations throughout the United States. Eighty-five percent were currently assigned to first-line supervisory positions on a full-time basis, and most of the remainder combined limited supervisory duties with the performance of some function involving technical or professional responsibilities. The work supervised spanned the entire range of company activities—production, receiving, warehousing, maintenance, engineering, accounting, quality control, work standards, computer operations, purchasing, sales, finance, insurance, accounts payable, material handling, medical, personnel, payroll, records retention, labor relations, and others.

The original intent was to obtain approximately equal-sized groups of males and females, minorities, and whites. An extended search for minority females, however, yielded only four, an insufficient number for analysis. Thus, the hypotheses remain untested insofar as this group is concerned, and these four females were not included in subsequent analyses. Data were obtained on seventy-five white males, thirty-six white females, and twenty-three minority males, mostly blacks. These groups were used to test the hypotheses through a comparison of mean item scores. In those instances in which this comprehensive item score analysis supported the hypotheses, subscale comparisons were made subsequently in an effort to identify those specific subscales that had contributed to the overall differences.

RESULTS

Table 8.2 presents the overall test of the hypotheses. Hypothesis 1 is supported by the data. On the standard MSCS, the minority male managers score significantly higher than the white males and also the white females. This is the main test of the hypothesis. However, data from

Table 8.2

Mean Scores on Miner Sentence Completion Scale Measures for Minority Male, White Female, and White Male Managers

MSCS Measures	Minority Males (N = 23)	White Females (N = 36)	White Males (N = 75)
Standard	5.26	1.18*	2.81*
Situation-specific	5.57	3.89	2.31*
Combined	10.83	5.69*	5.12*

Note: MSCS = Miner Sentence Completion Scale.
*$p < .05$ for comparison with minority males.

the situation-specific MSCS offer collaboration in that the significant difference between the two male samples is once again obtained; the difference between the minority males and the white females does not attain accepted levels of significance. When the two thirty-five-item measures are combined to produce a more reliable instrument, the data consistently support Hypothesis 1.

In contrast, Hypothesis 2 is not supported. The white females do not obtain an overall item score on the standard MSCS that is significantly below the white males. Furthermore, the situation-specific measure yields results that not only fail to attain significance but are in fact in a direction opposite to that hypothesized. The increased reliability provided by the combined measure does nothing to change the situation.

Table 8.3 provides information on the specific subscales contributing to the overall findings in support of Hypothesis 1. On the standard MSCS the minority males score significantly higher on the Competitive Situations, Assertive Role, and Routine Administrative Functions measures. In addition, there is corroboration for the Competitive Games and Imposing Wishes subscales from the other analyses. In general, these findings suggest that the greater motivation to manage of the minority males may be a consequence of their more pronounced willingness to compete, take charge, exercise power, and assert themselves.

DISCUSSION

With regard to the minority male findings, it is possible that prior discrimination has operated over the years to stockpile minority managerial talent at the first level of supervision, rather than spreading it evenly through all levels of management as deserved promotions occurred. Under this hypothesis, minorities with high motivation to manage scores would be blocked from further promotions and held at the first level, whereas their white counterparts would move up and therefore would not appear in the same numbers at the bottom of the managerial hierarchy.

Were this to be true, the minority males should be older than the other two groups of first-level supervisors, and one would also expect that the discrimination would be reflected in higher levels of education among minority managers at the same level as whites. This expectation is based on the over-qualification concept, which states that minorities must be better trained and educated than whites to reach the same position level (Fernandez 1975).

The data do not support either of these hypotheses. The mean age of the minority males is

Table 8.3

Mean Subscale Scores for Minority Male, White Female, and White Male Managers with Significance Levels for Hypothesized Differences

Measures	Minority Males (N = 23)	White Females (N = 36)	White Males (N = 75)
Authority Figures			
Standard MSCS	.78	1.08	.61
Situation-specific MSCS	1.43	1.25	.80
Combined	2.22	2.33	1.41
Competitive Games			
Standard MSCS	1.30	.64	1.49
Situation-specific MSCS	.74	–.44**	.05
Combined	2.04	.19*	1.55
Competitive Situations			
Standard MSCS	–.48	–.83	–1.25*
Situation-specific MSCS	1.13	1.64	1.09
Combined	.65	.81	–.16
Assertive Role			
Standard MSCS	.65	–.31*	.11
Situation-specific MSCS	.57	.19	–.04
Combined	1.22	–.11*	.07*
Imposing Wishes			
Standard MSCS	.96	.39	.44
Situation-specific MSCS	.91	.28*	–.09**
Combined	1.87	.67*	.35**
Standing Out from Group			
Standard MSCS	.78	.50	.84
Situation-specific MSCS	.26	.31	.27
Combined	1.04	.81	1.11
Routine Functions			
Standard MSCS	1.26	.33*	.57*
Situation-specific MSCS	.52	.67	.23
Combined	1.78	1.00	.80*

Note: MSCS = Miner Sentence Completion Scale.
*$p < .05$, **$p < .01$ for comparison with minority males

35.8 years, below the mean of 38.3 years for the white females and above that of 34.1 years for the white males. In neither case does the difference approach significance ($t = 1.09$ and 0.90, respectively). When education level is scored on a scale of 1 (less than high school graduate) to 5 (graduate study), the minority males obtain a mean value of 2.9, which is almost identical with that for the white males. The white female mean is 2.4, a value that approaches significance in comparison with the minority males ($t = 1.93$, $p < .10$). This trend, however, appears to be due to the relatively low educational level of the female group. In fact, the white females are both less well educated and older than the white males. These differences have no influence on the major findings, however, since age and education are uncorrelated with the MSCS.

The findings of this study are similar to those of two earlier investigations in that they provide no support for the view that females who enter upon a managerial career have less motivation to manage than males. They also provide the first evidence supporting the hypothesis that minorities who move into management have unusually strong motivation to manage. At least in terms of motivational requirements, the data indicate that the upgrading of minorities into positions of increased managerial responsibility represents a feasible solution to the twin pressures of compliance with equal employment opportunity legislation and managerial talent shortages. In addition, at least insofar as motivation to manage is concerned, there is nothing to indicate that a similar upgrading of female managers would yield consequences any different from those obtained with males. This latter conclusion is reinforced by assessment center data on male and female managerial candidates. The levels of managerial talent in the two sex groups as defined by this alternative method of evaluation have been found to be practically identical (Moses and Boehm 1975).

CHAPTER 9

ACADEMY OF MANAGEMENT MEMBERS AS PROFESSIONALS

INTRODUCTION

The Academy of Management research was carried out to provide data that would serve as a basis for my presidential address to that organization in 1978. These results represent an expanded version of that presentation. They were published in the *Academy of Management Journal* (Miner 1980a), although at the time such publication was not an automatic accoutrement of the presidential office in the Academy. In actual fact the manuscript was quite heavily reviewed and came very close to not appearing in the *Journal.*

This is the initial piece of research dealing with professionals, and accordingly introduced Form P of the Miner Sentence Completion Scale (MSCS). It thus fills the void made evident by the work with management consultants at McKinsey and Company (Chapter 5). In a very real sense it started a whole new thrust of role motivation theory, and indeed it introduced a new theory comparable to the hierarchical theory of Chapter 3. We will return to this professional theory and its measures in subsequent chapters.

* * *

The research reported here represents a test of one of four closely coordinated limited domain theories of organizational energy (Miner, 1976c; 1978b; 1980b). The first of these four, managerial role-motivation theory, is a theory of hierarchic inducement systems. It has been in existence for over twenty years and has generated a considerable body of research, most of which is supportive (Miner 1965a 1977b 1978c). The second theory, which applies to the domain of professional inducement systems, is of recent origin, at least in its present form, and was tested for the first time in this study. The remaining two theories, dealing with group inducement systems and task inducement systems, have not been directly tested as yet, primarily because measures to operationalize the variables have not been created. However, research related to McClelland's (1961, 1962) theory of the achievement situation does provide indirect support for the task inducement theory.

The guiding hypothesis for the research reported here is that the theory of professional inducement will more effectively predict professional career accomplishment than will the hierarchic inducement theory. The research itself has been conducted among professors employed in colleges and universities who are members of the Academy of Management.

The professional theory views work effort or energy as being induced as a result of the flow of role requirements from a profession and its norm transmitting association(s); thus, cosmopolitan rather than local methods of influence are emphasized (Gouldner 1957). At least five types of role prescriptions are hypothesized to combine with appropriate motivational patterns within the individual to induce work energy of the kind that powers organizations. The five role prescriptions of the professional theory were developed from various definitions of professionals and professional organizations such as those of Etzioni (1964), Satow (1975), and Vollmer and Mills (1966), and from certain research on professionals (Hall, 1967; Harrison, 1974; Sorensen and Sorensen, 1974):

1. Acquiring knowledge. In a profession technical expertise and knowledge must be developed, transmitted, and used in the service of clients. Thus, a professional should desire to learn and acquire the knowledge that permits providing an expert service.
2. Independent action. In a profession the individual has a private and personally responsible relationship with clients of a kind that typically requires autonomous action based on individual professional judgment. Thus, a professional should be an independent person and desire to act independently of others.
3. Accepting status. In a profession the successful provision of services to clients is predicated on client recognition of the existence of expert status. Thus, a professional needs to desire status in the eyes of others and the symbols of status in order that the available services be utilized. Involved here is a particular kind of visibility that not only attracts attention but also yields recognition and respect of a kind that will attract and retain clients.
4. Providing help. In a profession the client-professional relationship is central, and within that relationship the client should be assisted in achieving desired goals, or on occasion that which is considered by the profession to be in the client's best interest, even if not actually desired by the client. Thus, a professional must possess a desire to help others to achieve their best interests. This type of motivation, although normally described as a desire to serve others, is conceived as being conceptually comparable to the "helping power" construct as elaborated by McClelland (1975).
5. Professional commitment. In a profession there needs to be a strong tie to the profession, of a kind that keeps members responsive to ethical norms, and this tie typically is mediated through a sense of personal identification or commitment. Thus, a professional should possess a high level of value-based identification with the profession and commitment to it.

Among various hypotheses derivable from the professional theory (Miner 1980b) the one of significance for the present research is that within the domain of the theory *the individual who possesses the indicated motivational patterns at a high level will achieve generally accepted criteria of professional success more frequently than will the individual who lacks these motives.* The domain involved is defined by the various criteria of professional practice, including the acquisition of a set of specialized techniques supported by a body of theory, the development of a career supported and influenced by an association of colleagues, the establishment of a consensus within society that recognizes professional status, and the existence of a specified set of professional norms or ethics (Miner 1978b). Within this domain other types of motives having little or no conceptual relationship to specifically professional performance would not be expected to yield evidence of empirical relationships with success criteria.

Because of its parallel position to the theory of professional inducement systems, managerial role-motivation theory was selected to test the expectation of no relationship for theories dealing with domains other than the professional. This theory appears particularly germane because the sample studied consisted of professors of management who, however, were not actually managers of hierarchic systems. The sample falls within the professional domain, but within that space would appear to be conceptually closer to the hierarchic domain than would many other professions. Accordingly, a theoretical test against hierarchic predictors has something of the quality of a crucial experiment: if the differential prediction hypothesis is confirmed here at the boundary, it is very likely to be confirmed for more conceptually distant professions as well.

The hierarchic theory has been in the literature for many years, the first formal statement being in Miner (1965a). It is a theory for managers of bureaucracies large enough to require formalized written communication. As originally conceived, it was an extrapolation from the observations and clinical insights of the author as they applied to the Atlantic Refining Company in the late 1950s. Later the theory's domain was expanded to include large bureaucracies more generally. Its six role prescriptions have been expounded elsewhere (see, for example, Chapter 6).

METHOD

Sample

The subjects were 112 professors employed by colleges and universities in the United States. These individuals were the ones from an original randomly selected 10 percent sample of the Academy of Management's U.S. faculty membership who responded to a single mailing. The original sample contained 348 names; thus a response rate of 32 percent was achieved. The data were collected in early 1978. The Academy of Management's membership is predominantly made up of regular faculty members, most of them teaching one or more aspects of the management discipline in schools of business administration. Student members and members employed outside the academic setting were not included in the study. The mean age of the professor respondents was 43.5 years, with a standard deviation of 11.9.

It was possible to check on the representativeness of the respondent sample by comparing respondents and nonrespondents from the original 10 percent sample on several variables regularly entered into the professional organization's computer files. These included membership in the various professional divisions of the Academy, which numbered fourteen at the time of the study, area of the country broken down into eight regions, and whether membership dues were paid up or not. Of the twenty-three comparisons, only one yielded a significant difference—a disproportionately high number of members of the Social Issues Division in the respondent sample ($\chi^2 = 4.35$, $p < .05$). This one finding could well have occurred by chance. Thus the data do not provide evidence that would refute a claim of representativeness for the sample of 112. Comparisons with data from other, much larger samples (numbering over 1,000) of the Academy's membership also appear to indicate that representativeness was attained (Forsgren 1978; Wren, Atherton, and Michaelsen 1978). On the other hand, a number of management professors are not members of the Academy of Management, and those who are can be assumed to be among the professionally more active. Furthermore, it is entirely possible that the respondents are more active than the nonrespondents.

In general the nature, and limitations, of the sample would be expected to introduce a conservative bias in the results. Heterogeneity of organizations characteristically increases error variance over what would be anticipated from most single organization studies because the criteria are based on a more diverse set of considerations. Because the sample is probably more professionally active than the population it is intended to represent, some restriction of range and thus lower correlation values may result.

Predictor Measures

Miner Sentence Completion Scale (MSCS)–Form P

This instrument was devised specifically for this study. It is intended as a measure of the five motivational patterns specified by the professional theory. It contains forty sentence completion items, each of which is scored +1, 0, or –1 depending on whether the response indicates approach, unknown, or avoidance motivation. The total item score accordingly may vary from a possible high of +40 to a low of –40. In addition, subscale scores based on randomly distributed sets of eight items may be obtained. These subscales are intended to correspond to the five variables of the professional theory, and scores on each may range from +8 to –8; there are no filler items. As indicated in Table 9.1 all subscales correlate with the total item score in the range .48 to .69 in the study sample; the median correlation between the subscales of Form P is .16.

The specific items included in the final version of Form P were selected from a much larger item pool that had been pretested on an entirely independent sample from the one utilized in this study. This was the same approach utilized in developing Form H some twenty years ago. Within the subset of items established for each subscale those ultimately selected exhibited the closest relationship with a global rating of the relative professional accomplishments of the pretest subjects. In addition, to be used, items had to yield sufficiently high frequencies in both the approach and avoidance motivation categories so that they could in fact discriminate, rather than merely load a constant value into the scores. The specific scoring procedures or rules used to categorize completions also were established in advance from the pretest sample.

Although extensive analyses of the psychometric properties of Form P itself have not been carried out as yet, such analyses have been made using the original Miner Sentence Completion Scale (Form H), and various derivatives of it (Miner 1978d). In view of the virtually identical formats and scoring procedures used with the two instruments, there is reason to anticipate comparable psychometric results. However, in view of the greater number of items (eight rather than five) used in each subscale, Form P might yield somewhat higher subscale reliabilities. Such a result could introduce a differential advantage in favor of the Form P measures over Form H in predicting criteria.

In an effort to check on this possibility, the internal consistency (corrected odd-even) reliability of Form P was determined for the total sample of 112 professors. The total score value was .59, and the subscale coefficients ranged from .02 to .43 with a median of .31. These figures are substantially *below* the repeat administration reliability of Form H. They also are so low as to bring the use of Form P into serious question, based on traditional psychometric

Table 9.1

Intercorrelations among MSCS–Hierarchic (Form H) **and MSCS–Professional** (Form P) **Measures** (N = 112)

Within Instrument Correlations—MSCS–Professional

	Acquiring Knowledge	Independent Action	Accepting Status	Providing Help	Professional Commitment
Total Item Score	.58**	.48**	.69**	.57**	.60**
Acquiring Knowledge		.09	.33**	.19*	.08
Independent Action			.17	.13	.04
Accepting Status				.14	.29**
Providing Help					.32**

Within Instrument Correlations—MSCS–Hierarchic

	Authority Figures	Competitive Games	Competitive Situations	Assertive Role	Imposing Wishes	Standing Out from Group	Routine Administrative Functions
Total Item Score	.29**	.54**	.46**	.55**	.58**	.63**	.57**
Authority Figures		–.10	–.11	.07	.09	.04	.21*
Competitive Games			.30**	.19*	.11	.13	.17
Competitive Situations				.05	.20*	.27**	–.03
Assertive Role					.22*	.24*	.20*
Imposing Wishes						.30**	.18
Standing Out from Group							.29**

Note: MSCS = Miner Sentence Completion Scale.

Table 9.2

Intercorrelations Between MSCS–Hierarchic (Form H) **and MSCS–Professional** (Form P) **Measures** (N = 112)

Between Instrument Correlations

	MSCS–Professional					
MSCS–Hierarchic	Total Score	Acquiring Knowledge	Independent Action	Accepting Status	Providing Help	Professional Commitment
Total Item Score	.33**	.09	.15	.25**	.30**	.18
Authority Figures	.03	.04	−.02	−.05	.04	.07
Competitive Games	.21*	.10	.22*	.10	.15	.07
Competitive Situations	.05	.02	.14	.05	.00	−.05
Assertive Role	.25**	.06	.04	.27**	.20*	.15
Imposing Wishes	.20*	.05	.03	.14	.22*	.15
Standing Out from Group	.21*	.00	.09	.19*	.21*	.14
Routine Administrative Functions	.20*	.05	.01	.20*	.23*	.10

Note: MSCS = Miner Sentence Completion Scale.
$^{*}p < .05$; $^{**}p < .01$

assumptions. However, Atkinson (1977) reports several studies that lead him to conclude that when projective measures are used, substantial construct validity can be obtained even where there is no internal consistency reliability. Given these findings, and in the absence of the more appropriate repeat administration reliability measures, it seemed justified to proceed with the analysis of the Form P data.

Miner Sentence Completion Scale–Form H

This instrument is of the same type as Form P. However, it measures the six variables of the hierarchic theory with seven five-item subscales. In the management professor sample the seven subscales correlated with the total item score in the range .29 to .63, and the median correlation between subscales is .18 (see Table 9.1). In contrast, the median of the correlations between the subscales of Form P and Form H is .09, roughly half within the instrument values. To the extent the two comprehensive measures are significantly intercorrelated, this appears to be a function of low positive coefficients involving the Accepting Status and Providing Help subscales of the professional scale and the Assertive Role, Imposing Wishes, Standing Out from Group, and Routine Administrative Functions subscales of the hierarchic scale. The focused nature of these relationships argues against the existence of a pervasive response bias operating across both instruments; the correlation of .33 between the total item scores appears to be attributable to only six of the twelve subscales (see Table 9.2).

Criterion Measures

Compensation

As with all of the criterion measures, compensation was self-reported by the respondents. Nine different compensation measures were utilized.

1. University total. The regular yearly compensation from the employing organization reported, whether the typical mode of compensation was on an academic year or twelve-month basis. A figure below $10,000 was given a score of 1 and each successive $5,000 interval added an additional point.
2. University nine-month. For those who reported an academic year compensation figure, the value used was the same as for university total compensation. For those who reported a twelve-month figure this value was adjusted downward to 75 percent of the original and then the appropriate score was assigned based on the particular $5,000 range entered.
3. Management development. Additional income earned in the average year from the conduct of management development and other seminars. A score of 0 was assigned for values below $1,000, 1 for values in the $1,000 to $4,900 range, and each successive $5,000 interval added an additional point.
4. Consulting activities. Additional income earned in the average year from consulting activities. The scale was the same as for management development income.
5. Speaking engagements. Additional income earned in the average year from speaking engagements. Although the scale used for management development income was utilized initially, the values thus obtained were dichotomized as close to the median as possible and predictor-criterion relationships determined with biserial correlation due to the limited range.
6. Publishing royalties. Additional income earned in the average year from writing, including royalties and other earnings. Here, too, limitations in range required dichotomization of the scale and the use of biserial correlations.
7. Other nonuniversity. Additional income earned in the average year from sources other than management development, consulting activities, speaking engagements, and publishing royalties. Specifically noted were teaching at other educational institutions and operating a business, but other earned income sources were included as well, such as serving on boards of directors and doing labor arbitration. The scale was the same as for management development income.
8. Total nonuniversity. The sum of the scale values for 3 through 7 above.
9. Total professional. The sum of 1 or 2 and 8 above.

Academic Rank

Academic rank was recorded in terms of the following scale: Instructor—1, Assistant Professor—2, Associate Professor—3, Professor—4, Professor with endowed chair or similar appointment—5.

Publications

Three different measures of publication effectiveness were used.

1. Books. The number of books actually published, with subsequent editions after the first counted as 0.5. No correction for multiple authorship was used. Due to the large number of individuals who had not published any books, this measure was dichotomized and biserial correlations computed.
2. Journal articles. The total number of professional journal articles authored or coauthored.

3. Prestige articles. Articles authored or coauthored in the following publications: *Academy of Management Journal, Academy of Management Review, Administrative Science Quarterly, American Sociological Review, California Management Review, Harvard Business Review, Industrial Relations, Journal of Applied Psychology, Journal of Business* (Chicago), *Management Science, Organizational Behavior and Human Performance,* and *Personnel Psychology.*

The selection of these particular publications, although somewhat arbitrary, was influenced strongly by the results of a journal rating procedure developed by the management faculty at the University of Maryland. The journals included coincide closely with a listing of quality publications in the management field presented by Miller (1978), based on a survey of 208 management faculty members nationwide.

Professional Organizations

Measures in this area focused predominantly but not exclusively on the Academy of Management simply because it was known that all subjects belong to this organization:

1. Number of memberships. The reported number of *national* professional organizations in which the individual had achieved membership.
2. Attendance at meetings. The number of *national* Academy of Management meetings attended over the preceding ten years.
3. Participation in meetings. The number of *national* Academy of Management meetings in which the individual was a program participant over the preceding ten years.

Position Type

This measure was concerned with whether the individual had achieved an administrative or research appointment:

1. Administrative position. Of the twenty-eight individuals with administrative appointments, nineteen were department heads or in comparable positions, three were program chairpersons, four were associate deans, and two were deans. Analyses were carried out using an administrative-nonadministrative dichotomy and point biserial correlation.
2. Research position. Of the twenty-four individuals with research appointments, eight were on funded research grants, three were on institute research staffs, and thirteen had some release time from teaching, presumably primarily at institutional expense. Again predictor-criterion relationships were computed using the point biserial coefficient.

Doctoral Education

These indexes were included predicated on the assumption that greater professional prestige attaches to those most closely related to doctoral education and thus the perpetuation of the profession.

1. Department offers doctorate. Whether or not the department in which the professor worked had a doctoral program. This dichotomy was then used to calculate point biserial coefficients.

2. Supervises dissertations. Whether or not the individual supervises doctoral dissertations. These were primarily dissertations within the same department. However, in a few cases an individual in a department without a doctoral program nevertheless supervised dissertations in departments that did. Here, too, the point biserial correlation was used.

The twenty criteria tend to be quite closely related, as indicated in Table 9.3. Half of the variables are significantly related to 75 percent or more of the others. In order of the number of significant relationships, these are: total professional compensation, total nonuniversity compensation, journal articles, books, prestige articles, publishing royalties compensation, academic rank, university 9-month compensation, management development compensation, and supervises dissertations.

The pervasive role that publishing plays in the profession is clearly evident in these results. None of the publications measures appear in the following ranking of the more peripheral criteria: speaking engagements compensation, university total compensation, attendance at meetings, number of memberships, participation in meetings, consulting activities compensation, department offers doctorate, other nonuniversity compensation, administrative position, and research position.

Of the twenty criteria, only one—research position—is significantly related to less than 40 percent of the other measures. Research appointments appear to be associated only with being in a doctoral department and supervising dissertations. The implication is that there is a type of individual who, although research oriented, does not necessarily publish more, do more in professional organizations, or get paid more.

The criteria utilized certainly do not exhaust the possibilities available, and questions can be raised regarding the appropriateness of some of the measures. Yet the high degree of intercorrelation does suggest a common bond, and the measures do tap a wide range of professional activities. In deference to the fact that certain of the criteria may be viewed by some as irrelevant to professional success, only individual criterion relationships were calculated; thus no overall, composite criterion measure was utilized.

Because all measures (predictor and criterion) were collected at the same time from the same individuals, there is some possibility that method specificity might influence the results. Several considerations argue against this: The predictors are projective in nature; the criteria self-report. The projective approach used has proved relatively immune to falsification, and subjects typically have no knowledge of what they are revealing about themselves. There appears to be a consensus among those knowledgeable on the subject that the sentence completion method is the most valid of the projective techniques (Shouval, Duck, and Ginton 1975). The approach used to collect criterion data has been used widely in research for some time. See Porter (1964), for example. Although information of this kind often is distorted in the employment situation by applicants for lower level positions (Goldstein 1971), this seems much less likely to occur under the present circumstances, in which the benefits from portraying oneself favorably would be expected to be much less pronounced. The MSCS–Form P, MSCS–Form H, and the biographical questionnaire containing the criterion items were each presented separately and completed in whatever order the subject chose, presumably varying from subject to subject.

RESULTS

As indicated in Table 9.4, a number of the professional career success criteria are related to age. In general, these relationships are positive, and in the case of academic rank and several of

Table 9.3

Relationships among Criteria of Professional Success (N = 112)

	Correlations														
	Compensation									Publications			Professional Organizations		
	University														
	Total	9-month	Management Development	Consulting Activities	Speaking Engagements	Publishing Royalties	Other Non-university	Total Non-university	Academic Rank	Books	Journal Articles	Prestige Articles	Number of Memberships	Attendance at Meetings	Participation in Meetings
Compensation															
Total Professional	.72**	.69**	.71**	.58**	.43**	.73**	.34**	.92**	.64**	.70**	.61**	.49**	.33**	.34**	.29**
University—Total		.81**	.37**	.14	.18	.64**	.13	.40**	.78**	.61**	.38**	.35**	.23*	.37**	.16
University 9-month			.32**	.14	.37**	.69**	.20*	.47**	.77**	.61**	.50**	.43**	.23*	.42**	.23*
Management Development				.45**	.64**	.61**	-.06	.74**	.25**	.47**	.34**	.25**	.18	.25**	.36**
Consulting Activities					.57**	.33**	.10	.70**	.21*	.31**	.22*	.28**	.15	-.01	.07
Speaking Engagements						.22*	.32**	.51**	.28**	.38**	.82**	.68**	.30**	.37**	.50**
Publishing Royalties							.30**	.74**	.61**	.87**	.79**	.54**	.46**	.61**	.57**
Other Nonuniversity								.38**	.25**	.08	.41**	.05	.24*	-.08	-.05
Total Nonuniversity									.41**	.59**	.60**	.46**	.31**	.25**	.29**
Academic Rank										.56**	.41**	.30**	.21*	.30**	.10
Publications															
Books											.47**	.38**	.36**	.41**	.41**
Journal Articles												.57**	.48**	.21*	.31**
Prestige Articles													.19*	.30**	.40**
Professional Organizations															
Number of Memberships														.05	.09
Attendance at Meetings															.68**
Participation in Meetings															

(continued)

Table 9.3 *(continued)*

	t-tests Between Means											
	Administrative Position			*Research Appointment*			*Department Offers Doctorate*			*Supervises Dissertations*		
	Administrative	*Not Administrative*		*Research*	*Not Research*		*Doctorate*	*No Doctorate*		*Dissertations*	*No Dissertations*	
	(N = 28)	(N = 84)	*t*	(N = 24)	(N = 88)	*t*	(N = 43)	(N = 69)	*t*	(N = 31)	(N = 81)	*t*
Compensation												
Total Professional	8.3	5.7	4.18**	6.2	6.4	.76	7.3	5.8	2.36*	8.5	5.6	4.07**
University—Total	5.7	4.1	6.52**	4.7	4.5	.56	4.8	4.4	1.66	5.5	4.2	5.14**
University—9-month	4.6	3.7	4.27**	3.9	3.9	.16	4.1	3.8	1.48	4.6	3.6	4.06**
Management Development	1.0	.4	3.11**	.5	.6	.33	.7	.5	1.66	.8	.5	2.10*
Consulting Activities	.8	.7	.71	.6	.7	.68	.8	.6	1.03	1.1	.5	3.05**
Speaking Engagements	.1	0	.83	0	.1	.65	.1	0	1.36	.2	0	1.54
Publishing Royalties	.6	.3	1.31	.3	.3	.02	.6	.2	2.06*	.6	.2	1.58
Other Nonuniversity	.1	.2	.77	.1	.2	1.54	.3	.1	1.00	.3	.2	1.00
Total Nonuniversity	2.6	1.6	2.08*	1.5	1.9	.87	2.5	1.4	2.28*	3.0	1.4	2.75**
Academic Rank	3.6	3.0	4.79**	3.0	3.2	.61	3.2	3.1	.58	3.7	2.9	4.12**
Publications												
Books	1.6	.9	1.20	1.3	1.0	.60	2.1	.5	2.85**	2.7	.5	3.07**
Journal Articles	14.7	8.4	1.10	9.1	10.2	.32	17.0	5.6	2.41*	21.4	5.6	2.53*
Prestige Articles	1.3	1.2	.23	1.8	1.0	1.29	2.1	.6	2.76**	2.8	.6	3.26**
Professional Organizations												
Number of Memberships	3.4	3.0	1.11	3.3	3.1	.58	3.6	2.8	2.05*	3.9	2.8	2.24*
Attendance at Meetings	3.4	2.1	2.62**	2.3	2.4	.18	2.5	2.3	.36	2.7	2.3	.74
Participation in Meetings	1.3	.8	1.44	1.3	.9	1.35	1.4	.7	2.25*	1.5	.8	2.09*

	Chi Squares for Frequencies					
	Percent Research	χ^2	*Percent Doctorate*	χ^2	*Percent Dissertations*	χ^2
Administrative position						
Administration	18	.30	39	.07	43	4.40*
Not Administration	23		38		23	
Research appointment						
Research			63	7.53**	54	10.89**
Not Research			32		20	
Department offers doctorate						
Doctorate					65	48.87**
No Doctorate					4	

$*p < .05$; $**p < .01$

Table 9.4

Age Correlations for MSCS and Criterion Variables (N = 112)

MSCS	r	Criteria	r
Hierarchic		**Compensation**	
Total Item Score	.00	Total Professional	.48**
Authority Figures	.14	University—Total	.62**
Competitive Games	–.02	University—9-month	.67**
Competitive Situations	–.30**	Management Development	.06
Assertive Role	.20*	Consulting Activities	.09
Imposing Wishes	.00	Speaking Engagements	.24*
Standing Out from Group	–.06	Publishing Royalties	.43**
Routine Administrative Functions	.05	Other Nonuniversity	.28**
Professional		Total Nonuniversity	.30**
Total Item Score	.38**	**Academic Rank**	.76**
Acquiring Knowledge	.07	**Publications**	
Independent Action	.09	Books	.34**
Accepting Status	.24*	Journal Articles	.34**
Providing Help	.27**	Prestige Articles	.17
Professional Commitment	.45**	**Professional Organizations**	
		Number of Memberships	.14
		Attendance at Meetings	.20*
		Participation in Meetings	–.08
		Position Type	
		Administrative Position	.14
		Research Appointment	–.21*
		Doctoral Education	
		Department Offers Doctorate	–.13
		Supervises Dissertations	.09

Note: MSCS = Miner Sentence Completion Scale.
$*p < .05$; $**p < .01$

the compensation variables they are quite strong. The only significant negative relationship is for holding a research position—another indicator of the tangential nature of this variable.

On the other hand, the hierarchic MSCS yields no consistent pattern of relationship with age, a result consonant with that obtained in many other research studies. The professional MSCS differs in that some evidence of a positive relationship to age does appear for several subscales and, as a result, in the total score coefficient. The major source of this age relationship is the degree of professional commitment.

In view of these results it seemed important to determine whether significant predictor-criterion relationships would retain their significance with age effects removed. Accordingly, in Tables 9.5 and 9.6 the correlations obtained when age is partialed out are given in parentheses for all zero order correlations that reach significance.

Table 9.5 contains the findings bearing on the role of professional motivation in professional success. The median correlation of the total score measure with the twenty criteria is .35. All of the subscales appear to contribute to this result to a significant degree. The highest coefficient is .66 (for publishing royalties) and only seven negative values appear in the table—none even approaching significance. In all, 63 percent of the correlations are significant at the .05 level or better, and 80 percent of these (61 of 76) remain significant when age is partialed out.

Furthermore, the significant correlations tend to be concentrated among the more central

Table 9.5

Correlations between MSCS–Professional (Form P) **and Criterion Measures** (N = 112)

	MSCS Measures					
Criterion Measures	Total Score	Acquiring Knowledge	Independent Action	Accepting Status	Providing Help	Professional Commitment
Compensation						
Total Professional	.55**	.28**	.37**	.30**	.35**	.31**
	(.46**)	(.28**)	(.38**)	(.22*)	(.26**)	(.13)
University—Total	.57**	.35**	.21*	.39**	.36**	.36**
	(.47**)	(.39**)	(.19*)	(.32**)	(.25**)	(.11)
University—9-month	.48**	.19*	.23*	.32**	.27**	.41**
	(.33**)	(.19*)	(.23*)	(.22*)	(.13)	(.17)
Management Development	.30**	.13	.29**	.23*	.23*	.00
	(.30**)		(.28**)	(.23*)	(.22*)	
Consulting Activities	.23*	.17	.27**	.03	.20*	.03
	(.22*)		(.26**)		(.19*)	
Speaking Engagements	.28**	–.01	.16	–.08	.29**	.50**
	(.21*)				(.25**)	(.45**)
Publishing Royalties	.66**	.30**	.53**	.37**	.28**	.44**
	(.60**)	(.30**)	(.54**)	(.31**)	(.19*)	(.31**)
Other Nonuniversity	.12	.05	.06	–.02	.12	.16
Total Nonuniversity	.41**	.18	.37**	.18	.26**	.21*
	(.34**)		(.36**)		(.20*)	(.09)
Academic Rank	.51**	.17	.27**	.30**	.31**	.44**
	(.37**)		(.31**)	(.19*)	(.18)	(.17)
Publications						
Books	.53**	.17	.45**	.30**	.28**	.34**
	(.46**)		(.45**)	(.24*)	(.21*)	(.23*)
Journal Articles	.42**	.27**	.27**	.24*	.23*	.22*
	(.33**)	(.27**)	(.26**)	(.18)	(.16)	(.08)
Prestige Articles	.30**	.18	.27**	.19*	.11	.15
	(.26**)		(.25**)	(.16)		
Professional Organizations						
Number of Memberships	.30**	.18	.19*	.19*	.16	.17
	(.27**)		(.18)	(.17)		
Attendance at Meetings	.35**	.07	.29**	.25**	.07	.32**
	(.30**)		(.28**)	(.21*)		(.26**)
Participation in Meetings	.23*	.03	.29**	.16	.02	.16
	(.28**)		(.30**)			
Position Type						
Administrative Position	.43**	.26**	.22*	.37**	.21*	.19*
	(.41**)	(.25**)	(.21*)	(.35**)	(.18)	(.15)
Research Appointment	.02	–.02	.18	.02	.00	–.10
Doctoral Education						
Department Offers Doctorate	.08	.17	.11	.05	–.08	–.04
Supervises Dissertations	.35**	.24*	.33**	.16	.24*	.08
	(.35**)	(.23*)	(.32**)		(.23*)	
Median *r*	.35	.18	.27	.24	.23	.20

Note: MSCS = Miner Sentence Completion Scale. Figures in parentheses are partial correlations with age partialed out.

$*p < .05$; $**p < .01$

Table 9.6

Correlations between MSCS–Hierarchic (Form H) **and Criterion Measures** (N = 112)

	MSCS Measures							
Criterion Measures	Total Score	Authority Figures	Competitive Games	Competitive Situations	Assertive Role	Imposing Wishes	Standing Out from Group	Routine Administrative Functions
Compensation								
Total Professional	.08	−.01	.00	−.08	.06	−.01	.13	.19*
								(.19*)
University—Total	−.09	−.02	−.05	−.21*	.10	−.10	−.05	.00
				(−.03)				
University—9-month	−.10	−.05	−.02	−.21*	.06	−.10	−.07	.00
				(−.01)				
Management Development	.07	−.05	.01	.04	−.04	.01	.07	.22*
								(.22*)
Consulting Activities	.20*	.07	.04	.09	.06	.07	.20*	.20*
	(.20*)						(.21*)	(.20*)
Speaking Engagements	.15	.03	−.15	.03	.03	.10	.41**	.11
							(.43**)	
Publishing Royalties	.09	.02	.14	−.21*	−.01	−.06	.14	.24*
				(−.08)				(.24*)
Other Nonuniversity	.11	−.06	.04	.02	.08	.14	.13	.03
Total Nonuniversity	.16	.00	.03	.01	.03	.05	.19*	.25**
							(.22*)	(.24*)
Academic Rank	.02	.03	.06	−.18	.15	−.05	−.05	.08

(continued)

Table 9.6 *(continued)*

	MSCS Measures							
Criterion Measures	Total Score	Authority Figures	Competitive Games	Competitive Situations	Assertive Role	Imposing Wishes	Standing Out from Group	Routine Administrative Functions
Publications								
Books	.09	.04	.25** (.28**)	–.08	–.02	–.17	.07	.17
Journal Articles	.01	–.18	.04	–.05	.03	.00	.10	.07
Prestige Articles	–.07	–.09	–.06	–.17	–.03	–.02	.07	.01
Professional Organizations								
Number of Memberships	.17	–.07	.02	.03	.11	.13	.16	.24* (.23*)
Attendance at Meetings	.00	–.03	.05	–.10	.05	–.11	.08	.04
Participation in Meetings	.00	–.13	.07	.04	–.07	–.02	.07	–.01
Position Type								
Administrative Position	–.04	–.05	–.08	.02	.02	–.02	.04	–.08
Research Appointment	–.23* (–.23*)	–.11	–.13	–.05	–.10	–.15	–.14	–.15
Doctoral Education								
Department Offers Doctorate	–.05	–.01	–.04	.09	–.13	–.05	.01	–.05
Supervises Dissertations	–.02	.07	–.02	.04	–.06	–.02	.01	–.07
Median *r*	.02	–.02	.02	–.02	.03	–.02	.07	.06

Note: MSCS = Miner Sentence Completion Scale. Figures in parentheses are partial correlations with age partialed out.
$*p < .05$; $**p < .01$

criteria, as gauged by the high frequency of correlation of these criteria with other criteria. Among the ten criteria with 75 percent or more significant correlations of this type, 82 percent of the predictor-criterion relationships are significant at $p < .05$. Among the other, more peripheral criteria, this percentage is only 45. Three of the four most tangential criteria—research position, other nonuniversity compensation, and a department offering the doctorate—yield no significant correlations at all. Interestingly the fourth such criterion, holding an administrative position, is strongly and consistently related to professional motivation.

The data on hierarchic motivation given in Table 9.6 differ sharply from those of Table 9.5. The median total score predictor-criterion correlation is .02. None of the subscales show a consistent criterion relationship, although standing out from group does appear to be related to compensation from speaking engagements, as might be expected, and to a lesser degree to consulting income, and routine administrative functions is minimally related to several sources of nonuniversity income. The largest positive correlation is .41 and the largest negative –.23. In total, there are 15 significant correlations (9 percent), 11 of which are positive and 4 negative. As in the case of professional motivation, 80 percent of these remain significant when age is partialed out.

When the findings are broken down in terms of criterion centrality, the greater efficiency in predicting central criteria noted for the professional measure is not repeated. With the ten central criteria, 10 percent of the correlations are significant and with the remaining more peripheral criteria, 9 percent are. A large number of criteria, including appointment to an administrative position within a professional structure, do not yield any significant correlations at all, and several others produce only negative relationships.

DISCUSSION

The results obtained provide strong support for the hypotheses of this study and for the limited domain theory of professional inducement systems: Managerial role motivation theory does not work outside its own domain, in the professional arena, but the more appropriate professional theory does. There is little basis for attributing these differential results to differences in reliabilities or to other such design deficiencies. In fact, the subscale findings tend to support Atkinson's (1977) contention that internal consistency reliability is not a necessary condition for construct validity. Although partialling out the effects of age serves to reduce the number of significant correlations somewhat, it does so equally for both theories. There is no reason to believe that the professional theory results are either particularly or uniquely age dependent. The failure to find evidence of a relationship between MSCS–Form H variables and success indexes such as academic rank and administrative position is consistent with the results of an earlier, less well-controlled study of business school professors in various disciplines (Miner 1977b).

Another type of finding appears to give further support to the theoretical expectations. Inspection of the data of Table 9.7 suggests that management professors are consistently higher on professional than on managerial motivation—at least they are higher in this sample. The mean total scores for the sample as a whole are 5.57 and –2.31, respectively. Particularly noteworthy is the extremely low nature of the Form H scores. The mean total score of –2.31 contrasts sharply with the figure of roughly +5.00 which is typical for managerial samples (Miner 1977b). The Assertive Role and Competitive Games scores are particularly low. Standing Out from Group, which tends to be relatively high in teaching groups generally, is not depressed to any meaningful extent and the reduction in competitive situations

Table 9.7

Mean Scores for Miner Sentence Completion Scale–Forms P and H in Total Sample and in Administrative and Nonadministrative Samples

MSCS Measures	Total Sample (N = 112)	Administration (N = 28)	Non-administration (N = 84)	*t*
Professional				
Total Item Score	5.57	11.11	3.73	5.02**
Acquiring Knowledge	.41	1.57	.02	2.85**
Independent Action	2.01	2.96	1.69	2.40*
Accepting Status	1.29	3.04	.72	4.73**
Providing Help	1.69	2.50	1.42	2.27*
Professional Commitment	.17	1.04	–.12	2.05*
Hierarchic				
Total Item Score	–2.31	–2.82	–2.14	.46
Authority Figures	.42	.29	.46	.52
Competitive Games	–.17	–.47	–.07	.83
Competitive Situations	–.94	–.89	–.95	.16
Assertive Role	–1.44	–1.39	–1.47	.17
Imposing Wishes	–.36	–.43	–.33	.24
Standing Out from Group	.58	.71	.54	.43
Routine Administrative Functions	–.40	–.64	–.32	.69

Note: MSCS = Miner Sentence Completion Scale.
*$p < .05$; **$p < .01$

is not pronounced. Overall, the scores on the hierarchic measure are at a level that would be anticipated when the instrument is applied to a mature sample falling outside the appropriate theoretical domain. Although the findings as a whole do not necessarily support the construct validity of the separate subscale measures, they do yield credence to the view that Form P as a whole taps something closely akin to professional motivation and that this motivation is in turn a factor in professional success.

Table 9.7 also contains more detailed data on the administrative group. Those who take a universalistic view of the management process would anticipate that Form H, which differentiates managers from nonmanagers in hierarchic organizations, should do so in the professional context as well. The data do not support this expectation. Rather it is Form P that now differentiates the administrators, as the limited domain theories would anticipate. It should be emphasized, however, that the sample consists predominantly of low level administrators who are very close to the professional base in their organizations. Presumably they attain their positions because they closely approximate professional values and norms. Within the central administrations of large universities the hierarchic model may well be more applicable than the professional.

The data on academic administrators not only conflict with a universalistic conception of management process, but with certain findings derived from expectancy theory (Snyder, Howard, and Hammer 1978). These latter findings indicate that a desire for power and authority predominates among academic department chairmen, and professors who do not hold administrative aspirations have a strong desire for autonomy. In Table 9.7, however, the administrators are not high on the Imposing Wishes subscale, and they are significantly higher (not lower) on the Independent Action subscale. The major differentiating source of motivation for the administrators appears to be Accepting Status. A possible explanation is that these differences in results are attributable to the conscious process (Miner, 1980c) aspect of expectancy theory, and the theories utilized here deal with motives below the conscious level.

A finding of some significance is that although the Acquiring Knowledge, Accepting Status, Providing Help, and Professional Commitment measures of the professional scale tend to correlate highly with university compensation, the Independent Action subscale is more closely associated with nonuniversity compensation. This suggests that the Independent Action measure might be a particularly effective predictor of success in private practice and that the other subscales may be somewhat more relevant for professional organizations and professional components of hierarchic systems.

Another point relates to the unexpectedly high age correlation obtained with the Professional Commitment measure, which in turn contributes to the total score results. It would appear logical that individuals with low professional commitment might selectively leave a profession over time, and in particular a professional organization such as the Academy of Management, so that predominantly high commitment people would remain in the older age groups. This type of explanation emphasizes selective retention rather than motivational change.

On the other hand, the research of Bucher and Stelling (1977) indicates that at least within the training period actual role playing of professional activities is the major factor influencing the development of professional identity and commitment. The role playing contributes to a sense of mastery of professional skills and knowledge, which in turn fosters commitment. Extrapolating these results out beyond the training process into the professional career, it seems possible that with increasing levels of experience in the work, commitment might continue to increase as well. At present, without further research. it is not possible to reach a conclusion on this matter.

The strong relationship between professional motivation and publication is consistent with the academic nature of the profession studied. However, it is somewhat surprising that books and book royalties yield higher validities than do the more research oriented journal articles, especially those of a prestige nature. A possible explanation is that in this field at the present time being "professional" does not always equate with science, research, and the like; it still may be more closely allied with a strong teaching, communicating emphasis.

One way of looking at the results of this study is in terms of their implications for the operation of professional organizations. The role of such organizations should be to contribute to the satisfaction of motives that tend to be strong among their members and that are closely related to professional career success. In terms of the professional motivational model presented, tested, and supported in this paper, this means that to be successful themselves, professional organizations should:

1. Foster the development and dissemination of knowledge to members, thus meeting the need to acquire knowledge.
2. Protect the freedom of members to act with professional independence, thus meeting the need for independent action.
3. Foster the prestige and status of the profession and of its individual members, thus meeting the need to accept status.
4. Create opportunities for members to serve clients, thus meeting the need to provide help.
5. Define a full-fledged profession with appropriate norms and values, thus meeting the need for professional commitment (see Miner 2006a).

If one considers some of the more effective professional organizations currently in existence, it seems clear that the major activities of these organizations do indeed tend to mesh closely with these role prescriptions.

BIOGRAPHICAL FACTORS AS PREDICTORS

A subsequent analysis carried out on this same sample resulted in attempts to determine how well various biographical factors predicted success. Factors to be considered included experience in business and/or government, the unpleasantness of prior experience, career military service, age, gender, type of university where the degree was received, and type of degree. These analyses proved difficult to carry out due to small subsample sizes, age relationships, problems of interpretation, and the like. Although some significant findings were obtained, they were few in number and often not very strong. It is apparent that of the various factors considered in this research, professional motivation provides by far the closest approximations to a wide range of success criteria. Several of the biographical factors can prove useful, but they do not exhibit the strength or pervasiveness of the more immediate motivational effects.

ROLE-MOTIVATED LEADERSHIP IN PROFESSIONAL ORGANIZATIONS

A considerable number of years after the analyses described above, research was conducted to establish leadership within the Academy of Management sample. Discussion of this type of leadership may be found in Miner (2002a, 316–317) as follows:

> Professional, or intellectual, leadership has been given practically no attention by leadership theory, although within the sociological literature, the distinction between administrative elites and rank-and-file practitioners within a profession is discussed. It is these elites that the professional theory considers as its leaders. Intellectual leadership of this kind may be of either a cosmopolitan or local nature. In the former instance, the focus is on achieved professional status and recognition in the professional community as a whole; in the latter case, the focus is on achieved rank and status in the employing organization.
>
> Many professionals rise to leadership positions or status of both kinds. The key is that the person must be a professional and must have given evidence of high professional status, which often involves having rank-and-file professionals or pre-professionals who depend upon him or her in some manner. . . . Although the concept of mentoring has been studied most extensively within the hierarchic domain, it is an important function of professional leaders as well.
>
> Since acquiring knowledge is so important to becoming a professional, and takes considerable time as well, the professional career tends to extend across various degrees of training, to the early career stages, and then for some to true intellectual leadership. Thus, the idea of a continuum holds for professionals. Leadership tends to be defined by such factors as publications, professional compensation levels, professional rank, signs of recognition, administrative position, status within the educational context, professional organization activity, and the like, depending on the particular profession and its organizational context.

These are, of course, the kinds of criteria collected for the Academy of Management sample. In that sample forty-six individuals qualify as professional leaders and sixty-six do

Table 9.8

Relationships between MSCS Measures and Professional Leadership within the Academy of Management

MSCS Measures	Professional Leaders (N = 46)	Not Professional Leaders (N = 66)	t	r_{bis}
Professional				
Total Item Score	11.70	1.30	10.02**	.87
Acquiring Knowledge	1.46	–.32	3.81**	.43
Independent Action	3.17	1.20	4.48**	.49
Accepting Status	2.83	.21	5.51**	.58
Providing Help	2.72	.97	4.42**	.49
Professional Commitment	1.52	–.76	5.01**	.54
Hierarchic				
Total Item Score	–1.59	–2.80	.94	.11
Authority Figures	.48	.38	.33	.04
Competitive Games	.06	–.32	.97	.11
Competitive Situations	–1.13	–.80	1.02	–.12
Assertive Role	–1.04	–1.73	1.93	.23
Imposing Wishes	–.22	–.45	.67	.08
Standing Out from Group	.50	.64	.38	–.05
Routine Administrative Functions	–.24	–.52	.78	.09

Note: MSCS = Miner Sentence Completion Scale.
**$p < .01$

not, as indicated in Table 9.8. From the data given there it is evident that a huge difference in Form P scores exists between these two groups; all of these differences are highly significant at well beyond the $p < .01$ level. None of the Form H scores differentiate the two types of professionals. The leaders are compensated more highly with an $r_{bis} = .68$ for total professional compensation.

CHAPTER 10

GEORGIA STATE UNIVERSITY MBA STUDENTS ENROLLED IN A CAREER PLANNING COURSE

INTRODUCTION

The research described here was carried out with MBA students enrolled in night classes at Georgia State University when both of the authors were on the management faculty there. It was published in the *Academy of Management Journal* (Miner and Crane 1981). The career-planning course was taught by Donald Crane and the research component was a joint effort with John Miner doing the MSCS (Miner Sentence Completion Scale) scoring.

This article represents a considerable refinement of the thrust into the vocational guidance area described in Chapter 4. It is intended to provide information for career counseling relative to leadership careers of a hierarchic nature.

* * *

Prior research has indicated, as managerial role motivation theory would predict, that university students with higher levels of independently measured managerial motivation are more likely to cite some type of managerial activity as a career objective (Miner 1968a, 1968b; Miner and Smith 1969). Bedeian (1977) also has shown that various personality factors, self-esteem in particular, play a role in an individual's aspiring to prestigious occupations, including managing. Research by Schein (1975, 1978) indicates that certain motivational, attitudinal, and value syndromes tend to guide and influence people in decisions throughout their careers. Significantly for the present study, he has identified a managerial competence syndrome (or career anchor), which leads individuals to seek continually for positions with greater managerial responsibility. There is other evidence that expressed vocational choices of the kind utilized in these studies are in turn rather good predictors of subsequent employment (Wiggins and Weslander 1977).

Although none of the preceding research has employed formal career planning documents,

From John B. Miner and Donald P. Crane, "Motivation to Manage and the Manifestation of a Managerial Orientation in Career Planning," *Academy of Management Journal,* 24 (1981), 626–633.

it would appear appropriate to explore relationships between the content of such documents and managerial motivation as a next step. Accordingly the following hypothesis was formulated for test:

Individuals who have a stronger motivation to manage will manifest this motivation in their career planning—

1. by describing their present work as more managerial in nature.
2. by describing their planned work as more managerial in nature.
3. by planning a greater degree of future change in the direction of managerial work.

Although the essentially concurrent nature of this research precludes testing of causal relationships, the theoretical rationale underlying the hypothesis is that existing motivation to manage influences career planning statements regarding planned work. Furthermore, in the absence of special circumstances such as managerial role-motivation training that might intervene, it is assumed that motivation to manage is a generally stable characteristic. Accordingly, present motivation reflects past motivation, and that in turn exerts a causal impact on present work. Finally, it is assumed that a developmental process occurs whereby motivation to manage is increasingly likely to be tied to managerial work as an individual gains more experience in the world of work (usually with age). Thus, change from present to planned work also should reflect managerial motivation at least in the early phases of career development, before stabilization has occurred. In other words, a currently planned future position should more nearly reflect the base level of managerial motivation than a current position resulting from a decision made at some time in the past, when knowledge of work relationships would be expected to be less perfect.

METHOD

Sample

The subjects were fifty-six students enrolled in a graduate level management course taught by one of the authors. A major portion of the course was devoted to personal career and life planning. The mean age of the students was 30.2 years, with a standard deviation of 4.8 years. Practically all of the students were employed on a full time basis at the time the research was conducted. There were ten females.

The Course

The graduate course in management included a series of sessions on career planning, which were conducted as a pilot project for possible subsequent inclusion in the course. The Miner Sentence Completion Scale (MSCS) was administered in conjunction with the pilot module. Students completed the scale near the beginning of the course, and results were not reported until the end of the course after they submitted written career plans. This was to minimize contamination of the career plans that might result from knowledge of their MSCS scores. To test the hypotheses, the Miner Sentence Completion Scale scores were correlated with various indexes derived from the written planning documents.

The career planning portion of the course consisted of a series of lecturettes to establish a conceptual framework for career planning; a series of roundtable discussions to relate the philosophies of authors of management classics to the individual student's philosophy; several workshops on techniques pertinent to career planning; and "sharing" activities to enable the students to exchange thoughts and ideas. The end product of the course was a detailed document describing each student's life aspirations and employment plan extending at least five years into the future. This document included:

1. A detailed *analysis of personal values* that would become the basis for establishing personal life/career objectives;
2. A detailed articulation of *personal objectives* including a measure of attainment and a description of how these objectives were derived; and
3. *A personal development life/career plan* in which students analyzed their personal strengths that would help them meet objectives and identified shortcomings that would inhibit their achievement of objectives. They also delineated a plan to overcome their shortcomings and preserve their strengths.

Measures

Motivation to manage was measured using the Miner Sentence Completion Scale in the original free response format (Miner 1964).

To test the hypothesis the MSCS scores were correlated with various indexes derived from written planning documents prepared by the students toward the end of the course. The measures of managerial orientation in these documents were derived by one of the authors based on a thorough reading.

The second author was purposely not involved in this process because he had taught the career planning course and it was felt that his knowledge of the students could bias the measures. However, interrater reliability coefficients were obtained from a scoring of a random sample of twenty-one papers by the second author. The independently derived measures yielded coefficients in the range of .80 to .84, suggesting satisfactory reliability. Reliability coefficients were calculated for each of the four measures of managerial orientation in career planning. The measures and coefficients are as follows: (The four measures are described later in this paper.)

- present work—.83
- planned work—.82
- present and planned work—.84
- change from present to planned work—.80

Eliminating bias due to the fact that one of the authors taught the career planning course was a major concern. The other author had no contact with the students and thus could not introduce bias in assigning the measures of managerial orientation of present and planned work. However, the high reliability between the raters' measures suggests that possible bias of the author who taught the course did not, in fact, affect his scoring. The four measures obtained in this manner were:

Managerial Orientation of Present Work

Each subject's reported present employment was first scored on the following scale:

4. A manager of some kind in either a business or government bureaucracy.
3. A manager in an essentially professional organization.
2. A business entrepreneur.
1. A professional entrepreneur in either private practice or a professional partnership.
0. None of the above occupations mentioned, including not employed.

The value thus obtained was then multiplied by 2 if there was a clear indication that the individual liked the work or was satisfied in it. The final scores thus ranged from 0 to 8. The mean was 1.8 and the standard deviation was 2.7.

Managerial Orientation of Planned Work

Each subject's planned work history was evaluated using the same 0 to 4 scale as for present work. The highest possible score was assigned; thus the most managerial occupation noted, other than the present job, served as the basis for scoring. This value was then multiplied by 2 if there was evidence in the planning document of a high level of commitment to achieving the planned work. The mean was 3.8 and the standard deviation 2.5.

Managerial Orientation of Present and Planned Work

This measure was simply the sum of the present and planned work scores. It provided an overall index of managerial orientation and could, and did, range from 0 to 16. The mean was 5.5 and the standard deviation 4.1.

Change in Managerial Orientation from Present to Planned Work

This score was obtained by subtracting the managerial orientation of present work score from the managerial orientation of planned work; thus the possible range was –8 to +8. Minus values were in fact rather infrequent, however, and the mean change score was +2 with a standard deviation of 3.2. Because the magnitude of the change scores was strongly influenced by the size of the present work value ($r = -.64$), partial correlations were used to provide the basic test of the hypothesis.

The rationale underlying these measures derives from hierarchic role-motivation theory (Miner 1965a). It also derives from findings indicating a developmental sequence whereby existing managerial motivation levels are increasingly tied to managerial performance in large organizations of the bureaucratic form with increasing exposure to the world of work (Miner, 1968a; Miner and Smith 1969). The scale was originally constituted with reference to the managerial orientation of planned work, assuming that the process of tying motivation to manage to bureaucratic management is a gradual one, often moving through various stages of approximation to the theoretical ideal.

In this scale a 4 is assigned to managing in a large and bureaucratic organization, a 3 to managing in a large and nonbureaucratic organization, a 2 to managing in an organization that is neither large nor bureaucratic, a 1 to a potentially managerial position in an organization neither large nor bureaucratic, and a 0 to a position that in no way approaches the theoretical ideal. Because commitment level is a theoretically important consideration in evaluating career planning measures, it was decided that some index of this variable should be incorporated. A multiplicative formula was utilized in order to keep the score value of a complete departure from the theoretical ideal at 0. In the absence of any theoretical or empirical guidelines, a decision was made to minimize the amount of skewing and discontinuity at the upper score levels by using a multiplier of 2.

Having established such a scale for planned work, it seemed desirable to utilize a similar approach for present work in order to make the two measures essentially comparable. The basic 0 to 4 scale presented no problems in this regard. However, although commitment was relatively easy to determine for the planned positions (and satisfaction could not be determined because the position had not yet been occupied), the reverse was true for present positions. Invariably the planning documents discussed present work in terms of whether it was satisfying or not, rather than in terms of commitment, if this kind of consideration was discussed at all. Thus came about the decision to substitute satisfaction for commitment in the present work scale, assuming that the two variables play essentially similar roles vis-à-vis work motivation. The intercorrelations among the criterion measures are contained in Table 10.1.

RESULTS

As indicated in Table 10.2 the data support all aspects of the hypothesis with some consistency. In particular, it appears that the Imposing Wishes index of power motivation is related positively to exhibiting a managerial orientation in career planning.

A post hoc analysis was conducted to investigate those particular individuals for whom the managerial motivation scores did not predict managerial orientation levels in the career planning documents. The combined present and planned work managerial orientation score and the overall item score were used in this analysis, and each variable was split at the median to establish on and off quadrant cases. Using this criterion, thirty-nine subjects were correctly predicted and seventeen were not—eight with lower managerial orientations than their relatively high managerial motivation would suggest and nine with the reverse pattern. The only finding of significance emerging from this analysis was a higher level of competitiveness among the off quadrant subjects. This was characteristic of the group whose strong managerial motivation was not matched by a comparable level of managerial orientation only; the Competitive Situations score for the low motivation to manage and high managerial orientation subjects was not significantly different from that of the predicted subjects.

An analysis using the grade assigned to the career planning documents by the course instructor failed to reveal any significant relationships with either independent or dependent variables.

DISCUSSION

The results of this research offer considerable support to role motivation theory (Miner 1965a). This is most evident in the total score findings and in the Imposing Wishes subscale findings, but other subscales yield supporting data on occasion. The research also provides information extending prior findings regarding the role of personality factors, and motives in particular, in vocational choice directly to the career planning process. It now is apparent that strong motives can manifest themselves in career plans. Thus the study makes at least an initial contribution to an understanding of the dynamics of the career planning process.

The role that power motivation (Imposing Wishes) appears to play in planning for a managerial career, although not totally unexpected, emerged as much more significant than role motivation theory alone would have predicted. A check of prior studies in which managerial

Table 10.1

Correlation among Measures of Managerial Orientation in Career Plans

Managerial Orientation in Career Plans	Present Work	Planned Work	Present and Planned Work	Change from Present to Planned Work
Present Work	—	.25	.81**	–.64**
Planned Work		—	.78**	.58**
Present and Planned Work			—	–.07

*p < .05; **p < .01

Table 10.2

Correlations between Miner Sentence Completion Scale (MSCS) Measures and Managerial Orientation in Career Plans

MSCS Measures	Present Work	Planned Work	Present and Planned Work	Change from Present to Planned Work[a]
Total Scores				
Item	.35**	.40**	.48**	.02 (.33*)
Rare	.22	.42**	.40**	.15 (.39**)
Authority Figures	.03	.15	.11	.09 (.14)
Competitive Games	.17	–.07	.07	–.20 (–.12)
Competitive Situations	.03	.12	.09	.07 (.12)
Assertive Role	.31*	.19	.32*	–.11 (.12)
Imposing Wishes	.32*	.48**	.50**	.11 (.44**)
Standing Out from Group	.10	.17	.17	.05 (.15)
Routine Administrative Functions	.12	.27*	.24	.11 (.25)

Note: MSCS = Miner Sentence Completion Scale.
[a]Partial correlations holding managerial orientation in present work constant, are given in parentheses.
*p < .05; **p < .01

motivation was related to the choice of a managerial career, although not within a specifically career planning context, indicates that a similarly distinctive role for power motivation was not in evidence. However, in two of three studies the Imposing Wishes subscale, along with others, did differentiate those who expressed a preference for managing from those who did not (Miner 1968a, 1968b; Miner and Smith 1969). The samples in both instances in which differentiation did occur were made up of graduate students in their late twenties and early thirties having much in common with the present subjects. In contrast, the one case in which differentiation was not found involved undergraduates in their late teens and early twenties. On this evidence it would appear that power motivation comes to influence career processes, and managerial aspirations in particular, only at a rather late developmental stage (see Chapter 4).

The analysis intended to identify possible causes of failures in prediction from the managerial motivation measures suggests that certain individuals who have a relatively strong motive to manage and are very competitive may well plan on essentially nonmanagerial careers. The predominant orientation among these subjects is toward helping professions such as teaching and counseling. There also is a tendency to emphasize nonconfining activities of the type reflected in travel. Overall these data appear to suggest that other strong motives may conflict with the managerial motives and lead to a career planning objective outside the bureaucratic context. The other not predicted group—those with low managerial motivation, but unexpectedly high managerial orientations—are predominantly bureaucratic managers at present who are not too happy with their situation. It is entirely possible, given their lack of satisfaction in managerial work and low managerial motivation, that they are not very effective managers and may ultimately be forced out of their managerial roles.

In considering these conclusions and speculations from analyses of the off quadrant cases, the post hoc nature of the data should be emphasized. At best these represent hypotheses for future research. In no sense do they have the same status as the basic findings of this study, that indicate a clear relationship between motivation to manage and the manifestation of a managerial orientation in career planning documents. These latter findings provide further evidence of the construct validity of the motivation to manage variable.

CHAPTER 11

CHANGES IN THE MANAGERIAL MOTIVATION OF UNIVERSITY STUDENTS ACROSS THE 1960–1980 PERIOD

INTRODUCTION

This chapter presents three different pieces of research extending out over time across two decades. These studies have been published as follows:

Administrative Science Quarterly (Miner 1971d)*
Personnel Psychology (Miner 1974d)**
Journal of Applied Psychology (Miner and Smith 1982)***

---

* From John B. Miner, "Changes in Student Attitudes toward Bureaucratic Role Prescriptions during the 1960s," *Administrative Science Quarterly,* vol. 16 (September), 351–364. Copyright ©1971 Johnson Graduate School, Cornell University. Reproduced (or Adapted) with permission.

** From John B. Miner, "Students' Attitudes toward Bureaucratic Role Prescriptions and Prospects for Managerial Talent Shortages,"*Personnel Psychology,* vol. 27, no. 4, (December), 605–613. Copyright ©1974 by Blackwell Publishing. Reproduced (or Adapted) with permission.

*** From John B. Miner and Norman R. Smith, "Decline and Stabilization of Managerial Motivation Over a 20-year Period," *Journal of Applied Psychology,* vol. 67, no. 3, 297–305. Copyright © 1982 American Psychological Association. Reproduced (or Adapted) with permission.

Together these publications span the research on changes in attitudes and motives associated with the student activism of the 1960–1980 period. These are the core studies, but there have been other reports including (Miner 1973a, 1974a, 1977b, 1977c, 1979b, 1993) as well as (Miner and Smith 1981; Miner, Smith, and Ebrahimi 1985; Miner, Wachtel, and Ebrahimi 1989; and Miner, Ebrahimi, and Wachtel 1995). Several of these studies deal with international comparisons and the state of managerial talent supplies in countries beyond the United States.

I should note that the change discussed here was first identified during the research considered in Chapter 4. It was a happenstance finding, not an outgrowth of theory. Thus these data represent not so much a direct development from role motivation theory, but a side benefit related to it; if there had been no research on the theory, the changes considered would never have become evident.

* * *

The 1960s saw a drastic change in the behavior of university students throughout the United States. The first two years of the decade were an extension of the relatively quiescent 1950s, but, starting in 1962, with the peace demonstrations in Washington early in the year and the formation of Students for a Democratic Society during the summer, the pace of student activism and militancy began to quicken. By the fall of 1964, the Berkeley campus of the University of California was faced with large-scale demonstrations that then spread to most of the larger student bodies in the United States (Scott and El-Assal 1969). The last half of the decade witnessed widespread student behavior of a kind that was previously unheard of on most campuses at the beginning of the decade.

The hypothesis that these activities during the 1960s reflect a transitory process, derived from the actions of a small minority of students and devoid of any relationship to deeper social change, has been advanced by some of the most respected and knowledgeable scholars in the field of student politics (Lipset and Altbach 1967). On the other hand, were it conclusively demonstrated that these changed behavior patterns reflect the widespread emergence of new and relatively stable attitudes on a large number of college campuses, it would be difficult to argue that student activism in the 1960s was not an outgrowth of basic changes in American society.

Investigation of this problem requires a longitudinal analysis comparing data obtained before the advent of major student unrest with more recent data; however, an extensive literature search revealed no studies of this kind, although comparisons have been made based on longitudinal data that were first collected shortly after the Berkeley disorders of late 1964 (Peterson 1968a). The present study is an attempt to fill this void. Data on student attitudes and motives in the period 1960–61 are compared with data covering the period 1966–69.

MEASURE OF ATTITUDES

The data of this study were obtained using the Miner Sentence Completion Scale (MSCS), which was originally conceived as a measure of attitude toward the supervisory job (Miner 1960a). Subsequent studies have provided evidence of construct validity (Miner 1968a; Miner and Smith 1969).

Studies conducted with various groups since the scale was developed have increasingly suggested that it is best viewed as a measure of attitudes and motives associated with achieving success in meeting bureaucratic role prescriptions at the managerial level (see Chapters 3, 4, 6, 7, 8, and 10).

These data strongly support the conclusion that the MSCS measures—particularly the total score, attitude to authority, competitive motivation (games), competitive motivation (occupational), and power motivation measures—reflect attitudes toward the managerial role prescriptions of large bureaucratic organizations.

STUDENT SAMPLES

1960–61 Samples

The primary sample contained 287 students who completed the MSCS between September 1960 and September 1961. All were enrolled in a required, junior-level course in management conducted in the School of Business Administration at the University of Oregon. The course was offered four times in this period, and scales completed at the very beginning of the course were obtained from 88 percent of the total enrollment. The sample is representative of business students in junior courses at the University of Oregon during that period because the course was required, a high proportion of enrollment was involved, and very few students were majoring in subjects other than business. Only 14 percent of the students were females.

An additional early sample consisted of 143 students enrolled in a required, junior-level course, dealing with the school in its societal context, conducted in the School of Education at the University of Oregon. These students were given the MSCS as the course began in January 1961. A much higher proportion, 68 percent, of these students were females, but otherwise the education and business samples are comparable. The education sample is important because it extends the analyses beyond a single major. Samples were not obtained from other colleges and universities in the early years of the decade.

1966–69 Samples

The primary comparison sample for the latter part of the decade, when campus turmoil had become widespread, is representative of University of Oregon business students at the junior level. The 129 students completed the MSCS in a required, junior-level course in marketing during the 1967–68 academic year. The data were collected in November 1967 and January 1968 during two successive quarters. As with the 1960–61 business school sample, very few nonbusiness majors were included and only a small proportion of the students, 12 percent, were females. The mean age of the group was 20.9 years.

In addition to this direct comparison sample, two other samples have been studied in order to extend the generality of the findings. Like the University of Oregon, both colleges experienced student protests during the last half of the decade and both were under strong pressure for change from student groups. Neither, however, has experienced the degree of unrest that has characterized the University of Oregon.

The first of these samples contained 117 students enrolled in a lower-division management course conducted in the School of Business Administration at Portland State College. The course was not required and thus representativeness cannot be assumed. However, the sample was accumulated over three successive quarters from September 1966 to April 1967. Of the group studied, 20 percent were female.

The second supplementary sample from a school that had experienced disturbances was obtained at the University of Maryland. The MSCS was administered to 122 students in a required, junior-level course in management in the College of Business and Public Administration. The data were obtained in February and March 1969. This group appears to be similar to the University of Oregon business groups. The mean age is 21.7 years, but with 5 students in their thirties removed, it drops to the same level as the Oregon sample for 1968. Only 10 percent are females.

The three colleges and universities where data were obtained in the 1966–69 period are quite diverse except for the presence of student unrest and, of course, the fact of state support. Oregon is a medium-sized state university in a medium-sized city; Maryland is over twice as large, in the suburb of a large city; and Portland State College, primarily a commuter college in a large city, has a much smaller enrollment.

Partial data consisting only of MSCS total scores were also obtained for a sample of students in business courses at the University of Nevada. This school is unique among those studied in that it experienced practically no student unrest during the 1960s. The data were collected over six semesters during the years 1966 and 1967 from 202 undergraduate students enrolled in various courses in management and insurance conducted in the College of Business Administration.*

FINDINGS

Comparisons of Mean Scores

Although the primary comparison is that between the University of Oregon business students of 1960–61 and those of 1968, significance tests were carried out for all comparisons between sample means for all five samples on which complete data were available. The differences between the two 1960–61 groups and the three 1966–69 groups are most relevant and are presented in Table 11.1.

The data on MSCS total score differences indicate that the three more recent samples all have significantly and meaningfully lower mean values than the two samples from earlier in the decade. This indicates a marked shift in the direction of more negative attitudes toward meeting managerial role prescriptions in bureaucratic organizations.

The percentile values utilize the distribution of 1960–61 University of Oregon business student scores as a base. Because the mean and median are not identical, the mean for the base group falls at the 49th percentile rather than the 50th. The mean of the 1968 Oregon business sample falls at the 30th percentile on the 1960–61 Oregon business sample distribution, a decrease of 19 points. The score differences are not only marked in terms of statistical significance, but in terms of practical significance as well. There are no statistically significant differences between the two 1960–61 samples or among the three 1966–69 samples in total score.

Attitudes toward authority also became distinctly more negative over the decade. The Oregon business student mean was 19 percentile points lower in 1968 than in 1960–61. The decline relative to the education students of the earlier period was even more pronounced. Although the three more recent groups do not differ in their attitudes toward authority figures, there is a significant difference between the two 1960–61 Oregon samples ($t = 3.64, p < .01$). This difference cannot be accounted for in terms of the differing proportions of females in the two samples.

*MSCS data for the 1966–69 samples were collected by Norman R. Smith (Oregon), Robert D. Bowin (Portland State), John L. Kmetz (Maryland), and Alfred W. Stoess (Nevada). Bowin, Kmetz, and Stoess also scored their data.

Table 11.1

Shifts in MSCS Variables from 1960–61 to 1966–69

	MSCS Variables											
	Total MSCS Score			Attitude to Authority			Competitive Motivation (Games)			Competitive Motivation (Occupational)		
Group Studied	Mean Score	Percentile for Mean	Percent of Respondents with High Scores	Mean Score	Percentile for Mean	Percent of Respondents with High Scores	Mean Score	Percentile for Mean	Percent of Respondents with High Scores	Mean Score	Percentile for Mean	Percent of Respondents with High Scores
University of Oregon												
287 business students during 1960–61	3.33	49	22	1.17	49	15	1.18	47	26	–.55	49	26
143 education students during 1961	3.50	50	20	1.68	68	27	1.08	45	23	–.62	48	24
129 business students during 1967–68	.52	30	14	.47	30	7	.71	39	14	–1.04	38	16
Portland State College												
117 business students during 1966–67	–.03	27	11	.57	32	10	.78	40	19	–1.22	35	14
University of Maryland												
122 business students during 1969	.80	32	15	.46	29	11	1.09	45	24	–1.26	34	15

(continued)

Table 11.1 *(continued)*

	MCSC Variables							
	Total MSCS Score		Attitude to Authority		Competitive Motivation (Games)		Competitive Motivation (Occupational)	
Comparisons among Mean Scores of Studied Group	Student's t	Significance Level	Student's t	Significance Level	Student's t	Significance Level	Student's t	Significance Level
1960–61 Oregon Business Students Compared with								
1967–68 Oregon business students	4.61	$p < .01$	4.38	$p < .01$	2.47	$p < .01$	2.72	$p < .01$
1966–67 Portland State business students	5.25	$p < .01$	4.00	$p < .01$	2.00	$p < .05$	4.47	$p < .01$
1969 Maryland business students	3.61	$p < .01$	4.18	$p < .01$	.47	N.S.	3.74	$p < .01$
1961 Oregon Education Students Compared with								
1967–68 Oregon business students	4.52	$p < .01$	6.72	$p < .01$	1.68	$p < .05$	2.10	$p < .05$
1966–67 Portland State business students	5.12	$p < .01$	6.17	$p < .01$	1.30	N.S.	3.33	$p < .01$
1969 Maryland business students	3.62'	$p < .01$	6.42	$p < .01$	.05	N.S.	3.05	$p < .01$

	MSCS Variables											
	Attitude to Masculine (Assertive) Role			Power Motivation			Attitude to Differentiated Role			Attitude to Administrative Responsibility		
Group Studied	Mean Score	Percentile for Mean	Percent of Respondents with High Scores	Mean Score	Percentile for Mean	Percent of Respondents with High Scores	Mean Score	Percentile for Mean	Percent of Respondents with High Scores	Mean Score	Percentile for Mean	Percent of respondents with high scores
University of Oregon												
287 business students during 1960–61	.32	50	30	.37	53	22	.38	49	20	.45	46	27
143 education students during 1961	–.04	42	24	.23	49	14	.61	56	26	.57	49	30
129 business students during 1967–68	.00	43	16	.33	52	25	.26	46	16	–.20	33	19
Portland State College												
117 business students during 1966–67	–.05	42	19	.40	54	29	–.17	34	12	–.34	30	17
University of Maryland												
122 business students during 1969	–.11	40	21	.66	61	34	.23	45	20	–.26	32	20

(continued)

Table 11.1 *(continued)*

Comparisons among Mean Scores of Studied Group	MSCS Variables: Attitude to Masculine (Assertive) Role		Power Motivation		Attitude to Differentiated Role		Attitude to Administrative Responsibility	
	Student's t	Significance Level	Student's t	Significance Level	Student's t	Significance Level	Student's t	Significance Level
1960–61 Oregon Business Students Compared with								
1967–68 Oregon business students	1.78	$p < .05$	.24	N.S.	.80	N.S.	3.61	$p < .01$
1966–67 Portland State business students	1.95	$p < .05$	.18	N.S.	3.44	$p < .01$	4.16	$p < .01$
1969 Maryland business students	2.05	$p < .05$	1.53	N.S.	1.01	N.S.	3.55	$p < .01$
1961 Oregon Education Students Compared with								
1967–68 Oregon business students	.19	N.S.	.56	N.S.	2.06	$p < .05$	3.76	$p < .01$
1966–67 Portland State business students	.05	N.S.	.94	N.S.	4.22	$p < .01$	4.23	$p < .01$
1969 Maryland business students	.30	N.S.	2.15	$p < .05$	2.15	$p < .05$	3.77	$p < .01$

Note: MSCS = Miner Sentence Completion Scale.

The differences in competitive motivation as it relates to game performance are much less pronounced. The basic comparison between the two Oregon business student groups remains statistically significant, however, although the decrease of 8 percentile points suggests only limited practical significance. Comparisons involving the Oregon education students are of borderline statistical significance. There are no statistically significant differences within the early and late sample groupings on the games competition measure.

When the object of competitive motivation shifts from game performance to occupational performance, a more pronounced difference between the 1960–61 and the 1966–69 samples appears. All the comparisons are significant and in every instance the more recent students exhibit a lower level of competitive motivation. The percentile point decrease is only 11 points based on the two primary Oregon samples, but this rises to 15 points when the 1969 Maryland sample is used. The measure of occupational competitiveness used here is a general one and thus is not restricted to business occupations. The measure does not discriminate within the 1960–61 and 1966–69 groupings.

There was some change to more negative attitudes toward performing in accordance with the masculine (assertive) role although the shift on the percentile scale amounts to only 7 points when the two Oregon business samples are compared. Statistical significance is obtained only when the comparison involves the 1960–61 business students.

The education students scored significantly below the business students when the two Oregon samples from early in the decade are compared ($t = 2.03$, $p < .05$). This largely reflects the much higher proportion of females in the education sample. Thus, on this particular variable the results based on the education student data should be ignored.

In the case of power motivation there is no evidence of any decrease. The comparison of 1961 Oregon education students and 1969 Maryland business students suggests that an increase in power motivation may even have occurred at Maryland, although this cannot be established with any certainty in view of the limitations of the available data. In terms of power motivation, there are no statistically significant differences between the two 1960–61 samples or the three 1966–69 samples.

There is some shift to more negative attitudes toward assuming a differentiated role, but this shift is not in evidence when the early and late Oregon business samples are compared. There is only a decline of 3 percentile points, and this is far from statistically significant. There are consistent significant differences involving the 1960–61 Oregon education sample, but the high mean score here is almost certainly a reflection of the tendency for teachers generally to score at a differentially higher level on this particular measure (Miner 1965a).

There is a further basis for questioning whether a true shift to more negative attitudes toward standing out from a group has developed during the decade; it comes from the comparisons within the 1966–69 sample grouping. While the two early samples do not differ, the Portland State College mean is reliably below those for both the 1968 Oregon business students ($t = 2.39$, $p < .05$) and the 1969 Maryland business students ($t = 2.22$, $p < .05$). These are the only differences that reach significance among the three more recent samples, out of a total of twenty-four comparisons on the eight MSCS variables. The possibility of a random fluctuation here certainly cannot be ruled out, and with this and the other considerations noted—especially the lack of a significant difference between the two Oregon business samples—it is not possible to conclude with any certainty that a decline has occurred in the attitude toward a differentiated role measure.

The decline in the score on attitudes toward assuming administrative responsibility between 1960–61 and 1966–69 is significant for all comparisons, with the University of Oregon business students 13 percentile points lower in the later period. There are no significant differences in attitude to administrative responsibility within either the early or the more recent sample groupings.

A rough rank ordering of the eight variables in terms of the degree of negative shift in attitudes or motivational decrease is:

1. attitude toward authority figures;
2. general attitude toward managerial role prescriptions in bureaucracies;
3. attitude toward assuming administrative responsibility;
4. competitive motivation (occupational);
5. competitive motivation (games);
6. attitude toward assuming the masculine role;
7. attitude toward assuming a differentiated role; and
8. power motivation.

On the first four variables the change is pronounced, on the next two it is of considerably lower magnitude, and on the last two it is minimal. In the case of power motivation there is no evidence of a decline of any kind.

These findings involving colleges and universities that experienced student unrest should be compared with those for the University of Nevada, which was relatively free of such problems. One would anticipate that the Nevada data for 1966–67 would be more like that obtained earlier in the decade and that no decline would be in evidence. This is exactly what occurs. The mean MSCS total score for the 202 University of Nevada business students is 3.02, very close to the 3.33 obtained with the University of Oregon business students of 1960–61 and far removed from the 0.52 obtained at Oregon in 1968.

Comparisons of Distributions

The changes in mean scores reported might occur in two ways. One possibility is that a relatively small group of activists were added to the college population in the later years. These individuals with more negative attitudes and lower competitive motivation, when included with the existing stable student group, would be sufficient in and of themselves to account for the change in mean scores. Under this hypothesis one would expect larger standard deviations in the 1966–69 groups than in those of 1960–61 and roughly the same proportion of relatively high scores in both periods.

The other possibility is that in the later years the college population changed as a whole, that the students who arrived on campus tended to be different as a group, not just in the addition of a small number of activists. Under this hypothesis there should be no appreciable change in standard deviations and there should be a decline in the proportion of high scores. The whole distribution would shift downward carrying the mean with it, in contrast to the mean being pulled down by a small, dissimilar group.

The standard deviations for the two periods were compared using analysis of variance. On the MSCS total score measure, the comparison between the Oregon education student sample of 1961 and the Maryland business student sample of 1969 was significant ($F = 1.75$, $p < .01$), the standard deviation being larger in the more recent group.

In comparisons with both the 1960–61 Oregon business students ($F = 1.58$, $p < .01$) and the 1961 Oregon education students ($F = 1.57$, $p < .05$) on the attitude to authority measure, the 1969 Maryland sample also had a higher standard deviation. No other comparisons on this measure yielded significant results.

The only other significant findings occurred on the power motivation measure. The three later samples all had larger standard deviations than the two earlier samples, The *F* values were 1.65 ($p < .01$), 1.50 ($p < .05$), and 1.97 ($p < .01$) for respective comparisons of the 1960–61 Oregon business students with the later Oregon business, Portland State business, and Maryland business samples, and 1.96 ($p < .01$), 1.79 ($p < .01$), and 2.35 ($p < .01$) for respective comparisons involving the 1961 Oregon education students. Since power motivation was the variable on which no decline in mean scores occurred, the larger standard deviation in the more recent period cannot reflect the addition of an activist minority at the lower end of the score distribution only.

Data that permit a determination as to whether the proportion of high scores declined or remained much the same are also contained in Table 11.1. The cutting scores that serve to establish the definition of a high score were selected to give as close to 25 percent of the 1960–61 Oregon business students in the high category as possible.

When the 1960–61 and 1968 Oregon business samples are compared, decreases of 8 percent or more occur on all variables that exhibited a decrease in means. On power motivation there appears to have been a consistent and in some cases rather sizable increase in the number of strongly motivated individuals over the decade. This is consistent with the finding of an increased standard deviation.

The analyses of score distributions provide results that are much more consistent with the view that college student attitudes generally changed during the decade than with the view that the changes reflect the impact of a supplementary activist minority.

COMPARISON WITH ACTIVISTS

A comparison of the student samples used in this study with samples of student activists who are known to have participated in demonstrations reveals some striking differences. The present analysis focused on student groups that are typically least activist and least likely to be involved in demonstrations.

Unrest tended to be at very low levels among business school students. These students scored relatively low on measures of social conscience, cultural sophistication, and liberalism; they were not activists (Peterson 1968b). They tended to be more favorably disposed to business and business careers than most other student groups, particularly those majoring in the liberal arts (Dawson 1969). Studies at Berkeley and elsewhere consistently indicated that business students and education students were markedly underrepresented in demonstrations (Watts and Whittaker 1966; Solomon and Fishman 1964). Since all the samples studied, with the exception of the one containing education students, were comprised almost entirely of business students, these same nonactivist characteristics should also predominate.

As might be expected, the very few liberal arts students who were included in the samples studied did score consistently below the professional school students on the MSCS. The number of such cases was too small to permit statistical analysis, and liberal arts students—all were social science majors—who take business courses are certainly not typical; yet the reduction in scores was pronounced.

Studies of those who participated in demonstrations indicate a higher proportion of females than were included in the present samples, with the exception of the 1961 Oregon education students. The activists tended to be disproportionately female (Block, Haan, and Smith 1968), while the business students were largely male.

The reported age of demonstrators varied but the proportion of freshmen and sophomores who were not yet 20 is high (Lipset and Altbach 1967). At Berkeley the average age was somewhat higher (Watts and Whittaker 1966), but it still appears that the students included in this study were older.

Finally, the most desired occupation among activists, at least in the early college years, was university teaching (Lipset and Altbach 1967; Silver 1969). Among the Oregon business students of 1968 only 5 percent indicated teaching as career objectives, and the majority of these were considering positions below the college level.

On every dimension where information is available the students considered in this study were far removed from those who became activists and participated in demonstrations on university campuses.

IMPLICATIONS OF THE FINDINGS

In spite of the apparently quiescent character of the particular students studied, there was a clear shift toward attitudes more consistent with activist behavior. The most pronounced shift over the decade was in attitudes toward authority and authority figures. The more recent students typically are distinctly more negative in this regard.

Since demonstrations frequently involved confrontations with authority and on occasion physical attacks on authority figures, an obvious parallel does exist between the attitude changes identified and the changed patterns of behavior.

Studies of activist students have consistently provided evidence of a basic rebelliousness and restlessness (Block, Haan, and Smith 1968). The trend of student attitudes in general has been in the direction of the activist minority. In contrast to the student Left of the 1930s, the New Left rejected adult assistance and responded negatively to overtures from adult, leftist organizations (Lipset and Altbach 1967). The term "generation gap" appears to be a socially acceptable way of saying that many students in the late 1960s were antiadult and antiadult authority, irrespective of the form the authority took.

Closely allied to the finding of increased negativism to authority is the general shift to more negative attitudes toward managerial role prescriptions in large bureaucracies, reflected in the total score change. There is considerable evidence in support of this antibureaucratic trend from other sources, although much of this evidence has not been interpreted in terms of the bureaucracy concept. Thus, studies have repeatedly indicated that among the activists there was a strong tendency to reject formal religion (Watts and Whittaker 1966; Solomon and Fishman 1964; Lipset and Altbach 1967). The rule-oriented, authority-based nature of much formal religion and the church organizations that perpetuate it are probably a major factor.

Similarly, it was the very large and complex universities that experienced the greatest unrest and which appeared to be the focus of student protest (Scott and El-Assal 1969). Silver (1969) reported that half of all Columbia University students wanted to become professors before entering the university, but that only one-sixth indicated the same career choice during their senior year of college. He interpreted this change as reflecting a feeling—developing with increased exposure in the student role—that large universities are bureaucracies, coupled with a desire to avoid bureaucracies. A similar shift in a negative direction appears to occur insofar as attitudes toward a business career are concerned, at least within the liberal arts segment of the student population (Dawson 1969).

Finally, a major set of issues in student demonstrations throughout the country was the Vietnam War and the draft (Peterson 1968a). Although a number of students participated in demonstrations out of pacifist values and revulsion against physical violence, these factors seem inadequate to account for the extent and nature of the participation. In view of the present findings, a major factor in the war demonstrations may have been a rejection of bureaucracy and authoritarian systems as represented by military organizations. This suggests that the draft, rather than the war itself, was the major object of discontent and that antiwar sentiment represented, for many students, a displacement to a more acceptable object. These students not only did not want to fight in Vietnam, but they would really prefer not to enter the armed forces at all.

The third major change noted over the decade was a negative shift in attitude toward assuming administrative responsibility. This is consistent with the rejection of administration in general, at least as it is represented in bureaucracy. But perhaps even more significant is the rejection of responsibility to social systems implied by this finding. The increased appeal that hippy life and existentialism had for many young people in those years must almost certainly be associated with this shift in attitudes.

The final major change noted was the decline in competitive motivation. Other evidence suggests a similar pattern among activists. Studies indicate a limited commitment to the Protestant ethic. Achievement and success are of little concern (Block, Haan, and Smith 1968). Such a rejection of conventional competitive motivation in the economic sphere is consistent with the strong leftist orientation exhibited by most activists.

The stability and perhaps even the growth of power motivation represents a striking contrast. Yet evidence of strong power motivation within the activist sector parallels the findings obtained in this study. Activist students consistently demanded a greater voice in university affairs and greater power over decision-making processes (Soares 1967). At Columbia University surveys of student attitudes indicated widespread support for the view that students should exercise more control over university policy making (Barton 1968). The same result was obtained at Berkeley (Dubin and Beise 1967). A major source of student unrest throughout the country was the matter of campus governance (Peterson 1968a). Student power, as opposed to administrative or faculty power, grew as a major issue in demonstrations. Students seemed to have a need to exercise power over many aspects of university operations, not just over student behavior.

The significance of strong power motivation when stripped of interactions with positive attitudes to authority, strong competitive motivation, and favorable attitudes toward administrative responsibility is difficult to know. In the bureaucratic model for managerial success these factors move together; on the campus at the time they apparently did not. When all these motives and attitudes operate together, power motivation is muted and channeled to be consistent with organizational goals. The more naked power motivation that was prevalent among college students were not so restrained and controlled by other attitudes and motives within the individual.

SOURCES OF CHANGE

The more negative attitudes and lower levels of certain types of motives that have been found to characterize a large number of students in the last half of the 1960s were probably not in themselves a direct cause of demonstrations and activism. Groups with similarly low scores have previously been identified (Miner 1965a) without this particular behavior pattern being present, although in these cases power motivation has also typically been at a low level. On the other hand, such attitudes and motives provided both fertile ground for activist leadership to emerge and an environment that continued to nurture it. The data of this study are consistent with the view that demonstrations had strong support in the attitudes of student majorities, and that student unrest was not merely a product of a small dissident minority. Nor was it a temporary phenomenon. Student unrest has been viewed as a response to alienating forces in the university and to imperfections of the educational experience (Dubin and Beise 1967). Yet alienation was by no means a new phenomenon on the college campus (Jencks and Riesman 1968), and imperfections of the educational experience did not appear to be a major issue in demonstrations (Peterson 1968a; Lipset and Altbach 1967). The explanation most consonant with the findings reported here is that many of the students who entered colleges and universities at the time arrived with attitudes and motives that differed sharply from those of earlier generations. The new attitudes predisposed the individual against authority, bureaucracy, and the Protestant ethic. When such students faced the authority of large bureaucratic universities they generated leaders who epitomized the attitudes and motives of the majority, and activism appeared. In large, complex universities the new attitudes and motives did not need to be as prevalent or as widespread to produce demonstrations because bureaucratization was complete, at least from the vantage point of the student. In somewhat less bureaucratic educational organizations the student attitude base required to produce unrest was greater. This explanation assumes that different colleges attracted students with differing degrees of activist attitudes, and that these attitudes interacted with the degree of bureaucratization to produce activist behavior.

There has been some research into the family backgrounds of student activists that provides a possible clue to why the students of the late 1960s often had different attitudes and motives than their predecessors. The activists were typically reared in permissive homes with very little parental discipline (Flacks 1967; Block, Haan, and Smith 1968); that is, their parents rarely punished them, introduced few rules, and avoided intruding into the lives of their children.

Although data that would provide a certain link between these permissive practices and the attitudes identified in this study are lacking, it is likely that such a link does exist. It is a reasonable hypothesis that attitudes toward authority should be more negative, responsibility be valued less, and the desire to compete for rewards should decrease under such a permissive upbringing, while the desire to exercise power remains unaffected. If leftist activist students were reared in a family environment practically devoid of bureaucratic characteristics and sufficiently affluent to give them what is desired simply for the asking (Westby and Braungart 1966), it is not surprising that they would come into conflict with educational organizations. These organizations provided their first real experiences with bureaucratic processes.

These conflicts would represent the actions of an isolated minority to the extent permissiveness and affluence were characteristic of certain homes, but not of most. Such is not the case (Block, Haan, and Smith 1968). The findings of this study regard the attitudes and motives of the decade's generation of college students as probably reflecting these students' upbringing. Many were raised with few rules and little discipline. They often grew up with numerous labor-saving devices in the home, considerable economic security, and in an adult society which has given much while requiring little in return.

There is a certain parallel between the thesis developed here and the evidence McClelland (1961) presented regarding decreasing achievement motivation in the United States. McClelland's (1961) data and arguments suggest that this country may well have reached its economic peak, and that the process of decline already had set in. When achievement motivation is no longer passed on from parent to child, civilizations must inevitably start the process of decay. McClelland (1961) considered the advent of slavery associated with affluence as a major factor accounting for the failure to perpetuate achievement motivation. Slaves took over the childrearing chores and, being low on achievement motivation themselves, did not inculcate it in the children. In the United States of the 1960s, a similar disruption in the value-transmission process may have occurred, although not due to slavery. Permissiveness with its failure to use punishment and discipline may have resulted in attitudes being developed quite independent of parental influence. Achievement motivation and Protestant ethic values were transmitted less frequently because parents often stopped consciously transmitting values at all. In fact, they made a determined effort not to transmit values, on the theory that children should develop their own. In this vacuum other influences took over and a new set of attitudes and motives, antiauthority, antibureaucracy, anticompetition, antiresponsibility, and pro-power began to appear on the college campus. Parents did not intend this, but it was an inevitable consequence of their actions.

This very sketchy theoretical excursion is not proven by the data of this paper. The findings have been extended and extrapolated in numerous respects. But the views presented do not contradict the findings presented here, nor those of others. They do provide needed explanations. In a number of respects they are consistent with and supplement certain other theories and explanations of the origins of student activism (Block, Haan, and Smith 1968).

EXTENSIONS ACROSS THE 1970–72 PERIOD

The study below (Miner 1974d) extends the analysis into the 1970–72 period.

Procedure

The MSCS was administered to students from the University of Maryland in 1972, just three years after the earlier study. The 73 students were enrolled in the same required management course as the 1969 group, and thus can be assumed to be equally representative.

The Portland State University sample obtained in 1970 differed from that of 1966–67 in that the 65 students included 17, or 26 percent, who were thirty years of age or older. The average age of this 30 and over group was 36.8. Earlier results indicated that a change in student attitudes occurred in the mid-1960s. At that time, the age 30 and over students in the 1970 Portland State University sample were already beyond the usual age of college attendance. Accordingly one might expect them to be more like the students of the early 1960s than those of the latter half of the decade. To investigate this possibility separate analyses were carried out with the two age groups.

The third sample, obtained in 1971 at Western Michigan University, contained 349 students enrolled in a required, upper division management course, and can be assumed to be representative of business administration majors at the junior level (see Chapter 6).

The fourth sample was obtained at the University of South Florida in 1972. The 66 students were enrolled in 2 different upper division courses in the management area (see Chapter 6).

Findings

Comparisons of Combined Samples

The data thus available were combined to produce samples for three periods—1960–61 (Oregon), 1966–69 (Oregon, Maryland, Portland State) and 1970–72 (Maryland, Portland State, Western Michigan, South Florida). The results are given in Table 11.2.

Table 11.2

Shifts in Mean MSCS Scores for Combined Samples

MSCS Measures	Period Studied 1960–61 (N = 287)	1966–69 (N = 368)	1970–72 (N = 553)	t Values for Comparisons: 1960–61 vs. 1966–69	1960–61 vs. 1970–72	1966–69 vs. 1970–72
Total Score	3.33	.44	–.81	6.15**	9.86**	3.12**
Subscales						
Attitude to Authority	1.17	.50	.12	5.98**	9.81**	3.65**
Competitive Motivation (Games)	1.18	.86	.80	2.25*	2.86**	.50
Competitive Motivation (Occupational)	–.55	–1.17	–1.28	4.77**	6.08**	1.01
Attitude to Masculine (Assertive) Role	.32	–.05	–.66	2.64**	7.54**	5.00**
Power Motivation	.37	.46	.44	.75	.18	.70
Attitude to Differentiated Role	.38	.11	.27	2.41*	1.07	1.60
Attitude to Administrative Responsibility	.45	–.26	–.50	5.18**	7.85**	2.02*

Note: MSCS = Miner Sentence Completion Scale.
*$p < .05$; **$p < .01$

The findings when the 1960–61 scores are compared with those for 1966–69 are essentially the same as those reported previously. When the 1970–72 data are compared with those for 1960–61, the results serve to reinforce the prior conclusion that a real change did occur in the mid-1960s. The only apparent deviation from the earlier findings is the lack of a significant difference on the attitude toward a differentiated role measure. This failure to obtain significance with the 1970–72 data raises some questions regarding the generality of the earlier finding with this particular measure.

There is also evidence of a continued decline since the late 1960s on the total score index, in favorable attitudes to authority, in favorable attitudes to the masculine role, and in favorable attitudes to administrative responsibility. The decline in masculine identification is not due to an increase in females in the samples; in fact there has been a decrease since the 1966–69 period.

Comparison of Samples within Universities

Comparisons within universities permit a determination of change with specifically organization-based sources of sample fluctuation controlled. The University of Maryland data appear in Table 11.3.

The Maryland findings closely parallel those of Table 11.2. Attitudes to authority and the masculine role both show a decrease, as does the total score. However, a decline in attitude toward administrative responsibility is not found and there is a decrease in competitive motivation.

The Portland State University comparison is confounded by the possible influence of age-

Table 11.3

Shifts in Mean MSCS Scores for University of Maryland Samples

MSCS Measures	Period Studied 1969 (N = 122)	1972 (N = 73)	*t*
Total Score	.80	–.96	1.93*
Subscales			
Attitude to Authority	.46	–.08	2.25*
Competitive Motivation (Games)	1.09	.27	3.42**
Competitive Motivation (Occupational)	–1.26	–1.15	.44
Attitude to Masculine (Assertive) Role	–.11	–1.00	3.07**
Power Motivation	.66	.30	1.44
Attitude to Differentiated Role	.23	.56	1.64
Attitude to Administrative Responsibility	–.26	.14	1.48

Note: MSCS = Miner Sentence Completion Scale.
*$p < .05$, one-tailed; **$p < .01$, one-tailed

related factors. Thus comparisons were made initially between the students under 30 and those 30 or older. As indicated in Table 11.4 higher scores do occur among the older students. This is not a general phenomenon throughout the total age range. Studies of managers in the age range 30 to 65 have repeatedly indicated a lack of correlation between age and MSCS variables (Miner 1965a; 1967).

Because of the age differences identified, the comparison with the 1966–67 data utilized only the students under 30, thus making the two Portland State samples of comparable age. The resulting analysis produced evidence of differences on exactly the same variables as for the combined samples of Table 11.2.

Comparisons of Individual Samples

When each of the three 1966–69 samples is compared with each of the four 1970–72 samples differences in the expected direction at the $p < .05$ level or better occur on 37 of the 96 comparisons. In contrast, reversals involving higher scores in 1970–72 and yielding a comparable *t* value occur in only four cases.

There is a predominant tendency to decreasing scores on the same variables as in Table 11.2. When contrasted with differences *within periods,* those *between periods* that yield a decrease from 1966–69 to 1970–72 clearly predominate in the case of the total score, attitude toward authority, and attitude to the masculine role; data for attitude to administrative responsibility are less strong, but tend to support a similar interpretation.

Taking all three approaches to the analysis into account, the following conclusions regarding changes in the most recent period as they relate to those during the 1960s seem warranted:

- A marked decrease above and beyond those from 1960–61 to 1966–69
  —general attitude toward managerial role prescriptions in bureaucracies
  —attitude toward authority figures
  —attitude toward assuming the masculine role

Table 11.4

Shifts in Mean MSCS Scores for Portland State University Students

	Period Studied			*t* Values for Comparisons	
	1966–67	1970		1970–	1966–67 vs. 1970
MSCS Measure	(N = 117)	Age 30+ (N = 17)	Age < 30 (N = 48)	Age 30+ vs. Age < 30	Age < 30
Total Score	–.03	1.59	–1.81	2.00*	1.78*
Subscales					
Attitude to Authority	.57	1.06	–.25	3.97**	3.42**
Competitive Motivation (Games)	.78	1.41	.96	1.00	.56
Competitive Motivation (Occupational)	–1.22	–.59	–1.34	1.79*	.44
Attitude to Masculine (Assertive) Role	–.05	–.35	–.65	.49	1.88*
Power Motivation	.40	.65	.19	1.10	.81
Attitude to Differentiated Role	–.17	–.24	.16	.91	1.37
Attitude to Administrative Responsibility	–.34	–.35	–.88	1.10	1.74*

Note: MSCS = Miner Sentence Completion Scale.
*$p < .05$, one-tailed; **$p < .01$, one-tailed

- A somewhat less pronounced decrease above and beyond that from 1960–61 to 1966–69
  —attitude toward assuming administrative responsibility
- A decrease from 1960–61 to 1966–69 and little further change thereafter
  —competitive motivation (games and occupational)
- No definite evidence of generalized change over the period of study
  —attitude toward assuming a differentiated role
  —power motivation

EXTENSIONS TO 1980

Starting in the early 1970s, publications began to appear dealing with changing patterns of attitudes, values, and motives in the college population. In a number of instances, this research dealt with characteristics having implications for subsequent performance in a managerial capacity in bureaucratic organizations. Among these studies were investigations by Rotter (1971), Ondrack (1971), Morris and Small (1971), Ward and Athos (1972), in addition to the research by Miner and his colleagues. The results consistently portrayed a picture of declining managerial potential in the population segment from which future managers would be drawn, and thus presented the specter of future talent shortages to the country's major business and governmental organizations. Recent evidence from the corporate world itself has begun to substantiate these early predictions (Howard and Bray 1981; Opinion Research Corporation 1980).

The basic hypothesis under consideration here (in Miner and Smith 1982) states that if successive samples are taken from the same source at sufficient time intervals (four or five years), a significant decline in overall motivation to manage and its components from period to period will be found.

Method

The primary source of data was a series of samplings from required undergraduate core courses at the University of Oregon. Over the period of the study, four groups of students were measured as follows: (1) 287 students, 246 male and 41 (14 percent) female, in late 1960 and throughout 1961; (2) 129 students, 114 male and 15 (12 percent) female, in late 1967 and early 1968; (3) 86 students, 69 male and 17 (20 percent) female, in late 1972 and early 1973; and (4) 124 students, 71 male and 53 (43 percent) female, in early 1980.

There was very little age variation from sample to sample; the mean age was 21 and most of the students clustered in the early 20s. The changing proportion of females appeared to reflect the national experience in this regard.

Although, because of the time span covered, the University of Oregon data provided the best test of the successive declines hypothesis, an additional test for the most recent period was carried out utilizing students in required undergraduate core courses at Georgia State University. Two samples were employed as follows: (1) 74 students, 44 male and 30 (41 percent) female, in early 1975. This sample was collected in connection with a study by Singleton (1978) of student leaders and was employed as a control group in that research. (2) 51 students, 23 male and 28 (55 percent) female, in early 1979. The sample was collected by Bracker and Pearson (1982) as part of a more comprehensive investigation.

The Georgia State University students tended to be employed, often in full-time jobs, and the samples contained a larger proportion of older students than would have been typical at most other universities, including the University of Oregon. Comparisons between successive samples were carried out for each university using the various scores obtained from Form H of the Miner Sentence Completion Scale (MSCS).

All of the scales were scored by the first author except those contained in the 1975 Georgia State University sample (which were scored by Singleton 1978). Separate analyses designed to determine comparability among these two scorers produced a total score correlation of .95 and a median subscale correlation of .92 in a subsample of 12 students. Mean scores on the subscales showed no evidence of a significant variation between scorers, and no constant scoring bias was apparent.

Results

Data from the University of Oregon samples, as indicated in Table 11.5, characteristically supported the hypothesis from 1960–61 to 1967–68, and from 1967–68 to 1972–73, but not from 1972–73 to 1980. Among the subscales, significant declines in one or both of the early periods occurred for all measures except Imposing Wishes and Standing Out from Group. On these two indexes there was no evidence of any change over the full twenty years of the study. The evidence appears to indicate a general decline in managerial motivation over a roughly ten-year period from the early 1960s to the early 1970s and then a leveling off, but not a resurgence, through the remainder of the 1970s. In distinct contradiction to these statements are the Imposing Wishes and Standing Out from Group subscales that appear to have been immune to the change processes throughout the period.

The findings for male students, which predominate in the total sample, are essentially the same as in Table 11.5. The female data, however, present a much more unstable picture. There were meaningful increases in scores from period to period as well as decreases. However, statistical significance was obtained only by the decreases. Even so, the number of significant

Table 11.5

Pattern of Changes in MSCS (Form H) **Scores among University of Oregon Business Students Over 20 Years**

MSCS Measures	1960–1961 *M* scores (N = 287)	Δ/year	1967–1968 *M* scores (N = 129)	Δ/year	1972–1973 *M* scores (N = 86)	Δ/year	1980 *M* scores (N = 124)
Total Score	3.33	−.40**	.52	−.47**	−1.84	.00	−1.86
Authority Figures	1.17	−.10**	.47	−.06	.15	.00	.14
Competitive Games	1.18	−.07**	.71	−.06	.40	.00	.39
Competitive Situations	−.55	−.07**	−1.04	−.11**	−1.60	.05	−1.23
Assertive Role	.32	−.05*	.00	−.15**	−.77	−.03	−.99
Imposing Wishes	.37	−.01	.33	−.04	.15	−.01	.11
Standing Out from Group	.38	−.02	.26	−.01	.22	.01	.27
Routine Administrative Functions	.45	−.09**	−.20	−.04	−.38	−.02	−.55

Note: MSCS = Miner Sentence Completion Scale. Δ = rate of change. Rate of change values refer to the difference between the two adjacent mean scores; significance for these values was determined using *t* tests.

$^{*}p < .05$. $^{**}p < .01$

changes was sharply reduced (9 of 24 among the males, 3 of 24 among the females). None of the total score changes were significant for the females, although once again significant period-to-period changes on the subscales occurred from 1960–61 to 1967–68 and from 1967–68 to 1972–73, but not from 1972–73 to 1980.

In this instance, however, the findings appear to be influenced by the typical random fluctuations associated with small sample sizes. The 1967–68 and 1972–73 female samples are not of sufficient size to provide an adequate test of the hypothesis. When comparisons are made between the 1960–61 and 1980 female samples statistically significant declines appear for total score, $t(92) = 3.18$, $p < .01$; and on the Authority Figures, $t(92) = 3.04$, $p < .01$; Assertive Role, $t(92) = 2.68$, $p < .01$; and Routine Administrative Functions, $t(92) = 4.34$, $p < .01$, subscales. As in previous comparisons there is no evidence of change on Imposing Wishes or Standing Out from Group. In contradistinction to the males, the females of 1980 appear to have been just as competitive as the females of twenty years earlier. Overall, the forces for decline appear to have been somewhat muted as they influenced female college students.

The net effects of these processes are that in the early 1960s male business students characteristically had a stronger motivation to manage than did females. There were some reversals on individual subscales, but the overall trend throughout the decade and well into the 1970s favored the males (Miner 1974c). The 1980 data, however, indicated no significant differences at all, in spite of the entirely adequate sample sizes.

The Georgia State University data, coming from a diametrically opposite section of the country, were entirely consistent with those from the University of Oregon. As indicated in Table 11.6 little change occurred from the mid-1970s to the end of the decade. There was a statistically significant increase on Imposing Wishes, but there were no significant decreases. Even the one increase must be treated with caution. It was not replicated in the University of Oregon data nor was it sufficient to influence the total score comparison, and it occurred on a variable that previously had not been subject to change. If this finding should be substantiated by subsequent research it would reflect a new trend rather than an extension of past changes.

Table 11.6

Pattern of Changes in MSCS (Form H) **Scores among Georgia State University Business Students in the Recent Period**

MSCS Measures	*M* scores 1975 (N = 74)	Δ/year	*M* scores 1979 (N = 51)
Total Score	–.51	.14	.04
Authority Figures	.66	.00	.67
Competitive Games	.62	–.14	.06
Competitive Situations	–1.28	.04	–1.14
Assertive Role	–.31	–.10	–.71
Imposing Wishes	–.23	.22*	.65
Standing Out from Group	.15	.09	.49
Routine Administrative Functions	–.12	.03	.02

Note: MSCS = Miner Sentence Completion Scale. Δ = rate of change. Rate of change values refer to the difference between the two adjacent mean scores; significance for these values was determined using *t* tests.

*$p < .01$

Although the Georgia State University analyses of sex differences were based on rather small samples, they replicated those from the University of Oregon for the most recent period in every respect. In no instance was a significant difference between males and females subsequently obtained.

Discussion

The evidence identifies two major changes in the overall pattern of managerial motivation during the past few years. One is the general stabilization of motivational levels. The decline apparently has stopped. This conclusion is reinforced by data from other sources. Scales collected by Albert (1977) on 69 management majors at Georgia State University yielded a total score of –.12 in 1976. Southern (1977) obtained mean total scores of 1.54 and –.24 in two samples of 54 and 59 business students enrolled at junior colleges in the state of Georgia, also in 1976. All of these samples contained substantial numbers of higher scoring older students; the mean ages ran from 26 to 28, thus accounting for somewhat higher scores than were found at the University of Oregon in the more recent period. Muczyk and Schuler (1976) reported a mean total score of –.83 for 138 male students at Cleveland State University in 1974. Brief, Aldag, and Chacko (1977) provided data on 103 business students at a large southern university from which a mean total score of –.82 was computed.

Although the decline is not continuing, stabilization has occurred at a very low level and has remained at that point for seven or eight years. From the University of Oregon data it appears that MSCS scores currently are roughly one standard deviation below where they were twenty years ago, and they have been at that point for some time. Given that changes do not seem to occur as college students move on into the organizational world of business and government, at least without some specific intervention to that end, we face something like a fifteen-year deficit in managerial talent. Without a reversal, the deficit will extend over a much longer period.

Some years ago, there were sizable sex differences in the scores of business students, the great majority of whom were males. In the field of education, however, where more females enrolled, no sex differences were in evidence (Miner 1974c). Now with the influx of females into business courses there has been a shift to a pattern more consonant with the previous education findings. The sex differences have disappeared, not because the females failed to show a decline in MSCS scores during the 1960s and early 1970s; but because their rate of decline was less rapid than that of the males. Furthermore, the decrease in competitiveness that is so pronounced among the males is not apparent among the females. These changes are entirely consistent with the shifts in workforce composition that have occurred over the past twenty years, as increasing numbers of women have sought employment.

Contrary Evidence

The conclusions stated above have been challenged by certain research findings published by Bartol, Anderson, and Schneier (1980, 1981). Their evidence indicates that instead of stabilization, an acute reversal in scores occurred during the 1970s. In addition, they continued to find sex differences of the kind noted in the earlier research.

There were three samples involved in these studies, all obtained in 1977. One consisted of 108 students in basic management courses at the University of Maryland, 43 percent of whom were female. The second consisted of 108 students in basic management courses at Syracuse University, 32 percent of whom were female. The third consisted of 108 students in basic management courses at a "predominantly black university," variously reported as 32 percent and 39 percent female. Data on mean ages and the proportions of older students are not provided for these samples. The mean total scores were respectively 1.90, 3.50, and 1.00. It is difficult to evaluate the latter value, since data on black students have not been available previously, the scores are not so high as to be distinctly separable from the findings of the early 1970s, and the proportion of older students may be high in this sample. The University of Maryland and Syracuse University findings, on the other hand, clearly do appear to represent a departure from expectations. Furthermore, there is a consistent pattern of higher scores among males in all three samples; the Competitive Games subscale is the most pervasive contributor.

Questions about the Contrary Evidence

However, there is good reason to believe that this evidence is substantially compromised by scoring errors. To quote from the source, which reported this conclusion:

> Data are presented indicating substantial differences in scoring the Miner Sentence Completion Scales used in the Bartol et al. study between the original scorers and both Miner and Ebrahimi. These differences appear sufficient to account for the reversals and continued sex differences reported by Bartol et al. Analyses are presented to indicate that in all likelihood the Bartol et al. results are a consequence of scoring errors of a type often found among less experienced scorers (Miner, Smith, and Ebrahimi 1985, 290).

The sample on which these conclusions are based consisted of 23 MSCS protocols drawn by Bartol from the data bank used by Bartol, Anderson, and Schneier (1980, 1981) in their studies. These protocols were scored separately by both Miner and Ebrahimi. Both found the same sources of error, and their scorings correlated at .88. Concerning the reanalysis:

> It would have been desirable to know exactly how the sample of 23 records was selected from the larger group of 324, to have obtained a somewhat larger sample than 23, and to have been able to report the results of subscale analyses. Unfortunately, we were not able to obtain the necessary information and data. Yet we believe that what is available is sufficient to raise important questions regarding the Bartol et al. (1980, 1981) research (Miner, Smith, and Ebrahimi 1985, 297).

To my knowledge none of the contesting authors have conducted subsequent research on students at any of the three universities to further validate their initial findings. Thus these findings stand as single instances that do not measure change per se and, at the same time, seem fundamentally flawed.

CHAPTER 12

VARIED PERSONNEL FROM HIERARCHIC, PROFESSIONAL, TASK, AND GROUP SYSTEMS

AN INSTRUMENT FOR CLASSIFYING ORGANIZATIONS

JOHN E. OLIVER

INTRODUCTION

Research on the Oliver Organization Description Questionnaire was published in a Scoring Guide (Oliver 1981) and in the *Academy of Management Journal* (Oliver 1982). Thus began a series of studies devoted to establishing how four types of organizational forms underlying role motivation theory may be actually measured, and how they function.

The four forms were, of course, a product of my own theorizing, but beyond that John Oliver took over. We both agreed that some method of operationalizing the theoretical constructs was needed to establish what theoretical domain a given study was drawing upon. But beyond that, Oliver created the methodology, found the subjects, developed the procedures, and organized the results. As chairman of his dissertation committee, I found this to be one of the easiest such efforts I have ever "supervised." At most points it was clear that John understood a great deal more than I did.

* * *

Recent reviews of the literature on organizational taxonomies, typologies, or classifications express optimism in the potential usefulness of organizational classification as an aid to researchers and managers. According to these reviews, organizational classification can aid in the development of management theory beyond the contingency stage (McKelvey 1975), in refining hypotheses, investigating validity and utility of theories, and in predicting decision making and changes in behaviors (Haas, Hall, and Johnson 1966). Classification of organizations may permit better prescription of management styles (Filley and Aldag 1978) and the design of organization structures (Pugh, Hickson, and Hinings 1969), and it may facilitate the development of middle range theories of organizational behavior (Pinder and Moore 1979).

Carper and Snizek (1980) state that one of the most obvious benefits of a workable taxonomy is that it allows large amounts of information about various organizations to be collapsed into more convenient categories that are easier to process, store, and comprehend. It aids practitioners in the application of management knowledge in organizations as well.

McKelvey (1975) and Carper and Snizek (1980) have criticized the divorce of theory and empiricism in previous classification research. They conclude that multiple organizational dimensions must be simultaneously considered in a holistic framework in order to operationalize the theories. Operationalization of these multiple dimensions also will require valid and reliable measurements of classification variables.

The purpose of the present research is to combine organization theory (both micro and macro) with the empirical rigors of psychometrics in order to develop a valid and reliable instrument for classifying organizations and subunits of organizations. The theoretical base stems from Miner's (1979c) four limited domain theories of organization. In his role theory research, Miner identified four parsimonious domains: hierarchic (H), professional (P), task (T), and group (G). Each of these domains requires different types of behaviors, leaders, decision styles, controls, and organization designs. Most management research and literature can be classified as applicable to one of these four domains. The present research in organizational classification began with a study of the literature associated with each of these domains. The effort was to define precisely the four domains and set the stage for classifying organizations or subunits of organizations into one of the four domains, based on distinguishing attributes.

The resulting definitions constitute "ideal types" of organizations. As McKelvey has pointed out, "An ideal type concept, such as Weber's concept of bureaucracy, is used primarily for theory generation with little expectation that objects meeting all criteria of the ideal type will be found empirically" (1975, 510).

Hierarchic organizations are characterized by the distribution of impersonal, rational, legitimate authority among positions organized such that each lower position is controlled and supervised by a higher position. The responsibilities of each position are assigned by higher positions and are limited to a specific jurisdiction within a systematic division of labor. Rules regulate the activities and decisions of each position holder. Position holders are appointed and are remunerated by fixed salaries graded according to rank in the hierarchy. Promotion and discipline are dependent on the judgment of superiors. Loyalty to the organization and values congruent with organization goals are demanded of position holders. Power and prestige are distributed according to rank in the hierarchy. Freedom or discretion in decision making and communication is limited. Emphasis is placed on efficient performance of the duties assigned (Burns and Stalker 1961; Dubin 1949; Simon 1957; Weber 1947). Weber applied his definition to organizations, independent of goal or purpose, specifically including business, charities, hospitals, the Catholic Church, and modern armies.

Professional organizations are denoted by a preponderance of positions that are characterized by the presence of an abstract body of knowledge and theory, a self-governing association of peers, professional standards of workmanship and ethical conduct, and an orientation toward service to clients. The professional possesses an ideological commitment to the professional group and its norms, which determine the tasks that are appropriate for members, as well as how the tasks should be performed and evaluated. Moral norms exist to protect clients' welfare and are enforced through training, association, codes of ethics, and surveillance by colleagues. Thus, professions are self-governing and their members are relatively autonomous. Examples offered by Moore (1970) include organizations of physicians, lawyers, and professors at the highly professional end of the scale and skilled tradesmen such as carpenters at the lower end of the scale (Blau and Scott 1962; Elliott 1972; Moore 1970; Satow 1975; Vollmer and Mills 1966).

Task organizations are those in which most individual positions possess relatively large degrees of autonomy, skill variety, task identity and significance, and knowledge of results that are designed into the work. Individual goal-setting is used to induce commitment and performance. Success is achieved through the incumbent's own efforts, abilities, and motivation rather than by chance or compliance. Examples from literature include entrepreneurial organizations, venture teams, commissioned sales organizations, and enriched job settings (Collins, Moore, and Unwalla 1964; Hackman and Oldham 1976; Herzberg 1976; Locke 1967; McClelland, Atkinson, Clark, and Lowell 1953).

Organizations in the group domain exhibit democratic processes of decision making and task assignment, emergent situationally variable leadership that must conform to the will of the majority or group consensus, and interdependent tasks requiring cooperation and overlapping skills. Satisfying group relationships are coupled with work that would have little motivational potential if arranged as a set of individual tasks but that allows the group to assume total responsibility. Personnel selection and discipline are accomplished by the group, and compensation is based on group productivity (Bramlette, Jewell, and Mescon 1977; Trist and Bamforth 1951; Walton 1972).

It is not expected that all of the elements of a definition will apply to each organization classified. It thus should be possible to scale organizations within each category based on the number of defining elements found in each organization. For instance, not all professional organizations have an orientation toward service to clients. Professional research organizations might be an example.

It might also be expected that some organizations would score high on more than one scale. For example, the work of some professionals might be expected to have large degrees of autonomy, skill variety, task identity, significance, and knowledge of results, which are elements of the task domain.

In addition, some organizations may be mixed, such as the professional bureaucracy described by Mintzberg (1981). Mintzberg notes that the professional bureaucracy relies on the standardization of skills by trained professionals (rather than work processes or outputs used in a pure bureaucracy) for its coordination. This structure is very decentralized and democratic in nature for the professionals but contains a parallel autocratic (hierarchic) organization of support staff. One might expect to find significant degrees of both hierarchy and professionalism in such an organization.

METHOD

Instrument Development

The attributes generated in the literature review were used to create 100 forced-choice items of the following format:

In my work, duties are determined by

(a) management.
(b) my profession or occupation.
(c) my work group.
(d) me, based on the goal I am trying to accomplish.

Item responses were designed to describe possible states of each attribute in each of the four domains, based on the researcher's knowledge of the characteristics and the domains.

In order to reduce the transparency of the items, two techniques were used:

1. The wording of responses was varied, using synonyms found in dictionaries, a thesaurus, and in the literature.
2. Item response order was randomized from item to item so that there was no clear pattern of answers.

Instrument Pretest

Items were proofread for face validity, grammar, ambiguous wording, emotionally loaded words, and simplicity by six PhD judges from the fields of sociology, psychology, and management as well as two graduate student editors who were English and psychology majors. This edited instrument was administered to sixty employed MBA students who were instructed to complete the questionnaire for their work situations. Afterward, they were instructed in the purpose and theory underlying the instrument and were asked for feedback on the construction of the items, the accuracy of their scores, and difficulties encountered in answering. This field test led to several revisions.

Samples

The revised 100-item instrument was administered to purposive samples drawn from organizations or subgroups that were identified by the judges, on an a priori basis, as representative of one of the domains. The judges' expertise and the definitions previously developed were used as the criteria for selecting sample groups and for analyzing the item responses of the subjects.

When samples from a single organization or subunit did not contribute at least 100 subjects, samples from several organizations were combined to form the desired sample size from any one domain. The organizations sampled include both public and private sector organizations of various sizes and missions identified as fitting into one of the desired domains. Subjects were managers, owners, employees, or first level supervisors of the organizations sampled.

The hierarchic sample contained 107 subjects, composed of 24 production workers from a large multinational pharmaceutical manufacturer; 21 prison guards and working prisoners; 10 keypunch operators from a large air-conditioning manufacturer; 7 U.S. Civil Service clerical personnel, 38 U.S. Army officers, NCOs, and enlisted trainees; and 7 clerical workers from a large electric utility.

The professional sample of 105 subjects consisted of 23 members of three ministerial associations, 29 college professors, and 53 independent professionals, including 9 medical doctors, 7 pharmacists, 5 veterinarians, 2 professional engineers, 9 lawyers, 1 architect, 8 CPAs, and 4 medical technicians.

Table 12.1

Example Matrix for Selection of a Response (%)

Item 4 Response	Hierarchic Weighting Group	Professional Weighting Group	Task Weighting Group	Group Weighting Group
(a)	38	85	51	24
(b)	11	0	4	24
(c)	16	6	31	22
(d)	35	9	14	30

The 101 subjects of the task sample included 30 entrepreneurs, 19 real estate sales associates, 15 traveling commissioned sales representatives, and 37 undergraduate finance students.

The group sample was composed of 125 personnel from two sociotechnically designed container plants utilizing self-directed work groups.

Procedure

The data were collected in the winter of 1980. Questionnaires were administered at the work settings. Time required by a subject to complete the instrument varied from approximately 15 to 50 minutes, with a mean of 30 minutes. Participation was voluntary, and the usable response rate was 97 percent.

Keys for scoring each domain were based on the theorized, designed responses for each item. Four scores were computed by totaling the selected item responses keyed to each domain. An H score, P score, T score, and G score were computed for the hierarchic, professional, task, and group scales, respectively.

Each criterion group sample was divided into a weighting group of from 50 to 63 subjects and a holdout group of approximately the same size. This was done by alternately assigning questionnaires to each group as they were collected so that variance due to completion time was systematically distributed.

Item Selection

Each item was analyzed by creating a matrix showing the percentage of each domain's weighting sample that selected each response. The example matrix (Table 12.1) is for item number 4 of the initial instrument.

Because item response 4(a) was hypothesized to be a professional response, it was analyzed both vertically and horizontally. The vertical analysis indicated that 85 percent of the professional sample selected response 4(a). This is analogous to Berkshire's (1958) applicability index. The horizontal analysis indicates that significantly lower percentages of the other three samples selected response 4(a).

There were 43 items retained for further analysis. All items showed at least a 51 percent applicability index (vertically) and strong horizontal discrimination among domain samples. For simplicity in scoring, all items selected were given a weight of 1. Unit weights have been found to be as effective in discrimination as more complex weighting factors in previous research (Nunnally 1978). A total of 15 items are scored for each domain score so that possible scores range from 0 to + 15 for any given domain. Some items are scored on more than one response.

Table 12.2

Organization Scores and Classification

Organization	N	H Score	P Score	T Score	G Score	Classification
Undergraduate finance students	37	5.7	4.0	8.6	1.5	T
U.S. Army instructors	11	7.6	7.6	1.9	2.0	H/P
Prison guards and working prisoners	21	10.6	4.4	2.4	2.0	H
Independent professionals	46	1.0	11.8	4.9	1.9	P
Entrepreneurs	30	.9	5.3	10.2	1.5	T
Real estate sales firm	5	.4	7.8	11.0	2.4	T
Large air-conditioning manufacturer	10	10.4	4.3	.7	4.4	H
Large electric utility	7	10.0	5.1	3.0	1.2	H
Real estate sales firm	4	.3	6.3	15.0	1.0	T
Real estate sales firm	4	3.2	7.6	9.4	3.4	T
Commission salespeople (traveling)	9	6.8	6.5	9.8	1.1	T
Real estate sales firm	2	.5	10.0	8.5	1.5	P[a]
U.S. Army trainees	27	6.9	3.8	3.0	2.4	H
Real estate sales firm	4	2.5	6.7	8.5	1.7	T
Multinational drug manufacturer	24	11.9	2.5	2.1	3.4	H
Ministerial association	9	1.1	5.7	8.1	6.4	T[a]
State hospital chaplains	10	6.9	8.4	4.7	3.3	P
Certified public accountants	7	5.5	9.1	3.1	2.2	P
College professors	29	7.4	10.5	3.9	2.4	P
Large textile manufacturer	6	11.0	4.6	4.6	1.3	H
Ministerial association	4	4.5	7.2	5.5	1.7	P
U.S. Civil Service	7	10.1	5.7	3.5	2.0	H
Sociotechnical office unit	5	4.1	2.8	3.1	8.6	G
Sociotechnical manufacturing unit	21	4.2	1.4	2.7	9.3	G
Sociotechnical manufacturing unit	23	3.4	2.3	2.5	10.5	G
Sociotechnical manufacturing unit	18	3.6	2.0	2.5	10.5	G
Sociotechnical office unit	6	7.5	5.3	5.1	2.6	H[a]
Sociotechnical manufacturing unit	31	6.5	2.3	2.0	7.9	G
Sociotechnical manufacturing unit	21	5.2	3.0	2.5	10.3	G

[a]Unexpected classifications.

The classification ability of the selected items was determined by performing a fold-back classification on the weighting groups using highest score as the classification criterion. Of the weighting group subjects, 72 percent were correctly classified based on the 43 items retained.

To ensure that the 43 items selected were not spuriously related to the domain criterion, cross-validation was accomplished by classifying the holdout sample by highest score. Of the holdout subjects, 71 percent were classified correctly, indicating only a very slight degree of shrinkage.

If the items selected in the weighting groups had not been highly valid, the classification of the holdout groups would not have been equally successful. A chi-square goodness-of-fit test indicated that the distribution of scores in the holdout sample did not vary significantly from the distribution of scores in the weighting sample at the .01 significance level.

RESULTS

Unit or organization scores used for organizational classification are calculated by aggregating individual scores and computing the mean. Table 12.2 indicates the organization scores

Table 12.3

Subsample Means

Domain Group	H Score	P Score	T Score	G Score
Hierarchic (N = 107)	9.6	4.3	2.4	2.5
Professional (N = 105)	3.8	10.2	4.8	2.6
Task (N = 101)	3.8	5.3	9.3	1.6
Group (N = 125)	4.9	2.4	2.6	9.1
Total Sample (N = 438)	5.75	5.44	4.66	4.24

of the 29 organizations in the development sample. Of the organization classifications, 26 (or 90 percent) were in agreement with the hypothesized classifications.

Perhaps the most compelling evidence of criterion-related validity is presented in Table 12.3. The mean score for each scale is almost twice as high in its home domain as in the total sample and even higher when compared to other sample scores. Multivariate analysis of variance utilizing Winer's (1971) repeated measures model (BMD program P2V) and Sheffé tests indicate that these mean differences are significant at the .001 level.

Standard errors of measurement for the four scales are .20 for the hierarchic scale, .19 for the professional, .17 for the task scale, and .19 for the group scale, giving a high degree of confidence in the accuracy of mean scores.

Cronbach's alpha was used to estimate the internal consistencies of the scales. The values for the H score, P score, T score, and G score were .86, .84, .82, and .88, respectively.

Test-retest reliability was estimated by retesting 32 members of the original sample after a 30-day lapse. The Pearson Product Moment correlation coefficients between the first and second scores were .85 for the H scores, .87 for the P scores, .84 for the T scores, and .77 for the G scores. The smaller coefficient for the G scores is due, in part, to restricted range; none of the retests was from the group domain sample.

The four scales are negatively correlated to a slight degree (–.17 to –.43) with the exception of P scale and T scale, which are slightly positively correlated (.11) at the .018 significance level. These low correlations are assumed to have no practical significance even though they may aid in classification.

DISCUSSION

As hypothesized, the organizations scoring significantly high on the hierarchic scale were the manufacturers, government agencies, and prison workers. Those scoring highest on the professional scale were the independent professionals, such as MDs, CPAs, attorneys, college professors, and one real estate firm. The higher task scores were possessed by real estate sales firms, entrepreneurs, commissioned salesmen, and students. The only significant group scores were among the self-directed workgroups of the sociotechnically designed manufacturing plant and one ministerial association.

Subjects at all levels in the hierarchic samples described their positions in terms of being controlled and protected by superiors. Specifically, leaders were appointed, organization structure was set, work rules were established, and job duties were assigned by management. Individual freedom to act was limited by organizational guidelines, and both job results and worker competence were judged by supervisors. Pay was based on time worked or position in the organization, and punishments were decided by supervisors. Most meetings were called and conducted by management. Screening and selection of new employees was the responsibility of a personnel department, with counseling of problem employees and replacement of absent employees a responsibility of managers and supervisors. Resources were said to be allocated by management, and risk of failure was perceived as a concern of organization officials.

Members of professional organizations stressed knowledge, competence, and commitment in their descriptions. Most classified their position as a profession or occupation requiring specialized schooling and continued career development to increase knowledge and ability. They described their work as a central part of their life and part of their identity and status. Personal drive was seen as an aid in achieving professional or occupational goals, and some worked long hours due to professional commitment. Leaders were perceived to be most competent professionally, and loyalty was professed to the profession. Relationships with clients were reported to be based on both professional knowledge and trust. Most important day-to-day communication was with clients, customers, or colleagues, who also were said to receive most of the benefits of the professional's work.

The link between freedom and responsibility keynoted the task domain sample, who reported that risk taking is necessary for personal achievement but stressed that rewards are the result of task completion, with the most valued personal characteristic being a drive to achieve goals. Although freedom to make changes in their jobs without permission was reported, it was coupled with the need to establish work rules, take responsibility for daily workload, and work long hours to gain the rewards and achievements possible. Competence and job results were judged by the individual, and day-to-day decisions were determined by personal goals. Punishments reportedly stem from failure to achieve personal goals.

Members of the group sample reported that much of the organization's power resided in the work group rather than in individuals or in (non-existent) managers. Group members were said to share responsibility for daily workload, work problems, counseling employees, replacing absent employees, and performing housekeeping duties. Learning the jobs of the group required group effort to share skills and knowledge, and job rotation was encouraged to aid in learning. Competence of workers and job results were judged by the work group. Members reported that most important day-to-day communication was with other members of the work group. Conflicts between individuals were said to be resolved through group discussion and compromise. New members were screened and selected by the group. It, reportedly, was not uncommon for members to make sacrifices for the good of the group.

The positive correlation of the P scale and T scale along with the generally higher T scores in the professional sample indicate that the work in professional organizations has some of the characteristics of the work in task organizations.

A posteriori analysis of the organizations that were misclassified yielded interesting information. The ministerial association members who scored higher on the task scale than on the hypothesized professional scale were observed to be "more like commissioned salespeople than professionals" by a research assistant who knew quite well the evangelical fervor of her Baptist minister husband! It also should be noted that ministers assigned as chaplains in a large hierarchic state hospital scored higher on the professional scale and lower on the task scale. If any generalization could be made, it would be that independent, entrepreneurial ministers probably possess a higher degree of task motivation than do institutional chaplains. However, there is insufficient data to support this conclusion.

The office unit of the sociotechnical plant was examined more closely and found to work at the direction of the plant manager rather than as a cohesive self-directed work group. It appears that the sociotechnical intervention was unsuccessful or was not applied to this group as it was in the rest of the plant. That the army instructors scored equally high on the hierarchic and professional scales is not surprising. They are college professors as well as soldiers.

This a posteriori analysis indicates that the initial criterion group selection may have been in error, rather than the final instrument classification. For this reason, misclassified organizations were dropped from the samples and all analyses were rerun. The new analysis resulted in no change in the items selected even though some percentages changed slightly. Differences among domain scores increased even more dramatically, as would be expected.

It is important to note that the questionnaire was designed to classify organizations and subunits of organizations. The scores of an individual questionnaire represent a kind of position description. Hence one would expect considerably less than 100 percent of all individual positions to be correctly classified when the sample includes all the individuals from a selected group. The degree to which individual positions vary in a single group or organization may be one important way that organizations differ. Pinder and Moore (1979) have alluded to the value of operationalizing this variance concept in organizational analysis. It is beyond the scope of this paper and the available space to present individual position scores and detailed position descriptions that support the relevance of this variation.

USES FOR THE OODQ

The instrument developed yields a hierarchic score, a professional score, a task score, and a group score. These, taken together, will classify an organization or group into one or a combination of the four domains. The ability to measure an organization or unit on these four scales is important in a number of ways.

Considering the present knowledge of organizational typologies and contingencies, all research reports should identify and describe the domain of the research to ensure that findings are correctly catalogued and are applied only in the domain in which the research was conducted. One means of providing such identification and description is to use standardized, comparable measures of known relevance and reliability, such as those provided by the hierarchic, professional, task, and group scales developed here (the OODQ). Such scores are a potential guide to predict or prescribe behaviors, roles, or management styles needed to energize the organization and to manage conflict. The roles described by Miner (1979c) for each of these four domains can be prescribed only when the domain has been adequately identified. This study as well as those previously reported show that mis-classification of organizations results when only outsider observations are used in classification. Such rough measures must be replaced by more sensitive, accurate, valid, and reliable ones if parametric, multivariate statistical techniques are to be used to study organizations.

The measurements provided by such scores may aid in the design and selection of content and methods of training and organizational change programs by better describing the domain of the programs' intended impact. For instance, sensitivity training may be more applicable in some domains than in others. The evaluation of the effectiveness of training or change programs such as job enrichment, sociotechnical, or other organizational development interventions may be aided by using the questionnaire as a pre/post measure of domain states.

The scores may serve as criterion measures for testing the construct validity of theories and may add to the understanding of the relationship between domain characteristics, job satisfaction, individual differences, productivity, and the quality of work life. Work design and reward systems also may be studied using the instrument. Although intended as a research device,

Table 12.4

Normative Distributions

	Hierarchic Sample (N = 107)		Professional Sample (N = 105)		Task Sample (N = 101)		Group Sample (125)	
Score	Percent Obtaining	Percentile	Percent Obtaining	Percentile	Percent Obtaining	Percentile	Percent Obtaining	Percentile
15	1		8		5		3	
14	13	90th	15	90th	6	90th	4	
13	20	75th	10	75th	4		8	90th
12	14		11		13	75th	13	75th
11	13	50th	11	50th	13		11	
10	9		11		8		15	50th
9	14	25th	14	25th	16	50th	13	
8	4		11		9		8	
7	3		3		13	25th	4	25th
6	3		4		6		7	
5	3		1		3		5	
4	1		1		3		3	
3					1		2	
2							3	
1							2	

the questionnaire may have practical applications in organizations when used to evaluate the prior experience of job applicants for purposes of placement and career development.

More research needs to be done using the instrument in a variety of organizations for further test of its validity, reliability, and sensitivity. At present, the generalizability of these findings is limited because of the purposive nature of the sample selection, the limited geographic location of units studied, and the limited size of the sample, as well as the few types of organizations included. In fact, the a posteriori analysis was entered into only in an attempt to gain feedback for further development of the instrument and to test the construct validity of the theories.

This study tends to support the theory that several separate and independent domains or philosophies of management exist; that their characteristics can be effectively measured, scaled, and compared; and that organizations can be classified for both descriptive and normative purposes.

SCORING GUIDE FOR THE OODQ

A scoring sheet, and a scoring guide for the Oliver Organization Description Questionnaire (OODQ) have been created (Oliver 1981) that provide additional information beyond what is contained above. In particular normative distributions for the four scores are given. Table 12.4 indicates the distributions obtained from the standardization samples.

FACTOR STRUCTURE

Factor analysis of the OODQ carried out by Oliver and Fredenberger (1987) using data from 1,256 individuals in 113 different samples, produced strong support for the typology of role motivation theory. A three-factor solution proved optimal. The rotated factor matrix showed all 15 items of the task scale having a highest positive loading on one factor, all items of the group scale with a highest positive loading on another factor, and all items of the professional scale with a highest positive loading on the third factor. The items of the hierarchic scale were distinguished by the fact that they loaded negatively or zero on all three of these factors.

These results are consistent with the view that the professional, task, and group organizational forms are alternatives to hierarchy (Herbst 1976). They also fit well with the substitutes for leadership formulations (see Chapter 11 of Miner 2005). The factor analytic results indicate that hierarchy is in many respects antithetical to professional, task, and group forms. Information on the OODQ may be obtained from the publisher—Organizational Measurement Systems Press (P.O. Box 70586, Eugene, OR 97401).

CHAPTER 13

STUDENTS AT THE U. S. MILITARY ACADEMY (WEST POINT) AND AT THE BRANCH IMMATERIAL OFFICER CANDIDATE COURSE (FT. BENNING, GA)

INTRODUCTION

The military research consisting of two studies was published in the *Journal of Applied Psychology* (Butler, Lardent, and Miner 1983). Again, as in Chapter 6, research from separate sources was brought together to create synergy and thus added value. Richard Butler conducted Study 1 in connection with his institutional research activities at West Point. Charles Lardent carried out Study 2 at Ft. Benning as his PhD dissertation from the Department of Management at Georgia State University.

The latter study introduces several multiple-choice versions of the MSCS–Form H and accordingly picks up on the treatment in Chapter 8 of the research done with General Motors. My own reaction to moving to such a multiple-choice format has been ambivalent over the years. Doing so clearly dilutes the projective, and thus the unconscious, content of the MSCS, while at the same time making the scoring process much easier. I wish there were some way to "have our cake and eat it too" here, but I have not found one.

* * *

Recent reviews of turnover research and attempts to formulate models for the turnover process typically have given primary attention to satisfaction levels, attitudinal commitment, and similar variables. The idea that turnover may result from a lack of certain specific, strong motives

---

From Richard P. Butler, Charles L. Lardent, and John B. Miner, "A Motivational Basis for Turnover in Military Officer Education and Training," *Journal of Applied Psychology,* vol. 68, no. 3, 496–506.

or personality characteristics required for effective functioning in a particular organizational context, and thus from a lack of fit between individual motives and organizational structures, has received very little attention in this literature (Mobley, Griffeth, Hand, and Meglino 1979; Steers and Mowday 1981). A review by Muchinsky and Tuttle (1979) considered research using general, multivariable personality and interest measures and concluded that "personality differences have a very marginal impact on turnover" (48), whereas "there appears to be some negative relationship between vocational interest and turnover" (49). With only two exceptions, the studies noted by Muchinsky and Tuttle (1979) were conducted more than ten years before. Overall, the view that turnover may be due to certain motivational propensities of the individual (in interaction with aspects of organizational structure and process) appears to have received little empirical or theoretical attention, at least in recent years. The research presented here represents a return to this type of investigation, using a limited set of motivational constructs.

We propose that people are less likely to quit their jobs when their motives are consistent with the demands of their organizations. Among managers and those preparing to become managers in bureaucratic, hierarchical organizational structures, the people most likely to separate are the ones with low levels of managerial motivation; in professional systems, those with low professional motivation are most likely to separate; in group or sociotechnical systems, turnover is most likely among people with low group-oriented motives; in task (or entrepreneurial) systems, turnover is most likely among individuals who lack the needed task motives (Miner 1980b). We do not expect that these inconsistencies or incongruencies operate alone to determine turnover or that they necessarily override other factors. Turnover can occur for a variety of reasons (Steers and Mowday 1981). However, motivational-organizational fit is a factor that should be included in a comprehensive theory of the turnover process.

The particular hypothesis tested here is that within typically hierarchical military training institutions, turnover (attrition) among those preparing to become officers (managers) will be more frequent when the individual lacks motives that have been found to be congruent with hierarchical systems. More specifically, those who separate during training will be characterized by a lower initial level of overall motivation to manage and thus by more unfavorable attitudes toward authority, less competitiveness, more limited assertiveness, relatively little need for power, less desire to stand out from the group, and a more pronounced wish to avoid performing routine administrative functions.

MILITARY TRAINING INSTITUTIONS AS HIERARCHICAL

Research in developing the Oliver Organization Description Questionnaire (Oliver 1981, 1982) supports the view that a military training organization is hierarchical. (The questionnaire is a multiple-choice instrument measuring four comprehensive dimensions of organizational structure and process: hierarchical, professional, task, and group.)

Results derived from a group of infantry trainees indicate a predominantly hierarchical system. In a second sample of military personnel who were instructors at a military college, the pattern was similar, although both the hierarchical and professional scores were elevated to essentially the same degree. These findings may be contrasted with those for college professors in general, among whom the professional score tends to be the highest, with the hierarchical score elevated, but not nearly as much.

The task score predominates among college students. What differentiates students in military training institutions from other students is that they are in fact members of the military organization, just as participants in in-house management development programs are members of a corporate system. That military organizations as a whole are primarily hierarchical and represent typical bureaucracies has long been recognized (see, e.g., Weber 1968).

STUDY 1: THE MILITARY ACADEMY STUDY

Method

The sample consisted of 502 cadets, randomly selected, who entered the U.S. Military Academy at West Point, New York, in 1972. These 502 represent 36 percent of the entering class. Four years later, 313 graduated and became commissioned officers, whereas 189 left the Academy during the intervening years and did not graduate. This 38 percent turnover rate in the sample is almost identical to that for the class as a whole.

The major criterion for this study was the gross graduation-separation dichotomy. However, a second index of turnover was also used in an attempt to get at a more motivationally relevant component. This index contrasted the 313 individuals who graduated and the 136 who voluntarily resigned from the Academy. The 53 individuals who were forced to leave because of inability to meet requirements were not part of this analysis. Although not forced to withdraw, an unknown number of those who left voluntarily or who were motivated to leave might well have eventually been placed in the "forced out" category had they not chosen to resign. Thus the degree to which the voluntary resignation group was truly distinguishable from the total turnover group remains uncertain.

The MSCS–Form H was administered to all members of the sample at the time of admission to the Academy. All 502 scales were scored in accordance with the scoring guide (Miner 1964) by a single scorer at the United States Military Academy who had no knowledge of any criterion outcomes. Subsequently, a random sample of twenty records was rescored independently by Miner. From the results of this scorer-reliability analysis it appears that the primary scorer has introduced a sizable positive shift in scores in comparison with the more experienced reliability scorer. The differential is clearly evident in the total scores and in the Assertive Role and Imposing Wishes subscale scores, but there is a trend in the same direction on all subscales. The total score values are 5.6 vs. 3.0 ($t = 5.76$, $p < .01$). Evidence suggests that if a constant shift in scoring is present, it is particularly likely to be in a positive direction (Miner, 1978d; Miner and Smith 1982).

Because the scorer disagreements are consistent rather than random in direction, they do not appear to have had a major impact on the correlations. The correlation of .94 for the total scores is essentially the same as has been obtained in previous analyses involving experienced scorers (Miner 1978d). The subscale correlations are somewhat below a desirable level, but not substantially so. However, the percentage of agreement index, which reflects the constant differential as well as random error, is consistently below 90 and is particularly low on those measures with the greatest mean score differential.

These results indicate an undesirable degree of error in the predictor instrument. However, much of the error is systematic (i.e., represents a constant directional shift) and should have little impact on the relative graduate versus nongraduate comparisons; its major impact would be on the absolute level of scores in both groups. Accordingly, the scorer reliabilities were considered minimally acceptable. Although the sample on which this conclusion is based is not large (N = 20), it is representative of the larger group, is sufficient to identify significant mean differences, and yields scorer-reliability coefficients of essentially the same magnitude

Table 13.1

MSCS (Form H) **Free-Response Scores for Military Academy Graduates, Nongraduates, and Nongraduates Who Resigned Voluntarily**

	Graduates[a]	Nongraduates[b]	Voluntary resignations[c]	Graduates vs. Nongraduates	Graduates vs. Resigned
MSCS Measures (Form H)	*M*	*M*	*M*	*t*	*t*
Total Score	6.0	4.8	4.7	1.93* (.12)	2.20* (.13)
Authority Figures	1.7	1.6	1.7	.92	.06
Competitive Games	1.3	1.2	1.2	.42	.56
Competitive Situations	–.5	–.3	–.4	—	—
Assertive Role	.9	.6	.5	1.48	1.68* (.13)
Imposing Wishes	.9	.7	.6	1.36	1.90* (.13)
Standing Out from Group	1.0	.8	.9	1.06	.62
Routine Administrative Functions	.7	.2	.2	3.29** (.20)	2.78** (.19)

Note: The figures in parentheses are biserial correlations calculated with the higher values assigned to graduates. MSCS = Miner Sentence Completion Scale.

[a]N = 313. [b]N = 189. [c]N = 136.

$*p < .05$, one-tailed; $**p < .01$

as obtained in previous studies. Any random error would, of course, reduce the probability of obtaining significant findings and thus introduce a conservative bias.

Results

Table 13.1 contains the results of the first study. In general, the findings obtained using only voluntary resignations as a criterion follow the total turnover results, although they yield a larger number of significant values. Overall, there is a clear tendency for those who leave prior to graduation to score lower on the MSCS, but the magnitude of the difference is small, and the practical usefulness of this finding is limited. On the other hand, both the scorer-reliability problems in the predictor and the apparent heterogeneity encompassed by the criterion militate against obtaining sizable differences, as does the long time span of prediction. The findings support the hypotheses dealing with overall motivation to manage, assertiveness, power motivation, and the desire to perform routine administrative functions; the other four hypotheses are not supported.

STUDY 2: THE OFFICER CANDIDATE SCHOOL STUDY

Method

A second major source of military officers is the Branch Immaterial Officer Candidate Course at Fort Benning, Georgia. This training lasts approximately fifteen weeks and successful completion results in appointment as a commissioned officer. Two classes from this school provided the sample for the study.

The first class began training in October 1975, and predictor data were obtained three days after the program started. Of the 135 individuals scheduled to attend this class, 110 provided usable data. The remaining 25 either did not report for training, separated very early, were not available for testing, or provided unusable data. Of the 110, 91 graduated and 19 left prior to graduation.

The next class, which began in January 1976, provided the remainder of the sample. In this instance, data collection was delayed until thirteen days after training began. There were 205 candidates originally scheduled, but only 185 were officially enrolled. Of these, 141 provided usable data, with 131 graduating and 10 separating prior to graduation. The lower turnover rate in this group is attributable to the delay in testing; a number left before they could be included in the sample. Nevertheless, multiple discriminant function analyses indicated that the two classes were homogeneous in MSCS scores, and they were accordingly combined to produce a total graduate group of 222 and a turnover group of 29. Given the relatively small size of the turnover group, no further differentiation within was attempted. The inability to include certain early leavers in the study would be expected to produce more conservative tests of the study's hypotheses.

In this study, the problem of scorer disagreement did not exist. The primary instrument used was the multiple-choice version of the MSCS–Form H. This form presents the same 35 stems as the free-response version, but six multiple-choice alternatives—two positive, two neutral, and two negative—are provided in randomized order (Miner 1977b; 1978d). The provision of actual alternative completions appears to reduce the projective element; accordingly, positive-score escalation tends to occur. The amount of this escalation varies in different groups. The use of multiple-choice measurement introduces a much greater opportunity to present oneself favorably, in a more socially desirable manner, than does the free-response approach (Steger, Kelley, Chouiniere, and Goldenbaum 1975). Respondents can be much more consciously aware of negative portrayals and avoid them, since they can contrast alternatives.

Given this situation, the multiple-choice MSCS may measure a somewhat different construct, or group of constructs, than the free-response version. The degree to which this occurs should be reflected in the size of the correlations between theoretically comparable measures from the two instruments. Such information is not available for military samples, but it is available for a diversified group of managers, primarily at the first level, working for a hierarchical (see Oliver 1981) automobile company, General Motors, having much in common with the military (see Chapter 8). Of the 64 managers, 28 percent were minorities, and 42 percent were female; 56 percent were in production, and the remainder were in various office positions. To avoid possible distortion occasioned by prior knowledge of alternatives, the free-response measure was administered first, followed at a roughly three-month interval by the multiple-choice scale.

As indicated in the first two columns of figures in Table 13.2 many of the free-response versus multiple-choice correlation coefficients are at much the same level as the reported repeat reliabilities for the free-response instrument itself. The intervals between measurements in the reliability research and the automobile company study are essentially the same. However, the correlations for the Imposing Wishes and Routine Administrative Functions subscales are depressed, and this appears to have exerted some influence on the total score value as well. On this evidence, the multiple-choice versions of these two

Table 13.2

Correlations between Theoretically Comparable MSCS–Form H (Original Free-Response Version) **and Various Multiple-Choice MSCS Measures in a Sample of Automobile Company Managers** (N = 64)

		MSCS—Form H (Free response) vs.		
MSCS Measures	Repeat Reliability of Free-response Form H[a]	Form H Multiple Choice	Situation-specific Multiple Choice	Combined Multiple Choice
Total Score	.83**	.68**	.38**	.65**
Authority Figures	.55**	.48**	.31**	.50**
Competitive Games	.63**	.63**	.36**	.63**
Competitive Situations	.48**	.48**	–.05	.27*
Assertive Role	.59**	.54**	.25*	.49**
Imposing Wishes	.46**	–.02	–.10	–.11
Standing Out from Group	.44**	.29**	.07	.22*
Routine Administrative Functions	.45**	.07	.12	.13

Note. MSCS = Miner Sentence Completion Scale.
[a]See Miner (1965a).
$*p < .05$, one-tailed; $**p < .01$

subscales cannot be assumed to measure the same constructs as the free-response versions. On the other six indexes, the two instruments appear to be tapping essentially the same constructs, and comparability between the military academy and officer candidate school studies can be assumed.

In addition, a situation-specific, or face valid, sentence-completion measure (also multiple choice) developed originally for use in a manufacturing context (the automobile company) was used with the officer candidates. The thirty-five scorable items in this experimental instrument are intended to measure the same theoretical variables in the same basic manner but are completely nonoverlapping (Miner 1977b). The stems, although consistently and rather obviously relating to a specific work environment—that of manufacturing plants—do not focus on the particular specific situation that is relevant for military officers. Thus the measure is considered situation specific, but not directly for the situation of these subjects. Its relevance for this research derives entirely from the fact that it is intended to tap the same constructs as the other measures.

Certain evidence on the degree to which this objective was successfully achieved is given in Table 13.2. From the third column of correlations it is apparent that this situation-specific scale does not match the standard free-response Form H nearly as well as the multiple-choice Form H does. Yet half of the correlations are statistically significant, including the total score value. Note that Imposing Wishes and Routine Administrative Functions continue to show no relationships.

It is also possible to evaluate the experimental situation-specific measure by relating it to the multiple-choice Form H, thus correlating two multiple-choice scales administered at the same point in time. This analysis can be carried out using the officer candidate data. Table13.3 presents the results, which are contained in the first column of figures. The findings are much the same as those obtained using the free-response Form H. A similar analysis was

Table 13.3

Correlations between Theoretically Comparable MSCS Measures in Total Officer Candidate School Sample (N = 251)

MSCS Measures	Form H vs. Situation-specific	Form H vs. Combined	Situation-specific vs. Combined
Total Score	.47**	.87**	.84**
Authority Figures	.19**	.76**	.78**
Competitive Games	.24**	.80**	.77**
Competitive Situations	.30**	.83**	.77**
Assertive Role	.09	.75**	.73**
Imposing Wishes	–.01	.73**	.68**
Standing Out from Group	.13*	.68**	.77**
Routine Administrative Functions	.11	.78**	.71**

Note: MSCS = Miner Sentence Completion Scale.
*$p < .05$, one-tailed; **$p < .01$

Table 13.4

Correlations between Theoretically Comparable Multiple-Choice MSCS Measures in a Sample of Automobile Company Managers (N = 64)

MSCS Measures	Form H vs. Situation-specific	Form H vs. Combined	Situation-specific vs. Combined
Total Score	.46**	.90**	.80**
Authority Figures	.34**	.87**	.76**
Competitive Games	.30**	.85**	.75**
Competitive Situations	.25*	.80**	.78**
Assertive Role	.35**	.84**	.80**
Imposing Wishes	–.35	.54**	.60**
Standing Out from Group	.31**	.80**	.82**
Routine Administrative Functions	.06	.76**	.69**

Note: MSCS = Miner Sentence Completion Scale.
*$p < .05$, one-tailed; **$p < .01$

applied to the data for the automobile company managers and is reported in the first column of Table 13.4.

The pattern of findings remains essentially the same.

Whether these correlational data justify combining the two multiple-choice scales—Form H and the situation-specific—into a single composite measure is something of a judgment call; the answer is almost certainly *yes* for the total score and for some of the subscales, and definitely *no* for Imposing Wishes and Routine Administrative Functions. Our decision has been to present findings obtained using this combined index for all measures, with full understanding of its construct limitations, for those who might find them useful. The gain is in obtaining a longer, and presumably more reliable, measure of theoretically comparable variables in addition to the Form H and situation-specific measures. How this combined measure relates to the other MSCS measures is indicated in the right-hand columns of Tables 13.3 and 13.4. With the exception of our two consistently errant subscales, the correlation magnitudes support the decision to combine.

Results

The Officer Candidate School research overcomes certain of the difficulties inherent in the Academy study. The multiple-choice measurement eliminates problems of scorer reliability, although it may make for a greater degree of conscious intervention in the responses, and the time span of prediction is much less. However, the variety of causes inherent in the turnover criterion remains high, and the delay in testing the second class introduced some criterion restriction of range. In any event, the data of Table 13.5 support the hypotheses with regard to overall motivation to manage, competitiveness, assertiveness, and standing out from the group. The support involving attitudes toward authority figures is minimal at best ($p < .10$). There is no support for the hypotheses regarding power motivation and performing routine administrative functions, but the evidence considered previously suggests that these hypotheses were not actually tested in the Officer Candidate School study.

DISCUSSION

Motivational Patterns

Both studies support the view that relevant motivational variables make a difference in turnover, and they are consistent with the motivational-organizational system fit hypothesis. The total score results are significant in all instances—a total of five comparisons using four measures. The subscale findings are much less consistent, as might be expected given their lower reliabilities and the difficulties with the Imposing Wishes and Routine Administrative Functions measures in the multiple-choice format. Competitive Games yields the predicted results in two of five comparisons, Competitive Situations in three, Assertive Role in three, and Standing Out from Group in two. Excluding the multiple-choice measures, Imposing Wishes performs as predicted in one of two comparisons, and Routine Administrative Functions in both. In view of the variations in time, measures of theoretical constructs, and turnover rates, the overall consistency of the findings indicates a considerable degree of external and construct validity.

The total score results reflect a degree of relationship in the Officer Candidate School context comparable to that found in other validation research with the MSCS and at least equal to that typically found in the university context when first-year grades are predicted with mental ability tests (Powers and Hardy 1980). The degree of relationship found at the U.S. Military Academy is not as great. The much longer time span of prediction is without question a factor, and probably the scorer-reliability difficulties contribute as well. The important point, however, is that even so, a number of significant findings were obtained, and always when the total score was used. It is this fact that permits a conclusion of substantial external validity.

At the Academy, those who leave are characterized by less assertiveness, less power motivation, and in particular, less desire to perform routine managerial duties. The latter finding suggests that those who stay exhibit a type of mild compulsiveness that is lacking in those who leave. A similar finding emerged from a previous study of the leadership role in a simulated corporation organized along bureaucratic lines and used for training purposes at a business school (Miner, Rizzo, Harlow, and Hill 1974). To the extent that the Academy context simulates the hierarchical system of the Army as a whole, there would seem to be a parallel between the two studies. Simulated bureaucratic systems may have a special need for

Table 13.5

MSCS (Form H), **Situation-Specific** (Manufacturing), **and Combined Multiple-Choice Scores for Officer Candidate School Graduates** (N = 222) **and Nongraduates** (N = 29)

	Form H			Situation-specific			Combined		
	Graduates	Non-graduates		Graduates	Non-graduates		Graduates	Non-graduates	
MSCS Measures	*M*	*M*	*t*	*M*	*M*	*t*	*M*	*M*	*t*
Total Score	8.7	5.6	3.22** (.33)	8.5	6.1	2.32* (.26)	17.3	11.7	3.41** (.36)
Authority Figures	0.8	0.5	1.34	2.1	1.8	.94	3.0	2.3	1.52
Competitive Games	1.9	0.6	3.85** (.44)	.4	0.5	—	2.2	1.1	2.21* (.25)
Competitive Situations	1.4	0.8	1.67* (.20)	1.2	0.5	1.97* (.24)	2.6	1.3	2.32* (.26)
Assertive Role	1.2	0.6	2.11* (.25)	1.5	1.1	1.20	2.7	1.7	1.96* (.23)
Imposing Wishes	0.4	0.1	1.02	–.1	0.0	—	0.4	0.1	.62
Standing Out from Group	1.8	1.7	.45	1.8	1.0	2.55** (.32)	3.6	2.8	2.01* (.24)
Routine Administrative Functions	1.2	1.2	.00	1.6	1.2	1.65	2.8	2.5	.69

Note: The figures in parentheses are biserial correlations calculated with the higher values assigned to graduates. MSCS = Miner Sentence Completion Scale.

$*p < .05$, one-tailed; $**p < .01$

very conscientious, rather compulsive individuals who will maintain commitment and keep the simulation operating in spite of its relatively low "reality component."

The subscale findings in the Officer Candidate School study differ somewhat from those at the Academy, although this may be in part due to the lower construct validities of the multiple-choice versions of the Imposing Wishes and Routine Administrative Functions subscales. What is most pronounced, however, is the strong competitiveness of those who graduate as opposed to those who do not. Such a finding is not entirely unexpected because Officer Candidate School applicants are predominantly noncommissioned officers striving for promotion to the commissioned ranks. Apparently, those who are less competitively driven are also less likely to make it through the grueling training process. Taken as a whole, these subscale results suggest that the dynamics of the two types of military training institutions may differ while still producing, in both instances, a type of output selectively calculated to foster managerial efficiency in a hierarchical system.

Performance

The Steers and Mowday (1981) review concluded with a suggestion that greater emphasis in research be placed on the role of performance factors in the turnover process. Analyses to this end were carried out in both of the military training organizations, although, in certain respects, an unambiguous interpretation of the results is difficult. At the Academy, performance was measured using a single composite index called the Aptitude for the Service Rating. This leadership rating represents a weighted average of ratings derived from various sources: sociometric ratings by peers in the same class and company, sociometric ratings by members of the next most advanced class in the same company, a rating by the company tactical officer, and trait ratings by the cadet chain of command. Somewhat greater weight is given to the tactical officer component. These ratings were calculated at the end of each year at the Academy, so that for those who graduated, four ratings were available. Such ratings have been found to be valid predictors of subsequent officer performance as indicated by order of merit lists, promotion rates, and retention in the service. Reliability estimates are quite satisfactory, in the .90s (Priest 1975).

When we correlated the MSCS scores with the four sets of ratings (one for each year of residence), only one significant finding emerged: a correlation of .10 ($p < .05$) for Authority Figures in the first-year ratings. Overall, the correlations appear to be randomly distributed around a mean of .00. This is a rather surprising finding given the substantial amount of evidence for the validity of the MSCS using similar ratings in other settings (Miner, 1965a, 1977b). However, a likely explanation is inherent in the turnover data. The overall turnover rate for the four years is 38 percent, a sizable figure. Of this, 60 percent occurs before the first-year performance ratings are made, 85 percent before the second-year ratings, and almost 100 percent before the third-year ratings. If those who leave in a situation such as this are the poorer performers (which they are), turnover is substantial (which it is), and the predictor is related to turnover (which the MSCS is), then the turnover results can absorb the predictable criterion variance. This appears to be the case at the Academy, although alternative interpretations are possible.

At the Officer Candidate School, performance data were also obtained, but it is important to recognize that the overall turnover rate for the Officer Candidate School sample studied is only 12 percent. Thus we conducted the performance criteria analyses using a much larger proportion of the total research sample than at the Academy. (It is also true that substantial turnover occurred prior to the time this sample was established.) A variety of performance criteria were used, including peer ratings, tactical officer ratings, grades attained overall and in leadership subjects, and various evaluations of physical performance, including drill and physical training. To the extent these reflect intellectual and physical performances, there is little reason to expect the MSCS scores to be related; the ratings appear most relevant and they most closely approximate the Academy criterion. However, in this instance little is known regarding the psychometric properties of the measures, other than that they suffer from the score inflation and consequent restriction of range that historically have plagued many military performance evaluation procedures (Miner 1968c).

Once again, there is little evidence of a relationship between the MSCS measures and performance. Using the various ratings, the median correlation is .03; with a range from –.18 to .11; on the other, less motivational, criteria the median value is .00, with a range from –.19 to .12. To what extent these results may be due to absorption of criterion variance in turnover, as opposed to inadequacies in the criteria, is not known. In all probability both factors are involved. In any event, the sizable success achieved in predicting turnover is not repeated in the performance analyses.

A final point relates to the overall level of MSCS scores in the military samples. The Academy scores are extremely high for a college population of the early and mid-1970s (Miner and Smith 1982). In part this appears to be a consequence of a positive shift produced by the scorer, but even when reduced by the amount of the constant error, the scores are essentially at a level last obtained on most campuses in the early 1960s. The Officer Candidate School scores appear to be at a roughly comparable level, although perhaps somewhat higher. Data for comparison purposes are limited, but the students at Officer Candidate School score above the level obtained in a sample of predominantly first-line manufacturing company managers (Miner 1977b and Chapter 8).

Implications for Turnover Research

Two conclusions appear to stand out from the findings obtained. The first is that relevant motives and motivational fit deserve attention in turnover research. This is true at least in the military education and training context where the relevant motives define the motivation to manage. Generalization to other environments and motivational measures seems worth investigating. Insofar as overall motivation to manage is concerned, this finding seems quite robust, extending across variations in time, measurement procedures, turnover rates, and military training contexts. Second, the findings presented are consistent with a view that the prediction of performance and the prediction of turnover are intimately related, to the point where studying one without studying the other can well produce sizable errors of interpretation. At the very least it appears that this area needs intensive longitudinal study. A major change in current approaches to the design of validation research may very well be required.

CHAPTER 14

TOP EXECUTIVES FROM VARIED COMPANIES

INTRODUCTION

This article focuses on leadership, and thus top management, and hierarchic systems; it was published in *Personnel Psychology* (Berman and Miner 1985). It attempts to get at how managerial motivation operates among these types of leaders, and to establish the causal processes that are involved. Fred Berman conducted the research for his PhD dissertation at Georgia State University. Throughout this period he was actively involved in recruiting managers for company positions in the Atlanta area.

* * *

Observers of the top levels in large, bureaucratized corporations have emphasized the significant role personal characteristics play in determining aspects of organizational performance. The essentially qualitative studies of Glickman, Hahn, Fleishman, and Baxter (1968); Holden, Pederson, and Germane (1968); and more recently Steiner (1983) and Miles (1982), among others, attest to the influence that a single individual may exert. Weber (1968) appears to be subscribing to this same view when he discusses the use of bureaucratic mechanisms as tools by charismatic leaders and "the law of the small number." The increasing concern with corporate level decisions and strategy also reflects an appreciation of the role of individual differences at the top (Schendel and Hofer 1979; Steiner, Miner, and Gray 1986) although rejections of the individual level of explanation are still to be found in the literature (Aldrich 1979; Pfeffer and Salancik 1978).

Overall, one might anticipate the conduct of a sizable body of research dealing with personality and motivational patterns among top level executives. Yet in spite of a long history (Gardner 1948; Henry 1949), this type of research has been carried out only infrequently. Experience suggests that the problem is not so much a lack of researcher interest as it is a reluctance on the part of top executives to expose themselves to psychological inquiry.

In any event, relatively little is known about the personality characteristics of those who head large corporations, although there have been some studies. These studies have utilized

From Frederic. E. Berman and John. B. Miner, "Motivation to Manage at the Top Executive Level: A Test of the Hierarchic Role-motivation Theory," *Personnel Psychology,* 38 (1985), 377–391.

various projective measures such as the Rorschach (Piotrowski and Rock 1963), the Thematic Apperception Test (TAT) (Gardner 1948; Henry 1949), and the Tomkins-Horn Picture Arrangement Test (PAT) (Miner 1962b; Miner and Culver 1955). In other instances, self-report personality inventories have been employed (Grimsley and Jarrett 1973, 1975; Guilford 1952; Meyer and Pressel 1954; Wald and Doty 1954). The research typically has included functional vice presidents and even assistant vice presidents as well as those at higher levels.

One consistent pattern running through the cited studies involves a pervasive fear of negative outcomes—failure, illness, and the like. The executives appear to be striving for success to avoid these outcomes—or to convince themselves that their fears are not likely to be realized. A second consistent pattern reflects strivings for power and domination coupled with favorable attitudes toward father figures, a tendency to assert oneself, and a liking for administrative work. This latter set of findings, although derived from other sources, overlaps to a sizable extent the variables measured by the Miner Sentence Completion Scale–Form H (MSCS), and suggests that that instrument should prove fruitful in studying top executives. The same conclusion derives from statements of the role-motivation theory that provides the underlying rationale for the MSCS:

> The role requirements . . . are assumed to be among those which occur with high frequency in business firms organized in accordance with the scalar principle. . . . [They] would seem to have little relevance in those instances where promotion and evaluation within a hierarchy are not based primarily on considerations of administrative or managerial competence. When family membership, religious affiliation, sales ability, and the like are the crucial bases for reward . . . the theory is not pertinent (Miner 1965a, 42). . . .
>
> Those with high MSCS scores . . . would be expected to move more rapidly than others into higher level positions. The presence of a sizable concentration of this type of motivation at the upper levels of American industry should be entirely functional for the companies involved (Miner 1965a, 53).

In line with these statements of the hierarchic role-motivation theory, the hypothesis of this study is that those who reach the highest levels of large, bureaucratized business firms will have higher levels of motivation to manage, as measured by the MSCS, than individuals who have achieved less in these firms. It is anticipated that the scores of these top executives should average well above other groups. A subsidiary hypothesis is that the scores of top executives who have either founded their company or are related by blood or marriage to the founder should be below those of the other top executives.

Although prior research with the MSCS has on occasion incorporated individuals at the top management level—primarily vice presidents—the numbers have been small. In only one instance could a separate sample of such individuals be isolated, and that was in a study of personnel managers (Miner 1976a; Miner and Miner 1976). In this one instance the 22 vice presidents scored well above the remaining 79 personnel managers, most of whom were at a middle management level. Overall it has proved very difficult to obtain adequate samples of top level executives; others have also noted the difficulty of doing research in this area (see, for example, Cascio 1982).

METHOD

Samples and Procedures

Initially the MSCS was mailed to 300 large-company chief executive officers, along with a brief background questionnaire and a letter requesting their personal participation in the

Table 14.1

Characteristics of Top Executives and Comparison Samples

	Top Executives							
	Theory Congruent (N = 49)		Theory Incongruent (N = 26)		Total (N = 75)		Comparison Sample (N = 65)	
	M	*SD*	*M*	*SD*	*M*	*SD*	*M*	*SD*
Age	47.7	7.5	49.2	8.5	48.2	7.8	44.7	8.5
Years with Company	15.0	11.0	18.9	11.7	16.4	11.3	11.6	9.9
Years in Position	4.5	3.5	13.0	9.1	7.5	7.3	4.6	5.4
Education Level								
High School	2%		8%		4%		18%	
College	37%		73%		49%		54%	
Graduate Work	61%		19%		47%		28%	
Functional Specialization								
Marketing	57%		62%		59%		17%	
Finance	18%		12%		16%		9%	
Engineering	14%		8%		12%		9%	
Manufacturing	6%		4%		5%		14%	
Personnel	2%		8%		4%		23%	
Research	2%		4%		3%		3%	
Accounting	0%		4%		1%		17%	
None Given	—		—		—		8%	

research. Of the 300 individuals, 200 were identified from a list of the top public companies headquartered in the Southeast published by *South Magazine.* The remaining 100 were drawn from the client and prospect files of an Atlanta-based management consulting firm.

After various follow-ups by the first author, some by telephone and some in person, 83 completed responses were obtained. In 27 of these cases the respondents were not those to whom the materials had originally been sent. After deleting eight such respondents who were not at the top executive level, 75 individuals remained. Of these, 59 were chief executive and/or chief operating officers, and 16 were either executive vice presidents or group vice presidents. None were below that level. The 75 represented 68 companies, and thus, in a limited number of cases more than one top executive was included from the same firm. The number of employees working for these companies ranged from 110 to 40,000 with a mean of 4,824; their total revenues in the year of testing ranged from \$2.4 million to over \$6 billion. When the industry distribution for the responding firms was compared with that for the non-respondents, the distributions did not differ significantly ($\chi^2 = 9.92$, $df = 7$).

Information on characteristics of these top executives is given in the third column of Table 14.1. All were males.

To obtain a comparison sample, the senior personnel managers of the companies were contacted by telephone. Each personnel manager was asked to obtain a completed MSCS from an individual within the company who actually managed people, who was within plus or minus three years of the specified age of a previously tested top executive in the company, and who met one of four criteria, utilized in rotating order: was a lower level manager of average performance, was a lower level manager exhibiting good performance, was a middle level manager of average performance, or was a middle level manager exhibiting good performance.

The objective in using these criteria was to prevent obtaining a sample containing primarily high performers who were just below the top level. Available information on the top executives and their companies indicated that both good and average performers were included—really poor performers are unlikely to survive long at this level. After several follow-ups, 65 managers from 59 companies completed the MSCS. The characteristics of this comparison sample are given in the fourth column of Table 14.1. Four were females, and the average hierarchic level was roughly halfway up the scalar chain, i.e., middle management. Overall, there were 47 companies that provided at least one top executive and one member of the lower level comparison sample.

Toward the end of the telephone conversation with the senior personnel manager, information was solicited as to whether each top executive who had previously completed the MSCS was the founder of the company (the original entrepreneur) or was related by blood or by marriage to the founder. On the basis of answers to this question, 49 of the original 75 top executives were classified as congruent with the domain of the hierarchic role-motivation theory and 26 were not. Within the 26, 18 proved to be entrepreneurs who had headed their companies from the beginning, and 8 were relatives whose family memberships appeared to have exerted some influence on their assignments and current position level. The characteristics of these theoretically congruent and incongruent samples are given in columns 1 and 2 of Table 14.1. Although the theory-congruent group is better educated, this factor is unrelated to MSCS scores. Based on prior research, it was anticipated that the entrepreneurs would score well below the top corporate executives who had risen through the hierarchic ranks, presumably on the basis of merit (Smith and Miner 1983).

Measurement: The MSCS–Form H

The MSCS was used to measure motives related to six managerial role prescriptions (Miner 1978c, 741–742). All protocols were scored independently by the two authors, and where disagreements occurred, they were discussed with reference to the rationales and examples of the Scoring Guide (Miner 1964) until agreement was reached. The correlations between the two scorers, before any attempts at reconciliation occurred, were for the Total Score .94, Authority Figures .83, Competitive Games .93, Competitive Situations .87, Assertive Role .90, Imposing Wishes .82, Standing Out from Group .91, and Routine Administrative Functions .90.

These values are essentially the same as those previously obtained with experienced scorers (Miner 1978d; 1985b). The difference in mean Total Score between the two scorers before reconciliation was .35, a value which lacks both statistical and practical significance. Although it was not possible to achieve completely blind scoring—as between the top executives overall and the comparison managers—because of the content of the responses, whether the record came from theory-congruent or theory-incongruent top executives was not known when the records were scored. Furthermore, research comparing the result obtained when MSCS protocols are scored under blind and not-blind conditions has failed to yield evidence of a difference (Miner, Smith, and Ebrahimi 1985).

RESULTS

The results of a global analysis comparing MSCS scores for the total top executive and comparison samples given in Table 14.2 strongly support the basic hypothesis for the Total

Score and most, but not all, of the subscales. The Total Score provides the basic test of the theoretical hypothesis.

There are several potential sources of error in these global findings. The theory is limited to the domain of established bureaucracy (Weber 1968). It does not apply to entrepreneurial or familial organizational contexts, and thus a full test of the hypothesis should establish whether these theory-incongruent top executives are distinct from the bureaucratic managers and, if they are, remove them from the analysis.

A second problem relates to the age distributions in the two samples. In spite of considerable care in obtaining the comparison sample there is a difference in mean age between the total top executive and comparison samples of 3.5 years which, although relatively small, is statistically significant. An unknown number of lower level managers who will make it to the top by the time they reach the age of the present top executives may have been included in the comparison sample. Thus, a better age match is needed to provide an appropriate test of the hypothesis.

A comparison of the 49 bureaucratic managers with the 26 entrepreneurs and family managers, as noted in Table 14.2, produces significant results in spite of the reduced sample sizes. As anticipated, the theory-incongruent top executives do have less motivation to manage. When these individuals are excluded, the MSCS Total Score rises, and so do most of the subscales. In order to eliminate the age differential in the comparison sample, only the oldest 49 managers were retained in the analysis; the youngest 16 were deleted. The result was a revised comparison sample with a mean age of 48.3—almost identical to the 47.7 value in the revised top executive sample (t = .43, N.S.).

When the two previously noted sources of error are eliminated, the MSCS discriminates more sharply. However, the overall pattern of results is the same. The top executives are characterized overall by a stronger motivation to manage. They are also more positively disposed to authority figures, more competitive in an occupational sense, more desirous of power, more inclined to stand out from the group and attract attention, and more motivated to perform routine administrative functions. There is a continuing lack of evidence, however, that top managers in corporate bureaucracies are distinguished by greater competitiveness in the more occupationally distant sphere of sports and games or by a greater degree of assertiveness.

An additional point relates to the fact that the top executive samples, in relation to the comparison sample, have a higher percentage of individuals with a marketing functional specialization. Based on prior findings (Miner 1965a), this could in and of itself produce higher MSCS scores among the top executives. In the sample of 75 the Total Score for top executives who indicate a marketing specialization is 5.91, and for those indicating other specializations it is 5.29—not a significant difference. Within the theory-congruent sample of 49, those who have a marketing reference group have a mean Total Score of 6.61, and those who do not have a mean value of 6.95—a slight reversal. These data do not support the proposition that a difference in representation of those with a marketing functional specialization might account for the MSCS score differences between top executives and the comparison sample.

A second point at which sample differences might account for the results occurs in relation to the personnel functional specialization. The personnel area appears to be overrepresented, possibly because of the way the sample was chosen in the comparison sample, and this might account for the lower scores (Miner 1976a). Within the comparison sample of 65, those with a personnel referent have a mean Total Score of –.07 and those without 1.92—not a statistically significant difference. In the age-matched comparison sample, these values are .45 and 1.37 respectively—again not approaching statistical significance. When all personnel managers

Table 14.2

Mean MSCS–Form H Scores for Samples and Comparisons between Appropriate Samples

	Sample 1	Sample 1a	Sample 1b	Sample 2	Sample 2a	*t* values		
MSCS Measures	All Top Executives (N = 75)	Theory Congruent Top Executives (N = 49)	Theory Incongruent Top Executives (N = 26)	All Comparison Managers (N = 65)	Age-Matched Comparison Managers (N = 49)	Samples 1 vs. 2	Samples 1a vs. 1b	Samples 1a vs. 2a
Total Score	5.65	6.76	3.58	1.46	.86	4.75**	2.81**	5.99**
Authority Figures	1.55	1.88	.92	.85	.92	2.83**	2.55**	3.44**
Competitive Games	.76	.94	.42	.77	.67	.03	1.28	.77
Competitive Situations	–.33	–.33	–.35	–.94	–1.16	2.09*	.04	2.39**
Assertive Role	.08	.12	.00	–.35	–.16	1.32	.29	.76
Imposing Wishes	1.25	1.27	1.19	.43	.16	3.15**	.29	3.82**
Standing Out from Group	1.63	1.88	1.15	.57	.41	4.14**	1.85*	5.24**
Routine Administrative Functions	.71	.96	.23	.12	.00	1.89*	1.65	2.74**

Note: MSCS = Miner Sentence Completion Scale.
$*p < .05$; $**p < .01$

are removed from the comparison samples, the overall conclusions from the research do not change. Thus the representation of personnel managers in the comparison sample fails to account for the results obtained.

Within the very wide range of company sizes represented in the top executive sample there is no evidence of a relationship between size (number of employees) and MSCS Total Score. The correlation is .05.

DISCUSSION

Prior research has shown a consistent, positive relationship between MSCS scores and managerial promotion rates, grade level, and the choice of a managerial career (Miner 1978c; Miner and Crane 1981). The present research extends this relationship to the very highest executive levels and, thus, to a group that, although of considerable theoretical significance, has not been systematically studied previously. While the top executive MSCS scores are at a very high level, scores as high or higher are sometimes obtained after exposure to managerial role motivation training and in managerial groups preselected for high performance levels. In addition, scores above +7.0 have been obtained among MBA students of an early to mid 1960s vintage who were preparing themselves for specifically managerial careers and in samples which were exclusively or predominantly made up of sales managers (Miner 1965a; 1977b). It is apparent that the top managers would have obtained even higher Total Scores had they been differentiated on the Competitive Games and Assertive Role subscales in the same manner as they were on the other subscales. On these two subscales, and on Competitive Situations too, the top managers are not particularly high relative to the other samples that have been studied. The other subscale means are high, however.

In concurrent studies of this kind, the question of causality inevitably arises. If success serves to develop motivation to manage rather than the reverse, one might expect tenure at the top (and probably with the company) and age to be positively correlated with the MSCS scores. Data on this point are given in Table 14.3.

Contrary to this hypothesis, the trend of the data is toward lower MSCS score being associated with increasing tenure at the top; newly arrived top managers score somewhat higher than the sample as a whole. Thus, there is no support for the view that tenure at the top causes the higher MSCS scores, although the data of this study alone are insufficient to totally rule out this possibility. However, when these data are considered along with prior longitudinal findings that those with higher initial MSCS scores subsequently are promoted more rapidly in hierarchic systems (Miner 1965a), it becomes more certain that the causal arrow points from motivation to success, in line with theoretical predictions. The previous longitudinal research included a handful of individuals who actually were promoted into top management during the term of the study. Also, it should be noted that among the individual samples of this study and across the total group of managers tested, no significant relationships between age and motivation to manage were in evidence; this finding replicates those of numerous previous studies. It is possible that the process of moving up the ranks may contribute to increased motivation to manage, but the weight of the evidence suggests that a much stronger influence on the present results derives from the causal impact of motivation on behavior.

Another point relates to the relatively low scores in the comparison sample. The manner in which this sample was selected served to eliminate highly motivated younger managers, and it attracted somewhat less motivated individuals who probably now have dead-ended in their jobs. The net result is a set of lower mean scores than would be obtained from cross

Table 14.3

Relationships between MSCS Scores and Various Indexes Related to Top Management Longevity (N = 49)

MSCS Measures	Years in Position	Years with Company	Age
Total Score	–.23	–.40**	–.22
Authority Figures	–.01	.01	.38**
Competitive Games	.17	–.23	–.06
Competitive Situations	–.02	–.05	–.12
Assertive Role	–.30*	–.24	–.16
Imposing Wishes	–.32*	–.25	–.27
Standing Out from Group	–.14	–.20	–.05
Routine Administrative Functions	–.07	–.17	–.31*

Note: MSCS = Miner Sentence Completion Scale.
$*p < .05$; $**p < .01$

sections at these levels. This, however, is consistent with the objectives of the sample selection process: to compare those who had and those who had not succeeded on a major scale, within the same time frame.

Given that managerial motives do cause a rise to the very top levels of business hierarchies, how might this occur? There is little reason to believe that competitiveness and assertiveness, which on the evidence do matter at lower managerial levels, continue to exert the same influence in moving to the very top. A desire to perform the routine decision making and communication functions of managerial work appears to be a necessary but perhaps not sufficient condition for reaching the top; failure to perform these functions may only serve to eliminate such opportunities. On the other hand, favorable attitudes to superiors seem necessary if the sponsorship or mentor process is to operate, and surely many top executives have followed mobile superiors up the management hierarchy. As hypothesized, power motivation also appears to be important. Top management is a position of power that provides an opportunity to utilize the hierarchy and the tools of bureaucracy to implement policies and strategies. If one does not enjoy this use of power, survival at the top level may be short-lived. Also important is the desire to stand out and attract attention. In some respects this suggests Maccoby's (1977) gamesman, but a clearer parallel derives from Mintzberg's (1973) concept of the figurehead role. In this instance, however, the top executive is portrayed as providing a figurehead not only to external publics, but within the organization as well—there may well be an element of charisma involved at this point. Pfeffer and Salancik (1978) appear to have the same type of requirements in mind when they discuss the symbolic role of management.

Finally, it is important to recognize that although this research is described as a test of theory, the theory itself has considerable relevance for practice. If an organization is interested in attracting, selecting, and providing opportunity to individuals with top management potential, then the use of some measure of motivation to manage to identify these individuals recommends itself. The MSCS–Form H is obviously one such measure, and accordingly there appear to be good reasons to include it in selection batteries, psychological evaluation processes, assessment centers, and the like. However, the MSCS is not the construct; it is only one measure. Within AT&T, for example, the motivation to manage construct appears to have been tapped in several other ways (Howard and Wilson 1982; McClelland and Boyatzis 1982). The point is that some measure of motivation to manage increasingly seems to recommend

Table 14.4

Relationships between MSCS Measures and Hierarchic Leadership

MSCS Measures	Hierarchic Leaders (N = 49)	Not Hierarchic Leaders (N = 49)	t	r_{bis}
Total Score	6.76	.86	5.99**	.72
Authority Figures	1.88	.92	3.44**	.37
Competitive Games	.94	.67	.77	.09
Competitive Situations	–.33	–1.16	2.39**	.30
Assertive Role	.12	–.16	.76	.10
Imposing Wishes	1.27	.16	3.82**	.44
Standing Out from Group	1.88	.41	5.24**	.56
Routine Functions	.96	.00	2.74**	.33

Note: MSCS = Miner Sentence Completion Scale.
$*p < .05$; $**p < .01$

itself when there is a need to assess management potential. Companies should include the motivation to manage construct in their definitions of managerial talent.

ROLE-MOTIVATED LEADERSHIP IN HIERARCHIC ORGANIZATIONS

The data of Table 14.4, computed at a later date than the original analysis, are essentially those of Table 14.2 except that they are cast in correlational terms. The comparisons involve the congruent top executives (1a) and the age-matched comparison managers (2a from Table 14.2). The highest correlation is that for Total Score (.72) as one might expect from its greater reliability. Among the subscales Imposing Wishes (.44) and Standing Out from Group (.56) excel in the correlational analysis (r_{bis}).

CHAPTER 15

ENTREPRENEURS WHO APPLIED TO THE NATIONAL SCIENCE FOUNDATION FOR FUNDING OF HI-TECH INNOVATIONS

INTRODUCTION

This presents the lead article in the series on task role motivation; it was published in the *Journal of Applied Psychology* (Miner, Smith, and Bracker 1989), as was its follow-up study (Miner, Smith, and Bracker 1994). Further evidence on the follow-up results contained here is presented in Miner, Smith, and Bracker (1992a). All of this research deals with a sample of entrepreneurs obtained from the U.S. National Science Foundation. Smith was instrumental in securing this sample and in designing the research itself. Bracker contributed to the analysis. At the time he was employed at an entrepreneurial firm in the medical technology field located in Rochester, New York called Biosurge. He subsequently returned to a faculty position, one of several he held during his career. Smith, as previously, continued his long-term association with the marketing department at the University of Oregon where he specialized in entrepreneurship.

Also contained here is an introduction to the concept of entrepreneurial leadership, which will be considered further in subsequent studies. This approach to leadership, in addition to operationalizing the construct, supplements the work on hierarchic leadership and professional leadership noted previously.

* * *

In recent years, considerable research on the psychological characteristics of entrepreneurs has been conducted. Yet, despite many positive findings, a clear picture of the internal dynamics of the successful entrepreneur remains elusive. Reviews of the work in this area by Brockhaus and Horwitz (1986) and Begley and Boyd (1987) reinforce this conclusion.

One of the most promising theories dealing with the psychodynamics of entrepreneurship is McClelland's (1961, 1962) theory of achievement motivation. McClelland has taken several different positions at different times regarding the role of achievement motivation in corporate management, but he has consistently emphasized the close tie between entrepreneurship and the achievement motive (Miner 1980c). The primary work on this subject is the McClelland and Winter (1969) volume, which provides evidence indicating a causal impact of achievement motivation on firm growth.

McClelland's theory identifies an achievement situation in which achievement motivation is aroused and which people with a strong achievement motive prefer. The five features of this situation are (1) individual responsibility, (2) moderate risk taking as a function of skill, (3) knowledge of results of decisions, (4) novel instrumental activity, and (5) anticipation of future possibilities. In this view, the prospect of achievement satisfaction, not money, drives the successful entrepreneur; money is important primarily as a source of feedback on how well one is doing. Although in other contexts McClelland's theorizing considers power and affiliation motives also, the theory of entrepreneurship is concerned only with the achievement motive.

TASK MOTIVATION THEORY

Task motivation theory is largely synonymous with McClelland's achievement motivation theory. In fact, the original objective was simply to recast that theory in role-motivation format. In its final form, however, task theory appears to place somewhat greater emphasis on the concept of role and specifies five separate motive patterns rather than the single achievement motive. There are five distinct role prescriptions characterizing task systems, and a set of motive patterns matched to each role prescription. Thus, the theory does not use a single value, as in the case of need for achievement, but rather uses a complex of motive patterns that may substitute for one another in producing an overall index of task motivation (Locke and Henne 1986). These, and certain considerations involving the risk variable to be discussed shortly, differentiate the two theories. This research is presented as a test of task motivation theory, with full understanding that it also is a test of many aspects of achievement motivation theory. Certainly, the five aspects of the achievement situation and the role requirements of task theory have much in common.

Task theory involves a situation in which the pushes and pulls of sanctions are built into a task to be performed. This is a more circumscribed use of the task concept than is often found in the literature. Control over the person's behavior derives neither from superiors, nor professional norms, nor peer group members, but rather from the work itself and the way it is structured. One example of this type of inducement system is found in the entrepreneurial situation. Pulls or positive sanctions are inherent in the prospects for financial reward, community status, and personal satisfaction; at the same time, there are pushes to stay in the situation and to continue efforts, emanating from the threats of business failure and bankruptcy. These forces operate primarily on the individual entrepreneur (Collins, Moore, and Unwalla 1964). The entrepreneur is the individual closest to the task. The theory deals with motivation-organization fit. To the degree that this fit is off-center, the organization will fail to grow and prosper.

In addition to entrepreneurs, profit center managers, corporate venture managers, straight commission sales representatives of the kind found in real estate for example, and manufacturers' representatives may well have their jobs structured in a similar way. Much job enrichment engages the task domain; so too does the university grading system with its multi-input GPA, and varying consequences from high honors and Phi Beta Kappa to academic suspension and dismissal. Because of this broader area of application, task theory is not synonymous with a theory of entrepreneurship only.

As originally stated, task motivation theory first specified (1) a role the individual was expected to play, then (2) a motivational base or pattern relating to performing that role, and finally, (3) a rationale or explanation for positing the role and its related motive pattern. The roles, motivational bases, and rationales are as follows.

Self-Achievement

A desire to achieve through one's own efforts and to be able to clearly attribute any success to personal causation. In a task system, it is essential that individuals continually be pulled into the task situation so that they not simply avoid any pressures involved by escaping from the work context. The major source of this pull is an intrinsic desire to achieve through one's own efforts and ability and to experience the enhanced self-esteem that such achievement permits to be sure that one did it oneself.

Risk Taking

A desire to take moderate risks that can be handled through one's own efforts. In a task system, the individual must face considerable challenge and the prospect of being overextended, however briefly. Such a situation requires a desire to take risks; tasks that the individual considers easy and already knows how to deal with have little pull because there is no sense of achievement to be had in accomplishing them. However, desires to take high risks or to take risks related entirely to luck or fate (where one cannot ultimately reduce the risk through one's own effort) are not functional. In neither case can a sense of individual achievement be anticipated with any reasonable probability.

Feedback of Results

A desire for some clear index of the level of performance. In a task system, feedback on the level and results of one's performance are necessary to attribute any degree of success (or failure) to one's efforts; it is crucial to know whether one has succeeded or failed. Consequently, the individual must be motivated to actively seek out results-oriented feedback in terms of measures such as profitability, productive output, wastage, course grades, and so on.

Personal Innovation

A desire to introduce novel, innovative, or creative solutions. In a task system, the pull of individual achievement works only to the extent that the individual can attribute personal causation. Original or creative approaches have a distinctive quality that makes it easier to identify them as one's own and to take personal credit for them. A desire to introduce such approaches is more likely to make task inducement function properly.

Planning for the Future

A desire to think about the future and anticipate future possibilities including goal setting. In a task system, the individual must be pulled by the prospect of anticipated future rewards and therefore must approach life with a strong future orientation. There must be a desire to plan, to set personal goals that will signify achievement, and to plot paths to goal attainment: this in turn implies a minimal expectation, or fear, of future failure (Miner 1980b, 279–280).

Although entrepreneurs do manage businesses, the type of system that fits with task motivation is different from the one that matches hierarchic motivation, or motivation to manage. Entrepreneurial systems operate face-to-face rather than through the written communications of bureaucracy. Entrepreneurs are not constrained by the requirement that they operate within the hierarchy; they go wherever in the organization they are personally needed, to put out fires and handle crises. Given the differences in organizational systems involved, one would expect entrepreneurs to exhibit relatively low levels of hierarchic motivation, which includes motives related to dealing with authority above, competing with peers, and exercising power over subordinates. At the same time, managers would be expected to exhibit relatively low levels of task motivation relative to entrepreneurs.

Evidence on the first point is clear. Entrepreneurs consistently have been found to possess less hierarchic or managerial motivation than their counterparts in bureaucratic management (Berman and Miner, 1985; Smith and Miner 1983). The second point, involving the relative levels of task motivation, is considered by our research.

Two points emerge from this discussion. First, task motivation is a very different motivational constellation than managerial motivation, although the two theories are parallel in some respects. Second, task motivation, as the term is used here, refers to a specific set of motivational patterns that match or fit a particular type of task, that of the entrepreneur or one similar to it. We are not using the term task motivation in the more general sense of overall work motivation that is often encountered in the literature.

MODERATE RISK TAKING VERSUS RISK AVOIDANCE

Among the original role specifications of task theory, the one that seemed least certain from the beginning was the risk-taking role. Brockhaus (1980) reported results that questioned the significance of risk taking in entrepreneurial achievement. Raynor (1974) developed a theoretical rationale for a substantial risk-avoidance propensity among established entrepreneurs; his arguments run counter to the McClelland theory in this respect.

Even more unsettling was the fact that our initial pilot studies aimed at developing an instrument to measure task motivation indicated that risk avoidance was what characterized successful entrepreneurs (Miner 1985b), thus supporting Raynor (1974) and refuting McClelland (1961).

On the basis of these considerations, we made a decision at an early point to substitute a risk-avoidance role for the risk-taking role as stated previously. Consequently, the motivational base became a desire to avoid risks of any and all kinds. The rationale is that risk taking may result in the entrepreneur being forced out of the entrepreneurial situation because of business failure; to avoid this, the entrepreneur attempts to minimize risk. The actual process of measuring risk avoidance involved a change in scoring procedures only, not in the items themselves. This change in the theory occurred prior to the inception of this study, and this research provides a test of the revised theory.

HYPOTHESES

The overarching hypothesis behind this research has been stated as follows (Miner 1982):

> In task systems, task (achievement) motivation should be at a high level among task performers (entrepreneurs, for example), and it should be positively correlated with task success indexes; task motivation should not differentiate in these ways within other types of systems (298).

The latter part of this statement, "task motivation should not differentiate in these ways within other types of systems," is not considered in this research. Success is measured in terms of the firm's growth rate.

In addition, the task theory was extended by specifying certain hypotheses with regard to sources of capital used by entrepreneurs to start their businesses. It was expected that those who used personal savings would have low task motivation and those who did not would have high task motivation. This stems from the view that risk avoidance is part of high task motivation, and risk avoiders do not want to put their own money at risk. Moreover, we expected that the use of the Small Business Administration and banks or financial institutions as capital sources would characterize low task motivation individuals. These sources tend to be viewed as highly controlling of the entrepreneur, thus restricting the sense of self-achievement. On the other hand, venture capitalists are likely to be considered by entrepreneurs as more understanding of and compatible with successful entrepreneurship; thus, this source should be used by the high task motivation people. Friends and relatives and other business people also might be expected to be used as sources of capital by high task motivation entrepreneurs, although the rationale is somewhat less clear for using these individuals than for using the venture capital source. Wide variations among individuals within these latter two groups make prediction difficult.

METHOD

Samples

Surveys were sent to National Science Foundation (NSF) grant applicants. NSF and a number of other federal government agencies as well provide financial support to smaller firms to help them develop and bring to market various technological innovations. This program has consistently attracted a considerably larger number of grant applications than are funded. Funding, when it does occur, initially takes the form of a modest seed-money grant (Phase 1) and subsequently, in a much smaller number of cases, a more substantial financial commitment (Phase 2). Fostering technological advance along these lines has been a feature of government policy for some time (Hetzner, Tornatzky, and Klein 1983; National Science Foundation 1983).

The samples for this research were derived from Phase 1 awardees for the years 1979 through 1983 and from rejectees for 1982. There were insufficient rejectees to treat as a separate sample for analysis. Initial mailings were made to 631 individuals who had submitted grant applications. An effort was made to detect and delete all duplications resulting from multiple submissions within this group. A large number of envelopes were returned as undeliverable; presumably, these firms had either gone out of business or moved to a new location. Overall, there were 115 envelopes returned in this manner, bringing the effective size of the group contacted down to 516.

Two subsequent mailings were made after deleting prior respondents, refusals, and instances of failure to deliver. Partial or complete replies were received from 195 individuals, for an effective response rate of about 38 percent. Of these, 159 replies were fully usable, about 31 percent of the effective mailings. This response rate is 25 percent if the initial mailing total is used.

Although the definition of an entrepreneur is far from a settled issue (Brockhaus and Horwitz 1986), the concept of a firm founder is widely used. Accordingly, the following question was used to identify the entrepreneurs within the respondent group: "Were you involved in the original formation of your current company?" Those who responded *yes* were taken to be entrepreneurs. The respondents did not indicate any difficulty in answering this question. There were 150 in the respondent group as a whole and 118 in the fully usable sample. The entrepreneurs were predominantly men (there were only 6 women) and included relatively few who described themselves as minorities (14 in all). Almost 60 percent held doctoral degrees, and advanced degrees of some kind predominated among the others. The mean age was 47 years.

Forty-five subjects indicated that they were not involved in the original formation of their companies. Although not the entrepreneurs of their firms, these individuals were comparable with the entrepreneurs in numerous other respects. Of the 45, 41 provided fully usable data. Their positions in their firms varied considerably. Nine were presidents or chief executive officers who had assumed these positions subsequent to an entrepreneur. Another 24 held managerial titles from vice president, of whom there were 11, to program manager; almost all were in research. There were 7 people who had titles such as senior engineer, research scientist, senior associate, and so forth. These individuals may or may not have had some managerial responsibilities. In 5 cases, information on the positions held was not available. It appears that in many of these firms, the process of submitting applications to NSF had been delegated to persons with scientific backgrounds but who were below the very top levels of the firm. This nonentrepreneur sample was designated as *manager/scientists.* Being from comparable companies and having played similar roles in the NSF application process, the manager/scientists provided a useful comparison group for the entrepreneurs. The two samples were by no means matched, however. Three of the manager/scientists were women, and 1 selected the minority designation. The mean age was 46 years, and 36 percent held doctorates. Only 4 did not have training beyond the bachelor's level. The designation of manager/

scientist is not meant to indicate that the entrepreneurs were not manager/scientists as well; the difference is that the entrepreneurs were founders also, and the manager/scientists were not. These similarities and differences are exactly what made the manager/scientist sample a useful comparison group.

The entrepreneurial firms included in the analyses are located in 33 states, with only California and Massachusetts having more than 10 firms.

Measures

Two instruments were completed by the respondents. One, entitled the Innovative Technology Survey, contained questions dealing with individual demographics, the growth and success of the firm, and aspects of the firm's and entrepreneur's history. This was the source of the growth indexes used in this research. These indexes correlate .78 ($p < .01$) and are described as follows:

1. *Mean annual growth in number of employees:* The number of employees reported for the most recent year, divided by the number of years the firm has been in business.
2. *Mean annual growth in sales:* The dollar value of sales in thousands of dollars reported for the most recent year, divided by the number of years the firm has been in business.

From a research perspective, traditional measures such as return on investment, return on assets, and return on equity might easily have been used as well. The problem is that small entrepreneurs typically do not think in these terms and do not calculate these ratios. To ask for these figures might have precluded any response at all.

The second measure completed by respondents was the Miner Sentence Completion Scale (MSCS)–Form T. This is a measure of the components of the task motivation theory as previously stated (Miner 1986). It uses the sentence completion format, which has exhibited a number of positive qualities in recent studies (Rabin and Zltogorski 1985). Respondents complete 40 items, 8 for each of the theory's five components. An overall, total score for task motivation and five subscale scores is calculated. Each item is scored +, ?, or –, depending on whether the response is *consistent* with the theory's concept of effective task performance, *neutral* or unrevealing, or *inconsistent* with effective task performance. Items in each subscale are scattered throughout the instrument. Examples to facilitate scoring are available in the scoring guide (Miner 1986). The total score can vary from +40 to –40, and subscale scores can vary from +8 to –8.

All MSCS–Form T scoring was done by the first author. A check on the accuracy of this scoring, involving comparison with another, independent scorer on ten scales, yielded a total score correlation of .95 and subscale score correlations ranging from .91 to .96. No significant differences in the mean scores of the two scorers were found.

Table 15.1 contains the intercorrelations among the MSCS–Form T variables. All subscales correlate well with the total score because all are components of that score. The subscales exhibit a low positive correlation among themselves, with the median at .18. This figure is similar to what has been obtained with other sentence completion measures in the past. The MSCS–Form T is the measurement method of choice for task motivation theory. To the extent it may yield results differing from those obtained with the Thematic Apperception Test (McClelland's preferred measure of achievement motivation), the two theories must be incorporating different variables. This is an issue to investigate in future research.

Table 15.1

Correlations among MSCS–Form T Measures for Entrepreneurs and Manager/Scientists (N = 159)

	Subscale					
MSCS–T Measures	Self-Achievement	Avoiding Risks	Feedback of Results	Personal Innovation	Planning for the Future	Total score
Self-Achievement	—	.09	.31**	.37**	.09	.62**
Avoiding Risks		—	.15	.13	.15	.51**
Feedback of Results			—	.26**	.35**	.68**
Personal Innovation				—	.20*	.62**
Planning for the Future					—	.61**

Note: MSCS = Miner Sentence Completion Scale.
$*p < .05$; $**p < .01$

RESULTS

The results reported here provide a comprehensive statement of the findings from this research. Prior progress reports published in conference proceedings have dealt with smaller components of the overall efforts in terms of the samples considered, the analyses presented, or both (Smith, Bracker, and Miner 1987; Smith and Miner 1984, 1985).

The first part of the hypothesis states that task motivation will be higher among entrepreneurs than non-entrepreneurs (in this case, the manager/scientists). This hypothesis receives confirmation as indicated in Table 15.2. The total score difference of roughly 4 points is substantial, but two subscales—Personal Innovation and Planning for the Future—do not contribute to it to a significant degree. A two-group discriminant analysis applied to these data indicates that 64.15 percent of the cases are correctly classified by the discriminant function. The standardized canonical discriminant function coefficients for the subscales are .58 for Feedback of Results, .46 for Self-Achievement, and .41 for Avoiding Risks, but only .03 for Planning for the Future, and .02 for Personal Innovation.

It should be noted that the manager/scientists' firms have grown more rapidly than the entrepreneurs' firms. The mean annual growth in number of employees in manager/scientists' firms is approximately five employees greater, the mean annual growth in sales is almost $32,000 greater, and the manager/scientists' firms have existed roughly five years longer; these are statistically significant differences. What appears to be operating is that many of the manager/scientists work for entrepreneurial companies that have grown to the point where the grant application process frequently is delegated to someone below the top level in the organization. Unfortunately, the use of NSF lists for purposes of subject selection prevented our obtaining data from the original entrepreneurs in the firms of the manager/scientists. The theoretical hypotheses suggest that, had these data been available, the MSCS–Form T scores would have been quite high.

Table 15.3 contains the results of correlating the motivational measures with the firm growth measures in accordance with the second part of the hypothesis. The values reported are for Spearman's rho. This statistic has been used because both growth measures are seriously skewed, with a large number of firms experiencing low growth rates and a few having very high rates. Because Spearman's rho, in contrast with the Pearson *r*, does not assume normally distributed

Table 15.2

Comparison of Entrepreneurs (N = 118) **and Manager/Scientists** (N = 41) **on MSCS–Form T**

	Entrepreneurs		Manager/scientists		
MSCS–Form T Measure	*M*	*SD*	*M*	*SD*	*t*
Self-Achievement	1.64	2.76	.61	2.34	2.14*
Avoiding Risks	.80	2.58	.00	2.55	1.71*
Feedback of Results	–.54	2.27	–1.63	2.69	2.53**
Personal Innovation	2.88	2.41	2.37	1.91	1.24
Planning for the Future	1.15	2.89	.61	2.42	1.08
Total score	5.93	8.16	1.95	5.57	3.46**

Note: MSCS = Miner Sentence Completion Scale.
$^{*}p < .05$; $^{**}p < .01$

Table 15.3

Correlations between MSCS–Form T Measures and Indexes of Company Growth among Entrepreneurs

	Growth Measure	
MSCS–Form T Measures	Mean Annual Growth in Number of Employees	Mean Annual Growth in Sales
Self-Achievement	.49**	.35**
Avoiding Risks	.18*	.24*
Feedback of Results	.28**	.21*
Personal Innovation	.32**	.13
Planning for the Future	.24*	.25**
Total Score	.49**	.39**

Note: MSCS = Miner Sentence Completion Scale.
$^{*}p < .05$; $^{**}p < .01$

data, it is the statistic of choice in circumstances of this kind. When both statistics are computed from normally distributed data, rho tends to be only slightly lower than *r* (McNemar 1969).

Support for the theory comes from all of the MSCS–Form T subscales but is most pronounced in the case of the total score. The correlations compare favorably with those reported previously for Forms H and P of the MSCS within their respective domains (Miner 1985b).

As a check on the hypothesis that pronounced, rather than moderate, risk avoidance is associated with firm growth, the sample of entrepreneurs was split into high, medium, and low subgroups on risk scores; these groups were then compared on mean annual growth in number of employees and mean annual growth in sales. This analysis provides no support for a curvilinear relationship; the medium-risk group was not higher on the criterion measures.

The final analysis dealt with the relationship between task motivation and the use of various sources of capital. Considering only the directionality of the total score results in Table 15.4, the hypotheses are confirmed. However, only three of the differences are significant. Those entrepreneurs who use personal savings and seek capital from banks and financial institutions clearly do have less task motivation, and entrepreneurs who use venture capitalists have more.

Avoiding Risks and Personal Innovation play an important role in the decision not to use personal savings. Self-Achievement and Avoiding Risks play an important role in the decision not to use banks and financial institutions. A resort to venture capital sources is related to a desire for Feedback of Results and to Planning for the Future. Although these results do not match the hypothesized expectations in every respect, they are generally supportive.

DISCUSSION

This research does not permit definite conclusions to be reached regarding the direction of causality. The theory is causal in nature—from motivation to firm performance—but the MSCS–Form T administration did not precede the measures of performance. It is conceivable that recognized performance influenced the motivational findings, for instance.

Several considerations argue against this interpretation. In the research on achievement motivation, a causal impact from motivation to entrepreneurial outcomes has been demonstrated (McClelland and Winter 1969). Similarly, research on the hierarchic theory that is parallel to, and in many respects a sibling of, the task theory has demonstrated a causal flow from motivation to manage to managerial success (Miner 1985b). Finally, the MSCS–Form T is a projective device and respondents typically do not have an understanding of what is being measured. Accordingly, a conscious process of responding to recognition of their entrepreneurial success, by describing themselves as they perceive a successful entrepreneur should be, is unlikely to have produced the results obtained.

Generalizing the Results

Another question relates to whether the findings might be a specific consequence of those individuals who responded to the survey. This appears to be less of a problem than might otherwise be the case, because all comparisons were made within the survey samples. If biases were present, they should have affected all respondents in essentially the same manner, in the form of constant error. As a result, although absolute values might contain an unacceptable degree of error there is no reason to expect this error to transfer to relative or comparative results such as those reported in this article.

Further evidence related to the stability of the findings was obtained by conducting the analyses of Table 15.3 for the first 50 entrepreneur respondents and for the second 68. On 5 of the 6 MSCS variables there was no significant change in correlation coefficients; thus, the values reported in Table 15.3 are the best estimates of population values. Two subscales showed a consistent increase, and two a decrease. However, on the Self-Achievement measure, the correlation with mean annual growth in number of employees decreased from .67 to .34, and with mean annual growth in sales from .59 to .19. Both decreases are significant at $p < .05$. On the basis of this evidence, the correlations involving Self-Achievement in Table 15.3 are to a degree overestimates, although they remain significant. The high correlations on this variable in the initial sample suggest a substantial regression toward the mean.

The findings obtained from this research serve to substantiate earlier results dealing with the role of achievement motivation in entrepreneurial success. The measure of task motivation used, however, is new and has the advantage of being considerably less cumbersome than the Thematic Apperception Test, while retaining the advantages of projective measurement. There is also reason to believe that sentence completion measures of this kind possess considerably greater repeat reliability (Miner 1985b; Stahl 1986).

Table 15.4

Mean MSCS–Form T Scores for Entrepreneurs Using and Not Using Various Sources of Capital to Start the Business

	Personal Savings		Small Business Administration		Banks/Financial Institutions		Friends and Relations		Venture Capitalists		Other Business People	
	Used	Did not use	Used	Did not use	Used	Did not use	Used	Did not use	Used	Did not use	Used	Did not use
MSCS–Form T Measures	(N = 97)	(N = 21)	(N = 6)	(N = 112)	(N = 13)	(N = 105)	(N = 19)	(N = 99)	(N = 14)	(N = 104)	(N = 16)	(N = 102)
Self-Achievement	1.64	1.67	2.50	1.60	.31	1.81*	1.74	1.63	2.43	1.54	1.94	1.60
Avoiding Risks	.55	1.95*	–.33	.86	–.92	1.01**	1.58	.65	1.21	.74	1.38	.71
Feedback of Results	–.64	–.10	–.50	–.54	–1.08	–.48	.16	–.68	.43	–.67*	–1.13	–.45
Personal Innovation	2.70	3.71*	2.17	2.92	1.92	3.00	2.53	2.95	3.64	2.78	2.69	2.91
Planning for the Future	1.02	1.76	–.50	1.24	1.46	1.11	1.32	1.12	2.57	.96*	1.06	1.17
Total Score	5.27	9.00*	3.33	6.07	1.69	6.46*	7.32	5.67	10.29	5.35*	5.94	5.93

Note: MSCS = Miner Sentence Completion Scale.
$*p < .05$; $**p < .01$

Practical Usefulness

A large number of the firms studied had not grown to any significant degree and remained very small at the time they were involved in this research. This situation does not appear to be unique to high-technology companies, as the following quote from a multi-industry study (Birley 1987) indicates:

> Some firms had grown considerably but they were few in number, only four exceeding sales of $2.4 million, but they did not have any identifiable, external characteristics that would enable any focused strategy for picking high-growth firms ex ante. Thus, for example, they did not cluster in any particular industrial sector, nor did the founders have any specific incubator background. Some high-growth firms were formed with very close links to the previous employment of the owners; others had no apparent link whatsoever (163).

The need, from a practical viewpoint, is to identify in advance those entrepreneurs who will create high-growth firms. This is what investors want because these are the firms that accumulate substantial value. This is what government wants because these are the firms that expand employment and contribute to a prosperous economy. Entrepreneurs themselves would benefit because business failures could be reduced and the suffering that goes with failure could be avoided. Furthermore, the number of small firms that produce only a marginal income for their owners could be reduced. Technological innovations could be brought to the marketplace much more efficiently were it possible to identify those particular individuals able to do the job best.

The findings from this research represent a step toward achieving this kind of prediction through the early identification of entrepreneurial talent. Initial efforts in this research program dealt with managerial motivation, the thought being that high-motivation-to-manage founders would manage their firms into rapid growth in order to have more to manage (Smith and Miner 1983). It now appears that task motivation, not hierarchic motivation, is more likely to provide the key to understanding.

Using motivational measures for this purpose should be particularly fruitful for venture capitalists, because this source of capital tends to attract entrepreneurs with higher task motivation. However, banks and other financial institutions would benefit as well, even though they may have to search more widely to find the needed talent.

FOLLOW-UP OVER MORE THAN FIVE YEARS

The present research represents a follow-up of the concurrent study by introducing data on firm performance five and a half years after the entrepreneurs completed the MSCS–Form T. It thus permits a more informed test of the hypothesis that preexisting task motivation can serve to influence the level of success achieved by an entrepreneur's firm.

Method

Samples

The follow-up which, like the original study, involved three successive mailings, used data collected an average of five years and seven months after the initial measures were completed. The follow-up mailings were made to the last available address from the initial study or to a new address provided by the post office if the individual had moved and a new address was on file.

Of the 118 entrepreneurs whom we attempted to contact, 41 could not be located by the post office. The letters to these entrepreneurs were returned as undeliverable and unforwardable. In 7 cases, 3 mailings failed to produce any response; these people appeared to be located where the letters were sent, but they did not reply to any of 3 mailings. Finally, there were 11 instances in which the available data from the initial study or the follow-up were insufficient to reach a conclusion as to any improvement over the interval subsequent to testing. In 6 of these cases, the entrepreneur was no longer with the same firm. Although in 2 instances we learned that the individual was deceased, the remaining 4 situations simply were not explained.

This left 59 instances in which data sufficient to establish the extent of growth were available from the follow-up. For 49 of these firms, information on sales, number of employees, and the entrepreneur's income from the firm was provided, and the entrepreneur was still with the same organization. However, there were a number of instances of missing data on one or more of these measures, either at the time of testing or at follow-up. In addition, 10 entrepreneurs were no longer associated with their original firms, and data regarding the reason for separation were provided.

Measures

To categorize the 59 entrepreneurs in terms of the growth of their firms over the 5-plus years, we classified high-growth and low-growth samples. The high-growth sample contained 21 people whose firms had increased their sales by $1 million a year or more over the interim. In addition, there were 2 instances in which the necessary sales figures were not available, but either an increase in number of employees of 50 or more had occurred or the entrepreneur's income from the business had increased by $75,000 or more. Finally there was 1 case in which the original firm had been sold, but was known to be prospering at the time of sale. This high-growth sample of 24 entrepreneurs was contrasted with a low-growth sample of 35 individuals who did not meet the above criteria. In 26 of these cases, available measures of firm growth did not reach the specified levels. There were 7 instances in which the company was quite small, having less than 5 employees, and was simply discontinued at some point. The remaining 2 companies were doing poorly, and in each case the entrepreneur was forced to sell out. To our knowledge, there were no actual bankruptcies involved.

The two instruments completed by respondents at the time of initial contact were the MSCS–Form T and the innovative technology survey. The latter was designed in part to study a typology of entrepreneurs and their firms; the results obtained in this area have been reported in a previous paper (Miner, Smith, and Bracker 1992b). They bear primarily on the existence of an inventor-entrepreneur type and thus are tangential to the current research. However, the innovative technology survey does contain questions dealing with the company's annual sales in dollars for the most recent year, the number of people employed by the company in the most recent year, and the entrepreneur's current yearly income.

The follow-up questionnaire asked these same questions plus several others dealing with the individual's current work organization and position and whether any business failures had been experienced in the past five years. The questions were appended to a letter that introduced a reprint of the previous article (Miner, Smith, and Bracker 1989); this reprint was included with the letter.

As indicated in Table 15.5, the various criteria were highly intercorrelated at the initial point, at follow-up, and across the time gap from the initial period to follow-up. Furthermore,

Table 15.5

Relationships among Criteria and Means and Standard Deviations at Initial Testing and Follow-up

Measure	Growth in Number of Employees	Growth in Dollar Volume of Sales	Entrepreneur's Yearly Income from Position
Growth in number of employees	**.90**	.79*	.56
Growth in dollar volume of sales	.93*[a]	**.84***	.51*
Entrepreneur's yearly income from position	.58*[b]	.64*[c]	**.60**
Full sample at initial testing			
N	113	90	106
M	21.7	\$0.9 million	\$38,000
SD	31.1	\$1.2 million	\$29,400
Follow-up sample at initial testing			
n	53	46	40
M	23.6	\$1.2 million	\$51,500
SD	38.3	\$2.3 million	\$29,500
Follow-up sample at follow-up			
n	53	46	40
M	40.0	\$3.6 million	\$71,800
SD	71.6	\$7.6 million	\$46,600

Note: Values above the diagonal are for the full sample at the time of initial testing. Values below the diagonal are for the follow-up sample at the time of initial testing. Values on the diagonal in boldface are the test-retest correlations for the follow-up sample (at initial testing vs. at follow-up).

[a]For the follow-up sample at the time of follow-up, $r = .96$*. [b]For the follow-up sample at the time of follow-up, $r = .73$*. [c]For the follow-up sample at the time of follow-up, $r = .75$*.

*$p < .01$

although all three criteria showed substantial growth from one period to the other, part of this differential was attributable to the fact that the follow-up firms were somewhat larger than those not included in the follow-up in the first place.

Scorer reliability for the MSCS–Form T was supplemented by test-retest values measured over a period of one to two weeks. These figures were .96 for the total score and varied from .66 to .91 for subscales (Miner 1993).

The intercorrelations among MSCS–Form T measures, noted in Table 15.6, were very close to those obtained in the larger sample of 118 entrepreneurs (Miner, Smith, and Bracker 1989). The means in the follow-up sample were, more often than not, slightly lower than those in the total sample, but on two subscales the follow-up group was higher.

Results

The primary test of the hypothesis involved comparing the MSCS–Form T scores from the high-growth firms with those from the low-growth firms, high and low growth being defined in terms of changes over a 5-plus year period (the growth index). The results are given in the left-hand columns of Table 15.7. The total score findings were quite striking: A biserial correlation of .70 was obtained. On the subscales the relationships were somewhat less strong, presumably because of lower reliabilities, but they were substantial nevertheless in four of the five instances. Only with the Avoiding Risks variable did a significant relationship fail

Table 15.6

Means, Standard Deviations, and Correlations among MSCS–Form T Measures in the Follow-up Sample (N = 59)

	Subscale								Full
MSCS–Form T Measures	1	2	3	4	5	6	*M*	*SD*	Sample Mean
1. Self-Achievement	—	.04	.35**	.42**	.27*	.69**	1.08	2.79	1.64
2. Avoiding Risks		—	.13	.08	.22	.46**	.68	2.44	.80
3. Feedback of Results			—	.32*	.30**	.67**	–.42	2.44	–.54
4. Personal Innovation				—	.12	.60**	2.63	2.44	2.88
5. Planning for the Future					—	.66**	1.36	3.08	1.15
6. Total Score						—	5.32	8.17	5.93

Note: N = 118 for the full sample. MSCS—Form T = Miner Sentence Completion Scale—Form T. $*p < .05$; $**p < .01$

to emerge. The biserial correlation was used in these analyses on the assumption that the underlying performance dimension was, in fact, continuous and normally distributed.

Table 15.7 also presents the correlations between MSCS–Form T variables and the individual growth measures to the extent that the latter were available. The correlations at initial testing (concurrent) are given for the total sample and for the subset on which follow-up data were obtained. These concurrent findings may be compared with the predictive results obtained by using criteria provided at follow-up. There was nothing to suggest shrinkage in the correlations. The most frequent pattern is for the follow-up values to be somewhat higher than the concurrent values, but with only minimal differences when exactly the same samples are used in this comparison.

The total score results were quite consistent across all analyses, with correlations rising into the high .40s in the case of the follow-up data. Among the subscales, Self-Achievement and Planning for the Future were strong in both the concurrent and predictive analyses. Feedback of Results was significantly related to the criterion initially, but not at follow-up. However, this appears to be a consequence of sampling fluctuation. Personal Innovation was a significant predictor at follow-up, but was not significant in the initial concurrent study. Although Avoiding Risks produced a minimally significant correlation in the concurrent analysis, this relationship no longer obtained at follow-up. Taking the data of Table 15.7 overall, only Avoiding Risks can be questioned as a predictor.

Discussion

Support for the predictive validity of the MSCS is now strengthened substantially for the MSCS–Form T total score and four of its five subscales. In this sense, the hypotheses put forth in task theory receive greater support as well.

The lack of confirmation with regard to the Avoidance of Risk is puzzling, however. Concurrent analyses—and there have been a number of them—have consistently produced significant results when this measure was used (Miner 1993). This finding extends to the predecessor of this study (Miner, Smith, and Bracker 1989).

The literature dealing with the relationship between risk taking and entrepreneurial success indicates that when other measures of risk are used, a somewhat mixed pattern emerges, but that, in any event, the proverbial propensity of entrepreneurs to take high risks is not supported (Bird

1989). The present results are consistent with this latter conclusion. Why they do not go beyond this to support the avoidance hypothesis of task theory will have to be a matter for future research.

The Survival Criterion

A follow-up was also conducted to establish the relationship between the MSCS–Form T and firm survival (Miner, Smith, and Bracker 1992a). Of the 118 entrepreneurs in the concurrent sample, 16 had clearly gone separate ways from their original firm, 41 had moved with either themselves or their company and could no longer be located, and 61 remained with their original companies at follow-up. Comparing the first and third groups on years of education, age, annual sales, profit as percent of sales, annual growth in number of employees, and yearly income from their firm, all at the time of initial contact, yielded no evidence of differences, but there were MSCS–T differences as follows at follow-up:

	Failure to Survive (N = 16)	Survivors (N = 61)	
Total Score	1.94	7.72	$p < .01$
Avoiding Risks	0.06	1.25	$p < .05$
Personal Innovation	1.88	3.21	$p < .05$
Planning for the Future	–0.13	2.00	$p < .01$

In particular those who like to plan are much more likely to be in the survivors group. This represents a strong endorsement of planning, but only for those more highly motivated to plan.

As to the comparisons involving the second group, the following quote is relevant—

> Perhaps one of the most interesting findings occurs with the middle group—those whom we could not locate. In the past it has been common practice simply to drop such groups from the analyses. In contrast we developed certain assumptions about what might have caused the relocation and, based on these, hypothesized that this group should be intermediate in test score. Furthermore, because we expected problems to predominate over successes in this group, it seemed likely that they would score significantly below the survivors. These expectations proved to be true. The finding that test results for non-respondents of this type can be predicted is of some importance. It means that it is no longer necessary to delete such individuals from analyses. Accordingly sample sizes can be maintained at more respectable levels, and true differences are more likely to be identified (Miner, Smith, and Bracker 1992a, 152).

ROLE-MOTIVATED LEADERSHIP IN TASK ORGANIZATIONS

Some time after the follow-up analysis, further work was done to establish leadership within the NSF sample. Discussion of this particular kind of leadership may be found under task leadership in Miner (2002, 317–318) as follows:

> Task or entrepreneurial leadership involves the concept of a lead entrepreneur who typically owns a larger share of the venture or holds a more dominant position, and the existence of a growth orientation; both must be present for task leadership to occur. Entrepreneurs who are not leaders are venture team members who do not hold lead status and/or who are involved in ventures not evidencing commitment to organizational growth. The lead entrepreneur

Table 15.7

Relationships of MSCS–Form T Scores with Growth Index and with Measures of Company Success at the Time of Initial Testing and at Follow-up

	Growth Index Analyses			Growth in No. of Employees			Growth in Dollar Volume of Sales			Entrepreneur's Yearly Income from Position		
	Mean Score											
	High-growth Firms	Low-growth Firms	r_b	Initial		Follow-up	Initial		Follow-up	Initial		Follow-up
MSCS–Form T Measures	(n = 24)	(n = 35)	(n = 59)	(N = 113)	(n = 53)	(n = 53)	(N = 90)	(n = 46)	(n = 46)	(N = 106)	(n = 40)	(n = 40)
Self-Achievement	2.83	–.11**	.66**	.36**	.51**	.53**	.27**	.45**	.49**	.30**	.36**	.46**
Avoiding Risks	1.00	.46	.14	.11	.01	.05	.19*	.12	.07	.06	–.33	–.27
Feedback of Results	.46	–1.03*	.38**	.26**	.10	.14	.22*	.19	.17	.24*	.22	.10
Personal Innovation	3.79	1.83**	.49**	.16	.20	.25*	.08	.19	.26*	.09	.13	.16
Planning for the Future	2.71	.43**	.46**	.18*	.28*	.40**	.20*	.29*	.45**	.30**	.34*	.42**
Total Score	10.79	1.58**	.70**	.35**	.36**	.47**	.31**	.40**	.48**	.36**	.25	.32*

Note. MSCS–Form T = Miner Sentence Completion Scale–Form T. For initial testing, N = total sample size and n = subsample size. Subsample data were obtained for subsample sizes at follow-up.

*$p < .05$; **$p < .01$

Table 15.8

Relationships between MSCS–Form T Measures and Task Leadership in NSF Sample of Entrepreneurs

MSCS–Form T Measures	Task Leaders (N = 59)	Not Task Leaders (N = 59)	r_{bis}
Total Item Score	10.95	.92	.77**
Self-Achievement	3.10	.19	.66**
Avoiding Risks	1.56	.03	.37**
Feedback of Results	0.44	−1.53	.54**
Personal Innovation	3.98	1.78	.57**
Planning for the Future	1.86	.44	.31**

Note: MSCS = Miner Sentence Completion Scale.
$^{**}p < .01$

concept is especially important in team entrepreneurship of the kind that characterizes high technology ventures. In the team context, the concept of a lead entrepreneur has been shown to be a viable entity, and the vision of that person has been found to play an important strategic role (Ensley, Carland, and Carland 2000).

Growth orientation, the second requirement, has been operationalized as a demonstrated record of organizational growth (measured in years) over which the firm has increased substantially in number of employees and/or dollar volume of sales. This growth need not be maintained under all circumstances, such as during a period of recession, but it must have occurred, and under the guidance and vision of the same lead entrepreneur.

Entrepreneurial leadership is typically achieved following a period of educational experiences, part-time entrepreneurship, other employment, non-leader entrepreneurial work, and even other entrepreneurial leadership. Thus, a continuum of career development exists.

Table 15.8 deals with the relationship between this type of leadership and the MSCS–Form T scores with rather striking results.

CHAPTER 16

CONTRASTS AMONG ENTREPRENEURS AND MANAGERS

INTRODUCTION

The paper presented here was published in the *Journal of Business Venturing* (Miner 1990), intended to bring the task role motivation theory to the entrepreneurship scholarly community. Here for the first time the idea of a leadership role within entrepreneurship is broached. This presentation does not include an initial introduction to the conceptual development of role motivation theory, especially as applied to the hierarchic and task variants; however, this theorizing has been discussed previously, and may be assessed in the original article.

The research reported is couched in a theoretical framework developed by the author (Miner 1980b, 1982) and operationalized by Oliver (1981, 1982). This framework differentiates organizational forms in terms of the mechanisms used to elicit efforts from members. At various points these mechanisms have been referred to as "control systems" and as "inducement systems." It is also possible to view them as "power configurations," as Mintzberg (1983) has done. By whatever name, these organizational systems operate in their own specific ways to influence key performers who in turn orchestrate positive and negative sanctions to attain organizational goals. This paper focuses on hierarchic and task systems of this kind, on managers and entrepreneurs.

* * *

EMPIRICAL JOURNEYS

Tests of the premise that hierarchic motivation is positively related to managerial success—as reflected in performance appraisals, peer ratings, promotion rates, and managerial level at-

From John B. Miner, "Entrepreneurs, High Growth Entrepreneurs, and Managers: Contrasting and Overlapping Motivational Patterns," *Journal of Business Venturing,* vol. 5, 221–234.

tained in large bureaucratically organized firms—have produced positive results over many years. As anticipated, the theory generally has proved ineffective outside its intended domain of management (Miner 1985b; Nathan and Alexander 1985). Several studies are predictive in nature and are sufficiently controlled to justify a causal interpretation from motivation to performance. Hierarchic motivation also appears to contribute to the choice of a managerial career.

Using the Hierarchic Theory with Entrepreneurs

The initial research hypothesis regarding entrepreneurs was formulated at a time when the four role motivation theories were being developed and when the hierarchic theory was clearly dominant. The hypothesis was that people with strong managerial motivation would be prompted to found firms and create strategies for their growth in order to have something to manage. The first test of this proposition was carried out using a sample of 38 Oregon entrepreneur-founders (Smith and Miner 1983). As it turned out the data gave little support to the hypothesis.

A second opportunity to study these relationships arose in connection with a study of top level corporate executives (Berman and Miner 1985). Once again the entrepreneurs had the lower managerial motivation. The results gave no reason to believe that a desire to have something to manage was attracting large numbers of managerially motivated people into the ranks of entrepreneurs.

Research on the Task Theory

The next phase of the research introduced the by now, rather compelling hypothesis that task rather than hierarchic motivation should provide the key to understanding entrepreneurship. Miner, Smith, and Bracker (1989) compared 118 individuals who indicated they were involved in the founding of their companies with 41 manager-scientists who were not founders, but who worked in similar high technology firms. The sample of high technology entrepreneurs included substantial numbers of entrepreneurs who were not chief executive officers of their companies and/or who were not involved in major growth efforts—companies with very few employees. This latter consideration is particularly important given that entrepreneurs of low-growth companies—those that have increased their employment levels by less than 1.5 employees per year—constitute half of the high technology entrepreneur sample. The results of this study indicated a significant difference in task motivation favoring the entrepreneurs. In addition there was evidence that within the group of 118 entrepreneurs, task motivation was positively related to firm growth.

A second program of research comparing entrepreneurs and managers is that of Bellu (1988). His first study utilized groups of entrepreneurs from two geographical regions and managers at the vice-presidential level or above from the same two locations. The entrepreneurial firms tended to be consistently small, with over two-thirds having fewer than ten employees. Most were in retailing or services. The comparison managers were also working in small firms. A number of these comparison managers were operating in contexts that are essentially entrepreneurial. The net effects of these sample variations would be expected to be reduced task motivation in the entrepreneurial samples and perhaps increased task motivation in the managerial samples. Yet again there were consistent differences in favor of the entrepreneurs. Bellu, Davidsson, and Goldfarb (1989) subsequently extended this research to samples of entrepreneurs and managers from northern Italy, southern Italy, Israel, and Sweden. Three of the four comparisons produced clearly significant differences in favor of the entrepreneurs. In Sweden, although there was some supportive evidence, the entrepreneurs did not consistently have the higher task motivation.

A study by Jourdan (1987) compares the task motivation of entrepreneurs in bankruptcy with entrepreneurs who had achieved some level of success. No statistically significant differences between these criterion groups were identified. However, both groups had sufficiently high levels of task motivation to make it unlikely that differences would emerge. Furthermore, both groups appear to have had substantial records of both successes and failures in the past, thus bringing into question their designation as distinct criterion groups.

Research conducted by Bracker, Keats, Miner, and Pearson (1988) utilized a sample of entrepreneurs heading firms belonging to the American Electronics Association, in business for at least five years, and privately held. None had more than 100 employees, and the average revenues per year were just over $4 million. The task motivation of these entrepreneurs was also well above what has been found in managerial samples.

Overall, task theory research to date consistently supports the view that high task motivation people are attracted to entrepreneurship. However, there are clearly a number of entrepreneurial firms that grow so little as to exert only a very minimal influence on the employment statistics (Birley 1987). Removing these firms from the analyses, to focus on chief executive founders with larger enterprises, should help to provide greater insight into how task motivation operates; these are the entrepreneurial leaders.

RESEARCH DESIGN

Hypotheses

Based on the prior research, it seems reasonable to anticipate that task theory deals with constructs that play an important role in entrepreneurship. Accordingly, entrepreneurs can be expected to score high relative to non-entrepreneur managers on a measure of task motivation. The present research goes beyond past studies in testing the following major hypothesis:

Hypothesis 1(a). *The difference between entrepreneurs and managers (in favor of the former) on a measure of task motivation should be particularly pronounced when the group of entrepreneurs considered is limited to those operating in chief executive officer positions and to those heading firms that have grown significantly under the entrepreneurs (to at least 10 employees).*

Hyphothesis 1(b). *High growth founder-CEOs should obtain scores considerably higher than those obtained when a full range of entrepreneurs is studied.*

A second hypothesis derives from the differential patterns of results obtained when managerial and task motivation were studied among entrepreneurs and managers. This hypothesis may be stated in the null form as follows:

Hypothesis 2. *Within a diversified group containing substantial numbers of both entrepreneurs and managers, there should be no statistically significant relationship between measures of task motivation and managerial motivation. The two motive patterns are conceived as distinct entities.*

Measures

The Miner Sentence Completion Scale (MSCS)–Form T was used to test the initial, and major, hypothesis of this study. The MSCS–Form T and Form H were used to test the second hypothesis. In addition, various items of information were obtained from respondents regarding themselves and their firms.

Samples

The sample of high growth entrepreneurs used to test the first hypothesis was drawn from the author's files, built up over various previous studies. This sample contained all such individuals who were known to be founders and chief executives of their firms, and whose firms had grown to include at least 10 employees. In most instances this growth had occurred gradually, but there were several instances of quantum growth at a point very close to the inception of the firm. There were 65 individuals included. Four were women, the average educational level was one year of graduate work, and the average age was 46.1 years. The sample is very diverse both as to geographical location and area of entrepreneurial endeavor. The median number of employees achieved was 28 with the largest firm having 225. The median annual sales figure was $1.6 million; the largest such value was $14.5 million. These high growth entrepreneurs could be compared against the existing normative sample for the MSCS–T (Miner 1986). This sample contains 135 founder-entrepreneurs spread throughout the United States. Very small firms as well as larger ones are included, and the entrepreneurs may or may not be in a chief executive role. This normative sample appears to be quite typical, except for a heavy weighting on technologically innovative businesses.

The comparison managers were taken from the same source as the entrepreneurs, and represented all qualifying individuals. They numbered 71; of these 12 were chief executives (but not founders) and 24 reported directly to chief executives, primarily as vice presidents. The remainder were roughly equally distributed among middle and lower level managerial positions. Six were women; the average education level was virtually identical with that of the entrepreneurs, and the average age was 40.9 years. Like the entrepreneurs, the managers worked for a diverse array of companies both as to geographical location and industry. However, the managers were employed by much larger firms.

The sample used to test the second hypothesis contained a number of individuals drawn from the preceding samples, in fact, all 44 for whom both Form T and Form H protocols were available. There were 24 managers from 2 different companies, 20 entrepreneurs, and 23 students in a graduate entrepreneurship course—67 in all. The great majority lived in the Buffalo, New York area at the time of testing. There was substantial diversity across both the entrepreneurial and managerial domains.

RESULTS

As shown in Table 16.1 the high growth entrepreneurs studied have a Total Score mean of over 12, which places them at the 72nd percentile for entrepreneurs overall, using the published norms (Miner 1986). On the same scale the managers' score of less than 3 rates a percentile equivalent of 31. Thus there are roughly 40 percentile points between the two mean scores, over one and one-half standard deviations. For comparison purposes, it should be noted that the Total Score in the normative sample of entrepreneurs is 6.81. The growth-oriented, chief

Table 16.1

Miner Sentence Completion Scale–Form T Scores in Entrepreneur and Manager Samples

	High-Growth Entrepreneurs		Managers			
MSCS–T Measures	*M*	*SD*	*M*	*SD*	*t*	*p*
Total Score	12.14	6.10	2.66	5.75	9.32	< .01
Self-Achievement	3.54	2.22	.65	2.31	7.42	< .01
Avoiding Risks	1.68	2.15	–.20	2.71	4.48	< 01
Feedback of Results	.98	2.24	–.86	2.62	4.39	< .01
Personal Innovation	4.00	2.17	2.32	2.04	4.65	< .01
Planning for the Future	1.94	2.88	.75	2.45	2.61	< .01
N	65		71			

Note: MSCS–T = Miner Sentence Completion Scale–Form T.

executive entrepreneurs are distinctly more task motivated. The percentile equivalents for the subscales when comparisons are made with the normative sample are 69 for Self Achievement, 62 for Avoiding Risks, 67 for Feedback of Results, 64 for Personal Innovation, and 58 for Planning for the Future. The mean subscale scores in the normative sample are 1.91, .94, –.20, 2.99, and 1.17 respectively.

A two-group discriminant analysis applied to the data of Table 16.1 yields a canonical correlation of .66 with 84.56 percent of the cases correctly classified by the discriminant function. The standardized canonical discriminant function coefficients for the subscales are .59 for Self-Achievement, .49 for Avoiding Risks, .46 for Personal Innovation, .23 for Feedback of Results, and .17 for Planning for the Future.

These discriminant results can be compared with those obtained previously with an unselected sample of high technology entrepreneurs (Miner, Smith, and Bracker 1989). In that instance, when non-CEO founders and entrepreneurs with very small firms were included in the analysis, the canonical correlation was .25 and only 64.15 percent of the cases were correctly classified as entrepreneur or manager by Form T of the MSCS. The difference between the two correlation values of .41 points is highly significant ($t = 4.52, p < .01$). Thus, the hypothesized increase in discrimination anticipated when the analysis is restricted to chief executive entrepreneurs who have grown larger firms is in fact obtained. The effect size increases from 0.58 to 1.60.

Since the entrepreneurs and managers of Table 16.1 do not differ in educational level, the Form T results cannot be ascribed to that factor. However, the entrepreneurs are roughly five years older than the managers, a difference that is statistically significant ($t = 3.07, p < .01$). This difference is small in an absolute sense, and age correlates only .20 with Form T total score (due almost entirely to the greater risk taking propensity of younger subjects). Inspection of the Form T total score distributions indicates a very sizeable overconcentration of managers in the younger age categories, especially the 20s, and a similar overconcentration of entrepreneurs at the upper age levels, especially the 60s and 70s. When these two extreme groups are removed from the analysis to produce matched samples on age, with means at 43.7 and 43.5 years respectively for entrepreneurs and managers, the difference between the mean total scores for the two groups decreases by less than half a point. Clearly the age factor is not a meaningful contributor to the results in Table 16.1.

Table 16.2

Correlations between MSCS–T and MSCS–H Measures in a Sample of Managers and Entrepreneurs (N = 67)

	MSCS–T Measures					
MSCS–H Measures	Self-Achievement	Avoiding Risks	Feedback of Results	Personal Innovation	Planning for the Future	Total Score
Authority Figures	–.07	.13	–.13	–.11	.38**	.08
Competitive Games	.15	.06	.35**	.22	–.17	.22
Competitive Situations	.11	.05	.21	.16	.18	.26*
Assertive Role	–.21	.02	.00	–.20	.04	–.14
Imposing Wishes	.21	.01	.06	.06	.14	.19
Standing out from Group	–.10	.09	.11	.01	.24*	.12
Routine Administrative Functions	–.04	.19	.08	.15	.03	.16
Total Score	.04	.17	.25*	.12	.21	.29*

Note: MSCS = Miner Sentence Completion Scale.
$*p < .05$; $**p < .01$

The second hypothesis relates to the degree of association between the Form T and Form H measures. Are individuals with the motive patterns making for success in entrepreneurship also likely to be characterized by the motive patterns of effective managers? Table 16.2 contains the results obtained in this regard.

Of the forty-eight correlations in Table 16.2 only six achieve statistical significance at the .05 level or better. Although the two total scores are significantly related, the median correlation between measures from the two instruments is only .11. Clearly the relationship between task motivation and managerial motivation is not a strong one, but to the extent it exists, the association tends in a positive direction (there are only nine negative values in Table 16.2). Although these results should be treated with caution, because of the marginal significance, the data give some reason to believe that competitiveness (from managerial motivation) may enter into entrepreneurial motivation, and a desire for feedback (from task motivation) into managerial motivation.

RETURN TO CONCEPTUAL DEVELOPMENT

It is apparent that task motivation theory has its primary application in dealing with founders who head firms slated for growth. The theory has little relevance for the large number of organizations, such as those of a mom-and-pop nature or small professional practices, which never do and never were intended to achieve substantial growth. Probably it is the inclusion of large numbers of these non-growth or very slow growth firms in research samples that has produced the rather conflicting picture that currently exists insofar as entrepreneur personality dynamics are concerned (Brockhaus and Horwitz 1986; Begley and Boyd 1987). Certainly in the present instance, focusing on a more limited, growth-oriented group of entrepreneurs produced very strong evidence of distinctive personality patterns.

Given the very considerable attention focused on the entrepreneur-manager interface in the entrepreneurship literature, and the finding of some, although modest, positive relationship between entrepreneurial and managerial motivation in the present research, it appears that additional research journeys into this domain might well yield major new insights. Doing this, however, requires further conceptual development, beyond the theoretical framework considered previously.

The idea of an organizational life cycle owes a primary debt to Chandler (1962), although Chandler did not probe deeply into the early stages of his companies. Subsequently a number of life cycle concepts appeared with differentiations into a variety of stages. Among these are the formulations of Thain (1969), Steinmetz (1969), Greiner (1972), Scott (1973), Tuason (1973), and James (1973). In this period the major concern was with adding stages to those proposed by Chandler, particularly in the later, more mature period of a firm's existence. Where the earlier, more entrepreneurial, phases of firm development were considered in these theories, treatment was limited to a statement that the entrepreneur would have to shift to a more managerial style or actually relinquish leadership to a manager.

A decade later there was another burst of activity in the life cycle area, but again the emphasis was primarily on specifications regarding the states to be achieved at the mature end of the cycle (Galbraith and Nathanson 1978; Leontiades 1980; Kimberly and Miles 1980).

More recently there has been a shift to concentration on the entrepreneurial end of the life cycle. Typical formulations are those of Galbraith (1982), Churchill and Lewis (1983), and Mintzberg (1984). In these views the distinction between the early entrepreneurial stage and the later managerial one is clearly specified. For example (Galbraith 1982, 74):

> The task changes from: Invent and make it, to . . . Make it profitable.
>
> The people change from: Jacks of all trades, to . . . Business people, planners.
>
> The rewards change from: Equity, nonbureaucratic climate, make a mark, to . . . Career, salary.
>
> The processes change from: Informal, face-to-face contact, personal control, to . . . Formal control, planning and budget, information systems.
>
> The structure changes from: Informal, little needed, to . . . Functional with overlays, division of labor, decentralize.
>
> The leadership changes from: Quarterback, to . . . Manager.

Using hierarchic and task theory and assuming that motivation-organization fit is the key to effective pursuit of goals, the following propositions are set forth:

1. Many chief executive entrepreneurs will prefer the founder role and, following the corridor principle (Ronstadt 1988), will undertake a variety of new ventures. In such cases they are likely to turn over control of established ventures to managers to ensure growth. When this is done the managers will need high managerial motivation and will need to create a hierarchic system to work in, if the firm is to prosper. However, in the start-up stage of each enterprise the desired fit is that of a high task motivation entrepreneur and a task system.
2. Other entrepreneurs will prefer to found a company and steer it through major growth. For this to be possible one of two scenarios must be followed:
    a. The entrepreneur maintains a task system at the top of the organization, while gradually adding or getting others to add layers of hierarchy below as the company grows. These layers below will need to be staffed with high motivation to manage people and run as a bureaucracy. The resulting composite system can survive a transition from one entrepreneur to another, if the composite state is established, and stable, and if the new leader has high task motivation. Often these transitions will involve a relative.

b. The entrepreneur converts the system from a task to a hierarchic form as growth proceeds. At the same time the entrepreneur will need to shift from satisfying primarily task motives at work to satisfying primarily hierarchic motives. This is a situation where the chief executive entrepreneur needs to be high on both task and hierarchic motivation.

3. Inherent in the preceding propositions is the view that small organizations need task motivation in the chief executive to grow, and a task system to match, but that at some point size becomes such that the entrepreneur cannot control the system using face-to-face means. When exactly this point occurs depends on the capabilities of the entrepreneur and the degree of stress on the system. In any event, when the pure task system has been extended to its breaking point, hierarchy needs to be introduced in some form or the firm will either shrink or fail.
4. Many, in fact most, small firms are founded by entrepreneurs who lack the task motivation necessary to engineer growth. A task system exists, but there is insufficient energy to drive it. These firms are vulnerable to environmental stress, but barring acute stress may survive for long periods; they do not grow unless new leadership, and with it higher task motivation, is introduced.

This theoretical extension constitutes an agenda for the next stage of motivational research in entrepreneurship. It may suffer the fate of the original managerial motivation approach or it may prove as successful as the task motivation approach has to date.

The research results reported clearly establish the significance of task motivation for entrepreneurship. At the same time the domain in which the task theory best functions has been defined more precisely—entrepreneurs who are chief executives and thus wield substantial influence, organizations that have grown to some size at one time or another, and entrepreneurs with sufficiently high levels of education so that the necessary know-how for growth is present; these are what have been labeled high-growth entrepreneurs.

The discussion here has focused on managers and entrepreneurs, and the domains of hierarchic and task theories. However, work with a third parallel theory, that of professional motivation, suggests that at some point this theory too will need to be introduced into the theoretical mix (Miner 1980a). Many new start-ups are professional organizations. What effects do these professional considerations have on the relationships studied and hypothesized here? These are matters which extend beyond the purview of this article; yet it is well to recognize that they ultimately will need to be incorporated in a truly comprehensive theory.

CHAPTER 17

MANAGERS IN THE PEOPLE'S REPUBLIC OF CHINA

INTRODUCTION

The research on Chinese managers is contained in two articles published as follows:

- *Journal of Applied Psychology* (Miner, Chen, and Yu 1991)*
- *Journal of Applied Behavioral Science* (Chen, Yu, and Miner 1997)**

Chao C. Chen was born in China and came to this project as a graduate student at the State University of New York at Buffalo; he continued as a faculty member at Rutgers University. He participated in the first article (Miner, Chen, and Yu 1991) and led in spearheading the development and writing of the second (Chen, Yu, and Miner 1997) at a later date. K. C. Yu, a professor of human resources management and organizational behavior in the School of

* From John B. Miner, Chao-Chuan Chen, and K. C. Yu, "Theory Testing under Adverse Conditions: Motivation to Manage in the People's Republic of China," *Journal of Applied Psychology,* vol. 76, no. 3 (1991), 343–349. Copyright © 1991 American Psychological Association. Reprinted (or Adapted) with permission.

** From Chao-Chuan Chen, K. C. Yu, and John B. Miner, "Motivation to Manage: A Study of Women in Chinese State-owned Enterprises," *Journal of Applied Behavioral Science,* 33 (1997), 160–173. Copyright © 1997 NTL Institute, Inc. Reprinted (or Adapted) with permission.

Management at Dalian University of Technology, People's Republic of China served also as visiting professor at the State University of New York at Buffalo during the period in which the Miner Sentence Completion Scale (MSCS) tests were scored. He was instrumental in securing the MSCS and related data within China throughout. Yu's presence at Buffalo was part of an exchange program with Dalian, which operated over a number of years.

* * *

As described in hierarchic theory (Miner 1965a), managerial motivation ought to result in increased managerial success. Although managerial success may be measured in a variety of ways, the present research was concerned with the level of the management position attained—advancement into management, promotion rate within management ranks, achievement of a top management position, level in the management hierarchy, and the like. Above and beyond these considerations, managerial motivation is posited to be higher in the profit-oriented, corporate sector than in the nonprofit sector (that is, government, voluntary organizations, and the like).

These propositions have received considerable support from empirical research. However, this research has been conducted entirely within the United States. The present research extends the theory to the People's Republic of China. The hierarchic theory is rooted in the concept of bureaucracy (Weber 1968), and no major differences in its application across cultural boundaries was anticipated. Our assumption was that bureaucracy is bureaucracy wherever it is found and that, accordingly, the hypothesized relationships between motivation and success should hold within the appropriate organizational context irrespective of cultural differences. Such a view is consistent with the convergence hypothesis that there exists a managerial culture that transcends national cultural variations.

Research in the United States on the relationship between motivation to manage and hierarchic position has been reviewed previously (Miner 1965a, 1978c, 1985b). The data indicate substantial and consistent validity of both a concurrent and predictive nature. Initial research on different types of organizations (Miner 1974a) tended to support the view that profit-making organizations attract people with higher motivation to manage because such organizations offer higher pay and greater managerial discretion than do nonprofit organizations. A recent review of data from a large number of U.S. samples reinforced the conclusion that motivation to manage is lower in the nonprofit sector (Miner 1989).

CHINESE ORGANIZATIONAL FORMS

For motivation to manage to apply to Chinese organizations in the manner anticipated in hierarchic theory, it is essential that these organizations exhibit an essentially hierarchic form. If cultural influences, a socialist economy, a period of turbulent change, or other factors have produced organizational forms that deviate from the hierarchic bureaucracy to a substantial degree, then hierarchic theory and the concept of motivation to manage may not operate in the People's Republic of China as they do in the United States.

Only very limited research bearing on this question is available. The scientific fields involved are only just beginning to emerge within the People's Republic of China itself, and to date few researchers from the outside have conducted studies of Chinese organizations. Yet there are observational data that provide a sense of how organizational structures operate in modern China.

The Case for Hierarchy

In various lists of the primary features of Chinese culture, respect for hierarchic position and age is consistently emphasized (Boisot and Child 1988; Lockett 1988; Nevis 1983a). Weber used China as an example of a culture in which hierarchy has historically played a primary role (Gerth and Mills 1946). Within Chinese organizations, problems are continually referred upward, often to the point that upper-level managers are swamped with problems to be resolved (Lindsay and Dempsey 1983; Lockett 1988; Von Glinow and Teagarden 1988). Chinese society makes extensive use of centralized planning processes that require the use of hierarchic authority to achieve implementation (Holton 1985; Schermerhorn 1987). Chinese management is described as "basically hierarchical and very autocratic (Nelson and Reeder 1985, 24). In spite of periodic attacks on bureaucratic institutions, most notably during the Cultural Revolution, China appears to have retained the bureaucratic form in most of its organizations (Laaksonen 1988; Shenkar 1984).

These observations are consistent in their emphasis on the strong role that hierarchy plays in Chinese society. In addition, there is at least one, more systematic study that supports this conclusion. Laaksonen (1984) used the interview measures of relative influence developed by the IDE international research group staff (1981) to compare Chinese and European organizations. Workers, foremen, and middle managers in China were found to have less influence than their counterparts in Europe, but this difference disappeared at the top management level. The disparity between top management and workers was particularly large in China. In China, as in Europe, however, influence levels advanced steadily as managers moved up the organizational hierarchy.

The Case against Hierarchy

Although the evidence treated in the previous section holds out the prospect that the hypotheses derived from hierarchic theory will prove valid in the People's Republic of China, there are additional considerations and arguments that cloud this conclusion. One difficulty is that although Chinese culture is permeated by hierarchy, it also is permeated by collective orientations and groups. Small groups, or workshops, are used for socialization in organizations, but they also may undermine hierarchy (Lockett 1988; Myers 1987; Nevis 1983b). The Chinese have a strong predilection for meetings that are most consistent with power equalization (Nelson and Reeder 1985), and there has increasingly been a resort to some form of voting as a method of selecting people for supervisory responsibilities, following the Yugoslav model (Helburn and Shearer 1984; Warner 1986). Various informal, political relationships may also be detrimental to official, hierarchic authority (Lockett 1988).

Other forces thwarting hierarchy are inherent in Maoist ideology (Shenkar and Ronen 1987). Anything elitist tends to be opposed; this was especially true during the period of the Cultural Revolution. More recently, the emphasis on centralized planning has been joined by a shift toward a free-market economy (Holton 1985; Zhuang and Whitehill 1989). Although in other contexts such changes need not reflect a repudiation of hierarchy, given the highly planned socialistic system that has characterized China for so many years, a move to a more market-oriented approach does reflect a movement away from totally hierarchic forms. At one time, China's labor unions also represented a major threat to managerial hierarchies, and this no doubt continues to be true in some instances today. However, the Communist party has tended to assume the traditional union role so that the unions now appear to lack much influence (Hunt and Meindl 1988; Townsend, 1980).

The managerial role in China at the present time is clearly a confused one, as the following quote indicates:

> Managers . . . are given the responsibility for performance but denied the legitimate authority for achieving it. The increase in managerial rationality and autonomy that could result from reducing the involvement of the supervisory bureaucracy in a firm's operations and clarifying enterprise objectives is immediately drained away by a workforce that has secured for itself large tracts of managerial discretion. Chinese enterprise managers, in effect, are caught today in a pincer movement between the competing claims of a tax-maximizing state and a welfare-maximizing workforce (Boiset and Child 1988, 518).

China also has no clear model for the use of its managerial resources (Warner 1986). A central factor contributing to the confused managerial model is the parallel authority structure, consisting of the administrative system headed by the factory director on the one hand and the Communist party system headed by the first secretary of the branch committee on the other (Henley and Nyaw 1986; Schermerhorn 1987). In years past, the political party component was clearly dominant in organizations; authority was not blurred. But with recent changes this is no longer true. The situation may be described as follows:

> Currently the situation is confused. The unresolved tension between commercial and ideological values leaves authority relations uncertain. In a context of customary risk aversiveness, leadership and decision-making in China is therefore often slow and hesitant (Hunt and Meindl 1988, 10).

In short, there is some reason to believe that many Chinese organizations are characterized not so much by hierarchy as by what Mintzberg (1983) called a *political arena.* Accordingly, it becomes uncertain whether the hypotheses of hierarchic theory can be confirmed under the adverse conditions (for the theory) that exist in China today. Hierarchy may have become sufficiently blurred by competing forces as to become unrecognizable. Certainly there are enough arguments in favor of this view to give it some credibility (Townsend 1980; Wall 1990).

METHOD

Sample

Data were obtained from 170 employed individuals at locations in the vicinity of Dalian, People's Republic of China. Of these 55 were in managerial positions; 131 were men and 39 were women. The largest group (n = 112) worked in enterprises of a profit-making nature: 94 were employed by the Dalian Harbor Bureau, an organization now placed on a for-profit basis, and 18 worked for a diverse array of enterprises and were attending a management training program at the Managerial Cadre College in Dalian. The remaining subjects (n = 58) were employed in the nonprofit sector: 51 worked for the party committee of Dalian's city government, and the remaining 7 subjects were obtained from the management training program at the Managerial Cadre College.

Because of the concentration of Dalian Harbor Bureau employees in the enterprise sample, it is important to provide somewhat more detail on this organization. Admittedly, its classification as for-profit does not have quite the same meaning as it would within the Western market economy. In any planned economy, there are a wide range of institutional constraints on business organizations, private or public. However, the profit-nonprofit differentiation provides an important distinction within the Chinese context. As part of the reforms in the 1970s and early 1980s, some business organizations were granted sufficient managerial autonomy to allow them to retain part of their profits (Tan 1989). Certain of these enterprises opted to be fully responsible for their own profits and losses after paying all required taxes. Dalian Harbor Bureau was one of the latter. This managerial autonomy sets Dalian Harbor Bureau clearly apart from party and government institutions on the one hand and from business institutions with no autonomy on the other.

In its original form, Dalian Harbor Bureau was both an administrative unit and a production enterprise. As a consequence of reform, the administrative function was spun off and assumed by the Dalian Port Committee, a nonprofit organization. This separation of functions is a clear indication of the for-profit and nonprofit distinction. Although making a profit is the legitimate right of the for-profit enterprise, an emphasis on profits by party, government, or educational institutions would be considered dereliction of duty.

Measures

Respondents provided information on their position level, education level, and age. Alternatives for position level were party and government leader, middle-level cadre, professional, and administrative clerk. Alternatives for education level were university bachelor or above, college associate degree, senior middle school or secondary technical diploma, and junior middle school diploma.

A culturally adapted Chinese language version of the Miner Sentence Completion Scale–Form H (MSCS–H; Miner 1964) was used to measure motivation to manage. Cultural adaptation was deemed necessary in light of findings that Chinese values only partially overlap with Western values (Bond et al. 1987). The scale contains 40 items, only 35 of which are scored. The stems were selected to hide the true purposes of measurement. Consequently respondents are in no position to select their responses to present a consciously predetermined picture of their motivation with regard to managerial work.

Each individual response is scored as positive, neutral, or negative in accordance with guidelines and examples presented in the scoring guide (Miner 1964). The neutral category is used when, in extending the stem to make a complete sentence, the subject says nothing that would provide an indication of attitude or motivation with regard to the stem concept.

The subscales of the test are intended to measure the component variables of the role-motivation theory of managerial effectiveness (Miner 1965a). Subscale scores are obtained by subtracting the number of negatively scored responses within each set of five items from the number of positively scored items in that set. In all cases, subscale scores can vary from +5 to –5.

When all subscale scores are combined into a single index, the total score is obtained. This, of course, can vary from +35 to –35. The total score reflects the overall positive-versus-negative trend of the responses to the 35 scorable items and thus provides a measure of the extent to which an individual is motivated to manage.

In studies conducted with the standard MSCS–H, mean scores obtained independently by experienced scorers tended to be quite similar, and total scores correlated in the vicinity of .92 (Miner 1985b). Scorer reliability for the subscales is at essentially the same level.

Table 17.1

Changes in Wording Introduced in the Chinese Version of the Miner Sentence Completion Scale–Form H

Item no.	Original Scale	Chinese Version
1	family doctor	teacher
3	shooting a rifle	target shooting
10	political office	a top position
12	country club dances	dancing
14	federal	supreme court
16	dictating	drafting outlines
18	running my own business	in charge of my own affairs
24	golf	table tennis
32	driving a car	riding a motorcycle
39	yacht	boat

Note: Miner Sentence Completion Scale–Form H.

The culturally adapted scale used in this research contained twenty-five of the same items as the standard instrument. Eight items had been changed previously for use in a study of Chinese students (Singleton, Kelley, Yao, and White 1987). Two more items were changed in this study for essentially the same reasons—to make the instrument compatible with Chinese culture and the day-to-day experiences of Chinese people. The actual changes are noted in Table 17.1.

The culturally adapted instrument was translated into Chinese by Chao-Chuan Chen and translated back to English by K. C. Yu. Agreement was good, although a few adjustments in the translation to Chinese were made.

A problem unique to the sentence completion method of measurement is that if respondents complete the sentences in a language other than English, and actual scoring is to be done in English, a translation step must intervene. Because answers were scored by John B. Miner, who has no knowledge of Chinese, the responses had to be translated into English. John B. Miner did the scoring because he was already experienced with the procedure and his doing so would provide consistency between this study and many of the studies conducted in the United States.

As a check on the translation process, both Chinese-speaking authors independently translated 15 completed protocols into English: these 30 records were then scored by John B. Miner. The level of disagreement between the two translations was such that over 7 percent of the items were scored differently. Although discussion easily produced consensus on a translation and score, the original disagreement was greater than could be accepted if the translation task was to be divided. The disagreements were spread over 25 of the 35 items, and the consensus scores favored one translator as often as the other.

One benefit of the consensus discussions was that they produced a shared understanding of both the MSCS scoring process and areas of difficulty in translating from Chinese to English. It was hoped that this understanding would yield greater agreement subsequently. This proved to be the case. When a second set of 15 protocols was translated independently, disagreement was reduced to 3 percent—approximately one item per record. Again the disagreements were spread over a number of items (12 of the 35), and the scores emerging from a consensus discussion favored the two translations equally. Because the second round of consensus discussions had in all likelihood reduced disagreement even further, and because

Table 17.2

Comparison of the Miner Sentence Completion Scale–Form H (MSCS–H) **and Its Culturally Adapted Chinese Equivalent**

MSCS–H Measures	Correlation between Measures	MSCS–H		Chinese Equivalent		
		M	*SD*	*M*	*SD*	*t*
Total Score	.86**	–.40	4.66	1.20	4.62	4.08**
Authority Figures	.71**	.23	1.39	.10	1.34	.76
Competitive Games	.61**	.78	1.51	.73	1.84	.21
Competitive Situations	.58**	–1.23	1.75	–.73	1.68	2.02*
Assertive Role	.65**	–1.00	1.62	.00	1.74	4.47**
Imposing Wishes	.68**	.85	1.48	.68	1.46	.94
Standing Out from Group	.79**	.63	1.31	.43	1.50	1.35
Routine Administrative Functions	.73**	–.65	1.81	.00	1.75	3.13**

Note: N = 40. MSCS = Miner Sentence Completion Scale.
*$p < .05$; **$p < .01$

the level of measured disagreement was now quite low in any event, Chao-Chuan Chen and K. C. Yu each translated half of the remaining 140 protocols.

Comparability of the Culturally Adapted Scale

Changing almost 30 percent of the MSCS–H items to achieve a better cultural fit raises the possibility that construct validity may have suffered. Every effort was made to select revised stems that were conceptually similar to the ones replaced, and scoring of the 10 new items followed the same guidelines used previously. Still, there was a need to check empirically on the comparability of measures. Accordingly, English-language versions of the standard MSCS–H and of the culturally adapted Chinese equivalent were administered at a one-week interval to a sample of 40 graduate business students at the State University of New York at Buffalo. Half of the group completed the standard version first, and half completed the Chinese equivalent first.

RESULTS

Comparability Analysis

Because no order effects were identified, the total comparability sample of 40 subjects was used for analysis. The results are given in Table 17.2. The correlations between the two instruments are essentially what would be expected, given the interval between administrations and previous data on repeat reliability (Miner 1965a; Miner, Wachtel, and Ebrahimi 1989). On the basis of this criterion, the revisions do not appear to have altered the standard scale to any meaningful degree.

However, comparison of the means for the two measures yields a quite different conclusion. The Chinese equivalent total score is substantially higher, and three of the seven subscale scores are higher as well. These results are entirely attributable to the changed items. For the 25 items that remained the same, the mean total scores were .50 and .35 for the standard and Chinese versions, respectively, $t\,(39) = .41$, *ns*. For the 10 items that were changed, the mean

Table 17.3

Correlations between Culturally Adapted Miner Sentence Completion Scale–Form H (MSCS–H) and Position Level

MSCS–H Measures	Total Sample (N = 170)	For-profit Sample (N = 112)	Nonprofit Sample (N = 58)
Total Score	.35**	.40**	.25*
Authority Figures	.10	.18*	–.11
Competitive Games	.08	.18*	–.08
Competitive Situations	.19**	.17*	.22*
Assertive Role	.19**	.15	.22*
Imposing Wishes	.24**	.25**	.22*
Standing Out from Group	.09	.01	.22*
Routine Administrative Functions	.30**	.30**	.22*

*$p < .05$; **$p < .01$
Note: MSCS = Miner Sentence Completion Scale.

scores were –.90 and .85, for the standard and Chinese versions, respectively, $t\ (39) = 5.22$, $p < .01$. Overall, construct comparability was maintained, but direct comparisons between mean scores on the instruments are not justified.

Tests of Theory

Correlations between the adapted MSCS–H and the four-point position-level scale are presented in Table 17.3. The total-score findings are consistently positive and significant. The for-profit sample correlation was higher than that for the nonprofit sample, but not significantly so. The level of correlation is roughly equal to that obtained in the United States (Miner 1985b). With two exceptions, the subscale correlations were positive, and many were significant; the median correlation, however, was only .19.

The scores of managers (those in the two upper position levels) are compared with those of nonmanagers in Table 17.4. The results for position level closely parallel those presented in Table 17.3. Again the findings for the for-profit sample were more pronounced. The total-score effect size in favor of the for-profit managers was .85; for the nonprofit managers, it was .57.

Within the two-way analysis of variance (ANOVA) presented in Table 17.4, the for-profit sample scores were indeed higher, but only marginally so. The total-score figures in Table 17.4 approximate significance ($p < .07$), and two subscale values are clearly significant.

Analysis of the Twenty-five Unchanged Items

One way of substantiating the previous results was to conduct the same analyses with the 25 items that did not change when the culturally adapted Chinese equivalent was created. Such analyses were restricted to the total score because the subscales were affected unequally by the changes; one subscale was totally unaffected, whereas on another subscale three of the five stems were changed.

The test-retest reliability for the 25 unchanged items was .84. This contrasts with the total-score correlation between measures of .86 in Table 17.2 and a Spearman-Brown corrected estimate, when the 25 items were increased to the standard 35, of .88. Clearly the

Table 17.4

Analysis of Variance Results Comparing Managers and Nonmanagers in the For-Profit and Nonprofit Samples

		Mean Score			Mean Score		
MSCS–H Measures	Main Effect	Managers (N = 55)	Non-managers (N = 115)	*F*	For-profit Sample (N = 112)	Nonprofit Sample (N = 58)	*F*
Total Score	13.13**	4.95	1.45	23.12**	3.01	1.76	2.39
Authority Figures	2.31*	.78	.57	1.07	.76	.41	3.37*
Competitive Games	1.07	1.05	.63	2.05	.79	.71	.05
Competitive Situations	3.04*	.49	–.05	5.71**	.17	.03	.25
Assertive Role	2.58*	1.15	.55	4.29*	.83	.57	.70
Imposing Wishes	5.38**	.16	–.55	10.66**	–.29	–.36	.05
Standing Out from Group	.98	.20	.02	1.39	.04	.16	.66
Routine Administrative Functions	11.65**	1.11	.29	17.16**	.71	.24	5.21*

Note: MSCS—H = Miner Sentence Completion Scale—Form H.
$*p < .05$; $**p < .01$

25-item measure is psychometrically comparable to other versions, having essentially the same reliability. The 25-item measure correlated .89 with the Chinese equivalent in the total sample of 170.

Replicating the analyses of Table 17.3 with the 25 unchanged items produced a position-level correlation of .33 ($p < .01$) for the total sample, .40 ($p < .01$) for the enterprise sample, and .20 ($p < .07$) for the nonprofit sample. Conducting the same analyses presented in Table 17.4 yielded a main-effect F of 12.89 (*dfs* = 1, 169; $p < .01$). The manager–nonmanager comparison was replicated, $F(1, 169) = 23.52$, $p < .01$. The for-profit–nonprofit comparison remained below the level of significance, $F(1, 169) = 1.63$.

These analyses with the 25-item MSCS–H, in which changed items were not a factor, consistently support the results previously reported. The results do not appear to reflect some artifact of the measurement process.

DISCUSSION

The hypothesized relationships between motivation to manage and job level do appear to be in evidence in the People's Republic of China. MSCS–H scores were positively correlated with job level in two independent samples (from the profit and nonprofit sectors), and managers' scores exceeded those of sub-managerial workers in both samples. In spite of adverse conditions of no small magnitude, the data are consistent with the view that hierarchic systems are alive and well in China. The motivational patterns found are those that typically predominate when hierarchy prevails. Yet it would be premature to conclude that the question of the role of hierarchy in Chinese organizations is fully settled. The MSCS–H derives from Western culture, and the adaptations introduced here may well have been insufficient to fully remove that influence. Furthermore, little is known about such factors as instrument reliability and construct validity among Chinese subjects. Clearly, further research linking hierarchic motivation and hierarchic structure in China is needed.

The second hypothesis, that motivation to manage is higher when profit incentives are present than when profit considerations are lacking, was supported, but only weakly. The lack of substantial differences between the two sectors is not surprising. Profit-making has been a reality in China for only a short period of time and interorganizational job mobility tends to be discouraged. As a result, a major influx of highly motivated managers into the profit-oriented enterprises would not be expected. Moreover, managerial discretion in the enterprises is still by no means the equal of that in the United States, and substantial power can be exercised within the nonprofit sector. Thus, the differential attractiveness of the two sectors for a person who really likes to manage is unlikely in China to approximate the size it has attained in the United States.

Given the lack of an external managerial labor market and of interorganizational mobility generally in China, a question arises as to how the results reported here could have come about. Several considerations are relevant to this question (Von Glinow and Chung 1989). Chinese management is highly generalized, and as a result, horizontal mobility within organizations appears to be greater than in the United States. Furthermore, the lack of vertical movement across organizations fosters more such movement within them. When these factors are combined with the very labor intensive nature of Chinese organizations, it appears that movement within internal labor markets could be sufficient to account for the results obtained.

But why should this movement follow the dictates of hierarchic role-motivation theory? In China, moral and ideological purity historically have been the criteria for promotion, and thus the politically competent, much more than the managerially competent, often have moved up the hierarchic ladder most rapidly: For roughly ten years now, however, performance, knowledge, and merit have taken on considerably greater significance; this emphasis is clearly part of the move toward for-profit enterprises. Furthermore, the existence of production targets suggests that managerial competence cannot be completely ignored by Chinese organizations. Finally, although the relationship between hierarchic motivation and promotion is known to be mediated through performance in the United States, it is not known to what extent that is true in China. The motives explained in hierarchic theory are those likely to get people promoted even in the absence of outstanding performance; people with high motivation to manage tend to (1) make themselves visible to those who have the power to promote, (2) be highly adaptable, and (3) be politically astute. We suspect that those who progress in Chinese management are competent in both a political and performance sense, as are promotable managers in the United States, but we know nothing about the relative balance involved. This, too, is a research task for the future.

The results reported here derive from a sentence completion measure, which by its nature contains a potential for subjectivity. Could this subjectivity have influenced the results? One line of evidence involves the scorer reliability findings; coefficients in the .90s have been obtained in many studies, and mean scores have not differed significantly. Furthermore, research indicates that when the scorer is knowledgeable, and accordingly makes full use of the scoring guide, the comparability of the free-response and multiple-choice MSCS–H is very high (Perham 1989). In short, the standardized scoring procedures used with the MSCS substantially reduce subjectivity.

Another consideration in evaluating the possibility that subjectivity in scoring influenced the results is that we were open to any outcome. Arguments favoring hierarchic theory and those opposing it seemed equally convincing, as noted in the earlier discussion of Chinese organizational forms. There was no a priori expectation, and in fact the data do not fully support the hierarchic hypotheses; the for-profit/nonprofit differentiation was marginally significant at best.

Finally, there is ample evidence that the MSCS–H possesses common variance with a number of measures of what appear to be similar constructs, such as the dominance and low abasement measures in Gough's Adjective Check List and the self-assurance and decisiveness measures in Ghiselli's Self-Description Inventory (Miner 1977b, 1978c). The MSCS–H is not a measure in search of definition and thus highly dependent on support from alternative operationalizations. This does not preclude the desirability, as with any measure, of carrying out research with alternative indexes. There is a definite need for such research in China; unfortunately, at present this research is not possible.

A recent study of work goals in China (Shenkar and Ronen 1987) presented certain evidence consistent with the convergence hypothesis from a source not previously considered. The convergence hypothesis holds that processes inherent in economic development and industrialization lead to universal attitudes, values, and beliefs regardless of the national or cultural context. In particular a homogeneous managerial culture is hypothesized to develop as a function of industrial development and increasing international interaction. The present study appears to provide further evidence in support of the convergence hypothesis. In spite of the many differences between the United States and the People's Republic of China, and numerous arguments against convergence, the present data indicate many more similarities than differences.

EXTENSIONS TO CHINESE WOMEN MANAGERS

Managerial motivation has long been established as an important predictor of managerial effectiveness and success. In particular, organizational research on McClelland's needs theory and Miner's role motivation theory has shown that the need for power and the motivation to perform managerial roles predict the hierarchical level of managers both cross-sectionally and longitudinally (McClelland and Boyatzis 1982; Miner 1993). Those who possess stronger managerial motives were rated as more effective and rose faster and higher in the managerial hierarchy in large and bureaucratic organizations.

A number of questions can be raised regarding this line of research. First, how applicable are the managerial motivation theories applied to women, because "many of the existing theories of management were developed with male managers in mind" (Powell 1993, 152)? Second, how applicable are theories advanced in the West to nations that differ in economic development and cultural tradition? A combination of the two questions is the following: How applicable are these theories to women in different countries who participate in various degrees in employment and management? In this study we address this third question by testing Miner's role motivation theory on women employees in Chinese state-owned enterprises. On one hand, we examined the relationship between managerial motivation and managerial success among these women and, on the other hand, we compared them with Chinese men in their managerial motivation.

Assessing the level and the impact of managerial motivation of women is of particular importance in today's global business environment. Global competition has led to more attention to the utilization of women's work and managerial talents. Yet women's underrepresentation in work and management is a common finding all over the world, even though the degree may vary from country to country (Adler and Israeli 1994). This underrepresentation of women in management has been attributed to women's motivation to enter and succeed in managerial positions (Powell 1993). Findings about the strength of their managerial motivation provide empirical evidence regarding the validity of such attribution. Furthermore, companies could act upon the findings to better use women's existing strong motivation or to enhance that motivation by identifying factors that led to weak motivation. Knowledge of women's managerial motivation in different countries therefore can help global companies develop informed human resource policies for addressing the underutilization of women's talents.

Managerial Motivation and Success

The relationship between managerial motivation and success holds true for both men and women in real organizations (see Miner 1993 for a detailed report). These no-difference results were consistent with the conclusion that Powell (1993) reached upon reviewing the research literature on sex differences in managers. Powell concluded that U.S. women managers are as committed and as motivated as their male counterparts. Furthermore, there were findings that countered the stereotypical views of sex differences among American managers. "Female managers may conform more closely than male managers to the ideal motivation profile originally developed with male managers in mind" (Powell 1993, 164).

Applicability of Managerial Motivation Theory in China

Role motivation theories were not advanced from a cross-cultural perspective. Rather, their major premises were the role requirements of different types of organizations. Mainly because of the hierarchical nature of bureaucracy, managers have to respect authority and yet be willing to compete and become distinctive in order to advance in the system. Considerations in the applicability of managerial motivation theory to China lie primarily in the compatibility of the managerial motives to Chinese cultural norms.

Relevant to the concerns are the two cultural dimensions identified by Hofstede (1980): power distance and individualism versus collectivism. Power distance refers to the extent in which power inequality (for instance, between the supervisor and the subordinate) is accepted. On this dimension, China and overseas Chinese regions are classified as high in power distance, whereas the United States is considered low to medium in power distance (Hofstede 1980). Individualism versus collectivism refers to the extent to which individual goals take precedence over organizational goals. On the dichotomy of individualism versus collectivism, the United States is on the individualist end, whereas China is on the collectivist end.

Managerial motives of respect for authority and imposing wishes clearly are compatible with the large power distance aspect of Chinese culture. Hierarchy is one primary principle of Confucian social philosophy (Bond 1986). Indeed, ancient China was an example of bureaucratic hierarchy in Weber's theory of bureaucracy (Gerth and Mills 1946). More recent organizational studies by Western management scholars have reached a high consensus on the hierarchical nature of Chinese organizations (Boisot and Child 1988; Lockett 1988; Nelson and Reeder 1985; Shenkar 1984; Von Glinow and Teagarden 1988).

The compatibility with Chinese culture of other managerial motives, however, is open to question. Desires to assert oneself, to compete, and to be distinctive and different may seem to be individualistically oriented, and therefore not appropriate for the study of Chinese managers. This conclusion can be questioned with two counter-arguments. One is that collectivism and competitiveness are not necessarily incompatible. The Mandarin meritocratic tradition, still reflected in the fierce competition for college entrance in China, is one example of this. Collectivism does not preclude competition; so long as it is believed that competition is beneficial to the accomplishment of collective goals, it can be endorsed, as has been the case in recent Chinese enterprise reform (Chen, Meindl, and Hunt 1997; Jackson 1992).

The second counterargument is that cross-cultural differences do not automatically apply to within-culture variations. Compared with American managers, because of their differences in individualism-collectivism, Chinese managers may be less willing to be distinctive and to stand out from the group. However, this expectation does not necessarily mean that within China, managers will be less willing to stand out than will nonmanagers. Actually, there are reasons to expect the opposite to be true. First, managerial role performance itself involves being distinctive and standing out (Mintzberg 1973). It is hard to want to be a manager without wanting to be differentiated. Second, Triandis (1995) stated that within a culture, individualist values are correlated with class status, education, and modernity. On average, Chinese managers may be of a higher class, may be better educated, and may hold more modernistic views than do nonmanagerial employees. Finally, M. Chen (1995) differentiated Confucian cardinal relationships into predetermined (such as father and son) and voluntarily contracted types (such as friendship). In the former, the self is underdeveloped and constrained by the fixed status and responsibilities; in the latter, the self plays a more dynamic role. We would argue that the dynamic self is demonstrated in horizontal peer relationships, which include both competition and cooperation through horizontal network building (Redding 1993). In summary, collectivism is not necessarily incompatible with the motives prescribed by Miner for managers in bureaucratic organizations. It therefore remains an empirical question whether Chinese managers would be more or less competitive, assertive, and outstanding than are Chinese nonmanagerial employees.

Positioning the Study of Female Managers

Initial research in China yielded supporting evidence for the managerial role motivation theory. It has been found that within China, motivation to manage distinguished managers from nonmanagers. In particular, higher level managers were more likely to have stronger motives of competition, assertiveness, and imposing wishes. This study sought to contribute to the literature by replicating Miner, Chen, and Yu (1991) on the applicability of role motivation theory in China. More important, it examined whether such applicability holds for both men and women managers in China.

Chinese Women's Managerial Motivation

Management scholars have only recently begun to look at worldwide issues related to women in management (Adler and Israeli 1988, 1994). As there is little direct knowledge about the questions we raised, we were forced to resort to reports regarding the general status of Chinese women in the workplace to formulate our initial expectations for the conduct of this study. Korabik (1994) gave a comprehensive, albeit brief, review of the status of Chinese women in organizations and management. On the basis of this review, one could find reasons to expect that Chinese women may have either high or low motivation to manage and that this motivation may or may not affect women's advancement in management. Here we identify major arguments on each side.

There are a number of factors that may contribute to lower managerial motivation in Chinese working women. One is that China has one of the longest feudal histories in the world, and in that system women were in the bottom echelon of the hierarchy of power and authority. According to Confucian principles of governance and morality, the subservience of women to men (fathers, husbands, brothers, and sons) was a virtue. Dominance, ambition, and achievement were nonvirtuous desires for women to possess. To the extent that such traditional beliefs still persist, they should adversely affect the level of Chinese women's managerial motivation. Second, despite the fact that the Communist revolution ideologically promoted gender equality, men still dominate powerful positions in organizations of China's Communist party, governments, and businesses. Women therefore may be less motivated to pursue managerial careers. Third, negative stereotypes indicating that women are emotional, narrow-minded, and vengeful, and thus unfit or even dangerous when they occupy positions of power, are still widespread in China. Such stereotypes, when internalized by Chinese women, would inhibit them from seeking managerial positions.

Despite these possible negative impacts on Chinese women's managerial motivation, there are positive considerations as well. The first is the Maoist ideology of gender equality, which is diametrically contrary to the Confucian ideology of male superiority. Since the founding of the People's Republic of China (PRC), laws have been passed to ensure women's political, cultural, economic, and social equality. Although reaching gender equality has been a long and continuous process in China, the achievements during the last half century are tremendous compared with China's past, or even with developed countries such as the United States (Tien 1986). In 1949, when the PRC was founded, employed women accounted for only 7 percent of the workforce; in 1992, however, the figure was 38 percent. Women's contribution to family income went from 20 percent in the 1950s to 40 percent in the 1990s. In 1982, Chinese working women made up 43 percent of the total population, higher than the percentages enjoyed by American women (35.3 percent) or Japanese women (36 percent) ("Historic Liberation" 1995).

The second positive factor contributing to managerial motivation in Chinese women is the rapid increase in education among women since 1949. For instance, there were nine times as many women in college in 1983 as there were in 1949 (Hao and Zhou 1985). Female college students majoring in engineering in China accounted for 27 percent of university engineering graduates, compared with 15 percent in the United States; 37 percent of Chinese scientists and technicians were female, compared with 12.2 percent in the United States (Dong 1995). Because women with college degrees are the major source of female managers in China, increased education should directly stimulate Chinese women's motivation to pursue managerial occupations.

A third factor that boosted women's political and cultural equality with men is the Cultural Revolution, which occurred between 1966 and 1976, in which Mao's "women hold half the sky" was one of the most popular revolutionary slogans. The Cultural Revolution had a pervasive effect on young women in their formative years, from teenage to the early twenties. During this tumultuous period, women's femininity was criticized as a petty bourgeois characteristic, whereas their masculinity was praised. In this period, the models for women were revolutionary, militant, and ambitious. This defeminization of women can be seen in the masculine names given to many females born in this period. Indeed, many young women changed their names to sound more revolutionary, following the example of a famous Red Guard who changed her name from "Bin-bin" (gentle and courteous) to "Yao-wu" (Be militant) upon Mao's suggestion. During this period, there was a surge of heroines not only on the stages of the Peking Opera, where party leaders often were portrayed by women, but on the real-life political stage as well. Women appeared on the Revolutionary Committees in all organizations and at all government levels.

One final factor that may have had an effect on women's managerial motivation is the one-child-per-family policy enforced by the Chinese government. Although this policy is not without some negative effects on women, it does encourage women to pursue careers in the workplace by substantially freeing them from child care (Lu 1984).

The above review does not present a complete picture about women's managerial motivation. Nevertheless, it does suggest that women in China in the 1990s can no longer be stereotyped as content with being subordinate to men, or as lacking the motivation to exercise power and influence. After reviewing the various factors that have facilitated or hindered women's advancement in management, Korabik (1994) concluded that "it will probably be many years before Chinese women managers truly have the opportunity to 'hold up half the sky.' In the meantime, their 'long march' toward full equality with men continues" (125).

Method

Measures

In this study, respondents provided information on their job level, education, sex, age, and work unit. Job levels were top cadre, middle-level cadre, professional, and administrative clerk. Education had four levels: university bachelor or above, college associate decree, senior middle school or secondary technical diploma, and junior middle school diploma. Age was broken into four groups: 25 years or younger, 26 to 36 years, 37 to 49 years, and 50 years or older. Work unit had four types: party and governmental institutions, nonparty and nongovernment institutions, enterprises, and others.

Motivation to manage was measured using a culturally adapted Chinese language version of the Miner Sentence Completion Scale–Form H (MSCS–H; Miner 1964) that had been used by Miner, Chen, and Yu (1991) in the previous study of Chinese managers.

The projective method is especially desirable for measuring values and attitudes where social desirability is high. Triandis, Chen, and Chan (1996), for example, pointed out that the Likert-style value items of individualism and collectivism have the disadvantage of being confounded with social desirability. In addition, scholars doing research in China expressed the concern that Chinese respondents might not express their true attitudes and opinions when presented with straightforward survey questions (Adler, Campbell, and Laurent 1989; Korabik 1994).

One potential disadvantage of the projective method is the subjectivity of the researcher. To reduce this subjectivity of the scorer, detailed coding guidelines were developed for each item (Miner 1964, 1989). In addition, training and coaching by an experienced scorer were emphasized. A check on the accuracy of the scoring usually is conducted by comparing percentages of agreement in the scoring. In studies conducted with the standard MSCS–H, mean total scores obtained independently by experienced scorers tend to be quite similar, with an average correlation of .92 (Miner 1985b, 1993).

The three authors of this study worked closely at scoring the responses for the previous Chinese study (Miner 1991). Chen and Yu are bilingual in English and Chinese and had worked with Miner closely to translate and adapt the MSCS–H form for the Chinese study. A satisfactory interrater reliability (.90) had been obtained among the three authors in the 1991 study. The additional data collected for this study were scored in Chinese by Chen, who consulted with Yu and Miner only in cases of uncertainties. Chen was also blind to respondents' background information when he scored their protocols.

Sample

For the study of Chinese women, 85 protocols of managerial motivation were collected. Forty-seven were women who participated in managerial training classes conducted in

Table 17.5

ANCOVA[a] Results: Women's Managerial Motivation by Job Level

	Workers (n = 18)		Professionals (n = 43)		Middle Managers (n = 21)		
Managerial Motivation	*M*	*SD*	*M*	*SD*	*M*	*SD*	*F*
Total Score	1.55	4.79	3.18	4.54	5.71	5.15	3.58*
Authority Figures	.88	.96	.88	1.36	.95	1.74	.11
Competitive Games	.38	1.81	.55	1.89	1.09	1.99	.75
Competitive Situations	–.17	1.51	.00	1.79	.47	2.08	.74
Assertive Role	.77	1.30	.67	1.70	1.00	1.73	.35
Imposing Wishes	–.33	1.41	.07	1.42	.95	1.46	5.62**
Standing Out from Group	–.44	.92	.30	.83	.47	1.03	4.06*
Routine Administrative Functions	.44	1.54	.69	1.26	.76	1.44	.20

[a]ANCOVA = analysis of covariance.
*$p < .05$; **$p < .01$

Beijing, Shanghai, and Dalian in 1992 run by Yu, a professor of management in a Chinese university. Data for the rest of the women were taken from the (1991) study. These data were collected in 1989 in Dalian from two sources: managerial training classes and the Dalian Harbor Transportation Company. The data for gender comparisons comprised 121 men and 82 women who were workers, professionals, or middle-level managers. As there were too few top-level managers of either sex, they were excluded form the analysis. Although the respondents came from a wide range of organizations in terms of industry, all of the organizations were large, state-owned bureaucracies, and thus appropriate for testing Miner's hierarchical role motivation theory.

Analysis and Results

Women's Managerial Motivation and Job Level

In the female sample, the total score for managerial motivation was positively correlated with job level ($r = .25, p < .05$). Of the seven subscales, significant correlations with job level were obtained for imposing wishes ($r = .23, p < .05$) and standing out from the group ($r = .29, p < .01$). When analysis of covariance (ANCOVA) procedures were applied to the total and the subscale scores thus controlling for education, age, work unit, and training class (attendees vs. nonattendees), the scores for total managerial motivation, Imposing Wishes, and Standing Out from Group remained significantly related to job level (Table 17.5). As is evident in Table17.5, although the mean values for some subscales across job level failed to reach statistical significance, it is generally the case that motivation scores increased with job level.

Comparisons between Men and Women

To examine whether managerial motivation is related to job level differently for women than for men, we ran a parallel ANCOVA procedure on men's data taken from Miner, Chen, and Yu (1991), with job level as the main factor and age, education, work unit, and training class as the covariates. The results (Table 17.6) indicated that job level was significantly related to

Table 17.6

ANCOVA[a] Results: Men's Managerial Motivation by Job Level

	Workers (n = 43)		Professionals (n = 30)		Middle Managers (n = 48)		
Managerial Motivation	*M*	*SD*	*M*	*SD*	*M*	*SD*	*F*
Total Score	.72	4.95	2.20	4.12	4.81	4.28	7.48***
Authority Figures	.41	1.07	.80	1.15	.77	1.20	.18
Competitive Games	.74	1.81	.86	1.69	1.10	1.78	.90
Competitive Situations	–.23	1.36	.26	1.08	.52	1.35	2.97*
Assertive Role	.07	1.76	.67	1.88	1.02	1.78	2.69
Imposing Wishes	–.69	1.18	–.50	1.35	.12	1.39	3.94*
Standing Out from Group	.23	1.19	–.23	.77	.14	.94	.48
Routine Administrative Functions	.18	1.09	.33	1.44	1.12	1.29	5.37**

[a]ANCOVA = analysis of covariance.
$*p < .05$; $**p < .01$; $***p < .001$

the total score on managerial motivation, to Competitive Situations, to Imposing Wishes, and to Routine Administrative Functions. To further test the statistical significance of the pattern differences between men and women, an ANCOVA procedure was run with gender and job level as the main factors and the rest of the variables as covariates. A significant interaction between gender and job level was found for Standing Out from Group ($F = 5.74, p = .004$). As can be seen from the mean scores in Table 17.5 and 17.6, with respect to Standing Out from Group, female workers/clerks scored lower but female professionals and managers scored higher than their male counterparts, respectively.

To determine whether men and women, on average, scored differently on managerial motivation, we ran an ANCOVA procedure using gender as the main factor and controlling for education, age, job level, work unit, and training class. No differences emerged for either the total score or any of the subscale scores.

Discussion

The results of this study provide evidence that managerial motivation is positively related to the job level of Chinese women employees. It was found that the total score on managerial motivation distinguished Chinese women at higher job levels from those at lower levels. Of the seven component scores, Imposing Wishes and Standing Out from Group were significant predictors of the job level of women. In addition, we found that Chinese women had no less motivation to manage than did Chinese men. The relationships between managerial motivation and job level, however, suggest some sex differences. Although the overall motivation score and the subscore of Imposing Wishes significantly predicted job level for both sexes, motivations regarding competitive situations and routine administrative functions significantly predicted men's but not women's job level, and motivation to stand out from the group predicted women's but not men's job level.

The lack of a gender difference in overall motivation to manage suggests that Chinese women have come a long way psychologically toward gender equality and that the stereotype of Chinese women's lacking career and managerial motivation is unfounded. With economic reform, the one-child policy, and the increased education of women in China, we expect managerial motivation of Chinese women to increase. Organizations in China (domestic, foreign, and joint ventures) may not have fully recognized the motivational assets of women and therefore have not fully tapped this source of talents.

The significant interaction effect between gender and job level on standing out from the group may have two interpretations. One is that in Chinese organizations, female workers in general are more conformist than are male workers, but female cadres (in the Chinese personnel system, professionals and managers are cadres, whereas workers are not) are more individualistically oriented than are male cadres. The other possible interpretation is that individualistically minded Chinese women are more likely to climb up the corporate ladder, which is not necessarily the case for Chinese men. Future studies could explore the unique characteristics of the Chinese woman manager. In the United States, some researchers (e.g., Loden 1985; Rosener 1990) argued that as the proportion of women managers increases, they will be more likely to develop female ways of managing rather than conforming to a male model of management.

The results of this study provide further evidence in support of the applicability of the hierarchic role motivation theory in Chinese bureaucratic organizations. The finding that both men and women need the desire to exercise power to climb up the corporate ladder is consistent with findings in the United States from studies of the hierarchical motivation theory (Miner 1993), the need for power (McClelland and Boyatzis 1982), and Hofstede's (1980) power distance.

The competitive and differentiation motives of Chinese managers found in this and the previous Chinese study point to the important effects of organizational contingencies in shaping or reinforcing the motives and behaviors of organizational members. Current cross-cultural research predominantly focuses on patterned differences between cultures, yet organizational researchers should not ignore important cross-cultural commonalities. For instance, previous comparative research has found effects of organizational goal priorities and task interdependence on rewards distribution preferences in both Chinese and U.S. societies (C. C. Chen 1995; Chen, Meindl, and Hui 1998). Commonalities do not necessarily mean the absence of cultural effects but may result from within cultural variations that allow for selection and adaptation in response to situational contingencies. Our study suggests that in response to the hierarchical requirement, some Chinese employees (the managers) either learn to stand out from the group or are more inclined to do so and therefore get selected for managerial positions. It is worth pointing out that the same applies to the American managers. Strictly following the cross-cultural perspective and assuming that managers are more socialized into the norms of a culture, one would expect American managers to be less respectful of authority and less willing to impose wishes. Yet, they were more so, either because American managers learn to respect authority in bureaucratic organizations or because such organizations attract people with such attitudes. Future research could incorporate cultural, situational, and individual factors to examine how people of different cultural and individual background fit various organizational contingencies.

In view of the great difficulty in obtaining high-quality data because of political ups and downs and a general pressure to present a positive image to outsiders (Adler, Campbell, and Laurent 1989), the projective measurement of motivation used in this study has the great advantage of reducing artifacts of social desirability. This projective measurement and the objective criterion variable of job level make our study a robust test of the theory. Yet this same advantage could be a disadvantage if subjectivity in scoring influenced the results. As described in the Method section, we were confident that subjectivity was sufficiently controlled by standardized procedures, by training, and by blindness of the scorer to background information. Although the additional data (n = 47) were all scored by the first author, these comprised only 23 percent of the total sample (N = 203), and the rest of the data were scored by the whole research team.

This study was limited by the lack of top-level managers in both male and female samples and by the large proportion of the women recruited from training classes. Future assessments of the level and effects of managerial motivation might be conducted in large organizations with relatively equal proportions of men and women. A longitudinal design could further test the predictive power of managerial motivation for managerial success.

Despite the limitations, the current study represents an important step toward systematically assessing women's managerial motivation and its impact on women's advancement in organizations. Such findings can help organizations in China to identify and develop managerial talents in women. Continuing research in this area also can stimulate theory building and testing that is sensitive to cultural issues across gender and nationality.

CHAPTER 18

ACTIVE VOLUNTEERS WORKING IN VOLUNTARY ORGANIZATIONS IN WESTERN NEW YORK

INTRODUCTION

"Defining Voluntary Groups and Agencies within Organization Science" was published in *Organization Science* (Wilderom and Miner 1991). It represents the first application of the Oliver Organization Description Questionnaire (OODQ) as a stand alone instrument, and also the first study to consider voluntary organizations.

I met Celeste Wilderom when she came over from the psychology department at the State University of New York (SUNY) at Buffalo to attend a doctoral symposium in organizational behavior that I was conducting. As our research evolved she was associated with both SUNY/Buffalo and the Free University in Amsterdam, where she worked for a number of years subsequently. Celeste was the prime mover in our collaboration. She acquired the data, did the analyses, and wrote much of the published article. My contribution was primarily theoretical.

* * *

Although, as indicated in the title, this paper deals primarily with design issues related to voluntary organizations, it derives from a much broader concern with the specification of organizational types generally. There has been some tendency in the literature to consider organizations only in the bureaucratic form, and then to establish differentiations or subtypes *within* this bureaucratic framework. Yet Weber (1968) himself discusses several other

From Celeste P. M. Wilderom and John B. Miner, "Defining Voluntary Groups and Agencies within Organization Science," *Organization Science,* vol. 2, no. 4 (1991), 366–378.

organizational types, falling well outside the realm of bureaucracy. As specified throughout this paper, extra-bureaucratic forms are important; they occur frequently in society. Our theories may neglect them, but that is a deficiency of the theories. In the broadest sense this is a paper about the design of organizations that are not fully bureaucratic in nature, and an attempt to extend theory into domains beyond bureaucracy. We utilize a concentrated analysis of voluntary organizations to demonstrate the kind of work, at both the theoretical and empirical levels, that we believe needs to be done to build an organizational science that truly can guide practice.

Most writers on voluntary work systems describe them, usually without the help of empirical data, as significantly different from private firms and public agencies (e.g., Etzioni 1961, 1975; Gidron 1987; Harman 1982; Knoke and Prensky 1984; Mason 1984; Rothschild-Whitt 1979; Warner and Miller 1964; Walker 1975; Williamson and Ouchi 1981). Some scholars, however, imply that knowledge derived from nonvoluntary organizations is sufficient for managing voluntary work (e.g., Fulmer 1972; Wortman 1981).

Common in the literature on voluntary organizations are two opposing conceptual categories: "voluntary" and "nonvoluntary" organizations. The dichotomy is not derived from nor integrated with organization theory. More importantly, the two notions underlying the dichotomy, the absence of remuneration in the voluntary sector and the absence of altruistic or unremunerated contributions outside this sector, are antiquated. Many salaried people are employed by voluntary organizations. And unremunerated work is performed outside the voluntary sector as well (Organ 1988; Smith, Organ and Near 1983). The voluntary/nonvoluntary distinction may thus mislead organization scholars about current voluntary work. As a part of the discipline of organization science, a more accurate view on voluntary work settings is needed.

The view advanced in this paper is twofold: (1) voluntary work organizations vary in a number of significant ways from other types of organizations, and (2) a voluntary work organization that employs paid personnel behaves differently from a voluntary work organization in which no single individual is paid for his or her work efforts. Support for the first supposition stems from the organizational typology literature, support for the second primarily from the literature on voluntary work.

VOLUNTARY WORK AND GENERAL ORGANIZATIONAL TYPOLOGIES

Etzioni's (1961) typology of organizations comprises normative, coercive, and remunerative types. This typology is the oldest and best known classification scheme in which a voluntary or "normative" type is differentiated from other organizational species (Pearce 1983a). Current research on work values in profit-making organizations shows, however, that normative work motivation (Etzioni 1961) is not unique to voluntary work settings (Czarniawska-Joerges 1988; Organ 1988). Knoke and Prensky (1984, 6), for instance, note that commitment in nonvoluntary organizations "cannot simply be purchased but must also be induced through normative and affective means."

Not only Etzioni (1961) but also Mintzberg (1983) and Miner (1980b) build their typologies of organizations on the means of inducing work discipline. Unlike Etzioni and Mintzberg, Miner specifies *and* operationalizes central work motives of members of different organizational types. "Sociotechnical group inducements," for example, are to prevail in voluntary organizations. Members of three other types, that is, of either hierarchic, professional, or entrepreneurial types, tend to be motivated by qualitatively different inducements (Miner 1980b).

Overwhelming empirical support is found for the discriminating value of these three sets of inducements central to Miner's nonvoluntary types and thus for these three organizational systems (Berman and Miner 1985; Miner 1980a, 1990; Miner, Smith, and Bracker 1989; Smith and Miner 1983). Evidence is needed for the so-far untested assumption that work in voluntary organizations differs significantly from work in the three other organizational types. If such evidence can be found, significant aspects of Miner's (1980b, 1993) role motivation theory of organizations would be confirmed. Moreover, such evidence would show voluntary work settings to be unique, which would further legitimize research on the voluntary organization per se, and on its boundaries with other organizational types as well. It is here that the utility of the voluntary organization is found in supplementing organization science.

Miner's group system emphasizes five component role requirements. They are: (1) social interaction, supported by a desire to interact with others; (2) group acceptance, supported by a desire to belong to a group; (3) positive peer relations, supported by a desire to maintain good relations with group members: (4) cooperation, supported by a desire to work with others in a collaborative fashion; and (5) democracy, supported by a desire to participate in democratic decision-making processes (Miner 1980b). This study predicts that volunteers in voluntary organizations will score significantly higher on items related to the operation of all such group systems than on items derived from Miner's (1980b) theories of the other three organizational systems.

Hypothesis 1. *When asked about their work in voluntary organizations, volunteers score higher on measures describing group systems than they do on measures of the hierarchic, professional, or entrepreneurial types.*

PAID STAFF IN A VOLUNTARY ORGANIZATION

Support for the second supposition, that a voluntary organization employing paid staff is significantly different from a voluntary organization without paid staff, comes in part from Smith (1982). As one of the few behavioral scientists who has written extensively on voluntary work, Smith (1982) distinguishes two types of voluntary organizations: a "*volunteer* organization in which goals are mainly accomplished through the efforts of volunteers rather than paid staff" and a "*voluntary* organization" (Smith 1982, 32–34). He reserves the latter label for private, nonprofit organizations operating (never exclusively) with paid staff. Because no agreement exists on how to best measure "dependence on paid staff," Smith asserts that the distinction between paid-staff and pure voluntary work settings is blurred. He views voluntary organizations' "dependence on volunteer vs. paid employee efforts" (Smith 1982, 34) as a continuum. We propose nevertheless that the mere presence or absence of paid staff does, organizationally, make a difference.

Support for our categorical distinction is provided by extant typologies of voluntary organizations. For reviews of these typologies, generated since the 1950s primarily by sociologists, see, for instance, Amis and Stern (1974) and Palisi and Jacobson (1977). The gist of these typologies is that some voluntary organizations are oriented primarily to satisfactions of members deriving from group activity itself, while others are "associations oriented to accomplishing some task external to the group experience per se" (Amis and Stern 1974, 95). This distinction between essentially "expressive" and "instrumental" voluntary organizations runs parallel to our distinction between pure voluntary organizations or "voluntary groups" and voluntary organizations employing paid staff, "voluntary agencies."

The satisfaction of group needs in voluntary groups is central to their functioning, and concomitantly, most salient to their members. Volunteers in voluntary organizations with paid staff members, on the other hand, will emphasize organizational outcomes. The inclusion of paid staff in voluntary organizations is assumed to reduce the vitality of the group of volunteers as the primary means of organizational conduct (Pincus and Hermann-Kelling 1982; Reisch and Wenocur 1982; White 1982). Hence, whenever one or more members in a voluntary organization are paid, the system is believed to have less collective or group intensity; that is, the potential for unanimity among members of an organization is weakened. The literature on voluntary work improvement, furthermore, illustrates the prototypical latent conflict between volunteers and paid staff in voluntary work settings (Mason 1984; Scheier 1981; Selby 1978).

In sum, two voluntary organizational (sub)types are proposed: a type of organization operating with volunteers only, labeled "voluntary group," and a type in which a part of the membership is paid, labeled "voluntary agency." A final justification for our division of the population of voluntary organizations into "groups" and "agencies" is Blau and Scott's (1962) generic theory of organizations. Apart from private "businesses" and public or "commonweal" organizations, the theory proposes two private nonprofit types. While the prime beneficiary in the "mutual benefit" type is the organizational member, the client is the beneficiary in the "human service" type. It is reasonable to assume that the proportion of paid staff to volunteers in the latter type of organization is significantly larger. Hence, even though ostensibly differentiating between types on the basis of their cui bono principle, one could argue that Blau and Scott (1962) contrast professionalized nonprofit or voluntary agencies with pure voluntary groups.

Real-life examples of "voluntary groups" are mental or physical health-oriented support groups, hobby clubs, and small neighborhood, ethnic or protest groups. "Voluntary agencies" are mostly large or medium-sized nonprofit agencies, for example, for the aged or any other special population group. Note that "voluntary agencies" are typically larger in size—another potential justification for distinguishing them from "voluntary groups" (McPherson 1983).

Hypothesis 2. *Members of "voluntary groups" score differently on each of Miner's (1980b) four organizational system measures than volunteers in organizations that employ paid staff in addition to volunteers. Specifically, volunteers in "voluntary groups" will have a significantly lower hierarchic and professional score, and they will have a significantly higher entrepreneurial and group score.*

The reason for the direction of this hypothesis is as follows. Due to the influx of paid workers/professionals and the resulting increase in administrative or organizational complexity, volunteers in a voluntary agency will experience less group structuring of their work and less freedom to achieve on their own of the kinds reflected in Miner's (1980b, 1993) group and task systems. Both group interaction and highly individualized endeavor are believed to be dampened when group members are paid to do jobs that otherwise would be done by volunteers only.

That the task or entrepreneurial scores of volunteers in a pure voluntary system are expected to be significantly higher than those of individuals who work in a voluntary agency may not seem intuitively plausible. Yet contrary to popular belief and consistent with the nature of voluntary work, nontangible goals are more salient for an entrepreneur than tangible goals (McClelland and Winter 1969). Moreover, an entrepreneurial system often involves a group that is infused with inspirational energy. The same holds true for voluntary groups (Traunstein and Steinman 1973; Young 1983). Hence we expect members of voluntary groups to score higher on the entrepreneurial task score than members of voluntary agencies.

Differentiating *within* the population of voluntary organizations while overlooking possible similarities with organizations outside the voluntary sector can represent a problem in the study of voluntary work. Typologies of nonvoluntary organizations typically have not been empirically compared to those of the voluntary sector. When evaluating the role of the voluntary organization within the discipline of organization science, this position is not tenable. Our study, therefore, in addition to examining the variation within voluntary organizations empirically for the first time, contrasts the work structures of volunteer members of voluntary organizations against a known set of work structures of organizational members working outside the voluntary sector.

ROLE MOTIVATION THEORIES

Before describing the methodology of our research, it is important to consider the theories underlying the typology used. Role motivation theories deal with the relationships among organization types, role requirements for key performers (managers, professionals, entrepreneurs, or group members) that follow from these organizational forms, and motivational patterns that fit these roles. They are in effect *meso* theories that tie together the macro (organizational) and micro (individual) levels of organization science. The present research is concerned entirely with the macro or organizational level within the theories. In the context of the role motivation theories, this research represents an attempt to more firmly position and define the domain of group systems. Using two different ways in which voluntary work may be organized, we attempt to explore the limits of group systems and their relationships to hierarchic, professional, and task systems. From a practical, rather than theoretical, perspective, this issue translates into the following question: If one wishes to obtain whatever advantages are associated with a predominantly group-type of organization, how should a work system be structured?

METHODS

Sampling

Based on a definitional analysis carried out by the first author (Wilderom 1989), which corroborates the literature on the "distinctive nature of voluntary organizations" (e.g., Mason 1984; Warner 1972), a voluntary organization is distinguished from other, nonvoluntary organizations in at least two unique and essential characteristics. The market or economic value of its output is marginal, and the tangible benefits for its members are at most insecure. As a consequence, when sampling voluntary organizations for the purpose of comparative research involving voluntary and other organizations (e.g., Pearce 1983b), at least two factors have to be taken into account: the market value of outputs and the benefits resulting from member participation.

The two voluntary organization subtypes were identified as follows: whenever a voluntary organization employs one or more members who receive salary or wages, it is seen as a "voluntary agency." "Voluntary groups" are voluntary organizations operating with volunteers only. The two subsamples entail four voluntary agencies and six voluntary groups. The voluntary agencies are a United Way affiliated agency coordinating local voluntary work, a meals-on-wheels operation, a voluntary agency that works in a local hospital with patients, and an agency organizing assistance by the elderly in schools. The voluntary groups are a parent-teacher association, a mutual support group for widows, a group providing telephone assurance for home-bound elderly, a political lobbying and information dispersion committee concerned with protecting the legitimate use of firearms, a club for aspiring local musicians, and an ethnic neighborhood association.

In each participating organization the label as either a "voluntary group" or a "voluntary agency" was established on the basis of a priori knowledge of the organizations involved. This knowledge was corroborated using a question addressed to the executive director or coordinator of each organization in the sample: "How many people working in your organization are paid regular salaries or wages?"

The data used derive from ninety-one volunteers of the ten voluntary organizations, located in a northeastern metropolitan area in the United States. Respondents in this study are "active volunteers," defined as people who are regularly involved in unpaid work in the context of a nonfamilial group, sharing one or more goals. Each respondent in the study was drawn, in a systematic random fashion, from one of the ten participating voluntary organizations.

Measure

The Oliver Organization Description Questionnaire (OODQ) was developed to categorize individuals in terms of the extent to which they describe their work situations as primarily hierarchic or bureaucratic (the H scale), professional (the P scale), task or entrepreneurial (the T scale), and group or sociotechnical (the G scale) following Miner's (1980b, 1993) theory. Details of the development of the OODQ may be found in various works by Oliver (1980, 1981, 1982).

Data Collection

Each executive director or coordinator of the ten targeted organizations was called and asked to cooperate in this study. All of them reacted affirmatively. Apart from providing us with information on the total number of paid employees, directors were asked to be involved in two tasks: (1) the drawing of a systematic random sample of active volunteers within their organization and (2) the distribution of a copy of the OODQ to each such member in their organization. All selected respondents were asked to fill out the OODQ and return it to us anonymously in an attached pre-stamped, addressed envelope.

One hundred sixty questionnaires were sent out. The total yield of returned questionnaires was 91. The useable response rate is 57 percent. Except for one very large organization which distributed 25 questionnaires, 15 questionnaires were distributed per organization. The average return from voluntary agencies was 67 percent while that from voluntary groups was 47 percent.

Analyses

In order to test Hypothesis 1, an ANOVA (analysis of variance) procedure with repeated measures was carried out. Four *t* tests were used for the test of Hypothesis 2. In addition to testing the four raw scores, these scores were converted to standard scores, using means and standard deviations from Oliver's (1981, 1982) normative samples. This standardization of scores cancels out the inherent mean and standard deviation differences that exist between the raw scores as a function of item differences. All analyses are repeated using the standardized or normalized scores.

RESULTS

Table 18.1 shows the means and standard deviations of the four scores central to this study in both raw and normalized form. As hypothesized, the raw H, P, and T scores differ significantly from the G score. Also the three normalized scores differ significantly from the normalized G score. All reported F values are significant, confirming Hypothesis 1. In effect, they support Miner's thesis that the voluntary organization differs significantly from the three other organizational types. This result also provides evidence for the assumption voluntary organizations fit the "theory of group inducement systems" (Miner 1980b, 276). Of the four raw scores in Table 18.1 only the G score is large enough to indicate a significant presence of the organizational system using Oliver's (1981) cutting scores.

The variations obtained within voluntary organizations (Table 18.2) accord with Hypothesis 2. The stratification of voluntary organizations into the two types is supported. Volunteers working in voluntary organizations that employ paid personnel (voluntary agencies) have significantly higher H and P scores as well as significantly lower T and G scores in comparison with volunteers in voluntary groups. Of the eight raw scores in Table 18.2, only the T score and G score for the voluntary groups are large enough to indicate a significant presence using Oliver's (1981) criteria.

These results, obtained through tests of the two hypotheses, only approximate the recommended approach in comparative organizational research: "maximize differences between categories and . . . minimize differences within categories" (Pinder and Moore 1979, 101). We establish that the voluntary organization is distinctively a group system, but we also confirm significant differences *within* the voluntary organization category.

In order to examine more closely the variations within our set of voluntary organizations, the scores of the voluntary agencies and of the voluntary groups were subjected to a separate analysis utilizing the procedure with which we tested Hypothesis 1. The raw H, P, and T scores of members of voluntary groups do differ from their G scores as the Table 18.2 results would suggest. F values are 49.23, 47.33, and 11.65 respectively, all significant at $p < .001$. The same ANOVA procedure applied to the normalized scores for the voluntary groups yields a similar pattern of results. The G score is significantly higher at the $p < .001$ level with F values of 84.00, 74.04, and 15.15 respectively for the H, P, and T score comparisons.

Similar tests for the voluntary agencies under study reveal a less differentiated picture. Raw H, P, and T scores in fact do not differ significantly from the G score. The difference with the P and T scores is miniscule. The H score value is higher with an F of 3.86 and $p < .06$. Yet when the normalized scores are compared, the G score exceeds all others. However, with F values of 0.01, 3.20, and 0.85 for the H, P, and T scores respectively, no comparison is significant at $p < .05$. The data indicate that although the H score in voluntary agencies is higher than the G score, it is not significantly so, and the normalized H and G scores differ hardly at all.

These analyses confirm that voluntary organizations influenced primarily by group inducements are "voluntary groups," not "voluntary agencies." Our affirmation of Hypothesis 1 is thus clearly due to the impact of the voluntary groups' scores. It follows that voluntary organizations operating with paid workers cannot legitimately be defined as group organizations.

Table 18.1

Raw and Normalized[a] G Scores Compared to H, P, and T Scores of Volunteers in Ten Voluntary Organizations (N = 91)

Scores	Means	Comparisons	*Fs*
H Score		H Score vs. G Score	
Raw	3.945 (3.089)[b]	Raw	7.761**
Normalized	45.753 (7.268)	Normalized	27.781***
P Score		P Score vs. G Score	
Raw	3.319 (2.442)	Raw	18.502***
Normalized	44.657 (6.100)	Normalized	43.029***
T Score		T Score vs. G Score	
Raw	4.593 (2.417)	Raw	5.827*
Normalized	49.818 (6.605)	Normalized	11.019***
G Score			
Raw	5.615 (3.441)		
Normalized	53.439 (8.602)		

[a]Normalized scores are scores that are standardized based on the means and standard deviations of a weighted, normative sample provided by Oliver (1982).

[b]All parenthesized numbers in this table are the standard deviations of the preceding mean score.

$*p < .05$; $**p < .01$; $***p < .001$

Among voluntary organizations, only "voluntary groups" seem to be significantly different from hierarchic, professional, or entrepreneurial-type organizations. Voluntary organizations without paid personnel (together with sociotechnical units or autonomous work groups [see Oliver 1982]) differ significantly from hierarchic, professional, and entrepreneurial type organizations. In other words, voluntary organizations differ significantly from other organizational types only insofar as the voluntary organization is a "voluntary group."

How similar the organizational category comprised of "voluntary agencies" is to other organizational types needs further examination. The data suggest that voluntary agencies take on characteristics of all three nongroup organizational types, and perhaps somewhat more of the hierarchic. If further examination of unique characteristics of the "voluntary agency" should confirm our suspicion that the "voluntary agency" is not a purely hierarchic, professional, entrepreneurial, nor group type organization, a fifth organizational type may be plausible.

Such a fifth, "grab bag" category may well be comprised of organizations with characteristics that are either temporarily impure, as for instance some of Mintzberg's political arenas (1983), or permanently eclectic, as is perhaps the "voluntary agency." Further empirical tests of this are needed. Defenders of four instead of five classes of organizations may well argue that paid staff respondents of voluntary agencies as distinguished from the volunteers studied

Table 18.2

Raw and Normalized[a] G, H, P, and T Scores of Volunteers in Voluntary Agencies and Voluntary Groups

Scores	Means		
	Voluntary Agencies N = 46	Voluntary Groups N = 45	*t* values[b]
H Score			
Raw	5.391	2.467	5.11***
	(2.894)[c]	(2.555)	
Normalized	49.156	42.275	
	(6.810)	(6.011)	
P Score			
Raw	3.957	2.667	2.63**
	(2.538)	(2.132)	
Normalized	46.263	43.014	
	(6.394)	(5.370)	
T Score			
Raw	3.891	5.311	2.92**
	(2.523)	(2.098)	
Normalized	47.900	51.779	
	(6.894)	(5.732)	
G Score			
Raw	3.957	7.311	5.31***
	(3.091)	(2.937)	
Normalized	49.291	57.678	
	(7.727)	(7.344)	

[a]Normalized scores are scores that are standardized based on the means and standard deviations of a weighted, normative sample provided by Oliver (1982).

[b]The *t* values resulting from mean comparisons between the two subsamples for the raw scores are identical to those for the normalized scores.

[c]All parenthesized numbers in this table are the standard deviations of the preceding mean score.

$*p < .05$; $**p < .01$; $***p < .001$

here, would indicate their organization to be hierarchic. An intriguing empirical question thus is how paid staff would score in comparison to volunteers from the same voluntary agency on the OODQ. It also would be interesting to learn how tenure in the organization relates to the type of results we have obtained.

DISCUSSION: HOW VOLUNTARY ORGANIZATIONS CAN SUPPLEMENT ORGANIZATION SCIENCE

For no good reasons, organization science has neglected voluntary organizations, assuming them to be either similar to organizations in which most members are paid for their labor, or too different even to be a part of the discipline at all. Lack of definitional consensus (that is, not knowing what or what not to call a voluntary organization) may have stifled latent interest. Observations that few work settings are purely voluntary (Landsberger 1973; Warner

1972), plus the relatively large number of and high status associated with nonvoluntary work settings, may well have facilitated this convenience.

Nonetheless, a few organization scientists have introduced generic typologies in which voluntary organizations are explicitly included (Miner 1980b, Mintzberg 1983; for a conceptual comparison between Mintzberg's and Miner's typologies, see Miner 1993). In these typologies, voluntary work settings are not merely contrasted with all other organizations, as in the voluntary/nonvoluntary dichotomy, but with various specific other organizational types.

Even though research on voluntary work has been suggested to potentially add to the study of organizations (Fottler 1981; Heydebrand 1980; Likert 1961; Mason 1984; Pearce 1983b; Tomeh 1973, Weisbrod 1977), organization scientists have seldom sampled nonpublic, nonprofit organizational settings. This paper's results disconfirm the implicit belief prevalent in the organization science literature that voluntary work can only learn from organization science and not contribute to it. In fact, by showing that certain voluntary organizations are different from three other valid categories, this paper illustrates a supplementary role for voluntary organizations in the general study of organizational types. Furthermore, it indicates that if one wishes to design a group system, the voluntary group, along with sociotechnical, autonomous work groups, provides a useful prototype.

Finally, we would argue that organizational typologies should begin not only to incorporate all existing forms of voluntary organizations, but also to benefit from recent theoretical developments in organization science generally. For instance, population ecologists, occupying themselves with to-be-or-not-to-be types of issues, have resurrected the question of how systematic variations in organizational forms come about. They have also concerned themselves with the evolution of various forms, including hybrid stages and forms of the type represented by voluntary agencies.

Purists among the population ecologists often determine the extent to which various forms exist in different locations, and test their predictions using the total numbers of organizational subspecies that have survived and emerged (McKelvey and Aldrich 1983; Singh, House, and Tucker 1986). Others have extended the ecological perspective explicitly to voluntary organizations (McPherson and Smith-Lovin 1988). Issues such as the stages of the life cycle in organizations and the best economic parameters for predicting these stages may be of concern. Such a theoretical approach, and the type of research it spawns, appear ideally suited to determining whether (and how) voluntary organizations differ from and interact with other types. The possibility certainly exists that investigation from a population ecology perspective might produce evidence for a typology of organizations having much in common with the one considered in this paper.

The economic-theory-of-the-firm school of thought offers further insight into the role of voluntary organizations in organizational typology. Boisot and Child (1988) have added the concept of fief to the school's bureaucratic, market, and clan subspecies. Although by no means identical, this school's typology has accordingly come to increasingly parallel the views of Miner and Mintzberg. It is remarkable how, coming from diverse theoretical perspectives, various organizational scholars have arrived at a similar cross-cut of organizations. This situation must challenge not only population ecologists (Cafferata 1982), but organizational empiricists as well.

CHAPTER 19

LABOR ARBITRATORS NATIONWIDE (MANY OF THEM LAWYERS)

INTRODUCTION

Organization Science published this article as well (Miner, Crane, and Vandenberg 1994). The distinguishing characteristics are a return to the professional theory, and thus a follow-on to Chapter 9, and the use of the Oliver Organization Description Questionnaire (OODQ) (see Chapter 12) to establish a domain in which congruence would be anticipated. This domain-documentation role was what stimulated the development of the OODQ originally.

The authors had varying roles in constructing this research. Crane, a faculty member at Georgia State University, has had long experience as a labor arbitrator. He helped secure the arbitrator sample and to obtain the management performance ratings; he located the various union performance ratings, which were based primarily on data from the United Automobile Workers (UAW) and the Oil, Chemical, and Atomic Workers (OCAW), and ultimately obtained access to them. Vandenberg had worked with us in our research, specializing in statistics and design issues, and was heavily involved in this regard in this particular article. At the time he was on the faculty at Georgia State, but moved to the University of Georgia subsequently.

Closely related as to content is an article by Crane and Miner (1988) which deals with the relationship between management and union ratings of arbitrator performance.

* * *

A prior article in this journal presented an organizational typology that extends beyond bureaucracy to encompass professional, task or entrepreneurial, and group forms (Wilderom and Miner 1991). This article focused primarily on group systems of organization and dealt with the structure and process component of role motivation theory only, not the motivational. A major point made was that previous typologies have tended to consider organizations in the bureaucratic form only, and then to establish differentiations or subtypes within this same bureaucratic framework. A common ground emphasized in the Wilderom and Miner (1991) article and the present research is that extra-bureaucratic organizations are important and frequent. Here the focus shifts to professional forms, but the idea that organization theory must move beyond its preoccupation with bureaucracy remains. The managerial functions inherent in bureaucracy are performed by different people and in different ways in other organizational systems, and this creates a set of design considerations that make for substantial alterations in the way organizations should be structured.

This paper is concerned with professional organizations and with a theory related to their functioning—professional role motivation theory. Within the context of that theory it is also concerned with the concept of congruence or fit. This latter concept has had a long history in organization theory extending back at least to Chandler (1962). Since that time it has assumed an increasingly central position in the theoretical literature. The objective in what follows is to set forth the components of professional role motivation theory, to show how the congruence concept enters into that theory, to provide some empirical support for the theory in its congruence aspects, and to derive implications for practice from the theory and its supporting evidence.

ROLE MOTIVATION THEORIES

Four parallel, but distinct role-motivation theories have been proposed (Miner 1980b, 1982). Of these theories the one with the longest history and the greatest research support is the hierarchic theory which applies to managers in bureaucratic organizations (Miner 1965a, 1977b). Task theory has exhibited considerable validity in recent research on entrepreneurs (Miner, Smith, and Bracker 1989); the group theory has not been tested in its motivational aspects as yet. The remaining, professional theory, which is the subject of this article, has been studied previously using a sample of management professors, with very promising results (Miner 1980a).

PROFESSIONAL ORGANIZATION

Professional organization encompasses several different forms. The basic form is individual private practice. This may be expanded to group practice, and still further to professional organizations or units. As the number of professionals increases, the number of nonprofessional support personnel tends to increase also, these nonprofessionals may be organized in a hierarchic manner, and many features of bureaucracy may appear in these components, including managers. What is distinctive about professional organizations, however, is that authority remains in the hands of the professionals; ultimately they make the key decisions. If bureaucracy supersedes the professional form and managers assume the major role, as happens in many hospitals and scientific research units within corporations, true professional organization no longer exists (even though professionals are present).

In professional systems, role requirements derive from the values, norms, ethical precepts, and codes of the profession, rather than from a managerial hierarchy. They are transmitted through early professional training, by professional associations, and by colleagues. In professional organizations members of the core profession assume the key roles and perform many of the activities that managers perform in hierarchic organizations. In the conduct of their affairs the professionals use committees and voting procedures extensively. The overall structure tends to be flat with status differentiations based on professional expertise and experience.

Several distinctions from bureaucracy should be noted. Although sometimes given managerial titles, professionals with greater authority in professional organizations attain their authority because of their professional, not their managerial, skills; these professional skills include client development. Professional associations play a key role for professional organizations that is not replicated in the case of bureaucracies. These associations establish norms and role prescriptions for professionals. They play a particularly important role for private practitioners and small group practices where little or no organizational overlay exists. Finally, in professional organizations what are otherwise considered managerial functions are taken over by the professionals. These include such functions as strategic and structural planning, directing, coordinating, controlling, staffing, and representing, which have long been considered managerial in nature (Miner 1971b). In larger professional organizations certain aspects of these functions may be delegated to nonprofessionals. However, this delegation occurs within a context of professionally established policy guidelines and, like all delegations, it may be rescinded; the professionals may reassert their authority.

THE PROFESSIONAL THEORY

When a professional organization is present, certain roles need to be established for the professionals involved. These roles flow both from the organization and from the relevant professional associations.

Role Requirements and Motive Patterns

Professional role motivation theory hypothesizes five types of organizational role prescriptions that combine with appropriate motivational patterns as discussed in Chapter 9.

Highlighting Types of Congruence and Fit

A quote from Nadler and Tushman (1980, 45) will serve to define the concept of congruence or fit (the terms are typically used interchangeably):

> The congruence between two components is defined as the degree to which the needs, demands, goals, objectives, and/or structures of one component are consistent with the needs,

> demands, goals, objectives, and/or structures of another component. . . . Other things being equal, the greater the total degree of congruence or fit between the various components, the more effective will be the organization.

A major problem with this concept is that as it has evolved, it has taken a number of different forms. Thus, Galbraith and Kazanjian (1986) consider components that involve aspects of strategies, tasks, people, reward systems, information and decision processes, and structures. Mackenzie (1991) considers components falling within such categories as strategic conditions, organizational technology conditions, organizational results conditions, associates, position logic, and organizational/position reward systems. Nadler and Tushman (1988) utilize a component list of a still different type. A great many components have been proposed that need to be congruent with one another for effectiveness to occur.

A second problem with the congruence or fit concept is that, although considerable anecdotal evidence favors it (Miles and Snow 1984), empirical support for a number of versions of the concept has been mixed at best. It is entirely possible that certain types of fits are interchangeable one with another—one can do it either of several ways (Steiner, Miner, and Gray 1986). If so, testing these concepts becomes much more complex.

Professional role motivation theory, and in fact all four role motivation theories, deal with three component types. These are, first, an organization type with a characteristic set of structures and processes; second, a specific set of informal or formal role prescriptions that follow logically from the organization type and apply to key members (professionals, managers, and the like); and third, a set of motive patterns that follow logically from the roles. These three need to be congruent with one another for effectiveness to occur. Relative to other congruence theories, this is a more limited set of components, and the degree of specificity of the theoretical statements is relatively high. Once an organizational type is established, effectiveness will be compromised to the extent existing role prescriptions deviate from the theoretically appropriate *and* to the extent individual motive patterns deviate from what the roles would call for. Thus, two forms of congruence are anticipated. Professional role motivation theory predicts that the greater the degree of congruence or fit that is present, the greater the degree of effectiveness that will be found.

Empirical Support

Since the four role motivation theories are parallel in form, differing only in specific content and possessing the same patterns of congruence, evidence for one carries implications for the others. Substantial support is available for the hierarchic and task theories (Miner 1993). Hierarchic role motivation theory has been confirmed in 27 independent concurrent studies and 7 predictive studies. When the theory is applied outside its domain of managers in hierarchic systems, it should not work because the necessary congruence is lacking, and in fact it has failed to yield significant results in 17 concurrent and 4 predictive studies. Task role motivation theory has obtained support in 10 concurrent studies and 2 predictive studies (Miner 1993; Miner, Smith, and Bracker 1992a). When applied outside its domain of entrepreneurs in task systems, where congruence should not be present, it has failed to yield significant results in 3 concurrent studies.

While the importance of congruence or fit of the types hypothesized by the hierarchic and task theories seems to have been confirmed, this is not true for the group and professional theories. The motives of group role motivation theory remain unmeasured. Research to date on the professional theory is sparse. Initial research on the latter focused on the design of a measuring instrument (Miner 1981). This effort proved successful, and the instrument was then applied in the study of university professors in the field of management (Miner 1980a). The data obtained confirmed the professional theory within this particular sample, while indicating no validity for the hierarchic theory in the professional context. One objective of the research with labor arbitrators to be reported here was to extend this effort to determine whether the professional theory is applicable to another, different group of professionals, and thus to determine whether the congruencies involved are of wider significance.

A second objective of the research was to determine whether the professional form extends across multiple organizational contexts as the theory predicts. Professional role-motivation theory assumes that its measures of professional organizational structure and professional motivation will be at a high level irrespective of the organizational context in which the professional works. Thus it should not matter whether the professional is employed in a professional organization, a professional component of a larger, primarily bureaucratic organization, or in private professional practice. The labor arbitrator occupation is well suited to testing this hypothesis because arbitrators may have their primary employment in law firms, in the faculty components of universities which are organized at the top along bureaucratic lines, in legal or arbitration units within government at some level, or in the private practice of arbitration and/or law. The theory predicts that in all of these contexts arbitrators will perceive the organizational structure and process to be predominantly that of a professional system and for congruence to operate there should be evidence of strong professional motivation as well.

METHODOLOGY OF THE LABOR ARBITRATOR RESEARCH

The data used in this research derive from two sources. The arbitrators themselves provided information on their backgrounds and professional accomplishments; they also completed a measure of professional motivation and a questionnaire intended to establish the extent to which their work fell in the professional domain. A second source was a set of ratings of arbitrator performance made by management representatives who had been involved in the arbitration process with the arbitrator.

Miner Sentence Completion Scale (MSCS)–Form P

This instrument provides a measure of the five motivational patterns specified by the professional theory. The subscale scores obtained in this study correlate with the total score, of which each is a part, in the range .53 to .73. The median correlation between subscales is .26.

All MSCS–Form P scoring was done by the first author. A check on the accuracy of scoring, involving comparison with another, independent scorer on 10 scales, yielded a total score correlation of .98 and subscale correlations averaging .91 with none below .89. No significant differences in the mean scores of the two scorers were found. Detailed examples and information on scoring is contained in a Scoring Guide (Miner 1981).

Oliver Organization Description Questionnaire (OODQ)

This measure was developed by Oliver (1981, 1982) to categorize individuals in terms of the extent to which they describe their work situations as primarily hierarchic or bureaucratic (the H scale), professional (the P scale), task or entrepreneurial (the T scale), and group or sociotechnical (the G scale) following Miner's (1980b) theory of four basic types of organizational systems.

Among the labor arbitrators a high score on the P scale and relatively lower scores on the other three scales were anticipated as documentation that the research was being conducted within professional systems.

Arbitration Questionnaire

The arbitrators completed a questionnaire dealing with the details of their work. Included were the individual's primary occupation, degrees, age, memberships in professional organizations, and organizational context. Primary occupations noted were lawyer, professor, arbitrator, and very infrequently university administrator. Degrees were specified as a law degree, a PhD or equivalent in some field, a masters degree, a bachelors degree, and in some few cases no degree at all. Memberships in professional organizations was the number of organizations noted from a list of arbitration and labor relations associations and societies.

In the study of management professors (Miner 1980a), the number of professional memberships was significantly, positively related to a host of professional compensation measures including total professional compensation (.33), academic rank (.21), books published (.36), journal articles published (.48), and supervising doctoral dissertations. Thus it appears that the number of professional memberships can serve as a surrogate for other behavioral indexes of professional success. It is important to recognize that professional organizations play a particularly significant role in the professions. They serve to foster the development and dissemination of knowledge to members, protect the freedom of members to act with professional independence, foster the prestige and status of the profession and of individual members, create opportunities for members to serve clients, and define and enforce appropriate professional norms and values. Thus they serve to foster performance in the five professional roles. Accordingly, professional organization membership should contribute to more effective professional performance. This is a unique aspect of professional systems.

Performance Ratings by Management

The management evaluations were developed from current reports on each arbitrator prepared by a private arbitration reporting service. These reports are intended for the use of management clients. Management representatives and attorneys provide information after their cases are heard by a given arbitrator. This information includes a statement of either approval or disapproval regarding the arbitrator's performance in the case. Only very rarely does this evaluation take a neutral form.

Although the management representatives do not directly provide an overall evaluation of the arbitrator, the reporting service constructs such an evaluation in-house from all the data available to it. This consensus rating translates easily into a four-point scale (Heneman and Sandver 1983). Eighty-five percent of all arbitrators evaluated have received a consensus rating. Two management performance ratings were used:

1. The percentage of all positive and negative evaluations given the arbitrator that were stated as disapprovals; this is a percent negative rating. Low scores indicate effective rated performance and high scores poor rated performance.
2. The consensus rating developed by the reporting service. Low scores indicate good

rated performance and high scores poor rated performance. The scale points are 1—unqualified or general approval; 2—qualified approval; 3—controversial; and 4—highly controversial or unacceptable.

The nature of the management performance evaluations is such that a measure of rater agreement cannot be calculated. However, evidence from other sources suggests a reliability in the mid –.70s (Crane and Miner 1988). Given the common database, the correlation of .75 between the management percent negative ratings and the consensus ratings is not surprising. Neither is significantly related to the professional memberships index.

Data were also obtained from union representatives who rated the same arbitrators in much the same way the management representatives did. These data did not yield any statistically significant findings. However, there is reason to question their comparability to the data from the other effectiveness measures (Crane and Miner 1988), and consequently they are not considered further here.

Sample

The sampling process started with 386 arbitrators on whom performance ratings were available. These arbitrators were contacted by mail and asked to participate in the study. After two rounds of solicitation, 123 replies were received which contained some usable information. Most frequently this was the arbitration questionnaire. In 109 instances, the OODQ was completed and 100 completed MSCS–Form Ps were obtained. A number of undeliverable materials were returned and there were some deaths. However, using the 386 figure as a base, the calculated response rate varied from 26 to 32 percent for the different measures.

Do the respondents represent a typical group of arbitrators? Comparing the performance ratings obtained with those for the larger groups of 386, the respondents are consistently rated lower, more favorably, than the nonrespondents by the management representatives, but the difference is small. On the MSCS–Form P, the arbitrator respondents score above the level obtained in other professional groups where the mean total score is typically near +7 (Miner 1981). As indicated in Table 19.1, this value is +9.31 for the arbitrator respondents. On the OODQ, professionals typically have a P score of 10, a T score of 5, an H score of 4, and a G score of 3 (Oliver 1981). The arbitrators have somewhat higher P and T scores and lower H and G scores. Over 70 percent of the respondents are members of the National Academy of Arbitrators, where membership is generally a function of both professional respect and case load at the time of election.

On this evidence it seems likely that the respondents are somewhat more effective, more professional, and more successful than arbitrators in general. On the other hand, many arbitrators spend only a very small proportion of their professional time in the activity and earn only a small proportion of their income from it. To include large numbers of these individuals in the study would not speak to the profession as it is principally practiced and would dilute the reliability of the performance ratings when they could be obtained at all. Overall the sample appears well suited to the purposes at hand.

It is important to note, however, that the mean age in the arbitrator sample is 61.98 years with a standard deviation of 10.34. Age is unrelated to the criteria, and the only significant correlation with an MSCS–Form P variable involves professional commitment (.22). Thus age does not appear to be a factor in the current results, but the advanced age of the sample overall does affect the appropriateness of certain effectiveness criteria that might otherwise

Table 19.1

Correlations between MSCS–Form P and Effectiveness Measures, with Means and Standard Deviations, for Total Arbitrator Sample (N = 100), **Those with Law Degrees** (N = 63), **and Those for Whom Practicing Law Is the Primary Occupation** (N = 20)

	Effectiveness Measures										
				Management Ratings							
	No. Professional Memberships			Percent Negative			Consensus				
MSCS–P Measures	Total Sample	Law Degree	Legal Occupation	Total Sample	Law Degree	Legal Occupation	Total Sample	Law Degree	Legal Occupation	Mean	*SD*
Total Score	.29**	.21*	.24	–.26**	–.35**	–.42*	–.32**	–.38**	–.43*	9.31	7.69
Acquiring Knowledge	.24**	.23*	.19	–.14	–.12	–.35	–.21*	–.21*	–.34	0.81	2.25
Independent Action	.20*	.17	.44*	–.16	–.24*	–.39*	–.07	–.07	–.17	2.02	2.04
Accepting Status	.19*	.11	.11	–.10	–.23*	–.20	–.27**	–.38**	–.30	2.26	2.74
Providing Help	.29**	.22*	.26	–.20*	–.31**	–.35	–.24**	–.26*	–.30	2.25	2.59
Professional Commitment	.01	–.08	–.01	–.26**	–.24*	–.45*	–.25**	–.31**	–.68**	1.97	2.08
Mean	3.11			22.35			2.23				
SD	1.59			16.49			.67				

Note: Positive correlations involving number of professional memberships and negative correlations involving management ratings support the theory. MSCS = Miner Sentence Completion Scale.

$^*p < .05$; $^{**}p < .01$

Table 19.2

MSCS–P and OODQ Mean Score in Various Professional Organizational Contexts

	Organizational Contexts					
	University Faculty	Law Firm	Government	Private Practice	Private Practice (Retired from University)	*F*
N	28	27	6	34	14	
OODQ Measures						
P Score	9.68	11.11	11.00	11.18	11.57	1.90
T Score	6.57	6.33	4.83	6.26	5.00	1.17
H Score	3.64[a]	.81	1.00	.50	.64	15.14**
G Score	2.14	1.74	1.17	.44[b]	.43[c]	6.17**
MSCS–P Measures						
Total Score	11.33	7.58	13.00	8.21	10.50	1.29
Acquiring Knowledge	.71	.92	.80	.64	1.25	.19
Independent Action	2.08	1.23	2.40	2.33	2.58	1.47
Accepting Status	2.83	2.27	3.00	1.82	2.00	.59
Providing Help	3.25	1.54	4.00	1.82	2.25	2.31
Professional Commitment	2.46	1.62	2.80	1.61	2.42	1.11

Note: MSCS = Miner Sentence Completion Scale. OODQ = Oliver Organization Description Questionnaire.

$^{**}p < .01$

[a]Above all other groups at $p < .05$ or better.

[b]Below University Faculty and Law Firm at $p < .05$ or better.

[c]Below University Faculty at $p < .05$ or better.

have been used. A number of the arbitrators are partially retired, having retired fully from some other occupation and/or cut back on their arbitration caseload; some are doing more arbitration because they have left another professional activity. The net result is that such criterion measures as arbitrator or total professional income, caseload, and per diem charge for arbitration work are seriously contaminated as performance indexes. In contrast to younger professionals, these arbitrators are not necessarily attempting to maximize these outcomes. Many are receiving retirement income of some kind.

In terms of organizational context, 26 percent of the arbitrators hold university faculty appointments. Twenty-five percent are employed by law firms, 6 percent work in a professional unit of some kind within government, and 44 percent are in private professional practice (and thus fully self-employed). Within the latter group, 29 percent previously held full-time university positions from which they are now retired (see Table 19.2). In terms of both age and organizational context the sample appears to be typical of active arbitrators.

RESULTS OF THE ARBITRATOR ANALYSIS

It is apparent that the arbitrators do perceive their work as largely professional in nature. The mean P score on the OODQ is 10.82 and the standard deviation 2.64. Oliver (1981) notes that a P score of 6 or higher indicates a significant degree of professionalism. There are only four P scores below 6 in the entire sample. The mean value places the arbitrators at the 49th percentile for professionals and the 89th percentile in a balanced sample having equal representation from all four domains—professional, hierarchic, task, and group. Thus, it can be said that at the level of organizational structure and process the arbitrators work primarily in a professional context.

Total Sample Findings

Given the support for the professional nature of the organizational context, it is theoretically appropriate to test professional role-motivation theory, using Form P of the MSCS within the arbitrator sample. The results obtained in the total sample are given in Table 19.2. Congruence requires that the MSCS–Form P scores be high (to match the professional structure) and that they correlate significantly with the individual effectiveness indexes (to indicate that greater congruence produces greater success).

The MSCS total score of 9.31 is high, being at the 68th percentile for professionals using the published norms (Miner 1981). The mean score on the acquiring knowledge subscale is at the 62nd percentile, on independent action at the 50th percentile, on accepting status at the 61st percentile, on providing help at the 57th percentile, and on professional commitment at the 76th percentile. What is clearly most distinctive about these arbitrators in a motivational sense is their strong commitment to the profession. Considering the average age of the group, this finding is not surprising. Low commitment arbitrators would be expected to drop out of the profession at a younger age, leaving the high commitment individuals to work on into their seventies and even eighties (there are 30 arbitrators in the sample who are age 70 or older).

The total score correlations in Table 19.1 provide the most comprehensive test of the theory. The relationships with professional memberships and the two management ratings are highly significant and in the predicted directions. Among the subscales the most consistent support for the theory comes from the Providing Help measure; more successful arbitrators have a stronger desire to help others. However, all the other subscales show at least one significant relationship. On the evidence these findings support professional role motivation theory in its contention that congruence between organization type and individual motivation yields individual effectiveness. Since role prescriptions were not directly measured in this research, congruence at that level is only indirectly supported.

The Legal Profession

Within the arbitrator sample the only sizable group with professional training oriented to arbitration is the lawyers. Of the 100 individuals who completed the MSCS, 63 held law degrees. Another 21 had received doctoral degrees in some area, but in many of these cases there was little reason to believe arbitration was a major focus. Only three held doctoral degrees in industrial relations. The other doctorates were in economics, industrial engineering, business, sociology, education, and philosophy. The remaining subjects included 11 with master's degrees, three with bachelor's degrees, and two without a college degree at all. Only the 5 with master's degrees in labor or industrial relations could be considered to have an arbitration-related education, and this was not at the level of a terminal degree.

In short, the data indicate that the arbitration profession is not like medicine in having a single degree requirement and set of educational prerequisites. However there is what appears to be a strong core discipline—the law. Table 19.1 also provides data on the motivation-effectiveness relationships for those subjects with law degrees and for those who described their primary occupation as legal practice. These results for attorneys, whether defined in terms of original degree or professional practice, reinforce those for the total sample. All of the subscales appear to be related to at least one success index. From the perspective of this sample, professional role-motivation theory is supported for the legal profession as well as the arbitration profession as a whole. Given the traditional role accorded to the legal profession as a prototype of a professional system, this finding represents an important validation of professional role-motivation theory. The congruence relationships of Table 19.1 are clearly supportive of theory for the legal profession, even if the arbitration field as a whole is considered suspect as a full profession.

Variations with Organizational Context

Table 19.2 contains results related to the hypothesis of homogeneity across organizational contexts. Consistent with professional role-motivation theory, there is no evidence of a significant difference in OODQ–P score by organizational context. In all groups the P score levels are quite high, and the professional organizational type clearly prevails. T score levels do not vary by organizational context either. This is not true, however, of the remaining OODQ scores. The university faculty members experience a greater degree of hierarchy than the other groups—not a surprising finding given that universities typically take on a bureaucratic form above the level of direct faculty involvement. Also, the two private practice groups have very low G scores as would be expected in contexts such as these, where groups do not exist within the organization.

These OODQ findings suggest that when the respondents completed the instrument they were not just describing their arbitration work, but their work situation as a whole. Clearly the focus was on the arbitration context; the letter that went out with the various measures repeatedly addressed the respondents as arbitrators, and the arbitration questionnaire certainly served to reinforce that focus. Those whose only work activity was arbitration numbered just over 50 percent of the sample. However, the OODQ itself asks that the respondent select "the one answer which best describes your work situation." This would permit nonarbitration work to influence the responses, and from Table 19.2 it appears that this did happen. It is also apparent that the great majority of the work situations described were professional in nature whether or not arbitration was the sole focus.

The professional motivation scores in Table 19.2 fail to exhibit any statistically significant differences across organizational contexts. As noted previously, these MSCS–P measures are consistently high. Congruence between organization type (professional) and motivation pattern (professional) remains at the same elevated level irrespective of the organizational context.

IMPLICATIONS FOR THEORY

The findings of this study support professional role motivation theory and the congruence or fit relationships inherent in it. The professional form in its various manifestations emerges as a clear alternative to bureaucracy. As a test of theory the research proved successful. Furthermore the positive results were obtained using two measures that derive from completely different and independent sources—the arbitrators themselves in the case of the professional membership criterion and management representatives in the case of the management ratings. However, it is well to recognize that this research does not represent a test of the theory in its totality. The professional theory includes a role prescription component and a causal arrow from motivation to performance. These aspects of the theory have not been directly tested here. However, role-motivation fit must be present given the effectiveness correlations obtained with role-specific motivation measures noted in Table 19.1.

There are several considerations that should be taken into account in dealing with the matter of causality. Ample evidence exists that motives similar to those included in the professional theory can have a causal impact. For example, McClelland and Winter (1969) demonstrated this for achievement motivation, and McClelland and Boyatzis (1982) did the same for power motivation.

Even more significant is the fact that the motives of the two parallel theories—hierarchic theory and task theory—have been shown to have a causal relationship to performance. These theories were constructed along the same lines as the professional theory and the research utilized measures of the same type as the MSCS–Form P. As noted previously, the predictive validity of the hierarchic theory has been demonstrated in seven studies—three studies of R&D and marketing managers in an oil company (Miner 1965a); a study of scientists, engineers, and managers in a government R&D laboratory (Lacey 1974); a study of U.S. Army officer candidates at Ft. Benning, Georgia, and another study of U.S. Military Academy cadets (Butler, Lardent, and Miner 1983); and a study of graduate students in business (Bartol and Martin 1987). Similar results have been obtained using the task theory to predict entrepreneurial success in the electronics industry (Bracker, Pearson, Keats, and Miner 1991) and among technologically innovative entrepreneurs (Miner, Smith, and Bracker 1992a). One advantage of the use of parallel theorizing is that findings from one theory have potential for extrapolation to others. Given the fact that the professional theory has demonstrated concurrent validity comparable to that of the hierarchic and task theories, it seems appropriate to generalize the predictive feature from these other theories to the professional domain.

Another consideration is that the MSCS–Form P is a projective device, and accordingly respondents typically do not have an understanding of what is being measured. A conscious process of responding to recognition of their professional success, by describing themselves as they perceive a successful professional should be, is almost impossible. People do not know how to respond to produce a desired result, and consequently response bias is minimized. Finally, if effectiveness causes motivation and effectiveness takes time to achieve, as it does, there should be a positive correlation between age and professional motivation. This does not occur, except in the case of professional commitment, and the professional commitment measure does not yield consistently higher effectiveness correlations than the other subscales. In view of the age results and the fact that the effectiveness correlations in Table 19.1 involve motivational measures, it is difficult to argue for a causal process other than that posited by the theory.

At the same time it should be recognized that the correlations involved, though significant, are typically not large. This, however, is to be expected given that this research deals with congruence among only three types of components. A much larger proportion of variance presumably would be accounted for had the wide arrays of components proposed by Mackenzie (1991) or Galbraith and Kazanjian (1986) been studied.

IMPLICATIONS FOR PRACTICE

A significant feature of the arbitrator research is that it isolates the professional form as a separate and distinct organizational design. It engages a specific and unique set of motives, it is clearly differentiated by those participating in it, and it extends across a variety of organizational contexts having in common only their reliance on a professional system. This professional form is only tangentially related to bureaucracy at best, and then only mildly in the university context. It is a free-standing design in its own right. Those who confound it with bureaucracy may only confuse the system, introducing high levels of role conflict and making staffing extremely difficult. The distinct nature of a professional system was spelled out previously in the Professional Organization section. Those who design organizations should be aware of this alternative and know how to construct it; they should also be able to recognize it in a natural state. The OODQ is a useful aid for this purpose.

Secondly, the findings with regard to motivation-organization fit indicate that once one has established the fact that a professional system exists, it is important to staff the professional component of that system with high professional motivation people. Such people must be identified, selected, and appropriately placed. The MSCS–Form P is a useful aid for this purpose.

ADDENDUM ON PERFORMANCE RATINGS BY THE UNIONS

Previously noted was the fact that performance data were obtained from union sources, as well as from management. These union ratings were not reported because of lack of comparability with other data. An additional factor was that the *Organization Science* editor felt that the article was too long as submitted, and needed to be reduced in length. However, it may prove helpful to provide further information with regard to these ratings here:

> Analyses were carried out relating performance evaluations of labor arbitrators by union representatives to similar evaluations of the same arbitrators by management representatives. It was found that these evaluations are either unrelated or, in some cases, negatively related. An important consideration in the evaluations is whether an arbitrator's awards tend to favor union or management. These results are discussed in terms of the disparate values and "good arbitrator" views of arbitrator performance. Both views find some support (Crane and Miner 1988, 43).

Consonant with these results, the union evaluations were not significantly predicted by the MSCS–Form P in the same manner as the management evaluations were. This failure to validate instigated a search of the data with the objective of identifying anything that would explain this lack of hypothesized results. In cases of this kind there is always the possibility that unreliability in the criterion measure is to blame, but the evidence available did not support this interpretation.

One tack that was taken was to investigate those cases where the T score on the OODQ was high and either greater than the P score or very close to it. Operationally this meant a T score of 9 or more (at or above the entrepreneur mean) and a ratio of T score to P score of at least 80 percent. There were only eight such cases where the T score was above the P score, and another four where the two were equal. Adding the seven instances where the T score was within 80 percent of the P score produced a total of nineteen cases. The average P score was still 8.82. The group of nineteen is best described as working in a context that is balanced as to professional and entrepreneurial aspects, but the group is distinguished from the other arbitrators by its consistently high T scores. These arbitrators are spread across all five organizational context categories noted in Table 19.2 and do not concentrate in any one of them.

This group is important because within it significant correlations between the MSCS–Form P measures and the union ratings are obtained. The total score correlation is –.63 ($p < .01$). The subscale correlations are –.41 ($p < .05$) for Acquiring Knowledge, –.44 ($p < .05$) for Independent Action, –.40 ($p < .05$) for Accepting Status, –.59 ($p < .01$) for Providing Help, and –.47 ($p < .05$) for Professional Commitment. In this sample only the union rating success index produces significant results with any consistency. There appears to be nothing else distinctive about the group other than its entrepreneurial orientation.

It is important to recognize that this finding was not hypothesized, clearly involves a certain

Table 19.3

Relationships between MSCS–P Measures and Professional Leadership within the Labor Arbitrator Sample

MSCS–P Measures	Professional Leaders (N = 43)	Not Professional Leaders (N = 50)	t	r_{bis}
Total Item Score	14.07	5.54	6.21**	.68
Acquiring Knowledge	1.67	0.10	3.48**	.42
Independent Action	2.42	1.74	1.58	.21
Accepting Status	3.44	1.16	4.45**	.51
Providing Help	3.67	1.24	5.15**	.59
Professional Commitment	2.86	1.30	3.82**	.46

Note: MSCS = Miner Sentence Completion Scale.
$^{**}p < .01$

amount of capitalization on chance, and derives from a small sample where random fluctuations are most likely. A comprehensive study of the subject might well not support these results. The implication of the finding is that union evaluators do recognize and value professional motivation in an arbitrator, but only when that arbitrator views the job as one where professional and entrepreneurial factors both play an important role. A feasible interpretation is that the union ratings represent the preferences of the raters as well as the performance of the arbitrators. The union raters like more professionally motivated arbitrators, but only when those arbitrators see their work as somewhat entrepreneurial. This raises the possibility that the union ratings are to a degree contaminated by non-performance factors and should not be used in a test of the professional theory. The fact that the management rating results parallel those for number of professional memberships gives more confidence in the performance-based nature of the management ratings. Yet there is the possibility that there is something in this analysis of the union performance data that will provide a basis for a fruitful hypothesis for some future research investigation.

ROLE-MOTIVATED LEADERSHIP IN PROFESSIONAL ORGANIZATIONS

In the arbitrator sample seven individuals could not be classified as to whether they were leaders or not on the evidence available. However, the MSCS–P scores of these arbitrators were on the low side, approximating those of the non-leaders. Of the 93 arbitrators remaining, 43 were identified as leaders and 50 were not. The criteria used to make this identification are considered in Chapter 9. Key considerations used were professorial rank, partnership in a law firm, administrative position, publications, NLRB activities, and judicial service. In general these criteria followed the same pattern as the Academy of Management professors, and the proportion of leaders is much the same.

The data of Table 19.3 indicate a marked superiority of the MSCS–P scores of the leaders over those of arbitrators who were not leaders—following much the same pattern as the Academy of Management faculty members. On the subscales all give evidence of a similar strong relationship except that the independent action relationship fails to attain significance. It is not clear why this result occurs.

CHAPTER 20

ATTENDEES AT THE CENTER FOR ENTREPRENEURIAL LEADERSHIP PROGRAM OVER SEVEN YEARS

INTRODUCTION

This article was published in *Entrepreneurship and Regional Development* (Miner 1997b) with the objective of bringing the Center for Entrepreneurial Leadership research to the attention of a European audience. More extensive reports on this research had been published in book form in the United States—*The 4 Routes to Entrepreneurial Success* (Miner 1996b) for a trade audience and *A Psychological Typology of Successful Entrepreneurs* (Miner 1997a) for those with a more scholarly inclination. See also Miner 1997c.

The line of theorizing involved here diverges from what has characterized most other chapters of this book. This research is not based on role motivation theory (see Foti and Miner 2003), and thus departs from the programmatic format that has been typical previously in this book. However, it does utilize the MSCS in its various forms, with the result that many of the variables considered in the research are familiar. Accordingly ties to role motivation theory do exist. Also the chapter contains, at the end and after the article itself, certain material that is more consistent with the overall development of role motivation theory.

The Center for Entrepreneurial Leadership program conducted for many years by the School of Management at the State University of New York at Buffalo is the base from which this research gained its data. This program is described in considerable detail in Chapters 12 and 13 of Miner 1997a. I conducted the psychological assessments which contributed the test data, but a number of other people at the State University of New York at Buffalo made contributions to the research as well. In particular I want to acknowledge the assistance of John O'del, Chao-Chuan Chen, Eric Williams, Juan Carlos Pastor, Susan Stites-Doe, and Carol Newcomb.

* * *

It is widely recognized that entrepreneurs and their firms are spread over a broad range and that many different types exist. A number of different typologies have been proposed, although that of Smith (1967), which sets forth the craftsman and opportunistic types based on differences in education, social involvement, social competence, and time orientation, appears to have received the most attention. This typology now has been extended to incorporate inventor-entrepreneurs (Miner, Smith, and Bracker 1992b).

Discussions and evaluations of this and other typologies are provided by Bird (1989), Gartner (1985), Gartner, Mitchell, and Vesper (1989), Woo, Cooper, and Dunkelberg (1988, 1991), and Steiner, Miner, and Gray (1986). In some cases the typologies deal with successful entrepreneurs, either explicitly or implicitly, but many are concerned simply with existing ventures whether doing well or not. Although a few typologies relate to psychological characteristics of the entrepreneur to some extent, this is not the norm and none are focused entirely on differences in entrepreneurial personality make-up. The theory and research presented in the following pages, in contrast, are distinguished by an explicit focus on success, and on personality.

The literature on typologies is complex and disparate with no universal agreement on definitions or approaches (Rich 1992). Given this, those who work with typologies need to be quite specific regarding the approaches that they are following. The approach here is to treat typologies as theories that are subject to rigorous empirical testing (Doty and Glick 1994). They are not merely classification systems that specify decision rules for categorizing phenomena into mutually exclusive and exhaustive sets. Furthermore, typologies should be clearly distinguished from taxonomies. The former are conceptual in nature, and at their best have implications for important organizational outcomes (Miller 1996; Sanchez 1993). Taxonomies are derived from multivariate analyses of empirical data with the objective of identifying mutual clusters; they are empirically, not conceptually, based. Examples are provided in the use of cluster analysis for taxonomic purposes (Ketchen and Shook 1996) and in McKelvey's (1982) comprehensive treatment.

THEORETICAL FRAMEWORK

During the 1960s, research by McClelland and others dealing with the relationship between achievement motivation and entrepreneurship offered considerable promise (McClelland 1961, 1962, 1965; McClelland and Winter 1969). Yet by the 1990s Guth (1991) was disposed to write off the personality connection entirely, on the grounds that other more promising avenues for study existed. He was not alone in this conclusion. The early conference volumes edited by Kent, Sexton, and Vesper (1982) and Sexton and Smilor (1986) contained extensive discussions of personality factors and even chapters dealing with the subject. However, the third volume in the series (Sexton and Kasarda 1992) has much less to say on the topic. This pessimism regarding the value of personality factors as predictors of entrepreneurial success appears to carry up to the present (Eggers 1995).

Yet several lines of research have continued to yield support for the achievement motivation theme in one form or another. Among these are the work of Roberts (1991) on high technology entrepreneurship and the research on task motivation theory by Bellu and others (Bellu 1988, 1992, 1993; Bellu, Davidsson, and Goldfarb 1989, 1990; Bellu and Sherman 1993, 1995). In addition there are a series of studies in which the present author has been involved (Miner 1986, 1990, 1993; Miner, Smith, and Bracker 1989, 1992a, 1994; Smith, Bracker, and Miner 1987; Smith and Miner 1984, 1985). There have been some positive reviews of the research in recent years as well (Caird 1993; Naffziger 1995).

It appears that achievement motivation broadly defined continues to be an important consideration in predicting entrepreneurial success. The evidence to this effect is quite impressive overall, and in fact personality factors have been incorporated in several comprehensive theories of performance by entrepreneurial firms (Herron and Robinson 1993; Johnson 1990; Keats and Bracker 1988).

Yet there is an inconsistency between the typology literature and the personality research. The very concept of a typology assumes multiple types of entrepreneurs. The personality research to date has focused almost exclusively on a single type of personality. To bring these two approaches in line with one another requires hypothesizing multiple personality types, and thus differing patterns of behavior leading to entrepreneurial success—a psychological typology.

The *personal achiever* type is the closest to the classic pattern hypothesized and researched by McClelland and others. Ten conceptually related components may be involved; although all need not be present to define a personal achiever. The ten characteristics are:

1. Motivation for self-achievement.
2. Type A personality.
3. Desire for feedback on achievements.
4. Desire to plan and set goals for future achievements.
5. Strong personal initiative.
6. Strong personal commitment to their venture.
7. Desire to obtain information and learn.
8. Internal locus of control.
9. High value placed on careers in which personal goals, individual accomplishments, and the demands of the work itself govern.
10. Low value placed on careers in which peer groups govern.

The second, *real manager,* type derives from theory and observation, which suggest that there is a point on the entrepreneurial growth curve at which managers must take hold of a firm and introduce systematization into it (Galbraith 1982; Churchill and Lewis 1983; Mintzberg 1984). This organizational life cycle stage is discussed at length by Dyer (1992) who likens it to the point at which a marathon runner "hits the wall." It is one of the mid-career business dilemmas in his model of entrepreneurial careers (Dyer 1994). Real manager entrepreneurs possess certain essential characteristics of managers. Thirteen such characteristics are specified based on the research of Ghiselli (1971) and Miner (1993), although not all must be present in a person to identify that person as a real manager. The characteristics are:

1. High supervisory ability.
2. Strong self-assurance.
3. Strong need for occupational achievement.
4. Strong need for self-actualization.

5. Weak need for job security.
6. Strong personal decisiveness.
7. Positive attitudes towards authority.
8. Desire to compete with others.
9. Desire to assert oneself.
10. Desire to exercise power.
11. Directive in cognitive style.
12. Desire to stand out from the crowd.
13. Desire to perform managerial tasks.

The personal achiever and real manager types and the component characteristics that serve to define them were established a priori based on literature and research that preceded this study. This is only partially true of the third type—the *expert idea generators.* Aspects of this type derived from prior research (Miner, Smith, and Bracker 1992b; Roberts 1991), but other aspects only became evident during the early phases of the research. The five components of the expert idea generator type are as follows (again not all need to be present to establish the type):

1. Desire to personally innovate.
2. Conceptual in cognitive style.
3. Belief in new product development as a key element of company strategy.
4. High intelligence.
5. Desire to avoid taking risks.

The last two of these operate to embellish or control the first three. Intelligence aids the idea generation process. Risk avoidance serves to limit any excessive enthusiasm for ideas that might otherwise threaten a venture. In this latter connection it is important to note that, contrary to popular lore, entrepreneurs as a group are not pronounced risk-takers (Palich and Bagby 1995).

The fourth type, *empathic supersalespeople,* arose entirely from the early stages of the present research. Prior literature did not provide any basis for hypothesizing it. The five component characteristics, not all of which are required to identify the type, are:

1. Empathic in cognitive style.
2. Desire to help others.
3. High value attached to social processes.
4. Strong need for harmonious social relationships.
5. Belief in the sales force as a key element of company strategy.

Consistent with the author's approach to forming typologies, these four types need not be mutually exclusive in the sense that only one type may exist in a single person. In fact it is incumbent on theory to indicate what the consequences of a person's having more than one type might be. Thus, three hypotheses were tested in this research (Miner 1996a). They are as follows:

Hypothesis 1. *Personality characteristics of entrepreneurs, as measured by personality tests and questionnaires, are effective predictors of the subsequent success (growth) attained by the firms of these entrepreneurs.*

Hypothesis 2. *There are four types of entrepreneurs who can produce subsequent success (growth) in their firms—(a) personal achievers, (b) real managers, (c) expert idea generators, and (d) empathic supersalespeople—each of which may be defined in terms of a set of personality test and questionnaire results.*

Hypothesis 3. *The greater the number of key personality patterns present, defined by psychological tests and questionnaires and extending from 0 to 4, the more likely that subsequent entrepreneurial success (growth) will be attained.*

To the author's knowledge no such psychological typology of entrepreneurial success has been proposed previously. However, there is an uncanny similarity to the typology for large corporations in decline proposed by Miller (1990), which came to the author's attention well after these hypotheses were formulated. It appears that once again as science advances, the zeitgeist brings certain ideas into the window of creativity.

METHODOLOGY

Testing the hypotheses is best accomplished by using a longitudinal design in which personality measures are administered at T_1 and then follow-up measures are obtained to establish the success of firms (growth) at a later point in time (T_2).

Sample

The sample studied consisted of 100 entrepreneurs from ventures that had been in existence for some time, in the Buffalo, New York area. These entrepreneurs participated in an entrepreneurship development program sponsored by the State University of New York at Buffalo. The program was initiated to foster homegrown businesses in a region that had suffered from the withdrawal of large corporations headquartered elsewhere (Miner and Stites-Doe 1994). It involved presentations about their firms by the entrepreneurs themselves, presentations by various speakers including faculty members, psychological assessments utilizing tests and feedback sessions, and various social networking activities. The program extended through a single academic year. The sample was accumulated over a 7-year period; the numbers each year were 10, 9, 14, 14, 16, 19, 18, respectively—a total of 100. This was the Center for Entrepreneurial Leadership program.

The mean age of the entrepreneur sample was 41.9 years (SD = 9.4 years) with a range from 25 to 75 years; 9 percent were in their 20s and 4 percent were over 60 years of age. These figures were obtained as each cohort entered the program.

The mean years of education was 16—a college graduate (SD = 1.9 years); 4 percent had not attended college and 31 percent had some graduate study, including several with PhDs. Most had completed their formal education before entering the program.

The firms associated with these entrepreneurs extended over a wide range, including both service and manufacturing, although there were more of the former than the latter. In terms of origin, 49 percent were start-ups by the entrepreneur—21 percent without a partner and 21 percent with one or more partners. The remaining 7 percent of these start-ups were independent, but the firms are best described as sales or professional practices—small in scope and without a primary growth objective. In another 23 percent of the cases the entrepreneur was a member of a family business, and had either taken over leadership of the firm or was in line to do so. The entrepreneur had assumed ownership of the firm by purchasing it in 12 percent of the instances. The remaining 16 percent were involved in some type of corporate venturing or intrapreneurship—7 percent heading a corporate venture and 9 percent serving in a turnaround capacity to a corporate entity. This sample defines entrepreneurship quite broadly. However, no evidence was found that this fact hampered the research.

At the time these entrepreneurs entered the development program their firms had an average of 58.3 employees (SD = 93.3). The range was from 1 to 600, with 9 percent having 5 employees or less and 6 percent having 200 or more. The mean annual sales volume for the previous year was $4.4 million (SD = $6.2 million) and the range was from 0 to $37 million; 17 percent of the firms had sales of under half a million dollars and 12 percent had sales of $10 million or more. Profits on sales for the preceding year ranged from 0 to 27 percent, with the mean at 7 percent; 48 percent of the firms had profits of under 5 percent, and only 15 percent had profits above the 15 percent figure.

Personality Measures

The personality measures were administered during the early fall of each year to the program participants available at that time. Thus there were seven separate testing periods, each with its own cohort of subjects. Scores were clustered so as to operationalize each of the four personality types. The clustering was purely conceptual in nature. On each measure the total score distribution was segmented to yield three parts. Score levels expected to be most strongly associated with a type were set equal to 2, score levels expected to be somewhat less indicative were set equal to 1, and score levels not expected to contribute to the type at all were rated 0. These score levels were established using breaks in the normative score distributions indicated by the test authors. Thus each measure within a cluster of test scores had values assigned of 2, 1, or 0. The sum of these values across all component test measures was the cluster or type score.

The test components of the *personal achiever* pattern number 15. Thus the type score can range from 0 to 30. The actual range was from 5 to 24 (SD = 4.2) with a mean of 14.1. Scores of 17 or above were used to establish a personal achiever type. In the list that follows the test measures are preceded by a number from 1 to 10, which indicates the personality characteristics tapped (see the previous discussion).

(1) Lynn Achievement Motivation Questionnaire (Lynn 1969; Hines 1973). A score of 8 = 2, 6 or 7 = 1, and 0 to 5 = 0.
(2) Individual Behavior Activity Profile—abbreviated (Matteson and Ivancevich 1982a, b). Scores of 60 to 75 = 2, 45 to 59 = 1, and 0 to 44 = 0.
(2) Rose Tension Discharge Rate Scale (Rose, Jenkins, and Hurst 1978, Matteson and Ivancevich 1983). Scores of 31 to 42 = 2, 25 to 30 = 1, and 6 to 24 = 0.

Miner Sentence Completion Scale–Form T (Miner 1986, 1993).
(1) Self-achievement. Scores of 4 to 8 = 2, 2 or 3 = 1, and –8 to 1 = 0.
(3) Feedback of results. Scores of 2 to 8 = 2, 0 or 1 = 1, and –8 to –1 = 0.
(4) Planning for the future. Scores of 3 to 8 = 2, 1 or 2 = 1, and –8 to 0 = 0.
Ghiselli Self-description Inventory (Ghiselli 1971).
(5) Initiative. Scores of 41 to 47 = 2, 38 to 40 = 1, and 0 to 37 = 0.

Miner Sentence Completion Scale–Form P (Miner 1981, 1993).
(6) Professional commitment. Scores of 4 to 8 = 2, 2 or 3 = 1, and –8 to 1 = 0.
(7) Acquiring knowledge. Scores of 4 to 8 = 2, 2 or 3 = 1, and –8 to 1 = 0.
Levenson Internal-External Instrument (Levenson 1972, 1974).
(8) I (Internal) Scale. Scores of 43 to 48 = 2, 40 to 42 = 1, and 8 to 39 = 0.
(8) P (Powerful others) Scale. Scores of 8 to 13 = 2, 14 to 17 = 1, and 18 to 48 = 0.
(8) C (Chance) Scale. Scores of 8 to 12 = 2, 13 to 15 = 1, and 16 to 48 = 0.
(8) Matteson and Ivancevich Internal-External Scale (Matteson and Ivancevich 1982a). Scores of 0 to 2 = 2, 3 or 4 = 1, and 5 to 8 = 0.

Oliver Organization Description Questionnaire—completed for an ideal work situation (Oliver 1981, 1982; Miner 1993).
(9) T Score—ideal. Scores of 10 to 15 = 2, 5 to 9 = 1, and 0 to 4 = 0.
(10) G Score—ideal. Scores of 0 or 1 = 2, 2 to 4 = 1, and 5 to 15 = 0.

The test components of the *real manager* pattern number 14. Thus the type score can range from 0 to 28. The actual range was from 0 to 16 (SD = 3.6) with a mean of 5.9. Scores of 8 or above indicate a real manager type. In the following list the 13 characteristics measured are indicated by the parenthetic numbers.

Ghiselli Self-description Inventory (Ghiselli 1971).
(1) Supervisory ability. Scores of 40 to 47 = 2, 37 to 39 = 1, and 0 to 36 = 0.
(2) Self-assurance. Scores of 36 to 41 = 2, 33 to 35 = 1, and 0 to 32 = 0.
(3) Need for occupational achievement. Scores of 54 to 62 = 2, 50 to 53 = 1, and 0 to 49 = 0.
(4) Need for self-actualization. Scores of 16 to 18 = 2, 14 or 15 = 1, and 0 to 13 = 0.
(5) Need for job security. Scores of 0 to 6 = 2, 7 or 8 = 1, and 9 to 19 = 0.
(6) Decisiveness. Scores of 30 to 32 = 2, 27 to 29 = 1, and 0 to 26 = 0

Miner Sentence Completion Scale–Form H (Miner 1964, 1993)
(7) Authority figures. Scores of 3 to 5 = 2, 2 = 1, and –5 to 1 = 0.
(8) Competitive games. Scores of 4 or 5 = 2, 3 = 1, and –5 to 2 = 0.
(8) Competitive situations. Scores of 2 to 5 = 2, 1 = 1, and –5 to 0 = 0.
(9) Assertive role. Scores of 3 to 5 = 2, 2 = 1, and –5 to 1 = 0.
(10) Imposing wishes. Scores of 3 to 5 = 2, 2 = 1, and –5 to 1 = 0.
(12) Standing out from group. Scores of 3 to 5 = 2, 2 = 1, and –5 to 1 = 0.
(13) Routine administrative functions. Scores of 3 to 5 = 2, 2 = 1, and –5 to 1 = 0.

Decision Style Inventory (Rowe and Mason 1987).
(11) Directive style. Scores of 90 to 160 = 2, 82 to 89 = 1, and 20 to 81 = 0.

The test components of the *expert idea generator* pattern number 8. Thus the type score can range from 0 to 16. The actual range was 0 to 13 (SD = 2.6) with a mean of 4.9. Scores of 6 or above were used to indicate an expert idea generator type. The five inherent characteristics of the expert idea generator score are related to the test measures using parenthetic numbers as follows:

Miner Sentence Completion Scale–Form T (Miner 1986, 1993).
(1) Personal innovation. Scores of 5 to 8 = 2, 3 or 4 = 1, and –8 to 2 = 0.
(5) Avoiding risks. Scores of 3 to 8 = 2, 1 or 2 = 1, and –8 to 0 = 0.

Problem-solving Questionnaire (Slocum and Hellriegel 1983).
(2) Intuition style. Scores of 7 or 8 = 2, 5 or 6 = 1, and 0 to 4 = 0.

Decision Style Inventory (Rowe and Mason 1987).
(2) Conceptual style. Scores of 95 to 160 = 2, 87 to 94 = 1, and 20 to 86 = 0.
(3) Company Survey—Ranking of Competitive Strategies (Smith 1967; Miner, Smith, and Bracker 1992b). Ranking new product development 1 to 3 = 2; 4 to 6 = 1, 7 to 12 = 0.
(4) Vocabulary Test G-T–Forms A and B (Thorndike and Gallup 1944; Miner 1961a, 1973c). Scores of 34 to 40 = 2, 29 to 33 = 1, and 0 to 28 = 0.

Ghiselli Self-description Inventory (Ghiselli 1971).
(4) Intelligence. Scores of 52 to 57 = 2, 49 to 51 = 1, and 0 to 48 = 0.
(5) Shure and Meeker Risk Avoidance Scale (Shure and Meeker 1967; Harnett and Cummings 1980). Scores of 41 to 51 = 2, 37 to 40 = 1, and 17 to 36 = 0.

The test components of the *empathic supersalesperson* pattern number 6. Thus the type score can range from 0 to 12. The actual range was 0 to 11 (SD = 2.5) with a mean of 4.2. Scores of 6 or above establish an empathic supersalesperson type. The parenthetic numbers following indicate the particular one of the five inherent characteristics that is measured.

Problem-solving Questionnaire (Slocum and Hellriegel 1983).
(1) Feeling style. Scores of 6 to 8 = 2, 4 or 5 = 1, and 0 to 3 = 0.

Decision Style Inventory (Rowe and Mason 1987).
(1) Behavioral style. Scores of 70 to 160 = 2, 62 to 69 = 1, and 20 to 61 = 0.

Miner Sentence Completion Scale–Form P Miner (1981. 1993).
(2) Providing help. Scores of 5 to 8 = 2, 4 = 1, and –8 to 3 = 0.

Elizur Work Values Questionnaire (Elizur 1984; Meindl, Hunt, and Lee 1989).
(3) Social items (#5, 7, 8, 18, and 20 of the 24-item measure). Scores of 5 to 7 = 2, 8 or 9 = 1 and 10 to 30 = 0.
(4) Least Preferred Coworker (LPC) Scale (Fiedler and Chemers 1984). Scores of 73 to 144 = 2, 65 to 72 = 1, and 18 to 64 = 0.
(5) Company Survey—Ranking of Competitive Strategies (Smith 1967; Miner, Smith, and Bracker 1992a). Ranking sales force 1 to 3 = 2, 4 to 6 = 1, and 7 to 12 = 0.

Two approaches were used to measure the tendency to possess multiple patterns, and thus the extent to which a person may be described as being a complex entrepreneur. One was the number of entrepreneurial patterns an individual possessed, ranging from 0 to 4. Having two or more patterns defines a complex entrepreneur. The other score was the sum of the

Table 20.1

Intercorrelations of Pattern Scores

Pattern	Real Manager	Expert idea Generator	Emphatic Super-salesperson	Composite Score
Personal Achiever	.35**	.02	–.30**	.70**
Real Manager		.22*	–.24*	.74**
Expert Idea Generator			–.14	.47**
Emphatic Supersalesperson				.00

*Significant at $p < .05$; **Significant at $p < .01$

individual scores for personal achiever, real manager, expert idea generator, and empathic supersalesperson. This composite is based on 43 component scores and thus can range from 0 to 86. The actual range was from 15 to 47 (SD = 6.8) with a mean of 29.1. Scores of 33 or above serve to define a complex entrepreneur.

The intercorrelations of the scores are given in Table 20.1. All four type scores are free to vary in that no component of one pattern is determined by a component of another pattern. The median correlation between patterns is –.06. However, the empathic supersalespeople appear to be distinctly different from the other three types.

Success Measures

Success was determined by comparing information obtained when the entrepreneurs presented their firms during the entrepreneurship development program (T_1) with similar information obtained up to the end of the program seventh year (T_2). Thus success was defined in terms of growth, and the interval involved varied substantially depending on when the entrepreneur entered the program The range was from 6.7 years to 0.7 years; the average was 3.2 years. The follow-up process focused on annual dollar sales, number of employees, and profitability. Information was obtained also on whether the individual had remained with the same firm, and if not, what new employment was undertaken. Information regarding the effects of the economic recession that occurred in the Buffalo, New York area during the latter part of the 7-year period was recorded as well.

The follow-up process utilized a variety of sources. In most cases the entrepreneurs were interviewed at their places of business. There were two rounds of these interviews for the initial two years of the program. In some cases the entrepreneurs made later presentations regarding their firms to classes at the university and to other groups. There were numerous meetings at social events, in the airport, and the like. Sometimes information was provided in the Buffalo newspapers. Telephone interviews were conducted in those few cases where a face-to-face meeting could not be arranged. In one way or another, a considerable amount of follow-up information was obtained.

This information was sufficient to establish the success subsequent to testing of 84 of the 100 entrepreneurs. The remaining 16 people could not be evaluated in this manner for one of two reasons. In roughly a third of these cases the individual completed the tests, but did not make a company presentation, and did not complete the entrepreneurship development program. Thus, baseline data were not available. The remaining people were members of the seventh-year group, and the interval between their presentation of their firm and the termination of the study was insufficient to warrant determination of whether growth had occurred.

The follow-up data were used to classify the eighty-four entrepreneurs into one of six categories.

1. The individual had separated from the original firm at some point during the follow-up period, and had not undertaken subsequent employment of an entrepreneurial nature (7 percent).
2. The individual had left the original firm, but subsequently became engaged in another entrepreneurial venture; in all of these instances the individual then continued in an entrepreneurial role (7 percent).
3. The individual and the original firm remained together but the firm did not grow, and often in fact only barely survived (12 percent).
4. The individual and the original firm remained together, but although growth occurred at an early point, recession subsequently had a negative impact; some recovery occurred subsequently (13 percent).
5. The individual and the original firm remained together, but although growth occurred it was of a slow and steady nature overall, with some volatility (31 percent).
6. The individual and the original firm remained together, and growth was substantial (30 percent).

Business failure, if it occurs, would be found in the first two categories. However, there were no more than two or three such instances, and only one bankruptcy failure. For purposes of statistical analysis, categories 1 (no longer entrepreneuring) and 3 (firm did not grow) were combined under the "Little evidence of entrepreneurial success" designation. Categories 2 (re-involved in entrepreneurship), 4 (impacted by recession), and 5 (slow growth) were combined to produce the "Some evidence of entrepreneurial success" designation. Category 6 (the clear growth successes) constituted the "Substantial evidence of entrepreneurial success" designation.

RESULTS

The hypotheses underlying this research, and in particular Hypothesis 2, were not fully developed at the time the study was initiated. Half of the typology was in place—the *personal achiever* and *real manager* parts—but the *empathic supersalesperson* and to a large extent the *expert idea generator* types emerged out of experience during the early stages of the research itself; they did not have a solid basis in the pre-existing literature. This opens the possibility of confounding between theory forming and theory testing. Any results obtained from the research might reflect only a severe case of capitalization on chance.

The evidence indicates, however, that this is not the case. The complete theory, with all elements of the typology in place, was formulated during the fourth year of the entrepreneurship development program, when 47 entrepreneurs had entered the sample. Thus a comparison of the initial 47 subjects with the final 53 can be used to determine whether the capitalization on chance hypothesis is justified. This comparison is presented in Table 20.2.

Note that the theory forming and theory testing samples, for which there were a priori hypotheses applying to personal achievers and to real managers, yield much the same results in all of the comparisons. Expert idea generators and empathic supersalespeople operate in essentially the same way as personal achievers and real managers, and in no case does anything

Table 20.2

Relation of Patterns to Success among Theory Forming (N = 47) **and Theory Testing** (N = 53) **Subjects**

Pattern	Subjects	N†	Little Evidence of Entrepreneurial Success	Some Evidence of Entrepreneurial Success	Substantial Evidence of Entrepreneurial Success	χ^2 (df = 2)
Personal Achiever	Theory forming	12(1)	2	3	7	3.08
	Theory testing	14(2)	0	6	8	$p < .30$
Real Manager	Theory forming	13(1)	2	4	7	2.64
	Theory testing	14(5)	0	7	7	$p < .30$
Expert Idea Generator	Theory forming	13(2)	1	6	6	.04
	Theory testing	14(4)	1	7	6	$p < .98$
Empathic Super-salesperson	Theory forming	12(0)	0	7	5	1.06
	Theory testing	12(3)	1	8	3	$p < .70$
Multiple Patterns	Theory forming	14(1)	1	5	8	.27
	Theory testing	18(5)	1	8	9	$p < .90$
High Composite	Theory forming	12(2)	1	2	9	2.31
	Theory testing	13(4)	0	5	8	$p < .50$

†Numbers in parentheses indicate additional cases with no follow-up evidence.

approaching a significant difference between the theory forming and theory testing groups appear. Combining the two less successful categories to produce larger expected values, and df = 1, did not result in any meaningful change. On this evidence the two groups can be combined, and this is done in the following analyses. The fact that the personal achiever and real manager patterns contain 15 and 19 measures respectively, while the expert idea generator and empathic supersalesperson patterns contain 8 and 6 measures respectively reflects the fact that instruments were initially chosen with reference to the former types more than the latter.

To test the hypotheses, entrepreneurs who possessed a given pattern were compared, as to their subsequent success, with other entrepreneurs in the sample who had no pattern score high enough to exceed the cutting points. Thus, entrepreneurs with and without the specified pattern served as criterion groups. It is necessary to understand, however, that those who possessed a given pattern, and thus could be identified as of a particular type, often possessed other strong patterns as well. Thus, the differences observed cannot be attributed entirely to the particular pattern noted. Of the personal achievers 86 percent had at least one other strong pattern, and it was most frequently the real manager. Among the real managers 82 percent had one or more additional strong patterns, most frequently the personal achiever. The expert idea generators possessed some other strong pattern 67 percent of the time, with the real manager again being most likely. Finally, the empathic supersalespeople had at least one other strong pattern in 48 percent of the cases, with the expert idea generator being slightly more frequent.

Table 20.3 presents the results. All four of the personality patterns are associated with success levels that far exceed those for the entrepreneurs without any strong pattern. The results for the complex entrepreneur measures, however defined, are equally convincing. There can be no doubt that personality factors are associated with subsequent entrepreneurial success and that the four patterns hypothesized operated in this manner.

Table 20.3

Success Attained by Those Who Lack and Possess Patterns

Personality Make-up	N†	Little Evidence of Entrepreneurial Success	Some Evidence of Entrepreneurial Success	Substantial Evidence of Entrepreneurial Success	χ^2 (df = 2) vs. Those Who Lack Any Pattern
Lacks Any Pattern	21(6)	11	10	0	—
Possess Personal Achiever Pattern	26(3)	2	9	15	21.00 ($p < .001$)
Possess Real Manager Pattern	27(6)	2	11	14	19.71 ($p < .001$)
Possess Expert Idea Generator Pattern	27(6)	2	13	12	17.96 ($p < .001$)
Possess Emphatic Supersalesperson Pattern	24(3)	1	15	8	17.12 (p .001)
Possess Multiple Patterns	32(6)	2	13	17	21.99 ($p < .001$)
Possess High Composite Score	25(6)	1	7	17	25.82 ($p < .001$)

†Numbers in parentheses indicate additional cases with no follow-up evidence.

Table 20.4 presents the evidence of the relationship between the number of strong personality patterns possessed (complexity) and subsequent success. The data clearly support Hypothesis 3. The figures in the column farthest to the right show a steady progression with those who have no strong pattern having 0 percent of their members in the "Substantial evidence of entrepreneurial success" category and those who possess three (or in one case four) strong patterns having 78 percent of their members in that category.

The use of χ^2 analyses here provides a less powerful test than would be obtained with parametric procedures. Thus, the significance tests in Tables 20.3 and 20.4 may represent underestimates. Yet typologies by their nature serve to specify only that a type is or is not present, and in any event the differences using χ^2 are highly significant.

DISCUSSION

The research provides substantial support for the conclusion that personality patterns in an entrepreneur exert a dominant influence on the subsequent success of the entrepreneur's venture, that all four types of personalities studied operate in this manner, and that possessing a greater number of these patterns contributes to a greater likelihood of success. The four-way typology appears to have been confirmed.

Experience in working with entrepreneurs, and with the four-way personality-based model, indicates that each type must follow a particular career route that fits the type in order to reap the benefits inherent in the particular kind of entrepreneurial talent. People must actualize their specific potential, or potentials in the case of complex entrepreneurs. For the most part this was true of the 100 established entrepreneurs, although there were departures from time to time.

For *personal achievers* this means investing a great deal of energy in the business, constantly putting out fires and dealing with crises, wearing many hats depending on which crisis is paramount at the moment, and trying to be good at everything.

Table 20.4

Success Attained by Those with Various Numbers of Patterns

Number of Patterns Possessed	N†	Little Evidence of Entrepreneurial Success		Some Evidence of Entrepreneurial Success		Substantial Evidence of Entrepreneurial Success	
		N	%	N	%	N	%
0	21(6)	11	52	10	48	0	0
1	31(4)	3	10	20	65	8	25
2	23(4)	2	9	11	48	10	43
3 or 4	9(2)	0	0	2	22	7	78

χ^2 =34.14 (df = 6) $p < .001$

†Numbers in parentheses indicate additional cases with no follow-up evidence.

For *real managers* the appropriate route is to manage a business into major growth, serving as one's own general manager. To do this people need to find or start a business large enough to require their special managerial talents.

For *expert idea generators* the appropriate route is to invent new products, find new niches, develop new processes, and generally establish a way to outthink the competition. These people need to innovate, think their way through situations, and become visionaries for their firms.

For *empathic supersalespeople* the appropriate route is to spend as much time as possible selling, while getting someone else to handle internal administration and management.

Professional counselors who can provide valid career guidance based on the four-way typology, helping people to follow an appropriate route and to avoid diverting their energies to activities for which they have no talent, are needed. This matter of defining career routes and focusing energies appropriately is considered at length in Miner (1996b).

WOMEN IN THE CENTER FOR ENTREPRENEURIAL LEADERSHIP PROGRAM

Unfortunately only 12 women were contained in the Center for Entrepreneurial Leadership sample, to contrast with the 88 men. Thus any comparison of the sexes has to be considered tentative at best. However, the results of such a comparison can prove instructive, and therefore serve to refine hypotheses for future research (Miner 1997a).

Meaningful age and educational differences are not present between the women and men. On the other hand, the women are involved in somewhat smaller firms, and their companies are almost without exception within the service sector.

The conclusions from an analysis of the differences between the two groups have been set forth as follows in Miner 1996b, 152:

- Women are more likely to start businesses with partners, less likely to take over a family business, and less likely to be a turnaround person in a corporate venture.
- Complexity is more frequent among women entrepreneurs, and this contributes to somewhat higher levels of entrepreneurial achievement than among men.

Table 20.5

Data on the MSCS–Form T in the Center for Entrepreneurial Leadership Sample Including Correlations with Success and with Role-Motivated Leadership

MSCS–Form T Measures	Mean Score (N = 99)	Correlation with Success	Task Leaders (N = 45)	Not Task Leaders (N = 44)	r_{bis}
Total Item Score	10.11	.42**	12.93	7.11	.71**
Self-Achievement	3.09	.18*	3.87	2.38	.41**
Avoiding Risks	1.75	–.09	2.24	1.23	.26*
Feedback of Results	.69	.15	1.29	–.14	.42**
Personal Innovation	3.93	.44**	4.62	3.32	.38**
Planning for the Future	.65	.29**	.91	.32	.15

Note: MSCS = Miner Sentence Completion Scale.
*$p < .05$; **$p < .01$

- While women and men are equally likely to be Personal Achievers, Supersalespeople, and Real Managers, women do not possess the Expert Idea Generator pattern as often. This should make little difference as long as appropriate career routes are followed.

> . . . women do concentrate in the "substantial evidence of entrepreneurial success" category with 50 percent located there, in contrast to 28 percent of the men. The "same" and "little" follow-up categories both have proportionately fewer women. There is some reason to believe that the talents of these women. . . . are reflected in the success levels of their firms (Miner 1997a, 161).

RESULTS OBTAINED WITH THE MSCS–FORM T IN THE CENTER FOR ENTREPRENEURIAL LEADERSHIP SAMPLE INCLUDING IMPLICATIONS FOR ROLE-MOTIVATED LEADERSHIP IN TASK ORGANIZATIONS

The preceding article and analyses do not consider the task theory specifically, and thus the MSCS–Form T in its own right. Rather the concern is with patterns and types of a somewhat different nature than those involved in role motivation theory. However, the data collected with the Center for Entrepreneurial Leadership sample do encompass the MSCS–Form T as a stand alone measure and it is worthwhile considering these results in addition to the pattern data presented in Tables 20.3 and 20.4

These Form T findings are presented in Table 20.5. The mean MSCS–T scores for the total sample and for all subscales are above the 50th percentile points on the normative distributions (Miner 1986). Thus the Center for Entrepreneurial Leadership sample as a whole is consistently motivated by task factors congruent with its entrepreneurial origins. These scores look much like those of high growth entrepreneurs as presented in Table 15.7 for the hi-tech analyses.

The correlations in Table 20.5 for success indexes utilize the same criteria as noted previously for the patterns. As expected the total sample data are highly significant, and three of the five subscales are significant as well.

This analysis is extended in Table 20.5 to the leadership phenomenon in accordance with the guidelines set forth in Chapter 15. The total score correlation now rises to .71 and in addition four of the subscales attain significance. With only one exception the scores for task leaders in the Center for Entrepreneurial Leadership sample are somewhat *above* those of task leaders in the National Science Foundation sample (Chapter 15). Also, of theoretical importance, is the fact that when Form H and Form P scores are used to predict leadership no value exceeds a correlation of .37 and only five of the 14 correlations attain significance. The Form H total score value is .13 and that for Form P is .33. Presumably the Form P value is elevated because the Center for Entrepreneurial Leadership group contains a number of professionals. This interpretation is reinforced by the Oliver Organization Description Questionnaire (OODQ) scores; the mean T-score is 8.37, high as expected, the P-score is 4.80, consistent with the presence of a number of professionals, and the H- and G-scores are both 2.82, both on the low side.

CHAPTER 21

GRADUATE STUDENTS WHO ATTENDED AN ENTREPRENEURSHIP COURSE OVER FIVE YEARS

INTRODUCTION

The *Journal of Applied Behavioral Science* (Miner 2000) published this article. The major objective was to extend the line of research presented in Chapter 20 to the venture start-up phase, as well as to provide further insight into the value of the entrepreneurship typology identified previously. Other sources for information on this research are Miner 1996b and Miner 1997a.

As with the prior chapter, the thrust of the theorizing diverges from role motivation theory, and sets off in a new direction concerned specifically with a typology of entrepreneurship. As previously, however, I have attempted to deal with this factor by introducing at the end certain analyses that bring the student data reported here into a role motivation theory focus.

The course from which these data derive was initiated as an elective in both MBA and PhD programs at the School of Management in the State University of New York at Buffalo; it was in certain respects integrated with the Center for Entrepreneurial Leadership program and served for a number of years to broaden the generally corporate emphasis of the school's coursework. In conducting this research on entrepreneurship, I was aided in a number of ways by various graduate students and the staff at the Center for Entrepreneurial Leadership. I am indebted to these individuals; they have been noted previously in the Introduction to Chapter 20.

* * *

The research reported here was carried out with several purposes in mind. These relate to a theory of entrepreneurial personality and of the types of people who make effective entrepreneurs. This theory has been tested previously in a single sample of entrepreneurs with a view to determining whether the personality types specified contribute to firm growth and success. The results of this effort were encouraging (Miner 1996a, 1996b, 1997a, 1997b, 1997c). However, no single piece of research can fully confirm a theory, nor can a single study define the limits of the domain within which the theory applies.

This research is important for two reasons. First, it provides an opportunity to extend the domain of the theory from firm growth and success to include firm initiation—a crucial consideration when large corporations are downsizing and new sources of employment and capital creation are urgently needed. Second, the study serves as an expanded replication of the prior work, utilizing students rather than established entrepreneurs, and business initiation rather than firm growth as a criterion. In addition, the research permits a direct comparison of students who exhibit an interest in entrepreneurship, and who therefore are part of the talent pool for business creation, with practicing established entrepreneurs.

It has become evident that entrepreneurs and their firms are diverse and that many different types exist. Several typologies have been proposed; an example is Smith's (1967), which specifies craftsman and opportunistic entrepreneurs, based on differences in education, social involvement, social competence, and time orientation.

In general, this typological approach to theory construction has been favorably received within the field of entrepreneurship. Discussions of entrepreneurial typologies may be found in a number of sources (Bird 1989; Gartner 1985; Gartner, Mitchell, and Vesper 1989; Woo, Cooper, and Dunkelberg 1991). In some cases, these typologies consider certain psychological characteristics of the entrepreneur along with other factors. However, this is rare, and no previous typology has made differences in entrepreneurial personality its major concern. The present research focuses on four different personality types and relates these types to the business-founding activities of graduate business students.

The psychological typology investigated here differs from previous typologies and also from previous theorizing on the entrepreneurial personality, which has tended to focus narrowly on that aspect of personality related to achievement motivation. Thus, although types and personality have both been used before, they have been considered separately. The contribution to knowledge of the present approach is that it integrates these two aspects.

The literature on typologies lacks agreement on definitions and approaches (Rich 1992). Accordingly, those who use typologies need to be specific as to what they mean and intend. My approach is to treat typology as a theory, subject to rigorous empirical testing (Doty and Glick 1994). Typologies are not merely classification systems that establish decision rules for categorizing phenomena (data) into mutually exclusive and exhaustive sets. They must be clearly distinguished from taxonomies. Typologies are conceptual in nature, a priori, and at their best have implications for important organizational outcomes (Miller 1996; Sanchez 1993). Examples of such formulations are Mintzberg (1979), Miles and Snow (1978), Burns and Stalker (1994), and Miller (1990). Taxonomies on the other hand are derived from multivariate analysis of empirical data; the intent is to identify mutually exclusive clusters. Because these clusters are derived empirically, rather than conceptually, they are not a priori, and cross-validation on another sample is required. Cluster analysis is often employed (Ketchen and Shook 1996).

The status of research on entrepreneurial personalities also is somewhat muddied. During the 1960s, McClelland (1961, 1962, 1965) and McClelland and Winter (1969) developed a theory of achievement motivation that seemed to offer great promise for understanding entrepreneurship. However, this promise was not immediately fulfilled. There clearly has been some tendency to back away from the earlier optimism (see Low and MacMillan 1988).

Yet a rather sizable body of research has accumulated, lending considerable support to the early achievement motivation formulations (Bellu 1988, 1993; Bellu and Sherman 1995; Miner, Smith, and Bracker 1989, 1994; Roberts 1991). In addition there have been some rather positive reviews of the research on personality factors. Johnson (1990) notes twenty-three studies extended back to 1961 and concludes that a positive relationship between achievement motivation and some type of entrepreneurial behavior was found in twenty of the twenty-three studies. Reviews by Begley and Boyd (1987), Bird (1989), Timmons (1990), Cooper and Gascón (1992), Block and MacMillan (1993), Ray (1993), Caird (1993), and Naffziger (1995) all strike a positive tone. A major difficulty appears to have been that while the entrepreneurship field has increasingly come to embrace some kind of typological approach to theorizing, psychological theory and research have continued to focus on a single, highly achievement-oriented type of entrepreneur.

To deal with this problem, and expand theory in new directions, a four-way psychological typology has been proposed to predict venture growth and success (Miner 1996a, 1996b, 1997a, 1997b, 1997c). Previously reported research on this typology has concerned itself with the degree to which already established firms experienced growth over a period of time subsequent to the point at which an entrepreneur's typological position was determined via psychological testing. This research showed that all four psychological types have the capacity to grow ventures (as measured by larger numbers of employees and greater gross sales). This typology was developed insofar as possible through building upon existing knowledge in the field; thus, it extends what is already known in a cumulative manner, as a good theory should (Hartman 1988). Two of the types—the personal achiever and the real manager—were derived from the literature in this way. The remaining two—the expert idea generator and the empathic supersalesperson—were developed (partly in the former instance, and fully in the latter) from clinical analysis. This analysis was based on intensive study of individual entrepreneurs, their firms, and psychological test results over a number of years. The process attempted to link personality factors with firm outcomes and to establish the routes entrepreneurs follow in search of success and the traps they may fall into as well (Miner, 1996b).

As a consequence of this clinical approach to theory construction, which involved half of the participants in the study of established entrepreneurs (Miner 1997b), the possibility of confounding or fold-back existed in that study. Including the theory-forming participants in the analysis could create a self-fulfilling prophecy. Thus, an analysis comparing the theory-forming group with the remaining theory-testing group was required. When this was done, no evidence of capitalization on chance in the overall findings was obtained. Thus, the complete sample, containing both theory-finding and theory-testing participants, was used in the final analysis.

THEORETICAL FRAMEWORK

The typology applied in this research differed in some of its component characteristics from the one used previously to predict firm growth among established entrepreneurs. However, at least at the conceptual level, the revised theory closely approximates the original. The reasons for the change are explained in the Method section.

The Types and Their Component Characteristics

The *personal achiever* type is close to the classic pattern set forth by McClelland and others. An alternative term that has been considered for this type is "high-energy inputter." In this research, the type contained seven characteristics, whereas initially there were ten (Miner 1997a); in neither case do all characteristics need to be present to define a personal achiever. These seven were:

1. motivation for self-achievement,
2. type A personality,
3. desire for feedback on achievements,
4. desire to plan and set goals for future achievements,
5. strong personal commitment to their ventures,
6. desire to obtain information and learn, and
7. internal locus of control.

The version of the theory tested here did not give consideration to strong personal initiative; to high value placed on careers in which personal goals, individual accomplishments, and the demands of the work itself govern; or to low value placed on careers in which peer groups govern. Note, however, that deleting characteristics in this way is not unlike what happens when low scores are obtained on a particular test.

Motivation for self-achievement (1), desire for feedback on achievements (3), and desire to plan and set goals for future achievements (4) are all aspects of McClelland's (1961) global achievement motivation construct. Type A personality (2), as distinct from the more placid Type B, is a person who is aggressively involved in a chronic, incessant struggle to achieve more and more in less and less time and, if required to do so, against the opposing efforts of other things or persons. The link between type A personality and the personal achiever is evident in this definition.

Strong personal commitment to their ventures (5) is reflected in the value-based identification with their ventures that personal achievers experience. Mowday, Porter, and Steers (1982) say organizational commitment is characterized by a strong belief in and acceptance of the organization's goals and values, a willingness to exert considerable effort on behalf of the organization, and a strong desire to maintain membership in the organization. All three are congruent with the personal achiever type. Desire to obtain information and learn (6) is a very practical and pragmatic desire to acquire information that will make the venture successful. The importance of such learning as new ventures develop is emphasized by Woo, Daellenbach, and Nicholls-Nixon (1994). Internal locus of control (7) refers to people's belief that they control what happens to them in life and that this control resides within themselves. Such a belief makes planning feasible and facilitates throwing oneself into an endeavor as the personal achiever does.

The *real manager* type derives from theory and research indicating that, at some point on the entrepreneurial firm growth curve, managers must assume authority and introduce systematization (Churchill and Lewis 1983; Galbraith 1982; Mintzberg 1984). This organizational life-cycle stage is discussed in detail by Dyer (1992). Entrepreneurs of this type are characterized by a strong managerial identification. In this theoretical version, seven of the thirteen characteristics, posited based on research by Ghiselli (1971) and Miner (1993), were considered. In either version of the theory, a real manager may be defined by less than the full set of characteristics. These seven were:

1. positive attitudes toward authority,
2. desire to compete with others,
3. desire to assert oneself,
4. desire to exercise power,
5. directive in cognitive style,
6. desire to stand out from the crowd, and
7. desire to perform managerial tasks.

The remaining managerial characteristics not dealt with in this version of the theory were high supervisory ability, strong self-assurance, strong need for occupational achievement, strong need for self-actualization, weak need for job security, and strong personal decisiveness.

Six of these characteristics derive from hierarchic (managerial) role motivation theory—positive attitudes toward authority (1), desire to compete with others (2), desire to assert oneself (3), desire to exercise power (4), desire to stand out from the crowd (6), and desire to perform managerial tasks (7). These are all motivational factors involved in performing in the managerial role in bureaucratic contexts with their hierarchic, pyramidal structures, reliance on files, and family-like identity. People who are directive in cognitive style (5) fit well with structured, goal-oriented organizations where they can use power and authority to get things done quickly (Rowe and Mason 1987).

The *expert idea generator* type has its origins in research by Miner, Smith, and Bracker (1992b) and Roberts (1991), and also in the prior research on the typology itself (Miner 1996b, 1997a, 1997b). These entrepreneurs might also be called inventors, using that term in a broad sense to include innovators in any area. Four of the five characteristics originally specified for an expert idea generator were incorporated in the theory tested here. Again not all must be present for the type to be indicated. The four were:

1. desire to personally innovate,
2. conceptual in cognitive style,
3. high intelligence, and
4. desire to avoid taking risks.

The last two of these characteristics operate to embellish or control the initial two. Intelligence (3) fosters the idea-generation process. Desire to avoid taking risks (4) serves to hold back any excessive enthusiasm for ideas that might otherwise threaten an enterprise. It is important to note that contrary to popular lore, entrepreneurs as a group are not found to be great risk takers (see Palich and Bagby 1995). Desire to personally innovate (1) and managing risk are aspects of McClelland's global achievement motivation construct. People who are conceptual in cognitive style (2) love ideas and enjoy solving problems. This style plays an important role in how entrepreneurs approach their firms (Buttner and Gryskiewicz 1993). Belief in new product development as a key element of company strategy, which was specified previously, was not a component of the expert idea generator type in the present version of the theory.

The *empathic supersalesperson* type derives entirely from previous research on the typology (Miner 1996b, 1997a, 1997b). Another designation that would cover many entrepreneurs in this category would be empathic extravert. Of the five characteristics of an empathic supersalesperson indicated in the original theory, only two were given attention in the theory tested here. These two were:

1. empathic in cognitive style and
2. desire to help others.

High value attached to social processes, strong need for harmonious social relationships, and belief in the sales force as a key element of company strategy were not considered.

People who are empathic in cognitive style (1) are sociable, friendly, and supportive. They enjoy pleasing others and are responsive and sympathetic to other people's problems. Those who desire to help others (2) want to assist people with their problems and do for them what they cannot do for themselves; this is the kind of motivation that characterizes the helping professions. The personal concern and desire to help—the inherent empathy—come through, and customers are motivated to return the favor by buying the product or service the empathic supersalesperson is selling.

Hypotheses

The theory as set forth is about personality and its aspects. It identifies four types as its independent variables, each of which contains a number of component personality characteristics. Thus, a psychological typology is created that expands the horizon of entrepreneurship to include a much larger number of people than previously had been considered to be potential business founders. Although previous research has provided substantial support for the role of personality factors in predicting entrepreneurial criteria, there remains some skepticism on this score. Thus, one goal of this research is to shed light on this global question.

Hypothesis 1. *Personality characteristics, as measured by personality tests and questionnaires, are effective predictors of business-founding criteria.*

The theory as originally stated had reference to indexes of entrepreneurial success as operationalized by growth in employment, dollar sales, and profits. However, firms that grow in this manner must be founded; without founding, there can be no growth. Thus, it seems reasonable to test an expansion of the theory's domain to include founding as a predicted personality consequence. Because of business failures in the early period, one might expect founding to prove to be a somewhat weaker criterion than success, but nevertheless a significant one.

Hypothesis 2. *Four types of people are particularly likely to produce positive results on founding criteria—personal achievers, real managers, expert idea generators, and empathic supersalespeople—all of whom may be defined in terms of a set of personality test and questionnaire results.*

Typologies, being conceptual and a priori in nature (in contrast to taxonomies, which are empirically derived), need not be mutually exclusive in the sense that only one type may exist in a single person. Thus, theory must specify how the existence of more than one type in the same person might affect outcomes. Complexity has proven a powerful component of the theory, and complex entrepreneurs with multiple personality types within them should be particularly predisposed to founding.

Hypothesis 3. *The greater the number of these key personality types present in a person, defined by psychological tests and questionnaires and extending from 0 to 4, the more likely that that person will produce positive (entrepreneurial) results on business-founding criteria.*

In addition, the research seeks to compare data from the current student sample, which represents a source of entrepreneurial talent, with similar data from a group of already established entrepreneurs. Both samples are drawn from the same geographic locale.

How the Theory Speaks to Leadership

Some confusion exists in the literature regarding the use and meaning of the terms *manager, leader,* and *entrepreneur.* Accordingly, it seems important to clarify where the present theory stands in this regard, especially since the theory deals with entrepreneurs and a managerial type within that group and has had nothing to say to this point on the subject of leadership at all.

First, the reader should recognize that the present entrepreneurship typology exists within a broader role motivation theory typology dealing with (1) hierarchic (managerial), (2 professional (specialized), (3) group (team), and (4) task (entrepreneurial) organizations or components of organizations (see Miner 1993). Role motivation theory recently has been extended into the leadership domain. This extension holds a broad view of leadership, which contends that organizational leaders are the more successful key people in each of the four organizational domains—top managers in hierarchic systems, the intellectual elite within professional systems, emergent leaders within group systems, and lead entrepreneurs within growth-oriented task systems. Thus, organizational leadership roles take different forms in different organizational contexts, requiring different types of people to perform these roles effectively, and leadership careers vary in important ways with the organizational forms in which they occur.

One consequence of this way of thinking about leadership is that leaders in different organizational contexts are considered to be completely different types of people. Also, leaders in each organizational domain differ from rank-and-file managers, professionals, group members, and venture participants in that these leaders have more of the strong motives that tend to characterize the others as well; thus, they are different from the rank-and-file types in the degree, not the nature, of their motivation. Within the hierarchic domain, then, managers are those who hold managerial positions, normally with subordinates under them in the hierarchy. Hierarchic leaders are those who have achieved positions in the upper reaches of a hierarchic chain. This view should be distinguished from the heroic view of leaders, as opposed to managers, that others have endorsed (see Terry 1995; Zaleznik 1977). Leaders are both like managers in the strong motives that make them effective and unlike them in the strength of these motives.

Turning now to entrepreneurship and the present typology, leaders in this domain are lead entrepreneurs (see Timmons 1990) who head organizations committed to growth, a commitment that usually occurs in the form of an implicit or explicit vision statement (Baum, Locke, and Kirkpatrick 1998). Not being committed to growth, or possessing partner status are conditions that obviate the leader designation for an individual. Any one of the four types of entrepreneurs may become a leader; or more likely, this will be a complex entrepreneur who combines two or more types. The real manager type has no special advantage in this regard, because these people require a hierarchy to exercise their skills and thus an organization of some size—a large-scale start-up, a well-developed family business, a purchased firm that has already grown substantially, or the like. Real manager entrepreneurs typically do poorly at growing small firms if they do not possess the talents of some additional psychological type as well. Small, growing entrepreneurial firms tend to be somewhat organic in form (Burns and Stalker 1994) with little resort to hierarchic chains; the lead entrepreneur operates as an individual moving to deal with crises and grasp opportunities without reference to either hierarchic, professional, or group-based constraints. Often then, entrepreneurs are poor managers, but they do not need to be managers because they operate in organizational systems that do not require the managerial skills that hierarchies do. The term "real manager" was taken from Luthans, Hodgetts, and Rosenkrantz (1988) and carries the implication that the other three types of entrepreneurs, no matter what their titles, are not really managers.

Each of the four entrepreneurial types has his or her own preferred route to success, and each also faces certain traps or pitfalls that are uniquely associated with that particular route (see Miner 1996b). In large part, these traps that can lead to failure, or at least temporary failure, are self-created. They often stem from the special psychodynamics of the individual. Kets de Vries (1989) provides a particularly penetrating analysis of some of the ways in which entrepreneurs may thus lead themselves astray. Yet it is also true that the particular psychodynamics of entrepreneurs, such as their tendencies to distort perceptions of risk (Busenitz 1999), may yield positive consequences at certain points in the entrepreneurial firm cycle as well; without these distortions, many start-ups simply would not occur.

Since this research is concerned with the pre-start-up and venture initiation phases of entrepreneurship, not the subsequent processes of firm growth and success, most of this discussion of leadership and how it relates to managing and entrepreneurship is not immediately relevant. However, an understanding of how the theory deals with these issues should make the four-way theory both more meaningful and perhaps more comprehensible as well.

METHOD

The participants for this study were accumulated over a five-year period in a graduate entrepreneurship course at the State University of New York at Buffalo. The 159 students included 141 at the MBA level and 18 at the PhD level. The course was offered 6 times in the 5-year period with the following additions to the sample:

Year 1	26
Year 2	22
Year 3	30
Year 4 (1)	29
Year 4 (2)	22
Year 5	30

F values were computed across the six classes using a number of measures, including individual test scales, the type scores, the criteria, and a number of demographics. Four of twenty-six test measures yielded significant ($p < .05$) *F* values. These test measures consisted of the nine scales used to measure the personal achiever type, the eight scales used to measure the real manager type, the six scales used to measure the expert idea generator type, and the three scales used to measure the empathic supersalesperson type, as set forth in the following section dealing with predictor measures. The four that yielded significant class differences were the Individual Behavior Activity Profile (Matteson and Ivancevich 1982a, 1982b), where the one night class had a higher type A score; the Decision Style Inventory (Rowe and Mason 1987), including both the Conceptual and Behavioral scales; and the Miner Sentence Completion Scale–Form T: Avoiding Risks scale (Miner 1986, 1993). However, these differences were not sufficient to produce significant differences on any type score, nor were there significant differences on any of the criteria. There was an age difference: In one class, the night class, the students were approximately five years older than those in the other classes. Another class had significantly more PhD students. Given that none of the variables actually used in hypothesis testing produced a significant *F*, combining the six classes into a single sample for purposes of analysis was judged appropriate.

The course itself changed little during the five years. The textbooks did change; the instructor remained the same, namely this author, who did indeed become somewhat more experienced, however. The overall approach to the course, which was the only one in entrepreneurship offered at any point during the five-year period, remained unaltered. The primary source of attraction to the class was the opportunity to learn about entrepreneurship with the objective of evaluating the field as a career alternative. The course was entirely elective for both MBA and PhD students; it was not required as part of any major program of study. Although state and federal programs in support of entrepreneurship became more salient over the five years, these were rarely discussed in class and appear to have exerted little influence on these students.

Males outnumbered females by about 2 to 1—108 versus 51. The mean age was 27.4, with a standard deviation of 5.7. The most frequent major was marketing with 22 percent, followed by finance with 20 percent, human resources and organizational behavior with 18 percent, a general MBA with 15 percent, and systems and production at 11 percent. Beyond these, there was only a sprinkling of other majors.

The positioning of this sample in the wider entrepreneurial and student arena is important. The sample would appear to be typical of the kind of student who might enter upon an entrepreneurship major. There is no such major at the university involved, but such a major does exist at other universities. Just as one might study marketing majors to get a picture of the talent pool for sales and marketing management, it is appropriate to study a sample such as this to get at the talent pool for entrepreneurship. In both instances, the fact that career routes often do not lead through graduate study in business would be fully recognized.

It would have been impossible to conduct a study such as this using a representative sample of graduate students at the university simply because these students overall are predominantly corporate in orientation. There would have been few business start-ups, and any measure of entrepreneurial propensity would have yielded an overwhelming clustering at the very low end of the scale.

In terms of educational level, the sample may be compared with other groups I have studied (Miner 1997b; Miner, Smith, and Bracker 1989). The sample of established entrepreneurs, from the same geographical area as that in which the university is located, on the average had completed an undergraduate education. Thus, the current student sample is more educated than some, but it is also not nearly at the same high level that I have found among high-technology entrepreneurs where more than half hold doctorates.

Predictor Measures

The test battery was administered in class as the course began. Scores were clustered on an entirely conceptual basis to operationalize the four personality types. The total score distribution for each measure was segmented into three parts—score levels expected to be most strongly associated with a type (set equal to 2), score levels expected to be somewhat less indicative (set equal to 1), and score levels not expected to contribute to the type (set equal to 0). The score levels involved were established using guidance from test authors and the normative distributions they provided. The cluster or type score was the sum of the assigned values (0, 1, or 2) for all component measures.

The rationale for this approach derives from the fact that some of the measures had large standard deviations, whereas others showed less variability. It was necessary to combine the measures to obtain type scores but without allowing the large standard deviation measures to dominate the results. This situation would normally call for the use of standard scores; standardization could have been based on either the current, student data or the established entrepreneur data first used to test the theory. Because certain distributions from both samples were badly skewed, however, neither approach was attractive. The ideal would have been to use data for the population as a whole (or some approximation to it). This was not possible because neither distributions nor standard deviations of this type were available for ten of the measures (see Table 21.2).

The 0–1–2 approach was employed to capture the categories and normative information the test authors did provide. Some compression of variances may result for certain individual measures; however, individual measures were not used in the analyses, only type scores that sum the individual data. The result was type score standard deviations in the 1.7 to 3.1 range. If this procedure produces compression, the result should be a conservative bias that operates to reduce the likelihood of obtaining significance.

Only by using this procedure could comparisons be made with the established entrepreneur findings because that analysis was conducted in the same manner. These comparisons represent an important objective of the present research. Although not widely used in entrepreneurship research, the 0–1–2 procedure has been deemed acceptable in several prior applications (Miner, 1996a, 1996b, 1997b; Thayer 1997).

The rationale for reducing the number of characteristics studied in the present research as opposed to the number stated in the original version of the theory (see the theoretical framework discussion, above) and studied in previous research was compounded of several factors. From prior experience, it was apparent that administering the tests in class would assure a higher response rate than having the students take the tests home to complete; also, classroom testing provides a better protection against sharing of answers. However, the class time reasonably available was less than that needed to administer the full battery. Furthermore, four of the original measures assume present employment and thus are not suitable for a student population.

When the original test battery was developed, an attempt was made to introduce multiple measures of a construct wherever possible. This requirement was relaxed in the present study. Thus, many tests that were conceptually redundant with other tests were deleted. In this process, the tests removed in each instance were ones with less validity evidence and research in general, less reliability data, and the like. The net result was the deletion of thirteen more measures, for a total of seventeen.

In shortening the test battery in this manner, I was assuming that scores from the new battery would prove to be highly correlated with those from the original. If they were not, the research would be highly suspect as a test of the theory. Because all tests were included in the comprehensive battery used with the established entrepreneur group, it would be possible to test this expectation in the established entrepreneur sample once this sample was complete. The results are given in the first column of figures in Table 21.3. The correlations range from .72 to .94 with a median of .82, not far from the reliability of these measures. This result appears to legitimize the shortened battery. Details of the actual scoring of the various instruments are given in Chapter 20.

The seven characteristics of the personal achiever type were measured using nine test scales. Thus, the type score could range from 0 to 18. The mean actual score was 5.3 with a standard deviation of 3.1 and a range of 0 to 15. The 9 test measures contained 79 items. Scores of 10 or above established the type. In the listing of test scales that follows, each is preceded by a parenthetic number from 1 to 7 that indicates the specific personality characteristic tapped (see the previous listing in the Theoretical Framework section). The number (7) is repeated 3 times below because the Levenson instrument yields 3 usable measures of internal locus of control.

Miner Sentence Completion Scale–Form T (Miner 1986, 1993): (1) Self-Achievement, (3) Feedback of Results, (4) Planning for the Future.
(2) Individual Behavior Activity Profile—abbreviated (Matteson and Ivancevich 1982a 1982b).
Miner Sentence Completion Scale–Form P (Miner 1981, 1993): (5) Professional Commitment, (6) Acquiring Knowledge.
Levenson Internal-External Instrument (Levenson 1972, 1974): (7) (Internal scale), (7) (Powerful Others) scale, (7) (Chance) scale.

With regard to commitment (5), because of the projective nature of the instrument involved, the items are general in nature and would appear to deal with any type of commitment, including commitment to an organization or venture. This close association between professional and organizational commitment has been substantiated by Wallace (1993) and is consistent with my own clinical conclusions.

The seven characteristics of the real manager type were measured with eight scales. The type score could range from 0 to 16. The mean measured score was 2.4, the standard deviation 1.8, and the actual range 0 to 9. The 8 scales contained 55 test items. A type score of 5 or above defined a real manager. In the following, parenthetic numbers from 1 to 7 indicate the personality characteristic measured. The number (2) is repeated because the Miner Sentence Completion Scale–Form H yields two measures of desire to compete.

Miner Sentence Completion Scale–Form H (Miner 1964, 1993): (1) Authority Figures, (2) Competitive Games, (2) Competitive Situations, (3) Assertive Role, (4) Imposing Wishes, (6) Standing Out from the Group, (7) Routine Administrative Functions.
Decision Style Inventory (Rowe and Mason 1987): (5) Directive.

The four characteristics of the expert idea generator type were measured with six scales. The expert idea generator score can range from 0 to 12. The mean score was 3.2, the standard deviation 1.7, and the actual range 0 to 8. The six scales contain 101 test items. An expert idea generator is someone with a score of 5 or more. The characteristics measured are designated in the following list using parenthetic numbers from 1 to 4. The numbers (2) and (4) are both repeated because two measures of both conceptual cognitive style and desire to avoid risks remain in the battery.

Miner Sentence Completion Scale–Form T (Miner 1986, 1993): (1) Personal Innovation, (4) Avoiding Risks.
Decision Style Inventory (Rowe and Mason 1987): (2) Conceptual.
Problem-Solving Questionnaire (Slocum and Hellriegel 1983): (2) Intuition.

(3) Vocabulary Test GT: Forms A and B combined (Thorndike and Gallup 1944; Miner 1961a, 1973c).
(4) Shure and Meeker Risk Avoidance Scale (Shure and Meeker 1967; Harnettt and Cummings 1980).

With regard to intelligence, this particular vocabulary test (3) correlates in the .80s with the Wechsler Adult Intelligence Scale, the Terman Concept Mastery Test, and the Army General Classification Test in the general population (Miner 1961a). Vocabulary acquired is clearly a major component of general intelligence.

The two characteristics of the empathic supersalesperson type were measured with three scales. The type score could range from 0 to 6. The mean actual score was 2.1, the standard deviation 1.7, and the full possible range of scores was used. The three scales contained 36 test items. Any score of 3 or above is sufficient to identify the empathic supersalesperson. The inherent characteristics of the type are indicated in the following list using the parenthetic numbers 1 and 2. The number 1 is repeated because two measures of empathic cognitive style remain in the battery.

Decision Style Inventory (Rowe and Mason 1987): (1) Behavioral.
Problem-Solving Questionnaire (Slocum and Hellriegel 1983): (1) Feeling.
Miner Sentence Completion Scale–Form P (Miner 1981, 1993): (2) Providing Help.

Much greater detail on these tests and questionnaires may be found in the citations noted and in Miner (1997a).

Those people who possess multiple types from 2 to 4, called *complex entrepreneurs,* are not found as frequently among the students as among established entrepreneurs; there are 21 with 2 strong patterns, 3 with 3, and 1 with 4. In addition, a composite score was calculated as a second index of complexity by adding the 4 type scores. The mean score here was 12.9, the standard deviation 4.7, and the range 4 to 28, as against a possible 0 to 52. A composite score of 20 or more defined a complex entrepreneur.

The intercorrelations among independent variable measures are given in Table 20.1 All four type scores are free to vary in that no component test score of one type is directly determined by one single component, or combination of components, of another type. The median correlation between types is –.06, suggesting that as a whole the type scores are independent of one another.

Table 21.1 provides data on the reliabilities and validities of the individual test measures. More detailed information is contained in the citations noted previously for the different tests. Where possible, test-retest reliabilities are used; the alternatives are included only when test-retest studies have not been conducted. Several of the reliabilities are on the low side, but the median value is .77. Given that only type scores (based on from 36 to 101 items) are used in the analyses, not individual test scores, and increasing the number of items would be expected to increase reliability, the operative reliabilities should be in the vicinity of .85. The validity evidence represents a summation only. However, the term *substantial* is employed only when there are significant relationships extending across not only multiple criteria but also multiple samples, and often many of both.

The use of the 0–1–2 conversion scale in combining the test scores might be questioned on the grounds that it serves either to overcome and mask an inherent restriction of range in the raw scores or to produce an unnecessary degree of score compression. Both questions relate

Table 21.1

Reliability and Validity Evidence for Scales Used in the Research

Scale	Reliability Evidence	Validity Evidence
Miner Sentence Completion Scale–Form T (N = 39)		
Self-Achievement	.91 Test-retest	Substantial
Feedback of Results	.66 Test-retest	Substantial
Planning for the Future	.78 Test-retest	Substantial
Personal Innovation	.76 Test-retest	Substantial
Avoiding Risks	.86 Test-retest	Substantial
Individual Behavior Activity (N = 159)		
Profile-abbreviated	.80 Internal consistency	Face validity only
Miner Sentence Completion Scale–Form P (N = 10)		
Professional Commitment	.98 Scorer	Substantial
Acquiring Knowledge	.90 Scorer	Substantial
Providing Help	.91 Scorer	Substantial
Levenson Internal-External Instrument (N = 96)		
Internal	.64 Test-retest	Substantial
Powerful Others	.74 Test-retest	Substantial
Chance	.78 Test-retest	Substantial
Miner Sentence Completion Scale–Form H (N = 40)		
Authority Figures	.67 Test-retest	Substantial
Competitive Games	.79 Test-retest	Substantial
Competitive Situations	.76 Test-retest	Substantial
Assertive Role	.86 Test-retest	Substantial
Imposing Wishes	.75 Test-retest	Substantial
Standing Out from Group	.85 Test-retest	Substantial
Routine Administrative Functions	.86 Test-retest	Substantial
Decision Style Inventory (N = 428)		
Directive	.70 Test-retest	Some
Conceptual	.70 Test-retest	Some
Behavioral	.70 Test-retest	Some
Problem-Solving Questionnaire (N = 159)		
Intuition	.54 Internal consistency	Some
Feeling	.56 Internal consistency	Some
Vocabulary Test GT (N = 108)	.85 Test-retest	Substantial
Shure and Meeker Risk (N = 159)		
Avoidance Scale	.70 Internal consistency	Some

Note: The N values above apply only to the reliability evidence.

to the size of standard deviations in this as opposed to other samples. Data are not available for all measures, but they are available for 16 of the 26 test scale scores. As indicated in Table 21.2 mean standard deviation on these 16 measures in the current student sample is identical to that in the various normative samples available for comparative purposes.

Some discussion is required to explain how the cutting scores to establish the types and the complex entrepreneur were set using the test battery of this study. The procedure involved going back to the original study of established entrepreneurs and obtaining scores from that sample using only the test measures of the present study. To establish cutting points on the four type scores and on the composite score, I moved down the score distributions for established entrepreneurs by a percentage figure as close as possible to that used in the earlier study with a more comprehensive test battery. These identical cutting scores were then applied to the score distributions of this study. The results of this procedure are presented in

Table 21.2

Standard Deviations in Current Sample as Contrasted with Normative Samples

Scale	Current Sample	Normative Sample
Miner Sentence Completion Scale–Form T	(N = 159)	(N = 135)
Self-Achievement	2.58	2.76 High-technology entrepreneurs
Feedback of Results	2.35	2.27
Planning for the Future	2.46	2.89
Personal Innovation	2.42	2.41
Avoiding Risks	2.92	2.58
Miner Sentence Completion Scale–Form P	(N = 159)	(N = 125)
Professional Commitment	2.08	2.08 Professionals
Acquiring Knowledge	1.58	2.25
Providing Help	2.48	2.59
Miner Sentence Completion Scale–Form H	(N = 159)	(N = 695)
Authority Figures	1.42	1.49 Corporate managers
Competitive Games	1.94	1.77
Competitive Situations	1.72	1.65
Assertive Role	1.80	1.70
Imposing Wishes	1.63	1.46
Standing Out from Group	1.39	1.43
Routine Administrative Functions	1.80	1.64
Vocabulary Test GT	(N = 159)	(N = 108)
	4.19	3.77 Sales employees
Mean standard deviations	2.17	2.17

Note: Normative sample standard deviations are not available for the Individual Behavior Activity Profile, Levenson Internal-External Instrument, Decision Style Inventory, Problem-Solving Questionnaire, and Shure and Meeker Risk Avoidance Scale.

Table 21.3. In the established entrepreneur sample, the cutting score was set so as to define a type using a point as close as possible to the dividing line for the upper third of a score distribution. The net result of using this approach is that comparisons as to type frequencies can be made between established entrepreneurs and students; otherwise, such comparisons could not have been made.

Note first that the abbreviated battery of tests used here yields scores that approximate those obtained with the extended battery quite well. This is the conclusion noted previously. Second, in all instances except the empathic supersalesperson type, the students are less entrepreneurial than are the established entrepreneurs. There are, however, slightly more empathic supersalespeople in the student sample, and this type is concentrated among the marketing and human resource management majors. All in all, the version of the typology applied in this study appears to approximate that of the original theory rather well.

Business Founder Criterion Measures

The research strategy was to take criterion readings as the students began the entrepreneurship course, as they finished it, and finally after they had completed the educational process and became fully involved in the world of work. The reading of entrepreneurial propensity occurred as the course began, at the same time as the psychological testing, and thus was concurrent. The information was provided by the students themselves and dealt with past, present, and intended future entrepreneurial activity. This approach is well grounded in previous research

Table 21.3

Results of Analysis to Establish Cutting Scores Using Extended and Revised Test Batteries

	Correlation Between Extended and Revised Scores (established entrepreneur sample)	Score to Define Type Using Revised Battery	Percentage of Students with Type (N = 159)	Percentage of Established Entrepreneurs with Type (N = 100)
Personal Achiever Score	.89	10 or above	10	28
Real Manager Score	.72	5 or above	10	28
Expert Idea Generator Score	.94	5 or above	25	44
Empathic Supersalesperson Score	.81	3 or above	38	33
Composite Score (Complex Entrepreneur)	.82	20 or above	9	34

using student samples. The most frequent procedure has been to use questions regarding the likelihood of starting a business in the near future or at some point later on (Crant 1996; Koh 1996; Matthews and Moser 1995). Other approaches have dealt with an expanded concept of entrepreneurial career preference (Scherer, Brodzinski, and Wiebe 1991). Questions have been raised about using student participants in this manner (Robinson, Huefner, and Hunt 1991). Yet in conjunction with other criteria of entrepreneurial activity, the procedure seems justified.

As indicated in Table 21.4 the propensity measure responses were content analyzed to yield scores of 2, 1, or 0. Thus, with five questions, scores could range from 0 to 10; the higher scores were the more entrepreneurial. The mean score was 2.9 and the standard deviation 2.1. Only 10 percent of the students scored above the midpoint value of 5. With more knowledge, I could have made this a multiple-choice measure, but in the beginning, I did not have that knowledge. The internal consistency reliability was .67.

The second reading of the students' proclivity for entrepreneurship, the written business plan, came as they finished the course at the end of the semester. At this point, the students were required to submit a written business plan for a new venture, and the grade given on this project was the criterion measure. Thus, this phase of the research was predictive in design but only over the length of a semester. The rationale linking this index to business founding is that founding often involves some type of funding or investment on the part of banks, venture capitalists, angels, or the like, and these sources typically require a business plan. Thus, it seemed likely that students who wanted to be entrepreneurs and who were most likely to start new ventures would work harder on their plans and produce a superior product, all else being equal.

The students all had an outline or model to work from, although this varied somewhat at different times (Hisrich and Brush 1986; Timmons 1990), and they made an oral presentation to the class for critique prior to preparing the final written product. The plan was intended as a vehicle to obtain funding, an objective that prior research has shown is related to psychological factors (Pandey and Tewary 1979). All plans were graded by the same instructor using grades of A, A–, B+, B, B–, and C+. The mean value was in the B+ range. The grade distribution is typical of what might have been expected for a graduate course at this university. In 16 of the 159 cases, no business plan grade was available because the students left the course subsequent to testing without preparing plans. The type scores were not available in any way to the business

Table 21.4

Free Response Questions Used to Establish Entrepreneurial Propensity and Scores Assigned to Responses

Questions and Response Categories	Score
1. Are you working at present and if so, what are you doing?	
Fully self-employed in business	2
Partly self-employed and/or in what appears to be a small professional or sales practice	1
Not working or not self-employed	0
2. What is your immediate career objective after you leave school?	
Starting or buying a business	2
Mention of starting or buying a business, but with some uncertainty, or of starting what appears to be a small professional or sales practice	1
No mention of starting or buying any business	0
3. What is your long-range career objective?	
Starting or buying a business	2
Mention of starting or buying a business, but with some uncertainty, or of starting what appears to be a small professional or sales practice	1
No mention of starting or buying any business	0
4. Have you ever been involved in founding a business? If so, describe it.	
Founded a business that did not fail	2
Founded a business, but it was either very small, or a franchise, or failed	1
Never founded any business	0
5. What are your reasons for taking this course?	
Reason stated as learning how to start a business	2
Reason stated related to entrepreneurship, but not involving a full personal commitment to entrepreneurial activity	1
No reason related to starting a business	0

plan grading process; in fact, they had not even been calculated at that time. Being a one-item measure, estimates of reliability for the business plan index could not be calculated.

The third and ultimate criterion was evidence of entrepreneurial activity after leaving the university. Did the students go out and found businesses when first given an opportunity to do so? Or in some few cases, did they continue ventures that had been started prior to or during the time they were attending classes? To answer these questions, I waited until it was clear that the students had left the university (in almost all cases with a degree). On the average, contact occurred a year after leaving the university. Thus, the study was predictive in nature and extended over a period averaging more than two years. I obtained addresses and telephone numbers (parents' also) while the students were still in class, information from the registrar's office, and addresses and telephone numbers from the alumni office. At the time of follow-up, the students were located throughout the United States and in many parts of the world. I sent letters and follow-up letters, called them and their parents, asked friends about them, and followed every lead in an effort to contact them. A very thorough search was conducted.

Of the 159 students, 8 remained in student status at the conclusion of the study and thus could not be included in this phase of the research. Another 36 simply were lost, in that I was unable to determine their subsequent employment status. Thus the follow-up on entrepreneurial activity actually used a sample of 115. Within this group, my conclusions were as follows:

- No evidence of entrepreneurial activity at follow-up—85 cases (74 percent)
- Part-time participation in a business start-up (usually in conjunction with some other job)—17 cases (15 percent)

Table 21.5

Relationships among Entrepreneurial Criteria Using Categories Employed in Hypothesis Testing—Number and Percentage (in parentheses) **of Respondents**

Entrepreneurial Propensity Score	Business Plan Grade: B or Lower	B+	A or A–	Total	χ^2 (df = 4)
4–10	7 (15)	7 (15)	34 (70)	48 (100)	10.33, $p < .05$
2–3	21 (36)	12 (21)	25 (43)	58 (100)	
0–1	14 (38)	6 (16)	17 (46)	37 (100)	

Business Plan Grade	Evidence of Entrepreneurial Activity Postgraduation: No Evidence Present	Evidence Present	Total	χ^2 (df = 2)
A or A–	41 (65)	22 (35)	63 (100)	8.78, $p < .02$
B+	15 (83)	3 (17)	18 (100)	
B or lower	26 (93)	2 (7)	28 (100)	

Evidence of Entrepreneurial Activity Postgraduation	Entrepreneurial Propensity Score: 0–1	2–3	4–10	Total	χ^2 (df = 2)
Evidence present	7 (23)	7 (23)	16 (54)	30 (100)	9.30, $p < .01$
No evidence present	28 (33)	37 (44)	20 (23)	85 (100)	

- Full-time participation in a business start-up—8 cases (7 percent)
- Engaged in teaching and/or research in the entrepreneurship area—5 cases (4 percent)

The latter category served to accommodate those among the doctoral students who were in fact engaged in a type of entrepreneurial activity. It is apparent that many, if not most, professors in the entrepreneurship field enter into entrepreneurial ventures at some point in their careers. This category was added to recognize this fact. It reflects both that some type of entrepreneurial activity is manifest and that a propensity for venture founding is present.

Although the evidence indicates that the students studied are not unusually entrepreneurially active, the frequency clearly exceeds what would be expected from business students in general at this university. With more time, increased activity might be expected. Table 21.5 contains data on the relationships among all three entrepreneurial criteria, using the actual criterion categories employed in the subsequent analyses. With regard to the entrepreneurial propensity criterion, the categorization was guided by the fact that evidence of entrepreneurial activity postgraduation was a point distribution and by the need to have sufficient cell frequencies to compute χ^2. An attempt was made to approximate three equal categories. It is significant that both of the proximate criteria—the propensity score and the business plan grade—are positively related not only to one another but also to entrepreneurial activity postgraduation—the ultimate criterion of business founding. This is the pattern that would be desired when two of the criteria are proposed as intermediary proxies for the third—business founding. Evidence of significant intercorrelations among the three criteria supports construct validity. The use of chi-square procedures in this and subsequent analyses is appropriate to the typological approach.

Note that, consistent with the hypotheses, none of the criteria employed deal directly with entrepreneurial success, only with founding and, at least briefly, maintaining a business.

RESULTS

The following analyses compare those students who lack any strong pattern at all, and thus who possess none of the four types, with those who possess each of the types. Data are also presented related to the complex entrepreneur hypothesis. The findings are presented separately for the three criteria employed.

Entrepreneurial Propensity

Table 21.6 contains the findings using the concurrent entrepreneurial propensity criterion. The data are all in a direction consistent with the hypotheses, but the results are clearly significant only for the personal achiever and real manager types and for the composite score measure of complexity. The analysis using the number of strong patterns possessed suffers from the lack of multiple patterns at the 3 and above level; yet it approaches significance and in doing so reinforces the composite score findings. The failure to obtain significance for the expert idea generator and empathic supersalesperson types may reflect weaknesses in the entrepreneurial propensity criterion. The fact that the composite score relationship is significant provides evidence for the experiment-wise significance of the results.

Proficiency in Writing a Business Plan

Table 21.7 moves the analysis to a longitudinal, predictive design, using the grades applied to the students' business plans submitted at semester end. Again, the results are consistently in the predicted direction. They are clearly significant for the expert idea generator and empathic supersalesperson types and for both indexes of entrepreneurial complexity. The personal achiever results are marginally significant; only the real manager type is definitely devoid of significance. Again, the composite score findings support the experiment-wise nature of the findings.

Taking the two proximate criteria, entrepreneurial propensity and skill in writing a business plan, together, all of the four types yield significance in one analysis or another. Furthermore, the evidence in support of the complexity hypothesis is very strong, even though there is little complexity above two types in the student sample.

Entrepreneurial Founding Postgraduation

Table 21.8, which compares those who possess each of the strong patterns with those who lack strong patterns, supports Hypotheses 1 and 2 with considerable consistency. All of the four types yield significant results. The table also provides support for Hypothesis 3 in the last two comparisons. Complexity clearly accelerates founding a business. Note, however, that

Table 21.6

Tests of Hypotheses Using Entrepreneurial Propensity Criterion—Number and Percentage (in parentheses) **of Respondents**

Personality Makeup	Entrepreneurial Propensity Score 0–1	2–3	4–10	Total	χ^2 (df = 2) vs. Those Who Lack Any Pattern
Lack Any Strong Pattern	20 (36)	23 (41)	13 (23)	56 (100)	—
Possess Personal Achiever Pattern	1 (6)	3 (19)	12 (75)	16 (100)	15.34, $p < .01$
Possess Real Manager Pattern	3 (20)	3 (20)	9 (60)	15 (100)	7.70, $p < .05$
Possess Expert Idea Generator Pattern	11 (27)	14 (35)	15 (38)	40 (100)	2.30 Ns
Possess Empathic Supersalesperson Pattern	16 (29)	22 (39)	18 (32)	56 (100)	1.26 Ns
Possess High Composite Score	3 (23)	1 (8)	9 (69)	13 (100)	11.10, $p < .01$
Number of Strong Patterns Possessed					χ^2 (df = 4)
2–4	7 (28)	6 (24)	12 (48)	25 (100)	8.19, $p < .10$
1	14 (20)	30 (43)	26 (37)	70 (100)	
0	20 (36)	23 (41)	13 (23)	56 (100)	

entrepreneurial activity is more pronounced among personal achievers and real managers than among expert idea generators and empathic supersalespeople. This may be a function of the timing of the follow-up measure. The expert idea generators and the empathic supersalespeople may become more active as entrepreneurs later, after they have learned how to be experts or to sell with finesse. In any event, it is important to note that subsequent entrepreneurial activity increases from 5 percent with no strong pattern, to 28 percent with only one, to 68 percent with two (or, in a few cases, more) patterns.

DISCUSSION

All three of the theoretical hypotheses receive support from this research. These findings deal with the start-up phase and the initiation of a venture, thus extending previous research, which concentrated on the growth of existing enterprises. It is now apparent that the four types influence not only the growth of a previously existing firm but the proclivity for founding a firm in the first place. Second, proximate criteria such as past, present, and intended future entrepreneurial activity, as well as skill in constructing a business plan for a future start-up, are shown to be predictable in addition to actual venture initiation.

The proximate criteria do not yield quite the consistent results that actual entrepreneurial activity postgraduation does. Nevertheless, one or another of the proximate criteria produces significance in every single comparison. Accordingly, researchers should be encouraged to continue using criteria of this kind when the study design fosters it.

Table 21.7

Tests of Hypotheses Using Business Plan Grade Criterion—Number and Percentage (in parentheses) **of Respondents**

Personality Makeup	Business Plan Grade: B or Lower	B+	A or A–	Total	χ^2 (df = 2) vs. Those Who Lack Any Pattern
Lack Any Strong Pattern	20 (36)	15 (28)	20 (36)	55 (100)	—
Possess Personal Achiever Pattern	1 (8)	3 (23)	9 (69)	13 (100)	5.72, $p < .10$
Possess Real Manager Pattern	5 (38)	1 (8)	7 (54)	13 (100)	2.64 Ns
Possess Expert Idea Generator Pattern	7 (20)	3 (9)	24 (71)	34 (100)	10.28, $p < .01$
Possess Empathic Supersalesperson Pattern	13 (25)	7 (13)	32 (62)	52 (100)	7.03, $p < .05$
Possess High Composite Score	1 (8)	1 (8)	10 (84)	12 (100)	8.69, $p < .02$
Number of Strong Patterns Possessed					χ^2 (df = 4)
2–4	5 (23)	2 (9)	15 (68)	22 (100)	11.17, $p < .05$
1	16 (25)	8 (13)	40 (62)	64 (100)	
0	20 (36)	15 (28)	20 (36)	55 (100)	

An additional point relates to the minimal entrepreneurial potential inherent in this student sample. The students are engaged in a graduate program that has a primarily corporate emphasis, not unlike many other business management programs. The course is the only one dealing with entrepreneurship available to these students, and electing it is an entirely voluntary matter. There is every reason to believe that these student participants would be the most entrepreneurial of those in the graduate program as a whole. Yet even in a self-selected sample such as this, there are repeated indications that this is not a high-potential group insofar as entrepreneurial endeavor is concerned. In all likelihood, this situation is a product of the corporate emphasis and reputation of the overall program. A graduate program dedicated more fully to entrepreneurship would be expected to yield a larger pool of entrepreneurial talent. Yet this hypothesis has not been tested. That is part of a research agenda for the future.

At several points in this research, including the use of the 0–1–2 test score conversion that may result in some score compression, decisions have been made that, if anything, introduce a conservative bias in that the chances of obtaining significant results are reduced. This is particularly true of the use of a less powerful statistical procedure such as chi-square. This approach to analysis appears appropriate to the kinds of distributions produced by typologies. Furthermore, it follows the lead set by the prior study of established entrepreneurs and permits direct comparisons with that study. Nevertheless, it does introduce a further conservative bias. If significance had not been obtained frequently, there could be a question as to the meaning of the results. However, significance was obtained, and the fact that a conservative procedure was employed therefore serves only to yield more confidence in the results. We can now say

Table 21.8

Test of Hypotheses Using Evidence of Entrepreneurial Activity Postgraduation Criterion—Number and Percentage (in parentheses) **of Respondents**

	Evidence of Entrepreneurial Activity Postgraduation			
Personality Makeup	No Evidence Present	Evidence Present	Total	χ^2 (df = 1) vs. Those Who Lack Any Pattern
Lack Any Strong Pattern	36 (95)	2 (5)	38 (100)	—
Possess Personal Achiever Pattern	4 (31)	9 (69)	13 (100)	23.48, $p < .01$
Possess Real Manager Pattern	4 (36)	7 (64)	11 (100)	19.66, $p < .01$
Possess Expert Idea Generator Pattern	19 (61)	12 (39)	31 (100)	11.77, $p < .01$
Possess Empathic Supersalesperson Pattern	26 (63)	15 (37)	41 (100)	13.05, $p < .01$
Possess High Composite Score	1 (9)	10 (91)	11 (100)	33.75, $p < .01$
Number of strong patterns possessed				χ^2 (df = 2)
2–4	6 (32)	13 (68)	19 (100)	25.92, $p < .01$
1	39 (72)	15 (28)	54 (100)	
0	36 (95)	2 (5)	38 (100)	

that the four-way typology predicts not only entrepreneurial success but the more basic process of actually founding a firm in the beginning.

WOMEN IN THE STUDENT SAMPLE

On the variables with which this research has been concerned there is little to indicate a difference between women and men among the students (Miner 1997a). The women number 51, versus a male representation of 108, but even with these increased samples significance is rarely obtained. The women are not more likely to be complex entrepreneurs, nor to possess any particular patterns or types. On the criteria the only possible difference, at $p < .10$, is that the men are somewhat more likely to found a business shortly after graduation. Interpretation of these data becomes difficult, however, considering that most women enter upon their first entrepreneurial venture only after prior employment in a related area (Brush 1992), and thus at a somewhat more advanced age. There were no age differences within the student sample originally.

RESULTS OBTAINED WITH THE MSCS–FORM T IN THE STUDENT SAMPLE

As in Chapter 20, the preceding article and analyses do not consider the task theory specifically, and thus the MSCS–Form T results. This omission is corrected in Table 21.9. Using

Table 21.9

Correlations between MSCS–Form T and Business Founding Criteria in the Student Sample

MSCS—Form T Measures	Entrepreneurial Propensity Score (N = 159)	Proficiency in Writing a Business Plan (N = 143)	Entrepreneurial Founding Post-graduation (N = 115)
Total Item Score	.59**	.39**	.41**
Self-Achievement	.45**	.11	.27*
Avoiding Risks	.05	.13	–.04
Feedback of Results	.35**	.12	.17
Personal Innovation	.44**	.25**	.33**
Planning for the Future	.23**	.33**	.33**

Note: MSCS = Miner Sentence Completion Scale.
$^{*}p < .05$; $^{**}p < .01$

the same three business founding criteria as noted previously the correlations are consistently strong when the total score is the predictor. The Form T subscales yield significant correlations over half of the time, with the entrepreneurial propensity score producing the most pronounced results.

When the Form H and Form P measures are applied with these same criteria in this student sample some interesting results occur. Form H produces only one significant subscale finding (at the $p < .05$ level) among the 24 correlations. A similar picture emerges with Form P using both the entrepreneurial propensity and business plan measures. All this is predicable from theory. However, when Form P is applied to the entrepreneurial founding postgraduation criterion the results closely approximate those obtained with Form T. We do not have Oliver Organization Description Questionnaire (OODQ) scores here because these are students, and many are not employed, but with the doctoral students and the presence of a number of professionals, such as accountants and lawyers, the proportionate representation from the professions would appear to equal that from entrepreneurship in the student sample as a whole. Why this might result in the Form P pattern of relationships remains an enigma. That it does, however, remains a fact.

CHAPTER 22

PRINCETON UNIVERSITY ALUMNI (CLASS OF 1948), ON WHOM WHOLE CAREER DATA WERE AVAILABLE, AND THE SUBSEQUENT CREATION OF THE LEADERSHIP THEORY

INTRODUCTION

The Princeton study, and with it a more complete statement of the role motivation theory of leadership, was published as a chapter in a book (Miner 2002a). This book, entitled *Transformational and Charismatic Leadership: The Road Ahead* (Avolio and Yammarino 2002), was an outgrowth of a festschrift-conference held in Binghamton, New York to honor Bernard Bass. For this reason the chapter is somewhat skewed toward the transformational theory of

Published as John B. Miner, "The Role Motivation Theories of Organizational Leadership," in *Transformational and Charismatic Leadership: The Road Ahead,* ed. Bruce J. Avolio and Francis J. Yammarino (Amsterdam and New York: JAI, an imprint of Elsevier Science, 2002), pp. 309–338.

leadership that Bass created, especially in the later pages. Having known Bernie for a number of years, I was pleased to honor him.

However, this chapter also provided an opportunity to present my role motivation theory in a new light, and thus bring it into the leadership field much more specifically than had previously been possible. It also permitted a description of the Princeton University research, the most comprehensive investigation of my ideas on motivation and leadership that has been conducted to date. Here I am indebted to a large number of my classmates (1948) who so willingly completed the various questionnaires.

* * *

The purpose of this presentation is to demonstrate that macro-structural variables can be, and in fact should be, incorporated into leadership theories. The primary vehicle for this demonstration is an elaboration of role motivation theory extending beyond organizational motivation into the leadership domain, and the presentation of research on the theory as thus elaborated. At the same time, implications are drawn for the extension of the charismatic/transformational cluster of theories and how these theories might benefit from the inclusion of similar macro variables—consonant with the theme of this book, and looking to the "road ahead" for these theories.

Role motivation theory traces its origins back to the beginnings of organizational behavior. At that time, however, it was a theory with a rather small domain; it dealt only with managerial motivation and with managerial roles in hierarchic organizations. In the 1970s, this theoretical picture began to change, and a considerable expansion occurred. Consonant with this theoretical expansion, significant problems with the then-existing concept of leadership were raised, but not fully resolved. The essence of this critique was that " . . . our current theories of leadership tend to exist in an organizational vacuum. Some either explicitly or implicitly assume a bureaucratic context; some do not even do that . . . we have gone as far as is possible in the leadership area without forging a strong link between leadership on the one hand and the particular organizational context in which leadership behavior occurs on the other" (Miner 1982, 295).

Now, some twenty years later, I hope to cement this bonding of leadership with its various organizational forms—not to minimize the leadership construct, as was my original idea, but to give it additional strength by welding it on to the organizational context of which it is an inherent part. In the process, I present data from a previously unpublished study of former Princeton University undergraduates, which extends across their entire subsequent careers, and the findings from certain reanalyses of data from a number of other studies that were published previously in different forms.

THE CORE OF ROLE MOTIVATION THEORY

Role motivation theory's central constructs are four organizational forms, institutionalized role requirements for key performers (managers, professionals, entrepreneurs, and group members in good standing) that follow from these forms, and motivational patterns that are congruent with these roles. Each organizational type represents a theoretical domain; thus there are four parallel theories. The role requirements are derived logically and/or empirically from the form of organization involved and from the relationship the key performers have with that form. A matching set of motive patterns is posited, one for each role requirement. If the role-motive pattern match is congruent (theoretically specified), the likelihood that the role requirements will be carried out increases, and the potential for positive outcomes becomes greater.

The Four Organizational Forms

An organizational description questionnaire has been developed that participants may use to describe the unique features of an organization in which they work (see Oliver 1982). Although many organizations represent a mix of forms, it is typically true that one form predominates within a given work component or unit.

Hierarchic

Size is what most aptly characterizes hierarchic organizations. These are the bureaucratic forms that Weber (1968) describes. They possess multiple levels of hierarchy, and they often overlay other forms of organization. This mixing with professional, entrepreneurial, and group forms does not make the bureaucratic components any the less hierarchic. Typically, the hierarchic components appear at the top and assume control. However, hierarchic units may be embedded in other types of organizations, such as a hierarchic support staff unit in a professional organization. Wherever the hierarchic component is found, control resides in the managerial positions. The organization may be in the private sector, government, or the non-profit field.

Professional

The seminal type of professional system is individual private practice. This has increasingly expanded to group practice, and still further to professional organizations or units. The distinctive feature is that a substantial measure of control remains with the professionals. However, in many respects, this control reflects the external influence of professional associations. Service to some type of client is always involved. When professional components are embedded in hierarchic organizations, there is a single client—the surrounding organization—and given an absence of client diversification; in this case, the professional unit may face considerable competition for control, and thus substantial conflict.

Task

In the task form, key performers such as entrepreneurs are embedded directly in the pushes and pulls of the work system. Control resides in the task itself, which imposes the threat of business failure and offers the prospect of sizable financial reward. The prototype of a task system is the entrepreneurial start-up. However, growth is an essential component of this form, or at least intended growth. Thus, family businesses that pass from one generation to another and even purchased small businesses may be of a task nature. Within the task system, the entrepreneur operates as an individual moving to deal with crises and grasping opportunities without reference to hierarchic or professional constraints. The entrepreneur may be plural, but typically, a lead entrepreneur exists. Entrepreneurial components may be embedded in other organizational forms, and when this occurs, with the venture dependent on resources supplied by the surrounding organization, control conflicts may escalate.

Group

The group may be free-standing or embedded in some other type of organization. Examples are many voluntary organizations, musical groups, and autonomous or self-managing work teams. The key performers are members in good standing, leadership is emergent and at the will of the majority, and both cohesion and stability are important. Control resides in the group as a whole, and normative pressures derive from this source. As originally conceived, this form was envisioned as encompassing relatively small face-to-face groups. Nevertheless, town meetings, legislative components of government, and political parties including election campaign teams appear to share many features with these small groups.

Roles and Motive Patterns

The role motivation theories emerged over a considerable time span and the motivational variables have been operationalized, so that research could be conducted, at different points in time as well. There is as yet no motivational measure for the group theory; only the organizational level measure exists. The roles and their matching motive patterns have been the subject of substantial theoretical and empirical development (see Miner 1993 for an overview). It is important to note that the motives of role motivation theory are assumed to operate at below the conscious level on occasion.

Hypotheses

Using these concepts of organizational forms, their inherent roles, and the motive patterns that match them, four standing hypotheses have been formulated (Miner 1982, 1993). The first three of these hypotheses were tested in the present research.

Hypothesis 1. *In hierarchic systems, managerial motivation should be at a high level in top management, and it should be positively correlated with other managerial success indexes; managerial motivation should not differentiate in these ways within other types of systems.*

Hypothesis 2. *In professional systems, professional motivation should be at a high level among senior professionals, and it should be positively correlated with other professional success indexes; professional motivation should not differentiate in these ways within other types of systems.*

Hypothesis 3. *In task systems, task motivation should be at a high level among task performers (entrepreneurs), and it should be positively correlated with task-success indexes; task motivation should not differentiate in these ways within other types of systems.*

Hypothesis 4. *In group systems, group motivation should be at a high level among emergent leaders, and it should be positively correlated with other group-determined success indexes; group motivation should not differentiate in these ways within other types of systems.*

These hypotheses are domain-specific, and they reflect a causal effect from the appropriate motives to outcome variables. Within a theoretical domain, indexes of motive strength are combined additively to obtain comprehensive measures of managerial, professional, task, and group motivation. Thus, motivational deficiencies of one kind may be offset by high levels of motivation of some other type. In hypotheses 1 through 4, the assumption is that individuals with the appropriate motives will indicate a preference for work of a congruent kind and will make job and career choices accordingly. Those with higher congruent motives will perform better in these positions, will be more likely to stay in positions of the appropriate kind, and will achieve greater career success within the domain that best fits their motivational pattern.

DEVELOPMENT OF THE LEADERSHIP THEORY

The four standing hypotheses of role motivation theory make reference to top management in the case of the hierarchic theory and to emergent leadership in the case of the group theory, thus indicating a concern with leadership issues. Yet the professional theory hypothesis refers to senior professionals, not necessarily leaders among professionals, and in the case of task theory, entrepreneurs are mentioned, but without reference to entrepreneurial leadership. In fact, leadership theory to date has shown little inclination to incorporate entrepreneurship within its domain, and vice versa.

As noted previously, during the 1970s and into the early 1980s, I was quite critical of leadership theory, in part at least on the grounds that it was too narrowly defined to deal effectively with the phenomena that in my view should be its central focus. The problem as I saw it was inherent in the fact that the study of leadership had its origins within social psychology as a component of the larger field of group dynamics. Its major concerns in this early period were with the effects of leadership on small group performance, the emergence of leadership within such groups, and with the positive effects of democratic (as opposed to autocratic) leadership behavior. Much of the research was of a laboratory nature with extensions to the lower, work group levels of hierarchic organizations. This was a very narrow focus; yet it prevailed for a number of years, and served to limit the scope of leadership theory in a way that I believed (and still believe) made the field much less useful than it could have been. In particular, it failed to recognize that leadership is a function of the larger organizational form within which it operates. This seems like an obvious conclusion, especially for a field labeled organizational behavior, but it has continued to escape us to this day. Charismatic/transformational theory continues to show signs of its early origins in the group dynamics way of thinking up to the present; it needs to escape this bondage more fully.

Recently, however, a degree of broadening has taken hold within leadership, which, although still not sufficient, has the potential to move the field in the right direction. Thus:

> . . . a meeting of eighty-four scholars representing fifty-six countries from all regions of the world was conducted. In that meeting a consensus and universal definition of organizational leadership emerged: "the ability of an individual to influence, motivate, and enable others to contribute toward the effectiveness and success of the organizations of which they are members" (House, Wright, and Aditya 1997, 548).

Notice that this definition does not utilize the term "group" at all, and that it specifically engages the organizational context—although still failing to consider particular organizational forms.

In a previous publication, I have touched upon the ways in which my theoretical views speak to leadership (Miner 2000). As a prelude to the presentation of the research on this topic, let me now amplify this earlier discussion (Chapter 21).

Hierarchic Leadership

A frequent distinction in the leadership literature is between managers and leaders, with the former term often carrying negative connotations and the latter having something of a heroic quality (Terry 1995). This distinction goes back at least to Zaleznik (1977). Both terms tend to be used with reference to the hierarchic or bureaucratic domain. Given the variations in usage here, it seems essential to provide a view of role motivation theory's take on this issue.

Managers are those who hold managerial positions in hierarchic systems. In most cases, they have followers. Managers holding positions in the upper reaches of the hierarchic chain, often referred to as "top managers," are theoretically defined as organizational leaders. Attaining such positions represents the goal of hierarchic career success, only being more or less successful within a hierarchic system. These leaders may be heroic, but they need not be. In this context, managers below the top level are considered to be in a pre-leadership role, and of course many careers end in this zone. Hierarchic role motivation theory clearly indicates that, for its purposes, the study of top management should be the focus of leadership research (not the study of first level supervision). There is a managerial continuum extending from the early pre-leadership stages to the very top of the bureaucratic hierarchy. At some point in this continuum, an individual breaks into top management and is considered to be a hierarchic leader.

Since role motivation theory has been a theory of motivation and personality, it is important to specify how such a theory might relate to leadership *behavior*, a long-standing concern of leadership theory. Role motivation theory takes the position, consistent with Victor Vroom's normative decision process theory and Frank Heller's influence-power continuum theory but not with Fred Fiedler's contingency theory, that leaders are not tied to a single set of behaviors by their strong motives. Rather, each manager has the capability to vary his or her behaviors over a wide range, in pursuit of motivationally based goals, depending on the nature of the situations and constraints faced.

The research surrounding Vroom's and Heller's theories certainly supports this view, as does the research conducted by Zaccaro, Foti, and Kenny (1991). Thus, the hierarchic theory, and the other three theories as well, do not specify any particular behaviors (such as directive behavior), but they do anticipate that this behavior will be consistent with the goals inherent in the strong motives held by a person and with the demands of the situation faced. Note that, in contrast, existing charismatic/transformational theories have tended to continue to focus on explicit leader behaviors.

Professional Leadership

Professional, or intellectual, leadership has been given practically no attention by leadership theory, although within the sociological literature the distinction between administrative elites and rank-and-file practitioners within a profession is discussed. It is these elites that the professional theory considers as its leaders. Intellectual leadership of this kind may be of either a cosmopolitan or local nature. In the former instance, the focus is on achieved professional status and recognition in the professional community as a whole; in the latter case. the focus is on achieved rank and status in the employing organization.

Many professionals rise to leadership positions or status of both kinds. The key is that the person must be a professional and must have given evidence of high professional status, which often involves having rank-and-file professionals or pre-professionals who depend upon him or her in some manner. In hypothesis 2, the term "senior professionals" should be changed to "professional leaders" to make the statement consonant with the present view. Although the concept of mentoring has been studied most extensively within the hierarchic domain, it is an important function of professional leaders as well.

Since acquiring knowledge is so important to becoming a professional, and takes considerable time as well, the professional career tends to extend across various degrees of training, to the early career stages, and then for some to true intellectual leadership. Thus, the idea of a continuum holds for professionals, too. Leadership tends to be defined by such factors as publications, professional compensation levels, professional rank, signs of recognition, administrative position, status within the educational context, professional organization activity, and the like, depending on the particular profession and its organizational context.

Task Leadership

Task or entrepreneurial leadership involves the concept of a lead entrepreneur, who typically owns a larger share of the venture or holds a more dominant position, and the existence of a growth orientation; both must be present for task leadership to occur. Entrepreneurs who are not leaders are venture team members who do not hold lead status and/or who are involved in ventures not evidencing commitment to organizational growth. The lead entrepreneur concept is especially important in team entrepreneurship of the kind that characterizes high technology ventures. In the team context, the concept of a lead entrepreneur has been shown to be a viable entity, and the vision of that person has been found to play an important strategic role (Ensley, Carland, and Carland 2000).

Growth orientation, the second requirement, has been operationalized as a demonstrated record of organizational growth (measured in years) over which the firm has increased substantially in number of employees and/or dollar volume of sales. This growth need not be maintained under all circumstances, such as during a period of recession, but it must have occurred, and under the guidance and vision of the same lead entrepreneur.

Entrepreneurial leadership is typically achieved following a period of intentional and/or unintentional training for the position as reflected in educational experiences, part-time entrepreneurship, other employment, non-leader entrepreneurial work, and even other entrepreneurial leadership. Thus, again, a continuum of career development exists.

Group Leadership

For lack of an inductive empirical base from which to operate, defining group leadership in the manner of the other three types is difficult. Yet, some dimensions can be established to represent group leadership. Group leadership is emergent from within the group; it is not appointive from the outside, and it is not based on criteria held outside the group. It fits the model obtained from ad hoc laboratory groups, but it may appear in autonomous or self-managed teams as well, and in other similar settings. This is where leadership theory began, and it should be retained as a more limited domain of study.

Emergent leadership of this kind can be quite unstable in that group leaders may be replaced at any time by others who fit group norms better. Any group member in good standing is a potential candidate for group leadership. Group leaders receive a substantially greater amount of interaction with others than mere members (Cohen and Zhou 1991). Furthermore, a given group may well have several of these emergent leaders, each with a different role to play.

Hypothesis

Thus, we have four types of leadership based in four different organizational forms, with four different categories of institutionalized role prescriptions, and four different sets of motivational patterns needed in the leaders for effective performance to occur. This results in:

Hypothesis 5. *Leadership roles take different forms in different organizational contexts and require different types of people to perform in these roles effectively—people whose motives are strongly congruent with the particular organizational type involved; thus, leadership careers vary in important ways with the organizational forms in which they occur.*

Yet, in all instances, leadership involves the ability "to influence, motivate, and enable others to contribute toward the effectiveness and success of the organizations of which they are members." This is a very different, and much broader, concept of leadership than that with which leadership theory began, and in which it persevered for many years. Some time ago, however, Etzioni (1961) espoused a similar concept of leadership, covering both formal position holders and informal leaders, as well as power inherent in a position and personal power.

Leadership in any of its various organizational forms is essentially a developing process of career identification in which the individual increasingly takes on a set of institutionalized roles, which are viewed as personally compatible (Ashforth 2001). For some, a leadership career represents the whole or the major part of a total career. More frequently, a long period of career preparation and socialization precedes entering into the true leadership career.

METHOD

The primary source of data for the research reported here, although only part of the total, was a mail survey of the surviving members of the class of 1948 at Princeton University conducted on the occasion of the fiftieth anniversary of the class's graduation (1998). This was my class, and I am sure that facilitated data collection. However, the sample is important because it permitted studying careers across their full duration, contained a large number of leaders in the various domains, and represented a balanced sample in that hierarchic, professional, and task forms of organization were all well represented. In addition, a number of previously published studies yielded samples whose data were reanalyzed to provide findings relevant to the leadership hypotheses.

The Princeton Study

The addresses and much of the career data for this sample were obtained from a yearbook published to commemorate the class's fiftieth anniversary (Princeton University Class of 1948, 1998). This was a wartime class, and members actually graduated from college over a period starting in the latter 1940s and extending well into the 1950s; their ages spanned a roughly ten-year period.

The yearbook provided varying degrees of information on class members. Of the 778 individuals listed, 239 (31 percent) had no biographical data, or the career information was insufficient to make a career designation, or, less frequently, the apparent career did not fit into the manager, professional, or entrepreneur categories required by the research design. Another 143 of those listed had died at the time of mailing (plus 54 not listed). When eight honorary class members were subtracted, 388 individuals remained to whom the initial mailing was sent—just 50 percent of those listed. Subsequent information indicated that 17 more people could not have responded (owing to death, severe illness, or inadequate addresses), so the operative base sample was 371—and perhaps smaller, owing to deaths and illnesses of which we were unaware.

Through two rounds of mailings, 110 individuals provided usable data, for a 30 percent return rate. The response to the first mailing was 18 percent, and to the second mailing (sent roughly three months later) 12 percent. This reflects a reasonably good response rate, especially to the second mailing (Roth and BeVier 1998). A comparison of the first and second round respondents to check on the representativeness of the sample utilized (see Rogelberg and Luong 1998) was carried out, and the conclusions are reported subsequently.

The 110 members of the respondent sample are all male, reflecting the fact that Princeton did not admit females until a number of years later. Although this limitation of the sample's composition might seem to represent a deficiency, it may well have been fortuitous in that female career patterns have been found to differ substantially from those of males (Melamed 1996). In any event, it should be understood that the findings of this research are generalizable only to males.

The mean age of sample members at the time of response was 72 with a range of 70 to 80; however, almost three-quarters were either 71 or 72. Within the sample, 74 percent listed themselves as retired, meaning that they had passed the point of disengagement from their main careers. Nevertheless, considering the partially retired and the not-yet-retired numbers, a case can be made that the sample did not contain only individuals whose careers were completely behind them, and in that sense deal entirely with whole careers. Yet, whole careers were the prevailing mode, and all who were not fully disengaged were clearly in the last stages of their careers. For 44 percent of the sample, this career was managerial in nature, for another 34 percent, it was professional or highly specialized, and for 22 percent, it was entrepreneurial.

Motivational Measures

The independent variables of the research were the total scores and subscales of the Miner Sentence Completion Scales (MSCS)–Forms H, P, and T. When necessary for a given analysis, total scores for each sentence completion scale were converted to standard scores with a mean of 50 and the standard deviations set equal to 10. The appropriate normative sample data were used for the purpose of standardization. Scoring was done by the author in all cases.

The research design used would ideally call for administration of all three scales to all subjects. This, however, requires the completion of twelve pages of items, when evidence indicates that after four pages, the response rate to surveys begins to fall off substantially (Roth and BeVier 1998). To deal with this problem, subjects were initially sent only the MSCS form (hierarchic, professional, or task) that matched their career as initially determined from the yearbook information (Princeton University Class of 1948, 1998); they were also asked if they would be willing to complete the additional two forms.

The result of this process was that 51 first-wave respondents and 23 second-wave respondents, for a total of 74 out of the 110 subjects, completed all three forms. The remainder provided either one form (33) or, in a few cases, two (3). All in all, we received 92 Form Hs, 85 Form Ps, and 84 Form Ts. These represent the base data used in the analyses.

Outcome Measures

The analysis called for comparing the respondents with various career types on the motivational measures to provide a test of the core theoretical hypotheses; thus, managerial careers versus other careers on Form H, professional/specialists careers versus other careers on Form P, and entrepreneurial careers versus other careers on Form T. The theory, of course, would anticipate higher scores in the theoretically congruent samples than in the incongruent (other career) samples. In this design, the career is the dependent outcome variable.

Initially, as indicated previously, a career classification was made based on the yearbook information only. However, we solicited additional data of this nature in our letter to the subjects, and a number provided it. Furthermore, a twenty-fifth yearbook on the class (Princeton University Class of 1948, 1974), which contained biographical information, was located. With these latter data, career histories at two points in time at a twenty-five-year interval became available for 74 percent of the subjects. There were no significant differences among the three career types in this regard. When supplemented with *Who's Who* listings and subject-provided information, 80 percent of the subjects had career data from at least two sources. The consequence was that more precise career classifications became possible—91 percent of the respondents remained unchanged, but 9 percent were shifted to a new category.

The managerial career sample was constituted of 43 corporate managers and 5 non-profit managers. The managerial careers most typically started below the managerial level, but still in a hierarchic system. There were a few instances where the early period was spent in a professional capacity subsequent to a professional education before the move into hierarchic management.

The professional career sample of 38 was very diverse. Most frequently represented were the law, the clergy, teachers (at both the private school and university levels), and practicing physicians, but there were research scientists, professional engineers, librarians, accountants, and others as well. Also included with these professionals were certain individuals who had made a career of some specialty, which, although not generally recognized as a profession, involved advanced education and/or specialized experience. Included here were technical editors, writers, therapists, international specialists, and financial experts.

The entrepreneurial career sample contained 24 individuals who had developed a firm (usually one they had started) and often several firms, and spent most of their careers in this type of activity. The actual entrepreneurial careers more often than not were initiated after a stint in hierarchic or professional systems, but these stints may well have been part of the entrepreneurial careers in that they provided the learning needed to start a particular venture. These entrepreneurs invariably headed their firms, but the ventures themselves were quite varied in nature; the major concentrations were in oil and gas exploration and in the financial area.

Leadership Careers

In an effort to test theoretical expectations regarding leadership, those subjects who were leaders in their respective career fields were compared with those who did not achieve this status using the standardized total scores. The leaders were identified using the criteria presented previously.

Of the 48 managers, 38 achieved the status of hierarchic leader, and 10 had not. Of the 38 professionals and specialists, 27 were professional or intellectual leaders, and 11 were not. Of the 24 entrepreneurs, 19 were task leaders, and 5 were not. Overall, 76 percent of the subjects achieved a leader role in their careers and this was as likely to occur in one career domain as another. Among the leaders, 15 were listed in *Who's Who in America* at some point during the 1990s.

Sample Representativeness

Evidence on the probability of non-response bias in surveys such as this (where 70 percent did not respond) may be obtained by comparing the responses on the study variables of the first-wave respondents with those of the second-wave respondents. If differences were minimal, it is likely that no differences would be found comparing the respondents and non-respondents either. If differences were found from wave one to wave two, this trend should be perpetuated into the non-respondent group, and the representativeness of the respondent sample comes into serious question (Rogelberg and Luong 1998).

Comparisons were made between wave one and wave two data for all MSCS measures (numbering 20), age, retirement status, career type, and leadership status. There was only one significant difference, on value-based identification (professional commitment) at $p < .05$ with the second-round respondents scoring higher. This finding would have been anticipated on the basis of chance alone, given that 24 comparisons were made. Thus, the evidence obtained supports the representativeness of the respondent sample.

Intercorrelations

Within instruments, the subscales correlate significantly with the total scores of which they are part. These values range from .41 to .73 with an average of .58. The subscales themselves are generally positively correlated within instruments, with median values of .19, .22, and .18 for Forms H, P, and T, respectively—19 of these positive correlations are significant; almost half of the total. The same pattern occurs across all three measures—generally positive, but not large relationships. Comparing these findings with those from other studies (see Miner 1993), the present data appear entirely consistent with previous results, and with theoretical expectations.

Across instruments, where the theory would expect values close to .00, the three total score correlations are –.12, .04, and .12—none significant; the median subscale correlations across instruments in each data set are –.04, .02, and .07. Overall, there are 61 positive correlations and 67 negative, with 8 of the positive values significant and 6 of them negative. This looks very much like the total lack of relationships across instruments that was expected.

These results across measures stand in contrast to what has been obtained in previous studies (Miner 1993). There, a positive relationship, not large but consistent, has been obtained across all three measures. The present results, obtained with balanced samples and using whole career data that do not include any subjects who subsequently will be involved in career turnover are more compatible with theory and would seem to be more valid as well.

Other Leadership Data Sources

The samples used in these re-analyses all derive from previously published studies, which permit the leadership hypotheses to be investigated—that is, there are both leaders and members involved. Results were calculated in correlation form, whereas in the original publications, they typically were not. The re-analyses involve not only the calculation of these correlations, but also the actual establishment of criterion groups.

In addition to the Princeton study, two other investigations dealt with congruent hierarchic motivation. One was an analysis of human resource managers from a Bureau of National Affairs panel (see Chapter 7 and in particular Table 7.6). The other source utilizing congruent hierarchic motivation was Berman and Miner (1985), (see Chapter 14 and in particular Table 14.4).

Professional motivation was the focus of a study of Academy of Management members (see Chapter 9 and in particular Table 9.8). This sample provided information on hierarchic motivation as well, thus permitting non-congruent analyses (also Table 9.8).

Task motivation was studied in two entrepreneurial samples, the first of which yielded non-congruent data for both hierarchic and professional motivation, as well as congruent results for task motivation (see Chapter 20 and in particular Table 20.5). The sample contained 100 entrepreneurs, but in 11 cases the data available were insufficient to determine leadership status; comparisons indicated that these 11 cases did not differ from the others. The second entrepreneurial sample consisted of high-tech entrepreneurs who applied for National Science Foundation grants (see Chapter 15 and in particular Table 15.8).

A final leader analysis was conducted using hierarchic motivation as applied to non-congruent professional leadership (Miner 1977b). This sample of forty-nine professors was from three different business schools with a wide range of disciplines represented. Leadership level was determined using professorial rank and administrative position.

In two of these samples, the human resource managers and the Buffalo, NY area entrepreneurs, data could also be obtained on validities against the leader-member criterion using other predictors that have been supported in the literature; thus, an index of relative effectiveness versus the MSCS measures could be obtained in the same samples. Data on these instruments are reported in Miner 1977b and 1997a.

RESULTS

The findings that follow derive from the Princeton study, which provides a test of the core hypotheses of role motivation theory, and from a series of tests of the leadership hypothesis including one using the Princeton data.

The Princeton Study

Table 22.1 presents the Princeton results in correlational form. Significance was established using *t* tests to compare the means. All of the congruent findings are highly significant; none of the non-congruent findings were significant. When these congruent data are combined, using standard scores, the resulting correlation is .64. Given the comprehensiveness of the Princeton data, this appears to be the most definitive test of the core hypotheses of role motivation theory obtained to date; these total score findings are completely in accord with theory.

At the subscale level, the correlations characteristically substantiate the total score results. All five congruent Form T correlations are significant at $p < .01$ ranging from .32 to .53 (median .42). All five congruent Form P correlations are also similarly significant ranging from .24 to .43 (median .36). With Form H, the hierarchic chain subscales—authority (upward), competitiveness (lateral), and power (downward)—yield similar congruent correlations, significant at $p < .01$ and ranging from .41 to .53 (median .45). This is the pattern anticipated by Nystrom (1986). Consistent with Nystrom's hypothesis, the remaining Form H subscales yield correlations in the .10s, usually significant ($p < .05$), but relatively low. This type of finding has not been characteristic previously (Miner 1993).

Table 22.1

Relationships between MSCS Total Scores and Various Congruent and Noncongruent Career Indexes in the Princeton University Class of 1948 Sample

MSCS Form	Comparison	Point Biserial Correlation
Congruent Analysis		
H	Managers (n = 48); M = 6.65) vs. Professionals + Entrepreneurs (n = 44; M = –2.00)	.65**
P	Professionals (n = 38; M = 12.84) vs. Managers + Entrepreneurs (n = 47; M = 4.17)	.56**
T	Entrepreneurs (n = 24; M = 13.71) vs. Managers + Professionals (n = 60; M = .67)	.75**
Noncongruent Analysis		
H	Professionals (n = 28; M = –2.50) vs. Entrepreneurs (n = 16; M = –1.13)	–.11
P	Managers (n = 31; M = 2.81) vs. Entrepreneurs (n = 16; M = 6.81)	–.27
T	Managers (n = 32; M = 1.16) vs. Professionals (n = 28; M = .11)	.10

Note: MSCS = Miner Sentence Completion Scale.
$^{**}p < .01$

Tests of the Leadership Hypothesis

Table 22.2 contains descriptive data and correlations for the six studies in which congruent motives were related to a leadership measure. Two involve hierarchic systems, one professional, two task, and one all three combined. The latter, the Princeton University study, yields the lowest correlation, and that may be a function of using combined data standardized on different samples; however, the low proportion of non-leader, rank-and-file members may be a factor as well. In all three components, the directionality is as hypothesized. Note also that the member MSCS scores are still above the expected mean of 50, thus introducing some restriction of range.

Even with this relatively low correlation from the Princeton sample, the median value in Table 22.2 is in the low .70s. This is a very high figure for an uncorrected average validity coefficient. Something clearly quite important is going on here. The analyses that follow are intended to give some insight into what might be involved.

One possibility is that the MSCS measures inevitably yield such high correlations within their appropriate domains irrespective of the criterion. To determine whether this is the case, both the concurrent and predictive studies considered in Miner (1993), plus a few more recent studies, were culled. For Form H, dealing with hierarchic motivation, 50 relevant correlation coefficients were found; the median value was .24 (18 using a rating criterion for which the median was .24, 30 using a managerial level or compensation criterion for which the median was .25, and 2 using a job satisfaction criterion for which the median was .20). For Form P, dealing with professional motivation, there were 19 coefficients spread across a wide range of criteria, but with too few in any one category to break out separately; the median correlation was .35. For Form T, dealing with entrepreneurial motivation, the number of correlations found was down to 13; for these varied criteria, the median value was .36.

Table 22.2

Relationships between MSCS Total Scores and Various Congruent Leadership Forms

Sample (Prior Description)	MSCS Form	Leadership Form	Method of Analysis	Correlation
1. Princeton University class of 1948	H, P & T	Managerial, Professional & Entrepreneurial	Biserial correlation using combined standard scores Leaders—n = 84; M = 58.34 Members—n = 26; M = 52.45	.44**
2. Personnel and industrial relations managers (Miner 1977b)	H	Managerial	Biserial correlation using total scores Leaders—n = 41; M = 6.18 Members—n = 60; M = .95	.54**
3. Top managers and age-matched comparison managers (Berman & Miner 1985)	H	Managerial	Biserial correlation using total scores Leaders—n = 49; M = 6.76 Members—n = 49; M = .86	.72**
4. Academy of Management members (Miner 1980a)	P	Professional	Biserial correlation using total scores Leaders—n = 46; M = 11.70 Members—n = 66; M = 1.30	.87**
5. Buffalo, NY area entrepreneurs (Miner 1997)	T	Entrepreneurial	Biserial correlation using total scores Leaders—n = 45; M = 12.93 Members—n = 44; M = 7.11	.71**
6. High-technology entrepreneurs—NSF grant applicants (Miner,Smith, and Bracker 1989)	T	Entrepreneurial	Biserial correlation using total scores Leaders—n = 59; M = 10.95 Members—n = 59; M = .92	.77**
			Median value	.715

Note: MSCS = Miner Sentence Completion Scale.
**$p < .01$

Table 22.3

Relationships between MSCS Total Scores and Various Noncongruent Leadership Forms

Sample (Prior Description)	MSCS Form	Leadership Form	Method of Analysis	Correlation
Academy of Management members (Miner 1980a)	H	Professional	Biserial correlation using total scores Leaders—n = 46; M = –1.59 Members—n = 66; M = –2.80	.11
Buffalo, NY area entrepreneurs (Miner 1997a)	H	Entrepreneurial	Biserial correlation using total scores Leaders—n = 45; M = 3.18 Members—n = 44; M = 2.16	.13
	P	Entrepreneurial	Biserial correlation using total scores Leaders—n = 45; M = 11.13 Members—n = 44; M = 7.82	.33**
Business school faculty from three schools (Miner 1977b)	H	Professional	Pearson correlation with leadership level (n = 49)	.12

Note: MSCS = Miner Sentence Completion Scale.
** $p < .01$.

Taken as a whole, when leadership and career criteria are excluded, the average validity coefficient runs just under .30 for total scores—less than half of what Table 22.2 reports for leadership criteria. It seems evident that the MSCSs themselves do not invariably produce such high values.

Another question involves the extent to which various subscales may be operating. In this analysis, the Princeton study had to be excluded because of small Ns for individual subscales in the leadership analysis. The median correlation for the Form H subscales is somewhat lower, presumably because of the smaller number of items (5) in contrast to Forms P and T (8). Clearly, the limited reliability of the subscales (.65 on average) is a consideration throughout this analysis. Nevertheless, every single subscale yields at least one significant correlation; there are no non-contributing factors. The highest contributors to leadership appear to be attitude to authority within Form H, acquiring status within Form P, and achieving on one's own within Form T. The median subscale correlations with leadership for Forms H, P, and T, respectively are .30, .49, and .40. Of the 29 values, 24 are significant ($p < .05$ or better).

The Table 22.3 findings deal with the question of whether the results of Table 22.2 apply only to congruent relationships, or to non-congruent relationships as well (which they should not according to theory). The data overall are consistent with theoretical expectations—the median correlation is a non-significant .125. Yet there is one unexpected significant relationship, involving the prediction of entrepreneurial leadership from professional motivation; the significant subscales here are acquiring knowledge (.28*), acquiring status (.37**), and professional commitment (.29*). There are a number of professionals among the Buffalo area entrepreneurs, and the Form T versus Form P total score correlation is .26* (versus only .12 in the more balanced Princeton sample). When the effects from Form T are controlled, the resulting partial correlation of Form P with entrepreneurial leadership drops to a non-significant .21, a figure more consistent with theoretical expectations.

Table 22.4 presents information bearing on the question of whether the Table 22.2 findings might reflect something inherent in the samples involved. Although data are available for only two samples, the median correlation for the predictors studied is only .14 (versus .715 for the congruent MSCS predictors); there are only 2 of the 12 relationships that achieve significance. It seems unlikely that the samples utilized are in and of themselves particularly likely to yield high correlations.

Rather the implication of the data is that something about the match of the theoretical motives and their congruent indexes of organizational leadership is responsible for the very high validities obtained.

DISCUSSION

A considerable amount of evidence now exists to the effect that leadership is a set of organizational variables that often behave much like career variables. However, the really significant finding reported here is not that these motives predict; that had been reasonably well established previously. The major finding is that they can predict at a level well above that for other predictors, and above those obtained with non-leadership criteria. With these findings, a sizable proportion, although certainly not all, of the variance associated with leadership is accounted for.

How might this occur? To provide a possible explanation, I turn to a finding by Martell, Lane, and Emrich (1996), originally developed to explain the effects of sex bias on organizational careers. Using computer simulations, they were able to demonstrate that in hierarchic systems, very small relationships at the lowest levels tend to escalate, as multiple career decisions were made over time, into very large relationships at the top of the hierarchy. It would seem likely that in other types of organizations beyond the hierarchic, this same process may occur, at least to the extent that the organization is of substantial size, that leadership is a scarce commodity, and that an underlying leadership continuum exists.

If escalation of this kind does occur, it could well account for the high correlations reported for leadership variables. These relationships have been established well into the subjects' careers, and in some cases for whole careers, at a point where many career decisions have had an opportunity to compound. Whatever small advantage having a congruent motivational pattern may have given in the early years, and our data suggest that it is indeed small, is translated later into the results noted in Tables 22.1 and 22.2. What these leadership and career variables appear to measure is the end result of a career process, involving many decisions, that has unfolded over a considerable period of time.

Use of Organizational Forms in Leadership Theory

In a recent book (Miner, 2002b), I review, among other organizational behavior theories, sixteen major leadership theories. It may prove instructive to see how the constructs of the role motivation theories of leadership relate to this general body of knowledge in the field. See also Miner 2005.

One such question involves the extent to which the four forms or systems of role motivation theory enter into the theoretical formulations of these other leadership theories; to what degree are these theories organizationally based? A tabulation indicates that all sixteen utilize the hierarchic form in some manner, although this incorporation is frequently more implicit than explicit. The next most frequently incorporated is the group form, with half of the theo-

Table 22.4

Relationships between Various Predictors and Leadership Forms in Samples Where Congruent MSCS Correlations Are Available

Sample (Prior Description)	Predictor Measure	Leadership Form	Method of Analysis	Correlation
Personnel and Industrial Relations Managers (Miner 1977b)		Managerial	Biserial correlation Leader—n = 41; Member—n = 60	
	Ghiselli Self-Description Inventory—Supervisory Ability →		Leader—M = 30.39; Member—M = 28.19	.25*
	Adorno F-Scale →		Leader—M = 72.98; Member—M = 70.19	.14
	Kuder Preference Record Supervisory Interest		Leader—M = 35.73; Member—M = 34.33	.14
Buffalo, NY Area Entrepreneurs (Miner 1977a)		Entrepreneurial	Biserial correlation Leader—n = 45; Member—n = 44	
	Shure and Meeker Risk Avoidance Scale →		Leader—M = 31.87; Member—M = 32.14	–.03
	Gallup-Thorndike Vocabulary Test: Forms A & B		Leader—M = 25.02; Member—M = 25.43	–.06
	Matteson-Ivancevich Individual Behavior Activity Profile—Type A →		Leader—M = 54.15; Member—M = 57.20	–.17
	Levenson Instrument			
	Internal Control →		Leader—M = 40.73; Member—M = 38.98	.28*
	Powerful Other Control →		Leader—M = 18.87; Member—M = 20.16	–.14
	Chance Control →		Leader—M = 16.60; Member—M = 15.73	.11
	Rowe-Mason Decision Style Inventory			
	Directive Scale →		Leader—M = 79.91; Member—M = 79.43	.02
	Conceptual Scale →		Leader—M = 91.29; Member—M = 76.00	.21
	Behavioral Scale →		Leader—M = 60.44; Member—M = 60.34	.00

Note: MSCS = Miner Sentence Completion Scale.
$^*p < .05$

ries employing it. This is consistent with the group dynamics origins of leadership theory. Professional and task forms are embodied in several theories, but these types of organizational leadership play a much less significant role than do the other two.

The only theory that introduces constructs from all four organizational systems is substitutes for leadership theory—with professional, task, and group attributes appearing as substitutes for hierarchic leadership. This orientation is most manifest in a paper by Kerr and Slocum (1981).

The typical pattern is for two organizational forms to be incorporated in certain of their aspects. Among these forms the dominant combination is some mix of hierarchy and group variables. Fiedler's contingency theory illustrates this approach. The key LPC (Least Preferred Coworker) factor is at least on occasion viewed as an index of people-orientation on the high end, and thus contains a variable from group systems, as does the leader-member relations construct. Yet position power is construed as a hierarchic component (Fiedler and Chemers 1974). Fiedler's research, which provided the inductive base for theory development, has been conducted primarily within small groups and/or within the very hierarchic military. Other theories of the time often take this same tack, emphasizing both hierarchic and group forms.

Another approach in leadership theory has been to emphasize some construct, which by its nature cuts across the various organizational forms and could manifest itself in one form just as well as in another. Typically, however, these multi-organizational constructs are actually treated by the theory as present in hierarchic organizations and at best in one other form. Degrees of participation and/or delegation can be varied, for instance, in any type of organization, even the group form, where, under certain circumstances, the emergent leader can assume increasingly unilateral powers. Charismatic leadership behavior and its variants need not be limited to hierarchic systems but can appear through the visionary leadership of entrepreneurs, the god-like qualities of emergent sect leaders, and the intellectual brilliance of professional (intellectual) leaders.

Transformational leadership (Bass 1985) is generally treated as a factor that occurs in hierarchic systems or in the professional context, where empirically it has been found to act somewhat differently. Yet, there is no reason why entrepreneurial and group systems should not be permeated with the same type of leadership on occasion; in fact, we know that they often are, although transformational leadership has rarely been studied in these contexts.

My point here is that looking at leadership as it occurs in different organizational forms, as the role motivation theories of leadership do, could well extend the leadership field into new domains and new kinds of knowledge. The processes involved may not be unlike what has occurred as the multi-level approaches have come to permeate the field (Dansereau, Yammarino, and Markham 1995).

Implications for Charismatic/Transformational Theorizing

In closing, I want to extend these ideas with reference to the development of the charismatic/transformational cluster of theories. In doing so, I will draw on the literature review contained in Miner (2002b). Two points seem to be important. The first deals with the distinction between leader personality and leader behavior; the second with the extent to which charismatic/transformational leadership extends to lower levels of organization, or in role motivation theory terms into the ranks of organization members who are not leaders, at least as yet.

Both the House (1977) propositions and those that have followed, as well as the Bass (1985) propositions, are concerned with leader personality *and* leader behaviors. These represent two distinct levels within the individual level of analysis. They are not the same thing and, in fact, they would be expected to be only minimally correlated, because behavior (but less so personality) should be more strongly influenced by contextual forces and constraints. The House theory, especially in its research, has placed much more emphasis on personality; the Bass theory, using the Multi-factor Leadership Questionnaire (MLQ) and consistent with the theory's origins, has tended to focus primarily on behavior in the research conducted.

Research on charismatic personality in the context of the House theory has been concerned with executive leadership in hierarchic organizations and with laboratory studies. The latter, being short-term, have often lacked a strong organizational form induction of any kind. Within hierarchic organizations, the personality pattern that emerges in conjunction with charisma is very similar in a number of its aspects to that of the hierarchic leader. These are contexts, such as the U.S. presidency, where charismatic behaviors, if available to a leader, should work well; thus one cannot help wondering whether this research may only demonstrate the use of charismatic behavior by hierarchic leaders whose personalities are congruent with the organizational form in which they find themselves.

Charismatic leaders in other, non-bureaucratic contexts, according to this hypothesis, should prove to be very different types of people. But since we have only research, which looks at congruent leaders in one type of organization, it is easy to conclude that we have *the* charismatic personality. This is an alternative interpretation of the research, which needs testing. Will role motivation theory of leadership serve to explain the charismatic results in so far as personality is concerned?

Research on the Bass theory, as indicated, has had little to say about personality. It has focused on the *behaviors* of transformational leaders, again in hierarchic organizations, although many of these "leaders" are in what I would view as pre-leadership positions. There has been considerable focus on military organizations and business bureaucracies. On the few occasions when research has strayed outside the hierarchic form, to the professional for instance, it has not produced results that are as consistent with transformational leadership theory, even for behavior; there appears to be something operating behind the charismatic behavior that is different here (see Miner 2005). Again we need to conduct more research outside the bureaucratic form if we are to understand fully the nature of charismatic/transformational leadership. Do we simply have a cluster of theories dealing with a limited aspect of hierarchic leadership?

The second point I wish to raise also calls for research outside the hierarchic domain. Since Weber (1968), charisma has been associated with the upper levels of bureaucracies. Yet, Etzioni (1961) places it throughout all levels of normative (professional) systems as well, and Bass too has found charisma at lower (member) levels, although, in his view, it is identified primarily with lower levels of hierarchic systems. House appears to hold closer to the Weberian position. The role motivation view would be that charismatic behavior could be exhibited by leaders, or even pre-leaders, in any type of organization; its use would, however, be constrained by the potential willingness of those who are dependent on the leader to follow his or her dictates. Since potential follower responsiveness could vary across organization types, being greater for instance in certain professional systems, charismatic behavior could well exhibit an uneven pattern as it cuts across different kinds of organizations. In any event, there is a great need for research in multiple organizational domains to disentangle the existing theoretical perspectives here.

In a similar vein, we need to deal with the matter of the routinization of charisma. Routinization would seem to represent a normal leadership process, whatever accounts for the emergence of charisma. Thus, in role motivation theory terms, it should follow a different route in different types of organizations. There has been little research (or theory either) in this regard. Within task systems, however, it appears that hierarchy may be introduced to routinize the entrepreneur's vision (Miner 1997a). Perhaps similar phenomena operate in other organizational contexts as well. Again, the operation of charismatic/transformational processes within clearly specified organizational forms needs to be given much greater attention than it has been given in the past.

ADDENDUM ON TESTING THE LEADERSHIP THEORY

For several reasons the reported findings on other leadership data sources are incomplete. There are two additional studies that should be noted. These studies do little to change the conclusions, but they should be given attention. Professional motivation was considered in the study of labor arbitrators (see Chapter 19 and in particular Table 19.3). Task motivation was the subject of Chapter 16 contrasting entrepreneurs and managers. In particular the data of Table 16.1 are relevant, as are the discriminant findings. These two studies yield total score correlations of .68 and .66 respectively, which should be added to the correlations in Table 22.2. When this is done the new median value is .695, still a very high figure and indicative of a substantial relationship between leadership and the MSCSs.

FINDINGS FROM THE WHOLE CAREER DATA

The data on whole careers, or very near, indicate that career-relevant motivation survives and perhaps even prospers into the period normally considered to involve disengagement; certainly there is no evidence of decline with age. See Table 22.5. Career motivation levels do not appear to vary depending on whether the person is or is not retired ($t = .95$, p not significant); neither does age. What does seem to vary, however, is the type of career. Among those with managerial careers 85 percent were retired and this figure was only slightly lower (81 percent) among the professionals, but among the entrepreneurs only 39 percent were retired ($\chi^2 = 18.01, p < .01$ for df = 2). This finding takes on added meaning when placed in conjunction with the fact that the self-employed have generally been found to be particularly committed to their organizations and particularly satisfied with their jobs (Thompson, Kopelman, and Schriesheim 1992). They are less subject to pushes and pulls manipulated by others. Their failure to seek retirement may reflect the specific nature of their unique career motivation or it may reflect the nature of their work contexts; probably both are involved, but in any event these are people who tend not to seek early retirement.

There is in fact an item in Form T that allows us to sample how entrepreneurs feel about early retirement. This item, in sentence completion format, asks for reactions to "Retiring at an early age . . ." and is part of the achieving on one's own subscale. It is reverse scored. For the respondent group as a whole the percentage rejecting early retirement is 45; another 22 percent are equivocal on the matter; only 33 percent respond favorably to the idea. Among those not retired (and thus still working in their careers) these figures are 71 percent, 21 percent, and 8 percent respectively. Clearly there are few people still working in their 70s who long for retirement. When entrepreneurship is factored into this picture, entrepreneurs who are not retired and reject early retirement are overrepresented, as are managers and professionals who are retired and favor early retirement ($\chi^2 = 12.96, p < .05$ for df = 6). Thus entrepreneurship is both a source of continued employment and of attitudes unfavorable to retirement; but note

Table 22.5

Testing the Hypothesis that Career Motivation Declines with Age

MSCS Measures					Career Fit	*F*	*p*
Form H: Mean age	72		42		72		
N	44		695		48		
Total Score	–2.00	**	4.23	**	6.65	32.86	< .01
Authority Figures	–.07	**	1.17		1.40	14.08	< .01
Competitive Games	–.80	**	1.22		.85	23.07	< .01
Competitive Situations	–1.43	**	–.51	**	.48	16.25	< .01
Imposing Wishes	–.05	**	.71	**	1.73	16.62	< .01
Assertive Role	–.48		.14		.08	2.33	.10
Standing Out from Group	.45		.91		1.06	2.24	.11
Routine Administrative Functions	.36		.59		1.04	2.01	.14
Form P: Mean age	72		43		70		
N	47		125		38		
Total Score	4.17		5.74	**	12.84	17.61	< .01
Acquiring Knowledge	.36		.50	**	2.45	9.91	< .01
Independent Action	.98	**	2.02		2.34	4.22	.02
Accepting Status	.09	**	1.32		2.24	6.86	< .01
Providing Help	2.17		1.80	**	3.32	6.32	< .01
Professional Commitment	.57		.09	**	2.50	14.32	< .01
Form T: Mean age	72		47		72		
N	60		135		24		
Total Score	.67	**	6.81	**	13.71	30.01	< .01
Self-Achievement	.82	**	1.91	*	3.42	9.28	< .01
Avoiding Risks	.75		.94	**	3.25	9.31	< .01
Feedback of Results	–.78		–.20	*	1.04	4.64	.01
Personal Innovation	.97	**	2.99		3.71	16.11	< .01
Planning for the Future	–1.08	**	1.17		2.29	18.39	< .01

Note: MSCS = Miner Sentence Completion Scale.

Note: For Form H career fit = a hierarchic career; lack of career fit = professional or entrepreneurial career.

For Form P career fit = a professional career; lack of career fit = hierarchic or entrepreneurial career.

For Form T career fit = an entrepreneurial career; lack of career fit = hierarchic or professional career.

*p < .05 for adjacent means; **p < .01 for adjacent means.

also that in the group as a whole, where most have indeed retired and the average age is 72, there is substantial sentiment in favor of continuing employment at least beyond the "early out" period. Other data support this conclusion (McNaught, Barth, and Henderson 1989). There is good reason to believe that a substantial pool of older talent exists, which could be utilized to expand the workforce, and that achieving retirement in the 50s and even before, is not "the national goal."

CHAPTER 23

ADOLESCENTS IN ORANGE COUNTY, CA

FAMILY INFLUENCES ON THE DEVELOPMENT OF TASK MOTIVATION IN ADOLESCENTS

JENNIFER L. MINER

INTRODUCTION

Like several of the other chapters in this volume, this one is entirely original to this source. The ideas behind these analyses emerged as a result of discussions between the author, who is completing her PhD at the University of California, Irvine in child development/developmental psychology, and this volume's editor (the author's father). The paper has been facilitated by the access Jennifer had to longitudinal data on childrearing practices collected in connection with a national study (see National Institute for Child Health and Human Development Early Child Care Research Network 2001).

* * *

BACKGROUND AND HYPOTHESES

The study of achievement motivation can most directly be tied to the work of David McClelland (1961) in the 1950s and 1960s. McClelland proposed the concept of "need Achievement," (nAch, or *n* Achievement), an idea he defined as "behavior towards competition with a standard of excellence" (McClelland, Atkinson, Clark, and Lowell 1953). In his book, *The*

Achieving Society, McClelland provided a compelling argument that nAch drives individuals to succeed in entrepreneurial endeavors. In so doing, he laid the groundwork for future research into the role of achievement motivation in entrepreneurial behavior, and how this motivation develops in individuals.

Drawing upon McClelland's work, Miner (1993) reformulated the theory underlying nAch and entrepreneurial behavior into the task role motivation theory. As described more fully in Chapter 32, Miner proposed that individuals high in task motivation have a particular motivational pattern that serves them well in entrepreneurial environments. High achievers have a desire for achievement through personal effort; a desire to avoid risks; a desire for feedback on their performance; a tendency toward personal innovation; and a desire to plan and establish goals. To assess such a motivational pattern, the Miner Sentence Completion Scale–Form T(ask) (MSCS–T; Miner 1986) was developed. This measure has been successfully utilized in several studies (as described elsewhere in this volume), and results indicate that successful entrepreneurs exhibit higher levels of task motivation than less successful ones. Miner, Smith, and Bracker (1989; 1994), found for example, that entrepreneurs scored higher on the MSCS–T than non-entrepreneurs, and scores were also predictive of firm success over five years (see Chapter 15).

However, although research has suggested a link between task motivation and entrepreneurial behavior, studies on the development of this motive pattern in adolescents and adults are limited. As yet, no research is available on how parenting and early family relationships predict levels of task motivation, as formulated by Miner (1986; 1993). Knowledge of the family's influence on task motivation is likely to be both theoretically and practically important however, as it may shed light on how best to promote task motivation in children and adults. Furthermore, assessing task motivation in adolescents may aid in career counseling. The present study advances our current knowledge on task motivation on two levels. First, the current study utilized longitudinal data across two domains, family and child characteristics, to predict adolescent task motivation. Secondly, the sample consists of fifteen-year-old adolescents and thus represents the first study of adolescent task motivation using the MSCS–T.

Family Influences on Achievement Motivation

Because no research has examined the relationship between Miner's task motivation and early family relationships, it is necessary to take a step back in the theoretical lineage of task motivation to examine what research has suggested regarding the role of the early family environment in the development of need Achievement, the predecessor of the task role motivation theory.

In *The Achieving Society* McClelland (1961) suggests an important role for familial influences on the development of need Achievement in children, as it is within the context of family relationships that motives are learned. McClelland suggests that "something apparently happens in the family in childhood, beginning at least as early as the fourth or fifth year, which produces differences in *n* Achievement level" (341). This "something," he theorized, was a parenting style characterized by demands for independence and mastery within the context of warm parent-child interactions. Early research on this idea supported McClelland's proposal.

Rosen and D'Andrade (1959) conducted a study of forty families with nine, ten, or eleven-year-old boys, measuring the boys' *n* Achievement with the Thematic Apperception Test (TAT).

By observing both mother and father-child interactions across a variety of achievement tasks, the authors concluded that in general, mothers and fathers of high *n* Achievement boys set higher standards of excellence than did parents of children with low *n* Achievement; they were also more likely to exhibit positive affect and warmth in reaction to their sons' achievements. Additionally, the authors observed that mothers of high achieving sons tended to be more dominant and authoritarian, though also warmer in interactions with their sons. Fathers of high achievers tended to be less dominant and to stay out of the picture. Fathers of low achieving boys tended to exert their authority more frequently and to interfere with their son's activities. Taken as a whole, these results suggest that high achievement is fostered by a family environment in which standards of excellence are encouraged, and in which mothers are warm and involved but fathers are relatively non-interfering with their sons' achievement strivings.

Research since Rosen and D'Andrade's (1959) study has offered further support for the role of parenting from both mothers and fathers in the development of achievement motivation in children and adolescents. In a study of four-year-old children and their fathers, Epstein and Radin (1975) sought to test the theory that paternal warmth would provide the child with positive experiences, which in turn would lead the child to want to explore and master his or her environment. Using observational ratings of motivation during an IQ test, the authors observed that among middle- and working-class boys, the father's nurturance—including reinforcing the child, being verbally stimulating, and meeting the child's needs—enhanced motivation. For girls, restrictiveness and unpredictable parenting from the father interfered with task motivation.

In addition to father nurturance, mothers' sensitivity in interaction with their children has been shown to promote achievement motivation (Hokoda and Fincham 1995; Lakshmi and Arora 2006; Wigfield, Eccles, Schiefele, Roesser, and Davis-Kean 2006). Using the concept of helpless and mastery motivation in children, measured by both an attributional style questionnaire and observer ratings of behaviors during an achievement task, Hokoda and Fincham (1995) studied mother-child interactions among third-grade children. They observed that mothers of mastery children were more sensitive and affectively positive during achievement situations with their children, while mothers of helpless children showed less positive affect and were less encouraging of mastery.

Among adolescents, Lakshmi and Arora (2006) found that high need for achievement, measured via a modification of the TAT, was associated with high parental encouragement among Indian high school girls, and with high encouragement, acceptance, and autonomy granting among Indian boys. In a study of American adolescents, Steinberg, Elmen, and Mounts (1989) found that adolescents who reported their parents to be authoritative in their parenting style, defined as treating their children warmly, democratically, and firmly, were more likely to hold a healthy psychological orientation toward work, which in turn promoted academic achievement.

In sum, research on achievement motivation from a variety of theoretical traditions has offered general support for the premise that parents of high achieving children emphasize independence and mastery, show affection in interaction with their children, and are not overly controlling of their children's behavior (Lakshmi and Arora 2006; Epstein and Radin 1975; Winterbottom 1958). These findings appear to apply to both adolescents (Lakshmi and Arora 2006; Steinberg, Elmen, and Mounts 1989) and young children (Hokoda and Fincham 1995; Epstein and Radin 1975), and similar results are found whether achievement motivation is measured projectively (for instance, Rosen and D'Andrade 1959; Lakshmi and Arora 2006), or with observer- or self-report measures of motivation (Hokoda and Fincham 1995;

Steinberg, Elmen, and Mounts 1989). Therefore, the present study sought to explore whether a similar pattern of sensitive, child-centered parenting and demands for independence would predict higher levels of adolescent task motivation, as measured by the MSCS–T. Specifically, a series of hypotheses regarding the relations between parental behaviors and attitudes and task motivation were tested in the current study. These included:

Hypothesis 1. *Mothers and fathers who exhibited greater sensitivity and responsiveness toward their children in semi-structured interactions over the course of childhood would have children with higher levels of task motivation in adolescence.*

Hypothesis 2. *More traditional, authoritarian attitudes toward childrearing would be predictive of lower levels of adolescent task motivation.*

Hypothesis 3. *More frequent demands for independence from mothers early in childhood would predict higher levels of task motivation.*

In addition to these key hypotheses, predictive relations between these parenting variables and each of the subscales of the MSCS–T were also explored. No specific directional hypotheses were put forth for these subscales, as little theoretical or empirical work exists to support clear hypotheses in these areas.

Adolescent Characteristics and Achievement Motivation

A constellation of child characteristics, including birth order, gender and attachment security, has been indicated in the literature as relevant to the study of achievement motivation. Although not always consistently, researchers have often observed that firstborn children are higher in achievement motivation than later-borns (Snell, Hargrove, and Falbo 1986; Sulloway 1996; Jefferson, Herbst, and McCrae 1998). With regard to gender, the findings are mixed. Some researchers have observed girls to be higher in achievement motivation, while others have observed this trait to be characteristic of boys; the domain in which achievement is considered, such as math or verbal achievement, appears to be particularly important (Lueptow 1975; Wigfield, Eccles, Schiefele, Roesser, and Davis-Kean 2006). In the present study, both birth order and gender were included as potentially important predictors.

The last child characteristic examined in the present study was child attachment security (Bowlby 1969/1982). Although attachment security develops out of the relationship formed between a child and his or her caregiver, a cognitive model soon develops within the child. This cognitive model, known as the internal working model, is theorized to form a basis for the way the individual thinks about himself or herself and the relationships involved; it may therefore be considered a characteristic of the individual (Bowlby 1969).

Research on attachment and child development suggests that the more a child feels secure in relationship with a caregiver, the more the child will benefit both cognitively and socially (Belsky and Pasco Fearon 2002; Keller 2003). Such advantages include displaying higher self-esteem (Collins and Read 1990), and greater curiosity and more exploration of the environment (Bryant, Zvonkovic, and Reynolds 2006, 160). Attachment security in adults has also been theorized to significantly influence leader–follower relationships within organizational contexts (Keller 2003).

Elliot and Reis (2003) have proposed a theoretical model wherein a secure attachment,

> affords optimal, unimpeded exploration in achievement settings. The internalized representation of a secure base is presumed to serve as a resource that allows individuals to freely exercise their natural, approach-based motivational tendencies, and mastery pursuits in particular. For secure individuals, the possibility of failure is not an anxiety-provoking, distracting concern, because they expect attachment figures to be available, supportive, and reassuring, independent of their achievement outcomes (Elliot and Reis 2003, 319).

Thus, a secure attachment is theorized to provide an emotional context for a child wherein he or she feels comfortable exploring and gaining mastery over his or her environment. In support of this idea, Elliot and Reis (2003) report on a series of studies demonstrating a consistent link between attachment and achievement motivation in adulthood, such that individuals reporting a secure attachment style in adulthood had a higher need for achievement than insecurely attached individuals.

These findings clearly suggest a role for attachment security in achievement orientation; however, the results of Elliot and Reis' studies are limited by the lack of a longitudinal design. Specifically, both attachment and achievement motivation were assessed in adulthood using self-report measures, making it difficult to draw causal implications from the research. To improve upon this design, the current study used an observational measure of attachment when children were twenty-four months old to predict task motivation at age fifteen. This design allows for firmer causal conclusions to be drawn regarding the impact of attachment security on task motivation, as thirteen years separate the two measures. Furthermore, self-report bias is virtually non-existent in the present study, as the measure of attachment was assessed via trained observers in the home, and the projective quality of the MSCS–T ensured that participants had little idea what they were reporting about themselves.

Based upon the literature relating child characteristics to achievement motivation in children and adults, additional hypotheses were generated for the purposes of the current study. Specifically, it was hypothesized that:

Hypothesis 4. *Firstborn children would score higher on total task motivation than later-born children.*

Hypothesis 5. *A more secure attachment in infancy would be predictive of higher levels of task motivation in adolescence.*

Hypothesis 6. *A null hypothesis was put forth regarding the effect of a child's sex on task motivation. The mixed literature on this subject makes it difficult to ascertain whether males or females are more likely to exhibit this characteristic and therefore, no directional hypothesis was generated for this relationship.*

In addition to these hypotheses, the relationships between child characteristics and each of the subscales in the MSCS–T were also examined.

METHOD

Participants

In 2006, an opportunity arose for the author to collect data from a subset of adolescents involved in a longitudinal study of youth development begun in 1991. This study, known as the National Institute of Child Health and Human Development Study of Early Child Care and Youth Development (NICHD SECCYD), has gathered data from parents, caregivers, and the youth themselves since the birth of the child and continuing into the child's fifteenth year. Included in the data for the study are a wealth of information on the children and their families, including observations of parental behaviors, attitudinal measures from parents, assessments of attachment and parent-child relations, and a multitude of other socioemotional and cognitive measures gathered approximately every one to two years for the past fifteen years from the children and their families. The depth and quality of the data collected for the NICHD study provided a unique opportunity to examine the factors influencing the development of task motivation in the subsample of children involved.

For the current study, children residing at one site of the NICHD SECCYD were approached and asked to complete the MSCS–T as well as a personality measure, the Five Factor Model (John, Donohue, and Kentle 1991), which is based conceptually on Digman (1990). Recruitment procedures and characteristics of the NICHD SECCYD sample are described more fully in other publications (NICHD Early Child Care Research Network 2001). For the current study, 98 adolescents (47 males; 51 females) completed the measures of interest when they came to the university for an NICHD SECCYD lab visit. Visits occurred within one month of the adolescents' fifteenth birthday. Eight subjects were missing birth order data, and were excluded from the regression analyses. Of the remaining, most were either the second-born child in their family (45 percent) or the firstborn (31 percent); 14 percent were later-born. When children were one month of age, the average family income level was 4.1 times the poverty threshold. Seventy-three per cent of the children reported Caucasian ethnicity, with the remainder reporting "other" (20 percent), Hispanic (3 percent) or Asian (2 percent).

Procedure

Beginning when children were one month of age and continuing until they were fifteen years old, detailed measures of family demographics, parental attitudes and behaviors and child characteristics were assessed. At one month of age, parents reported on their child's gender and birth order. Parent-child interactions, from which a parental sensitivity code was derived, were assessed at multiple time points across childhood.

At 24 months, child attachment security to the mother was measured using an observational Q-sort instrument. When children were 54 months old, mothers completed a questionnaire measure assessing the frequency with which they made independence demands upon their children. When children were in grades 1 and 4, mothers and fathers completed a questionnaire assessing the extent to which they endorsed authoritarian attitudes toward childrearing.

Dependent measures were completed by adolescents when they visited the university lab to participate in the NICHD SECCYD Age 15 Lab Visit.

Measures

Demographics

When children were one month old, mothers reported on family income, child sex, and child birth order.

Maternal and Paternal Sensitivity

When children were 6, 15, 24, 36, and 54 months of age, and again when children were in grades 1, 3, and 5, mother-child interactions during semi-structured play scenarios and problem-solving activities were videotaped. Videotapes were coded at a central site with coders blind to other information about the families. At 6, 15 and 24 months, a maternal sensitivity composite score was computed consisting of the sum of three 4-point ratings [maternal sensitivity to child's non-distress signals, intrusiveness (reversed) and positive regard]. At 36 months to grade 5, sensitivity composites were computed as the sum of three 7-point ratings of supportive presence, respect for autonomy, and hostility (reversed). Intercoder reliability was established by having two coders assess approximately 20 percent of the tapes, randomly drawn from each assessment period. For the present study, individual dimensions were rescaled to a 7-point scale for all ages and then summed in a composite as described above, thus creating comparable measures at each time point. Reliability intra-class coefficients for the NICHD sample, from which the current subsample was drawn, ranged from .72 to .87; Cronbach's alphas ranged from .70 to .84.

Father-child interactions were assessed in a manner identical to the mother-child interactions when children were 54 months, and in grades 1, 3, and 5.

For analyses, an average score for mother and father sensitivity was computed. For mothers, this score consisted of the average level of sensitivity observed from 6 months to Grade 5. For fathers, the sensitivity score was computed as the average of scores from 54 months to Grade 5. Following this computation, 6 values were replaced with the mean for the paternal sensitivity variable. There were no missing values on the maternal sensitivity variable.

Attitudes Toward Childrearing

When children were in grades 1 and 4, mothers and fathers were administered the Parental Modernity Scale of Child-Rearing and Educational Beliefs (Schaefer and Edgerton 1985), which assesses the extent to which attitudes are traditional (strict, authoritarian, adult-centered) rather than modern (progressive, child-centered). For analyses, an average traditional attitudes score was computed (using the Traditional Attitudes scale) separately for mothers and fathers, as the average of scores from first and fourth grades. Higher scores reflect more traditional childrearing attitudes. It was necessary to replace 16 maternal scores and 12 paternal scores with the mean from the traditional attitudes scale.

Independence Demands

When children were 54 months old, mothers completed a modified form of the self-report measure developed by Greenberger and Goldberg (1989) to measure parental demands for mature child behavior. In the measure mothers are asked to respond to the question, "How often do you expect your child to . . ." with 32 items on a 7 point Likert scale, from 1 = "Never" to 7 = "Always." The scale has three subscales: demands for independence, demands for self-control, and demands for prosocial behavior. Only the Demands for Independence subscale was used in the present analyses, with higher scores reflecting greater frequency of independence demands. Sixteen missing values were replaced with the mean for the scale.

Child Attachment

The Attachment Behavior Q-Set (Bretherton and Waters 1985) was completed after a two-hour period of observation in the target child's home. The observer sorted the 90 items (cards) of the Attachment Behavior Q-Set into nine piles ranging from least characteristic to most characteristic of a particular subject. The final sort conformed to a symmetrical, unimodal distribution with specified numbers of items in each of the nine piles. Each item was given a final score in terms of its placement in the distribution. A correlation was then generated between the child's sort and a "criterion" sort representing a prototypically secure child. High reliability estimates for this measure were reported for the NICHD sample as a whole (r = .92). For purposes of analyses, 17 missing values were replaced with the mean correlation for the sample.

Task Motivation

The Miner Sentence Completion Scale–Form T (MSCS–T) was administered to adolescent participants to assess their level of task motivation. The measure consists of 40 sentence stems, which are coded along five dimensions and summed for a total score. The subscales of the measure include Self-Achievement, Planning for the Future, Personal Innovation, Avoiding Risks, and Feedback of Results. Total scores for the MSCS–T can range from –40 to +40. Subscale scores can range from –8 to +8.

Due to concerns that some of the vocabulary used in the measure may be inaccessible to adolescents, a definition sheet of commonly queried words (ascertained through pilot testing) was provided to the participants. The adolescents were also encouraged to ask any questions they may have about the items during the administration.

Scoring of the MSCS–T was done using the scoring guide for the instrument and was completed by the author (J. L. Miner). A subsample of 16 tests was scored by the measure's author (J. B. Miner) to assess scorer reliability. Scores as between the two raters were quite reliable, with 75 percent of the total scores on the MSCS–T agreeing within 1 point and 100 percent agreeing within 2 points. The correlation between the total scores obtained by the two raters was .98.

RESULTS

Descriptive statistics for dependent and predictor variables are presented in Table 23.1. Correlations between the MSCS–T subscales and the family and child variables are presented in Table 23.2. As seen in the table, children's birth order was positively associated with self-achievement in this sample. Additionally, maternal traditional attitudes toward childrearing were positively associated with scores on the Feedback of Results subscale. Finally, maternal sensitivity was positively related to the Total Score on the MSCS–T, as well as the subscales of Self-Achievement and Personal Innovation. Descriptive statistics and correlations were computed with missing data not imputed.

Key hypotheses were tested in a series of six simultaneous multiple regressions using the parenting and child variables (with missing values mean replaced) to predict the total and subscale scores of the MSCS–T.

Results of regression analyses are presented in Table 23.3. Before running regressions, intercorrelations among predictor variables were computed to address concerns about multicollinearity. These correlations were quite modest, averaging .17.

Table 23.1

Descriptive Statistics for Study Variables

Variable	n	*M*	*SD*
MSCS–T			
Total Score	98	7.14	6.43
Self-Achievement	98	1.07	2.45
Avoiding Risks	98	1.51	2.56
Feedback of Results	98	1.47	2.53
Personal Innovation	98	2.19	2.43
Planning for Future	98	.90	2.56
Child Sex			
Male	47		
Female	51		
Child Birth Order			
First	31		
Second	45		
Third	9		
Fourth	4		
Fifth	1		
Attachment Q-sort Correlation	81	.40	.24
Maternal Sensitivity	98	17.10	1.86
Paternal Sensitivity	92	17.35	1.74
Independence Demands	82	44.32	5.58
Maternal Traditional Attitudes	82	56.00	12.87
Paternal Traditional Attitudes	86	59.56	13.08

Note: MSCS = Miner Sentence Completion Scale.

Table 23.2

Zero-order Correlations between MSCS–T Scores and Predictor Variables

	Total Score	SA	AR	FR	PI	PF
Child Birth Order	.00	.26*	–.12	.05	–.02	–.18
Child Sex	.00	–.10	.16	–.15	.14	–.04
Paternal Traditional Attitudes	.11	.07	.05	.20	–.09	.05
Maternal Traditional Attitudes	–.03	–.14	–.17	.22*	–.10	.10
Independence Demands	.00	.19	.05	–.02	–.22	.01
Maternal Sensitivity	.27**	.19	.20*	–.01	.26*	.07
Paternal Sensitivity	–.02	.11	.08	–.05	–.01	–.18

Note: MSCS = Miner Sentence Completion Scale. SA = Self Achievement; AR = Avoiding Risks; FR = Feedback of Results; PI = Personal Innovation; PF = Planning for the Future. N's range from 82 to 98.
$^*p < .05$; $^{**}p < .01$

Regression models predicting the MSCS–T Total Score, Self-Achievement, and Personal Innovation were significant; models predicting the subscales of Avoiding Risks, Feedback of Results, and Planning for the Future were not. Of the parenting behaviors, higher levels of maternal sensitivity across childhood were found to predict higher total scores on the MSCS–T, after accounting for each of the other variables in the model. Additionally, more securely attached children scored higher on total task motivation.

Table 23.3

Regression Coefficients for the Prediction of MSCS–T Total and Subscale Scores from Parenting and Child Characteristics

	B	SE(b)	*B*
MSCS–T Total Score			
Maternal Sensitivity	1.66	.42	.49**
Paternal Sensitivity	–.75	.44	–.20
Maternal Traditional Attitudes	.017	.06	.03
Paternal Traditional Attitudes	.10	.06	.19
Independence Demands	–.06	.12	–.05
Child Sex (female)	–1.43	1.36	–.11
Child Birth Order	.48	.82	.06
Attachment Q-sort	6.5	2.93	.228*
Constant	–15.59	10.66	
F (df, df)		2.95 (8, 81)	
R^2		.23	
MSCS–T: Self-Achievement			
Maternal Sensitivity	.37	.15	.29*
Paternal Sensitivity	.10	.16	.07
Maternal Traditional Attitudes	–.04	.02	–.19
Paternal Traditional Attitudes	.01	.02	.05
Independence Demands	.05	.05	.12
Child Sex (female)	–1.05	.50	–.22*
Child Birth Order	1.11	.30	.39**
Attachment Q-sort	1.46	1.10	.14
Constant	–9.98	3.94*	
F (df, df)		3.55 (8, 81)	
R^2		.26	
MSCS–T: Personal Innovation			
Maternal Sensitivity	.57	.16	.44**
Paternal Sensitivity	–.42	.17	–.29*
Maternal Traditional Attitudes	.00	.02	.01
Paternal Traditional Attitudes	–.02	.02	–.10
Independence Demands	–.11	.05	–.24*
Child Sex (female)	.37	.53	.08
Child Birth Order	.36	.32	.13
Attachment Q-sort	.25	1.14	.02
Constant	4.82	4.15	
F (df, df)		2.49 (8, 81)	
R^2		.20	

Note: MSCS = Miner Sentence Completion Scale.
$^*p < .05$; $^{**}p < .001$

For the regression model predicting the subscale of Self-Achievement, maternal sensitivity was again found to be a significant predictor of higher levels of motivation. Additionally, being male (male $M = 1.32$; female $M = .84$) and a later-born child (firstborn $M = .10$; M of later borns = 1.72) was found to be predictive of higher levels of self achievement in this sample. These results were observed after accounting for the other variables in the model.

The last significant model to emerge in the analyses was for the prediction of the Personal Innovation subscale. Significant predictors in this model included independence demands, maternal sensitivity, and paternal sensitivity, after accounting for the remaining family and child variables in the model. Specifically, fewer independence demands from mothers and lower levels of paternal sensitivity predicted higher levels of innovation. Maternal sensitivity was found to positively predict an adolescents' personal innovation.

DISCUSSION

The primary goal of the current investigation was to test several hypotheses related to the development of task motivation in adolescents, and specifically to the role of the family environment in promoting task motivation. Towards this end, a longitudinal design was adopted to test the extent to which parental sensitivity and attitudes toward childrearing, independence demands, child attachment security, birth order and child sex would predict total task motivation. Also considered were the extent to which these characteristics would predict subscale scores on the MSCS–T.

Results from this study support the theoretical linkage between early parenting and family relationships and the development of task motivation. Specifically, total scores on the MSCS–T were predicted by both a more sensitive mother and a more secure attachment to the primary caregiver during childhood. However, other child and family characteristics, such as paternal sensitivity, traditional childrearing attitudes, demands for independence, and child sex and birth order were not predictive of overall task motivation in adolescence.

With regard to the analyses relating family and child characteristics and subscale scores on the MSCS–T, regression models for the prediction of Self-Achievement and Personal Innovation were significant. In particular, more sensitive mothering, being male, and being later-born, were related to higher self-achievement in this sample. Having a more responsive and sensitive mother during childhood was also related to a desire to innovate among the adolescents, as was lower paternal sensitivity, and fewer demands for independence from the mother.

One of the most consistent findings of the current study was for the role of maternal sensitivity in the development of task motivation. For both overall task motivation, and the closely associated subscale of Self-Achievement, maternal sensitivity was a significant factor. In this study, maternal sensitivity was defined as respect for the child's autonomy, positive regard, and a lack of hostility. As McClelland (1961) originally theorized about the development of need Achievement, a warm, supportive maternal figure in a child's life promotes the development of task motivation. It is likely that such a parent-child interaction pattern allows children to gain confidence in their abilities as they are granted greater autonomy, which in turn promotes a desire to achieve through one's own efforts. Indeed maternal sensitivity has been shown to promote a variety of positive outcomes in children, including scholastic achievement, behavioral control, and intellectual development (Belsky and Pasco Fearon 2002). Additionally, positive interactions with their mothers are likely to promote the internalization of parental norms in children, thus allowing achievement motives to be more easily learned (Wigfield, Eccles, Schiefele, Roesser, and Davis-Kean 2006).

In addition to predicting the Total and Self-Achievement scores of the MSCS–T, maternal sensitivity was also associated with the development of personal innovation, as was lower father sensitivity and fewer demands for independence from mothers when children were preschoolers. These findings appear to support two competing theories regarding the influence of the family on the development of creativity. Carl Rogers (as cited in Koestner, Walker, and Fincham 1999) proposed a theory of creativity wherein higher levels of creativity were fostered by a parenting style characterized by warmth and autonomy-granting. Harrington,

Block, and Block (1987) offered support for this idea in their results from a longitudinal study predicting adolescent creativity from early parenting attitudes.

In contrast, other authors have taken a behavioral view and have argued that creativity is fostered in family environments where children are specifically rewarded for creative endeavors, not necessarily where they experience unconditional positive regard. Gardner (1994) found, for example, that in studying the lives of exceptionally creative people, their home environments were more likely to be marked by strictness, discipline, and a lack of unconditional warmth. Koestner, Walker, and Fincham (1999) also observed that parental conflict during childhood related to creativity in adulthood, but that parental warmth did not.

With regard to the pattern of results observed in the present study, it appears that both Roger's and the behaviorist view of parenting and creativity were supported, but that the sex of the parent is critical. In particular, if sensitivity and a lack of demands come from the mother, this appears to promote innovation, whereas for fathers the opposite behaviors are important. It is significant to note however, that the research discussed thus far studied the development of observed creativity, whereas the current investigation considered only the motivation to behave in an innovative manner. Actual creativity levels were not measured in the current study, so links between the observed results and other empirical research about actual creativity are only suggestive at this point. Additional research is necessary to ascertain whether personal innovation as measured by the MSCS–T is in fact tied to higher levels of behavioral creativity in adolescents.

In addition to maternal sensitivity, attachment security also emerged as a significant predictor of overall task motivation in the current sample. Theory and research on the links between attachment and achievement motivation, especially the work conducted by Elliott and Reis (2003), provide support for the observed relationship. The current findings also extend previous work by using a longitudinal design. Results suggest that attachment security precedes the development of achievement motivation. Thus, having a secure attachment relationship with one's caregiver appears to allow children to feel safe in exploring their environments, and to develop the desire to achieve mastery through their own efforts.

Additional child characteristics, including birth order and child gender, were not predictive of overall achievement motivation, although they were found to relate to the Self-Achievement subscale. Contrary to the original hypothesis, self achievement scores were higher among later-born children, rather than among firstborns. Much of the literature on birth order effects suggests that firstborn children tend to be higher in achievement motives (Snell, Hargrove, and Falbo 1986; Sulloway 1996), but this finding is not always supported (Jefferson, Herbst, and McCrae 1998). Additional research using a larger sample of adolescents at differing birth orders may help to explain why later borns were found to be higher in task motivation than first borns. With regard to child sex, being male was found to positively relate to self achievement, a finding supported by various other studies of achievement motivation, though not all (see Wigfield, Eccles, Schiefele, Roesser, and Davis-Kean 2006 for a review).

Although several key parenting and child characteristics did emerge as significantly related to adolescent task motivation as discussed, other theoretically important variables did not. For example, maternal demands for independence were not found to relate to overall task motivation as hypothesized. McClelland and Franz (1992) have reported, for instance, that parental achievement pressure during the first two years of life is related to levels of need Achievement in adulthood. The null finding reported in this article may be due to the fact that the measure used did not tap demands for independence within mastery situations, but rather related to gaining independence in caregiving and social situations. Future research on this construct would likely benefit from an observational measure of parental demands for independence in an achievement context.

In addition to independence demands, parents' strict and authoritarian attitudes toward childrearing were not found to relate to lower levels of task motivation. It appears that this construct is not as critical in predicting task motivation in adolescents as having a positive, supportive presence in the mother. Furthermore, results suggest that it is sensitive, responsive parenting from the mother that is especially crucial to the development of task motivation, rather than paternal parenting. This finding may simply reflect the additional time that mothers spend with their children compared to fathers. Future work examining parenting by mothers and fathers specifically in an achievement situation may reveal more consistent links between fathering and task motivation.

Strengths, Limitations, and Future Directions

The study reported in this chapter had a variety of strengths. Of particular importance was its longitudinal, rather than concurrent design. All parenting and child characteristics were measured early in the adolescents' lives, increasing the author's ability to draw causal implications from the study. Furthermore, many characteristics, including parental sensitivity and childrearing attitudes were measured over several time points, thus increasing the reliability of the measures. Lastly, the current study benefited from the use of multiple-informants in its data collection. Parental sensitivity and child attachment, for example, was measured via observer ratings, childrearing attitudes were measured with a self-report instrument, and adolescent task motivation was measured via a projective measure. Indeed, it is quite remarkable that the observed associations did emerge so clearly, given the length of time over which data were collected, and the fact that study variables were assessed using such diverse methods.

However, although the current study benefited from several strengths in its design, it also had certain limitations. The sample consisted largely of white, middle-class adolescents in a particular region, therefore limiting the generalizability of the findings.

On a more conceptual level, the study was also limited by the fact that data on the adolescents' career aspirations were not collected. Specifically, a direct link between adolescent task motivation and entrepreneurial strivings could not be established in the current study, although Miner and his colleagues have specifically tied task motivation as measured with the MSCS–T to entrepreneurial behavior (1989; 1993; 1994). Indeed, considerable literature exists to suggest that task motivation is elevated among entrepreneurs, and furthermore, that parental behaviors can promote entrepreneurial interest and competence in children and adolescents (Lueptow 1975; Schmitt-Rodermund and Vondracek 2002; Schmitt-Rodermund 2004; Turner 1970). Schmitt-Rodermund (2004) found, for example, that an authoritative parenting style was linked to a measure of adolescents' entrepreneurial competence. In line with this as well, research on adolescent task motivation and entrepreneurial competence has the potential to inform career counseling for high schoolers, as those identified as having elevated task motivation may greatly benefit by knowledge about entrepreneurial careers.

Although the current study highlights the importance of parental and child behaviors and characteristics in the development of task motivation, future research should also explore the possibility of mediating relationships between parenting and adolescent achievement motivation. Research over the past two decades has begun to indicate, for example, that parenting has an effect upon child motivation through its impact on the child's emotional competence and ability to self-regulate (Wentzel and Feldman 1993). Thus, work on the development of

Table 23.4

Correlations (r) between the Miner Sentence Completion Scale–Form T and the Big Five Personality Characteristics in the Adolescent Sample (N = 97)

	Big Five Factors				
MSCS–T Variables	Extroversion	Conscientiousness	Neuroticism	Open to Experience	Agreeableness
Total Score	.03	.43**	–.20	.02	.29**
Self-Achievement	.06	.25*	–.05	–.01	.14
Avoiding Risks	–.12	.17	.10	–.21*	.00
Feedback of Results	–.06	.24*	–.32**	–.04	.21*
Personal Innovation	.22*	.15	–.08	.32**	.17
Planning for the Future	.00	.26*	–.15	.00	.20

**r is significant at the .01 level (2-tailed).
*r is significant at the .05 level (2-tailed).

task motivation in adolescents would benefit from longitudinal research modeling the complex relations between parental behaviors and attitudes, child socioemotional development, and task motivation.

RELATIONSHIPS BETWEEN THE MSCS–FORM T AND THE BIG FIVE CHARACTERISTICS

Information is available as well regarding how the MSCS–T relates to the factors of the big five model (John, Donahue, and Kentle 1991) in this adolescent sample. These data on relationships to a self-report measure (see Chapter 1) may prove helpful in interpreting the findings reported. Table 23.4 contains the correlations.

PART III

ANALYSES

CHAPTER 24

THE PSYCHOMETRIC SOUNDNESS OF THE MSCSs

INTRODUCTION

The article considered here was published in the *Academy of Management Journal* (Miner 1978d) in an attempt to redress certain conclusions that had been published previously regarding the Miner Sentence Completion Scale (MSCS)s. Although the data derive from various sources, a considerable contributor was a consulting engagement conducted at Lake Forest College in Illinois. Norris Love and Albert Furbay helped with this work.

* * *

A recent article in the *Academy of Management Journal* concluded with the following statement (Brief, Aldag, and Chacko 1977):

> . . . this paper has attempted to answer certain questions regarding the psychometric properties of the MSCS. The data reported do not argue strongly for continued use of the original version of the MSCS. The paper clearly demonstrates the importance of evaluating an instrument prior to its large-scale adoption by the research community. . . .

A similar statement appears in an earlier and shorter paper by the same authors (Brief, Aldag, and Chacko 1976).

The data brought to bear in reaching this conclusion suffer from serious shortcomings in conceptualization, differ sharply from the results obtained in other studies of similar phenomena, are not adequately integrated with the published literature, and raise certain questions regarding the authors' objectivity. It seems evident that certain properties of the MSCS need much more explanation than they have been given in the past.

From John B. Miner, "The Miner Sentence Completion Scale: A Reappraisal," *Academy of Management Journal,* 21 (1978), 283–294.

Table 24.1

Codings of Scorers in the Brief, Aldag, and Chacko Study (N = 101) **and Involving Experienced Scorers** (N = 12)

Intercorrelations

MSCS Measures	Brief, Aldag and Chacko Study			Experienced Scorers
	A vs. B	A vs. C	B vs. C	
Authority Figures	.71	.77	.77	.92
Competitive Games	.85	.91	.86	.98
Competitive Situations	.72	.60	.66	.89
Assertive Role	.74	.81	.79	.86
Imposing Wishes	.71	.66	.70	.83
Standing Out from Group	.58	.68	.65	.94
Routine Administrative Functions	.69	.76	.71	.96
Item Score	Not reported	Not reported	Not reported	.95
Median for Subscales	.71	.76	.71	.92

Mean Scores

MSCS Measures	Brief, Aldag, and Chaco Study			Experienced Scorers	
	Scorer A	Scorer B	Scorer C	ES1	ES2
Authority Figures	.16[a]	.84[b]	.26	.42	.58
Competitive Games	.92[ab]	1.49[b]	.66	.33	.50
Competitive Situations	–1.42[a]	–1.09[b]	–1.44	–1.25	–1.42
Assertive Role	–.61[b]	–.61[b]	–.91	–.75[c]	–1.42
Imposing Wishes	.29[ab]	.99[b]	.56	.67[c]	.17
Standing Out from Group	.29[ab]	1.59[b]	.73	.75	.92
Routine Administrative Functions	–.57[a]	–.28[b]	–.55	.25	.17
Item score	–.94[a]	2.93[b]	–.69	.42	–.50

Note: MSCS = Miner Sentence Completion Scale.
[a]Differs significantly ($p < .05$) from Scorer B mean.
[b]Differs significantly ($p < .05$) from Scorer C mean.
[c]Differs significantly ($p < .05$) from ES2 mean.

SCORER RELIABILITY

One line of argument advanced by Brief, Aldag, and Chacko is that agreement among scorers of the same MSCS protocols is low. Their data are given in Table 24.1 along with the results obtained with two known experienced scorers; all subjects are college students. These latter data, along with those contained in Tables 24.2 and 24.3, were generated quite recently (1975–77) and have not been published previously.

The scorer reliabilities noted in Table 24.1 for experienced scorers are consistently and sharply above those reported by Brief, Aldag, and Chacko. Furthermore, Scorer B appears to be out of line with A and C. Scorer B clearly gives much more positive scores. Brief, Aldag, and Chacko do not provide total score data, but item scores may easily be computed from the subscale means, and estimates of standard deviations are readily available. Overall the data strongly suggest a constant positive error in B's scoring. This conclusion derives not only from the actual data of Table 24.1 but from the fact that the mean scores for A and C are much more in line with previously published findings for

Table 24.2

Codings of a Learner and an Experienced Scorer at Different Stages of the Learning Process

Intercorrelations

MSCS Measures	Stage 1 (n = 25)	Stage 2 (n = 12)
Authority Figures	.86	.98
Competitive Games	.88	.95
Competitive Situations	.88	.95
Assertive Role	.92	.91
Imposing Wishes	.89	.66
Standing Out from Group	.83	.90
Routine Administrative Functions	.88	.97
Item Score	.91	.91
Median for Subscales	.88	.95

Mean Scores

	Stage 1 (n = 25)		Stage 2 (n = 12)	
MSCS Measures	$Learner_1$	Experienced $Scorer_1$	$Learner_2$	Experienced $Scorer_2$
Authority Figures	1.04	.88	1.50	1.33
Competitive Games	.92	1.00	1.17	.83
Competitive Situations	–1.08	–.92	–.42	–.50
Assertive Role	.40[a]	–.04	–.67	–.67
Imposing Wishes	.48[a]	.04	1.25	1.17
Standing Out from Group	–.04	.00	.08	–.08
Routine Administrative Functions	–.36	–.48	–.33	–.17
Item Score	1.36	.48	2.58	1.92

Note: MSCS = Miner Sentence Completion Scale.
[a]Differs significantly ($p < .05$) from Experienced Scorer mean.

college students (Miner 1977b, 142). Given the fact that Scorer B appears to derive from a different population of scorers than A and C, the procedure of "averaging the scores of the three coders" utilized by Brief, Aldag, and Chacko in conducting their analyses is not appropriate.

Even when B's scores are eliminated, however, there is a median subscale scorer reliability of .76 in the Brief, Aldag, and Chacko study and of .92 for the known experienced scorers. Why the difference? A partial explanation is provided by a study in which 25 protocols (8 managers, 17 college students) were scored first by a new scorer and then independently by an experienced scorer. The correlations are indicated under Stage 1 in Table 24.2. After an opportunity for further learning based on feedback of the original experienced scorer data, the new scorer scored 12 additional protocols (all managers) and the experienced scorer rescored them independently. The correlations are noted under Stage 2. Learning subsequent to feedback clearly has increased the scorer reliabilities. The single decline results almost entirely from a major discrepancy on one record among the 12. The same type of convergence with increased learning opportunity is in evidence for the means given in Table 24.2.

Table 24.3

Codings of Two Learners and an Experienced Scorer at Different Stages of the Learning Process

Intercorrelations

	Stage 1 (n = 25)			Stage 2 (n = 10)		
MSCS Measures	$L1_1$ vs. $L2_1$	$L1_1$ vs. ES_1	$L2_1$ vs. ES_1	$L1_2$ vs. $L2_2$	$L1_2$ vs. ES_2	$L2_2$ vs. ES_2
Authority Figures	.87	.90	.95	.76	.96	.86
Competitive Games	.72	.90	.82	.88	.94	.95
Competitive Situations	.87	.93	.94	.91	.91	.89
Assertive Role	.82	.93	.85	.82	.97	.91
Imposing Wishes	.69	.81	.68	.84	.78	.85
Standing Out from Group	.55	.75	.69	.82	.97	.90
Routine Administrative Functions	.90	.95	.95	.88	.97	.90
Item Score	.85	.88	.92	.88	.97	.86
Median for Subscales	.82	.90	.85	.84	.96	.90

Mean Scores

	Stage 1 (n = 25)			Stage 2 (n = 10)		
MSCS Measures	LI_1	$L2_1$	ES_1	$L1_1$	$L2_2$	ES_2
Authority Figures	.20	.60[b]	.24	.20	–.40	.00
Competitive Games	.92	.84	.88	1.60[ab]	.10[b]	1.00
Competitive Situations	–.80	–.96	–.80	–1.20	–1.40	–1.30
Assertive Role	–.44[ab]	–.84	–.84	–1.40	–1.00	–1.10
Imposing Wishes	.12	.52	.16	1.10[a]	.40[b]	1.20
Standing Out from Group	.40[ab]	1.56[b]	.76	1.20	.80	1.20
Routine Administrative Functions	.72	.76	.56	1.70[a]	.70[b]	1.50
Item Score	1.12[a]	2.48[b]	.96	3.20[a]	–.80[b]	2.50

Note: MSCS = Miner Sentence Completion Scale.
[a]Differs significantly ($p < .05$) from Learner 2 mean.
[b]Differs significantly ($p < .05$) from Experienced Scorer mean.

Table 24.3 provides data for a study utilizing the same feedback design with two learners. The subjects were graduate students in business, most of whom also held full-time jobs as managers. Initially, Learner 2 shows the same kind of constant positive error noted for Scorer B in the Brief, Aldag, and Chacko study. After feedback, Learner 1 achieves results that closely approximate those of the experienced scorer. However, the results of the increased learning opportunity for Learner 2 are not nearly as favorable. There appears to have been an overcompensation for the initial positive tendency in scoring such that now at Stage 2 a constant negative error is present. The number of significant differences in subscale comparisons with the experienced scorer actually increases. It appears that Learner 2 will require additional rounds of feedback before an acceptable level of scoring competence is attained.

These data indicate that MSCS scoring competence is a learned skill and that improvements can be expected with increased learning opportunities. In addition, there are sizable individual differences in the speed with which this type of learning occurs. Because the scorer is in fact part of the measuring instrument to a much greater degree when projective techniques, such as the MSCS, are used than with objective, forced choice tests, it is essential that research be conducted utilizing experienced scorers. Otherwise constant errors may distort the findings or a sizable random error may wash them out completely.

Given the available evidence, it is extremely difficult to understand Brief, Aldag, and Chacko's statement that "the scorers were advanced graduate students in organizational behavior and were *well versed* (italics added) in Miner's (1965a) scoring procedure." Reliabilities in the .90s have been obtained repeatedly with experienced scorers; there is only one such correlation among the 21 reproduced in Table 24.1 Even McClelland's complex procedures for scoring Thematic Apperception Test protocols for need achievement have yielded scorer reliabilities in the range of .80 to .90 or better when experienced scorers are used (Heckhausen 1967). Since the MSCS utilizes fewer scoring categories and is more directly stimulus-related, its somewhat higher scorer reliability would be anticipated.

CONSTRUCT VALIDITY

A second line of argument utilized by Brief, Aldag, and Chacko against the continued use of the MSCS involves their failure to establish convergence with certain other instruments and thus by implication the contention that the MSCS lacks construct validity. The Personal Values Questionnaire (PVQ) (England 1976) and the Self-Description Inventory (SDI) (Ghiselli 1971) were selected for use in this phase of the research because "the developers of both the PVQ and the SDI purport, like Miner, that their instruments can be used to predict managerial success. . . . Second, both the PVQ and the SDI appear to be relatively psychometrically sound." Although it would have been desirable for Brief, Aldag, and Chacko to devote greater effort to achieving more reliable measures before proceeding to these analyses, this was not done, thus sharply increasing the probability of nonsignificant results.

Comparisons with the Personal Values Questionnaire

The PVQ yields four basic categories of values into which individuals may be classified: pragmatic, ethical-moral, affect, and mixed. Of these it is the pragmatic values orientation that is positively associated with managerial success; the other three are not. Thus, one would expect, if anything, that the students with a primarily pragmatic value orientation would have higher MSCS scores. The reported results deal only with the MSCS item and rare scores, and no significant relationships are found. It would have been helpful to have the subscale data as well, but these are not given. Furthermore, Scorer B should have been excluded from the analyses (or handled separately), and probably, in view of the failure to obtain good agreement between A and C, the scores for each should be considered separately as well.

However, a much more important question concerns whether a failure to find significant relationships between the MSCS and the PVQ has anything to do with the construct validity of either instrument. One is a measure of motives, the other of values—two clearly distinct types of hypothetical constructs. Because two variables consistently correlate with a third is not reason to expect that they should necessarily correlate with each other. In fact, if the MSCS and the PVQ do turn out to be essentially unrelated, the two used in conjunction would be expected to provide particularly powerful predictions of managerial success. In any event, even if one feels for some reason that convergence should occur, the caution given by Brief, Aldag, and Chacko (and later ignored) still holds: "The evaluations of the MSCS involving the PVQ and SDI could, of course, be taken as providing unfavorable evidence concerning both of the latter scales rather than the MSCS." In this connection it would be interesting to know how the SDI fares in relation to the PVQ; the data are obviously available, but no such results are reported.

Comparisons with the Self-Description Inventory

The second instrument utilized by Brief, Aldag, and Chacko and considered to be "relatively psychometrically sound," is Ghiselli's SDI (1971). Three measures from the SDI are correlated with three subscales of the MSCS and with each other to provide data on both convergence and discrimination; no other data on either instrument are presented. The hypothesized convergent relationships are as follows:

1. MSCS Assertive Role versus SDI Masculinity (not supported, $r = .10$).
2. MSCS Imposing Wishes versus SDI Need for Power (not supported, $r = .10$).
3. MSCS Competitive Situations versus SDI Need for Occupational Achievement (supported, $r = .28$).

The Assertive Role measure was originally designated "Masculine Role," but this terminology was dropped a number of years ago (Miner 1973a). Although the measure was designed to tap motivation to behave in accordance with the traditional masculine role, it is evident that within some population groups this type of motivation is just as characteristic of females as of males—this is true of education majors, for instance (Miner 1977b, 162) and of public school administrators (Miner 1977b, 156). The studies demonstrating this are in fact referenced by Brief, Aldag, and Chacko.

These studies make it clear that motivation to achieve the traditional masculine role is not the same thing as maximally differentiating males from females, which is what the SDI scale indirectly does. This point is amply demonstrated by the fact that the MSCS Assertive Role measure is both theoretically and empirically an aspect of managerial talent while the SDI Masculinity-Femininity scale "plays no part in managerial talent" (Ghiselli 1971, 165). Brief, Aldag, and Chacko appear to assume that all the SDI measures are aspects of managerial talent; yet Ghiselli claims this designation for only 6 of his 13 scales. There is no reason to contend that known predictors of managerial success and known nonpredictors should be correlated.

Similarly, Ghiselli's Need for Power is not an aspect of managerial talent, whereas by the same criteria Imposing Wishes is. The distinction may be related to the socialized-personalized power differentiation noted by McClelland (1975). McClelland finds the two dimensions of the power motive often act reciprocally and are uncorrelated.

Need for Occupational Achievement does fall within the managerial talent definition proposed by Ghiselli; thus there is some basis for hypothesizing a relationship with the MSCS measure. The criterion groups utilized in empirically establishing this scale were men and women holding upper management and professional jobs versus men and women employed in semiskilled and unskilled work (Ghiselli 1971, 80). The inclusion of an unknown number of professionals in the upper level criterion group confounds the measure insofar as the MSCS is concerned because the MSCS is neither theoretically nor empirically related to professional status or success (Miner 1997b, 50–53). The significant correlation of .28 reported by Brief, Aldag, and Chacko with Competitive Situations is of interest, but does not bear on the construct validity of either instrument.

The most appropriate MSCS measures for establishing relationships with the SDI are the two total scores; they are more reliable than the individual subscales, and they overlap with and are empirically closely related to all of the subscales (see Table 24.4). Brief, Aldag, and Chacko did use these two MSCS measures in the PVQ comparisons. Why they rejected this approach and utilized only selected subscales in the SDI comparisons is not clear. Furthermore, the appropriate comparison measures on the SDI would have been all six indexes of managerial talent noted by Ghiselli (1971). These scales are highly correlated, and it is not certain that the separate designations refer to truly distinct characteristics. Previously unpublished data bearing on this point are given in Table 24.4 for a sample of students from diverse disciplines in an introductory psychology course at the University of Maryland and for a sample of personnel managers from as many companies distributed throughout the United States. The median SDI intercorrelation for the students is .36 and for the managers .43. In contrast, median MSCS subscale correlations in the same samples are .11 and .15 respectively (see also Chapter 7).

In commenting on their research with an earlier but comparable version of the SDI, focused primarily on the managerial talent variables, Frederiksen, Jensen, and Beaton (1972, 104) note:

> The reliabilities for the Ghiselli instrument ranged from .06 to .50 with a median of .36. The correlations of any score with other scores in the inventory were typically as high or higher than its reliability; the item overlap would of course tend to produce such high correlations. These results suggest that one factor would account for most of the reliable variance in the instrument. Because of the low reliabilities of most of the scales, the probability that they contained relatively little unique variance, and the uncertainty of the meaning of a single score based on all items, it was decided to drop the instrument from further analysis.

Of the six managerial talent measures, one—intelligence—has long been known to be unrelated to the MSCS (Miner 1965a, 92). The high correlations between Need for Occupational Achievement and intelligence in Table 24.4 raise further questions regarding that measure as well (academic grades may mediate the relationship between the two). In any event, Table 24.5 contains the relevant data (Miner 1977b, 62). These data, first published in mid-1976, are not referenced by Brief, Aldag, and Chacko.

There are 20 hypothesized correlations in the two samples (16 without Need for Occupational Achievement) and 12 of these are significant at $p < .10$ (two-tailed). In contrast, only 4 of 32 nonhypothesized correlations achieve the same level of significance, and 2 of these involve a lack of need for security—the next most likely candidate for designation as a managerial talent measure after the basic 6 (Ghiselli 1971, 165). Thus, contrary to the Brief, Aldag, and Chacko conclusion, the MSCS does appear to possess convergent and discriminant validity with the managerial talent scales of the SDI. The correlations are not high, probably due to the limited reliability of the SDI measures, but they are significant.

PSYCHOMETRIC SOUNDNESS

The stated conclusion of Brief, Aldag, and Chacko, both at the outset of their research and on its completion, is that there is insufficient basis for concluding that the MSCS is a psychometrically sound instrument. The PVQ and SDI, on the other hand, are held to be psychometrically sound. In support of the SDI, they note approvingly a reliability coefficient of .73 for the supervisory ability measure (a measure they did not use), while describing an

Table 24.4

Intercorrelations among SDI Indexes of Managerial Talent and among MSCS Measures in Student (N = 110) **and Personnel Manager** (N = 101) **Samples**[a]

	SDI Measures					
	Supervisory Ability	Need for Achievement	Intelligence	Self-actualization	Self-assurance	Decisiveness
Supervisory Ability		.38	.39	.22	.23	.19
Need for Achievement	.49		.67	.37	.39	.36
Intelligence	.26	.54		.36	.52	.09
Self-actualization	.20	.45	.39		.30	.30
Self-assurance	.43	.61	.47	.40		.24
Decisiveness	.46	.45	.00	.13	.42	

	MSCS Measures								
	Total Scores								
	Item	Rare	Authority Figures	Competitive Games	Competitive Situations	Assertive Role	Imposing Wishes	Standing Out from Group	Routine Administrative Functions
Total Scores									
Item		.79	.53	.43	.48	.42	.49	.56	.50
Rare	.88		.44	.24	.46	.42	.46	.44	.29
Authority Figures	.61	.59		.26	.18	.11	.09	.08	.09
Competitive Games	.61	.48	.37		.02	–.03	.01	.10	–.04
Competitive Situations	.54	.51	.10	.18		.05	.13	.24	.12
Assertive Role	.56	.56	.32	.20	.27		.21	.14	.04
Imposing Wishes	.47	.43	.20	.10	.15	.08		.16	.13
Standing Out from Group	.36	.20	–.01	.29	.11	–.13	.12		.25
Routine Administrative Functions	–.40	.35	.16	–.06	.03	.18	.19	–.01	

Note: MSCS = Miner Sentence Completion Scale.

[a]Correlations above diagonals are for the student sample and below diagonal for the personnel manager sample.

Table 24.5

Correlations between MSCS Total Scores (Item and Rare) **and Ghiselli SDI Measures of Managerial Talent in College Student** (N = 110) **and Personnel Manager** (N = 101) **Samples**

SDI Managerial Talent Measures	College Students				Personnel Managers			
	MSCS Item Score		MSCS Rare Score		MSCS Item Score		MSCS Rare Score	
	r	*p*	*r*	*p*	*r*	*p*	*r*	*p*
Supervisory Ability	.16	< .10	.21	< .05	.26	< .01	.24	< .05
Need for Occupational Achievement	.04	ns	.13	ns	.17	< .10	.15	ns
Intelligence	–.03	ns	.01	ns	–.08	ns	.00	ns
Self-actualization	.11	ns	.09	ns	.09	ns	.06	ns
Self-assurance	.16	< .10	.09	ns	.24	<.05	.18	< .10
Decisiveness	.27	< .01	.31	< .01	.35	< .01	.23	< .05

Note: MSCS = Miner Sentence Completion Scale. Ghiselli SDI = Self Description Index (Ghiselli 1971)

identical value, obtained in their own research, for the MSCS as reflecting an unnecessary degree of error. No reference is made to the disappointing reliabilities (ranging from .06 to .50) reported by Frederiksen, Jensen, and Beaton (1972) for the SDI, nor is there mention of Ghiselli's (1971, 33) own statement that the SDI scales are not sufficiently free of the effects of random factors to be used on an individual basis.

Test-retest reliabilities of .83 and .80 are reported for the PVQ, while the test-retest coefficients for the MSCS are described as exceeding .75. A more exact statement would be that in four separate samples, with the same experienced scorer used throughout, six of the eight total score repeat reliabilities exceeded .75, with the highest value .84 and the median .81 (Miner 1965a, 138). On the evidence, the MSCS, when coupled with an experienced scorer, is just as reliable as the PVQ and much more reliable than the SDI. In addition, correlations among subscales of the MSCS are well below the comparable values for the SDI (see Table 24.4 and Miner 1977b, 125).

Evidence of the MSCS's construct validity derives from its relationship with appropriate scales of the Strong Vocational Interest Blank (correlations ranging up to .51 with the credit manager scale), which Brief, Aldag, and Chacko appropriately note. However, they fail to note significant positive correlations with such scales as self-confidence, personal adjustment, achievement, and dominance from the Gough Adjective Check List, which are reported in the same article, and with a measure of supervisory interest derived from the Kuder Preference Record (Miner 1977b, 12–15, 92). This and other evidence (Miner 1965a, 1977b) consistently support the view that the MSCS is what it purports to be—a measure of motivation to manage.

In discussing validation research with the MSCS, Brief, Aldag, and Chacko report total score validity coefficients of .20 ($p < .10$) and .24 ($p < .05$) from one study and .29 ($p < .05$) and .25 ($p < .10$) from another; these are the only coefficients presented. In the first instance, the correlations have been selected from a table in which the other values, all involving equally theoretically relevant relationships, are .24 ($p < .05$), .31, .40, and .43 (all $p < .01$)

(Miner 1965a, 57). In the second instance, the correlations are selected from a chapter that also contains total score validity coefficients of .39 and .32 (both $p < .01$) and .69 and .57 (both $p < .01$) for other samples studied as part of the same overall predictive validation research effort (Miner 1965a, 62–66). Furthermore, in citing the study involving the Strong Vocational Interest Blank, Brief, Aldag, and Chacko fail to mention a validity coefficient of .55 obtained with the MSCS in that research (Miner 1977b, 17).

Although at the conclusion of their article the authors call for more validation research with the MSCS, especially predictive research, an entirely laudable objective, they appear not to recognize how much research already has been conducted over the past twenty years. There are at least twenty-one validity studies that have been carried out with different samples, five of them predictive in design. All twenty-one have yielded significant total score results. In the one instance that this author is aware of where the MSCS and the SDI were validated in the same sample against the same criteria, 24 percent of the criterion relationships for the MSCS were significant at $p = .05$ or better and 19 percent of the SDI relationships using the six indexes of managerial talent; for the other SDI scales, the percentage was 14, but of this figure 6 percent derives from the Need for Security measure (Miner 1977a, 75–77).

Overall, the research evidence appears to indicate that the MSCS is at least as psychometrically sound as the PVQ and SDI. One may prefer empirically derived measures such as the PVQ and SDI to theoretically derived measures such as the MSCS; in the same vein one may prefer objective tests, to projective ones. But these preferences should not blind one to the evidence. Theory-based, projective measures, like all other measures, should be evaluated in their own right on an individual basis. It is obvious that they can work.

THE MULTIPLE-CHOICE MSCS

Toward the end of their paper, Brief, Aldag, and Chacko do in fact argue for the replacement of the original version of the MSCS with a forced choice version and thus for a shift from projective to objective measurement. Thus it is relevant to note that a multiple-choice version of the original MSCS has been published (Miner 1977d). In three independent samples of managers, significant item score correlations were obtained between the two versions. The subscale correlations, however, are very unstable across samples, as indicated by the previously unpublished data of Table 24.6. The multiple-choice format appears to introduce some positive score inflation; thus the item scores moved from 3.12 to 4.73 and from 2.49 to 6.46 (both $p < .01$) in two samples (Miner 1977b, 208–209). This inflation was less pronounced, however, than what has been observed using a somewhat different method of multiple choicing; thus, for instance, one reported change was from 3.18 to 13.06 (Miner 1977b, 189).

Initial studies indicate that significant predictions of managerial success criteria may be made with the multiple-choice MSCS (see Chapter 13). However a troublesome finding appears to indicate that the significantly higher MSCS scores of black male managers, as contrasted with white males and white females, completely disappear when the multiple-choice format is used. In this instance, the two approaches simply do not have the same discriminatory power, and the data appear to favor the sentence completion procedure (Miner 1977b, 211–213).

On balance, at the present stage of research evidence, the original MSCS seems to be a somewhat superior instrument. However, this assumes an experienced and attentive scorer. With less experienced people or when an individual is having difficulty in learning the scoring procedure, the multiple-choice version would in fact appear preferable. In addition it may merely be much more practical when very large samples are involved.

Table 24.6

Correlations between MSCS and Multiple-Choice Version in Three Management Samples from a Manufacturing Company

MSCS Measures	Production Managers (n = 36)	Office Managers (n = 28)	Varied Managers (n = 35)
Authority Figures	.49	.49	.05
Competitive Games	.53	.75	.05
Competitive Situations	.52	.42	.10
Assertive Role	.54	.55	.30
Imposing Wishes	–.11	.12	.24
Standing Out from Group	.02	.55	.23
Routine Administrative Functions	.15	–.06	.21
Item Score	.68	.71	.38

Note: MSCS = Miner Sentence Completion Scale.

ON THE INCIDENCE OF FAULTY SCORING

How prevalent are errors in scoring the MSCS? Obviously we cannot know the answer to this question with any certainty, but from what has been noted throughout this book, and in Miner 1993, high levels of scorer reliability are entirely possible and occur frequently. Yet, as the evidence indicated in this chapter points up, errors occur too. Problems of the same kind are discussed in Chapter 11 and in Miner, Smith, and Ebrahimi 1985.

A third instance where faulty scoring seems to be involved occurs with regard to a dissertation conducted by Tracy (1992) in which I personally became involved and which has subsequently been cited rather extensively both in connection with meta-analyses (and reviews) and in various conference presentations. I was asked to help train Tracy in scoring the MSCS–Form T and completed one round of feedback where comparisons are possible on my part. My reaction in this instance is best indicated in the following letter—

> Dear Ms. Tracy:
>
> I am sorry for the delay. Dealing with multiple commitments does not appear to become any easier as one gets older.
>
> Let me offer you my reactions.
>
> 1. I am not sure how these cases were selected, but my feeling is that they are on the difficult side: perhaps you selected cases that were more difficult to score. That would not be representative.
> 2. Overall you seem to be exhibiting the common tendency to score more positively. People who are learning usually do this. This occurs in 7 of the 10 instances.
> 3. Overall I would have to say that you are not yet there; the reliability is not yet at the level I have achieved with others. But that could be because the cases are selected.
> 4. If these are all entrepreneurs, this is a weird group. The scores are low. Maybe there are many unsuccessful entrepreneurs. But these are not typical, growth-oriented entrepreneurs.

5. I have not checked out your item-by-item results (you should), but my impression is that there is a problem in the Personal Innovation area.

I do not know where we go from here, but I do think there is something of a problem with your current scoring.

Sincerely,
John B. Miner

The dissertation indicates that the scorer reliability is in the low .80s and the mean total Form T score is well below those noted in Chapters 14, 15, 16, 20, 21, and 22 for known entrepreneurs. I have numerous questions about this study, but have been unable to obtain answers.

In any event, it is evident that MSCS scoring can go awry on occasion, even though it need not do so. This can be caused by more clinically oriented individuals applying their idiosyncratic approaches to the protocols, thus ignoring the standardized approaches and the scoring guides. It can also be a consequence of a lack of desire or an inability to pay close attention to the standardized procedures available. For further discussion on this point see Miner 1993, 76–79, 215 and a study by Perham (1989) considered there.

CHAPTER 25

THE CONSTRUCT VALIDITY OF THE MSCS

KENNETH P. CARSON AND DEBORA J. GILLIARD

INTRODUCTION

This meta-analysis of Miner Sentence Completion Scale–Form H studies was published in the *Journal of Occupational and Organizational Psychology* (Carson and Gilliard 1993). Other than contributing a number of the studies involved, I had nothing to do with this analysis; it was prepared entirely by the authors. The MSCSs have been the subject of several other meta-analyses. Some of these are presented in subsequent chapters of this book. Others are contained in Nathan and Alexander (1985) for Form H and Collins, Hanges, and Locke (2004) for Form T.

* * *

While personality characteristics such as motivation, friendliness and extraversion are commonly thought to be reasonable predictors of job performance, personality measures suffer from general academic disfavor due to generally disappointing validity results in many selection situations (e.g., Schmitt, Gooding, Noe, and Kirsch 1984). However, some believe that this negative evaluation is premature (e.g., Barrick and Mount 1991). One of the more widely used measures of a specific personality construct for employee selection purposes is the Miner Sentence Completion Scale (MSCS; Miner 1964). The specific construct that the MSCS is intended to measure is labeled "motivation to manage." Its typical operational use is as a selection method of external applicants for managerial positions, or alternatively, as an assessment tool of current lower level managers who are being considered for positions at higher levels in the organization (Ryan and Sackett 1987). The purpose of the present study is to evaluate the construct validity of the MSCS through a meta-analytic examination of hypothesized relationships between the MSCS and three sets of theoretically relevant variables.

METHOD

A total of 26 studies were located that contained quantitative results pertinent to this investigation (see Appendix for a listing). Effects between the MSCS and other continuous measures (for instance, personality scales) reported as correlations were used as reported. Effects describing differences between two groups (for instance, upper and lower management) were usually reported as t statistics or F values. These were converted to their correlational equivalents using formulae given by Hunter and Schmidt (1990).

Effect sizes between MSCS item scores and nine dependent variables were used in this meta-analysis. The meta-analytic procedures described by Hunter and Schmidt (1990) were performed. Each effect was corrected for unreliability of the MSCS ($\alpha = .80$). The sample size weighted mean effects were then calculated for each of the following relationships: the MSCS with three personality dimensions, the MSCS with three performance measures, and the MSCS with three measures of career decisions. Credibility intervals were employed to test for the presence of moderated relationships, while confidence intervals were used to assess significance.

RESULTS AND DISCUSSION

The results are given in Table 25.1. The first hypothesis predicted that scores on the MSCS would be related to other measures of two personality constructs, conscientiousness and extraversion constructs, but not to the remaining "big five" dimensions of personality (Digman 1990). This is because both conscientiousness and extraversion overlap with the motivation to manage construct, but not the other three. The pattern of results was as predicted. The corrected correlation between the MSCS and other measures of conscientiousness was .20, which was significant, although the credibility interval includes zero, indicating that the effect is subject to further moderation. The corrected correlation for extraversion was .24, which was also significant, and not further moderated. The mean effect for openness to experience was .02, and was not significant. The remaining two big five dimensions, neuroticism and agreeableness, had only a single effect reported, and could not be meta-analyzed.

The second hypothesis stated that three different measures of managerial effectiveness would be related to the MSCS. The most direct measures of managerial effectiveness were actual performance measures. The mean effect here was .35, a value which was not further moderated and which was significant. The second measure was the level to which a manager has advanced in a hierarchical organization. The typical primary study contributing information to this analysis compared MSCS scores from two different positions in the organization. The mean effect for this variable was .13 which was subject to further moderation, but was significant. The mean effect for salary, another proxy for job performance, was also .13 and was also significant.

The third hypothesis predicted that persons who have made management-orientated career decisions should score higher on the MSCS than persons who intend to make or have made alternate career choices. Three comparisons were made to test this prediction. First, managers in line functions have been compared to similarly placed persons in staff roles. The mean effect for this comparison was .34, with no apparent moderation and the effect was significant. The second comparison has been to compare managers with entrepreneurs. The mean effect here was .09, and was not significant. The final analysis has been to compare the scores of persons who intend to pursue a career in management versus those who express alternate

Table 25.1

Meta-analytic Results

Variable	Number of Studies	Total Sample Size	Corrected Mean Effect[a]	Credibility Interval	Confidence Interval
Conscientiousness	7	851	.20 (.18)	–.05, .45	.09, .30[b]
Extraversion	5	684	.24 (.21)	.16, .33[d]	.17, .32[c]
Openness to Experience	4	581	.02 (.02)	–.13, .18	–.08, .13[b]
Performance Ratings	14	1,145	.35 (.31)	.17, .53	.30, .40[c]
Management Level	27	2,151	.13 (.12)	–.20, .45	.06, .20[b]
Salary	5	1,123	.13 (.12)	–.01, .27	.05, .21[b]
Line/staff	5	185	.34 (.30)	.28, .39	.20, .47[c]
Manager/entrepreneur	7	300	.09 (.08)	–.41, .60	–.11, .30[b]
Career Plan	5	319	.37 (.33)	—[d]	.27, .47[c]

Note: MSCS = Miner Sentence Completion Scale.
[a]Corrected for MSCS unreliability only; value in parenthesis is the uncorrected mean effect.
[b]Confidence interval for heterogeneous effects.
[c]Confidence interval for homogeneous effects.
[d]All variance is accounted for by sampling error.

career interests. The mean effect was .37, an effect which was not further moderated and is significant.

Thus, eight of the nine effects are in the expected direction. The one that was not, management versus entrepreneur, was not significant, and thus did not support the hypothesis. The explanation for this one contradictory finding is unclear. Possibly, entrepreneurs require a managerial motivation similar to that characteristic of managers in hierarchical positions. However, the results on average provide clear support for a conclusion that the MSCS is a construct valid measure of motivation to manage.

The present results were generally positive. The results reported here probably should be viewed as conservative estimates. Hunter and Schmidt (1990) list and discuss eleven artifacts that would generally have the effect of attenuating effect sizes. Only one of these, the reliability of the MSCS, could be accounted for in this investigation. Of the remaining ten, restriction of range (especially because many of the validity studies are concurrent) and criterion unreliability would be expected to have the largest effect on the results.

We confess to being somewhat surprised by the support found for the MSCS. In general, personality measures have not fared well in such investigations, and projective personality measures have suffered even more. However, recent research using the five-factor model and meta-analysis has led to a much more optimistic conclusion regarding the use of personality measures for personnel selection purposes (Barrick and Mount 1991). The present results perhaps represent another step toward renewed interest in personality characteristics as viable predictors of job performance.

APPENDIX: STUDIES INCLUDED IN THE META-ANALYSIS

Bartol and Martin (1987)
Berman and Miner (1985)
Brief, Aldag, and Chacko (1977)

Eberhardt, Yap, and Basuray (1988)
Gantz, Erickson, and Stephenson (1971)
Holland, Black, and Miner (1987)
Lacey (1974)
Miner (1968a)
Miner (1968b)
Miner (1971a)
Miner (1974b)
Miner (1974c)
Miner (1976a)
Miner (1977b)—Chapter 8 in Miner (1977b)
Miner (1977b)—Chapter 9 in Miner (1977b)
Miner (1977b)—Chapter 12 in Miner (1977b)
Miner (1977b)—Chapter 16 in Miner (1977b)
Miner (1977b)—Chapter 27 in Miner (1977b)
Miner and Crane (1981)
Miner and Miner (1976)—Chapter 10 in Miner (1977b)
Miner, Rizzo, Harlow, and Hill (1974)—Chapter 7 in Miner (1977b)
Miner and Smith (1969)
Muczyk and Schuler (1976)
Smith and Miner (1983)
Stahl, Grigsby, and Gulati (1985)
Steger, Kelley, Chouiniere, and Goldenbaum (1975)

CHAPTER 26

META-ANALYSIS OF GENDER DIFFERENCES IN RESPONSES TO THE MSCS–FORM H

INTRODUCTION

This approach to meta-analysis is somewhat different than the one in Chapter 25. It focused on gender differences in managerial motivation and was published in *The Leadership Quarterly* (Eagly, Karau, Miner, and Johnson 1994). This analysis was an outgrowth of a symposium presented at the Eastern Psychological Association in which Alice Eagly and I were involved. As our mutual project evolved, my role became primarily one of locating data sources for the meta-analysis. Many of these represented already published materials, but almost as many data sets were of a previously unpublished nature. The three others (Eagly, Karau, and Johnson) devoted their energies to the meta-analysis itself, and to the writing up of the results. Thus there was considerable similarity to Chapter 25 in that the actual analysis and presentation of the findings relied heavily on my research, but was carried out in large part independently

From Alice H. Eagly, Steven J. Karau, John B. Miner, and Blair T. Johnson, "Gender and Motivation to Manage in Hierarchic Organizations: A Meta-analysis," *Leadership Quarterly*, vol. 5, pp. 135–159.

of my own efforts. Certainly my input was important to the final product, but the other three, and in particular Alice, were much more knowledgeable about the procedures of meta-analysis and the literature on gender effects.

* * *

Women's participation in managerial roles is a topic of considerable interest in view of the growing number of women who occupy these roles, and many issues pertaining to gender and management have been considered by social scientists (e.g., Morrison and Von Glinow 1990; Morrison, White, and Van Velsor 1987; Powell 1993; Ragins and Sundstrom 1989; Riger and Galligan 1980). One important question is whether women and men have similar motivation to perform managerial roles. We approach this question in terms of Miner's construct of *motivation to manage,* which was derived from an analysis of the typical role requirements of managerial positions in business firms. Treated as a personality variable, motivation to manage is defined as the extent to which individuals desire to satisfy the requirements of the managerial role that has traditionally existed in a hierarchic organizational context, particularly within business firms (Miner 1977b, 1978c, 1993). Whether women and men differ in the strength of their motivation to manage within the constraints of this role and why any differences occur are the specific questions that this article is concerned with. To address these questions, we provide: (1) a theoretical analysis that focuses on the largely masculine definition of the traditional managerial role, and (2) a quantitative synthesis of the relevant research findings (see Hedges and Olkin 1985; Hunter and Schmidt 1990; Rosenthal 1991). The issues addressed in this article are consequential because of their implications for understanding the barriers that women have faced in entering managerial roles when they were defined in essentially masculine terms.

Given the potential relevance to equity issues of any sex differences in managerial motivation, it is not surprising that leadership researchers have shown considerable interest in the question of potential differences. Yet, they have expressed conflicting views (e.g., Bartol, Anderson, and Schneier 1981; Bartol and Martin 1987; Miner 1974b, 1974c, 1977a, 1977b, 1985b, 1993; Miner and Smith 1982; Miner, Smith, and Ebrahimi 1985). These earlier discussions are difficult to evaluate because they were based on informal, narrative reviewing of relevant findings and citations of only very few of the relatively large number of comparisons between men's and women's motivation to manage that are available from published and unpublished sources. Our project, which applied quantitative methods of research integration to the findings of a large number of studies, provides a much sounder basis for such discussions.

ANALYSIS OF THE GENDER-RELATED ASPECTS OF THE MANAGERIAL ROLE

Critical to understanding why women and men might differ in their motivation to manage is the hierarchic organizational context that business firms have traditionally provided. In such organizations, managers have considerable power over their subordinates and hold administrative positions that are associated with greater resources and rewards than the positions held by their subordinates. Organizations of this type can be contrasted with organizations that are based on principles other than hierarchy. For example, Miner (1993) considered professional, task, and group organizations, in addition to hierarchic organizations. Fiske (1992) considered social relationships based on principles of communal sharing, equality matching, and market pricing, in addition to the principle of authority ranking (or hierarchy).

Predictions concerning motivation to manage in hierarchic organizations must take into account the gender-related aspects of such hierarchies. One way that gender impacts on organizations is that men predominate in the upper levels of their managerial hierarchies. Despite the dramatic gains in women's representation in managerial careers in the last two decades (Jacobs 1992), women remain sparsely represented at the higher levels of organizations (Bergman 1986; Gutek 1993; Jacobs 1992; Powell 1993) and extraordinarily rare in top managerial positions of business firms (Ball, 1991; Fierman 1990).

A related aspect of gender's impact on organizational hierarchies is that managerial roles have been defined in largely masculine terms. Demonstrating this masculine definition are empirical studies of perceptions of the managerial role (e.g., Schein 1973), which have shown that people's expectations about the behaviors appropriate for managers match their expectations about men much more closely than their expectations about women. Contemporary research with male managers has confirmed these findings (Heilman, Block, Martell, and Simon 1989), but some recent studies suggest that women have evolved toward a relatively androgynous view of the qualities appropriate to managers (Brenner, Tomkiewicz, and Schein 1989; Frank 1988; Russell, Rush, and Herd 1988).

Although women's less frequent participation as managers in hierarchic organizations surely has a variety of causes, including gender discrimination (see Adler 1993; Martin 1992; O'Leary 1974), one reason for the scarcity of women could be that they have been less motivated than men to meet the requirements of the managerial role, as this role was traditionally defined in masculine terms. If we assume that, in general, people are motivated to engage in activities congruent with their culturally defined gender roles (see Eagly 1987), the definition of managerial roles as requiring mainly masculine qualities would itself constitute a barrier to women's participation in these roles. As Heilman (1983) has argued, a lack of fit would be perceived to exist between women's attributes and the requirements of the managerial role. Female managers would be vulnerable to role conflict, as many organizational theorists have argued (Bass 1990; Bayes and Newton 1978; Kruse and Wintermantel 1986; O'Leary 1974; Ragins and Sundstrom 1989). These women would risk violating conventions concerning appropriate female behavior by fulfilling people's expectations concerning managers.

Given this masculine definition of the managerial role, it would not be surprising to find that research assessing motivation to satisfy the requirements of this role would show a higher level of motivation among men. It would also make sense that as more women enter management, they would advocate change in how the managerial role is defined. Indeed, feminist writers and theorists have criticized the implicit masculine character of the administrative roles in hierarchic organizations (e.g., Acker 1991) and have contrasted hierarchic role definitions with alternative role definitions based on collaboration, participation, negotiation, and sharing of power and information (Helgesen 1990; Loden 1985; Rosener 1990).

Potential Moderating Variables

Pursuing our analysis of the managerial role in more depth suggests that whether sex differences in motivation to manage would be obtained in particular studies should depend on a number of their features. One very important consideration is the type of respondent population. Although in a general population, women may be less interested than men in roles that have been defined in primarily masculine terms, individual differences within each sex are no doubt large, and some women are at least as interested as typical men would be. Such relatively nontraditional women may be disproportionately represented in research on motivation to manage, given that most of the studies were conducted on business school students and business managers (see Results, below). Managers of both sexes have presumably selected themselves into this occupation based at least in part on their interest in managing (see Miner 1968a; Miner and Crane 1981; Miner and Smith 1969). Moreover, managers have been selected by organizations according to criteria that likely would include a demonstrated interest in and motivation for managerial work. In addition, managers appear to become socialized into their roles in the early stages of their experience in an organization (e.g., Wanous 1977), and this socialization could increase motivation to manage. As a consequence of these selection and socialization factors, which should operate similarly for female and male managers, they should differ relatively little in motivation to manage, even though sex differences may be obtained in less highly selected samples of respondents (see Eagly and Johnson 1990; Powell 1993, for related arguments).

This reasoning applies to a lesser extent to business school students. These students are interested in managerial careers, although of course they are not necessarily motivated by intrinsic interest in the role. Still, they should have already selected themselves at least to some degree on the basis of their motivation to manage. Such selection factors are presumably not relevant for respondent samples consisting of students who are not in business or employees who are not managers. In summary, consideration of the samples of respondents most commonly used in research on motivation to manage leads us to predict that any sex differences revealed should be rather small when aggregated across all of the available studies. Yet, classification of studies by type of subject population may shed some light on these selection and socialization issues.

Differences between men's and women's motivation to manage might also depend on when the data were collected, as Miner and Smith (1982) argued. When female managers were numerically very rare and expectations concerning appropriate female behavior were very restrictive (see Simon and Landis 1989), cultural barriers may have made it relatively difficult for women to develop a high level of managerial motivation. As the status of women has changed, many more women have aspired to manage in hierarchic organizations. Although this logic predicts a decline in any sex differences in managerial motivation, any predictions concerning secular trends would be highly speculative because women occupying managerial roles or choosing to study business in universities may have had relatively high motivation to manage in all historical periods, but may have possessed particularly high motivation when barriers that exclude women were stronger than they have been in recent years. To approach these issues on an exploratory basis, we examine secular trends in sex differences in motivation to manage. Fortunately, available data sets span approximately thirty years.

Miner's Measure of Motivation to Manage in Hierarchic Organizations

Miner's measure—the Miner Sentence Completion Scale (MSCS)—contains seven subscales, each of which represents a distinct aspect of the managerial role. Because these subscales appear to differ in the extent to which they emphasize male-stereotypic characteristics, sex differences in test performance might vary across the subscales of the instrument. A rationale for predicting such variation follows from research on gender stereotypes which shows that men are believed to have personalities characterized by assertive and controlling tendencies that are aptly described by Bakan's (1966) term "agentic" (e.g., Broverman,

Vogel, Broverman, Clarkson, and Rosenkrantz 1972; Spence, Helmreich and Stapp 1974; Williams and Best 1982). Men, thus, are believed to be more aggressive, assertive, ambitious, dominant, forceful, and leader-like than women. This agentic emphasis is reflected in most of the subscales of the MSCS—in particular, the subscales named Competitive Games, Competitive Situations, Assertive Role, Imposing Wishes, and Standing Out from the Group.

In contrast to these agentically toned subscales, the Authority Figures and Routine Administrative Functions subscales have quite a different emphasis. People who score high on the Authority Figures subscale are comfortable in a subordinate role vis-à-vis their organizational superiors. The association of characteristics such as "subordinates self to others" with the female stereotype (see Spence, Helmreich, and Holahan 1979) suggests that traditional female socialization may include preparation for occupying lower-status roles in society. If so, women may be especially good at maintaining relations with their superiors. In addition, achieving a high score on the Routine Administrative Functions subscale would seem to require a rather patient willingness to carry out everyday administrative activities. The association of traits such as "conscientious," "patient," and "painstaking" with the female stereotype in U.S. culture (see Williams and Best 1982) suggests that traditional female socialization may also include an emphasis on qualities represented in this subscale.

In summary, the majority of subscales of the MSCS are defined in terms of stereotypically masculine qualities, as would be expected from the greater similarity that people, especially men, perceive between managers and men than between managers and women. Nonetheless, two of the subscales, Authority Figures and Routine Administrative Functions, seem to emphasize aspects of the managerial role that could be considered stereotypically feminine. Based on this logic, the direction of any sex differences should differ across the subscales, with the predominant tendency for men to score higher probably reversing on the Authority Figures and Routine Administrative Functions subscales. This prediction is consistent with our prediction of a small difference favoring men on the overall scale, because men should score higher on five of the seven subscales.

Our gender analysis directs attention not only to the content of particular subscales of the MSCS but also to the content of particular items. This issue has already been raised by Bartol and Martin (1987), who suggested that some items on the MSCS (for instance, "athletic contests," "shooting a rifle") might produce sex differences because they require that respondents react to activities that are more typical of men than women but are not required by the managerial role. The fact that many of the sentence stems of the MSCS do not describe activities required by the managerial role follows from the indirect approach to assessment inherent in the projective method for assessing underlying motivation. Nonetheless, women may react differently (and less favorably) to such items, not because of a lower level of motivation to manage but because of gender-specific rules about appropriate behavior. Normative barriers to activities that are common among men but rare among women may cause items that name such activities to be poorer indicants for women of the general construct that the MSCS is intended to measure. Such items should produce distinctively larger sex differences than other items used in the instrument to measure the same constructs. In a preliminary effort to address this issue, we analyzed item-level data, which were available for several samples of respondents.

In summary, our purpose is to synthesize quantitatively all available comparisons between men's and women's performance on the MSCS. We examine sex differences on the subscales of the instrument as well as in the total score and consider the implications of these findings for women's participation in managerial roles in hierarchic organizations.

METHOD

Sample of Studies

Computer-based information searches were conducted using the keywords "motivation to manage" and "Miner Sentence Completion." These keywords were searched in the following databases: *Psychological Abstracts* (PsycLIT), *Dissertation Abstracts International* (DISS), *Educational Resources Information Center* (ERIC), and a worldwide business and management data base (ABI/INFORM). References were also located in earlier searches conducted for meta-analyses of sex differences in leadership style and the emergence of leaders (see Eagly and Johnson 1990; Eagly and Karau 1991). Finally, Miner provided unpublished data from a number of studies.

Studies were included if they compared men and women on the Miner Sentence Completion Scale–Form H in either its free-response or multiple-choice version. Studies conducted by Bartol, Anderson, and Schneier (1980, 1981) were not included. When more than one version of the MSCS was administered to the same sample of respondents, data from only the first administration were included, in order to avoid multiple-representation of the sample. For documents containing separate samples, which varied on characteristics such as race, occupation, nationality, geographical location, year of testing, or managerial or educational status, each sample was treated as a separate study. By this strategy, 35 documents produced 51 studies.

Variables Coded from Each Study

The following basic information was coded from each report: (1) year study was conducted; (2) publication form (journal article, dissertation, or unpublished document); (3) identity of authors (Miner or his associates, for example, his doctoral students; others); and (4) sex of first author (male, female). In addition, the following characteristics of the respondents were coded: (1) *n* (that is, sample size); (2) proportion of men, (3) age (estimated if not given); (4) status (business students, other students, business managers, other employees); (5) nationality (U.S., international); and (6) race or ethnicity (white, black, Asian, Latin American, other). Finally, the version of the MSCS (free response, multiple choice) was recorded.

All variables were coded independently by two of the authors. Given the objective nature of the coding categories, it is not surprising that the median agreement was 100 percent. The few disagreements were resolved by discussion.

Computation of Effect Sizes

The effect size calculated is *g,* the difference between the motivation to manage of women and men, divided by the pooled standard deviation (see Hedges and Olkin 1985). A positive sign was given to differences in the male direction (that is, men had a higher motivation to manage than women), and a negative sign to differences in the female direction.

To reduce computational error, two of the authors calculated these effect sizes independently with the aid of a computer program (Johnson 1989). If the data report was sufficient, effect sizes were calculated for the subscales of the MSCS as well as the total score.

Analysis of Effect Sizes

The analysis was based on Hedges and Olkin's (1985) presentation, which provides techniques appropriate for the project (see Johnson, Mullen, and Salas 1995). Before implementing these techniques, we corrected the *g*s for attenuation based on the test-retest reliabilities presented by Miner (1993), (see Hunter and Schmidt's 1990 discussion of such corrections). These *g*s were then converted to *d*s by correcting them for bias (that is, *g*'s overestimate of the population effect size, which occurs especially for small samples). To obtain an overall estimate of the sex difference reported in available research, we then combined the study outcomes by averaging the *d*s. All means were computed with each effect size weighted by the reciprocal of its variance, a procedure that gives more weight to effect sizes that are more reliably estimated. To determine whether the studies shared a common effect size (that is, were consistent across the studies), we calculated a homogeneity statistic, Q, which has an approximate chi-square distribution with $k-1$ degrees of freedom.

In the absence of homogeneity, we accounted for variability in the effect sizes for the MSCS total scores (but not the subscales) by relating them to the attributes of the studies using both categorical and continuous models. Categorical models, which are analogous to analyses of variance (ANOVAs), require that studies be assigned to classes based on study characteristics (for example, version of MSCS). The techniques for calculating categorical models provide a between-classes effect (analogous to a main effect in an ANOVA) and a test of the homogeneity of the effect sizes within each class. The between-classes effect is estimated by Q_B, which has an approximate chi-square distribution with $p-1$ degrees of freedom, where p is the number of classes. The homogeneity of the effect sizes within each class is estimated by Q_{wi}, which has an approximate chi-square distribution with $m-1$ degrees of freedom, where m is the number of effect sizes in the class. Continuous models, which are analogous to regression models, predict effect sizes from continuous study attributes (for example, subject age). These models are least-squares simple linear regressions, calculated with each effect size weighted by the reciprocal of its variance. Each such model yields a test of the significance of a predictor as well as a test of model specification, which evaluates whether significant systematic variation remains unexplained in the regression model (Hedges and Olkin 1985).

As a supplementary analysis, we attained homogeneity by identifying outliers among the effect sizes and sequentially removing those that reduced the homogeneity statistic by the largest amount. Using such a procedure, Hedges (1987) found for several meta-analyses on psychological topics that the removal of up to 20 percent of the outliers in a group of heterogeneous effects sizes usually resulted in a high degree of homogeneity. Inspection of the percentage of effect sizes removed to attain homogeneity allows us to determine whether the effect sizes are homogeneous aside from the presence of relatively few aberrant values. Under such circumstances, the mean attained after removal of such outliers may better represent the distribution of effect sizes than the mean based on all of the effect sizes.

RESULTS

Characteristics of the Studies

Before considering the sex comparisons reported in research on motivation to manage, we examine the characteristics of the studies from which conclusions about this research will be

Table 26.1

Summary of Study Characteristics

Variables	Values[a]
Mdn Year Study Conducted	1,979.00
Publication Form	
Journal Article	12
Book Chapter	5
Dissertation	17
Unpublished Data	17
Identity of Authors	
Miner or Associates	34
Others	17
Sex of First Author	
Male	44
Female	7
Mdn n of Respondents	89.00
M Proportion of Male Respondents	.62
Mdn Age of Respondents	26.30
Status of Respondents	
Business Students	32
Other Students	6
Business Managers	8
Other Employees	5
Nationality of Respondents	
United States	43
International	8
Race or Ethnicity of Respondents	
White	38
Black	4
Asian	4
Latin American	2
Other	3
Version of MSCS	
Free Response	37
Multiple Choice	14

Note: MSCS = Miner Sentence Completion Scale.
[a]Values presented to nearest hundredth are means or medians; integer values are numbers of studies found within each level of a variable.

drawn (see Table 26.1). As shown by the central tendencies of the variables given in Table 26.1, the studies generally: (1) were conducted relatively recently, (2) were dissertations and other unpublished documents with some journal articles, (3) were conducted by Miner or his associates, and (4) had male first authors. Studies also generally: (1) used a moderate number of respondents, (2) included more male than female respondents, (3) used a young-adult sample, and (4) used respondents who were business students, citizens of the United States, and white. In addition, most studies used the free-response version of the MSCS.

Overall Sex Differences in Motivation to Manage

The summary of the effect sizes given in Table 26.2 makes it possible to determine whether, on the whole, men and women differed on the MSCS and its seven subscales. This table

Table 26.2

Sex Differences for the Total Score and Subscales of the MSCS

	All Effect Sizes					Effect Sizes Excluding Outliers			
		M Weighted	95% CI for d_+		Homogeneity	n	M Weighted	95% CI for d_+	
Measure	Total n of Studies	Effect Size (d_+)[a]	Lower	Upper	(Q) of Effect Sizes[b]	Removed Outliers[c]	Effect Size (d_+)	Lower	Upper
Total Score	51	.22	.16	.27	103.77*	3 (.06)	.18	.11	.24
Subscales									
Authority Figures	45	$-.17_a$	–.24	–.11	122.76*	7 (.16)	–.24	–.31	–.17
Competitive Games	46	$.31_d$	.24	.37	110.28**	3 (.07)	.30	.24	.37
Competitive Situations	45	$.15_b$	.09	.21	91.48**	5 (.11)	.16	.09	.22
Assertive Role	45	$.27_{c,d}$	.21	.34	105.36**	5 (.11)	.25	.18	.32
Imposing Wishes	45	$.19_{b,c}$	.13	.26	97.98*	5 (.11)	.21	.14	.27
Standing Out from Group	45	$.12_b$	.05	.18	139.94*	7 (.16)	.18	.11	.26
Routine Administrative Functions	45	$-.09_a$	–.15	–.03	102.91*	3 (.07)	–.12	–.19	–.05

Note: MSCS = Miner Sentence Completion Scale. Positive effect sizes indicate that men have higher scores than women on motivation to manage, and negative effect sizes indicate that women have higher scores than men.

CI = confidence interval.

[a]Effect sizes were weighted by the reciprocal of the variance. Differences between subscale means that do not have a subscript in common are significant ($p < .05$, post-hoc contrasts).

[b]Significance indicates rejection of the hypothesis of homogeneity.

[c]The proportion appears in parentheses.

$^*p < .01$; $^{**}p < .001$

reports the mean effect size on the overall measure and each subscale, along with 95 percent confidence intervals for each mean. An overall sex difference is suggested by a mean effect size that differs significantly from the .00 value that indicates exactly no difference (that is, by a confidence interval that does not include .00).

As shown in Table 26.2, men had higher motivation to manage scores than women on the total score. Men also scored higher than women on the following five of the seven subscales: Competitive Games, Competitive Situations, Assertive Role, Imposing Wishes, and Standing Out from the Group. In contrast, women scored higher than men on the Authority Figures and Routine Administrative Functions subscales. Inspection of the confidence intervals for the total score and the subscales shows that all of these sex differences were significant.

As shown by the homogeneity statistics given in Table 26.2, the effect sizes were not homogeneous, for either the total score or any of the seven subscales. However, homogeneity was attained for the total score after the removal of only three outliers. [The removed studies were Dayani (1980), for which $d = -.62$; Bartol and Martin (1987), for which $d = .66$; and Nellen (1986), for which $d = .88$; the subject samples for these three studies were academic librarians, MBA students, and undergraduate business students at nine black colleges, respectively.] Homogeneity was attained for each of the seven subscales after removal of between three and seven outliers. The removal of these outliers did not substantially change the mean effect size on any of these measures. The outliers were returned to the data set for the subsequent calculation of models predicting the effect sizes.

Because the magnitude and direction of the sex differences appeared to vary depending on the subscale, we computed a categorical model to examine the between-classes effect of these subscales. (The categorical model uses non-independent effect sizes; most of the data sets contributed effect sizes for all seven of the subscales.) This model was highly significant, $Q_B(6) = 178.22, p < .001$, and post-hoc contrasts revealed that several of the subscales differed significantly from one another (see Table 26.2). These differences between subscales showed the same pattern when the free-response and multiple-choice versions of the MSCS were examined separately.

Models for Predicting Total Score from Study Attributes

The relative homogeneity of the effect sizes for the MSCS total score suggests that study attributes are unlikely to be powerful predictors of these effect sizes. Nonetheless, the study attributes were examined as potential moderators of sex differences in the total score. As shown by the model in Table 26.3, the version of the MSCS had a significant impact on sex differences in motivation to manage. The tendency for men to have higher motivation to manage scores than women was larger for studies that used the multiple-choice version than for studies that used the free-response version.

In Table 26.4 the effect sizes are classified by respondents' status as well as the version of the MSCS. This model also was significant, but contrary to our social-role hypothesis, there was no evidence for smaller sex differences among managers (and business school students) compared with other statuses of respondents. With the free-response version of the scale, the means for the various statuses were similar except for the heterogeneous class of other employees, which contained only two effect sizes. The means for the multiple-choice version of the scale were more variable across the statuses, but the small sample sizes within categories make these differences difficult to interpret. Post-hoc contrasts between the classes showed only that the multiple-choice version yielded a larger sex difference than the free-response version among business students, $p < .025$, and that the multiple-choice version yielded a

Table 26.3

Categorical Model for Version of MSCS

Variable and Class	Between-classes Effect	n	Mean Weighted Effect Size (d_{i+})	95% CI for d_{i+} Lower	95% CI for d_{i+} Upper	Homogeneity within Each Class (Q_{wi})[a]
Version of MSCS	7.40*					
Free Response		37	.15	.08	.23	46.48
Multiple Choice		14	.32	.22	.42	49.88**

Note: MSCS = Miner Sentence Completion Scale. Positive effect sizes indicate that men have higher total scores than women on motivation to manage. CI = confidence interval.

[a]Significance indicates rejection of the hypothesis of homogeneity.

*$p < .01$; **$p < .001$

larger sex difference among business students than among respondents in the other employees class, $p < .01$. No other differences between the classes were significant. In addition, the confidence intervals in Table 26.4 show that there is strong evidence for a sex difference in MSCS scores only for business students, but small sample sizes compromise the interpretability of the means reported for the other statuses.

Another model revealed that the tendency for men to have higher motivation to manage than women was especially large for the five studies that used samples of blacks ($p < .005$ for black versus white post-hoc contrast). In addition, a continuous model showed that age of respondents was inversely related to the effect sizes ($b = -.012$, $b^* = -.29$, $p < .005$; $Q_E(49) = 95.20$, $p < .001$); the tendency for men to have higher motivation to manage than women was smaller for older respondents. The confounding of respondents' age with their status (for example, student or employee) and other attributes of the studies renders this finding ambiguous. Yet, it should be noted that the younger subjects were predominately students and the older subjects were most frequently managers of some type.

Other models examined the relation between the year the study was conducted and the sex differences reported. There was no overall relation between year and the magnitude of the sex differences. Yet, when the relation between year and the effect sizes was examined separately for each version of the scale, a tendency for sex differences to decrease over time was significant for the multiple-choice version of the scale ($b = -.094$, $b^* = -.37$, $p < .01$; $Q_E(12) = 42.96$, $p < .001$), but not for the free-response version ($p = .22$). However, when performance on the free-response scale was examined separately among business school students, the decline was marginally significant ($p = .10$).

Finally, classifying effect sizes by other variables did not yield significant models. Among these null findings, it is of special interest that the effect sizes did not vary depending on whether studies were (1) conducted by Miner and his associates or by other investigators or (2) reported in articles authored by men or women.

Item-level Analyses

Item-level data were obtained for the free-response version of the scale for five samples: 124 U.S. undergraduate business students tested in 1980 (Miner and Smith 1982); 102 U.S.

Tab1e 26.4

Categorical Model for Version of MSCS and Status of Subjects

Variable and Class	Between-classes Effect	n	Mean Weighted Effect Size (d_{i+})	95% CI for d_{i+} Lower	Upper	Homogeneity within Each Class (Q_{wi})[a]
Version of MSCS and Status of Subjects	35.89**					
Free Response						
Business Students		24	.17	.07	.27	22.27
Other Students		4	.15	–.05	.35	3.06
Business Managers		7	.16	–.01	.34	12.54
Other Employees		2	–.08	–.37	.22	6.11*
Multiple Choice						
Business Students		8	.51	.38	.64	18.32*
Other Students		2	.16	–.14	.46	.17
Business Managers		1	1.09	.32	1.85	.00
Other Employees		3	.01	–.16	.18	5.42

Note: MSCS = Miner Sentence Completion Scale. Positive effect sizes indicate that men have higher total scores than women on motivation to manage. CI = confidence interval. The "other employees" classes include librarians, teachers, managers in academic libraries, managers in government agencies, and non-managerial business employees.

[a]Significance indicates rejection of the hypothesis of homogeneity.

$*p < .05$; $**p < .001$

graduate business students tested in 1987 (Miner 1993); 76 U.S. undergraduate liberal arts students tested in 1973 (Miner 1974c); 76 European business students tested in 1988 and 1990 (Miner, 1993); and 80 U.S. managers tested in 1974 (Miner 1977b). Items were scored as +1 (high motivation to manage), 0 (indeterminate motivation to manage), or –1 (low motivation to manage). Using a chi-square test, female and male distributions were compared both within samples and with the data pooled across the samples (see also Miner 1993).

Although none of the 35 items consistently produced significant differences within these five samples, a number of significant differences were obtained when the data were pooled across the samples. Some differences would of course be expected, given that all of the subscales produced significant sex differences when the entire sample of studies was considered (see Table 26.2). The items producing the largest sex differences ($p < .001$) were: (1) two items from the Assertive Role subscale—"shooting a rifle" and "wearing a necktie," and (2) two items from the Competitive Games subscale—"athletic contests" and "when running a race, I . . ." Although the rifle, necktie, and athletic contest items were noted by Bartol and Martin (1987), the necktie item produced a curvilinear distribution (with proportionally more men giving high and low responses to the item). The item about running a race was not noted by Bartol and Martin as potentially biased. Moreover, the three additional items that Bartol and Martin had noted as potentially stereotypic were not among the six other items that yielded significant sex differences ($p < .05$ or smaller) in the item-level analyses, which were "being interviewed for a job"; "giving orders"; "punishing children"; "when playing cards, I . . ."; "making introductions"; and "final examinations."

DISCUSSION

Magnitude of Tendency for Men to Score Higher Than Women on Motivation to Manage

Miner's instrument assessing motivation to manage in hierarchic organizations produced an overall sex difference in favor of men, a difference of about one-fifth of a standard deviation overall but about one-third of a standard deviation on the multiple-choice version of the scale. Interpretation of the magnitude of these mean effect sizes should take into account the fact that the measure was typically administered to relatively homogeneous samples of respondents (most often, business school students) in relatively controlled settings (for instance, a classroom). These features of the research may tend to reduce the variability of respondents' scores. In addition, respondents' total scores should be relatively reliable because their responses were aggregated over 35 items (and, moreover, the effect sizes were corrected for unreliability). Consequently, the magnitude of the effect sizes would not have been diminished by inflation of the standard deviation (which serves as the denominator of the effect sizes) due to uncontrolled variables or unreliable measures.

To facilitate interpretation of the magnitude of the average effect sizes obtained on the MSCS, they can be compared with average effect sizes produced by other quantitative reviews, especially by meta-analyses of sex differences in social behavior. Eagly's (1987) overview of some of these effect sizes suggested that they ranged from a low of 0.13 for helping behavior to a high of 1.19 for the use of pause fillers in vocal behavior. Eagly and Johnson's (1990) quantitative review of sex differences in leadership style found near-zero mean effect sizes for interpersonal and task styles, but a mean of .22 for the tendency for women to adopt a more democratic and participative style than men do. Eagly and Karau (1991) found a mean effect size of .32 representing the tendency for men to emerge more frequently than women as leaders in small groups. These bench marks suggest that the overall sex difference found for the MSCS (.22) is in line with some of the sex differences found in meta-analyses of social behavior. Yet, most of these other domains featured less controlled forms of research and less highly aggregated measures. Taking these various considerations into account, we suggest that the overall difference in women's and men's test performance is relatively small, as we expected in view of the selection of most respondents from populations of business managers and business students.

Moderators of Overall Sex Difference

Our most provocative findings emerged from the analysis of men's and women's performance on the subscales that are components of the total score. This analysis yielded significant sex differences on all seven subscales but, as we anticipated, the direction of these differences varied. Men scored higher than women on five subscales: Competitive Games, Competitive Situations, Assertive Role, Imposing Wishes, and Standing Out from the Group. Indeed, all of these subscales emphasize male-stereotypic agentic traits. Moreover, Eagly and Johnson's (1990) meta-analytic finding that male managers were somewhat more autocratic and directive in their leadership styles than female managers seems compatible with some of these subscale results—in particular, with the tendencies for men's motivation to be greater than women's on the Assertive Role and Imposing Wishes subscales. In contrast, women scored higher on two subscales: Authority Figures and Routine Administrative Functions. As we argued early in this article, these subscales emphasize certain female-stereotypic qualities. In general, these subscale analyses suggest that, despite the generally masculine definition of the traditional business manager role, women show a stronger motivation in relation to some aspects of the role.

It is quite interesting that the multiple-choice version of the scale yielded a significantly larger sex difference than the free-response version, even though the sentence stems used in the two versions are exactly the same and appear in the same order. Although the reasons for this finding are not clear, it may be that the free-response format allows women to express their managerial motivation in terms that are slightly different from those favored by men yet are still scored as manifesting a high level of motivation. Perhaps the high-motivation alternatives provided on the multiple-choice version of the scale are relatively less appealing to women because they are worded in a style that matches men's free responses somewhat more closely than women's free responses.

Contrary to our expectation that sex differences in motivation to manage might be smaller among people employed as managers than among other statuses of respondents, differences between these groups of respondents were not marked. Yet, the scarcity of samples from populations other than business managers and business students limits our ability to draw conclusions from these null findings. In addition, there is some evidence that sex differences in motivation may have declined over the years that the scale has been in use. Although there was no general decrease, a significant trend in this direction was obtained with the multiple-choice version of the scale, and a marginal trend with business school students using the free-response version of the scale.

Validity Issues

The findings of this review raise certain questions about the validity of the MSCS as a measure of managerial motivation among women. For the free-response measure, the limited data that are available on this question suggest similar validity among women and men (Miner 1974b, 1993). Not only have differential validity studies supported this conclusion, but substantial validities have been obtained using samples with a heavy representation of women. For the multiple-choice measure, a recent review of validities noted eight studies, six of which were concurrent and two predictive (Miner 1993). Three of these studies had samples that were totally or almost totally male, three more studies had samples that were known to be approximately 40 percent female (Bartol and Martin 1987; Stahl 1986), and the remaining two studies had samples that probably were around 40 percent female (Goldner 1986; Quigley 1979). Although these studies showed no relation between the proportion of women in these samples and the validity of the multiple-choice scale, validities have not been examined separately within male and female samples. Clearly, more attention should be given to the validity of the instrument for female managers, given our demonstration of a sex difference in test performance.

As a preliminary approach to investigating potential item bias in the MSCS, item-level analyses identified the stems that yielded the largest sex differences. Although these analyses were restricted by the limited availability of item-level data, it is interesting that of the six items that Bartol and Martin (1987) used to illustrate their thesis of item bias, only two produced significant sex differences in the predicted direction. This finding suggests that items appearing most gender-stereotypic do not necessarily yield large differences between women's and men's responses. Yet, further study of this matter is needed, especially in relation to the multiple-choice test. More formal methods should be used to examine possible item bias on the MSCS (see Drasgow and Hulin 1990), and the results of such analyses may suggest revisions in the items included in the scale.

Implications and Future Directions

In general, the findings of this quantitative synthesis, especially the interesting pattern of sex differences obtained on the subscales of the MSCS, are consistent with a generalization we emphasized early in this article—namely, that the role of business manager, as traditionally defined within hierarchic organizations, can be considered somewhat masculine in the sense that the majority of the qualities it requires are male-stereotypic. Moreover, the feminist critique of the managerial role is illuminated by findings suggesting that women may be less motivated than men to meet many of the expectations embodied in this classic definition of the role of business manager—in particular, the distinctively masculine aspects of the role. Nonetheless, the traditional managerial role may encompass a small number of female-stereotypic qualities, consistent with our findings on the Authority Figures and Routine Administrative Functions subscales. High total scores on the MSCS can of course reflect women's stronger motivation in these two areas.

Relevant to women's lesser motivation, as assessed by this measure, is evidence that women may often be penalized for adopting the autocratic and directive style that is reflected in Miner's (1993) description of the managerial role in hierarchic organizations. Specifically, in a meta-analysis of studies examining evaluations of female and male leaders whose behaviors were made equivalent by appropriate experimental procedures, Eagly, Makhijani, and Klonsky (1992) found that women were devalued, relative to men, for leadership behavior that was stylistically masculine, especially if it was autocratic or directive. Experience with this form of prejudice may deter many female managers from desiring to adopt the more directive and assertive features of the traditional managerial role.

Finally, we offer some cautions about our findings' implications for men's and women's effectiveness as managers. Some readers may wish to conclude that, however understandable it is that women would be somewhat less motivated than men to fulfill many of the role requirements represented in the MSCS, female managers may be less effective than male managers in hierarchic organizations, because of this lesser managerial motivation. This implication can be avoided by concluding that the mean effect size is too small to be meaningful or consequential. Although it is often tempting to dismiss relatively small effect sizes as unimportant, especially when they represent comparisons between the sexes, this stance may be inappropriate given that even rather small effects can be consequential, as many methodologists have argued (e.g., Abelson 1985; Rosenthal and Rubin 1979; Sechrest and Yeaton 1982).

Before concluding that women's somewhat lesser motivation to manage suggests lesser effectiveness, it is important to consider the chorus of voices calling for new definitions of the role of business manager. Quite a few management experts and organizational consultants have criticized the traditional managerial role for what they maintain are its overly hierarchical and rigidly bureaucratic role expectations (e.g., Foy 1980; Kanter 1983; Offerman and Gowing 1990; Ouchi 1981; Peters 1988). Moreover, some proposals for new models of management have advocated what might be termed a more feminine model of management. This alternative model emphasizes participatory decision making and democratic relationships and appears to be generally consistent with the leadership styles actually adopted by many female managers (see Eagly and Johnson 1990). For example, Loden (1985) advocated a *feminine leadership model* characterized by cooperativeness, collaboration of managers and subordinates, and lower control for the leader. Helgesen (1990) similarly argued for a *feminine principle in leadership* characterized by an emphasis on cooperation rather than competition and equality rather than a superior-subordinate hierarchy. Rosener (1990) claimed that many female managers favor an *interactive* form of leadership whose characteristics include encouragement of participation, sharing of power and information, and enhancing others' self-worth. Moreover, Miner (1993) discussed role motivation within group-based organizations in which decisions are made by consensus or majority vote. Before the implications of our findings for managers' effectiveness can be fully understood, two important questions remain to be addressed empirically: (1) is the managerial role truly evolving in the direction of the more feminine and participatory role requirements advocated by Loden (1985), Helgesen (1990), and Rosener (1990) and described by Miner (1993); and (2) are women more motivated than men to undertake these variants of the traditional managerial role? Should the answers to both of these questions be affirmative, women may be *more* effective managers than men for the contemporary conditions that exist in many organizations—in particular, in those organizations that have moved toward less hierarchic forms of organization. Miner's measure of motivation to manage can be considered a valid measure only in the hierarchic organizational environments in which it was designed. To the extent that business firms are evolving away from this form, new and different measures of motivation are required.

STUDIES USED IN THE META-ANALYSIS

Albert (1977)
Amaewhule (1982)
Arsan, Hunsicker, and Southern (1983)
Bartol and Martin (1987)
Bowin, Robert B.—Unpublished data—women managers—1977
Bracker, Jeffrey S., and Pearson, John—Unpublished data—undergraduate business students—1979
Dayani (1980)
Ebrahimi, Bahman—Unpublished data—Far Eastern graduate business students—1983
Ebrahimi (1984)
Harlan and Weiss (1982)
Hoffman (1983)
Love, Norris—Unpublished data—MBA students—1975
Love, Norris—Unpublished data—MBA students—1977
Miner, John B.—Unpublished data—University of Maryland undergraduate business students—1969
Miner, John B.—Unpublished data—undergraduate business students—1972
Miner (1974b)
Miner (1974c)
Miner (1977b)—Chapter 26
Miner, John B.—Unpublished data—MBA students—1987
Miner, John B.—Unpublished data—MBA students—1988
Miner and Smith (1982)
Miner, Chen, and Yu (1991)

Muczyk, Jan P., and Schuler, Randall S.—Unpublished data—undergraduate students—1978
Nellen (1986)
Overstreet (1980)
Rizzo, John R., Hill, James W., and Miner, John B.—Unpublished data—Western Michigan University undergraduate business students—1971
Singleton, Timothy M.—Unpublished data—Georgia State University undergraduate business students—1976
Southern, Lloyd J. F., and Pih, Peter—Unpublished data—Taiwanese, Turkish, and U.S. business students—1984
Stahl (1986)
Swisher, DuMont, and Boyer (1985)
Terrell, S. M.—Unpublished data—hospital administrators—1978
Wachtel (1986)
Wilderom, Celeste P. M., and Miner, John B.—Unpublished data—undergraduate economics students in the Netherlands—1988

CHAPTER 27

META-ANALYSIS OF RISK PROPENSITY DIFFERENCES BETWEEN MANAGERS AND ENTREPRENEURS ON THE MSCS–FORM T

INTRODUCTION

This article was published in the *Journal of Applied Psychology* (Miner and Raju 2004), achieving its final form only after a number of years. Thus, a bit of history is necessary to explain how the authors came to their various roles. As originally drafted, the paper was intended to point up certain omissions in the Stewart and Roth (2001) meta-analysis, and did not contain any meta-analytic findings of its own. On the recommendation of the then-editor of the *Journal of Applied Psychology* the conclusions were put in meta-analytic form and the second author was added for this purpose. As a result there was a considerable lapse of time; furthermore there was a change of editors, as well as many new directions in the focus of the article. Nam Raju did the meta-analyses and I gave him the data. Much of the write-up continued to use my original input, but Nam's quantitative expertise contributed a great deal to the final product.

I should note also that our second editor chose to solicit a "reply to our reply" which was published as Stewart and Roth (2004). Needless to say I do not endorse what these authors have to say about our work, but it is worth noting that their substantive conclusions actually match ours quite well; they too, now see a need for considerable additional research.

From John B. Miner and Nambury S. Raju, "Risk Propensity Differences Between Managers and Entrepreneurs and Between Low- and High-Growth Entrepreneurs: A Reply in a More Conservative Vein," *Journal of Applied Psychology,* vol. 89, no. 1, 3–13.

Although this article deals almost entirely with the Avoiding Risks subscale of the Miner Sentence Completion Scale–Form T (MSCS–T), the approach taken may also serve as a model for analyses that may focus on other subscales of Form T, and on subscales of Form H and Form P as well, to the extent sufficient data are available. Ultimately I believe this kind of investigation will be called for.

* * *

Stewart and Roth (2001) published a series of meta-analyses in the *Journal of Applied Psychology,* the results of which led them to conclude that the risk propensity of entrepreneurs is greater than that of managers. They also concluded from the data they presented that entrepreneurs with venture growth as their primary goal have a greater risk propensity than entrepreneurs who have as their objective producing family income (low growth).

We disagree with these conclusions on the basis of findings from additional studies not included in the Stewart and Roth (2001) meta-analyses. In what follows we present these additional findings, and some meta-analyses of our own, toward the end of refuting the broad conclusions set forth by Stewart and Roth (2001) and restoring a more conservative position to this debate. The conclusions with which we disagree are best stated in the authors' own words:

> Results indicate that the risk propensity of entrepreneurs is greater than that of managers. Moreover, there are larger differences between entrepreneurs whose primary goal is venture growth versus those whose focus is on producing family income. (145)
>
> Entrepreneurs have a somewhat higher risk propensity than do managers. . . . If we focus on entrepreneurs with growth aspirations versus managers, the differences in risk propensity becomes very large indeed. (150)

This position takes issue with McClelland's (1961) achievement motivation theory view that differences between entrepreneurs and managers in this area are small or nonexistent and affirms that, on the basis of available research, entrepreneurs actually have a higher risk propensity. Furthermore, entrepreneurs who are predisposed to growth, and presumably those with a record of growth, are found to have a particularly high propensity to take risks. On the basis of this evidence, Stewart and Roth proposed that "risk propensity appears to lie at the crux of a constellation of constructs that form an interconnected situation-trait rubric of entrepreneurial behavior" (151). Thus, they see risk taking as a key variable at the core of future theorizing on the process of entrepreneurship.

To restate: The question addressed by the present article is whether these conclusions regarding the facts of the matter are justified or whether we would do better to view these conclusions as premature and thus to retain the more conservative position held previously—to continue to respond "I don't know" and seek further research evidence in this area.

THE CONSERVATIVE POSITION IN SCIENCE

In adopting a more conservative position on this issue, we hold more closely to the view that ideally a scientist remains neutral until a convincing body of evidence is amassed; this is an inherent aspect of scientific objectivity. In accordance, "I don't know" becomes not only an acceptable answer to a scientific question but in many cases a highly valued one as well. By admitting that adequate knowledge to solve a problem is lacking, science opens the door to scientific investigation. The greatest error is the one that occurs when inadequate or insufficient data are overinterpreted or overgeneralized with the result that an unsolved problem is accepted as solved. Errors of this kind block scientific progress because the identification of problems is made extremely difficult, if not completely foreclosed.

It is in this sense that Brown and Ghiselli (1955) described the scientist as conservative. He or she remains open to new facts until the weight of the evidence demands change. The key to scientific decision making is that all the facts be evaluated, and that sufficient evidence clearly is available. "When there is no doubt, there can be no science" (Brown and Ghiselli 1955, 13). In this same vein, theories that are in error, if they are nevertheless accepted as true, can have substantial negative consequences for science (Miner 2002b; Webster and Starbuck 1988). They can sustain themselves for considerable periods of time and lead science off along paths that ultimately prove unfruitful and make for invalid practice.

The role of risk propensity in the behavior of entrepreneurs has until recently been an open issue. Questions in this regard have typically been met with the "I don't know" response—based on an assessment of what was believed to be the diversity of research findings available in the literature. The Stewart and Roth (2001) review, however, holds that "We do know." It is that position with which we take issue.

ADDITIONAL EVIDENCE

The questions we raise rest on the adequacy and the comprehensiveness of the Stewart and Roth (2001) meta-analyses. To this end it is important to consider any additional studies and results that might prove relevant. Relevance here means having a bearing on (1) the relationship between risk propensity and the entrepreneur-manager criterion and on (2) the relationship between risk propensity and a criterion, which pits growth-oriented entrepreneurs against either their nongrowth-oriented (current income-oriented) counterparts or managers. In actual fact, as the previous quote indicates, Stewart and Roth reached conclusions from their meta-analyses on both of these matters, although the former is presented as the major thrust of the analyses.

Are there additional studies that should be brought to bear? We believe that there are, and in what follows we cite 14 studies that deal with one or the other, or both, of the conclusions that Stewart and Roth (2001) reached. In this connection, note that the Stewart and Roth meta-analyses appear to be based on 14 studies contained in 11 publications; only 3 of these studies bear on the growth-orientation conclusion.

The Measures

The additional evidence that we wish to cite is described in the following. The great majority of these studies involved the Risk Avoidance subscale of the Miner Sentence Completion Scale–Form T (MSCS–T). The MSCS–T was conceptually derived and does not assume a particular factor structure. The components, such as "avoiding risks," measure motivational counterparts of perceiver prototypes (role prescriptions) as explicated in Foti and Miner (2003).

The Risk Avoidance subscale, like the other MSCS measures, is a projective instrument and thus permits the incorporation of motives below the level of consciousness in the measurement process. Projective measures such as this have been shown to yield outcome correlations that are significantly larger than those obtained with self-report measures intended to measure the same variables (Spangler 1992). Sentence completion indexes are widely used by clinical psychologists (Holaday, Smith, and Sherry 2000). A recent major review of projective technique validities (Lilienfeld, Wood, and Garb 2000) noted that a sentence completion measure, developed and scored in much the same manner as the MSCS, proved far superior to other projective measures (including most indexes from the Rorschach and the Thematic Apperception Test [TAT]) when based on sound psychometric procedures; such approaches can yield substantial validities.

Whether the risk construct thus specified is the same as that identified by Stewart and Roth (2001) is not easily answered. In fact, Stewart and Roth indicated that among the six self-report instruments they studied, they found differences of a kind that raise questions regarding the extent of construct homogeneity within their own analyses. The stems of the MSCS–T items are much the same as those included in many self-report measures, but the free-response format facilitates the expression of unconscious material in that respondents often are unaware of the meanings indicated. However, both the MSCS–T measure and those self-report instruments noted by Stewart and Roth (2001) all appear to tap some aspect of risk. A likely explanation of what is involved is that various types of measures, including the MSCS–T, are concerned with different facets of the risk-taking–risk-avoidance construct. This idea is developed more fully in the Discussion below, in the section dealing with the role of implicit and self-attributed motives. In any event, it is safe to say that the nature and structure of the risk construct remain an unanswered question at the present time, one of many questions that require keeping the door open to further research in this area.

In 2 of the 14 studies (Studies 1 and 2), in addition to the MSCS–T, a version of the Shure and Meeker (1967) Risk Avoidance Scale (Miner 1997a) was used. This measure derives from factor analysis and uses 17 items to which responses are made on a scale of 1 to 3, with the highest scores indicating the most risk avoidance; thus, the possible score range is 17–51. The items are of a self-report nature and deal with material and physical risk taking. Four items from the scale as printed in Harnett and Cummings (1980, 95–97) were not used. The scale is part of a much larger instrument that has been employed widely in studies of bargaining behavior (Shure and Meeker 1967). Internal consistency reliability has been reported at .70 (Miner 2000). This instrument, although similar to those used in the Stewart and Roth (2001) analyses, was not actually used in any of the studies on which they report, nor is it mentioned in their article.

The Studies

The studies that follow were not necessarily selected on the same basis as those used by Stewart and Roth (2001); the primary focus was on obtaining adequate tests of their conclusions, not merely on replicating their procedures. Thus, any study that gave any indication of providing information on the risk propensities of growth-oriented entrepreneurs was included. In this respect, the present analysis attempts to move beyond the analysis of three meta-analytic studies reported in Stewart and Roth. In addition, although the experimental, entrepreneurial samples used here are essentially the same as those used by Stewart and Roth, the control comparison samples are not necessarily identical. The latter differ in that in certain instances they contain entrepreneurs who lack a growth orientation in order to make comparisons on the growth variable. Also, in some cases, professionals of various kinds were included with the managerial subjects; this appears justified given that, in terms of risk avoidance as measured by the MSCS–T, managers and professionals do not differ (see Study 3 below), and adding

Table 27.1

Summary Data for Studies Included in the Initial Meta-Analysis

		Experimental Group			Control Group				Effect Size
Study	Scale	N	*M*	*SD*	*N*	*M*	*SD*	*t*	(*d*)
1	MSCS–T	45	2.24	2.60	44	1.23	2.12	–2.01*	–.422
2	MSCS–T	30	–1.47	3.49	85	–1.25	2.53	.37	.078
3	MSCS–T	24	3.25	2.44	60	.75	2.58	–4.07*	–.975
4	MSCS–T	65	1.68	2.15	71	–.20	2.71	–4.46*	–.760
5	MSCS–T	59	1.56	2.58	59	.03	2.58	–3.22*	–.589
6	MSCS–T	24	1.12	2.67	24	1.08	2.24	–.06	–.016
7	MSCS–T	41	1.09	2.16	10	–.50	1.22	–2.23*	–.775
8a	MSCS–T	34	1.59	2.82	34	.15	2.52	–2.22*	–.532
8b	MSCS–T	36	.17	2.87	33	.00	2.40	–.27	–.063
9	MSCS–T	31	2.58	7.23	33	.12	3.66	–1.73	–.428
10	MSCS–T	34	2.82	5.26	33	–.48	4.67	–2.71*	–.655
11	MSCS–T	35	1.87	5.11	36	–.09	3.10	–1.96	–.460
12	MSCS–T	31	1.12	2.69	26	1.00	2.80	–.17	–.043
13	MSCS–T	47	.87	2.69	66	.36	2.42	–1.05	–.200
1	SM	45	31.87	5.35	44	32.14	5.01	.25	.052
2	SM	30	30.83	6.56	85	32.55	5.95	1.33	.280

Note: MSCS–T = Miner Sentence Completion Scale—Form T; SM = Shure and Meeker Scale.
$*p < .05$

the professionals expands the analysis considerably. In any event, Stewart and Roth's criteria for inclusion-exclusion do not make reference to projective techniques in any way.

Many of the studies that follow, and the risk-related data that they contain, were in the published literature at the time the Stewart and Roth (2001) analyses were carried out, although none of these citations are listed by these authors. Where published data were not available—and thus Stewart and Roth cannot be faulted for failing to include them—we have so indicated in discussing that study.

Study 1 *[See Chapter 20]*

This Buffalo, New York area sample is described in detail in Miner (1997a, 1997b); results related to risk avoidance are given in Miner (2002a). These latter studies involve both the Risk Avoidance subscale of the MSCS–T and the Shure and Meeker Risk Avoidance Scale. The MSCS–T analysis focuses on the relation between risk and the extent to which entrepreneurs are growth-oriented. In Table 27.1 the experimental group consists of entrepreneurial leaders specified as both (1) lead entrepreneurs and (2) growth-oriented. The control group contains entrepreneurs lacking in one or both of these characteristics.

Table 27.1 shows the sample sizes, means, and standard deviations for the experimental and control groups, separately, by study. Also shown in this table are the *t* test results and effect sizes. It should be noted that in the *t* test and effect size computations, the mean of the experimental group was subtracted from the mean of the control group in order to make the metric of our effect sizes correspond to the metric underlying Stewart and Roth's (2001) effect sizes. This sign reversal was introduced only for meta-analytic purposes, not in the calculations reported in the text of this section.

As indicated by the *t* test results, the experimental group scored significantly higher than the control group on the MSCS–T in Study 1. An analysis relating risk avoidance to firm success data (from growth to failure and leaving the field) obtained from 1 to 7 years after testing produced an *r* of –.09. Results from this additional analysis were not included in the reported meta-analysis because the same samples were involved in both analyses.

Data from the Shure and Meeker (SM, 1967) Scale were obtained using the same samples as above. Means and standard deviations based on the SM Scale are shown separately at the bottom of Table 27.1. Unlike the MSCS–T, the means for the experimental and control groups on the SM Scale were not significantly different from each other in this study. With respect to the additional analysis involving risk avoidance and firm growth (success), the obtained correlation of .10 was also not significant for the SM Scale. These, and the MSCS–T, findings were not available in the published literature when the Stewart and Roth (2001) analyses were published.

Study 2 *[See Chapter 21]*

This sample of State University of New York—Buffalo graduate students in an entrepreneurship course is described in Miner (1997a, 2000); risk avoidance results are contained in Miner (2002b) and include data from both the MSCS–T and SM Scale measures of risk avoidance. An entrepreneurial propensity score was derived dealing with current self-employment, previous business founding, and career objectives in the entrepreneurship field; high scores indicate a proclivity for an entrepreneurial career. Analyses involving this score could not be included in the meta-analyses because clearly defined experimental and control groups were not available and because of the independence requirements. However, the correlation was .05 with the MSCS–T and–.21 with the SM Scale, which is statistically significant.

Entrepreneurial activity also was established based on employment source after graduation; graduates were identified as either engaged in some type of entrepreneurial activity or not so engaged. In Table 27.1 the experimental group contains those who became engaged in entrepreneurial activity, and the control subjects were the otherwise employed. As shown the experimental and control group means did not differ significantly on both the MSCS and SM Scales. Both sets of findings were not published at the time Stewart and Roth (2001) appeared.

Study 3 *[See Chapter 22]*

Information on the following sample and the risk avoidance results is discussed in Miner (2002a) and thus was not available when Stewart and Roth (2001) published their study. Data on the whole careers of members of the class of 1948 from Princeton University were analyzed to identify those with an entrepreneurial career pattern and those whose careers were more appropriately classified as managerial or professional. Given that the 32 managers and 28 professionals did not differ significantly on the MSCS–T Risk Avoidance subscale, it seemed appropriate to combine these samples. In Table 27.1, those with an entrepreneurial career pattern were the experimental group, and those with managerial or professional careers were the control group; the mean difference was statistically significant, with the experimental group receiving a higher score than the control group on the MSCS–T.

Study 4 *[See Chapter 16]*

Information on the following sample and the risk avoidance results are discussed in Miner (1990). The entrepreneurial leaders in this study met both the lead entrepreneur criterion and the criterion of heading high-growth firms. Both samples were constituted from the author's files, built up over various studies and consulting engagements. The results reflect on the relationship of risk both to an entrepreneur-manager criterion and to one involving high-growth entrepreneurs. The experimental group in Table 27.1 contains the entrepreneurial leaders, the control group contains the managers. The experimental group scored significantly higher than the control group. The data of this study initially appeared to be independent (Miner 1990); however, some overlap is indicated in Miner (1993). Data to determine which report is correct are currently unavailable, and in the interest of inclusiveness, the initial conclusion was accepted. All other samples in Table 27.1 are clearly independent of one another.

Study 5 *[See Chapter 15]*

The following samples have been subjected to a variety of analyses that have been published in a number of sources. Concurrent results appear in Miner (1993, 2002a). Miner, Smith, and Bracker (1989), and Smith, Bracker, and Miner (1987). The follow-up predictive findings, obtained roughly five years later, appear in Miner, Smith, and Bracker (1992a, 1994). The subjects were high-technology entrepreneurs who applied for National Science Foundation (NSF) grants. All subjects were lead entrepreneurs, but the leaders (in Table 27.1 the experimental group), in contrast to the control group, all shared in common the fact that they were above the median in firm growth. Again, the experimental group scored higher than the control group.

A sample of manager-scientists, also NSF grant applicants who completed the MSCS–T, from similar high-technology firms to the entrepreneurs, also was used for comparison purposes (N = 41). Within this sample, at least 75 percent held managerial positions. When all 118 entrepreneurs were compared with these manager-scientists, a standardized canonical discriminant function coefficient of .41 was obtained. This analysis, although significant, and those analyses that followed as a result, could not be included in our meta-analysis due to the independence requirement.

We obtained a number of correlations relating risk avoidance (from the MSCS–T) to various indexes of firm growth, both at the time of the initial data collection and at follow-up. These analyses were restricted to the entrepreneurial subjects. Risk avoidance was related to mean annual growth in number of employees with a statistically significant rank-order correlation (r_s = 18; N = 113); to mean annual growth in sales (r_s = .24; N = 90), which was statistically significant: to overall growth at follow-up (r_b = .14; N = 59); to growth in number of employees at follow-up (r_s = .05; N = 53); and to growth in sales at follow-up (r_s = .07; N = 46).

A comparison of entrepreneurs remaining with their firms at follow-up (N = 61) versus those who did not remain (N = 16) should also capture something of the growth dynamic. When a sample of nonrespondents was included in this analysis, no significance was obtained, $F(2, 115) = 2.05$, but the two samples of interest differed significantly, $p < .05$ (remaining $M = 1.25$, not remaining $M = .06$). Except for the comparison involving the manager-scientists, all of the analyses in Study 5 involved the relationship of risk to high growth.

Study 6

This study by Jourdan (1987) is an analysis that used entrepreneurs from Atlanta, Georgia. The successful entrepreneurs were in business at the time of testing and presumably had experienced some growth, although many had experienced bankruptcy in the past, often several times. The entrepreneurs who had become bankrupt were located at their original places of business and were either in Chapter 11 or in the same business with a new name: thus, they were not typical of business failures, although some differential in growth orientation between these two samples was to be expected. In Table 27.1, the experimental group is the successful entrepreneurs and the control group is the bankrupt entrepreneurs: comparison of the means yielded no significant results.

Study 7

The unpublished study by Bracker, Pearson, Keats, and Miner (1991) is discussed in Miner (1993). This study involved owner-managed firms in the electronics industry that were in business at least five years and had less than one hundred employees. Follow-up over a five-year period subsequent to testing was able to establish definitive data on the status of all entrepreneurs in the sample. To the extent that growth was involved it would have to have been within the "firm survived" sample. In Table 27.1 the experimental group is the survivors and the control group is those whose firms did not survive (t testing [$df = 49$] of the difference yielded a value of 2.23, $p < .05$).

Study 8

These data derive from research conducted and published by Bellu (1988). The entrepreneur and manager (top level) samples were from comparable firms in two geographic locations—Brooklyn, New York (labeled 8a in Table 27.1) and Rutland, Vermont (labeled 8b in Table 27.1); the numbers for each sample were essentially the same in each locale. As in most of Bellu's other studies (Bellu 1993; Bellu, Davidsson, and Goldfarb 1990; Bellu and Sherman 1995), correlations are not reported; the entrepreneurs are in the experimental group and the managers are in the control group. All samples are independent of one another. As indicated in Table 27.1, the 8a results are significant, but the 8b results are not.

Study 9

The study of Bellu, Davidsson, and Goldfarb (1990) involved managers who were all at the top level and who did not hold any ownership interest in the company. Firm sizes of the two samples were both under 50 employees. The MSCS–T was administered in person by an author who was fluent in English and Italian.

Two rounds of double translations were necessary to assure cultural homogeneity. For a few items, paraphrases were used to convey the same concepts as in the English original. In Table 27.1, the entrepreneurs are the experimental group and the managers are the control group, with no significant mean difference. All subjects were from northern Italy (Lombardy). Note that Stewart and Roth (2001) did not exclude non-U.S. samples from their meta-analyses (Ahmed 1985; Richard 1989).

Study 10

In the study by Bellu, Davidsson, and Goldfarb (1990), samples were established much as in Study 9. Both entrepreneurs and managers came from southern Italy (Sicily).

Two rounds of translations were required—back and forth, and paraphrasing was needed to obtain cultural homogeneity. As stated previously, in Table 27.1 the entrepreneurs are the experimental group and the managers are the control group; the experimental group had a significantly higher mean than the control group.

Study 11

In the study by Bellu, Davidsson, and Goldfarb (1990), samples were established much as in Studies 9 and 10, but in this instance, subjects were from Tel Aviv, Israel. Homogeneity was established as previously for the MSCS–T. The Table 27.1 data reflect the entrepreneurs in the experimental group and the managers in the control group; the difference between the two groups was not significant.

Study 12

The study by Bellu, Davidsson, and Goldfarb (1990) also involved Swedish firms (from the Stockholm area) that were somewhat larger. Within the manager sample, some of the subjects had had prior entrepreneurial experience.

Homogeneity proved less difficult to obtain with the Swedish MSCS–T, although again a bilingual author provided the translation. In Table 27.1, the experimental group is the entrepreneurs and the control group is the managers; there was no significant mean difference between the two groups.

Study 13

These samples from the New York City area are described and the results are reported in Bellu (1993). The managerial sample consisted of women at the middle level of management and above. These are the only samples of Bellu's that are entirely female in nature. The means in Table 27.1 reflect the entrepreneurs in the experimental group and the managers in the control group, $t(111) = 1.05$.

In another study described in Bellu and Sherman (1995), the sample of entrepreneurs from New York City consisted of participants in an entrepreneurship development program who indicated a desire for firm growth and an interest in developing a formal strategic plan for that purpose. The follow-up (N = 43) occurred five years after the MSCS–T was administered, and the criterion measures reflect changes over that five-year period. The correlation with growth in sales was $r = .12$ and with growth in profits was $r = .35$, $p < .01$.

Because these data came entirely from entrepreneurial leaders with a growth orientation, and no control group was established, they were not used in the meta-analysis. However, they do suggest that the degree of risk avoidance may contribute to increasing growth, even among the already growth-oriented.

Of the 23 statistical results noted for Studies 1–13 involving the MSCS–T in Table 27.1 and discussed previously, 11 are significant ($p < .05$ or better), and 21 positively associate risk avoidance with the fact of entrepreneurship or growth-oriented entrepreneurship. These analyses, of course, are not always independent, but according to the *t* test results in Table 27.1, 7 of 14 MSCS–T findings are statistically significant, and these analyses are independent. There are no findings available that support the Stewart and Roth (2001) conclusions other than those involving the SM Scale measure, although as with their analysis there are a substantial number of nonsignificant results.

The results obtained with the SM measure are nonsignificant in three of the four instances reported, but the one significant finding reflects an association between entrepreneurial activity and risk taking. The overall pattern of results with this measure is much like what was reported in Stewart and Roth (2001); it varies sharply from the pattern obtained with the MSCS–T.

META-ANALYSES

To provide consistency between the Stewart and Roth (2001) analyses and what is reported here, various meta-analyses were carried out. For this purpose, all data were converted to the form used by Stewart and Roth, with positive values indicating risk taking and negative values (–) indicating risk avoidance; this was done in the meta-analyses only.

Study Identification and Screening Criteria

The studies used in the initial meta-analysis are shown in Table 27.1. The procedures used for identifying studies not previously included in Stewart and Roth (2001) and the criteria for their inclusion in this analysis are that either entrepreneurs and managers (or their equivalent) are compared, or growth-oriented lead entrepreneurs (entrepreneurial leaders) are compared with other groups of entrepreneurs. Only studies that were independent from other studies within a set of studies, and with complete information for computing the effect size, were included in the current investigation. This resulted in 16 data sets, as shown in Table 27.1.

The last column of Table 27.1 shows the unbiased effect size (*d*) for each study. The computation of *d* followed the procedures described in Hedges and Olkin (1985) and Hunter and Schmidt (1990): The mean difference was divided by the pooled standard deviation. In most meta-analyses, the mean of the control group is subtracted from the mean of the experimental group. In our study, the mean of the experimental group was subtracted from the mean of the control group so that the resulting effect sizes (*d*s) are on the same metric as the effect sizes in Stewart and Roth (2001). In Stewart and Roth, a positive difference (*d*) indicates a propensity for risk taking, which is also true of the effect sizes shown in Table 27.1. The fact that most of the effect sizes are negative in the table implies that entrepreneurs (or entrepreneurial leaders) are less likely to take risks than the control subjects.

The Initial Meta-Analysis

The Hunter and Schmidt (1990) procedure was used in the current investigation. The mean effect size was computed as the sample-size weighted average of the available effect sizes. The same weights were also used in computing the standard deviation of effect sizes. Given the current emphasis on the random-effects model in meta-analysis (Hedges and Vevea 1998; Hunter and Schmidt 2000), only the standard errors based on the random-effects model were reported for the mean effect sizes. It should be noted that the standard errors based on the fixed-effects model will always be less than or equal to the standard errors on the random-effects model. The 95 percent confidence intervals (CIs) for mean effect sizes were constructed

Table 27.2

Results from the Initial Meta-Analysis

Study	N	K	$\bar{d}$	SD of *d*	SD of $\bar{d}$ (random)	CI	SD of δ
MSCS–T	1,150	14	–.429	.316	.084	(–.594, –.264)	.221
SM	204	2	.181	.114	.141	(–.095, .457)	.000

Note: *K* = number of studies; $\bar{d}$ = mean of d; CI = confidence interval; MSCS–T = Miner Sentence Completion Scale-Form T; SM = Shure and Meeker Scale.

using these standard errors. Because *d* is viewed as an estimate of the population effect size (denoted as δ), an estimate of the standard deviation of δs was also computed using the procedures described in Hunter and Schmidt (1990). No corrections were made for unreliability in the risk propensity measures.

Initial Results

The meta-analytic results from the current investigation are shown in Table 27.2 separately for the 14 studies using the MSCS–T and the 2 studies using the SM Scale. As previously noted, these 2 sets of studies are not independent, and hence a combined meta-analysis was not performed. According to the data in Table 27.2, the total sample size for the first set of 14 studies is 1,150, with a mean effect size of –.429 and a standard deviation of 0.316. The standard deviation (SD) for the mean effect size is 0.084. The standard deviation of population effect sizes is estimated at 0.205, indicating substantial variability in population effect sizes. The 95 percent CI for the mean effect size varies between –.594 and –.264. Because this interval does not include the zero point, one is 95 percent confident that the (population) mean effect size is different from zero. Substantively, this significant negative effect size implies that entrepreneurs are less likely to be risk prone than are their control subjects. This result, based on the MSCS–T, is the direct opposite of what Stewart and Roth (2001) reported.

The SM Scale analysis (also reported in Table 27.2) was based on only two studies, with a mean effect size of .181 and a standard deviation of 0.114 This mean effect size is not statistically significant because the 95 percent CI varies between –.095 and .457. This result is consistent with the statistically nonsignificant *d* values reported in Table 27.1 for the two studies included in this analysis. Again, it should be noted that the SM Scale analysis was based only on two studies and therefore should be interpreted with caution.

90 Percent Credibility Values

Because estimates of the standard deviations of population effect sizes are known for the meta-analyses reported in Table 27.2 it is possible to compute the 90 percent credibility values. The mean effect size for the 14 MSCS–T studies is –.429 with a standard deviation of δ equal to .221. Therefore the 90 percent credibility value may be computed as follows: –.429 + (1.28 x .221) = –.146. This means that 90 percent of the population effect sizes will fall below –.146, provided that δs are normally distributed. That is, it is very likely that, in most populations (90 percent or more) in the MSCS–T-based study, entrepreneurs are less likely to indulge in risk-taking behavior than are their control subjects. In the SM Scale-based

Table 27.3

Meta-Analysis Results for the Combined Data

Meta-analysis	N	K	$\bar{d}$	SD of $\bar{d}$ (random)	CI
MSCS only	1,150	14	–.429	.084	(–.594, –.264)
Stewart & Roth (2001)	3,338	14	.313	.032	(.250, .375)
Combined	4,488	28	.123	.071	(–.016, .262)

Note: K = number of studies; $\bar{d}$ = mean of d; CI = confidence interval; MSCS = Miner Sentence Completion Scale–Form T.

study, the estimated standard deviation of population effect sizes is 0.0, which means that the effect size is the same across populations, and the best estimate of that common effect size is .181. Again, it is worth noting that this particular meta-analysis is based on only two studies with a total sample size of 204 cases, and therefore, the mean effect size of .181 should be interpreted with caution.

Incorporating the Stewart and Roth Findings

Stewart and Roth's (2001) meta-analysis, based on studies using self-report measures of risk-proneness, shows that entrepreneurs are risk-prone, whereas the current meta-analysis, based on the MSCS–T, a projective measure of risk proneness, shows that entrepreneurs are risk avoidant. These results, which are opposite in explaining the relationship between entrepreneurship and risk-proneness, may be reflecting more than the true relationship between the two. That is, these results may also be reflecting the effect of the type of psychometric measure used for assessing risk-proneness: self-report measures versus a projective measure. The type of risk-proneness measure used probably moderates the relationship between entrepreneurship and risk-proneness. At the least, the current meta-analytic results, and those from Stewart and Roth, appear to suggest this hypothesis. Despite this probable explanation for the observed discrepancy between the results from the two meta-analytic studies, we wanted to conduct a meta-analysis combining the data from both investigations for the following reason: Because our effect size was negative and the effect size from Stewart and Roth was positive, we wanted to know the degree to which the sign and magnitude of the effect size would change in a combined analysis. Results from such an analysis would hopefully help us to understand better the true relationship between entrepreneurship and risk-proneness, as well as suggest some viable hypotheses for future research.

Results from the combined meta-analysis are shown in Table 27.3. This table also shows the meta-analytic results based only on Stewart and Roth's (2001) 14 studies, as reported in their Table 2. Our recomputed mean effect size for their studies is .313 (P. L. Roth, personal communication, March 24, 2003), whereas their published mean effect size is .300. The very small difference between these two estimates appears to be simply a function of rounding. The (random effects) standard error and 95 percent CI for their recomputed mean effect size of .313 are .032 and (.250, .375), respectively.

As shown in Table 27.3, the combined mean effect size is .123, with a (random effects) standard error of .071. The associated 95 percent CI is (–.016, .262), which includes the zero point. This means that the population effect size may not be different from zero. That is, the combined meta-analytic result suggests that entrepreneurs may not have a propensity for risk. This conclusion is at variance with the conclusions derived from two meta-analyses: One meta-analysis including only the MSCS–T studies and the other meta-analysis including only the studies from Stewart and Roth (2001). As previously noted, these two substudies reach opposite conclusions. The fact that the combined meta-analysis supports neither of these two conclusions argues for a more conservative stance in this matter. The next section elaborates on this point, including a discussion of moderator effects.

DISCUSSION

A possible limitation of the MSCS–T data we marshal to reach our conclusions is that our Studies 9–12 are international in nature and involve the use of translations, yet with no measurement equivalence work being reported. Although adequate professionally accepted linguistic procedures appear to have been followed in these studies, no psychometric assessments of the fidelity of these translations are reported. Such a methodology could potentially identify certain items as having measurement inequivalence but would not necessarily pinpoint measurement inequivalence at the scale level, which is basic to the current investigation (Budgell, Raju, and Quartetti 1995; Collins, Raju, and Edwards 2000; Raju, Laffitte, and Byrne 2002).

To deal with this issue, we conducted two separate meta-analyses. The first considered the data of Studies 1–8 and 13, in which no translation factors were involved. The second dealt with the data of Studies 9–12, in which translations were used. The mean effect size for the first analysis was –.434 with a (random effects) standard error of .110; in the second analysis these values were –.411 and .126. Although the estimated mean effect sizes were not identical, the difference was small and within statistical sampling error. It does not appear that the translated MSCS–T measures introduced moderator effects of any meaningful magnitude.

Potential problems also exist with the data used by Stewart and Roth (2001). For one thing, the studies as listed in their Table 1 (*Sample Studies of Entrepreneurial Risk Taking Propensity*) do not match up either with those included in the References and designated as used in the meta-analysis or with those used in the meta-analyses of their Table 2 (P. L. Roth, personal communication, March 24, 2003). It appears in the latter instance that a sizable portion of the material intended for their Table 1 was in fact omitted. Furthermore, the reference provided for one meta-analytic study (Begley and Boyd 1987) does not contain any mention of risk or risk measurement at all. A study by Sexton and Bowman (1983) contains data using several measures of risk taking; in their Table 1, under *Sample,* data are presented on one measure (which did not yield significant results), but under *Results* they present data on a different measure (which are significant). In addition, the standard deviation for nonbusiness majors is reported as 63.74, whereas in the original it is 13.74.

We believe that these departures from expectation quite possibly could be explained away, although we do not know with certainty what the explanations might be or who might be responsible, and/or the deviations are such as to have a relatively small overall effect; accordingly we feel that for some set of studies the direction of the results reported by Stewart and Roth (2001) is reasonably accurate. This conclusion regarding the direction of results is reinforced by our own findings with the self-report SM Scale, although the mean differences (as shown in Table 27.1) lacked statistical significance in both studies. On balance, then, it seems appropriate to go along with the general thrust of the Stewart and Roth findings without supporting their specifics and certainly with the proviso that they apply only to a set of studies that do not include projective techniques. It appears that the type of scale (self-report versus projective) used may moderate the relationship between entrepreneurship and risk propensity.

Stewart and Roth's (2001) analysis is restricted to a rather small sample of studies using self-report measures of risk taking; it does not include an equal number of studies that use projective measurement procedures. This appears to have been a consequence in some instances of exclusion on methodological grounds, but in most cases these latter studies were omitted because they did not come to the authors' attention or because they were not readily available. One might hypothesize that such oversights as occurred did so because risk is not noted in the titles of the publications involved; however, the MSCS–T measure and some of the research on it were known to Stewart and Roth at the time of their meta-analyses (W. H. Stewart, personal communication, April 18, 2001).

This limitation of the Stewart and Roth (2001) analysis would have been less of a problem if the included and omitted studies had produced similar results, but as we have seen, this is not the case. The failure to deal with the literature as a whole yielded a conclusion that the problem had been solved, when in fact the "I don't know" response seems more appropriate to the data. This interpretation is reinforced by certain findings, derived from interview results provided by managers, to the effect that the decision making of these subjects is in fact characterized by considerable risk taking. The managers resorted to cognitive processing, which involved

> focusing on a few discrete values (events) in the outcome distribution; sequentially attending to critical performance targets . . . ; dealing with risk in a dynamic process in which estimates are modified, parameters are changed, and the problem is restructured in an active manner (Shapira 1995, 17).

In thus rejecting a normative approach, the managers were quite insensitive to estimates of the probabilities of possible outcomes.

Although the Shapira (1995) study dealt only with managers, not entrepreneurs, it argues for a much more risk-accepting view of managerial decision making than do the Stewart and Roth (2001) results. It also introduces certain concepts of decision making under risk that do not fit well with the rational model. A somewhat similar type of cognitive processing has been noted as well among entrepreneurs and may help to explain why such people can emerge as risk avoidant in nature although making certain startup and investment decisions that give every objective appearance of possessing high risk.

Biases and Heuristics in Entrepreneurial Decisions

A growing body of literature indicates that entrepreneurs are characterized by a proclivity for using biases and heuristics in their approach to business decisions. A series of reports (Busenitz 1999; Busenitz and Barney 1994, 1997) demonstrated that overconfidence prevails among entrepreneurs, as well as a tendency to base decisions on evidence from case examples and small samples (representativeness). These biases and simplifying heuristics are characteristic of entrepreneurs much more than of general managers within large firms. Other studies have found a similar tendency to overestimate the chances of success (Cooper, Woo, and Dunkelburg 1988; Palich and Bagby 1995). Another study differentiates the heuristics used by innovative as opposed to less innovative entrepreneurs (Manimala 1992).

The relevance of research in this area for an understanding of entrepreneurial risk propensities is apparent, but there is a need for much more of the same. Other biases and heuristics may well be operative, and in any event the processes involved need to be tied much more closely to what happens when risky entrepreneurial decisions are made. For instance, the use of heuristics may well be as much a function of the stresses inherent in the entrepreneurial situation as of individual differences associated with being an entrepreneur. There is a great deal that we do not know. The existing studies use a wide range of measurement procedures, making it difficult to compare results across studies. It looks, for instance, as if managers tend to believe in their ability to exercise postdecisional control and thus avoid risk in this manner (Shapira 1995). The research on entrepreneurs, on the other hand, suggests a belief in predecisional control, which means that risk is removed in a completely different manner. However, because the measures used in the two domains are different, it is impossible to know whether this is really what is happening. It is certainly not the time to close the book on entrepreneur-manager differences in risk propensity; we do not even know for sure what risk is in the minds of those involved.

The Role of Implicit and Self-Attributed Motives

Another issue that requires exploration involves the differences between the results of the Stewart and Roth (2001) analysis and those obtained with the MSCS–T, as well as between the MSCS–T and SM Scale findings. The evidence here tends to indicate that entrepreneurs are both risk takers and risk avoiders, depending on the type of measurement procedures employed. Why might such contradictory results occur?

A possible approach to solving this conundrum involves the differentiation between implicit (measured by projective techniques) and self-attributed (measured by self-report tests) motives. These two concepts have been referred to as "the most differentiated and advanced theorizing about cross-method disparities" (Meyer 1996, 575). The author then goes on to provide definitions as follows:

> Implicit motivations are viewed as being more unconscious and physiologically related, as developing earlier in life and not requiring language and verbal mediation to solidify, and as being more strongly associated with long-term spontaneous behavioral trends. In contrast, self-attributed motives are understood as having different historical antecedents and as being better predictors of conscious choices and immediate, situationally defined behaviors. . . . Cross-method disagreement is thus not a question of test invalidity. Rather it is a phenomenon that can lead to a more refined identification of people and more accurate behavioral predictions (Meyer 1996, 575).

Formulations of this type began with McClelland (1961) and are most fully explicated in McClelland, Koestner, and Weinberger (1989). The research shows that implicit motives have a relationship with memories of affective experiences congruent with a particular goal state, whereas self-attributed motives relate to memories of routine experiences (Woike 1995). Implicit motives seem to operate to produce more personally meaningful memories (McAdams 1982). They play an important role in determining the content and structure of events represented in episodic memory and operate at a level that taps into less conscious aspects of personality (Woike, Gershkovich, Piorkowski, and Polo 1999).

In this research, the stimulus for projective response has been some type of picture cue, whereas self-attributed motives have been measured with multiple-choice items and true-false variants such as those contained in the Jackson Personality Inventory (Jackson 1989). However, there have been instances that have moved beyond the domain of the TAT to use other projective procedures such as sentence cues (see, for example, French 1958).

Will the implicit-self-attributed distinction handle the conundrum? It clearly would have the best chance of doing so if the correlation between implicit (projective) measures and self-attributed (self-report) measures were essentially .00. Then, it would be most likely that the projective approach could yield a number of associations between risk avoidance and entrepreneurship, and the self-attributed approach could produce an equal number of associations between risk taking and entrepreneurship. This essentially uncorrelated nature of the relationship involved is what McClelland, Koestner, and Weinberger (1989) hypothesized originally, and they cite data to this effect for achievement motivation overall. Using a wider range of motives, Schultheiss and Brunstein (2001) also failed to find any overlap when the same characteristics measured in different ways were correlated. However, a meta-analysis based on 36 correlations conducted by Spangler (1992) for achievement motivation as a whole produced a significant, although small, positive relationship.

All of these analyses used TAT indexes of implicit motivation. There are also relevant data from Form H of the MSCS, the form that measures managerial motivation, although there are no relevant data from Form T, the form that includes the Risk Avoidance subscale (Miner 1993). The Form H correlations with self-report measures of the same constructs across 10 samples that yield meaningful data average .15. However, this same median value obtained when the correlations are calculated using dissimilar constructs is .10. Thus, using the latter data as a base, there appears to be a positive relationship, although it is small and certainly below .10.

On the basis of the evidence, an average positive relationship between implicit and self-attributed measures does appear to exist, but it is of such small magnitude that it does not seem to preclude the disparate pattern of results that has been obtained. Nevertheless, we do not have data on the specific risk-related motives that are at issue here, and to have the two types of motives produce results that are directly antithetical is not exactly what one might have expected. (See for instance Bornstein 2002, for data on the way in which similar research on interpersonal dependency has evolved over time, producing a substantially different pattern.)

RESEARCH FOR THE FUTURE

It is tempting to conclude that projective techniques (and implicit motives) produce one result, whereas self-report measures (and self-attributed motives) yield something completely different. However, the relationships between these two in general are far from being well established, and in any event, in the case of risk, we have data on the projective side for only one instrument. What would happen if another sentence completion measure were used, or some different type of projective technique? It is too early to say that we have a clear example of the operation of a projective-self-report moderator. Something is moderating the risk relationship, but we do not know as yet exactly how to define it.

A possible moderator of the relationship is the stage of the entrepreneurial firm's development as it progresses through the growth cycle, often moving from a small entrepreneurial organization to a large bureaucratic one (see Miner 1997a). Yet we know little about how risk operates in this framework. A possibility is that it diminishes, with risk pervasive in the start-up and minimal in the managed hierarchy, matching some of the Stewart and Roth (2001) findings. However, one is also reminded of the many instances in which start-ups involve part-time work by the entrepreneur (while holding a full-time job), a "garage" setting, and little initial capital outlay, that is, low risk. Conversely, many growth situations move to aggrandizement that involves changing product lines, new markets, and investment decisions dealing with expanded capital outlays, that is, high risk. A case can clearly be made that managing risk can be essential throughout all stages of the entrepreneurial process. This ubiquity would appear to call for much more study of risk in whatever form it may take and at whatever stage. It does not seem wise to close the book on the relationship between risk propensity and entrepreneurial status or firm growth.

This call for future research on risk should not be construed as being at the expense of other studies dealing with other skills, abilities, motives, cognitions, and cognitive styles; a balanced approach seems preferable. Concepts of risk came to entrepreneurship early through economic theory and because McClelland (1961) included risk in his achievement motivation syndrome. However, economic theory is not always relevant to all entrepreneurship questions, and McClelland's view of achievement striving included much more than his formulations regarding risk. Furthermore, research with the MSCS–T indicates that motives such as a desire to achieve through one's own efforts, a desire to introduce innovative solutions, a desire to receive feedback on performance, and a desire to think about the future and establish goals are somewhat more powerful than the desire to minimize risk. In view of these considerations, we are far less sanguine than Stewart and Roth (2001) appear to be regarding the potential of risk propensity to operate as the key variable in any future theory of entrepreneurship. It may ultimately come to serve in this role, but its current position is far removed from such status. We need to be open to a great deal more research on other constructs, as well as on risk propensity.

To these areas for future research we would add the matters discussed previously—biases and heuristics as well as the implicit-self-attributed differential. These appear to be promising approaches to obtaining an understanding of how risk propensity operates in the entrepreneurship domain, and that is why they are given attention here. Yet the questions involved have not been solved, and in fact we appear to be at a point in this area of study in which the number of questions is actually increasing as more research is conducted. It is not yet time to shut down the research engine. The conservative alternative, the "I don't know" response, needs to be kept open, perhaps for a long time.

CHAPTER 28

RELATIONSHIPS INVOLVING PROJECTIVE TECHNIQUES, SELF-REPORT MEASURES, AND CRITERIA

INTRODUCTION

The selection contained here was published as part of a review article entitled "Role Motivation Theories" contained in a handbook presentation edited by Jay C. Thomas and Daniel L. Segal (Miner 2006b). The material represents the first one-fourth of the published chapter. The remainder contains material on role motivation theory that closely parallels much of the preceding content of this volume.

The analysis was initially carried out for presentation as part of a symposium on unconscious motivation held in 2005 at a meeting of the Society for Industrial/Organizational Psychology (SIOP). This represented one of the few such treatments—if not the only one—of unconscious motivation within organizational behavior.

* * *

ROLE MOTIVATION DATA

My thought in introducing the subject of role motivation theory is to provide certain data derived from the theory—data that are thus emblematic of the type of ideas the theory can generate. These data are given in Table 28.1 and Table 28.2; they deal with findings from four studies, two of which utilize entrepreneurs as subjects and two involving managers. The former are longitudinal in nature and draw upon follow-up analyses to establish criterion relationships; the latter are concurrent.

These are all the data I know of that compare the Miner Sentence Completion Scales (MSCSs) with various self-report measures using similar constructs. The MSCSs represent

From John B. Miner, "Role Motivation Theories," in John. C. Thomas and Daniel L. Segal (Eds.), *Comprehensive Handbook of Personality and Psychopathology*. Volume 1. *Personality and Everyday Functioning* (Hoboken, NJ: John Wiley & Sons 2006), 233–237.

Table 28.1

Correlations between Projective Techniques and Self-Report Measures and Criteria (Plus Intercorrelations) **Involving Similar and Overlapping Constructs for Theoretically Congruent Situations**

	Criterion Correlations	Intercorrelations		Summaries	
Measures	Follow-up Success as Entrepreneur	(a)	(b)	Median Correlation	No. with $p < .05$
Study 1—Buffalo, NY Area Entrepreneurs					
N = 100 (Miner 1997a)					
Achievement Motivation					
Projective Techniques					
MSCS–Form T					
(a) Total Score	.42**			.30	2 (100%)
(b) Self-Achievement Subscale	.18*				
Self-report Measures					
(c) Lynn Achievement Motivation Questionnaire	.14	.17	.19	.10	0 (0%)
(d) Elizur Achievement Motivation Index	.09	.14	–.04		
(e) Ghiselli SDI–Need for Occupational Achievement	.10	.08	–.03	.11 for intercorrelations	
Desire to Innovate					
Projective Techniques					
MSCS–Form T					
(a) Total Score	.42**			.43	2 (100%)
(b) Personal Innovation Subscale	.44**				
Self-report Measures					
(c) Rowe/Mason DSI–Conceptual	–.01	.17	.21*	.13	1 (33%)
(d) Slocum/Hellriegel PSQ–Intuition	.13	.14	.36**	.18 for intercorrelations	
(e) Ghiselli SDI–Initiative	.22*	.19	.15		
Desire to Avoid Risks					
Projective Techniques					
MSCS–Form T					
(a) Total Score	.42**			.43	2 (100%)
(b) Avoiding Risks Subscale	.44**				
Self-report Measures					
(c) Shure/Meeker Risk Avoidance Scale	–.10	.01	.07	–.10	0 (0%)
				.04 for intercorrelations	

	Criterion Correlations			Intercorrelations		Summaries	
Measures	Entrepreneurial Propensity Score	Business Plan Grade	Follow-up Behavior as Entrepreneur	(a)	(b)	Median Correlation	No. with $p < .05$
Study 2—SUNY/Buffalo Graduate Students in Entrepreneurship							
N = 159 (Miner 1997a)							
Achievement Motivation							
Projective Techniques							
MSCS–Form T							
(a) Total Score	.59**	.38**	.41**			.395	5 (83%)
(b) Self-Achievement Subscale	.45**	.11	.27*				
Self-report Measures	(None available)						
Desire to Innovate							
Projective Techniques							
MSCS–Form T							
(a) Total Score	.59**	.38**	.41**			.395	6 (100%)
(b) Personal Innovation Subscale	.44**	.24**	.33**				
Self-report Measures							
(c) Rowe/Mason DSI–Conceptual	.14	.13	.12	.07	.12	.125	1 (17%)
(d) Slocum/Hellriegel PSQ–Intuition	.01	.08	.23*	–.02	.12	.095 for intercorrelations	
Desire to Avoid Risks							
Projective Techniques							
MSCS–Form T							
(a) Total Score	.59**	.38**	.41**			.26	3 (50%)
(b) Avoiding Risks Subscale	.05	.14	–.04				
Self-report Measures							
(c) Shure/Meeker Risk Avoidance Scale	–.21**	–.05	–.17	–.01	.30**	–.17	1 (33%)
						.145 for intercorrelations	

(continued)

Table 28.1 (*continued*)

Measures	Criterion Correlations		Intercorrelations		Summaries	
	Management Performance	Appraisals Potential	(a)	(b)	Median Correlation	No. with $p < .05$
Study 3—Business Managers from a Single Firm						
N = 420 (Miner 1965a)						
Power Motivation						
Projective Techniques						
MSCS–Form H						
(a) Total Score	.24*	.43**			.265	4 (100%)
(b) Imposing Wishes subscale	.29**	.24*				
Self-report Measures						
(c) Kuder Preference Record-Vocational-Supervisory Scale	.14**	.24**	.45**	.32**	.19	2 (100%)
					.385 for intercorrelations	
	Composite Success Score					
Study 4—Human Resource Managers from Varied Firms						
N = 101 (Miner 1977b)						
Power Motivation						
Projective Techniques						
MSCS–Form H						
(a) Total Score	.28**				.195	1 (50%)
(b) Imposing Wishes Subscale	.11					
Self-report Measures						
(c) Ghiselli SDI–Supervisory Ability	.18*		.26**	NS	.08	1 (33%)
(d) Ghiselli SDI–Need for Power	.08		NS	NS	.11 (est.) for intercorrelations	
(e) Kuder Preference Record-Vocational-Supervisory Scale	.08		.38**	.12		
Summary of Summaries						
Projective Techniques					.35	85%
Self-report Measures					.10	31%
Intercorrelations					.11	

Note: The Composite Success Score criterion reflects the position level attained in the hierarchy ($r = .80$) and the income from that position ($r = .71$). The three criteria are all significantly related (at $p < .05$) in the range .22 to .54.

MSCS = Miner Sentence Completion Scale.

Lynn Achievement Motivation Questionnaire (Lynn 1969); Elizur Achievement Motivation Index (Elizur 1984); Ghiselli SDI = Self Description Index (Ghiselli 1971); Rowe/Mason DSI = Decision Style Inventory (Rowe and Mason 1987); Slocum/Hellriegel PSQ = Problem Solving Questionnaire (Slocum and Hellriegel 1983); Shure/Meeker Risk Avoidance Scale (Shure and Meeker 1967); Kuder Preference Record-Vocational-Supervisory Scale (Miner 1977b)

$*p < .05$; $**p < .01$

Table 28.2

Correlations between Projective Techniques and Self-Report Measures and Criteria (Plus Intercorrelations) **Involving Similar and Overlapping Constructs for Theoretically Noncongruent Situations**

	Criterion Correlations	Intercorrelations		Summaries	
Measures	Follow-up Success as Entrepreneur	(a)	(b)	Median Correlation	No. with $p < .05$
Study 1					
Power Motivation					
Projective Techniques					
MSCS–Form H					
(a) Total Score	.21*			.19	1 (50%)
(b) Imposing Wishes Subscale	.17				
Self-report Measures					
(c) Rowe/Mason DSI–Directive	.16	.18	.25*	.085	1 (25%)
(d) Slocum/Hellriegel PSQ-Thinking	–.08	.16	.24*	.15 for intercorrelations	
Ghiselli SDI–					
(e) Supervisory Ability	.01	.03	–.06		
(f) Need for Power	.22*	.14	.05		
Affiliation Motivation					
Projective Techniques					
MSCS–Form P					
(a) Total Score	.24*			.155	1 (50%)
(b) Providing Help Subscale	.07				
Self-report Measures					
(c) Rowe/Mason DSI–Behavioral	–.09	.20*	.15	.085	0 (0%)
(d) Slocum/Hellriegel PSQ–Feeling	.08	.08	.24*	.17 for intercorrelations	
(e) Fiedler's LPC Score	.09	–.09	.19		
(f) Elizur Work Values Questionnaire–Social Values Items	.10	.30**	.02		

(*continued*)

Table 28.2 (*continued*)

Measures	Criterion Correlations			Intercorrelations		Summaries	
	Entrepreneurial Propensity Score	Business Plan Grade	Follow-up Behavior as Entrepreneur	(a)	(b)	Median Correlation	No. with $p < .05$
Study 2							
Power Motivation							
Projective Techniques							
MSCS–Form H							
(a) Total Score	.11	.14	.12			.115	1 (17%)
(b) Imposing Wishes Subscale	.17*	–.06	–.01				
Self-report Measures							
(c) Rowe/Mason DSI–Directive	.07	–.07	–.07	.05	–.07	–.07	1 (17%)
(d) Slocum/Hellriegel PSQ–Thinking	.09	–.21*	–.13	.15	.17*	.10 for intercorrelations	
Affiliation Motivation							
Projective Techniques							
MSCS–Form P							
(a) Total Score	.08	.02	.42**			.11	2 (33%)
(b) Providing Help Subscale	.14	.06	.31*				
Self-report Measures							
(c) Rowe/Mason DSI–Behavioral	–.21*	–.01	–.10	–.06	.02	–.05	2 (33%)
(d) Slocum/Hellriegel PSQ–Feeling	–.09	.21*	.13	.06	.29**	.04 for intercorrelations	
Summary of Summaries							
Projective Techniques						.135	(37%)
Self-report Measures						.02	(19%)
Intercorrelations						.12	

Note: MSCS = Miner Sentence Completion Scale; Ghiselli SDI = Self Description Index (Ghiselli 1971); Fiedler's LPC Score = Least Preferred Coworker Score (Fiedler 1967); Elizur Work Values Questionnaire (Elizur 1984).

$^*p < .05$; $^{**}p < .01$

the preferred procedure for measuring the constructs of role motivation theory and thus are projective in nature. Projective techniques such as the MSCSs unearth both conscious and unconscious motives, but with a heavy emphasis on the latter; self-report measures deal entirely with the conscious level. Projective techniques accomplish their measurement processes by eliciting typical samples of cognitive, emotional, and perceptual content in response to ambiguous—or, as in the case of the MSCSs, more content-focused—stimuli that are then analyzed to determine meanings and motives. In contrast, self-report indexes insert meanings and motives into multiple-choice alternatives, so that responses are predetermined and channeled into what the investigator is looking for. In the first instance the really difficult work begins after a response occurs, whereas in the latter instance it occurs in the item-development phase. Errors in projective measurement tend to occur because of failures in interpretation; errors in self-report measurement are usually attributable to inappropriate item specification.

Projective techniques are said to measure implicit motives, whereas self-report approaches measure self-attributed motives. According to this distinction the two types of motives are quite different in origin and yield substantial cross-method disparities. Meyer (1996) provides the following definitions and theoretical elaborations:

> Implicit motivations are viewed as being more unconscious and physiologically related, as developing earlier in life and not requiring language and verbal mediation to solidify, and as being more strongly associated with long-term spontaneous behavioral trends. In contrast, self-attributed motives are understood as having different historical antecedents and as being better predictors of conscious choices and immediate, situationally defined behaviors. . . . Cross-method disagreement is thus not a question of test invalidity. Rather it is a phenomenon that can lead to a more refined identification of people and more accurate behavioral predictions. (Meyer 1996, 575)

The cross-method disagreement has been hypothesized to result in a correlation between projective and self-report measures of essentially .00, and early data supported that conclusion (McClelland, Koestner, and Weinberger 1989). However, more recent and comprehensive findings suggest a small positive relationship (Spangler 1992). Other results that focused more specifically on the MSCSs yield this same positive conclusion (Miner and Raju 2004), and indeed that is what the data of Tables 28.1 and 28.2 indicate, with median intercorrelations of .11 and .12, respectively.

Thus, one thing that can be learned from these tables is that correlations between projective and self-report measures are indeed low, as expected, and accordingly that it matters which type of measure is used to validate role motivation theory. The theoretical approach of choice involves some type of projective index because the theory posits that unconscious (implicit) motives are crucial.

Congruent Situations

In both Tables 28.1 and 28.2 criterion relationships are given for both projective techniques and self-report measures, and in both instances the median value is higher for projectives and the number of significant findings is higher as well. Yet what is really meaningful here is the comparison of the Table 28.1 data with those of Table 28.2: the comparison under theoretically congruent conditions with theoretically noncongruent conditions. In the former instance the projective technique correlations average .35 with 85 percent significant at $p < .05$ or better and values as high as .59 with numerous findings in the .40s.

Noncongruent Situations

In the situation where role motivation theory does not anticipate many sizable criteria relationships, these correlations are much lower and much less frequently significant as well; they top out in the low .20s. Thus, it is not only the difference between projective and self-report measurement, unconscious versus conscious, that matters but the difference between research situations where a theoretical fit, or congruence, exists between the individual's predominant motives and the work context. It requires considerable elaboration to discover what this theoretical fit means—elaboration that has been provided in previous chapters of this book.

COMPARING PROJECTIVE AND SELF-REPORT MEASURES

Any such comparative analysis depends upon the legitimacy of the procedures used to classify the measurement instruments involved. Are the MSCSs truly projective techniques and are the Lynn, Elizur, Ghiselli, Rowe/Mason, Slocum/Hellriegel, Shure/Meeker, Kuder, and Fiedler instruments legitimate instances of the self-report genre? With regard to the former instance sentence completion measures have long been accepted as projective techniques (see Bell 1948). The self-report measures have a common factor in that they deal with situations where the person describes himself or herself, and does so in some type of multiple-choice context. The one such instance that does not clearly meet this criterion is the LPC (least preferred coworker) measure from Fiedler (1967).

LPC as a Special Case

LPC asks the individual to "describe the person with whom you can work least well" in terms of a set of adjectives. As such it concerns both the person and an ambiguous "other." There is both a self-report and a projective element as well. According to Ayman (2002) "the LPC scale . . . is not a self-report measure of behaviors or personal values of a respondent. It is an indirect measure of the leader's inner needs or orientation, similar to a projective test like the Thematic Apperception Test (200)." Elsewhere, "Its lack of relationship with most other measures of similar constructs may be due to its quasi-projective nature (205)." This semi-projective aspect deserves consideration; yet Ayman (2002) acknowledges that LPC is usually considered as a self-report measure. In any event this one disclaimer should be recognized; otherwise the self-report indexes are quite compatible.

Differences in Reliability

Another consideration is that the self-report measures might be less reliable than the MSCS indexes thus diluting validity to a point where the differences reported in Tables 28.1 and 28.2 are obtained. On this score all of the measures noted appear to meet generally accepted levels of reliability—both projective and self-report—but not to the same degree. The median reliability coefficient for the MSCS indexes in the tables is a clear .81. The data available on the self-report measures are less precise, however. The best estimate available would place the median at around .70 (excluding the LPC value of .67) (Ayman 2002). Thus, there does appear to be some leverage that would inflate the projective criterion relationships relative to those of the self-report findings. However, this effect is insufficient to account for the results presented in Table 28.1, which do not include LPC at all.

CHAPTER 29

CONGRUENCE AND THE SIGNIFICANCE OF CAREERS IN TESTING ROLE MOTIVATION THEORY

USING TASK MOTIVE PATTERNS

INTRODUCTION

The analysis presented here was included in a Society for Industrial/Organizational Psychology (SIOP) symposium in 2003, but it has not been published previously. Comments by Edwin A. Locke who served as a discussant at the symposium are gratefully acknowledged and have been incorporated into the article.

The approach I have taken here is applicable not only to the task theory and to Form T of the Miner Sentence Completion Scale (MSCS), but to the other role motivation theories as well. The reason for starting with task theory is that there are more studies, and thus more data, to be considered within the task domain. Subsequent chapters will take up hierarchic theory, and then professional theory, using this same approach. Much of what is considered here is refocused to apply subsequently to the hierarchic and professional domain; thus this will serve as an introduction and model for a subset containing Chapters 30 and 31 as well.

* * *

The major concern here is with task organizations, task theory, task motivation, and task roles. For present purposes this means entrepreneurial roles in business contexts, although task theory can apply beyond the entrepreneurial world, extending even to non-business organizations; it has been found to operate in the religious sphere, for example (Osborne 2003).

Although research on role motivation theories previously has had implications for career choice (see for instance Miner 1974b), what is distinctive about the analyses of the present research is that they focus specifically on the dynamics of careers and on careers that extend into the leadership context. In the past, entrepreneurial careers have been treated as one among several possible outcomes from a fit between task motivation and task roles (Miner 1993; 1997a) and entrepreneurial leadership careers have been given only limited attention (Miner 2002a).

In this chapter careers as the outcome or criterion variable become the special concern of the analyses. The hypotheses to be investigated involve a combining of this career emphasis with the fit or congruence formulations that have characterized role motivation theory from its beginnings.

HYPOTHESIS GENERATION

For the organizations involved, the theory expects that given appropriate staffing, and thus motivational congruence, an organization of a particular type will run smoothly and produce desired outcomes (see Jones and Lichtenstein 2000). For *individuals* possessing the appropriate motives, a career in an organizational unit congruent with those motives will lead to a variety of positive personal outcomes, including an extended career in the type (or form) of organization specified. Within a task system an entrepreneur operates as an individual moving to deal with crises and grasping opportunities with relatively less reference to hierarchic regulations, professional constraints, or group norms. In a very real sense entrepreneurial careers exhibit those characteristics that exemplify the protean career (see Hall 2002).

The standing hypothesis from theory that applies in these contexts is to the effect that in task systems task (achievement) motivation should be at a high level among task performers (entrepreneurs), and it should be positively correlated with task success indexes; task motivation should not differentiate in these ways within other types of systems (Miner 1993, 25–26).

Roles and Careers

For role motivation theory, roles are institutionalized and they are informal; they are also a function of leadership prototypes and implicit theories (Lord and Maher 1991). With regard to this latter point, Hunt, Boal, and Sorensen (1990) note that organizational structure tends to influence the development of leadership prototypes and they cite the Miner (1980b) typology in this regard. Thus task organizations should elicit a particular set of leadership prototypes not only from followers, but from any observer (or role-set member, or stakeholder). Leadership in organizational contexts, and careers as well, would appear to be phenomena that exist in the perceptions of beholders, subject to the same biasing and stereotyping processes that characterize perceptions in general. As a result observers of entrepreneurs and entrepreneurial leaders send roles and role prescriptions; those people with the motives needed to match these role expectations tend to be judged favorably and to experience positive affect in the task roles.

But the role prescriptions or prototypes involved are also institutionalized. Institutions establish cultural rules that give collective meaning and value to phenomena such as perceptions. Institutionalization is the process through which these perceptions are normatively and cognitively held in place and thus come to be taken for granted (Scott 2001). Institutionalized perceptions (like actions) are not a matter of individual choice, but rather function in accordance with broad social scripts. Task role prescriptions (or prototypes) have this driven, socially conforming quality; they tend to be held in common by most observers, although not necessarily consciously so.

Institutionalization may be informal. If this is the case, it tends to operate in the manner of rules, based on implicit understanding, primarily socially derived rather than sanctioned by formal position. Such informal institutions serve to influence the ways in which organizational forms function (Zenger, Lazzarini, and Poppo 2002). Thus the perceptual prototypes (role prescriptions) of observers create the informal expectations according to which entrepreneurs (and their firms) operate throughout their careers. If they have the matching motives (in some mix), they tend to play their roles very well, and are thus apt to be frequently reinforced by themselves and others. Thus, their decisions and actions are perpetuated; they stay in their careers.

Role motivation theory, as it has been extended to encompass leadership and leadership careers (Miner 2002a; Foti and Miner 2003), takes the position that understanding leadership requires that the processes involved be couched in the institutionalized roles established by the particular type of organizational form operating. Thus leadership differs in hierarchic, professional, group, and task systems. The present paper focuses on the task or entrepreneurial context for leadership and leadership careers.

The standing hypothesis from theory is to the effect that leadership roles take different forms in different organizational contexts and require different types of people to perform in these roles effectively—people whose motives are strongly congruent with the particular organizational type involved; thus, leadership careers vary in important ways with the organizational forms in which they occur (Miner 2002a, 318). In all instances, leadership involves the ability "to influence, motivate, and enable others to contribute toward the effectiveness and success of the organizations of which they are members" (House, Wright, and Aditya 1997, 548).

In invoking the concept of a leadership career, however, the theory views leadership in a somewhat different manner than has been typical in the past. In this view leadership is an activity to which people devote their energies for long periods of their lives; it is comparable to any other career. It is not merely a stage in career development, as has often been claimed in the vocational psychology literature (see Leong and Serafica 2001); it is a type of career to which some individuals aspire in the first place, and toward which a developmental experience may be devoted.

The Concept of Fit

Tinsley (2000a; 2000b) has provided a comprehensive review of the person-environment fit (or congruence) literature and concludes that this model yields a valid and useful approach to theory. Dawis (2000) goes beyond Tinsley, contending that the person-environment fit model provides the paradigm par excellence for psychology. Thus, there is reason to couch a psychological theory in terms of the person-environment fit model if it is at all possible to do so.

Role motivation theory does in fact have many characteristics of the congruence model as set forth by Tinsley, and thus may be viewed as a variant on that theoretical theme. The *desires* component, reflecting the person, is inherent in the "matching motive patterns." These would appear to be comparable to needs, goals, values, interests, and preferences, although rarely specified in these exact terms.

The *supplies* component, reflecting the environment, is inherent in the role requirements. These role specifications are not designated as reinforcers, benefits, satisfiers, or payoffs, but they have the capacity to produce all of these. When behavior generated by strong motives matches the role expectations of role senders in the environment, positive supplies are generated. These role expectations differ, however, depending on the type of organization involved.

The congruence between motives and roles is expected to generate outcomes that in role motivation theory research have included turnover intentions and actual turnover, vocational choice and entry, performance, occupational success, tenure, and job satisfaction. The career that a person has chosen and followed over a period of years, extending up to the whole career bounded by retirement, is such an outcome; it may or may not be a leadership career. Tinsley (2000b) calls for more longitudinal research using the person-environment fit model, and thus more extensive coverage of careers. Role motivation theory research has utilized predictions out to a seven year maximum, and has involved studies on whole careers extending beyond the age of seventy. These analyses are included in what follows.

The Route to Hypotheses

The hypotheses that guide the research reported here were developed out of a synthesis of the (1) congruence or fit formulations of the role motivation theory; (2) the concept of entrepreneurial leadership; and (3) a focus on careers, including entrepreneurial leadership careers, as the outcome to be given special attention and thus distinguished from other outcomes or criteria. The first two of these have been treated previously, but it remains to be explained how this research came to focus on careers.

For many years it had been evident that the Miner Sentence Completion Scale, in some form, is significantly correlated with measures of matching occupational interests derived from the Kuder Preference Record (Miner, 1960b; 1977b) and the Strong Vocational Interest Blank (Gantz, Erickson, and Stephenson 1971). These correlations are in the high .30s and .40s—substantial, but not unusually large (see Table 29.1 for examples).

However, a recent investigation of the risk taking and risk avoidant tendencies of entrepreneurs (Miner and Raju 2004) yielded the finding that while entrepreneurial leaders and entrepreneurs in general tended to be *risk avoidant* as assessed by the Miner Sentence Completion Scale–Form T (a projective technique), these groups tended to emerge as *risk prone* when various self-report indexes were used. These findings are consistent with the distinction between implicit motives and self-attributed motives first proposed by McClelland, Koestner, and Weinberger (1989). These authors indicate that correlations extending across measurement methods (projective and self-report) may be expected to be much lower than correlations within methods. Accordingly a reassessment of the MSCS-interest inventory results should produce much larger correlations, if the same type of measurement process were employed, restricting the data either to implicit or self-attributed motives; the use of different measurement procedures may well have limited the size of the correlations obtained in the early research.

A number of recent findings give further credibility to the view that interest inventories

Table 29.1

Correlations between Task Role Motivation Theory Variables and *Congruent* Careers (Including Leadership Careers) **as Entrepreneurs**

	N		Motive Patterns					
Samples and Analyses	Congruent Condition	Non-congruent Condition	Total Task	Achieving on One's Own	Minimizing Risks	Receiving Feedback	Introducing Innovations	Planning and Establishing Goals
Princeton Graduates (class of 1948)								
Entrepreneurial career vs. other	24	60	.75**	.48*	.42**	.32**	.42**	.53**
Entrepreneurial leadership career								
vs. non leader entrepreneurs	19	5	.67**	.53*	–.36	.61*	.46	.21
vs. non-entrepreneurs	19	60	.76*	.51**	.35**	.37**	.45**	.52**
High Technology Entrepreneurs								
Initial								
Entrepreneurial career vs. other	118	41	.25*	.46*	.41*	.58**	.02	.03
Entrepreneurial leadership career								
vs. non-leader entrepreneurs	59	59	.77**	.66**	.37**	.54**	.57**	.31**
vs. non-entrepreneurs	59	41	.58**	.47**	.30**	.40**	.38**	.23**
Follow-up								
Entrepreneurial leadership career								
vs. non-leader entrepreneurs	24	35	.70**	.66**	.14	.38**	.49**	.46**
vs. non-entrepreneurs	24	41	.57**	.41**	.18	.36**	.35**	.37**
Buffalo, NY Area Entrepreneurs								
Career success level	84	—	.42**	.18*	–.09	.15	.44**	.29**
Entrepreneurial leadership career vs. non-leader entrepreneurs	45	44	.71**	.41**	.26*	.42**	.38**	.15
SUNY/Buffalo Graduate Students								
Projected propensity for an entrepreneurial career	159	—	.59**	.45**	.05	.35**	.44**	.23**
Actual entrepreneurial career (early) vs. other	30	85	.41**	.27*	–.04	.17	.33**	.33**
File Samples								
Entrepreneurial leadership career vs. managerial career	65	71	.66**	.59**	.49**	.23**	.46**	.17**

$^{**}p < .01$; $^{*}p < .05$

may converge both with the MSCSs and with individual career choices to a substantial degree. This three-way convergence suggests that career variables may well be embedded not only in the various occupational interest indexes, but in the various role motivation scales as well. Paramount among these findings are data indicating that interest inventories yield effective predictions of career choice, entry, and to a degree career stability (Meir and Tziner 2001). Career commitment involves a wide-ranging constellation of variables, which would appear to include relevant interests (Goulet and Singh 2002). Interest inventories, such as the Kuder and the Strong, tend to exhibit considerable convergent validity with one another in spite of the diversity of measurement approaches involved (Savickas, Taber, and Spokane 2002). Like the MSCSs, interest inventories may be viewed as indexes of personality (Tinsley 2000a). Interest measures should generally be considered as reflecting emotions caused by cognitive mechanisms (Barak 2001); the same may be said of the MSCSs. Barak (2001) also advocates a more comprehensive, open-ended and general approach that appears to be of the kind inherent in sentence completion measurement.

Thus, the unique facets that ultimately come to characterize this research are as follows:

- Using a measure of task motivation to predict career patterns (congruent versus noncongruent).
- Comparing the prediction of career-related outcomes with other more traditional outcomes.
- Comparing the effectiveness of a measure of task motivation with alternative predictors of entrepreneural outcomes.
- Applying a role motivation perspective to entrepreneurial leadership.

The two hypotheses (and their components) follow.

Hypothesis 1. *Congruent analyses, which are conducted comparing those with careers inside the task domain against those having careers outside that domain on measures of task motivation, should produce correlations that—*

a) exceed correlations obtained using only those having careers outside the task domain;

b) exceed correlations obtained using criterion variables other than career status, but still appropriate to the task domain, such as performance indexes;

c) exceed correlations obtained using predictors other than measures of task motivation, but still appropriate to the task domain, such as locus of control indexes.

Hypothesis 2. *Congruent analyses, which are conducted comparing those with leadership careers inside the task domain against either those having non-leader careers inside the task domain or those having careers outside the domain on measures of task motivation, should produce correlations that—*

a) exceed correlations obtained using only those having careers outside the task domain;

b) exceed correlations obtained using criterion variables other than career status, but still appropriate to the task domain, such as performance indexes;

c) exceed correlations obtained using predictors other than measures of task motivation, but still appropriate to the task domain, such as locus of control indexes.

Thus, task leadership careers should operate in terms of these correlational analyses in the same manner as specified in Hypothesis 1 for other task careers.

METHOD

Measures

The measure of task motivation used in this investigation was the Miner Sentence Completion Scale–Form T (MSCS–T) (Miner 1986; 1993). The major dependent variable of this research was the career—entrepreneurial or otherwise—undertaken by the respondent. Ideally this would be reflected in a whole career extending up to final retirement. In actual practice it is more frequently reflected in the position held at some mid-career point when testing occurs. The stability of the career within a domain and the length of its duration are important criteria in assessing any such career index. As indicated previously, organizational leadership is viewed as a career phenomenon; in the entrepreneurial context leaders may be compared with non-leader entrepreneurs, who do not meet the leadership criteria, or they may be compared against respondents in other than entrepreneurial careers.

In several of the study samples it was possible to obtain data using an organizational description questionnaire, the Oliver Organization Description Questionnaire (OODQ) (Oliver 1981; 1982). This measure was used to verify the organizations used in the research as entrepreneurial or task, and thus to confirm a priori domain designations. The OODQ scores were not used in the actual selection of study participants or to provide moderator variables.

Studies

Presenting correlations is inherent in the hypotheses and a key aspect of this article; all of the analyses utilize this statistical form. The five studies represent all of the currently existing research conducted by the author that is relevant to the stated hypotheses. The focus on the strength of relationships, rather than the significance of differences, is in line with recent recommendations in the literature and seems best calculated to communicate effectively with the audience (Breaugh 2003; Mitchell and James 2001). Alternative indexes could have been used in certain instances, but in the interest of consistency correlations are reported throughout.

In evaluating the correlation coefficients that emerge from this research, it is helpful to employ the guidelines proposed by Hemphill (2003), using data marshaled from meta-analysis: lower third = < .20, middle third = .20 to .30, and upper third = > .30. Any correlation of .50 or above is considered quite large.

In what follows, the correlational methods utilized were Pearson *r* where both distributions were continuous and approximated normality, biserial *r* where one distribution had those qualities and the other (the careers) was dichotomous but with an underlying continuous distribution, and point biserial *r* where the dichotomous variable was clearly of a point nature (yes or no).

Princeton Graduates—Class of 1948 [See Chapter 22]

This study utilized 50-year career data and thus dealt with employment up to retirement, or very close to it (whole careers). It is described in Miner (2002a), although the data presented there are far less than what are included in the present analyses. The entrepreneurial sample numbers 24, 19 of whom had careers in entrepreneurial leadership. For purposes of analysis those participants who had entrepreneurial careers or entrepreneurial leadership careers were considered to be in the congruent condition and those who did not meet these requirements were in the noncongruent condition.

High Technology Entrepreneurs [See Chapter 15]

The subjects of this study were applicants for National Science Foundation grants to develop innovative technologies. Prior publications dealing with this sample include Miner (1993; 2002a), Miner, Smith, and Bracker (1989), and Smith, Bracker, and Miner (1987), plus a 5-year follow-up (Miner, Smith, and Bracker 1992a; 1994). The base sample of entrepreneurs had an N of 118, half of whom were identified as leaders; the follow-up group numbered 59, with 24 being leaders (see Table 15.8). A sample of grant applicants who were managers and/or scientists, but not entrepreneurs, was also established and used for noncongruent comparison purposes (N = 41). The follow-up data are distinctive in that they extend out over time and thus come closer to approximating whole careers. Most of the analyses reported relate to leadership careers, and individuals of this type were always assigned to the congruent condition. The noncongruent condition contained the managers/scientists or the non-leader entrepreneurs depending on the analysis. Only the entrepreneurial career versus manager/scientist correlations were reported in the original studies.

Buffalo, NY Area Entrepreneurs [See Chapter 20]

Information on this sample of 100 largely male entrepreneurs is contained in Miner (1996b; 1997a; 1997b; 1997c). Roughly half of the entrepreneurs were in leadership careers (see Table 20.5). Several other alternative predictor instruments were incorporated in this study. These measures were used to test Hypotheses 1c and 2c. Evidence that this is indeed an entrepreneurial sample is available from the OODQ.

One of the analyses with this sample utilized the continuous follow-up data on career success level on the assumption that those with lower scores were less attached to entrepreneurship; the other analysis compared leader and non-leader entrepreneurs. Thus the correlations were Pearson r and biserial r respectively.

SUNY/Buffalo Graduate Students [See Chapter 21]

These were 159 graduate students at the State University of New York (SUNY) at Buffalo who registered for a course in entrepreneurship taught by the author. Data on this sample are given in Miner (1997a; 2000). A follow-up was carried out shortly after graduation to the extent possible, for the purpose of establishing whether any entrepreneurial activity had occurred. Data collection focused throughout the period of contact with this group on past, present, and anticipated future entrepreneurial efforts. Thus, although there were students in the sample who clearly were not on an entrepreneurial route, it was not possible at this early point to establish with any certainty any specific non-entrepreneurial career groupings or to assess leadership. The same instruments above and beyond the MSCS–T as noted for the Buffalo, New York area entrepreneurs were included as alternative measures in this study as well. The follow-up was successful in contacting 115 of the 159, of whom 30 were found to be engaged in entrepreneurial activity of some kind (congruent condition).

A projected entrepreneurial career propensity score was developed dealing with current self-employment, previous business founding, and career objectives in entrepreneurship, with high scores indicating a proclivity for an entrepreneurial career. A sizable number of the students had very low scores; the mean was 2.9 out of a possible 10. This score was used in the analysis on the assumption that it differentiates those more likely to take up entrepreneurial careers from those who will pursue other careers; on the evidence this assumption proved correct. Given the continuous nature of this measure, it was possible to calculate Pearson *r* using it (see Table 21.9).

Because these were largely day students without regular employment, it was not possible to obtain OODQ reports on their organizational employment contexts. However, there was one group of 28 night students, who were all employed and who did complete the OODQ. Evidence as to the entrepreneurial relevance of this study is inherent in the fact that the 3 students who filled out the OODQ from entrepreneurial positions had a task score mean of 10.7; the other 25 (non-entrepreneurs) had a mean task score of 4.3.

Although the analyses reported for this study were intended at the time the author scored the MSCS–Ts, correlations were not derived. Thus the correlational analyses are original to the current investigation.

File Samples—Entrepreneurs and Managers [See Chapter 16]

This study is reported in Miner (1990) and included data from both research and consulting sources. Subjects having an entrepreneurial leadership career (congruent condition) were compared with others whose careers had been in management within hierarchic organizations (noncongruent condition); there were 65 of the former and 71 of the latter (see Table 16.1). MSCS–Ts were scored by the author for purposes other than that of the Miner (1990) study, although the analyses reported here were conducted for the 1990 study.

RESULTS

Congruent Careers

Table 29.1 contains correlations relevant to Hypotheses 1a and 2a from the five studies. The congruent values presented for the total task score are the most important since they deal with the theory as a whole, and also are based on the most reliable measurement. Not surprisingly, they are the highest as well, but there are a few comparable values among the subscale correlations. Thus, the total task correlations range from .25 to .77 with the majority of the 13 values falling in the .60s and .70s. Using a .50 criterion, 77 percent of the total score correlations in Table 29.1 would qualify as large. The subscale correlations span a range from .66 down to a negative figure of –.36; a majority are in the upper .30s and above, but only a few extend into the .60s.

Noncongruent Careers

In Table 29.2 certain noncongruent correlations are considered that represent all of the correlations of this type that could be computed from the available data (all from the Princeton sample). These data also relate to Hypotheses 1a and 2a. Note that in this instance the correlations tend to be much lower than in Table 29.1 and fewer are significant, as postulated by role motivation theory, and in accord with the hypotheses. The leadership careers noted in Table 29.2 utilize different criteria than in the entrepreneurial context, employing leaders appropriate to the hierarchic and professional domains as reflected in top management status and intellectual leadership respectively. To obtain non-congruent results the MSCS–T was applied to these groups. The total task correlations are all positive, but with a majority in the .10s. The subscale correlations extend into the negative range in a third of the cases, but vary upward to the .20s and even .30s as well. None of the correlations in Table 29.2 qualify as large.

Congruent and Noncongruent Careers Compared

A summary of the differences between the data of Tables 29.1 and 29.2 is contained in Table 29.3, again bearing on Hypotheses 1a and 2a. Here actual comparisons between matching correlation sets from the two tables are presented, as well as median correlations and counts of significance levels. The data, especially for total task, indicate high levels of correlation for the congruent analyses when careers are used as the dependent variable. Note, however, that all five subscales contribute to this result. However, the minimizing risks subscale yields the lowest median value and the fewest significant results while producing only one significant difference in the Princeton sample comparisons. These data on the role of risk propensity in predicting career decisions align well with the judgment made in a previous article (Miner and Raju 2004) [Chapter 27] that risk considerations do not at present indicate the potential to operate as key factors in any future theory of entrepreneurship.

Homogeneity of Career Predictions

Table 29.4 tests the expectation that leadership careers will operate in the same manner as other careers in congruent validity analyses; thus the concluding sentence of Hypothesis 2.

Here, the five samples each provide one set of correlations from Table 29.1 in such a manner as to maximize the wholeness of the career, and to include at least two instances that involve comparing leadership careers with others and two dealing with career data unspecified as to leadership considerations. With regard to total task and three of the subscales the correlations are homogeneous (as indicated by the χ^2 values), and thus leadership careers are seen to operate in the same manner as entrepreneurial careers generally. On the minimizing risks and planning and establishing goals subscales this appears not to be the case, in that certain correlations are lower than is generally true otherwise.

When comparisons are made within the total set of correlations, significant differences emerge on minimizing risks between the low values of .05, .14, and in one instance .26 and the high values of .42 and .49. However, both the low and high correlations include non-leadership as well as leadership career comparisons. Similarly, on planning and establishing goals the low correlations of .15, .17, and .23 are significantly below the high values of .46 and .53. Again these two groupings each include both non-leadership and leadership career comparisons. Thus, in neither instance is the negative deviation associated specifically with a leadership or non-leadership career comparison. Factors other than leadership appear to account for the heterogeneity of the correlations. Leadership careers in entrepreneurship behave in much the same manner as other congruent careers; most importantly, however, they typically operate as careers with similar correlations. Also note that the combined task correlations of Table 29.4 are about the same as the median correlations reported for all congruent analyses in Table 29.3. Overall the data appear to offer strong support for Hypothesis 2.

Table 29.2

Correlations between Task Role Motivation Theory Variables and *Noncongruent* Careers (Including Leadership Careers)

	N		Motive Patterns					
Samples and Analyses	First Mentioned Condition	Second Mentioned Condition	Total Task	Achieving on One's Own	Minimizing Risks	Receiving Feedback	Introducing Innovations	Planning and Establishing Goals
Princeton Graduates (class of 1948)								
Managerial career vs. professional career	32	28	.10	.27*	–.14	.17	–.04	–.02
Managerial leadership career vs. non-leader managers	26	6	.12	–.04	.16	.24	–.28	.24
Professional leadership career vs. non-leader managers	18	10	.48*	.18	.05	.18	.27	.35

*$p < .05$

Table 29.3

Data Bearing on the Differences between the Results of Congruent (N = 13) **and Noncongruent** (N = 3) **Career Analyses for Task Theory**

	Motive Patterns					
Comparison Factors	Total Task	Achieving on One's Own	Minimizing Risks	Receiving Feedback	Introducing Innovations	Planning and Establishing Goals
Median Correlations						
Congruent analyses	.66	.47	.26	.37	.44	.29
Noncongruent analyses	.12	.18	.05	.18	–.04	.24
Percent significant ($p < .05$)						
Congruent analyses	100	100	54	85	85	77
Noncongruent analyses	33	33	0	0	0	0
Comparison of Correlations in Princeton Sample						
Congruent	.75	.48	.42	.32	.42	.53
Noncongruent	.10	.27	–.14	.17	–.04	–.02
p	< .01	NS	< .01	NS	< .01	< .01
Congruent	.67	.53	–.36	.61	.46	.21
Noncongruent	.12	–.04	.16	.24	–.28	.24
p	< .05	<.05	NS	NS	< .01	NS
Congruent	.76	.51	.35	.37	.45	.52
Noncongruent	.48	.18	.05	.18	.27	.35
p	< .05	<.05	NS	NS	NS	NS

NS = not significant at $p < .05$

Congruent Careers Compared with Other Criteria

Table 29.5 deals with the question of whether the results obtained for congruent career analyses differ from those obtained where the dependent variable is not of a career nature, though still congruent, thus with Hypotheses 1b and 2b. The latter include entrepreneurial success criteria, performance, and efficiency. The "other congruent analyses" in Table 29.5 are primarily studies noted in Miner (1993). However, this category also includes certain analyses taken from Tracy's (1992) doctoral dissertation, a study whose inclusion raises serious questions. This study contains mean MSCS–T scores well below the level obtained in any other entrepreneurial group, the subscale means (reported in multiple locations) add to 1.5 less than the reported total task score (when these values should be equal), and one subscale (avoiding risks) produces a significant *negative* correlation with the total score (even though all previous studies have yielded substantial positive correlations), a very unlikely finding given that all subscales represent components of the total score. There are problems with the criteria as well, in that relationships that logically should occur do not. In the interest of inclusiveness, data from this study were retained, with the predominant effect that median values are reduced, but the limitations thus introduced should be recognized.

In any event the data of Table 29.5, with the exception of the planning and establishing goals subscale, provide evidence that, holding congruence constant, career analyses produce

Table 29.4

Tests for Homogeneity of Validity Coefficients Involving *Congruent* Career and Leadership Relationships (Independent Samples)—**Task Theory**

		Motive Patterns					
Sample Designation	Career Comparison	Total Task	Achieving on One's Own	Minimizing Risks	Receiving Feedback	Introducing Innovations	Planning and Establishing Goals
Princeton 1948	Non-leadership	.75	.48	.42	.32	.42	.53
High technology	Leadership	.70	.66	.14	.38	.49	.46
Buffalo, NY	Leadership	.71	.41	.26	.42	.38	.15
SUNY/Buffalo students	Non-leadership	.59	.45	.05	.35	.44	.23
File samples	Leadership	.66	.59	.49	.23	.46	.17
x^2 (for df = 4)		6.00	4.19	20.34	2.79	.80	13.68
p		NS	NS	< .01	NS	NS	< .01
Combined r (weighted)		.67	.51	.28	.33	.44	.28

NS = not significant at $p < .05$

Table 29.5

Data Bearing on the Differences between the Results of Congruent Career Analyses (N = 13) **and Congruent Analyses Involving Other Outcomes** (N = 17) **for Task Theory**

	Motive Patterns					
Comparison Factors	Total Task	Achieving on One's own	Minimizing Risks	Receiving Feedback	Introducing Innovations	Planning and Establishing Goals
Median correlations						
Congruent career analyses	.66	.47	.26	.37	.44	.29
Other congruent analyses	.35	.27	.07	.14	.13	.24
Percent significant ($p < .05$)						
Congruent career analyses	100	100	54	85	85	77
Other congruent analyses	65	59	29	35	29	65
Comparison of correlations in samples where appropriate data were available:						
High technology follow-up						
Career—leader vs. non-leader	.70	.66	.14	.38	.49	.46
Other—yearly income	.32	.46	–.27	.10	.16	.42
p	< .01	NS	< .05	NS	< .05	NS
SUNY/Buffalo graduate students						
Career—projected propensity for entrepreneurship	.59	.45	.05	.35	.44	.23
Other—skill in preparing a business plan	.39	.11	.13	.12	.25	.33
p	< .05	< .01	NS	< .05	< .05	NS

NS = not significant at $p < .05$

higher correlations than do other outcome criteria. In both the high technology and SUNY/Buffalo student samples it was possible to compare matching data sets; the specific analyses were selected so as to approach the median total task values as closely as possible. These comparisons both indicate a significantly higher total score correlation for the career criterion, and either one or two significant differences for all subscales except planning and establishing goals. In this latter instance there is nothing to suggest the superiority of the career index; prediction is reasonably effective irrespective of the criterion employed. Overall, however, it appears that although other criteria are predicted reasonably well by task theory, especially by the total task score, entrepreneurial career identifications are predicted at a considerably higher level. The median career correlation is well up into the large range for total score, and the subscale correlations are in the middle or upper range; for the other congruent analyses these values are in the upper third, and the middle third or below respectively.

Alternative Instruments

Table 29.6 contains what evidence is available on the predictive power of alternative instruments in situations where the samples and analyses are identical to those reported for the MSCS–T. This analysis bears on Hypotheses lc and 2c. All of the nine alternative measures have been associated with entrepreneurial criteria in some way in the past (Miner 1997a). The median absolute value in Table 29.6 is .15, but other than a sprinkling of significant correlations elsewhere, real predictive power appears to be concentrated in the Levenson (1974) measures of locus of control where the median correlation is .28 and the maximum value is .36. Even in this instance, however, the career correlations involving the MSCS–T are clearly much higher (see Table 29.1).

An additional question relates to the effectiveness of Forms H and P of the MSCS in predicting entrepreneurial career indexes, where any association would appear to be a noncongruent one (Miner 1993). For Form H, which should do its best predicting in the hierarchic domain, the median total score correlation from five analyses is .12. Quite apparently the hierarchic theory shows only very minimal evidence of contributing to predictions of entrepreneurial careers. For Form P, however, this median correlation rises to .27. This finding is due to the results in the two Buffalo samples where proclivities for entrepreneurial careers are quite frequently matched by a strong professional orientation as well. This is a situation that occurs often in high technology entrepreneurship, and probably in these contexts Form P would be expected to emerge often as a predictor as well as Form T. In the full Buffalo entrepreneur sample the second highest OODQ score was the professional (4.8); there were 18 individuals who appeared to be professionals also in the sample of 100, and these 18 had a mean professional score on the OODQ of 8.3. In the Buffalo student sample there were 18 PhD students (11 percent of the sample), who were clearly preparing for professional careers, plus several other established professionals as well (including lawyers and accountants). Although entrepreneurial careers clearly predominate in these samples, and the MSCS–T results reflect this, professional careers are a strong undercurrent, and that appears to be why the MSCS–P results are as strong as they are.

DISCUSSION

These findings provide strong support for the congruent hypothesis of task role motivation theory, and for the view that entrepreneurial leadership careers are indeed careers, operating

Table 29.6

Correlations between Alternative Predictor Measures and Career Indexes in Various Buffalo, NY Samples

	Alternative Measures								
				Levenson Instrument			Decision Style Inventory		
Samples and Analyses	Shure & Meeker	Vocabulary Test G-T	Individual Behavior Activity	Internal	Powerful Other	Chance	Directive	Conceptual	Behavioral
Buffalo, NY area entrepreneurs									
Career success level	–.10	–.12	.05	.20*	–.32**	–.07	.16	–.01	–.10
Entrepreneurial leadership career vs. non-leaders	–.03	–.06	–.17	.28*	–.14	.11	.02	.21	.00
SUNY/Buffalo graduate students									
Projected propensity for an entrepreneurial career	–.21**	–.06	.32**	.28**	–.26**	–.28**	.07	.15	–.21**
Actual entrepreneurial career (early) vs. other career	–.17	.10	.15	.31*	–.36**	–.27*	–.07	.12	–.10

Note: Shure & Meeker = Shure/Meeker Risk Avoidance Scale (Shure and Meeker 1967); Vocabulary Test G-T = Forms A and B combined (Thorndike and Gallup 1944; Miner 1961); Individual Behavior Activity = Individual Behavior Activity Profile—a measure of type A behavior (Matteson and Ivancevich 1982a; 1982b); Levenson Instrument = Levenson Internal-External Control Instrument (Levenson 1972; 1974); Decision Style Inventory (Rowe and Mason 1987).

$^{*}p < .05$; $^{**}p < .01$

in essentially the same manner as other entrepreneurial careers. However, the truly significant new finding from this research is that the motives of task theory predict career identifications at a level well above what has been found with other criteria and predictors; correlations averaging in the .60s, and often extending well up in to the .70s, give considerable credence to the hypotheses of this study. These results are not a consequence of statistical artifacts; they derive from a theory that appears to be quite powerful, at least as it applies to such matters as career choice and perseverance.

Scorer Diversity and Additional Findings

As indicated previously, the MSCS–T data in all five of the studies utilized in the preceding analyses resulted from scoring by the author; there are no data from more diverse sources. This has the advantage that the scorer is held constant, and that an experienced scorer, who in fact devised the scoring system, is employed throughout. Yet there is a possibility that in some manner a bias (either conscious or unconscious) in favor of the hypotheses was introduced by this process.

One argument against this latter supposition is that in most instances the actual scoring of the MSCS–Ts was done in the context of hypotheses other than those tested in the current analyses. In all cases the leadership career hypothesis came on the scene well after the test scores were already established, as did the expectation that career correlations would be exceptionally high.

Another approach to this issue is to consider data from sources where the MSCS–T scoring was done by someone other than the author. Studies of this kind do not contain correlational findings per se, but in a number of instances it was possible to convert *t* values to correlations (see Hunter, Schmidt, and Jackson 1982). These studies do not test the leadership career hypotheses in any instance, although in one case it was possible to deduce data of this kind from what was presented. In general the sample sizes in these studies are relatively small.

Bellu (1988) carried out analyses of MCST–T scores comparing samples (with Ns in the mid-30s) of entrepreneurs and managers in two geographical locations within the United States. In the first location an entrepreneurial career was correlated with the total task score at .37. Three subscales were similarly significant and the median subscale correlation was .25 with achieving on one's own yielding the highest value ($r = .34$). In the second location the total task correlation was .38 and only one subscale (planning and establishing goals) was similarly significant with $r = .49$. The median subscale correlation was only .14.

Studies utilizing this same design with sample Ns ranging from 26 to 36 were also conducted outside the United States (Bellu, Davidsson, and Goldfarb 1990). The first study, using samples from northern Italy, produced a total task correlation of .38, a median subscale correlation of .25 (with three subscales similarly significant), and a maximum subscale value of .38 for minimizing risks. The samples from southern Italy yielded a total task correlation with entrepreneurial careers of .61. Here all of the subscale differences were similarly significant, and the median correlation was .50 with a high value of .55 for introducing innovations. In Israel the relationship between total task and an entrepreneurial career yielded $r = .50$. Three of the subscales were similarly significant and the median subscale correlation was .37 with a high value of .50 for minimizing risks.

The final samples in the Bellu, Davidsson, and Goldfarb (1990) article came from Sweden; the results there were substantially different from the others. Neither the total score nor four of the MSCS–T subscales yielded significant findings. The only significant value was a correlation with entrepreneurial careers of .29 for achieving on one's own. Several aspects of the Swedish study should be noted, however. The Ns are the smallest of any in which Bellu was involved. The samples are less well matched than in the other studies in that the managers are preponderately in sales and marketing, with a number having had previous entrepreneurial experience, while the entrepreneurs are concentrated in service firms, with a number being professionals. The fact that Sweden is a union-controlled socialist economy with very high tax rates and substantial governmental mandating of time off from work (see Begin 1991)—not the ideal environment for entrepreneurship—may well have contributed to the findings as well.

Bellu (1993) also conducted a study in the New York City area using entirely female samples of entrepreneurs (N = 47) and managers (N = 66). In spite of the somewhat larger Ns, significance was reported only for the total score and for one subscale (achieving on one's own). These correlations with an entrepreneurial career were .21 and .24 respectively. The median subscale value was $r = .10$. These findings are considered further in a later section.

All of the studies considered to this point involved MSCS–T scoring by someone other than the author, often by Bellu. All compared entrepreneurial with managerial careers, required that correlations be determined from t values, and contained insufficient information to permit the identification of entrepreneurial leadership careers. Three other studies utilized entrepreneurial samples only and thus do not allow for career comparisons, other than for leadership careers.

The first of these studies was conducted by Bracker, Pearson, Keats, and Miner (1991) and reported in Miner (1993); Bracker did the scoring of the MSCS–Ts. Within this study of 51 electronics industry entrepreneurs 9 could be identified as engaging in structured strategic planning and accordingly appeared to be involved in entrepreneurial leadership careers. Another 10 had firms that did not survive over a 5-year period subsequent to testing, and thus would not qualify for designation as entrepreneurial leaders. The remaining 32 entrepreneurs did not provide the information needed to classify them as to leader status, and thus were dropped from this analysis. Using the 19 individuals that were retained, a correlation of .72 was obtained between total task and leadership career and 4 of the subscale r's were similarly significant; the median subscale value was .43 and the highest of these (receiving feedback) was .51.

A study conducted by—and with the MSCS–Ts scored by—Jourdan (1987) compared two groups of 24 entrepreneurs each, both of which had persevered in entrepreneurial activity. No significant differences were found between groups and the information needed to designate any entrepreneurs as leaders was unavailable. However, the combined total score (N = 48) was +9.57, which would place this group at the 61st percentile among the normative sample of entrepreneurs (Miner 1986). All of the subscale means were above the 50th percentile, except personal innovation which was close. These entrepreneurs had MSCS–T scores at a level sufficiently high so that if it had been possible to compare them with others on a non-entrepreneurial career trajectory, a quite substantial career correlation would be expected to emerge in all likelihood. In contrast, Bellu and Sherman (1995) carried out a study of 43 entrepreneurs in which all participants qualified as leaders. The total score value was +9.04 which placed these entrepreneurs at the 60th percentile in the normative sample. All subscale means were above the 50th percentile with the exception of personal innovation. Again the scores were sufficiently high so that, had comparison groups been available, the correlations probably would have been quite large.

Although the findings reported in this section do not permit direct comparisons with the results from the author's studies, evidence for concluding that the two data sets differ substantially does not appear to exist. MSCS–T scoring by someone other than the author often yields correlations in the upper third of values, extending into the large range and up to the low .70s for total score. Although some of the Bellu studies yield unexpected results, others produce sizable correlations. Overall these additional findings would seem to add support for the hypotheses.

Female Careers

A question, however, is introduced by the Bellu (1993) study noted previously. In this instance entrepreneur-manager comparisons were made using entirely female samples, as distinct from the occasional female characterizing the samples studied previously. The total task comparison was significant, but the correlation was only .21 and the subscale findings were equally low. This is not the striking career effect that had predominated in most of the previously reported analyses. It may be that what is reflected here is the gender-specific consequence that others have noted in the past (see Melamed 1996); females have been found to exhibit very different career patterns than males. Thus, the finding of very high career correlations indicated throughout this article may reflect the fact that all of the analyses involved predominantly male samples.

To check this possibility, small samples of females were gleaned from the five studies, which form the body of this chapter. The intent was to test the entrepreneurial leadership career hypothesis in samples that were entirely female. The consequence of this process was that groups of eight female leaders and ten female non-leaders were constituted. The total task mean for leaders was +13.25 (77th percentile), yielding a correlation of .89, $p < .01$ with entrepreneurial leadership career. The subscale correlations were as follows:

Achieving on one's own	.73, $p < .05$
Minimizing risks	.70, $p < .05$
Receiving feedback	.38, NS
Introducing innovations	.31, NS
Planning and establishing goals	.14, NS

Certainly these results demonstrate the volatility inherent in small samples, but they provide no evidence to support the view that female careers, or at least female leadership careers in the entrepreneurship area, operate differently from those of males. Other research with the MSCS–T suggests minimal, if any, gender differences (Miner 1993). However, there is clearly a need for further research on this topic, and on female careers.

Why the Large Correlation?

Is there anything in role motivation theory that would serve to explain the strong support for the hypotheses? One answer to this question appears to lie in the concept of role. That certain patterns of motives predict, in the present instance the motives of task theory, seems to be because, among particular people, motives exist that match well with a given set of organizational roles (Foti and Miner 2003). These roles are characterized by the fact that they are institutionalized and thus yield a minimum of role conflict; the role senders in the environment tend to be in considerable agreement simply as a function of the fact that institutionalization is operating. With roles this stable, those who have matching motives are likely to experience many positive outcomes and to stay in the careers that give them these positive outcomes.

These formulations need to be melded with some additional ideas derived from results reported by Martell, Lane, and Emrich (1996) in order to provide an answer to the question: Why the high correlations? The Martell et al (1996) investigation was a computer simulation which can be interpreted as demonstrating that very small relationships early in one's career can well escalate, as multiple career-related decisions (Hall 2002) are made, into very large relationships later in that same career. Thus, the existence of a small profit margin in a small local business can provide a basis for substantial earnings later on in an entrepreneur's career as repeated business expansion decisions are compounded over time and geographical locations.

A key factor here appears to be that later in a single career trajectory, and particularly with movement up into leadership status, many more career-related decisions are made both by the entrepreneur and by stakeholders. These multiple decisions have the quality of creating reliability for the career index, much in the same manner that adding construct-related items to a test increases the reliability of that test. This criterion reliability effect cannot be the total explanation of the results reported here, because that would imply that all predictors should yield such high correlations when coupled with career indexes. This is not the case (see Table 29.6). However, when a powerful theory, which role motivation theory appears to be, guides the predictor, and this is then married with a highly reliable criterion measure, as entrepreneurial careers appear to be, the consequences—in the form of very high correlations and substantial criterion variance accounted for—would seem to be well on the way to being explained. This does not mean, however, that such conditions are unique to role motivation theory. For instance, career-related decisions have been found to be predictable from expectancy theory (see Miner 2005) with a value of .72 (Wanous, Keon, and Latack 1983).

CHAPTER 30

CONGRUENCE AND THE SIGNIFICANCE OF CAREERS IN TESTING ROLE MOTIVATION THEORY

USING HIERARCHIC MOTIVE PATTERNS

INTRODUCTION

This chapter represents the application of Chapter 29's model to the hierarchic domain and Form H of the Miner Sentence Completion Scale (MSCS). The material presented has not been published, or even presented, previously; it is original to this volume.

* * *

In this chapter the major concern is with hierarchic organizations, hierarchic theory, hierarchic motivation, and hierarchic roles. The discussion of hypothesis generation in Chapter 29 is applicable, but now with an emphasis on hierarchic organizations and managers. The standing hypothesis from theory that applies is to the effect that in hierarchic systems hierarchic motivation should be at a high level among top managers, and it should be positively correlated with managerial success indexes; hierarchic motivation should not differentiate in these ways within other types of systems.

For the reasons specified in Chapter 29 for task theory, the hierarchic theory operates according to the following hypotheses:

Hypothesis 1. *Congruent analyses, which are conducted comparing those with careers inside the hierarchic domain against those having careers outside that domain on measures of hierarchic motivation, should produce correlations that—*

a) exceed correlations obtained using only those having careers outside the hierarchic domain;

b) exceed correlations obtained using criterion variables other than career status, but still appropriate to the hierarchic domain, such as performance indexes;

c) exceed correlations obtained using predictors other than measures of hierarchic motivation, but still appropriate to the hierarchic domain, such as the Ghiselli Self-Description Inventory-Supervisory Ability.

Hypothesis 2. *Congruent analyses, which are conducted comparing those with leadership careers inside the hierarchic domain against either those having non-leader careers inside the hierarchic domain or those having careers outside the domain on measures of hierarchic motivation, should produce correlations that—*

a) exceed correlations obtained using only those having careers outside the hierarchic domain;

b) exceed correlations obtained using criterion variables other than career status, but still appropriate to the hierarchic domain, such as performance indexes;

c) exceed correlations obtained using predictors other than measures of hierarchic motivation, but still appropriate to the hierarchic domain, such as the Ghiselli SDI (1971).

Thus, hierarchic leadership careers should operate in terms of these correlational analyses in the same manner as specified in Hypothesis 1 for other managerial careers.

METHOD

Measures

The measure of hierarchic motivation used in this investigation was the Miner Sentence Completion Scale–Form H (Miner 1964; 1993).

The major dependent variable of this research was the career—managerial or otherwise—undertaken by the respondent. Organizational leadership is viewed as a career phenomenon; in the hierarchic context leaders may be compared with non-leader managers, who do not meet the top management leadership criteria, or they may be compared against respondents in other than managerial careers.

Studies

Presenting correlations is inherent in the hypotheses and a key aspect of this chapter; all of the analyses utilize this statistical form. The four studies represent all of the currently existing research conducted by the author that is relevant to the stated hypotheses.

Princeton Graduates—Class of 1948 [See Chapter 22]

This study utilized whole career data and is described in Miner 2002a. The managerial sample numbers 48, of whom 38 qualify as leaders. For purposes of analysis those participants who had managerial careers or managerial leadership careers were considered to be in the congruent condition.

Human Resource Managers [See Chapter 7]

These are the members of the Bureau of National Affairs (BNA) panel. Prior publications on this panel are Miner (1976a; 1976b; 1979a) and Miner and Miner (1976). The base sample of human resource managers numbered 101. Among these, 41 qualified as hierarchic leaders and 60 did not, using the most stringent leadership criteria available (see Table 7.6). Several other alternative predictor instruments were incorporated in this study. These measures were used to test Hypotheses 1c and 2c.

Top Level Executives [See Chapter 14]

Berman (see Berman and Miner 1985) collected the MSCS–Form H data used in this study. There were 49 top executives, and thus hierarchic leaders, and 49 managers who were age-matched to these leaders and also congruent, but not leaders (see Table 14.4). The data for the 26 noncongruent top executives were not utilized.

University of Oregon Graduate Students [See Chapter 4]

These students indicated various career goals associated with their studies at the same time as they completed the MSCS–Form H (Miner 1968a). There were 41 such students who indicated managerial goals; 68 students noted goals other than managerial—various specialist careers, teaching, etc. (see Table 4.4). Leadership was not involved in this study in that the data were collected long before such matters were at issue.

RESULTS

Congruent Careers

Table 30.1 contains correlations relevant to Hypotheses 1a and 2a from the four studies. The congruent values for the total hierarchic score are the most important and they are also the highest. The total hierarchic correlations range from .13 to .72 with 83 percent above .50 and thus designated as large. The subscale correlations span a range from .56 to –.40 with the majority above .25 and 27 significant. In general, these correlations are at the same level as in Table 29.1 for Form T, but diluted somewhat by the lower number of items in Form H.

Noncongruent Careers

In Table 30.2 certain noncongruent correlations are considered which represent all of the correlations of this type that could be computed from the available data. The samples involved are described in various sources—in order of presentation within Table 30.2:

- The Princeton class [see Chapter 22].
- The Academy of Management members [see Chapter 9].
- The business faculty [see Miner 1977b (Chapter 8)].

Table 30.1

Correlations between Hierarchic Role Motivation Theory Variables and *Congruent* Careers (Including Leadership Careers) **as Managers**

	N		Motive Patterns							
Samples and Analyses	Congruent Condition	Non-congruent Condition	Total Hierarchic	Attitude to Authority	Competing Games	Competing Situation	Asserting Oneself	Exercising Power	Assuming Distinctive Status	Performing Routine Duties
Princeton Graduates (class of 1948)										
Managerial career vs. other	48	44	.65**	.42**	.41**	.53**	.16	.48**	.19*	.19*
Hierarchic leadership career										
vs. non-leader managers	38	10	.13	.13	–.40	–.01	.17	.06	.08	.34
vs. non-managers	38	44	.64**	.43**	.35**	.53**	.18	.48**	.20	.24*
Human Resource Managers										
Hierarchic leadership career vs. non-leader managers	41	60	.54**	.49**	.41**	.29*	.25*	.13	.07	.25*
Top Level Executives										
Hierarchic leadership career vs. non-leader managers	49	49	.72**	.37**	.09	.30**	.10	.44**	.56**	.33**
University of Oregon Graduate Students										
Projected managerial career	41	68	.52**	.34**	.19*	.38**	.36**	.30**	.10	.29**

*$p < .05$; **$p < .01$

- The Buffalo, New York entrepreneurs [see Chapter 20].
- The SUNY/Buffalo graduate students [see Chapter 21].

These data also relate to Hypotheses 1a and 2a. The correlations are much lower than in Table 30.1 and fewer are significant (a total of 5 of 72). The leadership careers noted in Table 30.2 utilize different criteria than in the hierarchic context, employing leaders appropriate to the task and professional domains. To obtain noncongruent results, the MSCS–Form H was applied to these groups. All but one of the nine total hierarchic correlations were positive, but only one of these was significant (at the $p < .05$ level); most were in the .10s. Just under a third of the subscale correlations extend into the negative range. There is considerable volatility due to some small Ns. Comparing these results with those of Table 29.2, obtained with Form T, the parallels are striking.

Congruent and Noncongruent Careers Compared

A summary of the differences between the data of Table 30.1 and 30.2 is contained in Table 30.3, again bearing on Hypotheses 1a and 2a. The data, especially for total hierarchic, indicate high levels of correlation for the congruent analyses when careers are used as the dependent variable. This is consistently supported for 4 of the 5 subscales. However, Standing Out from the Group, and thus assuming a distinctive status, does not operate in the same manner. It is not apparent why this anomaly occurs; it is associated with high noncongruent correlations in the Princeton sample where very small Ns are involved, however, and this may be a factor.

Homogeneity of Career Predictions

Table 30.4 tests the expectation that leadership careers will operate in the same manner as other careers in congruent validity analyses; thus the concluding sentence of Hypothesis 2. The four samples include two instances that involve comparing leadership careers with others and two dealing with career data unspecified as to leadership considerations. With regard to total hierarchic and four of the subscales the correlations are homogeneous (as indicated by the χ^2 values) and thus leadership careers are seen to operate in the same manner as managerial careers generally. On the Competitive Games and Exercising Power subscales there are outliers on the low end while with assuming a distinctive status this occurs on the high end.

No differences in correlation size can be attributed specifically to the leadership or nonleadership samples. Thus, where heterogeneity does occur, it cannot be attributed directly to the leadership factor. Leadership careers in hierarchic organizations behave in much the same manner as other congruent careers. Also note that the combined hierarchic correlations in Table 30.4 are much the same as the median correlations for all congruent analyses in Table 30.3. Overall the data appear to offer strong support for Hypothesis 2, as was the case for task motivation in Chapter 29.

Congruent Careers Compared with Other Criteria

Table 30.5 deals with the question of whether the results obtained for congruent career analyses differ from those obtained where the dependent variable is not of a career nature, though still congruent—thus with Hypotheses 1b and 2b. These "other" criteria include such outcomes as performance ratings, position level, compensation, promotion, success indexes,

Table 30.2

Correlations between Hierarchic Role Motivation Theory Variables and *Noncongruent* Careers (Including Leadership Careers) **as Managers**

	N		Motive Patterns							
Samples and Analyses	First Mentioned Condition	Second Mentioned Condition	Total Hierarchic	Attitude to Authority	Competing Games	Competing Situation	Asserting oneself	Exercising Power	Assuming Distinctive Status	Performing Routine Duties
Princeton Graduates (class of 1948)										
Professional vs. Entrepreneurial career	28	16	–.11	.06	–.20	–.24	.08	.11	–.19	.18
Professional leadership career vs. non-leaders	18	10	.29	.16	–.06	.18	–.19	.37	.60*	.04
Entrepreneurial leadership career vs. non-leaders	13	3	.49	.45	.52	.47	–.01	–.07	.55	–.02
Academy of Management Members										
Professional leadership career vs. non-leaders	46	66	.11	.04	.11	–.12	.23	.08	–.05	.09
Business Faculties										
Professional leadership career level	49	—	.12	.17	.08	–.04	.05	–.08	.16	.17
Buffalo, NY Entrepreneurs										
Entrepreneurial leadership career vs. non-leaders	45	44	.13	–.10	.15	.02	–.01	.15	.32*	–.12
Career success level	84	—	.21*	.12	.11	.00	–.01	.17	.25*	.01
Buffalo Graduate Students										
Projected propensity for an entrepreneurial career	159	—	.11	–.04	.08	.07	.02	.17*	–.04	.08
Actual entrepreneurial career (early) vs. other	30	85	.12	.04	.09	.12	–.11	–.01	.18	.07

$*p < .05$; $**p < .01$

Table 30.3

Data Bearing on the Differences between the Results of Congruent (N = 6) **and Noncongruent** (N = 9) **Career Analyses for the Hierarchic Theory**

	Motive Patterns							
Comparison Factors	Total Hierarchic	Attitude to Authority	Competing Games	Competing Situation	Asserting Oneself	Exercising Power	Assuming Distinctive Status	Performing Routine Duties
Median correlations								
Congruent analyses	.59	.40	.27	.34	.18	.37	.15	.27
Noncongruent analyses	.12	.06	.09	.02	–.01	.11	.18	.07
Percent Significant (*p* < .05)								
Congruent analyses	83	83	67	83	33	67	33	83
Noncongruent analyses	11	0	0	0	0	11	33	0
Comparison of Correlations in Princeton Sample								
Congruent	.65	.42	.41	.53	.16	.48	.19	.19
Noncongruent	–.11	.06	–.20	–.24	.08	.11	–.19	.18
p	< .01	< .05	< .01	< .01	NS	< .05	< .05	NS
Congruent	.13	.13	–.40	–.01	.17	.06	.08	.34
Noncongruent	.29	.16	–.06	.18	–.19	.37	.60	.04
p	NS	NS	NS	NS	NS	NS	< .05	NS
Congruent	.64	.43	.35	.53	.18	.48	.20	.24
Noncongruent	.49	.45	.52	.47	–.01	–.07	.55	–.02
p	NS	NS	NS	NS	NS	< .05	NS	NS

NS = not significant at $p < .05$

Table 30.4

Tests for Homogeneity of Validity Coefficients Involving *Congruent* Career and Leadership Relationships (Independent Samples)—**Hierarchic Theory**

		Motive Patterns							
Sample Designation	Career Comparison	Total Hierarchic	Attitude to Authority	Competing Games	Competing Situation	Asserting Oneself	Exercising Power	Assuming Distinctive Status	Perform-ing Routine Duties
Princeton 1948	Non-leadership	.65	.42	.41	.53	.16	.48	.19	.19
Human resource	Leadership	.54	.49	.41	.29	.25	.13	.07	.25
Top executives	Leadership	.72	.37	.09	.30	.10	.44	.56	.33
Oregon students	Non-leadership	.52	.34	.19	.38	.36	.30	.10	.29
	χ^2 (for df = 3)	7.09	1.91	8.80	7.07	4.39	8.99	19.78	1.15
	p	NS	NS	< .05	NS	NS	< .05	< .01	NS
	combined r (weighted)	.61	.40	.28	.37	.22	.34	.24	.27
	distinctive value			.09 (low)			.13 (low)	.56 (high)	

NS = not significant at $p < .05$

job satisfaction, and turnover. The research does not appear to isolate any type of outcome (other than careers) as particularly likely to produce more valid results. These "other congruent analyses" in Table 30.5 are primarily from studies noted in Miner (1993). However, data are also included from Schneider, Ehrhart, and Ehrhart (2002), updated to include recently available information (see Chapter 4 and Table 4.6).

The data of Table 30.5 provide evidence that, holding congruence constant, career analyses produce higher correlations than do other outcome criteria. Yet certain explanations are clearly required. The total hierarchic data do not fulfill expectations insofar as percent significant are concerned, but this is because at the correlation levels involved, both career and "other" criteria produce over 80 percent significance. Clearly it is at the upper reaches of validities that differences begin to emerge. Thus subscale significance appears on only five of the seven subscales; the two that clearly do not yield significant results (Asserting Oneself and Standing Out) are indeed not replicated within the human resources managers from the BNA panel. In fact in that analysis only the Imposing Wishes findings are not supportive of the hypotheses. Yet that subscale produces the greatest difference in median correlations between career and other analyses, some .25 correlation points. It is apparent that higher correlations are associated with the congruent career situation when the total score for Form H is applied—in the .50s when the criterion is a career and in the .20s when it is not. This conclusion is reinforced by the subscale analyses in practically all, if not all, cases.

Alternative Instruments

Table 30.6 contains what evidence is available on the predictive power of alternative instruments in situations where the samples and analyses are identical to those reported for the MSCS–H. This analysis bears on Hypothesis 1c and 2c. The nine alternative predictors have been associated with managerial criteria in some way in the past. The median absolute value in Table 30.6 is .22 and significance is concentrated in the various indexes of managerial talent from the Ghiselli Self-Description Inventory (1971); significance is lacking for the Kuder measure (Miner 1960b) and for the F–Scale (Adorno, Frenkel-Brunswik, Levinson, and Sanford 1950). Note that prior results for the SDI measures reported in this volume do not utilize the leadership criterion, as reported here, but rather some other criterion index.

The data of Table 30.6 need to be compared with MSCS–H data to test the hypotheses. When this is done for the subscales of the MSCS and for the SDI indexes both yield a median validity of .25 (see Table 30.1, also 30.4 and 30.5); there is little to indicate a difference at this level. But when the total hierarchic measure is brought to bear the results are as indicated in the right hand column of Table 30.6; all of the alternative predictors yield correlations well below the MSCS–H total score of .54 at $p < .05$ or better, thus supporting Hypothesis 2c. These utilize all the alternative predictor data available. Perhaps other alternative findings would produce results more compatible with those for the MSCS–H. However, any such analysis needs to hold constant the factors considered here.

Forms T and P do not work well in the hierarchic domain. The available evidence stems from the Princeton sample (see Chapter 22).

DISCUSSION

The findings provide strong support for the congruent hypothesis of hierarchic role motivation theory and for the view that managerial leadership careers are indeed careers, operating much

Table 30.5

Data Bearing on the Differences between the Results of Congruent Career Analyses (N = 6) **and Congruent Analyses Involving Other Outcomes** (N = 36) **for Hierarchic Theory**

	Motive Patterns							
Comparison Factors	Total Hierarchic	Attitude to Authority	Competing Games	Competing Situation	Asserting Oneself	Exercising Power	Assuming Distinctive Status	Performing Routine Duties
Median Correlations								
Congruent career analyses	.59	.40	.27	.34	.18	.37	.15	.27
Other congruent analyses	.29	.13	.12	.18	.15	.12	.14	.13
Percent Significant (p < .05)								
Congruent career analyses	83	83	67	83	33	67	33	83
Other congruent analyses	86	34	28	45	34	48	31	31
Comparison of Correlations where Appropriate Data Were Available:								
Human resource managers								
Career leader vs. nonleader	.54	.49	.41	.29	.25	.13	.07	.25
Other—successes index (position level + income)	.28	.30	.13	.18	.04	.11	-.06	.13
p	<.01	<.01	<.01	<.05	<.01	NS	<.05	<.05

NS = not significant at $p < .05$

Table 30.6

Correlations between Alternative Predictor Measures and a Leadership Career Index in the BNA Panel of Human Resource Managers (N = 101)

Alternative Measures	Hierarchic Leadership Career vs. Non-leader Managers	Significance of Differences from Total Hierarchic (.54)
Kuder Preference Record-Supervisory Index	.14	< .01
Adorno, Frenkel-Brunswik, Levinson, and Sanford F-Scale	.14	< .01
Ghiselli SDI		
Supervisory Ability	.25*	< .01
Occupational Achievement	.31**	< .05
Intelligence	.22*	< .01
Self-actualization	.22*	< .01
Self-assurance	.28*	< .01
Decisiveness	.17	< .01
Need for Security	–.36**	< .05

Ghiselli SDI = Self Description Index (Ghiselli 1971).

as do other managerial careers. However, the truly significant finding is that the hierarchic theory's motives predict career identifications at a level well above that found with other criteria and predictors; correlations often rise into the .60s and .70s, as they did with the task theory (see Chapter 29).

As indicated previously, these same results were obtained from one contributing sample in which scoring of Form H was done by a co-author (Fred Berman in Chapter 14). In this instance, at least, the results obtained did not permit the possibility that bias on the part of the author entered into the scoring process. It is unlikely, accordingly, that author bias influenced the other studies of Table 30.1. In addition, as with the data reported in Chapter 29, much of the scoring of the MSCSs was done in the context of hypotheses other than those tested in the current analyses.

With regard to gender differences, the findings for Form H are just as unrevealing as for Form T. The expectation that at least the University of Oregon graduate students might produce a gender difference was not fulfilled. In this sample none of the managerial goals group and only three of those with non-managerial goals (see Table 4.4) were females. This was the mid-1960s and such situations were the norm. In any event no evidence could be adduced as to career relationships involving female managers. A need for further research on female careers remains just as much in evidence for the hierarchic theory as it was for the task theory.

The two theories would appear to be equally subject to explanation of the large correlations obtained from the career analyses. Early career decisions in the hierarchic domain, though producing small effects at the beginning, can escalate as many decisions pile up, so that ultimately leadership status and top management careers are the result. This explanation is just as applicable to movement up the hierarchic chain as it is to aggrandizement of an entrepreneurial venture.

CHAPTER 31

CONGRUENCE AND THE SIGNIFICANCE OF CAREERS IN TESTING ROLE MOTIVATION THEORY

USING PROFESSIONAL MOTIVE PATTERNS

INTRODUCTION

Chapter 31 represents the application of the model from Chapter 29 to the professional domain and Form P of the Miner Sentence Completion Scale (MSCS). This particular ordering of these chapters has been dictated by the number of studies that are applicable. The material presented has not been published previously; it is original to this volume.

* * *

In this chapter the major concern is with professional organizations, professional theory, professional motivation, and professional roles. The discussion of hypothesis generation in Chapter 29 is applicable, but now with an emphasis on professional organizations and professionals. The standing hypothesis from theory is to the effect that in professional systems professional motivation should be at a high level among professional leaders, and it should be positively correlated with other professional success indexes; professional (intellectual) motivation should not differentiate in these ways within other types of systems.

For the reason specified in Chapter 29 for task theory, the professional theory operates according to the following hypotheses:

Hypothesis 1. *Congruent analyses, which are conducted comparing those with careers inside the professional domain against those having careers outside that domain on measures of professional motivation, should produce correlations that—*

a) exceed correlations obtained using only those having careers outside the professional domain;

b) exceed correlations obtained using criterion variables other than career status, but still appropriate to the professional domain, such as performance indexes;

c) exceed correlations obtained using predictors other than measures of professional motivation, but still appropriate to the professional domain.

Hypothesis 2. *Congruent analyses, which are conducted comparing those with leadership careers inside the professional domain against either those having non-leader careers inside the professional domain or those having careers outside the domain on measures of professional motivation, should produce correlations that—*

a) exceed correlations obtained using only those having careers outside the professional domain;

b) exceed correlations obtained using criterion variables other than career status, but still appropriate to the professional domain, such as performance indexes;

c) exceed correlations obtained using predictors other than measures of professional motivation, but still appropriate to the professional domain.

Thus, professional leadership careers should operate in terms of these correlational analyses in the same manner as specified in Hypothesis 1 for other professional careers.

METHOD

Measures

The measure of professional motivation used in this investigation was the Miner Sentence Completion Scale–Form P (Miner 1981; 1993).

The major dependent variable of this research was the career—professional or otherwise—undertaken by the respondent. Organizational leadership is viewed as a career phenomenon; in the professional context leaders may be compared with non-leader professionals, who do not meet the elite leadership criteria, or they may be compared against respondents in other than professional careers.

Studies

A key aspect of this chapter is the presentation of correlations; all of the analyses use this statistical form to test the hypotheses. The three studies represent all of the existing research that has been conducted by the author and that is relevant to the stated hypotheses.

Princeton Graduates—Class of 1948 [See Chapter 22]

This study draws upon whole career data and is described in Miner 2002a. The professional sample included a number of specialists who qualified by virtue of advanced education or special experience. The sample contained 38 individuals, 27 of whom qualified as leaders. For purposes of analysis those participants who had either professional careers or professional leadership careers were considered to be in the congruent condition.

Academy of Management Members [See Chapter 9]

The Academy of Management members served as faculty members in the management discipline, broadly defined, at universities and colleges in the United States. There were 112 such individuals; of these 46 qualified as leaders (see Table 9.8). The respondents completed the MSCS–Form P and also the MSCS–Form H, but no other alternative measures. The sample is described in Miner 1980a.

Labor Arbitrators [See Chapter 19]

The labor arbitrators, many of whom were also lawyers, numbered 100, although different subsamples were comprised of somewhat smaller components. There were 43 who were identified as leaders, and 50 who were not (see Table 19.3). Of the group of 100, 63 held law degrees. The primary source of information is Miner, Crane, and Vandenberg (1994), but also see Crane and Miner (1988).

On the Oliver Organization Description Questionnaire (OODQ) the P score is consistently elevated in all groups of arbitrators. The T score is up, but not nearly to the same extent; the scores by organizational context run around 5 or slightly above. H scores and G scores are consistently the lowest (see Table 19.2). This is distinctly a professional sample.

RESULTS

Congruent Careers

Table 31.1 contains correlations relevant to Hypotheses 1a and 2a from the three studies. The congruent values for the total professional score are the most important and they are also the highest. The total professional correlations range from .56 to .87 with all above .50 and thus designated as large. The subscale correlations span a range from .64 to .21, with 23 of the 25 significant. The high level of the correlations continues, now across all three of the analyses, and chapters.

Noncongruent Careers

In Table 31.2 certain noncongruent correlations are considered, which represent all of the correlations of this type that could be computed from the available data. The samples involved are described in prior chapters, as within Table 31.2, as follows:

- The Princeton class [see Chapter 22]
- The Buffalo, New York entrepreneurs [see Chapter 20]
- The SUNY/Buffalo graduate students [see Chapter 21]

These data also relate to Hypotheses 1a and 2a. The correlations are well below those of Table 31.1, and few are significant (a total of 11 out of a possible 42) with less than a majority

Table 31.1

Correlations between Professional Role Motivation Theory Variables and *Congruent* Careers (Including Leadership Careers) **as Professionals**

	N		Motive Patterns					
Samples and Analyses	Congruent Condition	Non-congruent Condition	Total Professional	Acquiring Knowledge	Exhibiting In-dependence	Acquiring Status	Helping Others	Identifying with a Profession
Princeton Graduates (Class of 1948)								
Professional career vs. other	38	47	.56**	.43**	.28**	.36**	.24**	.42**
Professional leadership career								
vs. non-leader professionals	27	11	.82**	.56**	.30	.37*	.64**	.41*
vs. non-professionals	27	47	.65**	.51**	.33**	.42**	.34**	.49**
Academy of Management Members								
Professional leadership career vs. non-leader professionals	46	66	.87**	.43**	.49**	.58**	.49**	.54**
Labor Arbitrators								
Professional leadership career vs. non-leader professionals	43	50	.68**	.42**	.21	.51**	.59**	.46**

*$p < .05$; **$p < .01$

Table 31.2

Correlations between Professional Role Motivation Theory Variables and *Noncongruent* Careers (Including Leadership Careers)

	N		Motive Patterns					
Samples and Analyses	First Mentioned Condition	Second Mentioned Condition	Total Professional	Acquiring Knowledge	Exhibiting Independence	Acquiring Status	Helping Others	Identify-ing with a Profession
Princeton Graduates (class of 1948)								
Managerial vs. entrepreneurial career	31	16	–.27	–.14	–.18	–.18	–.16	–.08
Hierarchic leadership career vs. non-leaders	25	6	.22	.04	.27	–.03	.02	.36
Entrepreneurial leadership career vs. non-leaders	13	3	.30	–.20	.51	–.14	.18	.48
Buffalo, NY Entrepreneurs								
Entrepreneurial leadership career vs. non-leaders	45	44	.33**	.28*	–.01	.37**	–.15	.29*
Career success level	84	—	.24*	.13	.02	.16	.07	.22*
SUNY/Buffalo Graduate Students								
Projected propensity for an entrepre-neurial career	159	—	.08	.00	.19*	–.15	.14	.09
Actual entrepreneurial career (early) vs. other	30	85	.42**	.19	.30*	–.02	.31*	.42**

$*p < .05$; $**p < .01$

Table 31.3

Data Bearing on the Differences between the Results of Congruent (N = 5) **and Noncongruent** (N = 7) **Career Analyses for the Professional Theory**

	Motive Patterns					
Comparison Factors	Total Professional	Acquiring Knowledge	Exhibiting Independence	Acquiring Status	Helping Others	Identifying with a Profession
Median Correlations						
Congruent analyses	.68	.43	.30	.42	.49	.46
Noncongruent analyses	.24	.04	.19	–.03	.07	.29
Percent significant ($p < .05$)						
Congruent analyses	100	100	60	100	100	100
Noncongruent analyses	43	14	29	14	14	43
Comparison of Correlations in Princeton Sample						
Congruent	.56	.43	.28	.36	.24	.42
Noncongruent	–.27	–.14	–.18	–.18	–.16	–.08
p	< .01	< .01	< .01	< .01	< .05	< .01
Congruent	.82	.56	.30	.37	.64	.41
Noncongruent	.22	.04	.27	–.03	.02	.36
p	< .01	< .01	NS	< .05	< .01	NS
Congruent	.65	.51	.33	.42	.34	.49
Noncongruent	.30	–.20	.51	–.14	.18	.48
p	NS	< .01	NS	< .05	NS	NS

NS = not significant at $p < .05$

of the total professional score correlations significant. The leadership careers noted in Table 31.2 use different criteria than in the professional context, employing leaders appropriate to the task and hierarchic domains. To obtain noncongruent results the MSCS–P was applied to these groups. Over a third of the subscale correlations are negative. Especially in the Princeton samples small Ns tend to predominate. Comparing Table 31.2 with Tables 29.2 and 30.2 the results all show the same pattern in that they underperform those for the congruent findings by a considerable amount.

Note that some confounding of professional and task motivation, as noted in the Alternative Instruments section of Chapter 29, is evident in the two Buffalo samples of Table 31.2. That is where the significant correlations occur, and it is due to the fact that although these samples are basically entrepreneurial they contain substantial professional components.

Congruent and Noncongruent Careers Compared

A summary of the differences between the data of Table 31.1 and 31.2 is contained in Table 31.3, again bearing on Hypotheses 1a and 2a. The data, especially for total professional, indicate high levels of correlation for the congruent analyses when careers are used as the dependent variable. All of the subscales appear to contribute to this result. When the Princeton data are used to check on the significance of this finding, one of the three analyses does not yield significance for total professional in spite of a sizable difference in the expected direction; as previously, the small N involved appears to be a contributing factor. Yet two of the subscales do produce a significant supportive result here.

Homogeneity of Career Predictions

Table 31.4 tests the expectation that leadership careers will operate in the same manner as other careers in congruent validity analyses; thus the concluding sentence of Hypothesis 2. The three samples include two instances which involve comparing leadership careers with others and one instance where career is considered independent of leadership considerations. The majority of the correlations are homogeneous (as indicated by the χ^2 values) consistent with the hypothesis. However, there are two instances where this is not the case; total professional motivation yields an outlier in the Academy of Management sample at the high end, and helping others deviates on the low end in the Princeton sample. The total professional finding is not supported in the labor arbitrator sample, and thus does not appear to be distinctive to a leadership career. Since only one non-leadership sample is available for the helping others subscale analysis, no such comparison can be made in this instance. Overall, however, the data support a position indicating that careers are careers, irrespective of whether leadership is involved or not. Also the combined professional correlations in Table 31.4 do not differ substantially from the median correlations for all congruent analyses in Table 30.3. The data from Chapters 29, 30, and 31 consistently indicate essentially the same thing—each reinforces its own unique version of Hypothesis 2.

Congruent Careers Compared with Other Criteria

Table 31.5 deals with whether the results obtained for congruent career analyses differ from those obtained when the dependent variable is not of a career nature, though still congruent. Thus Table 31.5 serves to test Hypotheses 1b and 2b. These other outcomes, beyond careers, include performance ratings, job satisfaction, compensation, position level, and professional behavior (such as publications, professional association activities, and the like). The research does not appear to isolate any of these "other" criteria as particularly likely to yield more valid results. The "other congruent analyses" of Table 31.5 are primarily from Miner (1993), most of which are published in this volume, but also include several unpublished dissertations (see Pilgrim 1986 and Al-Kelabi 1991).

The data of Table 31.5 provide evidence that, holding congruence constant, career analyses produce higher correlations than do other outcome criteria. The total professional data do not fulfill expectations insofar as percent significant are concerned, but this once again is because at the correlation levels involved, both career and "other" criteria yield a large percentage of significance. Clearly it is at the upper levels of validities that *differences* in significance begin to appear.

The subscale analyses of Table 31.5 are consistently supportive of theory in all instances except Independent Action; there the data do not yield the expected results except for the one finding of a significant difference among the Academy of Management members. No explanation for this one subscale failure comes readily to mind. Overall, however, the median career correlation is well up into the large range for total score, and the subscale correlations are generally in the .40s. These congruent findings are set against values of .35 for the "other" criteria with the total score and correlations that average in the .20s for the subscales. Thus the results with Form P are much like those with Forms T and H.

Table 31.4

Tests for Homogeneity of Validity Coefficients Involving *Congruent* Career and Leadership Relationships (Independent Samples)—**Professional Theory**

		Motive Patterns					
Sample Designation	Career Comparison	Total Professional	Acquiring Knowledge	Exhibiting Independence	Acquiring Status	Helping Others	Identifying with a Profession
Princeton class of 1948	Non-leadership	.56	.43	.28	.36	.24	.42
Academy of Management	Leadership	.87	.43	.49	.58	.49	.54
Labor arbitrators	Leadership	.68	.42	.21	.51	.59	.46
χ^2 (for df = 2)		25.45	0	5.75	3.84	8.33	1.22
p		< .01	NS	NS	NS	< .05	NS
combined r (weighted)		.75	.43	.35	.50	.46	.48
distinctive value		.87 (high)				.24 (low)	

NS = not significant at $p < .05$.

Table 31.5

Data Bearing on the Differences between the Results of Congruent Careers Analyses (N = 5) **and Congruent Analyses Involving Other Outcomes** (N = 19) **for the Professional Theory**

	Motive Patterns					
Comparison Factors	Total Professional	Acquiring Knowledge	Exhibiting Independence	Acquiring Status	Helping Others	Identifying with a Profession
Median Correlations						
Congruent career analyses	.68	.43	.30	.42	.49	.46
Other congruent analyses	.35	.18	.22	.20	.21	.22
Percent Significant ($p < .05$)						
Congruent career analyses	100	100	60	100	100	100
Other congruent analyses	79	42	68	53	58	58
Comparison of Correlations in Samples Where Appropriate Data were Available:						
Academy of Management Members						
Career-Leader vs. non-leader	.87	.43	.49	.58	.49	.54
Other—frequency of meeting attendance	.35	.07	.29	.25	.07	.32
p	< .01	< .01	< .05	< .01	< .01	< .05
Labor Arbitrators						
Career-Leader vs. non-leader	.68	.42	.21	.51	.59	.46
Other-management consensus rating	.32	.21	.07	.27	.24	.25
p	< .01	NS	NS	< .05	< .01	< .05

NS = not significant at $p < .05$

Alternative Instruments

The data testing Hypotheses 1c and 2c are deficient in most respects; there simply are not sufficient alternative instruments to bring to bear. In part this is because such instruments that would be applicable in the professional domain are few in number; psychometric research in this area has been limited. Furthermore, our own studies have been deficient in this regard.

The best evidence with regard to using Form H as a predictor within the professional domain comes from Chapter 9, where both Forms P and H were used. Whereas the former predicted a leadership career with a value of .87 using the total score, the Form H total score predicts with a coefficient of .11 (see Table 9.8); the subscales of Form P average .49, while those of the incongruent Form H correlate with the professional criterion at .06. Additional data are given in Table 22.3, pointing to the same conclusion.

Analyses from Chapter 22 do nothing to indicate that Forms T and H do anything to extend what has been said previously on this score.

DISCUSSION

The findings provide strong support for the congruent hypothesis of professional role motivation theory and for the view that professional leadership careers are indeed careers, operating much as do other professional careers. However, the truly significant finding is that the professional theory's motives predict career identification at a level well above that found with other criteria and predictors; correlations that rise into the .80s are obtained. All in all the findings in this regard obtained with the task theory (Chapter 29) continue into the hierarchic theory (Chapter 30) and now on into the professional theory (Chapter 31).

Scorer Diversity

All of the MSCS data of this chapter were scored directly by the author. Thus Table 31.1 does not contain any Form P scorings of a kind that might provide for diversity in this regard. However, the two dissertations noted previously do provide for some check on author bias.

In the Pilgrim (1986) instance, Form P was administered to 90 special education program personnel (mostly teachers) who as a group had an H-score of 7.3 and a P-score of 8.9 on the OODQ. When compared to the OODQ norms (see Chapter 12) they were higher on the hierarchic scale and lower on the professional scale, but still predominantly professionals. After instruction from the author, Pilgrim scored the 90 Form Ps. Subsequently 10 protocols were selected at random and rescored by the author. Comparison of the Pilgrim data with those provided by the author resulted in the following—

Total score—percent agreement 94.9 ($r = .98$)
Acquiring knowledge—percent agreement 91.5 ($r = .90$)
Independent action—percent agreement 93.9 ($r = .89$)
Accepting status—percent agreement 100.0 ($r = 1.00$)
Providing help—percent agreement 93.9 ($r = .91$)
Professional commitment—percent agreement 96.4 ($r = .98$) (Pilgrim 1986, 58).

The reported point-by-point agreement was 95.5 percent.

In the Al-Kelabi (1991) instance, Form P was administered to 301 individuals from a hospital (145), an office automation company (112) and a computer services company (44) in Saudi Arabia. The OODQ results for the total sample were 7.0 for the P-score and 8.4 for the H-score with professionals predominating in the hospital. The scoring of the MSCS–Ps was done by Al-Kelabi after extensive training by the author described as follows—

> The training was given face-to-face in a form of feedback on results and discussion of the rationale of scoring the items. For each session the researcher prepared a long list of items, along with their scores, which he perceived as difficult. Each item was discussed and the rationale of scoring each was emphasized. . . . Along with this training the experienced scorer (Miner) independently scored 14 MSCS–P forms. . . . Three weeks after completion the researcher rescored the 14 reports and yielded almost identical results to that of the experienced scorer (Al-Kelabi 1991, 83).

Based on these two results it appears unlikely that any author bias entered into the findings of Table 31.1. In addition, as with the data reported in Chapters 29 and 30, much of the scoring of these MSCSs was done in the context of hypotheses other than those tested in the current analyses. The Pilgrim and Al-Kelabi studies were not included in the Table 31.1 analyses because I do not have access to leadership or career data for them.

Female Careers

As in other instances, data that would permit separate analyses of female careers are limited. In the Princeton sample there are, of course, no females; in the Academy of Management sample, there are 9 females (4 leaders and 5 not); in the arbitrator sample there are 2 females (1 leader and 1 not). These results are much too small to warrant any analysis of MSCS–Form P findings for females. Yet a comparison of leader total scores with non-leader values yields means of 11.40 and 1.17 respectively; this is in contrast with total sample means of 11.70 and 1.30 (see Table 9.8). These data are surprisingly consistent. On what limited evidence exists female leadership careers are much like male careers, but the need for findings based on much larger samples continues, as with Forms T and H.

Why the Large Correlations?

Again I believe that the process described previously is brought into play, so that small decisions made early in the career escalate along the career track, and following the direction prescribed by a given set of roles, to a point where intellectual leadership status is achieved. Thus the model provided by Martell, Lane, and Emrich (1996) and the reliability achieved through the making of multiple decisions in the same mode is again brought to bear—but this time in the professional domain, rather than the task or hierarchic.

CHAPTER 32

FACTOR ANALYSIS OF THE MINER SENTENCE COMPLETION SCALES

JENNIFER L. MINER

INTRODUCTION

The Miner Sentence Completion Scales (MSCSs) were developed on a conceptual basis, not using factor analysis to specify their constructs. This was an intentional strategy, and it assumes that factor pure constructs are not a requirement for reliability and validity; the Wechsler instruments are offered as a case in point (Miner 1993). Yet there remains a question as to how the MSCS measures would fare at the hands of factor analysis—not because such an approach is required to create effective instruments or to aid in the development of tests with appropriate item structures, but to see how closely the MSCS instruments do in fact, given their conceptual origins, conform to the dictates of factor analysis. To what extent has a meeting of the minds actually occurred here, in spite of the wide diversity in origins?

An opportunity to assess this question developed as the data of Chapter 22 became available, and as Jennifer Miner became educated in the intricacies of factor analysis. This article is indeed a reality because she was able to bring to bear a type of knowledge of both the MSCS measures and of factor analysis that had not previously existed among those working on the role motivation theories. She is to be credited with utilizing her unique combination of skills to produce the following analysis. At the same time she has compiled a fitting overview of the key components of this volume.

* * *

Assessing an employee's propensity to succeed within a particular organization is a critical priority for businesses; developing measures for this purpose is a main concern of organizational behavior. One such set of instruments were the Miner Sentence Completion Scales (MSCSs). These scales, consisting of three parallel forms intended for use in the hierarchical (Form H), professional (Form P) and task (Form T) domains, have proven useful over the years in predicting both concurrent and longitudinal successes of persons operating within these organizational arenas (see Miner 1993, for a review; Miner 1980; Miner, Smith, and Bracker 1989, 1994). However, these instruments have received somewhat mixed reviews in the literature primarily because researchers have questioned the statistical soundness of the measures (Brief, Aldag, and Chacko 1977; Eberhardt, Yap, and Basuray 1988; Stahl 1986), although their validities have been demonstrated many times in practice both in the United States and abroad (Al-Kelabi 1991; Carson and Gilliard 1993; Ebrahimi 1997; Miner 1980, 1993, and in the present volume; Tullar 2001). The present study sought to assess the construct validity of the measures through an exploratory factor analysis to determine whether the obtained factor structure would support the hypothesized theoretical structure of the instruments. Furthermore, the analyses used a sample of established, older adults, rather than college students, who completed all three measures. Such a study has never been carried out previously.

The three instruments share many structural characteristics in common, making it possible to discuss the general format of the measures first, before delving into the specific theories underlying each form. Each of the forms derives from one of the role motivation theories developed by Miner (1993). The set of theories, which parallel one another in their underlying structure and logic, posit a set of role requirements that derive from the particular form of an organization. Organizations can assume one of four types—that of a hierarchic, professional, task, or group form. Corresponding to each organizational structure is a unique set of informal and institutionalized roles that must be fulfilled by leaders. Derived from these roles is a set of motives that match the role requirements. If the fit between the role requirement and the person's motivation is optimal, the likelihood increases that the person will not only fulfill the role requirement, but will be successful in doing so. This goodness-of-fit model between the prescribed roles and motive patterns underlies all of the Miner Sentence Completion Scales.

A second aspect common to the three instruments is their projective nature (see Chapter 1). Each of the Miner Sentence Completion Scales is intended to assess largely unconscious motivations. There were several reasons for taking this direction when the measures were designed. Firstly, by utilizing a projective approach, people completing the measures would have very little idea as to what they were revealing about themselves, and could not, therefore, hide socially undesirable aspects of their behavior. This is a particularly relevant concern in applied settings where supervisors are utilizing the instruments to assess an employee's motivations in light of a potential promotion. Secondly, the use of the projective technique allows for the measurement of motives that are, in fact, largely unconscious to the subject, thereby making them unavailable for conscious self-reporting (Miner 1993).

MSCS–Form H

Research on the first of the measures to be developed, Form H (for hierarchical), was originally published in 1960 (Miner 1960a). The measure was intended to assess the motive patterns of individuals working within typically large, bureaucratic organizations in which power is hierarchically organized and management sets forth job duties and oversees promotions (Miner 1993). The role requirements and matching motive patterns of the hierarchical role motivation theory were developed largely out of the author's experience observing and working within a large corporation and can thus be best characterized as emerging from a grounded theory approach.

Form H was originally designed as a means of assessing the success of an experimental course offered within the Research and Development Department of a large corporation to 72 supervisors (see Chapter 3). The course was intended to increase what later came to be known as "motivation to manage." From both personal insight and contributions from the empirical literature, Miner posited six role requirements and their corresponding motivation patterns as being particularly important to performance within a hierarchical organization. Of the six role requirements, the first role prescribed by the theory was positive relations with authority that matched with the motive pattern of favorable attitudes toward superiors. The second role, competing with peers, and the matching motive pattern of desire to compete, represents the desire and ability to compete with others in order to advance and win status within the organization's hierarchy. The third role, imposing wishes on subordinates, is associated with the desire to exercise power and denotes the ability and desire to give others in subordinate positions directives and to act in a position of authority. The fourth role, behaving assertively, matches with the desire to assert oneself. This role is characterized by taking charge, making decisions, and protecting one's group and was historically known as the masculine role. The fifth role, standing out from the group, matches with a desire to be distinct and different and corresponds to a person's tendency to assume a position of high visibility and to deviate from common group practices. Finally, the sixth role, performing routine administrative functions, matches with a desire to perform routine duties responsibly and relates to a person's attitude toward performing routine tasks required by the managerial job.

To best operationalize the constructs arising from the hierarchic role motivation theory, a projective, sentence-completion scale was designed. The stems for the instrument were originally piloted on a set of 21 managers and those items that were most likely to elicit a range of responses and to best distinguish successful from less successful managers were selected (Miner 1993). A final set of 35 items made up the instrument, with 5 filler items added to help disguise the purpose involved. Thus, as will be seen with the other MSCSs, a role motivation theory was developed out of a need to understand a particular phenomenon, in this case the motivation to manage, and the theory was then translated into an appropriate assessment measure. As a result of this process, the subscales of Form H closely approximate the role requirements detailed by the hierarchic role motivation theory. These subscales include Authority Figures, Imposing Wishes, Routine Administrative Functions, Assertive Role, and Standing Out from the Group. Items measuring the desire to compete were divided into two subscales, Competitive Games and Competitive Situations. Thus the hierarchic role motivation measure (and its subscales) extends back some 48 years.

Research using Form H, since its inception in the 1960s, has provided empirical data on the validity of the instrument in a variety of settings (see Miner 1993, for a review; Carson and Gilliard 1993; Nystrom 1986). For example, Carson and Gilliard (1993) conducted a meta-analysis of 26 studies utilizing the MSCS–H, and reported that the measure correlated with personality measures, such as the Big Five (extraversion, agreeableness, conscientiousness, emotional stability, and openness to experience (intellect), as predicted. They also found that it was positively related to managerial effectiveness, and that the scale adequately predicted career choices in management. The only apparent anomaly in the study was that there was not a significant difference between managers and entrepreneurs on Form H. Furthermore, in the most comprehensive presentation of research on Form H, Miner (1993) indicates that there is strong concurrent and predictive validity for the instrument, especially the total score, from a range of studies. In terms of the subscale validities, Nystrom (1986) indicated that three of the original seven subscales have demonstrated particularly high validity coefficients in research. These subscales dealt with authority figures, competitive situations, and imposing wishes. This modification to the original hierarchic theory was incorporated in role motivation theory as of that time—more than 20 years ago.

In spite of the apparent validity of the MSCS-H in a variety of studies, some have criticized the instrument on the basis of its low internal consistencies, especially of the subscales (Eberhardt, Yap, and Basuray 1988; Stahl 1986). However, given the way the measure was designed, with reference to external validity but not internal consistency, it is not surprising that it has shown limited internal consistency reliability (Miner 1993). Additionally, it has been argued that strong internal consistency, such as that measured by coefficient alpha, may not be a necessary, or even an appropriate measure for some instruments, depending on how the measure was constructed (see Streiner 2003). Atkinson (1977) argues that internal consistency reliability is not a necessary condition for construct validity when projective measures are involved. In the present study, we explored the internal consistencies of each of the Miner scales to determine whether the particular sample utilized in this study would shed any further light on the issue of the internal consistencies of the MSCSs.

MSCS–Form P

The MSCS–Form P (for professional) followed Form H by approximately twenty years (Miner 1980) and was guided by the professional role motivation theory, which specified a set of five role requirements and their matching motive patterns. In professional systems, in contrast to hierarchical organizations, the overall structure tends to be flat, rather than pyramidal, with stature differentiations based upon professional expertise and experience. Professional systems tend to require extensive training for one to enter into the system, goals are largely set by individuals, and members typically exhibit a high level of commitment and identification with the profession. The seminal type of professional system is individual private practice, though this has increasingly expanded to group practices, and professional organizations or units.

As with Form H, the role requirements for the professional role motivation theory were largely developed out of both the author's personal experience as a university professor and through explorations into the literature on professions and professional organizations. Guided by the professional role motivation theory, he generated and selected items in a manner that paralleled the approach taken for Form H. A large pool of sample items was pre-tested on a sample of professors and advanced doctoral students, and those items that best discriminated between more and less successful professionals and provided variability in response patterns were selected (Miner 1993). The first role requirement specified by the professional role motivation theory was acquiring knowledge, which matched with the motive of a desire to learn and acquire knowledge. Within a professional organization, it is critical to seek to acquire knowledge that can be used in providing an expert service. The second role, independent action, matches with a desire to exhibit independence. Autonomous decision-making and action are necessary for professionals who must keep their clients' interests as a focus. A third role within the professional domain is accepting status, which is associated with the desire to acquire status. According to this role, professionals must be willing to promote themselves and achieve status in order to achieve recognition and meet requests for service from clients. A fourth role requirement, providing help, corresponds to a desire to help others. In the professional domain, services of one sort or another are typically provided to others, and indeed successful professionals will likely enjoy providing help that advances their clients' best interests. Finally, the fifth role requirement is exhibiting professional commitment, where the corresponding motive pattern is achieving a value-based identification with the profession. Such an identification typically works to retain members in the profession and to promote adherence to the set of ethical principles established by the profession.

The first empirical tests of the professional role motivation theory and its corresponding measure, Form P, were conducted with a sample of management professors (Miner 1980) (see Chapter 9). As prescribed by the theory, the author hypothesized that those professionals indicating a generally good fit with the professional motive patterns would be more likely to evidence success in their careers than those whose motive patterns were a poor fit. Additionally, as the role motivation theories are domain limited theories, the author hypothesized that scores on Form H would have little relationship to professional success. Both hypotheses were supported by the research. Management professors in the sample scored consistently higher on professional than managerial motivation. Additionally, subscale and total scores from Form P were significantly correlated with measures of professional success, such as salary level and number of books published. Conversely, this pattern of results was not obtained for the Form H subscales or total score, indicating that the professional theory operates within the professional domain, but the hierarchical theory is largely not relevant (Miner 1980). This validation study of Form P suggests that the theoretical underpinnings of the measure are sound, but never before has this instrument been subjected to a factor analysis to determine whether the statistical structure also supports the theoretical configuration of subscales, as posited by the 1980 theory.

MSCS–Form T

The final organizational form for which an MSCS measure has been designed is for the task domain. The task motivation theory, which is operationalized in Form T, corresponds to an organizational environment in which the pushes and pulls of sanctions are built into a task to be performed (Miner, Smith, and Bracker 1989). Unlike in the hierarchical or professional domains, control over the actor's behavior derives neither from superiors nor from professional norms or organizations, but from the work itself and the individual's motivation. One common example of the task environment is the entrepreneurial situation (see Chapter 15).

The task motivation theory draws heavily upon McClelland's (1961, 1962) achievement motivation theory, and can be seen as an extension and reformulation of that theory within a role motivation framework (Miner 1993). McClelland's theory identifies an achievement situation in which achievement motivation is aroused and which people with a strong achievement motive prefer. The key features of the achievement situation are (1) individual responsibility, (2) moderate risk taking as a function of skill, (3) knowledge of results of situations, (4) novel instrumental activity, and (5) anticipation of future possibilities.

With these components from McClelland's theory guiding the formulation of the task motivation theory, five roles and their corresponding motive patterns were theorized as operating within the task domain. The first of these roles is self-achievement, which is associated with a desire to achieve through one's own efforts and to be able to attribute success to personal behavior. The second role is avoiding risk, which reduces the entrepreneur's likelihood of being pushed out of the task situation through failure. The third role in task motivation theory is seeking results of behavior (or feedback of results), which matches with the motivation to gain a clear understanding of the level of performance achieved. A fourth role is personal innovation, which is associated with a desire to introduce novel, innovative, or creative solutions. Lastly, the fifth role, planning for the future, corresponds to a desire to think about and anticipate future possibilities. As a whole these five roles and their matching motive patterns make up the five subscales of the MSCS–Form T. As with the previous two measures, items were first written and divided into subscales along conceptual lines and then piloted with a sample of entrepreneurs and non-entrepreneurs to determine the best set of items for the scale (Miner 1989, 1993). Thus the theory in its present form with the stated subscales extends back some 18 years.

In a test of the task motivation theory, Miner, Smith, and Bracker (1989) hypothesized that task motivation would be at a high level among entrepreneurs involved in an entrepreneurial situation, and would correlate with indices of success such as firm growth and income. Using a sample of 118 entrepreneurs who had founded a business and a comparison group of 41 manager/scientists who were not founders, the authors observed that entrepreneurs scored significantly higher on the MSCS–Form T than nonentrepreneurs. Task motivation also correlated positively with indexes of firm growth. In a follow-up study with the same sample over 5 years later, it was further demonstrated that those entrepreneurs heading high-growth firms scored significantly higher on the MSCS–T than those leading low-growth firms, with the exception of the risk avoidance subscale (Miner, Smith, and Bracker 1994).

As can be seen in the previous discussion of Form T, as well as with the other MSCSs, one noteworthy aspect of the development of the measures was the manner in which a clear theory preceded the creation of the scales. Rather than being ad hoc, the theories were deliberately developed to explain particular behavior patterns, and this led to the formation of specific scales intended to measure the constructs of each role motivation theory. For example, the professional theory was first considered in 1975, and more fully explicated in the literature in 1980 (Miner 1980). The MSCS–Form P followed a year later (Miner 1981).

Also noteworthy is that in addition to being guided by a clear theory, the MSCSs were conceptually rather than statistically derived. Thus, the measures did not assume a particular factor structure at their inception (Miner 1993; Miner and Raju 2004). With this in mind, the present undertaking in which we sought to apply factor analytic techniques to the three MSCSs was truly exploratory. Although we had specific theoretical reasons for expecting a particular factor structure to emerge, should there be one, it was not clear precisely what would happen in the data. However, such an examination of the MSCSs could conceivably yield important additional information about the psychometric properties and especially construct validity of the instruments; aspects that several have argued have been insufficiently addressed (Brief, Aldag, and Chacko 1977; Eberhardt, Yap, and Basuray 1988; Stahl 1986).

Previous Factor Analyses with the MSCS

Although few attempts have been made to apply factor analytic techniques to the MSCSs, two separate instances do appear in the literature (Eberhardt, Yap, and Basuray 1988; Stahl 1986).

Both analyses deal with the multiple choice version of Form H which was published in 1977. The multiple choice version presents six possible completions for each stem, two that are positive, two that are negative, and two that are neutral. The first factor analysis, conducted by Stahl (1986), utilized a sample of 111 undergraduate students at Clemson University, of which 46 were female. Items from Form H were then scored and factor analyzed via an orthogonally rotated principle components analysis. After retaining factors with Eigen values greater than 1, Stahl reported a total of 14 factors, none of which were interpretable. With these results, Stahl concluded that the factor structure of Form H did not support a 7 factor solution as theorized by the role motivation theory.

A second study, conducted by Eberhardt and colleagues (1988), revealed a much different factor structure within the multiple choice version of Form H than the one obtained by Stahl (1986). In their study, 189 male and 82 female senior business students completed the MSCS–Form H (multiple choice). Again, Eberhardt and his colleagues conducted a principle components analysis on the items from the scale, with an orthogonal rotation. Results yielded 3, rather than 7 factors. The resulting factors were named Being in Front of Groups, Sports, and Image, and comprised items from a variety of the original subscales. With these results the authors, like Stahl (1986), called into question the use of the multiple choice version of Form H.

Taken together, the results of the two factor analyses of the multiple choice version of Form H argue against a clear 7 factor solution as hypothesized by role motivation theory. However, there are several issues that must be considered when examining these results. Firstly, both studies reported factor analyses of Form H at an item level; there was no attempt to factor analyze subscale scores to see if they loaded in a theoretically consistent manner across the three instruments. Such an approach may be more reliable, as the item level reliabilities of the measures have been shown to be quite low (Miner 1993).

Secondly, both factor analyses were conducted using the multiple choice version of Form H, about which Miner (1993) has specifically expressed concerns, as a multiple choice format turns a projective measure into essentially a self-report measure. Data obtained from the multiple-choice version may be impacted by the response format. In particular, score inflation appears to be a problem, though the amount of inflation varies from sample to sample (Miner 1993; Steger, Kelley, Chouiniere, and Goldenbaum 1975). There is a tendency for participants to fail to endorse negative stems as frequently in the multiple-choice version. Together, these factors can influence the quality of the data available for factor analysis; the free-response format would be preferable, as it represents the role motivation theory as originally stated.

A final point to make regarding the Stahl (1986) and Eberhardt, Yap, and Basuray (1988) factor analyses is that both studies utilized student samples of both genders, which can influence the structure of the data obtained. There is some indication in the literature that the scores of males and females may differ on Form H (Bartol, Anderson, and Schneier 1981; Thornton, Hollenshead, and Larson 1997; Eagly, Karau, Miner, and Johnson 1994), but in both factor analyses scores of males and females were combined without consideration of possible gender differences. Interestingly, in the study in which the respondents were predominantly male, the factor structure was somewhat clearer (Eberhardt, Yap, and Basuray 1988) than when the division between males and females was approximately equal. Further research is needed to address whether the factor structure apparent in the measures applies more or less well to samples of men or women.

It is also important to note that both samples were relatively young. College students completing the MSCS may not yet have reached full maturity in their motive patterns, thus creating a hodgepodge of data, which essentially seems to be what Stahl reports. Research on the factor structure of the instruments may benefit from the use of an older group of participants, many of whom have demonstrated leadership roles in their careers, to determine if the factor structure that emerges in such a sample is more likely to be amenable to interpretation.

The Current Study

The current study sought to explore the factor structure of the Miner Sentence Completion Scales in a sample of older adult males who completed all three of the instruments through a mailed survey. Although previous factor analyses looked at the item-level structure of a single instrument (Form H-multiple choice), the present study examined the factor structure of the subscales across the three instruments. One advantage of such an approach is that it can address whether the roles theorized for each domain are statistically confirmed as belonging to their specific domains, or whether some roles are better considered to belong within some different domain. Such a study has never been conducted to our knowledge, but the results do have the potential to improve understanding of the psychometric properties and construct validity of the Miner Sentence Completion Scales.

As each instrument has a specific role motivation theory underlying it, it was hypothesized that the subscales from Form H would load on a single hierarchical factor, that the subscales of Form P would load significantly on a professional factor, and that the Form T subscales would load together on a task factor. Thus, we hypothesized three primary factors, with the subscales from each measure constituting each factor.

METHOD

Procedure

For the purposes of this study, a mail survey was conducted with the surviving members of the class of 1948 at Princeton University conducted on the occasion of the fiftieth anniversary of the class's graduation (1998). This sample permitted the study of a large number of careers in the various domains, which were approximately balanced across the hierarchic, professional, and task domains. Furthermore, the sample had a large proportion of leaders in all three career groups, thus extending the variance in the scores and permitting a better test of our hypotheses.

Participant's names and addresses were obtained from a yearbook published to commemorate the class's fiftieth anniversary (Princeton University Class of 1948 1998). The samples were developed as specified in Chapter 22. Overall, with two mailings, a 30 percent return rate was obtained, which is quite good for a mailed survey in which respondents did not receive any form of reimbursement (James and Bolstein 1990; Roth and BeVier 1998). After the two mailings, the sample consisted of 110 participants, 74 of whom completed all three measures. The remainder provided either one form (n = 33), or two forms (n = 3). In total, 92 Form Hs were received, 85 Form Ps, and 84 Form Ts.

Participants

All participants were male, a result of the fact that Princeton did not admit females until several years after the class graduated. The mean age of the sample was 72, with a range of 70 to 80; three-quarters of the respondents were either 71 or 72. Within the sample, 72 percent listed themselves as retired, thus the sample represents predominately whole careers. Designations regarding career types were made from class yearbooks and other sources, as discussed in Chapter 22. The final sample consisted of 48 managers of whom 38 were classified as hierarchic leaders, 38 professionals and specialists of whom 27 were leaders, and 24 entrepreneurs, of whom 19 were task leaders.

Sample Representativeness

Concerns about sample representativeness led to the conduct of analyses to determine whether respondents differed significantly from non-respondents. By comparing the responses on the study variables of the first-wave respondents with those of the second-wave, evidence on the probability of non-response bias can be obtained in surveys such as this where approximately 70 percent did not respond. The evidence as set forth in Chapter 22 substantially supports the representativeness of the respondent sample.

MEASURES

Demographics

Included in the mailings sent to participants was a questionnaire requesting information about participants' age, education, and current employment status.

Miner Sentence Completion Scales

The three instruments comprising the Miner Sentence Completion Scales are intended for use within the hierarchic, professional, and task domains, as described previously. For each measure, a set of sentence stems are presented, which participants complete in a manner that "expresses their real feelings." Each item was scored by John B. Miner using the corresponding scoring guide for each instrument (Form H: Miner 1964; Form P: Miner 1981; Form T: Miner 1986). Previous assessments on the reliability of scoring—where the person who devised the instruments and the scoring procedures was one participant, and a trained scorer was the other—suggest a high degree of reliability in the scoring procedures. With only a few exceptions, scorer reliabilities are in the .90s; the total score medians are all .95 or above, and the subscale median is .91 or higher (Miner 1993; 2002).

Statistical Analysis

In the present study, an exploratory principle components factor analysis utilizing the subscale scores from each instrument was undertaken. One primary reason for taking this approach was that we sought to do a factor analysis of the three instruments in combination, and using the item scores would have resulted in 115 items in the factor analysis. When considering our sample size of 110, this would have resulted in a prohibitively large number of items to factor analyze given the restrictions imposed by the sample size. The use of subscale scores was also advantageous in that these are much more reliable measures than are the individual items.

Secondly, we chose an exploratory analysis rather than a confirmatory factor analysis for two reasons. First, our study was truly exploratory in nature. The MSCSs were not developed with factor analysis in mind, as has been discussed, and therefore the author was uncertain what would emerge in the data. Secondly, a confirmatory factor analysis requires a much larger sample size than we had at our disposal.

To test the factor structure of the subscales of the three Miner Sentence Completion Scales, two analyses were performed. The first was the extraction and rotation of three principal components to determine whether the subscales adhered to the hypothesized three factors (hierarchical, professional, and task). Following this, an additional analysis was conducted by extracting, rotating, and interpreting all factors with an Eigen value greater than one. This exploratory analysis was undertaken to assess whether additional, unthought-of, factors would emerge in the data. Varimax rotations were utilized in each factor analysis undertaken. Lastly, we calculated the difference in internal consistency reliabilities of the scales based on their original subscale configurations, and then based upon their structure as suggested by the factor analysis.

RESULTS

Prior to conducting the factor analyses, descriptive statistics were calculated for each of the subscales that comprised Forms H, P, and T of the Miner Sentence Completion Scales (Table 32.1). Following this, subscale scores were converted to standardized scores, and missing values were substituted using the mean of the subscale for the sample. The amount of missing data for the forms was 16.4 percent, 23.6 percent, and 22.7 percent for Forms H, P, and T, respectively. Analyses were conducted using both the mean-substituted data and the original data, and results were consistently in the same direction, although the use of the mean-substituted data allowed for greater power in the analyses.

Results of the initial extraction and rotation of three primary factors revealed that the subscales of the Hierarchic Form of the MSCS loaded primarily on Factor 1, the subscales of the Professional Form loaded predominately on Factor 2, and the subscales of Form T loaded highest on Factor 3. Specific data on the three factors is presented in Table 32.2. Cumulatively, the three factors explained 37.05 percent of the variance, with Factor 1 contributing 14.54 percent, Factor 2, 12.60 percent; and Factor 3, 9.91 percent.

Using the convention of interpreting a factor based on items that load above .40, the Form H subscales of Competitive Situations, Competitive Games, Imposing Wishes, Authority Figures, and Standing Out from the Group can be seen as belonging to the Hierarchic factor. Additionally, the Form T subscale of Avoiding Risks loaded negatively on this first factor. The Form H subscales of Routine Administrative Functions and Assertive Role did not approach the critical value of .40.

The second factor, best characterizing the Professional Form of the MSCS, includes 4 of the 5 subscales from Form P. These subscales include Professional Commitment, Accepting Status, Acquiring Knowledge, and Providing Help; the Form P subscale of Independent Action had a factor loading value below .40. No additional subscales from the other MSCSs loaded on this Professional factor. Similarly, the Task Factor (Factor 3), includes 4 of the 5 subscales from Form T. Specifically, Self-Achievement, Feedback of Results, Personal Innovation, and Planning for the Future loaded on Factor 3. The only subscale from Form T that did not load on this factor was Avoiding Risks, which was found to load negatively on the Hierarchic factor. Of the 17 subscales analyzed, 13 loaded on a factor as hypothesized, for a 76 percent hit rate overall.

Given the exploratory nature of the present study, we also submitted the data to a principal

Table 32.1

Descriptive Statistics for the MSCS Subscales

	M	*SD*
MSCS–Form H (n = 92)		
Authority Figures	.70	1.76
Competitive Games	.07	2.02
Competitive Situations	–.43	1.79
Assertive Role	–.18	1.80
Imposing Wishes	.88	1.86
Standing Out from Group	.77	1.60
Routine Administrative Functions	.72	1.81
MSCS–Form P (n = 85)		
Acquiring Knowledge	1.30	2.40
Independent Action	1.59	2.44
Accepting Status	1.05	2.98
Providing Help	2.68	2.44
Professional Commitment	1.44	2.27
MSCS–Form T (n = 84)		
Self-Achievement	1.55	2.50
Avoiding Risks	1.46	2.77
Feedback of Results	–.26	2.64
Personal Innovation	1.75	3.01
Planning for the Future	–.13	2.91

Note: MSCS = Miner Sentence Completion Scale.

components analysis in which all factors with an Eigen value greater than 1 were extracted and rotated. This was done to determine if any unthought-of factors would emerge in the data allowing for a better characterization of the structure of the MSCS subscales. When this analysis was completed, there were a total of 6 factors, explaining approximately 59 percent of the total variance. In examining the highest loading subscales, Factor 1 best resembled the professional factor from the first analysis. Loading on this factor were Acquiring Knowledge (.66), Accepting Status (.62), Providing Help (.62) and Professional Commitment (.65). An attempt was made to interpret the remaining factors, but no clear patterns were evident. The lack of interpretability of these remaining factors suggests that a three-factor solution is best at characterizing the structure of the MSCS subscales in this sample.

Based on the results of the three-factor solution, steps were undertaken to assess the extent to which the internal consistency reliabilities of the Professional, Hierarchic, and Task scales improved when constrained to only those subscales shown to load highly on their corresponding factors. For example, for the Professional scale, a Cronbach's alpha was computed based on all of the original subscales in the measure, and then a modified Cronbach's alpha including only the subscales of Acquiring Knowledge, Accepting Status, Providing Help, and Professional Commitment as these were the subscales that loaded above .40 on the Professional factor. Using Alsawalmeh and Feldt's (1994) test of the equality of two dependent alpha coefficients, it was found that the difference between the original Form P alpha coefficient (.586) and the modified Form P alpha (.599) was not statistically significant. Similar non-significant results were obtained for the Form T (original $\alpha = .491$; modified $\alpha = .520$) and Form H alpha coefficients (original $\alpha = .568$; modified $\alpha = .620$). However, when a modified alpha was computed for Form H with the addition of Avoiding Risks (reversed) from Form

Table 32.2

Rotated Factor Matrix of MSCS Subscales with Varimax Rotation

Subscale Name	Factor 1	Factor 2	Factor 3
MSCS—Form P			
Acquiring Knowledge	−.178	**.649**	−.146
Independent Action	−.140	**.228**	.139
Accepting Status	.023	**.660**	.109
Providing Help	.015	**.564**	.330
Professional Commitment	−.036	**.731**	−.144
MSCS—Form T			
Self-Achievement	.051	−.218	**.652**
Avoiding Risks	**−.463**	.065	.189
Feedback of Results	.336	.171	**.519**
Personal Innovation	−.167	.002	**.598**
Planning for the Future	−.084	.158	**.674**
MSCS—Form H			
Authority Figures	**.569**	.241	−.199
Competitive Games	**.618**	.019	.146
Competitive Situations	**.684**	−.168	.187
Assertive Role	**.188**	−.076	−.084
Imposing Wishes	**.587**	−.191	.136
Standing Out from Group	**.484**	.169	.352
Routine Administrative Functions	**.265**	−.091	−.137

Note: MSCS = Miner Sentence Completion Scale. N = 110. Highest factor loadings are given in bold.

T, the resulting internal consistency value was marginally improved from the original scale (original α = .568; modified α = .642; $F_{173, 227} = 1.207$, $p < .10$).

DISCUSSION

The results of this factor analysis of the Miner Sentence Completion Scales substantially support the theorized structure of the instruments in this sample. When constrained to three factors, which is the number of components suggested by the role motivation theories, a clear structure emerged in which the subscales loaded on their theoretically relevant components. In the analysis using all factors with an Eigen value greater than 1, six factors emerged, but these were largely not interpretable. However, using the Eigen values > 1 approach has been soundly criticized in the past, suggesting that it is not always an appropriate method for correctly identifying factors (Cudek 2000; Steger 2006; Tabachnick and Fidell 2001). In the present study, a theory-guided approach yielded the clearest and most interpretable results.

In the three factor solution, five of the hypothesized seven subscales loaded on a Hierarchic component (Factor 1), four of the five hypothesized subscales loaded on a Professional factor, and similarly four of the five subscales from Form T loaded together on a Task factor. Furthermore, where subscales could not be said to load substantially on a particular factor (< .40), they still loaded most highly on the factor to which they were hypothesized to belong. For example, the Routine Administrative Functions subscale from Form H loaded at approximately .30 on the Hierarchic component, which is greater than its loadings on either of the other two factors. The only exception to this rule was in the case of Avoiding Risks from Form T; this subscale loaded most highly on the Hierarchic factor (negatively). Overall, however, a preponderance of the evidence strongly supports the composition of the three role motivation theories. A discussion of the specific findings of the study follows, along with an assessment of the advantages and limitations involved and future directions for research.

The structure of the Hierarchic factor was found to consist of the subscales of Authority Figures, Competitive Games, Competitive Situations, Imposing Wishes, and Standing Out from the Group from Form H; the Avoiding Risk subscale Form T loaded negatively on this component in this sample. It is particularly noteworthy that the subscales of Authority Figures, Competitive Situations, and Imposing Wishes all loaded highly on this factor, as it has been argued in the literature that these three can be expected to have the highest validity coefficients of the Form H subscales (Nystrom 1986). The results of the present analyses further validate the use of these subscales. Note that these are most consistent with the hierarchic chain of a bureaucracy.

The subscales that did not appear to be important contributors to the Hierarchic factor—Assertive Role and Routine Administrative Functions—would appear to be less central to the Hierarchic role motivation theory (as anticipated).

The one unusual finding that emerged in connection with the Hierarchic factor was the suggestion that managers tend to be risk takers, as indicated by the negative loading of the avoiding risks subscale from Form T on the Hierarchic factor. Although this result would certainly require replication before more can be made of it, there are reasons to believe that risk taking may be a characteristic of high-level managers. In a study of top-level executives, for example, MacCrimmon and Wehrung (1990) found that the trait of "success" differentiated the risk takers from the risk averters. Specifically, those who were wealthier, had a higher position in the company, and had the greatest authority over employees, were more likely to be risk takers. In contrast, those high on the trait of maturity (older, longer seniority, fewer dependents) were found to be more risk averse. In relation to the present study, the sample of managers consisted largely of "hierarchic leaders," having many traits in common with the successful executives studied by MacCrimmon and Wehrung. Thus, our results are in line with the view that managers are more likely to take risks, especially if they are successful.

Others have similarly argued that managers may have a propensity for risk taking. Miner and Raju (2004) (see Chapter 27), for example, suggest that "the decision making of these subjects [managers] is in fact characterized by considerable risk taking." Their argument is supported by research conducted by Shapira (1995) indicating that managers often resort to cognitive processing in which they fail to adequately perceive the probabilities of possible outcomes, making them more likely to accept risk. There is thus support for the current finding that risk taking may be a characteristic of the hierarchic role. However, additional research is needed to substantiate this possibility, especially with regard to the MSCS–Form H.

Complementary to the finding that the avoiding risk subscale from Form T loaded negatively on a Hierarchic factor is the result that this subscale did not load positively on the Task factor. In this factor analysis, risk avoidance apparently is not highly associated with the other behavior patterns of the task role motivation theory. There has been much debate in the literature regarding the role of risk taking among entrepreneurs (Miner and Raju 2004; Norton and Moore 2002; Stewart and Roth 2001; Xu and Ruef 2004) and as yet no clear consensus has emerged. When originally developed, the MSCS–Form T drew extensively from McClellannd's theory of achievement motivation, which stressed a moderate level of risk taking among entrepreneurs. However, in testing the measure, it became evident that business founders in fact scored in the direction of risk avoidance, and hence this aspect became incorporated into the task role motivation theory and its corresponding measure (Miner 1989). Results of the current factor analysis suggest that risk avoidance may be less centrally associated with the theorized behavior pattern described by the task role motivation theory; yet these results also do not indicate that the theory is better characterized by a risk-taking propensity among entrepreneurs. Many questions still remain regarding the role of risk taking among entrepreneurs (Miner and Raju 2004), and the current findings only highlight the need to delve more deeply into this issue.

The results of the three factor principle components analysis further indicate that the subscale of Independent Action does not load highly on the Professional factor. Although the tendency to exhibit independence of thought and action regardless of the opinions of others is considered a central component of the professional role motivation theory, it may be most applicable to private practitioners (Miner 1993). Professionals in the role of private practitioners, such as therapists and lawyers, must ascertain the best interests of their clients and then act to serve those interests, even in the face of opposition from social norms, other interested parties, or the clients themselves (Miner 1993). In the current study, although about a third of the sample could be characterized as having a professional occupation, only seven of these were in private practice. Therefore, the result obtained may be partially related to the sample utilized. In a sample of proportionally greater private practitioners, the role of Independent Action may be more highly associated with professional role motivation. On the other hand it is also possible that this subscale lacks applicability to certain professional contexts.

The purpose of the current study was to conduct a factor analysis utilizing the subscale scores from the Miner Sentence Completion Scales to better understand the statistical structure of the instruments. It was hypothesized that a three factor solution would best represent the structure of the three MSCS forms, and our hypotheses in this regard were substantially supported.

In conducting the present study, there are some limitations that are necessary to address. In particular, the results presented are specific to the sample utilized. By utilizing a sample of largely retired Princeton graduates, the study was able to remove the influences of a variety of demographic factors, but this in turn limits the generalizability of the findings. However, there were many advantages to the current sample as well. One such advantage was that the sample consisted of older participants who had whole career data available, which represents an ideal sample in which to test the structure of the role motivation theories. Because their motive patterns have been strengthened over time as a result of occupational experiences, older participants provide a potentially more valid test of the tenets of the role motivation theories, than, for example, a student sample would. Secondly, by having a sample characterized by a substantial number of career leaders, the range of scores obtained on the MSCSs is extended, since high level scores become more common. Lastly, research suggests that the careers and motive patterns of females may differ substantially from those of males, thus making the use of an entirely male sample advantageous (Melamed 1996; Miner, this volume). In future research, however, it would be useful to assess the factor structure of the MSCSs in a similar sample of females.

One other limitation of the present study was its relatively small sample size, which restricted any ability to test the structure of the scales using item scores. Such an exploration would provide a finer-grained assessment of the empirical structure of the MSCSs. However, the items tend to be unreliable; thus the use of the subscale scores appears to have been beneficial, in that the subscales are generally more reliable than are the items (Miner 1993).

The results of the present study largely support the theoretical structure of the Miner Sentence Completion Scales; thus they contribute to the construct validity of these measures. Overall, the majority of the subscales hypothesized to load together on a particular factor did so. Of the 17 subscales analyzed, only the subscales of Avoiding Risks (Form T), Independent Action (Form P), Routine Administrative Functions (Form H), and Assertive Role (Form H) did not operate as anticipated. Where theory was not clearly supported, further investigation seems warranted to better understand the motives involved.

REFERENCES

Abelson, Robert P. (1985). A Variance Explanation Paradox: When a Little is a Lot. *Psychological Bulletin,* 97, 128–133.

Acker, J. (1991). Hierarchies, Jobs, Bodies: A Theory of Gendered Organizations. In J. Lorber and S. A. Farrell (Eds.), *The Social Construction of Gender.* Newbury Park, CA: Sage, 162–179.

Adler, Nancy J. (1993). An International Perspective on the Barriers to the Advancement of Women Managers. *Applied Psychology: An International Review,* 42, 289–300.

Adler, Nancy J., Campbell, N., and Laurent, A. (1989). In Search of Appropriate Methodology: From Outside the People's Republic of China Looking in. *Journal of International Business Studies,* 20(1), 61–74.

Adler, Nancy J., and Israeli, D. N. (Eds.) (1988). *Women in Management Worldwide.* Armonk, NY: M.E. Sharpe.

Adler, Nancy J., and Israeli, D. N. (Eds.) (1994). *Competitive Frontiers: Women Managers in a Global Economy.* Cambridge, UK: Blackwell.

Adorno, Theodore W., Frenkel-Brunswik, Else, Levinson, Daniel J., and Sanford, R. Nevitt (1950). *The Authoritarian Personality.* New York: Harper and Row.

Ahmed, S. U. (1985). nAch, Risk-taking Propensity, Locus of Control, and Entrepreneurship. *Personality and Individual Differences,* 6, 781–782.

Aiken, L. R. (1994). *Psychological Testing and Assessment.* Needham Heights, MA: Allyn & Bacon.

Albert, Michael (1977). An Investigation of the Relationship between Creative Ability and Managerial Motivation. Doctoral dissertation, Georgia State University, Atlanta, GA.

Aldrich, Howard E. (1979). *Organizations and Environments.* Englewood Cliffs, NJ: Prentice-Hall.

Al-Kelabi, Saad A. (1991). A Multiple Level, Limited Domains Theory of Leadership in Professional and Hierarchic Domains. PhD dissertation, State University of New York, Buffalo, NY.

Alsawalmeh, Y., and Feldt, L. S. (1994). A Modification of Feldt's Test of the Equality of Two Dependent Alpha Coefficients. *Psychometrica,* 59, 49–57.

Amaewhule, Weyebo A. (1982). Managerial Motivation among Females: A Status Study of Black American Females. PhD dissertation, Georgia State University, Atlanta, GA.

Amis, W. D., and Stern, S. E. (1974). A Critical Examination of Theory and Function of Voluntary Associations. *Journal of Voluntary Action Research,* 3, 91–99.

Anastasi, Ann (1982). *Psychological Testing.* New York: Macmillan.

Anderson, Michael C. (2003). Rethinking Interference Theory: Executive Control and the Mechanisms of Forgetting. *Journal of Memory and Language,* 49, 415–445.

Anderson, Michael C. (2005). The Role of Inhibitory Control in Forgetting Unwanted Memories. A Consideration of Three Methods. In C. MacLeod and B. Uttl (Eds.), *Dynamic Cognitive Processes.* Tokyo, Japan: Springer-Verlag, 159–190.

Anderson, Michael C. (2006). Repression: A Cognitive Neuroscience Approach. In M. Mancia (Ed.), *Neuroscience and Psychoanalysis.* Milan, Italy: Springer, 327–350.

Anderson, Michael C., and Green, Collin (2001). Suppressing Unwanted Memories by Executive Control. *Nature,* 410, 366–369.

Anderson, Michael C., and Levy, Benjamin J. (2002). Repression Can (and Should) Be Studied Empirically. *Trends in Cognitive Science,* 6, 502–503.

Anderson, Michael C., and Levy, Benjamin J. (2006). Encouraging the Nascent Cognitive Neuroscience of Repression. *Behavioral and Brain Sciences,* 29, 511–513.

Anderson, Michael C., Ochsner, K. N., Kuhl, B., Cooper, J., Robertson, E., Gabrieli, S. W., Glover, G. H., and Gabrieli, J. D. E. (2004). Neural Systems Underlying the Suppression of Unwanted Memories. *Science,* 303, 232–235.

Arsan, Noyan, Hunsicker, Frank R., and Southern, Lloyd J. F. (1983). A Comparative Study of the Motivation to Manage of Turkish and U.S. Business Students. *Southern Management Association Proceedings,* 222–224.

Asch, Morton J. (1951). Nondirective Teaching in Psychology: An Experimental Study. *Psychological Monographs,* 65 (4, Whole No. 321).

Ashforth, Blake E. (2001). *Role Transitions in Organizational Life: An Identity-based Perspective.* Mahwah, NJ: Lawrence Erlbaum.

Association for Research in Nervous and Mental Disease (1950). *Life Stress and Bodily Disease.* Baltimore, MD: Williams and Wilkins.

Atkinson, John W. (1977). Motivation for Achievement. In T. Blass (Ed.), *Personality Variables in Social Behavior.* Hillsdale, NJ: Erlbaum Associates, 25–108.

Avolio, Bruce J. (2007). Promoting More Integrative Strategies for Leadership Theory-building. *American Psychologist,* 62, 25–33.

Avolio, Bruce J., and Yammarino, Francis J. (Ed.) (2002). *Transformational and Charismatic Leadership: The Road Ahead.* New York: Elsevier Science.

Ayman, Roya (2002). Contingency Model of Leadership Effectiveness: Challenges and Achievements. In Linda L. Neider and Chester A. Schriesheim (Eds.), *Leadership.* Greenwich, CT: Information Age Publishing, 197–228.

Bakan, D. (1966). *The Duality of Human Existence: An Essay on Psychology and Religion.* Chicago, IL: Rand McNally.

Ball, K. (1991). Study Finds Few Women Hold Top Executive Jobs. *Washington Post,* Aug. 26, A-11.

Barak, Azy (2001). A Cognitive View of the Nature of Vocational Interests: Implications for Career Assessment, Counseling, and Research. In Frederick T. L. Leong and Azy Barak (Eds.), *Contemporary Models in Vocational Psychology: A Volume in Honor of Samuel H. Osipow.* Mahwah, NJ: Lawrence Erlbaum, 97–131.

Bargh, John A. (1990). Auto-motives: Preconscious Determinants of Social Interaction. In E. T. Higgins and R. M. Sorrentino (Eds.), *Handbook of Motivation and Cognition, Volume 2: Foundations of Social Behavior.* New York: Guilford, 93–130.

Bargh, John A. (2007). *Social Psychology and the Unconscious: The Automaticity of Higher Mental Processes.* New York: Psychology Press.

Bargh, John A., and Chartrand, Tanya L. (2000). The Mind in the Middle: A Practical Guide for Priming and Automaticity Research. In H. T. Reis and C. M. Judd (Eds.), *Handbook of Research Methods in Social and Personality Psychology.* New York: Cambridge University Press, 253–285.

Bargh, John A., Gollwitzer, Peter M., Lee-Chai, Annette, Barndollar, Kimberly, and Trötschel, Roman (2001). The Automated Will: Nonconscious Activation and Pursuit of Behavioral Goals. *Journal of Personality and Social Psychology,* 81, 1014–1027.

Bargh, John A., and Pietromonaco, P. (1982). Automatic Information Processing and Social Perception: The Influence of Trait Information Presented Outside of Conscious Awareness on Impression Formation. *Journal of Personality and Social Psychology,* 43, 437–449.

Bargh, John A., and Williams, Erin L. (2006). The Automaticity of Social Life. *Current Directions in Psychological Science,* 15, 1–4.

Barrick, Murray R., and Mount, Michael K. (1991). The Big Five Personality Dimensions and Job Performance: A Meta-Analysis. *Personnel Psychology,* 44, 1–26.

Bartol, Kathryn M., Anderson, Carl R., and Schneier, Craig E. (1980). Motivation to Manage among College Business Students: A Reassessment. *Journal of Vocational Behavior,* 17, 22–32.

Bartol, Kathryn M., Anderson, Carl R., and Schneier, Craig E. (1981). Sex and Ethnic Effects on Motivation to Manage among College Business Students. *Journal of Applied Psychology,* 66, 40–44.

Bartol, Kathryn M., and Martin, David C. (1987). Managerial Motivation among MBA Students: A Longitudinal Assessment. *Journal of Occupational Psychology,* 60, 1–12.

Barton, Allen H. (1968). The Columbia Crisis: Campus, Vietnam, and the Ghetto. *Public Opinion Quarterly,* 32, 333–351.

Bass, Bernard M. (1985). *Leadership and Performance beyond Expectations.* New York: Free Press.

Bass, Bernard M. (1990). *Bass and Stogdill's Handbook of Leadership: Theory, Research, and Managerial Applications.* New York: Free Press.

Baum, J. Robert, Locke, Edwin A., and Kirkpatrick, Shelley A. (1998). A Longitudinal Study of the Relation of Vision and Vision Communication to Venture Growth in Entrepreneurial Firms. *Journal of Applied Psychology,* 83, 43–54.

Bayes, M., and Newton, P. M. (1978). Women in Authority: A Sociopsychological Analysis. *Journal of Applied Behavioral Science,* 154, 7–20.

Beach, Lee Roy (1998). *Image Theory: Theoretical and Empirical Foundations.* Mahwah, NJ: Lawrence Erlbaum.

Bedeian, Arthur G. (1977). The Role of Self-esteem and n Achievement in Aspiring to Prestigious Vocations. *Journal of Vocational Behavior,* 11, 109–119.

Begin, James P. (1991). *Strategic Employment Policy: An Organizational Systems Perspective.* Englewood Cliffs, NJ: Prentice-Hall.

Begley, Thomas M., and Boyd, David P. (1987). Psychological Characteristics Associated with Performance in Entrepreneurial Firms and Smaller Businesses. *Journal of Business Venturing,* 2, 79–93.

Bell, John E. (1948). *Projective Techniques.* New York: Longmans, Green.

Bellu, Renato R. (1988). Entrepreneurs and Managers: Are They Different? *Frontiers of Entrepreneurship Research,* 8, 16–30.

Bellu, Renato R. (1992). Toward a Theory of Entrepreneurial Motivation: Evidence from Female Entrepreneurs. *International Council for Small Business Proceedings,* 37, 195–213.

Bellu, Renato R. (1993). Task Role Motivation and Attributional Style as Predictors of Entrepreneurial Performance: Female Sample Findings. *Entrepreneurship and Regional Development,* 5, 331–344.

Bellu, Renato R., Davidsson, Per, and Goldfarb, Connie (1989). Motivational Characteristics of Small Firm Entrepreneurs in Israel, Italy, and Sweden: A Cross-cultural Study. *Proceedings of the International Council for Small Business,* 34, 349–364.

Bellu, Renato R., Davidsson, Per, and Goldfarb, Connie (1990). Toward a Theory of Entrepreneurial Behavior: Empirical Evidence from Israel, Italy, and Sweden. *Entrepreneurship and Regional Development,* 2, 195–209.

Bellu, Renato R., and Sherman, Herbert (1993). Predicting Entrepreneurial Success from Task Motivation and Attributional Study: A Longitudinal Study. *Proceedings of the United States Association for Small Business and Entrepreneurship,* 8, 16–23.

Bellu, Renato R., and Sherman, Herbert (1995). Predicting Firm Success from Task Motivation and Attributional Style: A Longitudinal Study. *Entrepreneurship and Regional Development,* 7, 349–363.

Belsky, J., and Pasco Fearon, R. (2002). Early Attachment Security, Subsequent Maternal Sensitivity, and Later Child Development: Does Continuity in Development Depend upon Continuity of Caregiving? *Attachment & Human Development,* 4, 361–387.

Bennis, Warren (2007). The Challenge of Leadership in the Modern World. *American Psychologist,* 62, 2–5.

Berant, Ety, Mikulincer, Mario, Shaver, Phillip R., and Segal, Yaacov (2005). Rorschach Correlates of Self-reported Attachment Dimensions: Dynamic Manifestations of Hyperactivating and Deactivating Strategies. *Journal of Personality Assessment,* 84, 70–81.

Bergman, Barbara R. (1986). *The Economic Emergence of Women.* New York: Basic Books.

Berkshire, J. R. (1958). Comparisons of Five Forced-choice Indices. *Educational and Psychological Measurement,* 18, 553–561.

Berman, Frederic E., and Miner, John B. (1985). Motivation to Manage at the Top Executive Level: A Test of the Hierarchic Role-motivation Theory. *Personnel Psychology,* 38, 377–391.

Bird, Barbara J. (1989). *Entrepreneurial Behavior.* Glenview, IL: Scott, Foresman.

Birley, Sue (1987). New Ventures and Employment Growth. *Journal of Business Venturing,* 2, 155–165.

Blankenship, Virginia, Vega, Christopher M., Ramos, Erica, Romero, Katherine, Warren, Kenneth, Keenan, Kathleen, Rosenow, Valery, Vasquez, Jennifer, and Sullivan, Amanda (2006). Using the Multifaceted Rasch Model to Improve the TAT/PSE Measure of Need for Achievement. *Journal of Personality Assessment,* 86, 100–114.

Blau, Peter M., and Scott, W. Richard (1962). *Formal Organizations.* San Francisco, CA: Chandler.

Block, Jeanne H., Haan, Norma, and Smith, M. Brewster (1968). Activism and Apathy in Contemporary Adolescents. In James F. Adams (Ed.), *Understanding Adolescence—Current Developments in Adolescent Psychology.* Boston, MA: Allyn and Bacon, 198–231.

Block, Zenas, and MacMillan, Ian C. (1993). *Corporate Venturing: Creating New Businesses within the Firm.* Boston, MA; Harvard Business School Press.

Boal, Kimberly B., and Hooijberg, Robert (2000). Strategic Leadership Research: Moving On. *Leadership Quarterly,* 11, 515–549.

Boisot, Max, and Child, John (1988). The Iron Law of Fiefs: Bureaucratic Failure and the Problems of Governance in the Chinese Economic Reforms. *Administrative Science Quarterly,* 33, 507–527.

Bond, M. H. (1986). *The Psychology of the Chinese People.* New York: Oxford University Press.

Bond, M. H., et al. (1987). Chinese Values and the Search for Culture-free Dimensions of Culture. *Journal of Cross-cultural Psychology,* 18, 143–164.

Bornstein, Robert F. (2002). A Process Dissociation Approach to Objective-projective Test Score Interrelationships. *Journal of Personality Assessment,* 78, 47–68.

Bowlby, John (1969/1982). *Attachment and Loss: Vol. 1. Attachment.* New York: Basic Books.

Bracker, Jeffrey S., Keats, Barbara, Miner, John B., and Pearson, John N. (1988). Task Motivation, Planning Orientation, and Firm Performance. Working paper, Arizona State University.

Bracker, Jeffrey S., and Pearson, John (1982). *Hierarchic and Professional Motivation among College Students.* Unpublished manuscript.

Bracker, Jeffrey S., Pearson, John N., Keats, Barbara W., and Miner, John B. (1991). Entrepreneurial Intensity, Strategic Planning Process Sophistication, and Firm Performance in a Dynamic Environment. Unpublished paper, University of Louisville. (In Miner 1993, 155–156).

Bramlette, Carl A., Jewell, Donald O., and Mescon, Michael H. (1977). Designing for Organizational Effectiveness: A Better Way; How it Works. *Atlanta Economic Review,* 27(5,6) 35–41, 10–15.

Breaugh, James A. (2003). Effect Size Estimation: Factors to Consider and Mistakes to Avoid. *Journal of Management,* 29, 79–97.

Brenner, O. C., Tomkiewicz, Joseph, and Schein, Virginia E. (1989). The Relationship between Sex Role Stereotypes and Requisite Management Characteristics Revisited. *Academy of Management Journal,* 32, 662–669.

Bretherton, Inge, and Waters, Everett (1985). Growing Points of Attachment Theory and Research. *Monograph of the Society for Research in Child Development,* 50 (1–2, Serial No. 209).

Brief, Arthur P., Aldag, Ramon, J., and Chacko, Thomas I. (1976). The Miner Sentence Completion Scale: A Psychometric Appraisal. *American Institute for Decision Sciences Proceedings,* 171–172.

Brief, Arthur P., Aldag, Ramon J., and Chacko, Thomas I. (1977). The Miner Sentence Completion Scale: An Appraisal. *Academy of Management Journal,* 20, 635–643.

Brockhaus, Robert H. (1980). Risk Taking Propensity of Entrepreneurs. *Academy of Management Journal,* 23, 509–520.

Brockhaus, Robert H., and Horwitz, Pamela S. (1986). The Psychology of the Entrepreneur. In Donald L. Sexton and Raymond W. Smilor (Eds.), *The Art and Science of Entrepreneurship.* Cambridge, MA: Ballinger, 25–48.

Broverman, I. K., Vogel, S. R., Broverman, D. M., Clarkson, F. E., and Rosenkrantz, P. S. (1972). Sex-role Stereotypes: A Current Appraisal. *Journal of Social Issues,* 28(2), 59–78.

Brown, Clarence W., and Ghiselli, Edwin E. (1955). *Scientific Method in Psychology.* New York: McGraw-Hill.

Brown, James A. C. (1954). *The Social Psychology of Industry.* Baltimore, MD: Penguin Books.

Brush, Candida G. (1992). Research on Women Business Owners: Past Trends, A New Perspective and Future Directions. *Entrepreneurship Theory and Practice,* 16, 5–30.

Bryant, Brenda K., Zvonkovic, Anisa M., and Reynolds, Paula (2006). Parenting in Relation to Child and Adolescent Vocational Development. *Journal of Vocational Behavior,* 69 149–175.

Bucher, Rue, and Stelling, Joan G. (1977). *Becoming Professional.* Beverly Hills, CA: Sage.

Budgell, G. R., Raju, Nambury, S., and Quartetti, D. A. (1995). Analysis of Differential Item Functioning in Translated Assessment Instruments. *Applied Psychological Measurement,* 19, 309–321.

Burns, Tom, and Stalker, G. M. (1961, 1994). *The Management of Innovation.* Chicago, IL; Quadrangle.

Busenitz, Lowell W. (1999). Entrepreneurial Risk and Strategic Decision Making: It's a Matter of Perspective. *Journal of Applied Behavioral Science,* 35, 325–340.

Busenitz, Lowell W., and Barney, Jay B. (1994). Biases and Heuristics in Strategic Decision Making: Differences between Entrepreneurs and Managers in Large Organizations. *Academy of Management Proceedings,* 54, 85–89.

Busenitz, Lowell W., and Barney, Jay B. (1997). Differences between Entrepreneurs and Managers in Large Organizations: Biases and Heuristics in Strategic Decision Making. *Journal of Business Venturing,* 12, 9–30.

Butler, Richard P., Lardent, Charles L., and Miner, John B. (1983). A Motivational Basis for Turnover in Military Officer Education and Training. *Journal of Applied Psychology,* 68, 496–506.

Buttner, E. Holly, and Gryskiewicz, Nur (1993). Entrepreneurs' Problem Solving Styles: An Empirical Study Using the Kirton Adaptation/Innovation Theory. *Journal of Small Business Management,* 31(1), 22–31.

Cafferata, G. L. (1982). The Building of Democratic Organizations: An Embryological Metaphor. *Administrative Science Quarterly,* 27, 280–303.

Caird, Sally P. (1993). What Do Psychological Tests Suggest About Entrepreneurs? *Journal of Managerial Psychology,* 8(6) 11–20.

Carper, W. B., and Snizek, William E. (1980). The Nature and Types of Organizational Taxonomies: An Overview. *Academy of Management Review,* 5, 65–75.

Carr, Adrian (2002). Managing in a Psychoanalytically Informed Manner. *Journal of Managerial Psychology,* 17, 343–347.

Carson, Kenneth P., and Gilliard, Debora J. (1993). Construct Validity of the Miner Sentence Completion Scale. *Journal of Occupational and Organizational Psychology,* 66, 171–175.

Cascio, Wayne F. (1982). *Applied Psychology in Personnel Management.* Reston, VA: Reston.

Chandler, Alfred D. (1962). *Strategy and Structure: Chapters in the History of the American Industrial Enterprise.* Cambridge, MA: MIT Press.

Chen, Chao C. (1995). New Trends in Rewards Allocation Preferences: A Sino-U.S. Comparison. *Academy of Management Journal,* 38, 408–428.

Chen, Chao C., Meindl, James R., and Hui, Harry (1998). Deciding on Equity or Parity: A Test of Situational, Cultural, and Individual Factors. *Journal of Organizational Behavior,* 19(2), 115–129.

Chen, Chao C., Meindl, James R., and Hunt, Raymond G. (1997). Testing the Effects of Vertical and Horizontal Collectivism. *Journal of Cross-Cultural Psychology,* 28(1), 44–70.

Chen, Chao C., Yu, K. C., and Miner, John B. (1997). Motivation to Manage: A Study of Women in Chinese State-owned Enterprises. *Journal of Applied Behavioral Science,* 33, 160–173.

Chen, M. (1995). *Asian Management Systems.* New York: Routledge.

Churchill, Neil C., and Lewis, Virginia L. (1983). The Five Stages of Small Business Growth. *Harvard Business Review,* 61(3), 30–50.

Cohen, Bernard P., and Zhou, Xueguang (1991). Status Processes in Enduring Work Groups. *American Sociological Review,* 56, 179–188.

Collins, Christopher J., Hanges, Paul J., and Locke, Edwin A. (2004). The Relationship of Need for Achievement to Entrepreneurial Behavior: A Meta-analysis. *Human Performance,* 17, 95–117.

Collins, Nancy L., and Read, Stephen J. (1990). Adult Attachment, Working Models and Relationship Quality in Dating Couples. *Journal of Personality and Social Psychology,* 58, 644–663.

Collins, Orvis F., Moore, David G., and Unwalla, Darab B. (1964). *The Enterprising Man.* East Lansing, MI: Bureau of Business and Economic Research, Michigan State University.

Collins, William C., Raju, Nambury S., and Edwards, Jack E. (2000). Assessing Differential Functioning in a Satisfaction Scale. *Journal of Applied Psychology,* 85, 451–461.

Cooper, Arnold C., and Gascón, F. Javier Gimeno (1992). Entrepreneurs, Processes of Founding, and New-firm Performance. In Donald L. Sexton and John P. Kasarda (Eds.), *The State of the Art of Entrepreneurship.* Boston, MA: PWS-Kent, 301–340.

Cooper, Arnold C., Woo, Carolyn Y., and Dunkelberg, William C. (1988). Entrepreneurs' Perceived Chances for Success. *Journal of Business Venturing,* 3, 97–108.

Coutu, Diane L. (2004). Putting Leaders on the Couch—A Conversation with Manfred F. R. Kets de Vries. *Harvard Business Review,* 82(1), 65–71.

Crane, Donald P. (1971). How Blacks Become Managers in Atlanta, Georgia Companies. *Training in Business and Industry,* 8(6), 21–26.

Crane, Donald P., and Miner, John B. (1988). Labor Arbitrators' Performance: Views from Union and Management Perspectives. *Journal of Labor Research,* 9, 43–54.

Crant, J. Michael (1996). The Proactive Personality Scale as a Predictor of Entrepreneurial Intention. *Journal of Small Business Management,* 34(3), 42–49.

Cudeck, R. (2000). Exploratory Factor Analysis. In H. E. A. Tinsley and S. D. Brown (Eds.), *Handbook of Applied Multivariate Statistics and Mathematical Modeling.* Mahwah, NJ: Lawrence Erlbaum Associates, 237–259.

Czarniawska-Joerges, B. (1988). *Ideological Control in Nonideological Organizations.* London: Freemond Press.

Dansereau, Fred, Yammarino, Francis J., and Markham, Steven E. (1995). Leadership: The Multiple-level Approaches. *Leadership Quarterly,* 6, 97–109, 251–263.

Dao, Tom K., and Prevatt, Frances (2006). The Psychometric Evaluation of the Rorschach Comprehensive System's Perceptual Thinking Index. *Journal of Personality Assessment,* 86, 180–189.

Dawis, Rene V. (2000). P-E Fit as a Paradigm: Comment on Tinsley (2000). *Journal of Vocational Behavior,* 56, 180–183.

Dawson, Leslie M. (1969). Campus Attitudes toward Business. *MSU Business Topics,* 17, 36–46.

Dayani, Mohammad H. (1980). Academic Library Managers and Their Motivation to Manage. PhD dissertation. Rutgers University, New Brunswick, NJ.

Digman, John M. (1990). Personality Structure: Emergence of the Five-Factor Model. *Annual Review of Psychology,* 41, 417–440.

Dijksterhuis, Ap, and Nordgren, Loran F. (2006). A Theory of Unconscious Thought. *Perspectives on Psychological Science,* 1, 95–109.

DiVesta, Francis J. (1954). Instructor-centered and Student-centered Approaches in Teaching a Human Relations Course. *Journal of Applied Psychology,* 38, 329–335.

Dong, Y. H. (1995). Differing Status of Chinese and American Women. *Beijing Review,* September 4–10, 13–18.

Doty, D. Harold, and Glick, William H. (1994). Typologies as a Unique Form of Theory Building: Toward Improved Understanding and Modeling. *Academy of Management Review,* 19, 230–251.

Drasgow, Fritz, and Hulin, Charles L. (1990). Item Response Theory. In Marvin D. Dunnette and Leaetta M. Hough (Eds.), *Handbook of Industrial and Organizational Psychology,* Vol. 1, Palo Alto, CA: Consulting Psychologists Press, 577–636.

Dubin, Robert (1949). Decision-making by Management in Industrial Relations. *American Journal of Sociology,* 54, 292–297.

Dubin, Robert, and Beise, Fredric (1967). The Assistant: Academic Subaltern. *Administrative Science Quarterly,* 11, 521–547.

Dunning, David, Heath, Chip, and Suls, Jerry M. (2004). Flawed Self-assessment: Implications for Health, Education, and the Workplace. *Psychological Science in the Public Interest,* 5, 69–106.

Dyer, W. Gibb (1992). *The Entrepreneurial Experience: Confronting Career Dilemmas of the Start-up Executive.* San Francisco, CA: Jossey-Bass.

Dyer, W. Gibb (1994). Toward a Theory of Entrepreneurial Careers. *Entrepreneurship Theory and Practice.* 19(2), 7–21.

Eagly, Alice H. (1987). *Sex Differences in Social Behavior: A Social-role Interpretation.* Hillsdale, NJ: Erlbaum.

Eagly, Alice H., and Johnson, Blair T. (1990). Gender and Leadership Style: A Meta-analysis. *Psychological Bulletin,* 108, 233–256.

Eagly, Alice H., and Karau, Steven J. (1991). Gender and the Emergence of Leaders: A Meta-analysis. *Journal of Personality and Social Psychology,* 60, 685–710.

Eagly, Alice H., Karau, Steven J., Miner, John B., and Johnson, Blair T. (1994). Gender and Motivation to Manage in Hierarchic Organizations: A Meta-analysis. *Leadership Quarterly,* 5, 135–159.

Eagly, Alice H., Makhijani, Mona G., and Klonsky, Bruce G. (1992). Gender and the Evaluation of Leaders: A Meta-analysis. *Psychological Bulletin,* 111, 3–22.

Eberhardt, Bruce J., Yap, Choon K., and Basuray, M. Tom (1988). A Psychometric Evaluation of the Multiple Choice Version of the Miner Sentence Completion Scale. *Educational and Psychological Measurement,* 48, 119–126.

Ebrahimi, Bahman (1984). Measuring the Effects of Cultural and Other Explanatory Variables on Motivation to Manage of Potential Managers from Five Countries: A Case of Theory Building and Theory Testing in Cross-cultural Research. PhD dissertation. Georgia State University, Atlanta, GA.

Ebrahimi, Bahman (1997). Motivation to Manage in Hong Kong: Modification and Test of Miner Sentence Completion Scale–H. *Journal of Managerial Psychology,* 12, 401–414.

Eggers, John H. (1995). Developing Entrepreneurs: Skills for the "Wanna Be," "Gonna Be," and "Gotta Be Better" Employees. In Manual London (Ed.), *Employees, Careers, and Job Creation.* San Francisco, CA: Jossey-Bass, 165–184.

Elfhag, Kristina, Rössner, Stephan, Lindgren, Thomas, Andersson, Ingalena, and Carlsson, Anna M. (2004). Rorschach Personality Predictors of Weight Loss with Behavior Modification in Obesity Treatment. *Journal of Personality Assessment,* 83, 293–305.

Elizur, Dov (1984). Facets of Work Values: A Structural Analysis of Work Outcomes. *Journal of Applied Psychology,* 69, 379–389.

Ellingson, Jill E., Sackett, Paul R., and Connelly, Brian S. (2007). Personality Assessment across Selection and Development Contexts: Insights into Response Distortion. *Journal of Applied Psychology,* 92, 386–395.

Elliott, Andrew J., and Reis, Harry T. (2003). Attachment and Exploration in Adulthood. *Journal of Personality and Social Psychology,* 85, 317–331.

Elliott, P. (1972). *The Sociology of the Professions.* London: Macmillan.

England, George W. (1976). *The Manager and His Values: An International Perspective.* Cambridge, MA: Ballinger.

Ensley, Michael D., Carland, James W., and Carland, Jo Ann C. (2000). Investigating the Existence of the Lead Entrepreneur. *Journal of Small Business Management,* 38(4), 59–77.

Epstein, Ann S., and Radin, Norma (1975). Motivational Components Related to Father Behavior and Cognitive Functioning in Preschoolers. *Child Development,* 46, 831–839.

Erdberg, Philip, and Weiner, Irving B. (2007). John E. Exner Jr. (1928–2006). *American Psychologist,* 62, 54.

Etzioni, Amitai (1961, 1975). *A Comparative Analysis of Complex Organizations.* New York: Free Press.

Etzioni, Amitai (1964). *Modern Organizations.* Englewood Cliffs, NJ: Prentice-Hall.

Exner, John E. (1974). *The Rorschach: A Comprehensive System, Volume 1.* New York: John Wiley.

Fernandez, John P. (1975). *Black Managers in White Corporations.* New York: Wiley.

Fiedler, Fred E. (1969). *A Theory of Leadership Effectiveness.* New York: McGraw-Hill.

Fiedler, Fred E., and Chemers, Martin M. (1974). *Leadership and Effective Management.* Glenview, IL: Scott, Foresman.

Fiedler, Fred E., and Chemers, Martin M. (1984). *Improving Leadership Effectiveness: The Leader Match Concept.* New York: Wiley.

Fierman, J. (1990). Why Women Still Don't Hit the Top. *Fortune,* July 30, 40–62.

Filley, Alan C., and Aldag, Ramon J. (1978). Characteristics and Measurement of an Organizational Typology. *Academy of Management Journal,* 21, 578–591.

Fiske, A. P. (1992). The Four Elementary Forms of Sociality: Framework for a Unified Theory of Social Relations. *Psychological Review,* 99, 689–723.

Fitzsimons, Gráinne M., and Bargh, John A. (2004). Automatic Self-regulation. In R. F. Baumeister and K. D. Vohs (Eds.), *Handbook of Self-Regulation.* New York: Guilford, 151–170.

Flacks, Richard (1967). The Liberated Generation: Explanation of the Roots of Student Protest. *Journal of Social Issues,* 23, 52–75.

Fleishman, Edwin A., Harris, Edwin F., and Burtt, Harold E. (1955). *Leadership and Supervision in Industry: An Evaluation of a Supervisory Training Program.* Columbus, OH: Bureau of Educational Research, Ohio State University.

Forsgren, R. A. (1978). *Characteristics of the Academy Member.* Unpublished paper, Department of Management, University of Maine, Orono.

Foti, Roseanne J., and Miner, John B. (2003). Individual Differences and Organizational Forms in the Leadership Process. *Leadership Quarterly,* 14, 83–112.

Fottler, M. D. (1981). Is Management Really Generic? *Academy of Management Review,* 6, 1–12.

Foy, N. (1980). *The Yin and Yang of Organizations.* New York: Morrow.

Frank, E. J. (1988). Business Students' Perceptions of Women in Management. *Sex Roles,* 19, 107–118.

Frederiksen, Norman O., Jensen, Ollie, and Beaton, Albert E. (1972). *Prediction of Organizational Behavior.* Elmsford, NY: Pergamon Press.

French, E. G. (1958). Development of a Measure of Complex Motivation. In John W. Atkinson (Ed.), *Motives in Fantasy, Action, and Society.* Princeton, NJ: Van Nostrand, 242–248.

Fulmer, R. M. (1972). *Managing Associations for the 1980's.* Washington, DC: Foundation of the American Society of Association Executives.

Gabriel, Yiannis (1999). *Organizations in Depth.* London, UK: Sage.

Galbraith, Jay R. (1982). New Venture Planning—The Stages of Growth. *Journal of Business Strategy,* 3(1), 70–79.

Galbraith, Jay R., and Kazanjian, Robert K. (1986). *Strategy Implementation: Structure, Systems, and Process.* St. Paul, MN: West.

Galbraith, Jay R., and Nathanson, Daniel A. (1978). *Strategy Implementation: The Role of Structure and Process.* St. Paul, MN: West.

Gantz, Benjamin S., Erickson, Clara O., and Stephenson, Robert W. (1971). Measuring the Motivation to Manage in a Research and Development Population. *Proceedings of the 79th Annual Convention, American Psychological Association,* 6, 129–130. (Also in John B. Miner (Ed.), *Motivation to Manage: A Ten-year Update on the "Studies in Management Education" Research.* Atlanta, GA: Organizational Measurement Systems Press, 11–17).

Gantz, Benjamin S., Erickson, Clara O., and Stephenson, Robert W. (1972). Some Determinants of Promotion in a Research and Development Population. *Proceedings of the 80th Annual Convention, American Psychological Association,* 7, 451–452. (Also in John B. Miner (Ed.), *Motivation to Manage: A Ten-year Update on the "Studies in Management Education" Research.* Atlanta, GA: Organizational Measurement Systems Press, 18–22).

Gardner, Burleigh B. (1948). What Makes Successful and Unsuccessful Executives? *Advanced Management,* 13, 116–123.

Gardner, Howard (1994). *Creating Minds.* New York: Basic Books.

Gartner, William B. (1985). A Conceptual Framework for Describing the Phenomenon of New Venture Creation. *Academy of Management Review,* 10, 696–706.

Gartner, William B., Mitchell, Terence R., and Vesper, Karl H. (1989). A Taxonomy of New Business Ventures. *Journal of Business Venturing,* 4, 169–186.

Gerth, Hans H., and Mills, C. Wright. (Eds. and trans.) (1946). *From Max Weber: Essays in Sociology.* New York: Oxford University Press.

Ghiselli, Edwin E. (1971). *Explorations in Managerial Talent.* Pacific Palisades, CA: Goodyear.

Ghiselli, Edwin E., and Lodahl, Thomas M. (1958). Patterns of Managerial Traits and Group Effectiveness. *Journal of Abnormal and Social Psychology,* 57, 61–66.

Gidron, B. (1987). Integration of Volunteer Workers into Formal Human Service Agencies: An Organizational Theory Perspective. *Journal of Applied Social Sciences,* 11(2), 191–205.

Ginzberg, Eli, Miner, John B., Anderson, James K., Ginsburg, Sol W., and Herma, John L. (1959). *The Ineffective Soldier, Vol. II: Breakdown and Recovery.* New York: Columbia University Press.

Glaser, Barney G., and Strauss, Anselm L. (1967). *The Discovery of Grounded Theory.* Chicago, IL: Aldine.

Glickman, Albert S., Hahn, Clifford P., Fleishman, Edwin A., and Baxter, Brent (1968). *Top Management Development and Succession: An Exploratory Study.* New York: Macmillan.

Goldner, Jane S. (1986). *Type A Behavior and the Motivation to Manage among Postsecondary Vocational Educators in Georgia.* PhD dissertation, Georgia State University, Atlanta, GA.

Goldstein, Irvin L. (1971). The Application Blank: How Honest Are the Responses? *Journal of Applied Psychology,* 55, 491–492.

Gough, Harrison G. (1965). *The Adjective Check List.* Palo Alto, CA: Consulting Psychologists Press.

Gouldner, Alvin W. (1957). Cosmos and Locals: Toward an Analysis of Latent Social Roles. *Administrative Science Quarterly,* 2, 281–306, 444–480.

Goulet, Laurel R., and Singh, Parbudyal (2002). Career Commitment: A Reexamination and an Extension. *Journal of Vocational Behavior,* 61, 73–96.

Greenberger, Ellen, and Goldberg, Wendy (1989). Work, Parenting and the Socialization of Children. *Developmental Psychology,* 25, 22–35.

Greiner, Larry E. (1972). Evolution and Revolution as Organizations Grow. *Harvard Business Review,* 50(4), 37–46.

Grimsley, Glen, and Jarrett, Hilton F. (1973). The Relation of Past Managerial Achievement to Test Measures Obtained in the Employment Situation: Methodology and Results. *Personnel Psychology,* 26, 31–48.

Grimsley, Glen, and Jarrett, Hilton F. (1975). The Relation of Past Managerial Achievement to Test Measures Obtained in the Employment Situation: Methodology and Results—II. *Personnel Psychology,* 28, 215–231.

Grønnerød, Cato (2004). Rorschach Assessment of Changes Following Psychotherapy: A Meta-analytic Review. *Journal of Personality Assessment,* 83, 256–276.

Grønnerød, Cato (2006). Reanalysis of the Grønnerød (2003) Rorschach Temporal Stability Meta-analysis Data Set. *Journal of Personality Assessment,* 86, 222–225.

Guilford, J. S. (1952). Temperament Traits of Executives and Supervisors Measured by the Guilford Personality Inventories. *Journal of Applied Psychology,* 36, 228–233.

Gutek, B. A. (1993). Changing the Status of Women in Management. *Applied Psychology: An International Review,* 42, 301–311.

Guth, William (1991). Director's Corner—Research in Entrepreneurship. *The Entrepreneurship Forum,* Winter, 11.

Haas, J. E., Hall, J. H., and Johnson, N. J. (1966). In R. V. Bowers (Ed.), *Studies on Behavior in Organizations.* Athens, GA: University of Georgia Press, 157–180.

Hackman, J. Richard, and Oldham, Greg R. (1976). Motivation through the Design of Work: Test of a Theory. *Organizational Behavior and Human Performance,* 16, 250–279.

Hackman, J. Richard, and Wageman, Ruth (2007). Asking the Right Questions About Leadership. *American Psychologist,* 62, 43–47.

Haire, Mason (1956). *Psychology in Management.* New York: McGraw-Hill.

Hall, Douglas T. (2002). *Careers In and Out of Organizations.* Thousand Oaks, CA: Sage.

Hall, Richard H. (1967). Some Organizational Considerations in the Professional-organizational Relationship. *Administrative Science Quarterly,* 12, 461–478.

Hao, K., and Zhou, Y. (1985). Growth of Women's Education. *Women of China,* April, 2–3.

Harlan, Anne, and Weiss, Carol L. (1982). Sex Differences in Factors Affecting Managerial Career Advancement. In Phyllis A. Wallace (Ed.), *Women in the Workplace.* Boston, MA: Auburn House, 59–100.

Harman, J. D. (Ed.) (1982). *Volunteering in the Eighties: Fundamental Issues in Voluntary Action.* Washington, DC: University Press of America.

Harnett, Donald L., and Cummings, Larry L. (1980). *Bargaining Behavior: An International Study.* Houston, TX: Dame.

Harrington, David M., Block, Jeanne H., and Block, Jack (1987). Testing Aspects of Carl Rogers's Theory of Creative Environments: Child-rearing Antecedents of Creative Potential in Young Adolescents. *Journal of Personality and Social Psychology,* 52, 851–856.

Harrison, Frank (1974). The Management of Scientists' Determinants of Perceived Role Performance. *Academy of Management Journal,* 17, 234–241.

Hartman, Edwin (1988). *Conceptual Foundations of Organization Theory.* Cambridge, MA: Ballinger.

Hartmann, Ellen, Wang, Catharina E., Berg, Marit, and Saether, Line (2003). Depression and Vulnerability as Assessed by the Rorschach Method. *Journal of Personality Assessment,* 81, 242–255.

Hassin, Ran R., Uleman, James S., and Bargh, John A. (2005). *The New Unconscious.* New York: Oxford University Press.

Heckhausen, Heinz (1967). *The Anatomy of Achievement Motivation.* New York: Academic Press.

Hedges, Larry V. (1987). How Hard is Hard Science, How Soft is Soft Science? The Empirical Cumulativeness of Research. *American Psychologist,* 42, 443–455.

Hedges, Larry V., and Olkin, I. (1985). *Statistical Methods for Meta-analysis.* Orlando, FL: Academic Press.

Hedges, Larry V., and Vevea, J. L. (1998). Fixed and Random-effects Models in Meta-analysis. *Psychological Methods,* 3, 486–504.

Heilman, Madeline E. (1983). Sex Differences in Work Settings: The Lack of Fit Model. *Research in Organizational Behavior,* 5, 269–298.

Heilman, Madeline E., Block, Caryn J., Martell, Richard F., and Simon, Michael C. (1989). Has Anything Changed? Current Characteristics of Men, Women, and Managers. *Journal of Applied Psychology,* 74, 935–942.

Helburn, I. B., and Shearer, John C. (1984). Human Resources and Industrial Relations in China: A Time of Ferment. *Industrial and Labor Relations Review,* 38, 3–15.

Helgesen, S. (1990). *The Female Advantage: Women's Ways of Leadership.* New York: Doubleday/Currency.

Hemphill, James F. (2003). Interpreting the Magnitude of Correlation Coefficients. *American Psychologist,* 58, 78–79.

Heneman, Herbert G., and Sandver, Marcus H. (1983). Arbitrators' Backgrounds and Behaviors. *Journal of Labor Research,* 4, 115–124.

Henley, John S., and Nyaw, Mee Kau (1986). Introducing Market Forces into Managerial Decision-making in Chinese Industrial Enterprises. *Journal of Management Studies,* 23, 635–656.

Henry, William E. (1949). The Business Executive: The Psychodynamics of a Social Role. *American Journal of Sociology,* 54, 286–291.

Herbst, P. G. (1976). *Alternatives to Hierarchies.* Leiden, Netherlands: Martinus Nijhoff.

Herron, Lanny, and Robinson, Richard B. (1993). A Structural Model of the Effects of Entrepreneurial Characteristics on Venture Performance. *Journal of Business Venturing,* 8, 281–294.

Herzberg, Frederick (1976). *The Managerial Choice: To Be Efficient and To Be Human.* Homewood, IL: Dow-Jones-Irwin.

Hetzner, William A., Tornatzky, Louis G., and Klein, K. J. (1983). Manufacturing Technology in the 1980s: A Survey of Federal Programs and Practices. *Management Science,* 29, 951–961.

Heydebrand, W. (1980). A Marxist Critique of Organization Theory. In William M. Evan (Ed.), *Frontiers in Organization and Management.* New York: Praeger, 125–150.

Hibbard, Stephen (2003). A Critique of Lilienfeld et al's (2000) "The Scientific Status of Projective Techniques." *Journal of Personality Assessment,* 80, 260–271.

Higdon, Hal (1969). *The Business Healers.* New York: Random House.

Hilsenroth, Mark J., and Strickler, George (2004). A Consideration of Challenges to Psychological Assessment Instruments Used in Forensic Settings: Rorschach as Exemplar. *Journal of Personality Assessment,* 83, 141–152.

Hines, George H. (1973). Achievement Motivation, Occupations, and Labor Turnover in New Zealand. *Journal of Applied Psychology,* 58, 313–317.

Hisrich, Robert D., and Brush, Candida G. (1986). *The Woman Entrepreneur: Starting, Financing, and Managing a Successful New Business.* Lexington, MA: Lexington Books.

Historic Liberation of Chinese Women. (1995). *Beijing Review,* September 4–10, 6–9.

Hoffman, Robin W. (1983). A Study of Motivation to Manage: Selected Post-secondary Vocational Educators in Georgia. PhD dissertation. Georgia State University, Atlanta, GA.

Hofstede, Geert (1980). *Culture's Consequences: International Differences in Work-related Values.* Beverly Hills, CA: Sage.

Hokada, Audrey, and Fincham, Frank D. (1995). Origins of Children's Helpless and Mastery Achievement Patterns in the Family. *Journal of Educational Psychology,* 87, 375–385.

Holaday, Margot, Smith, Debra A., and Sherry, Alissa (2000). Sentence Completion Tests: A Review of the Literature and Results of a Survey of Members of the Society for Personality Assessment. *Journal of Personality Assessment,* 74, 371–383.

Holden, Paul E., Pederson, Carlton A., and Germane, Gayton E. (1968). *Top Management.* New York: McGraw-Hill.

Holland, Max G., Black, Cameron H., and Miner, John B. (1987). Using Managerial Role Motivation Theory to Predict Career Success. *Health Care Management Review,* 12, 57–64.

Holton, Richard H. (1985). Marketing and the Modernization of China. *California Management Review,* 27(4), 33–45.

House, Robert J. (1977). A 1976 Theory of Charismatic Leadership. In James G. Hunt, and Lars L. Larson (Eds.), *Leadership: The Cutting Edge.* Carbondale, IL: Southern Illinois University Press, 189–207.

House, Robert J., Wright, N. S., and Aditya, Ram N. (1997). Cross-cultural Research on Organizational Leadership: A Critical Analysis and a Proposed Theory. In P. Christopher Earley and Miriam Erez (Eds.), *New Perspectives on International Industrial/Organizational Psychology.* San Francisco, CA: New Lexington Press, 535–625.

Howard, Ann, and Bray, Douglas W. (1981). Today's Young Managers: They Can Do It, But Will They? *Wharton Magazine,* 5(4), 23–28.

Howard, Ann, and Wilson, James A. (1982). Leadership in a Declining Work Ethic. *California Management Review,* 24(4), 33–46.

Hunt, James G., Boal, Kimberly, B., and Sorensen, R. L. (1990). Top Management Leadership: Inside the Black Box. *Leadership Quarterly,* 1, 41–65.

Hunt, Raymond G., and Meindl, James R. (1988). Chinese Economic Reforms and the Problem of Legitimizing Leader Roles. In Edwin P. Hollander (chair), *New Developments in the Psychology of Leadership.* Symposium conducted at the annual meeting of the Eastern Psychological Association, Buffalo, NY.

Hunter, John E., and Schmidt, Frank L. (1990). *Meta-analysis: Correcting Bias and Error in Research Findings.* Newbury Park, CA: Sage.

Hunter, John E., and Schmidt, Frank L. (2000). Fixed Effects and Random Effects Meta-analysis Models: Implications for Cumulative Research Knowledge. *International Journal of Selection and Assessment,* 8, 275–292.

Hunter, John E., Schmidt, Frank L., and Jackson, Gregg B. (1982). *Meta-analysis: Cumulating Findings Across Studies.* Beverly Hills: Sage.

Huprich, Steven K. (2006). *Rorschach Assessment of the Personality Disorders.* Mahwah, NJ: Lawrence Erlbaum Associates.

IDE International Research Group Staff (1981). *Industrial Democracy in Europe.* Oxford, UK: Clarendon Press.

Jackson, D.N. (1989). *Personality Research Form Manual.* Port Huron, MI: Research Psychologists Press.

Jackson, S. (1992). *Chinese Enterprise Management.* New York: deGruyter.

Jacobs, Jerry A. (1992). Women's Entry into Management: Trends in Earnings, Authority, and Values among Salaried Managers. *Administrative Science Quarterly,* 37, 282–301.

James, Barrie G. (1973). The Theory of the Corporate Life Cycle. *Long Range Planning,* June.

James, J. M., and Bolstein, R. (1990). The Effects of Monetary Incentives and Follow-up Mailings on the Response Rate and Response Quality in Mail Surveys. *Public Opinion Quarterly,* 54, 346–361.

James, Lawrence R., and Mazerolle, Michelle D. (2002). *Personality in Work Organizations.* Thousand Oaks, CA: Sage.

Janson, Harald, and Stattin, Håkan (2003). Predictions of Adolescent and Adult Delinquency from Childhood Rorschach Ratings. *Journal of Personality Assessment,* 81, 51–63.

Jefferson, Tyrone, Herbst, Jeffrey H., and McCrae, Robert R. (1998). Associations between Birth Order and Personality Traits: Evidence from Self-reports and Observer-ratings. *Journal of Research in Personality,* 32, 498–509.

Jencks, Christopher, and Riesman, David (1968). *The Academic Revolution.* Garden City, NY: Doubleday.

John, O. P., Donahue, E. M., and Kentle, R. (1991). The "Big Five" Inventory-Versions 4a and 54. Technical Report, Institute of Personality and Social Research, University of California/Berkeley.

Johns, Gary (2006). The Essential Impact of Context on Organizational Behavior. *Academy of Management Review,* 31, 386–408.

Johnson, Blair T. (1989). *DSTAT: Software for the Meta-analytic Review of Research Literatures.* Hillsdale, NJ: Erlbaum.

Johnson, Blair T., Mullen, Brian, and Salas, Eduardo (1995). Comparison of Three Major Meta-analytic Approaches. *Journal of Applied Psychology,* 80, 94–106.

Johnson, Bradley R. (1990). Toward a Multidimensional Model of Entrepreneurship: The Case of Achievement Motivation and the Entrepreneur. *Entrepreneurship Theory and Practice,* 14(3), 39–54.

Johnson, Sarah K., and Anderson, Michael C. (2004). The Role of Inhibitory Control in Forgetting Semantic Knowledge. *Psychological Science,* 15, 448–453.

Jones, Candace, and Lichtenstein, Benyamin M. B. (2000). The "Architecture" of Careers: How Career Competencies Reveal Firm Dominant Logic in Professional Services. In Maury A. Peiperl, Michael B. Aurthur, Rob Goffee, and Timothy Morris (Eds.), *Career Frontiers: New Conceptions of Working Lives.* Oxford, UK: Oxford University Press, 153–176.

Jourdan, Louis F. (1987). Differentiating between Successful and Unsuccessful Entrepreneurs. PhD dissertation, Georgia State University, Atlanta, GA.

Judge, Timothy A., Bono, Joyce E., Ilies, Remus, and Gerhardt, Megan W. (2002). Personality and Leadership: A Qualitative and Quantitative Review. *Journal of Applied Psychology,* 87, 765–780.

Kahn, Robert L. (1956). *Employee Motivation.* Ann Arbor, MI: Bureau of Industrial Relations, University of Michigan.

Kahn, Robert L., and Katz, Daniel (1953). Leadership Practices in Relation to Productivity and Morale. In Dorwin Cartwright and Alvin Zander (Eds.), *Group Dynamics: Research and Theory.* Evanston, IL: Row, Peterson, 612–628.

Kanter, Rosabeth M. (1983). *The Change Masters: Innovations for Productivity in the American Corporation.* New York: Simon and Schuster.

Karon, Bertram P. (1958). *The Negro Personality: A Rigorous Investigation of the Effects of Culture.* New York: Springer Publishing.

Karon, Bertram P. (1973). The Price of Privilege: The Effects of the American Caste System on the Deep South White. *Social Behavior and Personality,* 1, 161–168.

Kawada, Christie L. K., Oettingen, Gabriele, Gollwitzer, Peter M., and Bargh, John A. (2004). The Projection of Implicit and Explicit Goals. *Journal of Personality and Social Psychology,* 86, 545–559.

Keats, Barbara W., and Bracker, Jeffrey S. (1988). Toward a Theory of Small Firm Performance: A Conceptual Model. *American Journal of Small Business,* 12(4), 41–58.

Keller, Tiffany (2003). Parental Images as a Guide to Leadership Sensemaking: An Attachment Perspective on Implicit Leadership Theories. *Leadership Quarterly,* 14, 141–160.

Kent, Calvin A., Sexton, Donald L., and Vesper, Karl H. (1982). *Encyclopedia of Entrepreneurship.* Englewood Cliffs, NJ: Prentice Hall.

Kerr, Steven, and Slocum, John W. (1981). Controlling the Performance of People in Organizations. In Paul C. Nystrom and William H. Starbuck (Eds.), *Handbook of Organizational Design,* Volume 2. New York: Oxford University Press, 116–134.

Ketchen, David J., and Shook, Christopher L. (1996). The Application of Cluster Analysis in Strategic Management Research: An Analysis and Critique. *Strategic Management Journal,* 17, 441–458.

Kets de Vries, Manfred F. R. (1989). *Prisoners of Leadership.* New York: Wiley.

Kihlstrom, John F. (2002). No Need for Repression. *Trends in Cognitive Science,* 6, 502.

Kimberly, John R., and Miles, Robert H. (1980). *The Organizational Life Cycle.* San Francisco, CA: Jossey-Bass.

Knoke, D., and Prensky, D. (1984). What Relevance Do Organization Theories Have for Voluntary Associations? *Social Science Quarterly,* 65, 3–20.

Koestner, Richard, Walker, Marie, and Fincham, Laura (1999). Childhood Parenting Experiences and Adult Creativity. *Journal of Research in Personality,* 33, 92–107.

Koh, Hian Chye (1996). Testing Hypotheses of Entrepreneurial Characteristics: A Study of Hong Kong MBA Students. *Journal of Managerial Psychology,* 11(3), 12–25.

Korabik, K. (1994). Managerial Women in the People's Republic of China: The Long March Continues. In Nancy J. Adler and D. N. Israeli (Eds.), *Competitive Frontiers: Women Managers in a Global Economy.* Cambridge, UK: Blackwell, 114–126.

Krizan, Zlatan, and Windschitl, Paul D. (2007). The Influence of Outcome Desirability on Optimism. *Psychological Bulletin,* 133, 95–121.

Kruse, L., and Wintermantel, M. (1986). Leadership Ms.-qualified: I. The Gender Bias in Everyday and Scientific Thinking. In C. F. Granmann and S. Moscovici (Eds.), *Changing Conceptions of Leadership.* New York: Springer-Verlag, 171–197.

Laaksonen, Oiva (1984). The Management and Power Structure of Chinese Enterprises During and After the Cultural Revolution: Empirical Data Comparing Chinese and European Enterprises. *Organization Studies,* 5, 1–21.

Laaksonen, Oiva (1988). *Management in China During and After Mao in Enterprises, Government, and Party.* New York: deGruyter.

Lacey, Lynn A. (1974). Discriminability of the Miner Sentence Completion Scale among Supervisory and Nonsupervisory Scientists and Engineers. *Academy of Management Journal,* 17, 354–358.

Lakshmi, Aishwarya R., and Arora, Meenakshi (2006). Promoting Achievement Orientation among Adolescents: Role of Parental Behaviors. *Psychological Studies,* 51, 228–231.

Landsberger, H. (1973). Labor and Peasant Movements as Sources of Voluntary Organizations and Instruments of Class Mobility. In D. H. Smith (Ed.), *Voluntary Action Research: 1973.* Lexington, MA: Lexington Books. 363–385.

Langan-Fox, Janice, and Grant, Sharon (2006). The Thematic Apperception Test: Toward a Standard Measure of the Big Three Motives. *Journal of Personality Assessment,* 87, 277–291.

Latham, Gary P. (2007). *Work Motivation: History, Theory, Research, and Practice.* Thousand Oaks, CA: Sage.

Laughlin, H. P. (1954). A Group Approach to Management Improvement. *International Journal of Group Psychology,* 4, 165–171.

Leana, Carrie R., and Rousseau, Denise M. (2000). *Relational Wealth: The Advantages of Stability in a Changing Economy.* New York: Oxford University Press.

Leong, Frederick T. L., and Serafica, Felicisima C. (2001). Cross-cultural Perspective on Super's Career Development Theory: Career Maturity and Cultural Accommodation. In Frederick T. L. Leong and Azy Barak (Eds.), *Contemporary Models in Vocational Psychology: A Volume in Honor of Samuel H. Osipow.* Mahwah, NJ: Lawrence Erlbaum, 167–205.

Leontiades, Milton (1980). *Strategies for Diversification and Change.* Boston, MA: Little, Brown.

Levenson, Hanna (1972). Distinctions within the Concept of Internal-External Control: Development of a New Scale. *Proceedings, American Psychological Association Annual Convention,* 80, 261–262.

Levenson, Hanna (1974). Activism and Powerful Others: Distinctions within the Concept of Internal-External Control. *Journal of Personality Assessment,* 38, 377–383.

Levinson, Harry (1973). *The Great Jackass Fallacy.* Boston, MA: Graduate School of Business Administration, Harvard University.

Levinson, Harry (1998). A Clinical Approach to Executive Selection. In Richard Jeanneret and Rob Silzer (Eds.), *Individual Psychological Assessment: Predicting Behavior in Organizational Settings.* San Francisco, CA: Jossey-Bass, 228–242.

Levy, Benjamin J., and Anderson, Michael C. (2002). Inhibitory Processes and the Control of Memory Retrieval. *Trends in Cognitive Sciences,* 6, 299–305.

Levy, Benjamin J., McVeigh, Nathan D., Marful, Alejandra, and Anderson, Michael C. (2007). Inhibiting Your Native Language: The Role of Retrieval-Induced Forgetting During Second-Language Acquisition. *Psychological Science,* 18, 29–34.

Liebman, Samuel J., Porcerelli, John, and Abell, Steven C. (2005). Reliability and Validity of Rorschach Aggression Variables with a Sample of Adjudicated Adolescents. *Journal of Personality Assessment,* 85, 33–39.

Likert, Rensis (1961). *New Patterns of Management.* New York: McGraw-Hill.

Lilienfeld, Scott O., Wood, James M., and Garb, Howard N. (2000). The Scientific Status of Projective Techniques. *Psychological Science in the Public Interest,* 1, 27–66.

Lindsay, Cindy P., and Dempsey, Bobby L. (1983). Ten Painful Learned Lessons from Working in China: The Insights of Two American Behavioral Scientists. *Journal of Applied Behavioral Science,* 19, 265–276.

Ling, Cyril C. (1965). *The Management of Personnel Relations: History and Origins.* Homewood, IL: Irwin.

Lipset, Seymour M., and Altbach, Philip G. (1967). Student Politics and Higher Education in the United States. In Seymour M. Lipset (Ed.), *Student Politics.* New York: Basic Books, 199–252.

Livingston, J. Sterling (1971). Myth of the Well-educated Manager. *Harvard Business Review,* 49(1), 79–89.

Locke, Edwin A. (1967). Motivational Effects of Knowledge and Goal Setting. *Journal of Applied Psychology,* 51, 324–329.

Locke, Edwin A., and Henne, Douglas (1986). Work Motivation Theories. *International Review of Industrial and Organizational Psychology,* 1, 1–35.

Locke, Edwin A., and Latham, Gary P. (2002). Building a Practically Useful Theory of Goal Setting and Task Motivation: A 35-year Odyssey. *American Psychologist,* 57, 705–717.

Locke, Edwin A., and Latham, Gary P. (2004). What Should We Do about Motivation Theory? Six Recommendations for the Twenty-first Century. *Academy of Management Review,* 29, 388–403.

Locke, Edwin A., and Latham, Gary P. (2006). New Directions in Goal-setting Theory. *Current Directions in Psychological Science,* 15, 265–268.

Locke, Karen (2001). *Grounded Theory in Management Research.* Thousand Oaks, CA: Sage.

Lockett, Martin (1988). Culture and Problems of Chinese Management. *Organization Studies,* 9, 475–496.

Lockwood, Howard C. (1974). Equal Employment Opportunities. In Dale Yoder and Herbert G. Heneman (Eds.), *Staffing Policies and Strategies.* Washington, DC: BNA Books, 245–287.

Loden, M. (1985). *Feminine Leadership: or How to Succeed in Business without Being One of the Boys.* New York: Times Books.

Loevinger, Jane (1998). *Technical Foundations for Measuring Ego Development: The Washington University Sentence Completion Test.* Mahwah, NJ: Lawrence Erlbaum.

Loevinger, Jane (2002). Confessions of an Iconoclast: At Home on the Fringe. *Journal of Personality Assessment,* 78, 195–208.

Logan, Richard E., and Wachler, Charles A. (2001). The Rotter Incomplete Sentences Blank: Examining Potential Race Differences. *Journal of Personality Assessment,* 76, 448–460.

Lord, Robert G., and Maher, Karen J. (1991). *Leadership and Information Processing: Linking Perceptions and Performance.* Boston, MA: Unwin, Hyman.

Low, Murray S., and MacMillan, Ian C. (1988). Entrepreneurship: Past Research and Future Challenges. *Journal of Management,* 14, 139–161.

Lu, X. (1984). China: Feudal Attitudes, Party Control, and Half the Sky. In R. Morgan (Ed.), *Sisterhood is Global: The International Women's Movement Anthology.* Garden City, NY: Anchor Books, 151–156.

Lueptow, Lloyd B. (1975). Parental Status and Influence and the Achievement Orientations of High School Seniors. *Sociology of Education,* 48, 91–110.

Luthans, Fred, Hodgetts, Richard M., and Rosenkrantz, Stuart A. (1988). *Real Managers.* Cambridge, MA: Ballinger.

Lynn, Richard (1969). An Achievement Motivation Questionnaire. *British Journal of Psychology,* 60, 529–534.

Maccoby, Michael (1977). *The Gamesman.* New York: Simon and Schuster.

MacCrimmon, K. R., and Wehrung, D. A. (1990). Characteristics of Risk Taking Executives. *Management Science,* 36, 422–435.

MacKenzie, Kenneth D. (1991). *The Organizational Hologram: The Effective Management of Organizational Change.* Boston, MA: Kluwer.

Manimala, Mathew J. (1992). Entrepreneurial Heuristics: A Comparison between High PI (Pioneering-Innovative) and Low PI Ventures. *Journal of Business Venturing,* 7, 477–504.

Mann, Floyd C. (1957). Studying and Creating Change: A Means to Understanding Social Organization.

In Conrad M. Arensberg, Solomon Barkin, William E. Chalmers, H. L. Wilensky, James C. Worthy, and Barbara D. Dennis (Eds.), *Research in Industrial Human Relations.* New York: Harper, 146–157.

Manners, John, and Durkin, Kevin (2001). A Critical Review of the Validity of the Ego Development Theory and Its Measurement. *Journal of Personality Assessment,* 77, 541–567.

March, James G. (1988). *Decisions and Organizations.* Oxford, UK: Blackwell.

March, James G. (1999). *The Pursuit of Organizational Intelligence.* Oxford, UK: Blackwell.

Markowe, Morris (1953). Occupational Psychiatry: A Historical Survey and Some Recent Researches. *Journal of Mental Science,* 99, 92–101.

Martell, Richard F., Lane, David M., and Emrich, Cynthia (1996). Male-female Differences: A Computer Simulation. *American Psychologist,* 51, 157–158.

Martin, P. Y. (1992). Gender, Interaction, and Inequality. In C. L. Ridgeway (Ed.), *Gender, Interaction, and Inequality.* New York: Springer-Verlag, 208–231.

Masling, Joseph (2006). When Homer Nods: An Examination of Some Systematic Errors in Rorschach Scholarship. *Journal of Personality Assessment,* 87, 62–73.

Mason, D. E. (1984). *Voluntary Nonprofit Enterprise Management.* New York: Plenum Press.

Matteson, Michael T., and Ivancevich, John M. (1982a). *Managing Job Stress and Health: The Intelligent Person's Guide.* New York: Free Press.

Matteson, Michael T., and Ivancevich, John M. (1982b). Type A and B Behavior Patterns and Self-reported Health Symptoms and Stress: Examining Individual and Organizational Fit. *Journal of Occupational Medicine,* 24, 585–589.

Matteson, Michael T., and Ivancevich, John M. (1983). Note on Tension Discharge Rate as an Employee Health Status Predictor. *Academy of Management Journal,* 26, 540–545.

Matthews, Charles H., and Moser, Steven B. (1995). Family Background and Gender: Implications for Interest in Small Firm Ownership. *Entrepreneurship and Regional Development,* 7, 365–377.

McAdams, Dan P. (1982). Experiences of Intimacy and Power: Relationships between Social Motives and Autobiographical Memory. *Journal of Personality and Social Psychology,* 42, 292–302.

McClelland, David C. (1961). *The Achieving Society.* Princeton, NJ: Van Nostrand.

McClelland, David C. (1962). Business Drive and National Achievement. *Harvard Business Review,* 40(4), 99–112.

McClelland, David C. (1965). N Achievement and Entrepreneurship: A Longitudinal Study. *Journal of Personality and Social Psychology,* 1, 389–392.

McClelland, David C. (1975). *Power: The Inner Experience.* New York: Irvington.

McClelland, David C., Atkinson, John W., Clark, Russell A., and Lowell, Edgar L. (1953). *The Achievement Motive.* New York: Appleton-Century-Croft.

McClelland, David C., and Boyatzis, Richard E. (1982). Leadership Motive Pattern and Long-term Success in Management. *Journal of Applied Psychology,* 67, 737–743.

McClelland, David C., and Franz, Carol E. (1992). Motivational and Other Sources of Work Accomplishments in Mid-Life: A Longitudinal Study. *Journal of Personality,* 60, 679–707.

McClelland, David C., Koestner, Richard, and Weinberger, Joel (1989). How Do Self-attributed and Implicit Motives Differ? *Psychological Review,* 96, 690–702.

McClelland, David C., and Winter, David G. (1969). *Motivating Economic Achievement.* New York: Free Press.

McGrath, Robert E. (2005). Conceptual Complexity and Construct Validity. *Journal of Personality Assessment,* 85, 112–124.

McKelvey, Bill (1975). Guidelines for the Empirical Classification of Organizations. *Administrative Science Quarterly,* 20, 509–524.

McKelvey, Bill (1982). *Organizational Systematics: Taxonomy, Evolution, Classification.* Berkeley, CA: University of California Press.

McKelvey, Bill, and Aldrich, Howard (1983). Populations, Natural Selection, and Applied Organizational Science. *Administrative Science Quarterly,* 28, 101–128.

McNaught, William, Barth, Michael C., and Henderson, Peter H. (1989). The Human Resource Potential of Americans over 50. *Human Resource Management,* 28, 455–473.

McNemar, Quinn (1969). *Psychological Statistics.* New York: Wiley.

McPherson, J. Miller, and Smith-Lovin, Lynn (1988). A Comparative Ecology of Five Nations: Testing a Model of Competition among Voluntary Organizations. In Glenn R. Carroll (Ed.), *Ecological Models of Organizations.* Cambridge, MA: Ballinger, 85–109.

McPherson, M. (1983). The Size of Voluntary Organizations. *Social Forces,* 61(4), 1044–1063.

Meckler, Mark, Drake, Bruce H., and Levinson, Harry (2003). Putting Psychology Back into Psychological Contracts. *Journal of Management Inquiry,* 12, 217–228.

Meindl, James R., Hunt, Raymond G., and Lee, Wonsick (1989). Individualism-collectivism and Work Values: Data from the United States, China, Taiwan, Korea, and Hong Kong. *Research in Personnel and Human Resource Management,* Supplement 1, 59–77.

Meir, Elchanan I., and Tziner, Aharon (2001). Cross-cultural Assessment of Interests. In Frederick T. L. Leong and Azy Barak (Eds.), *Contemporary Models in Vocational Psychology: A Volume in Honor of Samuel H. Osipow.* Mahwah, NJ: Lawrence Erlbaum, 133–166.

Melamed, Tuvia (1996). Career Success: An Assessment of a Gender-specific Model. *Journal of Occupational and Organizational Psychology,* 69, 217–242.

Meyer, Gregory J. (1996). The Rorschach and MMPI: Toward a More Scientifically Differentiated Understanding of Cross-method Assessment. *Journal of Personality Assessment,* 67, 558–578.

Meyer, Gregory J. (2006). Special Issue: The MMPI-2 Restructured Clinical Scales—Introduction. *Journal of Personality Assessment,* 89, 119–120.

Meyer, Gregory J., Finn, Stephen E., Eyde, Lorraine D., Kay, Gary G., Moreland, Kevin L., Dies, Robert R., Eisman, Elena J., Kubiszyn, Tom W., and Reed, Geoffrey M. (2001). Psychological Testing and Psychological Assessment: A Review of Evidence and Issues. *American Psychologist,* 56, 128–165.

Meyer, Gregory J., and Kurtz, John E. (2006). Advancing Personality Assessment Terminology: Time to Retire "Objective" and "Projective" as Personality Test Descriptors. *Journal of Personality Assessment,* 87, 223–225.

Meyer, Gregory J., Mihura, Joni L., and Smith, Bruce L. (2005). The Interclinician Reliability of Rorschach Interpretation in Four Data Sets. *Journal of Personality Assessment,* 84, 296–314.

Meyer, Henry D., and Pressel, G. L. (1954). Personality Test Scores in the Management Hierarchy. *Journal of Applied Psychology,* 38, 73–80.

Miles, Raymond E., and Snow, Charles C. (1978). *Organizational Strategy: Structure and Process.* New York: McGraw-Hill.

Miles, Raymond E., and Snow, Charles C. (1984). Fit, Failure, and the Hall of Fame. *California Management Review,* 26(3), 10–28.

Miles, Robert H. (1982). *Coffin Nails and Corporate Strategies.* Englewood Cliffs, NJ: Prentice-Hall.

Miller, Danny (1990). *The Icarus Paradox: How Exceptional Companies Bring About Their Own Downfall.* New York: Harper Business.

Miller, Danny (1996). Configurations Revisited. *Strategic Management Journal,* 17, 505–512.

Miller, Joshua D., and Lynam, Donald R. (2003). Psychopathy and the Five Factor Model of Personality: A Replication and Extension. *Journal of Personality Assessment,* 81, 168–178.

Miller, T. R. (1978). *Average Ratings of Management Publications.* Unpublished paper, Department of Management, Memphis State University.

Milton, Charles R. (1970). *Ethics and Expediency in Personnel Management: A Critical History of Personnel Philosophy.* Columbia, SC: University of South Carolina Press.

Miner, John B. (1957). *Intelligence in the United States.* New York: Springer.

Miner, John B. (1960a). The Effect of a Course in Psychology on the Attitudes of Research and Development Supervisors. *Journal of Applied Psychology,* 44, 224–232.

Miner, John B. (1960b). The Kuder Preference Record in Management Appraisal. *Personnel Psychology,* 13, 187–196.

Miner, John B. (1960c). The Concurrent Validity of the PAT in the Selection of Tabulating Machine Operators. *Journal of Projective Techniques,* 24, 409–418.

Miner, John B. (1961a). On the Use of a Short Vocabulary Test to Measure General Intelligence. *Journal of Educational Psychology,* 52, 157–160.

Miner, John B. (1961b). The Validity of the PAT in the Selection of Tabulating Machine Operators: An Analysis of Predictive Power. *Journal of Projective Techniques,* 25, 330–333.

Miner, John B. (1962a). Personality and Ability Factors in Sales Performance. *Journal of Applied Psychology,* 46, 6–13.

Miner, John B. (1962b). Conformity among University Professors and Business Executives. *Administrative Science Quarterly,* 7, 96–109.

Miner, John B. (1963). *The Management of Ineffective Performance.* New York: McGraw-Hill.

Miner, John B. (1964). *Scoring Guide for the Miner Sentence Completion Scale.* New York: Springer.

Miner, John B. (1965a). *Studies in Management Education.* New York: Springer.

Miner, John B. (1965b). The Prediction of Managerial and Research Success. *Personnel Administration,* 28(5), 12–16.

Miner, John B. (1966). *Introduction to Industrial Clinical Psychology.* New York: McGraw-Hill.

Miner, John B. (1967). *The School Administrator and Organizational Character.* Eugene, OR: University of Oregon Press.

Miner, John B. (1968a). The Early Identification of Managerial Talent. *Personnel and Guidance Journal,* 46, 586–591.

Miner, John B. (1968b). The Managerial Motivation of School Administrators. *Educational Administration Quarterly,* 4, 55–71.

Miner, John B. (1968c). Management Appraisal: A Capsule Review and Current References. *Business Horizons,* 11(5), 83–96.

Miner, John B. (1970a). Psychological Evaluations as Predictors of Consulting Success. *Personnel Psychology,* 23, 393–405.

Miner, John B. (1970b). Executive and Personnel Interviews as Predictors of Consulting Success. *Personnel Psychology,* 23, 521–538.

Miner, John B. (1971a). Personality Tests as Predictors of Consulting Success. *Personnel Psychology,* 24, 191–204.

Miner, John B. (1971b). *Management Theory.* New York: Macmillan.

Miner, John B. (1971c). Success in Management Consulting and the Concept of Eliteness Motivation. *Academy of Management Journal,* 14, 367–378.

Miner, John B. (1971d). Changes in Student Attitudes toward Bureaucratic Role Prescriptions During the 1960s. *Administrative Science Quarterly,* 16, 351–364.

Miner, John B. (1973a). The Real Crunch in Managerial Manpower. *Harvard Business Review,* 51(6), 146–158.

Miner, John B. (1973b). The Management Consulting Firm as a Source of High Level Managerial Talent. *Academy of Management Journal,* 16, 253–264.

Miner, John B. (1973c). *Intelligence in the United States.* Westport, CT: Greenwood.

Miner, John B. (1974a). *The Human Constraint: The Coming Shortage of Managerial Talent.* Washington, DC: BNA Books.

Miner, John B. (1974b). Motivation to Manage among Women: Studies of Business Managers and Educational Administrators. *Journal of Vocational Behavior,* 5, 197–208.

Miner, John B. (1974c). Motivation to Manage among Women: Studies of College Students. *Journal of Vocational Behavior,* 5, 241–250.

Miner, John B. (1974d). Student Attitudes toward Bureaucratic Role Prescriptions and Prospects for Managerial Talent Shortages. *Personnel Psychology,* 27, 605–613.

Miner, John B. (1975). *The Challenge of Managing.* Philadelphia, PA: W. B. Saunders.

Miner, John B. (1976a). Levels of Motivation to Manage among Personnel and Industrial Relations Managers. *Journal of Applied Psychology,* 61, 419–427.

Miner, John B. (1976b). Relationships among Measures of Managerial Personality Traits. *Journal of Personality Assessment,* 40, 383–397.

Miner, John B. (1976c). The Uncertain Future of the Leadership Concept: An Overview. In James G. Hunt and Lars L. Larson (Eds.), *Leadership Frontiers.* Kent, OH: Kent State University Press, 197–208.

Miner, John B. (1977a). Motivational Potential for Upgrading among Minority and Female Managers. *Journal of Applied Psychology,* 62, 691–697.

Miner, John B. (1977b). *Motivation to Manage: A Ten-year Update on the "Studies in Management Education" Research.* Eugene, OR: Organizational Measurement Systems Press.

Miner, John B. (1977c). Implications of Managerial Talent Projections for Management Education. *Academy of Management Review,* 2, 412–420.

Miner, John B. (1977d). *1977 Supplement-Scoring Guide for the Miner Sentence Completion Scale.* Eugene, OR: Organizational Measurement Systems Press.

Miner, John B. (1978a). Validation Study of Mental Ability Tests. Chapter 13 in Miner, Mary G., and Miner, John B. (Eds.), *Employee Selection Within the Law.* Washington, DC: The Bureau of National Affairs, 202–207.

Miner, John B. (1978b). *The Management Process.* New York: Macmillan.

Miner, John B. (1978c). Twenty Years of Research on Role Motivation Theory of Managerial Effectiveness. *Personnel Psychology,* 31, 739–760.

Miner, John B. (1978d). The Miner Sentence Completion Scale: A Reappraisal. *Academy of Management Journal,* 21, 283–294.
Miner, John B. (1979a). Managerial Talent in Personnel. *Business Horizons,* 22(6), 10–20.
Miner, John B. (1979b). Leadership: Our Nation's Most Critical Shortage. In Frank E. Kuzmits (Ed.), *Leadership in a Dynamic Society.* Indianapolis, IN: Bobbs-Merrill, 1–13.
Miner, John B. (1980a). The Role of Managerial and Professional Motivation in the Career Success of Management Professors. *Academy of Management Journal,* 23, 487–508.
Miner, John B. (1980b). Limited Domain Theories of Organizational Energy. In Craig C. Pinder and Larry F. Moore (Eds.), *Middle Range Theory and the Study of Organizations.* Leiden, Netherlands: Martinus Nijhoff, 273–286.
Miner, John B. (1980c). *Theories of Organizational Behavior.* Hinsdale, IL: Dryden.
Miner, John B. (1981). *Scoring Guide for the Miner Sentence Completion Scale—Form P.* Eugene, OR: Organizational Measurement Systems Press.
Miner, John B. (1982). The Uncertain Future of the Leadership Concept: Revisions and Clarifications. *Journal of Applied Behavioral Science,* 18, 293–307.
Miner, John B. (1985a). *People Problems: The Executive Answer Book.* New York: Random House.
Miner, John B. (1985b). Sentence Completion Measures in Personnel Research: The Development and Validation of the Miner Sentence Completion Scales. In H. John Bernardin and David A. Bownas (Eds.), *Personality Assessment in Organizations.* New York: Praeger, 145–176.
Miner, John B. (1986). *Scoring Guide for the Miner Sentence Completion Scale—Form T.* Eugene, OR: Organizational Measurement Systems Press.
Miner, John B. (1989). *1989 Supplement—Scoring Guide for the Miner Sentence Completion Scale: Form H.* Eugene, OR: Organizational Measurement Systems Press.
Miner, John B. (1990). Entrepreneurs, High Growth Entrepreneurs, and Managers: Contrasting and Overlapping Motivational Patterns. *Journal of Business Venturing,* 5, 221–234.
Miner, John B. (1993). *Role Motivation Theories.* New York: Routledge.
Miner, John B. (1996a). Evidence for the Existence of a Set of Personality Types, Defined by Psychological Tests, that Predict Entrepreneurial Success. *Frontiers of Entrepreneurship Research,* 16, 62–76.
Miner, John B. (1996b). *The 4 Routes to Entrepreneurial Success.* San Francisco, CA: Berrett-Koehler.
Miner, John B. (1997a). *A Psychological Typology of Successful Entrepreneurs.* Westport, CT: Quorum.
Miner, John B. (1997b). A Psychological Typology and Its Relationship to Entrepreneurial Success. *Entrepreneurship and Regional Development,* 9, 319–334.
Miner, John B. (1997c). The Expanded Horizon for Achieving Entrepreneurial Success. *Organizational Dynamics,* 25(3), 54–67.
Miner, John B. (2000). Testing a Psychological Typology of Entrepreneurship Using Business Founders. *Journal of Applied Behavioral Science,* 36, 43–69.
Miner, John B. (2002a). The Role Motivation Theories of Organizational Leadership. In Bruce J. Avolio and Francis Yammarino (Eds.), *Transformational and Charismatic Leadership: The Road Ahead.* New York: Elsevier Science, 309–338.
Miner, John B. (2002b). *Organizational Behavior: Foundations, Theories, and Analyses.* New York: Oxford University Press.
Miner, John B. (2005). *Organizational Behavior: Essential Theories of Motivation and Leadership.* Armonk, NY: M.E. Sharpe.
Miner, John B. (2006a). *Organizational Behavior 3: Historical Origins, Theoretical Foundations, and the Future.* Armonk, NY: M.E. Sharpe.
Miner, John B. (2006b). Role Motivation Theories. In Jay C. Thomas and Daniel L. Segal (Eds.), *Comprehensive Handbook of Personality and Psychopathology. Volume 1: Personality and Everyday Functioning.* Hoboken, NJ: John Wiley, 233–250.
Miner, John B. (2007). *Organizational Behavior 4: From Theory to Practice.* Armonk, NY: M.E. Sharpe.
Miner, John B., and Anderson, James K. (1958). The Postwar Occupational Adjustment of Emotionally Disturbed Soldiers. *Journal of Applied Psychology,* 42, 317–322.
Miner, John B., Chen, Chao C., and Yu, K. C. (1991). Theory Testing under Adverse Conditions: Motivation to Manage in the People's Republic of China. *Journal of Applied Psychology,* 76, 343–349.
Miner, John B., and Crane, Donald P. (1981). Motivation to Manage and the Manifestation of a Managerial Orientation in Career Planning. *Academy of Management Journal,* 24, 626–633.

Miner, John B., Crane, Donald P., and Vandenberg, Robert J. (1994). Congruence and Fit in Professional Role Motivation Theory. *Organization Science,* 5, 86–97.

Miner, John B., and Culver, John E. (1955). Some Aspects of the Executive Personality. *Journal of Applied Psychology,* 39, 348–353.

Miner, John B., and Dachler, H. Peter (1973). Personnel Attitudes and Motivation. *Annual Review of Psychology,* 24, 379–402.

Miner, John B., Ebrahimi, Bahman, and Wachtel, Jeffrey (1995). How Deficiencies in Motivation to Manage Contribute to the United States' Competitiveness Problem (and What Can Be Done About It). *Human Resource Management,* 34, 363–387.

Miner, John B., and Miner, Mary G. (1976). Managerial Characteristics of Personnel Managers. *Industrial Relations,* 15, 225–234.

Miner, John B., and Raju, Nambury S. (2004). Risk Propensity Differences between Managers and Entrepreneurs and between Low- and High-Growth Entrepreneurs: A Reply in a More Conservative Vein. *Journal of Applied Psychology,* 89, 303–313.

Miner, John B., Rizzo, John R., Harlow, Dorothy N., and Hill, James W. (1974). Role Motivation Theory of Managerial Effectiveness in Simulated Organizations of Varying Degrees of Structure. *Journal of Applied Psychology,* 59, 31–37.

Miner, John B., and Smith, Norman R. (1969). Managerial Talent among Undergraduate and Graduate Business Students. *Personnel and Guidance Journal,* 47, 995–1000.

Miner, John B., and Smith, Norman R. (1981). Can Organizational Design Make up for Organizational Decline? *The Wharton Magazine,* 5(4), 29–35.

Miner, John B., and Smith, Norman R. (1982). Decline and Stabilization of Managerial Motivation Over a 20-year Period. *Journal of Applied Psychology,* 67, 297–305.

Miner, John B., Smith, Norman R., and Bracker, Jeffrey S. (1989). Role of Entrepreneurial Task Motivation in the Growth of Technologically Innovative Firms. *Journal of Applied Psychology,* 74, 554–560.

Miner, John B., Smith, Norman R., and Bracker, Jeffrey S. (1992a). Predicting Firm Survival from a Knowledge of Entrepreneur Task Motivation. *Entrepreneurship and Regional Development,* 4, 145–153.

Miner, John B., Smith, Norman R., and Bracker, Jeffrey S. (1992b). Defining the Inventor-Entrepreneur in the Context of Established Typologies. *Journal of Business Venturing,* 7, 103–113.

Miner, John B., Smith, Norman R., and Bracker, Jeffrey S. (1994). Role of Entrepreneurial Task Motivation in the Growth of Technologically Innovative Firms: Interpretations from Follow-up Data. *Journal of Applied Psychology,* 79, 627–630.

Miner, John B., Smith, Norman R., and Ebrahimi, Bahman (1985). Further Considerations in the Decline and Stabilization of Managerial Motivation: A Rejoinder to Bartol, Anderson, and Schneier (1980). *Journal of Vocational Behavior,* 26, 290–298.

Miner, John B., and Stites-Doe, Susan (1994). Applying an Entrepreneurship Development Program to Economic Problems in the Buffalo Area. In Abraham K. Korman (Ed.), *Human Dilemmas in Work Organizations: Strategies for Resolution.* New York: Guilford, 243–271.

Miner, John B., Wachtel, Jeffrey, and Ebrahimi, Bahman (1989). The Managerial Motivation of Potential Managers in the United States and Other Countries of the World: Implications for National Competitiveness and the Productivity Problem. *Advances in International Comparative Management,* 4, 147–170.

Mintzberg, Henry (1973). *The Nature of Managerial Work.* New York: Harper and Row.

Mintzberg, Henry (1979). *The Structuring of Organizations.* Englewood Cliffs, NJ: Prentice-Hall.

Mintzberg, Henry T. (1981). Organization Design: Fashion or Fit? *Harvard Business Review,* 59(1), 103–116.

Mintzberg, Henry (1983). *Power in and around Organizations.* Englewood Cliffs, NJ: Prentice-Hall.

Mintzberg, Henry (1984). Power and Organization Life Cycles. *Academy of Management Review,* 9, 207–224.

Mitchell, David B. (2006). Nonconscious Priming after 17 Years: Invulnerable Implicit Memory? *Psychological Science,* 17, 925–929.

Mitchell, Terence R., and James, Lawrence R. (2001). Building Better Theory: Time and the Specification of When Things Happen. *Academy of Management Review,* 26, 530–547.

Mobley, William H., Griffeth, Roger W., Hand, Herbert H., and Meglino, Bruce M. (1979). Review and Conceptual Analysis of the Employee Turnover Process. *Psychological Bulletin,* 86, 493–522.

Moore, Wilbert E. (1970). *The Professions: Roles and Rules.* New York: Russell Sage Foundation.

Morgan, Wesley G. (2002). Origin and History of the Earliest Thematic Apperception Test Pictures. *Journal of Personality Assessment,* 79, 422–445.

Morgan, Wesley G. (2005). Origin and History of the "Series B" and "Series C" TAT Pictures. *Journal of Personality Assessment,* 81, 133–148.

Morris, Charles, and Small, Linwood (1971). Changes in Conceptions of the Good Life by American College Students from 1950 to 1970. *Journal of Personality and Social Psychology,* 20, 254–260.

Morrison, Ann M., and Von Glinow, Mary Ann (1990). Women and Minorities in Management. *American Psychologist,* 45, 200–208.

Morrison, Ann M., White, R. P., and Van Velsor, Ellen (1987). *Breaking the Glass Ceiling: Can Women Reach the Top of America's Largest Corporations?* Reading, MA: Addison-Wesley.

Moses, Joseph L., and Boehm, Virginia R. (1975). Relationships of Assessment-center Performance to Management Progress of Women. *Journal of Applied Psychology,* 60, 527–529.

Mowday, Richard T., Porter, Lyman W., and Steers, Richard M. (1982). *Employee-Organization Linkages: The Psychology of Commitment, Absenteeism, and Turnover.* New York: Academic Press.

Muchinsky, Paul M., and Tuttle, M. L. (1979). Employee Turnover: An Empirical and Methodological Assessment. *Journal of Vocational Behavior,* 14, 43–77.

Muczyk, Jan P., and Schuler, Randall S. (1976). The Management Motive among Male College Students. *Academy of Management Proceedings,* 36, 311–315.

Murray, Henry A. (1943). *Thematic Apperception Test: Manual.* Cambridge, MA: Harvard University Press.

Myers, Howard (1987). The China Business Puzzle. *Business Horizons,* 30(4), 25–28.

Myers, Isabel B. (1962). *The Myers-Briggs Type Indicator Manual.* Princeton, NJ: Educational Testing Service.

Nadler, David A., and Tushman, Michael L. (1980). A Model for Diagnosing Organizational Behavior. *Organizational Dynamics,* 9(2), 35–51.

Nadler, David A., and Tushman, Michael L. (1988). *Strategic Organization Design.* Glenview, IL: Scott, Foresman.

Naffzinger, Douglas (1995). Entrepreneurship: A Person Based Theory Approach. *Advances in Entrepreneurship, Firm Emergence and Growth,* 2, 21–50.

Nash, Allan N., and Miner, John B. (1973). *Personnel and Labor Relations: An Evolutionary Approach.* New York: Macmillan.

Nathan, Barry R., and Alexander, Ralph A. (1985). An Application of Meta-analysis to Theory Building and Construct Validation. *Academy of Management Proceedings,* 45, 224–228.

National Institute for Child Health and Human Development Early Child Care Research Network (2001). Nonmaternal Care and Family Factors in Early Development: An Overview of the NICHD Study of Early Child Care. *Applied Developmental Psychology,* 22, 457–492.

National Science Foundation (1983). *The Process of Technological Innovation: Reviewing the Literature.* Washington, DC: The Foundation.

Nellen, Eugene H. (1986). Motivation to Manage of Black College Students Aspiring to Careers in Business Management: An Application of Miner's Role Motivation Theory. DPS dissertation, Pace University, New York, NY.

Nelson, James A., and Reeder, John A. (1985). Labor Relations in China. *California Management Review,* 27(4), 13–32.

Nevis, Edwin C. (1983a). Cultural Assumptions and Productivity: The United States and China. *Sloan Management Review,* 24(3), 17–29.

Nevis, Edwin C. (1983b). Using an American Perspective in Understanding Another Culture: Toward a Hierarchy of Needs for the People's Republic of China. *Journal of Applied Behavioral Science,* 19, 249–264.

Nichols, David S. (2006). The Trials of Separating Bath Water from Baby: A Review and Critique of the MMPI-2 Restructured Clinical Scales. *Journal of Personality Assessment,* 87, 121–128.

Norton, W. I., and Moore, W. T. (2002). Entrepreneurial Risk: Have We Been Asking the Wrong Question? *Small Business Economics,* 18, 281–287.

Nunnally, J. C. (1978). *Psychometric Theory.* New York: McGraw-Hill.

Nystrom, Paul C. (1986). Comparing Beliefs of Line and Technostructure Managers. *Academy of Management Journal,* 29 812–819.

Offerman, L. R., and Gowing, M. K. (1990). Organizations of the Future: Changes and Challenges. *American Psychologist,* 45, 95–108.

O'Connor, Anahad (2004). Theory Given on Burying of Memories by People. *The New York Times,* January 9.
O'Leary, V. E. (1974). Some Attitudinal Barriers to Occupational Aspirations in Women. *Psychological Bulletin,* 81, 809–826.
Oliver, John E. (1980). The Development of an Instrument for Describing Organizational Energy Domains. PhD dissertation. Georgia State University, Atlanta, GA.
Oliver, John E. (1981). *Scoring Guide for the Oliver Organization Description Questionnaire.* Eugene, OR: Organizational Measurement Systems Press.
Oliver, John E. (1982). An Instrument for Classifying Organizations. *Academy of Management Journal,* 25, 855–866.
Oliver, John E., and Fredenberger, William B. (1987). Factor Structure of an Organizational Taxonomy. Unpublished paper, School of Business Administration, Valdosta State College, Valdosta, GA.
Ondrack, Daniel A. (1971). Attitudes toward Authority. *Personnel Administration,* 34(3), 8–17.
Opinion Research Corporation (1980). *Strategic Planning for Human Resources: 1980 and Beyond.* Princeton, NJ: Author.
Organ, Dennis W. (1988). *Organizational Citizenship Behavior: The Good Soldier Syndrome.* Lexington, MA: Lexington Books.
Osborne, Gwen (2003). Are Apostles Entrepreneurs? The Need for Achievement as a Common Trait between Entrepreneurs and Apostles in the International Coalition of Apostles (ICA). PhD dissertation. Regent University, Virginia Beach, VA.
Ouchi, William G. (1981). *Theory Z: How American Business Can Meet the Japanese Challenge.* Reading, MA: Addison-Wesley.
Overstreet, James S. (1980). Managerial Motivation of Government Managers: A Comparison of Business and State Government Managers Using Miner's Role Motivation Theory. DBA dissertation. Florida State University, Tallahassee, FL.
Palich, Leslie E., and Bagdy, D. Ray (1995). Using Cognitive Theory to Explain Entrepreneurial Risk-taking: Challenging Conventional Wisdom. *Journal of Business Venturing,* 10, 425–438.
Palisi, B. J., and Jacobson, P. E. (1977). Dominant Statuses and Involvement in Types of Instrumental and Expressive Voluntary Associations. *Journal of Voluntary Action Research,* 6, 80–88.
Pandey, Janek, and Tewary, N. B. (1979). Locus of Control and Achievement Values of Entrepreneurs. *Journal of Occupational Psychology,* 52, Part 2.
Patten, Thomas H. (1972). Personnel Administration and the Will to Manage. *Human Resource Management,* 11(3), 4–9.
Paunonen, Sampo V., and Nicol, Adelheid A. A. M. (2001). The Personality Hierarchy and the Prediction of Work Behaviors. In Brent W. Roberts and Robert Hogan (Eds.), *Personality Psychology in the Workplace.* Washington, DC: American Psychological Association, 161–191.
Pearce, Jone L. (1983a). Comparing Volunteers and Employees in a Test of Etzioni's Compliance Typology. *Journal of Voluntary Action Research,* 12, 22–30.
Pearce, Jone L. (1983b). Job Attitudes and Motivation Differences between Volunteers and Employees from Comparable Organizations. *Journal of Applied Psychology,* 68, 646–652.
Pederson-Krag, Geraldine (1955). *Personality Factors in Work and Employment.* New York: Funk and Wagnalls.
Perham, Roy G. (1989). The Effect of Relevant and Irrelevant Information on Miner Sentence Completion Scale Scoring Accuracy. PhD dissertation. Stevens Institute of Technology, Hoboken, NJ.
Peters, Thomas J. (1988). Restoring American Competitiveness: Looking for New Models of Organizations. *Academy of Management Executive,* 2, 103–109.
Peterson, Richard E. (1968a). *The Scope of Organized Student Protest in 1967–68.* Princeton, NJ: Educational Testing Service.
Peterson, Richard E. (1968b). The Student Left in American Higher Education. *Daedulus,* 97, 293–317.
Pfeffer, Jeffrey, and Salancik, Gerald R. (1978). *The External Control of Organizations: A Resource Dependence Perspective.* New York: Harper and Row.
Pilgrim, Martha S. (1986). Development of a Professional Role-Motivation Training Package for Special Educators. PhD dissertation, Georgia State University, Atlanta, GA.
Pincus, C. S., and Hermann-Kelling, E. (1982). Self-Help Systems and the Professional as Volunteer: Threat or Solution? *Journal of Voluntary Action Research,* 11, 86–96.
Pinder, Craig C., and Moore, Larry F. (1979). The Resurrection of Taxonomy to Aid the Development of Middle Range Theories of Organizational Behavior. *Administratiave Science Quarterly,* 24, 99–119.

Piotrowski, Zygmunt A., and Rock, Milton R. (1963). *The Perceptanalytic Executive Scale: A Tool for the Selection of Top Managers.* New York: Grune and Stratton.

Porter, Lyman W. (1964). *Organizational Patterns of Managerial Job Attitudes.* New York: American Foundation for Management Research.

Porter, Lyman W., and McLaughlin, Grace B. (2006). Leadership and the Organizational Context: Like the Weather? *Leadership Quarterly,* 17, 559–576.

Powell, Gary (1993). *Women and Men in Management.* Newbury Park, CA: Sage.

Powers, D. E., and Hardy, F. M. (1980). *A Summary of Results of the Graduate Management Admission Council (GMAC) Validity Service for 1979.* Princeton, NJ: Educational Testing Service.

Priest, R. F. (1975). *Improving Prediction of Fourth Class Leadership by Reweighting Components.* (Report No. 75–019). West Point, NY: United States Military Academy.

Princeton University Class of 1948 (1974). *The Book of the Princeton University Class of 1948 on the Occasion of Its Twenty-fifth Anniversary.* Princeton, NJ: Princeton University.

Princeton University Class of 1948 (1998). *Going Back: 50 Years of the Class of 1948.* Princeton, NJ: Princeton University.

Pugh, Derek S., Hickson, David J., and Hinings, C. Robert (1969). An Empirical Taxonomy of Structures of Work Organizations. *Administrative Science Quarterly,* 14, 115–126.

Quigley, John V. (1979). Predicting Managerial Success in the Public Sector: Concurrent Validation of Biodata and the Miner Sentence Completion Scale in the Georgia Department of Human Resources. PhD dissertation, Georgia State University, Atlanta, GA.

Rabin, Albert I., and Zltogorski, Zoli (1985). The Sentence Completion Method—Recent Research. *Journal of Personality Assessment,* 49, 641–647.

Ragins, Belle R., and Sundstrom, Eric (1989). Gender and Power in Organizations: A Longitudinal Perspective. *Psychological Bulletin,* 105, 51–88.

Raju, Nambury S., Laffitte, Larry J., and Byrne, Barbara M. (2002). Measurement Equivalence: A Comparison of Methods Based on Confirmatory Factor Analysis and Item Response Theory. *Journal of Applied Psychology,* 87, 517–529.

Ray, Dennis M. (1993). Understanding the Entrepreneur: Entrepreneurial Attributes, Experience and Skills. *Entrepreneurship and Regional Development,* 5, 345–357.

Raynor, Joel O. (1974). Future Orientation in the Study of Achievement Motivation. In John W. Atkinson and Joel O. Raynor (Eds.), *Motivation and Achievement.* New York: Wiley, 121–154.

Redding, S. G. (1993). *The Spirit of Chinese Capitalism.* New York: deGruyter.

Reisch, M., and Wenocur, S. (1982). Professionalization and Volunteerism in Social Welfare: Changing Roles and Functions. *Journal of Voluntary Action Research,* 11, 11–31.

Reiser, Morton F. (1990). *Memory in Mind and Brain: What Dream Imagery Reveals.* New York: Basic Books.

Rich, Philip (1992). The Organizational Taxonomy: Definition and Design. *Academy of Management Review,* 17, 758–781.

Richard, J. C. (1989). A Comparison of the Social Characteristics, Personalities, and Managerial Styles of Managers and Entrepreneurs. PhD dissertation. University of Windsor, Windsor, Ontario, Canada.

Riger, Stephanie, and Galligan, Pat (1980). Women in Management: An Exploration of Competing Paradigms. *American Psychologist,* 35, 902–910.

Ritsher, Jennifer B. (2004). Association of Rorschach and MMPI Psychosis Indicators and Schizophrenia Spectrum Diagnoses in a Russian Clinical Sample. *Journal of Personality Assessment,* 83, 46–63.

Roberts, Brent W., Walton, Kate E., and Viechtbauer, Wolfgang (2006). Personality Traits Change in Adulthood: Reply to Costa and McCrae (2006). *Psychological Bulletin,* 132, 29–32.

Roberts, Edward B. (1991). *Entrepreneurs in High Technology: Lessons from MIT and Beyond.* New York: Oxford University Press.

Robinson, Peter B., Huefner, Jonathan C., and Hunt, H. Keith (1991). Entrepreneurial Research on Student Subjects Does Not Generalize to Real World Entrepreneurs. *Journal of Small Business Management,* 29(2), 42–50.

Rogelberg, Steven G., and Luong, Alexandra (1998). Nonresponse to Mailed Surveys: A Review and Guide. *Current Directions in Psychological Science,* 7, 60–65.

Ronstadt, Robert (1988). The Corridor Principle. *Journal of Business Venturing,* 3, 31–40.

Rorschach, Herman (1942). *Psychodiagnostics: A Diagnostic Test Based on Perception.* Bern, Switzerland: Hans Huber.

Rose, R. M., Jenkins, C. D., and Hurst, M. W. (1978). *Air Traffic Controller Health Change Study: A Prospective Investigation of Physical, Psychological, and Work-related Changes.* Austin: University of Texas Press.

Rosen, Bernard C., and D'Andrade, Roy (1959). The Psychological Origins of Achievement Motivation. *Sociometry,* 22, 185–218.

Rosener, Judy B. (1990). Ways Women Lead. *Harvard Business Review,* 68(6), 119–125.

Rosenthal, R. (1991). *Meta-analytic Procedures for Social Research.* Newbury Park, CA: Sage.

Rosenthal, R., and Rubin, D. B. (1979). A Note on Percent Variance Explained as Measure of the Importance of Effects. *Journal of Applied Social Psychology,* 9, 395–396.

Roth, Philip L., and BeVier, Craig A. (1998). Response Rates in HRM/OB Survey Research: Norms and Correlates, 1990–1994. *Journal of Management,* 24, 97–117.

Rothschild-Whitt, J. (1979). The Collectivist Organization: An Alternative to Rational-Bureaucratic Models. *American Sociological Review,* 44, 509–517.

Rotter, Julian B. (1971). Generalized Expectancies for Interpersonal Trust. *American Psychologist,* 26, 443–452.

Rowe, Alan J., and Mason, Richard O. (1987). *Managing with Style: A Guide to Understanding, Assessing, and Improving Decision Making.* San Francisco, CA: Jossey-Bass.

Rudman, Laurie A. (2004). Sources of Implicit Attitudes. *Current Directions in Psychological Science,* 13, 79–82.

Russell, J. E. A., Rush, M. C., and Herd, A. M. (1988). An Exploration of Women's Expectations of Effective Male and Female Leadership. *Sex Roles,* 18, 279–287.

Ryan, Ann M., and Sackett, Paul R. (1987). A Survey of Individual Assessment Practices by I/O Psychologists. *Personnel Psychology,* 40, 455–488.

Sanchez, Julio C. (1993). The Long and Thorny Way to an Organizational Taxonomy. *Organization Studies,* 14, 73–92.

Satow, Roberta L. (1975). Value Rational Authority and Professional Organizations: Weber's Missing Type. *Administrative Science Quarterly,* 20, 526–536.

Saucier, Gerard, and Goldberg, Lewis R. (2003). The Structure of Personality Attributes. In Murray R. Barrick and Ann Marie Ryan (Eds.), *Personality and Work: Reconsidering the Role of Personality in Organizations.* San Francisco, CA: Jossey-Bass, 1–29.

Savickas, Mark L., Taber, Brian J., and Spokane, Arnold R. (2002). Convergent and Discriminant Validity of Five Interest Inventories. *Journal of Vocational Behavior,* 61, 139–184.

Schaefer, E. S., and Edgerton, M. (1985). Parent and Child Correlates of Parental Modernity. In I. E. Sigel (Ed.), *Parental Belief Systems.* Hillsdale, NJ: Lawrence Erlbaum, 287–318.

Schafer, Roy (1967). *Projective Testing and Psychoanalysis.* New York: International Universities Press.

Schafer, Roy (2006). My Life in Testing. *Journal of Personality Assessment,* 86, 235–241.

Scheier, I. (1981). Positive Staff Attitude Can Ease Recruiting Pinch for Volunteers. *The Volunteer Leader,* 22, 1–7.

Schein, Edgar H. (1975). How "Career Anchors" Hold Executives to Their Paths. *Personnel,* 52(3), 11–24.

Schein, Edgar H. (1978). *Career Dynamics: Matching Individual and Organizational Needs.* Reading, MA: Addison-Wesley.

Schein, Virginia E. (1973). The Relationship between Sex Role Stereotypes and Requisite Management Characteristics. *Journal of Applied Psychology,* 57, 95–100.

Schendel, Dan E., and Hofer, Charles W. (1979). *Strategic Management: A New View of Business Policy and Planning.* Boston, MA: Little, Brown.

Scherer, Robert F., Brodzinski, James D., and Wiebe, Frank A. (1991). Examining the Relationship between Personality and Entrepreneurial Career Preference. *Entrepreneurship and Regional Development,* 3, 195–206.

Schermerhorn, John R. (1987). Organizational Features of Chinese Industrial Enterprise: Paradoxes of Stability in Times of Change. *Academy of Management Executive,* 1, 345–349.

Schmalt, Heinz-Dieter (2005). Validity of a Short Form of the Achievement-Motive Grid (AMG-S): Evidence for the Three-Factor Structure Emphasizing Active and Passive Forms of Fear of Failure. *Journal of Personality Assessment,* 84, 172–184.

Schmitt, Neal, Gooding, Richard Z., Noe, Raymond D., and Kirsch, Michael (1984). Meta-analyses of Validity Studies Published between 1964 and 1982 and the Investigation of Study Characteristics. *Personnel Psychology,* 37, 407–422.

Schmitt-Rodermund, Eva (2004). Pathways to Successful Entrepreneurship: Parenting, Personality, Early Entrepreneurial Competence, and Interests. *Journal of Vocational Behavior,* 65, 498–518.

Schmitt-Rodermund, Eva, and Vondracek, Fred W. (2002). Occupational Dreams, Choices and Aspirations: Adolescents' Entrepreneurial Prospects and Orientations. *Journal of Adolescence,* 25, 65–78.

Schneider, Benjamin, Ehrhart, Karen H., and Ehrhart, Mark G. (2002). Understanding High School Student Leaders II. Peer Nominations of Leaders and Their Correlates. *Leadership Quarterly,* 13, 275–299.

Schneider, Benjamin, Paul, Michelle C., White, Susan S., and Holcombe, Karen M. (1999). Understanding High School Student Leaders, 1: Predicting Teacher Ratings of Leader Behavior. *Leadership Quarterly,* 10, 609–636.

Schultheiss, Oliver C., and Brunstein, Joachim C. (2001). Assessment of Implicit Motives with a Research Version of the TAT: Picture Profiles, Gender Differences, and Relations to Other Personality Measures. *Journal of Personality Assessment,* 77, 71–86.

Scott, Bruce R. (1973). The Industrial State: Old Myth and New Realities. *Harvard Business Review,* 51(2), 133–148.

Scott, Joseph W., and El-Assal, Mohamed (1969). Multiversity, University Size, University Quality and Student Protest: An Empirical Study. *American Sociological Review,* 34, 702–709.

Scott, W. Richard (2001). *Institutions and Organizations.* Thousand Oaks, CA: Sage.

Scott, W. Richard, and Meyer, John W. (1994). *Institutional Environments and Organizations.* Thousand Oaks, CA: Sage.

Sears, Robert R. (1943). *Survey of Objective Studies of Psychoanalytic Concepts: A Report Prepared for the Committee on Social Adjustment.* New York: Social Science Research Council.

Sears, Robert R. (1944). Experimental Analysis of Psychoanalytic Phenomena. In J. McV. Hunt (Ed.), *Personality and the Behavior Disorders: A Handbook Based on Experimental and Clinical Research.* New York: Ronald Press, 306–332.

Sechrest, L., and Yeaton, W. H. (1982). Magnitudes of Experimental Effects in Social Science Research. *Evaluation Review,* 6, 579–600.

Selby, C. C. (1978). Better Performance for Nonprofits. *Harvard Business Review,* 56(5), 92–98.

Sexton, Donald L., and Bowman, Nancy B. (1983). Comparative Entrepreneurship Characteristics of Students: Preliminary Results. *Frontiers of Entrepreneurship Research,* 3, 213–232.

Sexton, Donald L., and Kasarda, John D. (1992). *The State of the Art of Entrepreneurship.* Boston, MA: PWS-Kent.

Sexton, Donald L., and Smilor, Raymond W. (1986). *The Art and Science of Entrepreneurship.* Cambridge, MA: Ballinger.

Shapira, Zur (1995). *Risk Taking: A Managerial Perspective.* New York: Russell Sage Foundation.

Shenkar, Oded (1984). Is Bureaucracy Inevitable: The Chinese Experience. *Organization Studies,* 5, 289–308.

Shenkar, Oded, and Ronen, Simcha (1987). Structure and Importance of Work Goals among Managers in the People's Republic of China. *Academy of Management Journal,* 30, 564–576.

Shouval, Ron, Duck, Edmund, and Ginton, Avital (1975). A Multiple Choice Version of the Sentence Completion Method. *Journal of Personality Assessment,* 39, 41–49.

Shure, G. H., and Meeker, J. P. (1967). A Personality Attitude Schedule for Use in Experimental Bargaining Studies. *Journal of Psychology,* 65, 233–252.

Silver, Allan (1969). Who Cares for Columbia? *New York Review of Books,* 12, 15–19, 22–24.

Simms, Leonard J. (2006). Bridging the Divide: Comments on the Restructured Clinical Scales of the MMPI-2. *Journal of Personality Assessment,* 87, 211–216.

Simon, Herbert A. (1957). *Administrative Behavior.* New York: Macmillan.

Simon, R. J., and Landis, J. M. (1989). Women's and Men's Attitudes about a Woman's Place and Role. *Public Opinion Quarterly,* 53, 265–276.

Singh, Jitendra V., House, Robert J., and Tucker, David J. (1986). Organizational Change and Organizational Mortality. *Administrative Science Quarterly,* 31, 587–611.

Singleton, Timothy M. (1978). Managerial Motivation Development: A Study of College Student Leaders. *Academy of Management Journal,* 21, 493–498.

Singleton, Timothy M., Kelley C. Aaron, Yao, Ester, and White, Louis P. (1987). Motivation to Manage: People's Republic of China and Hong Kong. *Southern Management Association Proceedings,* 34–36.

Slocum, John W., and Hellriegel, Don (1983). A Look at How Managers' Minds Work. *Business Horizons,* 26(4), 58–68.

Smith, C. A., Organ, Dennis W., and Near, Janet (1983). Organizational Citizenship Behavior: Its Nature and Antecedents. *Journal of Applied Psychology,* 68, 653–663.

Smith, D. H. (1982). Altruism, Volunteers, and Volunteerism. In J. D. Harman (Ed.), *Volunteering in the Eighties: Fundamental Issues in Voluntary Action.* Washington, DC: University Press of America, 23–44.

Smith, Norman R. (1967). *The Entrepreneur and His Firm: The Relationship between Type of Man and Type of Company.* East Lansing, MI: Bureau of Business and Economic Research, Michigan State University.

Smith, Norman R., Bracker, Jeffrey S., and Miner, John B. (1987). Correlates of Firm and Entrepreneur Success in Technologically Innovative Companies. *Frontiers of Entrepreneurship Research,* 7, 737–753.

Smith, Norman R., and Miner, John B. (1983). Type of Entrepreneur, Type of Firm, and Managerial Motivation: Implications for Organizational Life Cycle Theory. *Strategic Management Journal,* 4, 325–340.

Smith, Norman R., and Miner, John B. (1984). Motivational Considerations in the Success of Technologically Innovative Entrepreneurs. *Frontiers of Entrepreneurship Research,* 4, 488–495.

Smith, Norman R., and Miner, John B. (1985). Motivational Considerations in the Success of Technologically Innovative Entrepreneurs: Extended Sample Findings. *Frontiers of Entrepreneurship Research,* 5, 482–488.

Snell, William E., Hargrove, Linda, and Falbo, Toni (1986). Birth Order and Achievement Motivation Configurations in Women and Men. *Individual Psychology,* 42, 428–438.

Snyder, Robert A., Howard, Ann, and Hammer, Tove H. (1978). Mid-career Change in Academia: The Decision to Become an Administrator. *Journal of Vocational Behavior,* 13, 229–241.

Soares, Glaucio A. D. (1967). The Active Few: Student Ideology and Participation in Developing Countries. In Seymour M. Lipset (Ed.), *Student Politics.* New York: Basic Books, 124–147.

Society for Personality Assessment (2005). The Status of the Rorschach in Clinical and Forensic Practice: An Official Statement by the Board of Trustees. *Journal of Personality Assessment,* 85, 219–237.

Solomon, Frederic, and Fishman, Jacob R. (1964). Youth and Peace: A Psychological Study of Peace Demonstrators in Washington, D.C. *Journal of Social Issues,* 20, 54–73.

Sorensen, James E., and Sorensen, Thomas L. (1974). The Conflict of Professionals in Bureaucratic Organizations. *Administrative Science Quarterly,* 19, 98–105.

Southern, Lloyd J. F. (1977). An Analysis of Motivation to Manage in the Tufted Carpet and Textile Industry of Northwest Georgia (Doctoral dissertation, Georgia State University). *Dissertation Abstracts International,* 38, 2917A.

Spangler, William D. (1992). Validity of Questionnaire and TAT Measures of Need for Achievement: Two Meta-analyses. *Psychological Bulletin,* 112, 140–154.

Spence, Janet T., Helmreich, R. L., and Holahan, C. K. (1979). Negative and Positive Components of Psychological Masculinity and Femininity and Their Relationships to Self-reports of Neurotic and Acting Out Behaviors. *Journal of Personality and Social Psychology,* 37, 1673–1682.

Spence, Janet T., Helmreich, R. L., and Stapp, J. (1974). The Personal Attributes Questionnaire: A Measure of Sex-role Stereotypes and Masculinity-femininity (Ms. No. 617). *JSAS: Catalog of Selected Documents in Psychology,* 4(43).

Stahl, Michael J. (1986). *Managerial and Technical Motivation: Assessing Needs for Achievement, Power, and Affiliation.* New York: Praeger.

Stahl, Michael J., Grigsby, David W., and Gulati, Anil (1985). Comparing the Job Choice Exercise and the Multiple Choice Version of the Miner Sentence Completion Scale. *Journal of Applied Psychology,* 70, 228–232.

Stajkovic, Alexander D., Locke, Edwin A., and Blair, Eden S. (2006). A First Examination of the Relationships between Primed Subconscious Goals, Assigned Conscious Goals, and Task Performance. *Journal of Applied Psychology,* 91, 1172–1180.

Steers, Richard M., and Mowday, Richard T. (1981). Employee Turnover and Post-decision Accommodation Processes. *Research in Organizational Behavior,* 3, 235–281.

Steger, Joseph A., Kelley, Winslow B., Chouiniere, Gregory, and Goldenbaum, Arnold (1975). A Forced Choice Version of the MSCS and How It Discriminates Campus Leaders and Nonleaders. *Academy of Management Journal,* 18, 435–460.

Steger, M. F. (2006). An Illustration of Issues in Factor Extraction and Identification of Dimensionality in Psychological Assessment Data. *Journal of Personality Assessment,* 86, 263–272.

Steinberg, Laurence, Elmen, Julie D., and Mounts, Nina S. (1989). Authoritative Parenting, Psychosocial Maturity, and Academic Success among Adolescents. *Child Development,* 60, 1424–1436.

Steiner, George A. (1983). *The New CEO.* New York: Macmillan.

Steiner, George A., Miner, John B., and Gray, Edmund R. (1986). *Management Policy and Strategy.* New York: Macmillan.

Steinmetz, Lawrence L. (1969). Critical Stages of Small Business Growth: When They Occur and How to Survive Them. *Business Horizons,* 12(1), 29–36.

Sternberg, Robert J. (2007). A Systems Model of Leadership. *American Psychologist,* 62, 34–42.

Stewart, Wayne H., and Roth, Philip L. (2001). Risk Propensity Differences between Entrepreneurs and Managers: A Meta-analytic Review. *Journal of Applied Psychology,* 86, 145–153.

Stewart, Wayne H., and Roth, Philip L. (2004). Data Quality Affects Meta-analytic Conclusions: A Response to Miner and Raju (2004) Concerning Entrepreneurial Risk Propensity. *Journal of Applied Psychology,* 89, 14–21.

Streiner, David L. (2003). Being Inconsistent about Consistency: When Coefficient Alpha Does and Doesn't Matter. *Journal of Personality Assessment,* 80, 217–222.

Strong, E. K., and Campbell, D. P. (1966). *The Strong Vocational Interest Blank Manual.* Stanford, CA: Stanford University Press.

Sulloway, Frank J. (1996). *Born to Rebel.* New York: Patheon.

Swisher, Robert, DuMont, Rosemary R., and Boyer, Calvin J. (1985). The Motivation to Manage: A Study of Academic Librarians and Library Science Students. *Library Trends,* 34, 219–234.

Tabachnick, B. G., and Fidell, L. S. (2001). Principle Components and Factor Analysis. In B. G. Tabachnick and L. S. Fidell (Eds.), *Using Multivariate Statistics.* Boston, MA: Allyn and Bacon, 582–652.

Tan, C-H (1989). Human Resource Management Reforms in the People's Republic of China. *Research in Personnel and Human Resource Management.* Supplement 1, 45–58.

Terry, Larry D. (1995). The Leadership-management Distinction: The Domination and Displacement of Mechanistic and Organismic Theories. *Leadership Quarterly,* 6, 515–527.

Thain, Donald H. (1969). Stages of Business Development. *Business Quarterly,* 34, 32–45.

Thayer, Paul W. (1997). Review of *The 4 Routes to Entrepreneurial Success. Personnel Psychology,* 50, 517–520.

Thompson, Cynthia A., Kopelman, Richard E., and Schriesheim, Chester A. (1992). Putting All One's Eggs in the Same Basket: A Comparison of Commitment and Satisfaction among Self- and Organizationally Employed Men. *Journal of Applied Psychology,* 77, 738–743.

Thorndike, Robert L., and Gallup, George H. (1944). Verbal Intelligence of the American Adult. *Journal of General Psychology,* 30, 75–85.

Thornton, G., Hollenshead, J., and Larson, S. (1997). Comparisons of Two Measures of Motivation to Manage: Ethnic and Gender Differences. *Educational and Psychological Measurement,* 57, 241–253.

Tien, J. S. (1986). A Long and Winding Road: Chinese Women and Judith Stacey's Patriarchy and Socialist Revolution in China. *US-China Review,* 10(2), 10–12.

Timmons, Jeffrey A. (1990). *New Venture Creation: Entrepreneurship in the 1990s.* Homewood, IL: Irwin.

Tinsley, Howard E. A. (2000a). The Congruence Myth: An Analysis of the Efficacy of the Personality-Environment Fit Model. *Journal of Vocational Behavior,* 56, 147–179.

Tinsley, Howard E. A. (2000b). The Congruence Myth Revisited. *Journal of Vocational Behavior,* 56, 405–423.

Tomeh, A. K. (1973). Formal Voluntary Organizations: Participation, Correlates, and Interrelationship. *Sociological Inquiry,* 43, 89–122.

Tomkins, Silvan S., and Miner, John B. (1957). *The Tomkins-Horn Picture Arrangement Test.* New York: Springer.

Tomkins, Silvan S., and Miner, John B. (1959). *PAT Interpretation: Scope and Technique.* New York: Springer.

Townsend, J. R. (1980). *Politics in China.* Boston, MA: Little, Brown.

Tracy, Kay B. (1992). *Effects of Need for Achievement, Task Motivation, Goal Setting and Planning on the Performance of the Entrepreneurial Firm.* PhD dissertation, University of Maryland, College Park.

Traunstein, D. M., and Steinman, R. (1973). Voluntary Self-Help Organizations: An Exploratory Study. *Journal of Voluntary Action Research,* 2, 230–239.

Triandis, Harry C. (1995). *Individualism-collectivism.* Boulder, Co: Westview.

Triandis, Harry C., Chen, X. P., and Chan, D. K.-S. (1996). *Scenarios for the Measurement of Collectivism and Individualism.* Unpublished working paper.

Trist, Eric L., and Bamforth, K. W. (1951). Some Social and Psychological Consequences of the Longwall Method of Coal-getting. *Human Relations,* 4, 3–38.

Tuason, Roman V. (1973). Corporate Life Cycle and the Evolution of Corporate Strategy. *Academy of Management Proceedings,* 35–40.

Tullar, W. (2001). Russian Entrepreneurial Motive Patterns: A Validation of the Miner Sentence Completion Scale in Russia. *Applied Psychology: An International Review,* 50, 422–435.

Turner, Jonathan H. (1970). Entrepreneurial Environments and the Emergence of Achievement Motivation in Adolescent Males. *Sociometry,* 33, 147–165.

Vernon, Philip E. (1950). *The Structure of Human Abilities.* New York: Wiley.

Viglione, Donald J., Perry, William, and Meyer, Gregory (2003). Refinements in the Rorschach Ego Impairment Index Incorporating the Human Representational Variable. *Journal of Personality Assessment,* 81, 149–156.

Vollmer, Howard M., and Mills, Donald L. (1966). *Professionalization.* Englewood Cliffs, NJ: Prentice-Hall.

Von Glinow, Mary Ann, and Chung, Bjung J. (1989). Comparative Human Resource Management Practices in the United States, Japan, Korea, and the People's Republic of China. *Research in Personnel and Human Resource Management,* Supplement 1, 153–176.

Von Glinow, Mary Ann, and Teagarden, Mary B. (1988). The Transfer of Human Resource Management Technology in Sino-U.S. Cooperative Ventures: Problems and Solutions. *Human Resource Management,* 27, 201–229.

Vroom, Victor H., and Jago, Arthur G. (2007). The Role of the Situation in Leadership. *American Psychologist,* 62, 17–24.

Wachtel, Jeffrey M. (1986). A Cross-Cultural Comparative Management Study Measuring the Differences in Managerial Motivation and the Effects of Cultural and Other Explanatory Variables of Potential Managers from Mexico and the United States. PhD dissertation. Georgia State University, Atlanta, GA.

Wald, Robert M., and Doty, Roy A. (1954). The Top Executive: A Firsthand Profile. *Harvard Business Review,* 32(4), 45–54.

Walker, J. M. (1975). Organizational Change: Citizen Participation and Voluntary Action. *Journal of Voluntary Action Research,* 4, 4–22.

Wall, James A. (1990). Managers in the People's Republic of China. *Academy of Management Executive,* 4(2), 19–32.

Wallace, Jean E. (1993). Professional and Organizational Commitment: Compatible or Incompatible? *Journal of Vocational Behavior,* 42, 323–349.

Walton, Richard E. (1972). How to Counter Alienation in the Plant. *Harvard Business Review,* 50(6), 70–81.

Wanous, John P. (1977). Organizational Entry: Newcomers Moving from Outside to Inside. *Psychological Bulletin,* 84, 601–618.

Wanous, John P., Keon, Thomas L., and Latack, Janina C. (1983). Expectancy Theory and Occupational/Organizational Choices: A Review and Test. *Organizational Behavior and Human Performance,* 32, 66–86.

Ward, Lewis B., and Athos, Anthony, G. (1972). *Student Expectations of Corporate Life: Implications for Management Recruiting.* Boston, MA: Graduate School of Business Administration, Harvard University.

Warner, Malcolm (1986). Managing Human Resources in China. *Organization Studies,* 7, 353–366.

Warner, W. K., (1972). Major Conceptual Elements of Voluntary Associations. In D. H. Smith, R. D. Reddy, and B. R. Baldwin (Eds.), *Voluntary Action Research: 1972.* Lexington, MA: Lexington Books, 71–80.

Warner, W. K., and Miller, S. (1964). Organizational Problems in Two Types of Voluntary Associations. *American Journal of Sociology,* 70, 654–684.

Watts, William A., and Whittaker, David (1966). Free Speech Advocates at Berkeley. *Journal of Applied Behavioral Science,* 2, 41–62.

Weber, Max (1947). *The Theory of Social and Economic Organization.* (A. M. Henderson and T. Parsons, trans.) Oxford, UK: Oxford University Press.

Weber, Max (1968). *Economy and Society.* (G. Roth and C. Wittich, Eds. and trans.) New York: Bedminster Press.

Webster, Jane, and Starbuck, William H. (1988). Theory Building in Industrial and Organizational Psychology. *International Review of Industrial and Organizational Psychology,* 3, 93–138.

Weick, Karl E. (2001). *Making Sense of Organization.* Oxford, UK: Blackwell.

Weisbrod, B. A. (1977). *The Private Non-Profit Sector: An Economic Analysis.* Lexington, MA: Lexington Books.

Wentzel, Kathryn R., and Feldman, S. Shirley (1993). Parental Predictors of Boys' Self-restraining and Motivation to Achieve at School: A Longitudinal Study. *Journal of Early Adolesence,* 13, 183–203.

Westby, David L., and Braungart, Richard G. (1966). Class and Politics in the Family Backgrounds of Student Political Activists. *American Sociological Review,* 31, 690–692.

Westen, Drew (1998). The Scientific Legacy of Sigmund Freud: Toward a Psychodynamically Informed Psychological Science. *Psychological Bulletin,* 124, 333–371.

White, O. F. (1982). Professionalization of Volunteer Organizations as a 'Problem' in the Theory of Human Action. In J. D. Harman (Ed.), *Volunteering in the Eighties: Fundamental Issues in Voluntary Action.* Washington, DC: University Press of America, 125–157.

Wigfield, Allan, Eccles, Jacquelynne S., Schiefele, Ulrich, Roesser, Robert, and Davis-Kean, Pamela (2006). Development of Achievement Motivation. In W. Damon, R. Lerner, and N. Eisenberg (Eds.), *Handbook of Child Psychology: Vol. 3. Social, Emotional, and Personality Development.* New York: Wiley, 933–1002.

Wiggins, J. D., and Weslander, Darrell (1977). Expressed Vocational Choices and Later Employment Compared with Vocational Preference Inventory and Kuder Preference Record-vocational Scores. *Journal of Vocational Behavior,* 11, 158–165.

Wilderom, Celeste P. M. (1989). On Defining Voluntary Work Within Organizational Science. Working paper, State University of New York at Buffalo and Free University, The Netherlands.

Wilderom, Celeste P. M., and Miner, John B. (1991). Defining Voluntary Groups and Agencies within Organization Science. *Organization Science,* 2, 366–378.

Williams, J. E., and Best, D. L. (1982). *Measuring Sex Stereotypes: A Thirty-nation Study.* Newbury Park, CA: Sage.

Williamson, Oliver E., and Ouchi, William G. (1981). The Markets and Hierarchies and Visible Hand Perspectives. In Andrew H. Van de Ven and William F. Joyce (Eds.), *Perspectives in Organizational Design and Behavior.* New York: Wiley.

Willis, Janine, and Todorov, Alexander (2006). First Impressions: Making Up Your Mind After a 100-Ms Exposure to a Face. *Psychological Science,* 17, 592–598.

Winer, B. J. (1971). *Statistical Principles in Experimental Design.* New York: McGraw-Hill.

Winerman, Lea (2005). Can You Force Yourself to Forget? *Monitor on Psychology*¸36(8), 52–57.

Winterbottom, Marian R. (1958). The Relation of Need for Achievement to Learning Experiences, Independence and Mastery. In John W. Atkinson (Ed.), *Motives in Fantasy, Action, and Society.* Princeton, NJ: Van Nostrand.

Woike, Barbara A. (1995). Most-memorable Experiences: Evidence for a Link between Implicit and Explicit Motives and Social Cognitive Processes in Everyday Life. *Journal of Personality and Social Psychology,* 68, 1081–1091.

Woike, Barbara A., Gershkovich, Irina, Piorkowski, Rebecca, and Polo, Marilyn (1999). The Role of Motives in the Content and Structure of Autobiographical Memory. *Journal of Personality and Social Psychology,* 76, 600–612.

Woo, Carolyn Y., Cooper, Arnold C., and Dunkelberg, William C. (1988). Entrepreneurial Typologies: Definitions and Implications. *Frontiers of Entrepreneurship Research,* 8, 165–176.

Woo, Carolyn Y., Cooper, Arnold C., and Dunkelberg, William C. (1991). The Development and Interpretation of Entrepreneurial Typologies. *Journal of Business Venturing,* 6, 93–114.

Woo, Carolyn, Daellenbach, Urs, and Nichols-Nixon, Charlene (1994). Theory Building in the Presence of "Randomness": The Case of Venture Creation and Performance. *Journal of Management Studies,* 31, 507–524.

Wood, James M., Garb, Howard N., Lilienfeld, Scott O., and Nezworski, M. Teresa (2002). Clinical Assessment. *Annual Review of Psychology,* 53, 519–543.

Wood, James M., Nezworski, M. Teresa, Lilienfeld, Scott O., and Garb, Howard N. (2003). *What's Wrong with the Rorschach?* San Francisco, CA: Jossey-Bass.

Wortman, M. S. (1981). A Radical Shift from Bureaucratic to Strategic Management in Voluntary Organizations. *Journal of Voluntary Action Research,* 10, 62–81.

Wren, Daniel A., Atherton, Roger M., and Michaelsen, Larry K. (1978). The Managerial Experience of Management Professors: Are the Blind Leading the Blind? *Journal of Management,* 4, 75–83.

Xu, H., and Ruef, M. (2004). The Myth of the Risk-tolerant Entrepreneur. *Strategic Organization,* 2, 331–355.

Young, D. R. (1983). *If Not for Profit, for What? A Behavioral Theory of the Nonprofit Sector Based on Entrepreneurship.* Lexington, MA: Lexington Books.

Zaccaro, Stephen J. (2007). Trait-based Perspectives of Leadership. *American Psychologist,* 62, 6–16.

Zaccaro, Stephen J., Foti, Roseanne J., and Kenny, David A. (1991). Self-monitoring and Trait-based Variance in Leadership: An Investigation of Leader Flexibility Across Multiple Group Situations. *Journal of Applied Psychology,* 76, 308–315.

Zaleznick, Abraham (1977). Managers and Leaders: Are They Different? *Harvard Business Review,* 55(3), 67–78.

Zenger, Todd R., Lazzarini, Sergio G., and Poppo, Laura (2002). Informal and Formal Organization in New Institutional Economics. *Advances in Strategic Management,* 19, 277–305.

Zhuang, Shirley C., and Whitehill, Arthur M. (1989). Will China Adopt Western Management Practices? *Business Horizons,* 32(2), 58–64.

NAME INDEX

C

D

H

SUBJECT INDEX

T

ABOUT THE AUTHOR

John B. Miner has a professional practice in Eugene, Oregon. He held the Donald S. Carmichael Chair in Human Resources at the State University of New York–Buffalo and was faculty director of the Center for Entrepreneurial Leadership there. Previously he was Research Professor of Management at Georgia State University. He has written 56 books and over 140 other publications.